Gabriel Hoo~~~~ ~3

SO-ACW-964

# Our Changing Population

**RICHARD T. GILL (ECONOMICS)**
*Former Master of Leverett House, Harvard University*

**NATHAN GLAZER (SOCIOLOGY)**
*Professor of Sociology and Education, Harvard University*

**STEPHAN A. THERNSTROM (HISTORY)**
*Winthrop Professor of History, Harvard University*

WITH SPECIAL CONTRIBUTIONS BY:
    HARRIETTE McADOO  (Sociology), *Howard University*
    SHIRLEY SMITH  (Demography), *Bureau of Labor Statistics*
    MARTA TIENDA  (Sociology), *University of Chicago*
    REED UEDA  (History), *Tufts University*

**PRENTICE HALL, ENGLEWOOD CLIFFS, NEW JERSEY 07632**

Library of Congress Cataloging-in-Publication Data

Gill, Richard T.
    Our changing population / Richard T. Gill, Nathan Glazer, Stephan
A. Thernstrom ; with special contributions by Harriette McAdoo ...
[et al.].
        p.     cm.
    Includes bibliographical references and index.
    ISBN 0-13-642661-1
    1. United States--Population--History.     I. Glazer, Nathan.
II. Thernstrom, Stephan.   III. Title.
HB3505.G55  1992
304.6'0973--dc20                                            91-30137
                                                              CIP

Acquisitions editor: Nancy Roberts
Editorial/production supervision and
   interior design: Serena Hoffman
Cover design: Wanda Lubelska
Prepress buyer: Kelly Behr
Manufacturing buyer: Mary Ann Gloriande
Copy editor: Judith Ashkenaz
Supplements editor: Sharon Chambliss

© 1992 by Richard T. Gill, Nathan Glazer, Stephan A. Thernstrom

All rights reserved. No part of this book may be
reproduced, in any form or by any means,
without permission in writing from the publisher.

Printed in the United States of America
10  9  8  7  6  5  4  3

ISBN 0-13-642661-1

Prentice-Hall International (UK) Limited,London
Prentice-Hall of Australia Pty. Limited, Sydney
Prentice-Hall Canada Inc., Toronto
Prentice-Hall Hispanoamericana, S.A., Mexico
Prentice-Hall of India Private Limited, New Delhi
Prentice-Hall of Japan, Inc., Tokyo
Pearson Education Asia Pte. Ltd., Singapore
Editora Prentice-Hall do Brasil, Ltda., Rio de Janeiro

# Contents

## Part II:  THE OLDER GENERATION  73

## 7  To Work or To Retire?   109

## 8  Health Care and the Elderly   125

## Part III:   ADULTS: YOUNG AND MIDDLE AGED   141

## 9  The "Traditional" American Family   143

## 10  A Tale of Two Generations   161

**Part VI: OUR POSTERITY 387**

# Preface

We are living much longer. We are having fewer children. The racial and ethnic composition of our population is changing. Demographic trends—as they have developed historically and as they are continuing to transform prospects for the decades ahead—are central to some of the deepest social and economic phenomena of our time. *Our Changing Population* charts these trends in the United States and examines their profound consequences for the present and future state of American society.

## FOCAL ISSUES

Although there is necessarily some formal demography in this text, most of the demographic commentary is confined to the first few chapters and a technical appendix. The focus of the book lies elsewhere: namely, in an effort to trace the dramatic effects of U.S. population change on crucial aspects of our common life. After outlining the historical development of population trends in the United States, the book takes up the consequences of a number of significant developments.

*The Aging of Our Population.* What is the effect of the increased proportion of older Americans relative to children and those of working age on our Social Security system, retirement prospects, and health care burdens? Americans live longer today, especially women, who increasingly face old age alone, sometimes in infirmity, often in poverty. Meanwhile, men are retiring earlier. Between 1970 and 1986, the average number of years a U.S. male could expect to spend in retirement increased by an estimated 31 percent! Such changes represent potentially revolutionary transformations in the way we lead our lives.

*The Changing Structures of Our Families.* Family life in the United States both deeply affects and is deeply affected by population change. Reduced fertility combined with increased longevity has substantially influenced child-bearing and child-rearing in the U.S. family. Women's careers are increasingly focused on the world outside the family, raising the issue of a gender gap in wages, and also the important question of day care in the case of dual-earner or single-parent families. While some men have taken an increased interest in the home, a surprising number have avoided family commitments altogether. It is estimated that a third or more of today's fathers of young children are not living with their natural children. The younger generation seems to be beset by profound problems of poverty, inadequate attention, and educational deficiency. How well, one wonders, will this generation fare when it comes to supporting the heavy burden as the Baby Boomers begin to retire in the early decades of the next century?

*Changes in Ethnic and Racial Structure.* Because of differential fertility and immigration, both legal and illegal, the racial and ethnic mix of the American population will change considerably over the coming decades. The increase will be largely in minority groups, especially Hispanics, Asians, and blacks. Whether this change will increase the numbers of lower-income and less well-educated Americans over time, or whether these minority groups will, on average, repeat the success stories of many earlier immigrant and racial groups will have profound effects on the future quality of American life. It will also have a clear bearing on the issues of sustaining the costs of an aging society and the future structure of American families.

*Issues for the Distant Future.* Although the subjects just mentioned are all concerned with the future to a degree, *Our Changing Population* makes a specific effort, in its final chapters, to suggest possibly momentous changes that could affect us in the decades ahead. Suppose there were changes in maximum human life span? What of the effect on the United States of dramatic increases in Third World populations? Will biogenetic engineering enable us to choose what the next generation will be like, and even alter the basic ways in which babies are conceived and borne? Given the pace of demographic changes that have already occurred, speculation about such matters is no longer fanciful but required for any serious student of modern populations.

## USING THIS TEXTBOOK

*Our Changing Population* has been designed as a textbook for a one-semester course in the general field of population analysis. Supplemented by other readings, it could also, of course, serve as the basic text for a full-year course.

In the course of preparing the manuscript, the authors benefited from an independent survey of universities, four-year colleges, and community colleges. In the majority of cases, respondents indicated that courses that dealt with these topics were located in sociology departments; however, it was also noted that comparable courses were given in other departments: history, American studies, general education, core curricula, and, less frequently, economics.

Another point that emerged from the survey was that multitudes of courses in these various institutions dealt with *parts* of the materials presented in the text. Courses dealing with aging, the family, children, minority relations, international and internal migrations, and even more specific topics like the Baby Boom were found in great numbers. With this in mind, *Our Changing Population* was written so that instructors can make module-like selections from its parts and/or chapters. To take three examples: a course on aging might focus on Chapters 1–3, Part II, and Chapter 22. A course on the family might choose Chapters 1–3, Parts III and IV, and Chapters 23 and 26. And a course on minority relations might focus on Chapter 4, Chapter 13, Part V, and Chapters 23 and 24.

Survey responses also confirmed the judgment of the authors that the problems studied: (a) are of great importance; and

(b) can only be studied through an interdisciplinary lens. Consequently, the book is interdisciplinary in approach. The authors' disciplines are sociology, history, and economics. Furthermore, the efforts of the three authors were assisted by other scholars, including those from the field of demography.

In order to facilitate the difficult teaching task that any interdisciplinary material commonly involves, a special effort has gone into making the complementary Instructor's Manual, Study Guide, and Test Bank as practically useful as possible.

## ACKNOWLEDGMENTS

As mentioned above, your authors benefited from the assistance of many scholars. Of particular note are those listed on the title page as having made "special contributions": Harriette McAdoo (Sociology) Howard University, who read and sent in very helpful comments on chapters dealing with black Americans; Shirley Smith (Demography) Bureau of Labor Statistics, who drafted the appendix on demographic analysis; Marta Tienda (Sociology) University of Chicago, who drafted Chapter 21; and Reed Ueda (History) Tufts University, who drafted Chapters 18 and 19. In order to preserve the continuity of the book as a whole, the authors edited these drafts, thus absolving the contributors from responsibility for what finally appears here. The help that these contributors provided, however, was truly exceptional.

Exceptional also was the help that the authors received from representatives of the Bureau of the Census. A constant flow of vital documents was provided in a very timely fashion. A special note of gratitude is due Cynthia Taeuber, who, despite an extremely busy schedule of official work, went out of her way to respond to all requests for help. It is fair to say that the publication of the book would have occurred at a much later date had it not been for her speedy and highly professional assistance.

The list of scholars who, in one way or another, have personally influenced the structure of this textbook is a long one. Even a short list would have to include: Henry Aaron, Donald Addison, Brigitte Berger, Barbara Bergmann, William P. Butz, Eileen Crimmins, Jacques Dubois, Richard Easterlin, Charles Longino, Jr., Reynolds Farley, Frank Levy, Stanford Lyman, Richard M. Suzman, Earnestine Thomas-Robertson, and William Armando Vega.

Special thanks are due to Stephanie Ventura for her aid in tracking down documents at the National Center for Health Statistics, and also to Ken Kochanek of NCHS, and John Bregger of the BLS. Prentice Hall has been unfailingly cooperative in the preparation of this manuscript, and the authors are particularly indebted to Nancy Roberts, whose commitment to *Our Changing Population* extends back in time to the virtual beginning of the entire project. Others at Prentice Hall who have made this book possible are our production editor, Serena Hoffman, and our supplements editor, Sharon Chambliss.

Finally, we collectively thank our wives, who have been patient and supportive over the months and actually years that were required to bring this book to fruition.

Richard T. Gill
Nathan Glazer
Stephan A. Thernstrom

# Part I
# HISTORIC POPULATION TRENDS IN AMERICA

**1**

# Too Many People, or Too Few?

When the first images of the earth were beamed back from space, many Americans had two reactions. One was pride in the beauty of our planet: We were not desolate, cratered and forbidding like the moon or Mars, but an inviting blue with a splendid white tracery from our life-giving atmosphere.

The second reaction was concern: Viewed from this grand prospect, we seemed so small and vulnerable. Was this all there was to our planet? Did all those immense areas—forests, deserts, steppes, oceans, polar regions—add up only to this attractive but rather diminutive spaceship? And this led immediately to another question: How many travelers could this pleasant vehicle actually carry over time? Five billion? Ten billion? A trillion? Were we nearing earth's carrying capacity? Or very far from it? Or was this even the right way to put the question?

However the question is put, there is no doubt that, from a world point of view, one of the most intriguing issues of our time is what is happening to the population of the species *Homo sapiens*. Have human beings created a "population bomb" ready to explode? Or is the bomb already defused? Are we in imminent danger, or simply on the crest of a new wave of continuing human progress?

## THE STUDY OF POPULATION— WHY IT MATTERS

In this book, we shall be largely concerned with the changing population of one country, the United States. However, we shall have many occasions to refer to the worldwide population concerns we have just mentioned. We shall find in all cases that they provide a context in which our own population problems are illuminated.

Sometimes this illumination takes the form of deep similarities. Our own population expansion during the past two centuries is part and parcel of a general worldwide population expansion during this same period. Table 1-1 and Figure 1-1 show how dramatic the world's modern population expansion has been. This recent growth has no real parallel in earlier human history. In the year 1 A.D. estimated world population was around 300 million; it took nearly 1,700

**TABLE 1-1: World Population Growth, 1500–1990**

| Year | Population | Year | Population |
|------|-----------|------|-----------|
| 1500 | 475,000,000 | 1950 | 2,486,000,000 |
| 1650 | 500,000,000 | 1960 | 3,049,000,000 |
| 1750 | 700,000,000 | 1970 | 3,575,000,000 |
| 1800 | 900,000,000 | 1980 | 4,453,000,000 |
| 1850 | 1,171,000,000 | 1990[a] | 5,319,719,000 |
| 1900 | 1,608,000,000 | | |

[a] Projected, *World Population Profile, 1987*, WP-87, U.S. Department of Commerce, Bureau of the Census.

*Sources:* United Nations; U.S. Bureau of the Census.

**TABLE 1-2: U.S. Population Growth, 1790–1990**

| Year | Population (thousands) | Percentage Increase per Decade |
|------|----------------------|-------------------------------|
| 1790 | 3,929 | — |
| 1800 | 5,308 | 35.1 |
| 1810 | 7,240 | 36.4 |
| 1820 | 9,638 | 33.1 |
| 1830 | 12,866 | 33.5 |
| 1840 | 17,069 | 32.7 |
| 1850 | 23,192 | 35.9 |
| 1860 | 31,443 | 35.6 |
| 1870 | 39,818 | 26.6 |
| 1880 | 50,156 | 26.0 |
| 1890 | 62,948 | 25.5 |
| 1900 | 75,995 | 20.7 |
| 1910 | 91,972 | 21.0 |
| 1920 | 105,711 | 14.9 |
| 1930 | 122,775 | 16.1 |
| 1940 | 131,669 | 7.2 |
| 1950 | 150,697 | 14.5 |
| 1960 | 179,323 | 19.0 |
| 1970 | 203,235 | 13.3 |
| 1980 | 226,546 | 11.5 |
| 1990 | 248,710[a] | 9.8 |

[a] Unadjusted; see Appendix, pp. 475–478.

*Source:* U.S. Bureau of the Census.

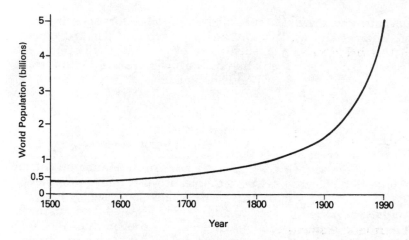

**FIGURE 1–1: Estimated World Population Growth, 1500–1990**

years for it to double. Between 1950 and 1990, world population also doubled, accomplishing in forty years what had earlier taken 17 centuries.

Table 1-2 and Figure 1-2 show that the United States, with its more than sixtyfold population increase over the past two hundred years, was no laggard in this process of expansion. In this respect, our population history is very similar to that of the world in general.

In other respects, however, it is often very useful to *contrast* the United States'

population history with that of other nations. Thus, to take an obvious (and very important) illustration, our population growth during the modern period started earlier, decelerated sooner, and had a vastly different relationship to the general processes of industrialization and economic growth than did the population growth of much of the less developed world where the majority of the earth's population currently lives.

Speaking quite generally, however, we can find three reasons that the study of

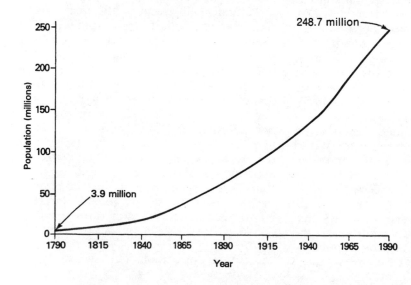

**FIGURE 1–2: U.S. Population Growth, 1790–1990**

*Source:* U.S. Bureau of the Census.

population change is important, and these apply equally to the United States and to other nations.

### Populations Change in Unexpected Ways

The first general point is that the populations of the various countries of the world not only change over time but often change in quite unexpected ways.

This is an extremely important point to keep in mind because there is a general tendency in the population field simply to project into the future the patterns of the past. This tendency was already apparent in the work of Thomas Robert Malthus (1766–1834) whose **geometric** growth of population versus an **arithmetic** growth of food supplies we'll discuss in a moment. It appeared much more recently in the so-called Doomsday growth models popular in the early 1970s. Let any variable—population, pollution, fossil fuel consumption, nuclear waste—grow at a compound interest rate over a sufficient period of time and the system is virtually guaranteed to break down.[1]

The fact is that we often get changes in the rates of change of these variables, and sometimes changes in the direction of these changes, and that these variations in both rates and directions of change are often quite unexpected. In the case of population change, this point is obvious, sometimes embarrassingly so for the professional prognosticators. In the United States, for example, most observers failed to anticipate the Baby Boom that occurred after World War II—a major phenomenon—and then went on to fail to predict the severity of the Baby Bust that followed immediately thereafter.

This first point suggests, negatively, that simple projections of past trends into the future are always suspect in the population field. More positively, it suggests that a deeper analysis of the factors affecting population can lead to substantial improvements on such naive projections. Developing such an analysis is a major reason for the study of population change.

### Human Decisions Affect Population Change

A deeper analysis of population change is also required because, unlike the rotation of the planets and stars, such change is clearly and deeply affected by **human decisions.** Indeed, it is probably possible to go even further and argue that it is, in our age, *increasingly* affected by such decisions.

We shall have countless occasions in later chapters to point out the ways in which human decisions can affect the rate and direction of population trends. Sometimes these decisions are highly personal. Will we get married? At what age? How many children will we want to have? Collective

At other times, the decisions are made collectively. What level of immigration should be permitted? How stringently should prohibitions against illegal immigrants be enforced? In this case, the issues typically involve some form of legislation or other public action.

Often **private** and **public** decisions become intertwined. Indeed, sometimes the issue is precisely whether a decision is appropriately a private *or* a public one. Abortion is a prime case in point. At one extreme, the abortion decision is argued to be wholly that of the pregnant woman, no matter what her age or circumstances, no matter what her parents, husband, boyfriend, community, or state think about the decision. At the other extreme, some believe that the abortion decision is wholly public and that there is no private right to have an abortion even when rape, incest, genetic defect, or any other mitigating factor is involved.

Whether private, public, or a mixture of the two, our decisions will largely shape our future population. Thus, we study population change to ensure that these decisions will be intelligent and informed.

### The Deep Consequences of Those Decisions

A major reason for wanting those decisions to be wise ones is that population changes have such *deep effects* on our society, and ultimately on ourselves, our children, and our children's children.

Take, for example, a decision that young adults have been making in the United States over the past two centuries—to have fewer babies. If we compared the 1980s with the 1780s, we would find that modern American women on the average were having *only a quarter of the number of babies* they were having two centuries earlier. We shall be investigating this "flight from fertility," as we call it, at length during the course of this book.

For the moment, we notice only the profound consequences of this decision on U.S. society. For one thing, it leads quite directly to a general *aging* of the society. Fewer babies mean fewer young people and an increase in the average age of our population. The implications of this societal aging are everywhere around us. Fewer young people could, for example, mean less crime. On the other hand, we have to consider the financing of Social Security, the mounting burden of health care costs, the possible extension of that burden into long-term nursing home care and catastrophic care. As the proportion of the young in the society declines and the proportion of the elderly rises, all such issues take on a greater weight and significance.

But there is also the question of younger people themselves. Without question, a primary function of the family in Western civilization has been to rear children and prepare them for entry into adulthood. But if young adults are deciding to have very few children, perhaps one or two only, perhaps none at all, what then happens to

the family unit? Does it lose its point and purpose?

Our decisions about having babies may also affect our immigration policies, for the decline in the number of young people is bound to have some impact on the labor force with which our society provides incomes to all its members, young and old. If we have too few young workers coming up through the pipeline, will we be tempted to fill the gap by importing cheap labor from abroad? But if we open our borders wide, what effect will this have on our political, social, and cultural future?

In short, population decisions will have a bearing on the future of U.S. society at the most fundamental level. And this is the final, and ultimately the most important, reason that a careful study of those issues is now a requirement for a truly educated citizenry.

### THE HISTORIC DRIVE FOR MORE PEOPLE

One of these issues is a quite obvious one: How big a population do we want to have? Would we like ideally to have more people than we now have? Or fewer? Related to this question, but not exactly the same, is the issue of the *rate of population growth.* Do we consider it to be an advantage to have a population that is expanding, or one that is contracting? Or is the ideal stability, as many Americans in the 1960s and 1970s began to say—that is, **Zero Population Growth (ZPG)?**

Even to think about these questions will require most of us to pull back a little from the mood that was established in the 1960s–1970s period and that was reinforced by those pictures of the earth from space we referred to earlier. And, in pulling back, we will be forced to recognize that during most of human history on this planet, large and growing populations were considered an unqualifiedly desirable objective. This was so for a variety of reasons.

*[handwritten margin notes: "man made to control pop. war also pop-control"]*

### The Smallness of World Population in Premodern Times

As Table 1-1 indicates, as recently as 1650 the entire world's population probably did not exceed 500 million people—less than half the current population of China alone. This figure already represents a substantial advance over the population in prehistoric times. There has been, on average, a slow expansion of the world's population over the millennia since the appearance of *Homo sapiens*, an advance that was accelerated by the development of settled agriculture and the domestication of animals some ten thousand years ago. By modern standards, however, this earlier rate of expansion was extremely slow.[2] We are currently *adding* to the world's population an equivalent of the *entire 1650 world population* every five years or so!

### The Vulnerability of Premodern Populations

It wasn't just that premodern populations were small; they were also quite capable of getting smaller. Periods of advance were frequently followed by periods of decline as a consequence of war, plague, pestilence, drought, flood, famine, earthquake, and other natural and man-made disasters. During the course of the fourteenth century, it is estimated that Europe's population was reduced 40 percent by the Black Death. Even before this, European populations had been on something of a roller-coaster, rising during the height of the Roman Empire, then declining again as Europe entered the Dark Ages; rising again until the fourteenth century, then declining; then rising again after A.D. 1500, now persistently, as we come to the modern period. Warfare could be disastrous, as in the predations of Ghengis Khan, or in the Thirty Years' War (1618–1648), which wiped out a huge fraction of the population of Germany. Famines in Egypt, China, and India took the lives of millions of people. Even as late as the 1870s, a famine in the northern Chinese provinces is estimated to have taken 10 million or more lives.

Of course, famines still occur today. Massive epidemics like acquired immune deficiency syndrome (AIDS) could sweep the earth. Furthermore, modern warfare has potentialities for destruction that could dwarf all ancient disasters.

The fact of the matter, however, is that the forces of population growth since 1650, and particularly since the Industrial Revolution of the eighteenth and nineteenth centuries, have been so powerful that even major catastrophes—like World Wars I and II—have scarcely made a dent in, and certainly have not reversed, the world's burgeoning numbers.

### Large Populations Were Considered National Assets

Not only was there little to fear from large populations in earlier centuries, there was, or was believed to be, much good to be derived from them. This was especially true at the beginning of the modern period in Europe, when centralized states were emerging from the more fragmented political structure of medieval life. The so-called mercantilist statesmen and philosophers of the sixteenth and seventeenth centuries were uniformly devoted to population growth, sometimes passionately. Whether to increase the tax base, the military power of the sovereign, or the general glory of the state, mercantilist governments would often explicitly adopt "pro-natalist" policies, exempting married men from certain taxes, granting special pensions to parents, and placing surtaxes on the single and childless.

Thus, as the Western world entered the era of the Industrial Revolution, the predominant view remained that vigorous population growth was an asset rather than a liability. Emerging from a much smaller world, where life was "nasty, brutish and short," where national survival, power, and prestige could depend on the sheer weight of one's numbers, who could possibly question this central proposition?

## THE DISMAL SCIENCE
## OF MALTHUS AND RICARDO

But, of course, that proposition could be questioned. And it was questioned emphatically toward the end of the 18th century. The questioner was Thomas Robert Malthus, and his dramatic theory was presented to the world in *An Essay on the Principle of Population as It Affects the Future Improvement of Society,* the first edition of which was published in 1798.

### The Malthusian Ratios

There are many ironies connected with the timing of Malthus's *Essay.* One is that he brought a pessimistic attitude to bear on humanity's economic future just at the time when the Industrial Revolution was making possible the first real breakthrough into what would become "the affluent society." Another is that, particularly in his first edition, he emphasized the unbridled power of population growth just as the Western world was about to enter an age of unprecedented population control. Still, the Malthusian approach has, at least in spirit, many advocates to this day.

As we have already mentioned, Malthus put the problem in terms of two **ratios.** Population, unless checked, had a natural tendency to double every 25 years, thus growing at a **geometric ratio:** 1, 2, 4, 8, 16, 32, . . . Food production, however, could at best be expected to grow at an **arithmetic ratio:** 1, 2, 3, 4, 5, 6, . . . Thus, unless checked, population growth would soon outpace any conceivable increase in food supplies.

Malthusian pessimism consisted in the belief that the likely checks to population growth would be "positive"—that is, those that raised the death rate. The general term Malthus used was "misery."

There were, admittedly, other possible checks of a "preventive" nature. These were those that lowered the birth rate. As a minister of the cloth, Parson Malthus nat-urally approved of "moral restraint," which was defined as "restraint from marriage which is not followed by irregular gratifications." As a practical matter, however, he feared that preventive restraints might quickly descend to the level of "vice." "Vice" consisted of "promiscuous intercourse, unnatural passions, violations of the marriage bed, and improper arts to conceal the consequences of irregular connections." Translated: Malthus was no fan of prostitution, homosexuality, adultery, or birth control.[3]

Thus, in Malthus's view, the greater likelihood was that the effective checks on population would be positive rather than preventive. Instead of lowered birth rates we would have higher mortality rates as a result of plague, famine, war, and the general tendency of the population to expand quickly and fill up any available economic space.

### The Ricardian Systemization

This general view was systematized and incorporated into the structure of British political economy by Malthus's good friend David Ricardo (1782–1823). Actually, Ricardo and Malthus often disagreed on economic issues, particularly on the possibility of depressions in an industrial society. (Malthus believed that frequent "universal gluts" were possible; Ricardo, on theoretical grounds, denied this.) On the matter of population, however, they were of one mind.

In his *Principles of Political Economy and Taxation* (1817), Ricardo put the whole issue in terms of the supply and demand for labor. When farmers or industrialists— "capitalists" in Ricardian terminology— have high profits, they try to hire more laborers. This increased demand for labor will bid up the wage rate. But now the Malthusian principle comes into play. As soon as wages are bid up above a low "subsistence level," people begin to marry earlier, to have more surviving babies, and in general to expand their numbers. This increase in the supply of labor, however, will force the wage back down to the "subsistence level" once again. The population is larger, but the wage has returned to the level from which it started.

But if wages are lower again, does this mean that the capitalists' profits are going up? Not necessarily. For there is an underlying constraint operating here: the fundamentally limited quantity of available agricultural land and, indeed, of natural resources generally. Each time population expands, we are forced to cultivate this limited land more and more intensively or, alternatively, to have recourse to marginal lands of poorer quality.

In either case, we face what is the real limiting factor in the Malthus-Ricardo world: *the law of diminishing returns.* We get less and less additional output as we cultivate our land more intensively or use inferior lands. This is the fundamental reason that a *geometrically* growing population can only bring (at best) an *arithmetically* growing food supply. It is also the reason that population is virtually bound to bump up against the positive check of famine and below-subsistence wages, and that profits as well as wages end up getting squeezed.

Finally, one might add, it is also the reason that Malthus and Ricardo earned for their subject the name "the dismal science," a designation that has clung to economics ever since.[4]

## FILLING UP A CONTINENT

This emphasis on limited land and "diminishing returns" will explain immediately why the Malthus-Ricardo population doctrine had relatively little resonance in the United States of that period, and even less in colonial times. From the beginning, and well into the twentieth century, our national interest seemed clearly identified with population growth.

### The Smallness of Our Early Population

Anyone who visits the reconstructed Plimoth Plantation in Massachusetts at Thanksgiving time will see a parade—a very *small* parade—representing individually each of the settlers and their families who survived the first cruel winter in New England. Considering the vastness of the wilderness about them, one has to be impressed by the immensity of the challenge that this tiny band of survivors had undertaken to face. In 1650 there were probably no more than 50,000 settlers in the colonies; by a century later, perhaps around 1.2 million. At the time of our first census in 1790, the count was still under 4 million.

Of course, new settlers were not the only inhabitants of the North American continent. Although the Native American population was much denser in areas south of what is today the continental United States, there were substantial numbers of Native Americans in the areas that were eventually colonized. Unfortunately, the number is difficult to determine, with estimates for the area that was to become the United States ranging from a low of 750,000 to as many as 10 to 12 million Native Americans. What is not difficult to determine, however, is that the appearance of Europeans in North America, and even more strikingly in Central and South America, was an unmitigated demographic disaster for many different tribes. Their numbers were radically reduced, especially by disease and epidemic, and it has only been during the last century that the Native American population of the United States has begun to grow again.[5]

Under any circumstances, even counting the Native American population, the number of people inhabiting our continent was small by the standards of Europe and Asia of the day, and certainly by reference to the massive population increase we have experienced subsequently.

## Our Effective Land Resources Were Increasing

Not only was our population small in relation to our land area, but we were constantly adding to that area. The Malthus-Ricardo picture of population pressing against a relatively fixed natural resource base had little relevance to a nation where land acquisitions were constantly expanding our domain. We virtually doubled our land area with the Louisiana Purchase (1803) alone, and further acquisitions before the Civil War added over a million square miles to the nation's lands. Despite our rapid population growth, these added lands meant that the number of Americans per square mile was actually *declining* between 1800 and 1820; between 1800 and 1860, this number rose only slightly, from 6.1 to 10.6—both extremely small numbers, and certainly representing no excessive pressure on our agricultural base.

## Population Growth as a Positive Asset

Not only did our historic population growth create very little pressure on our natural resources, it had, or was certainly believed to have, many decidedly *favorable* effects on our society. Three factors might be mentioned:

1. *The national market and economies of scale.* As the size of our nation grew, we developed a very large national market. This made it possible for U.S. firms to enjoy economies of scale—the benefits of mass production—in many different industries. These economies were so great that they were widely thought to be a major advantage that we had over the much more nationally fragmented European markets. The development of the European Common Market in our own era has been to a large degree an effort to compensate for this U.S. advantage. Thus, it can be said that, during much of our history, population growth was leading to increasing rather than diminishing returns.

2. *Population growth versus economic stagnation.* Many people also believed that population *growth* (as distinguished from population *size*) could be a major factor in promoting a vigorous, high-employment economy. This line of thought was developed primarily during the Great Depression of the 1930s, when it was noticed that (a) our rate of population growth was declining and (b) we were facing the worst unemployment condition in U.S. history. One might have thought it would work the other way—the more you added to your population, the harder it would be to find jobs for the added workers. However, according to the theories of John Maynard Keynes (1883–1946), high levels of employment depended on high levels of business **investment,** and population growth could be a major factor stimulating this investment. Thus, the argument was made that our prosperity during the eighteenth and nineteenth centuries had been greatly aided by our rapid population growth; by the same token, the fear developed that, if the declining rate of growth of our population in the twentieth century continued, we might be facing a future of economic stagnation.[6]

3. *The melting pot as a source of national pride and strength.* Although the greater part of our historic population growth resulted from an excess of births over deaths, the United States was also the beneficiary of massive immigration during much of its national existence. Not only did the immigrants add greatly to the economic strength of our country (because, for example, they were heavily weighted towards the working-age groups compared with the native population), but they also added a social and cultural dimension that, many observers believe, made our society more fluid, open, pluralistic, and democratic than the more structured societies of Europe and Asia. Despite many outcries against immigration

at various times in our history, there is little doubt that most Americans have taken pride in the fact that we are a "nation of immigrants" and that our society has been flexible enough to preserve both a national identity and the richness of ethnic and cultural **diversity.**

In total, it can be said that a large and expanding population was considered a favorable condition during most of our life as a nation. Americans took pride in the growing national census tallies just as, at the local level, did most towns and cities take pride in their growing numbers. Until World War II at least, it would have been a rare Chamber of Commerce that would have bragged about the declining population of its region.

## ENTER THE POPULATION EXPLOSION

And then quite suddenly the mood shifted. Certainly by the 1960s, both in the United States and abroad, a revolution in our thinking about population growth had taken place. If the historic answer to the title of this chapter had characteristically been "Too few people," the answer in the 1960s and early 1970s was almost uniformly, "Too many," and "Growing much too fast!"

### The Population Revolution in the LDCs

From a worldwide point of view, this seemed virtually self-evident. Here is the assessment of Dr. Paul R. Ehrlich in his book *The Population Bomb*, which sold two million copies in the decade following its first publication in 1968:

> The battle to feed all humanity is over. In the 1970s and 1980s hundreds of millions of people will starve to death in spite of any crash programs embarked upon now. . . . The current situation of global overpopulation is so serious, and the built-in potential for further population increase is so great, that the only sensible strategy for humanity

today is to *end population growth and start population decline as rapidly as is humanely possible.* . . .[7]

A major factor in this reversal of attitudes was, of course, the extraordinary developments that were taking place in the less developed countries of the world (the LDCs). Putting the global situation in its most dramatic form, we could make a convincing case for the following propositions:

1. *The current rate of world population growth is unsustainable.* As already mentioned, the population of the world roughly doubled from 1950 to 1990. Even a somewhat lower rate of increase would lead to a world population of 9 billion by the year 2030, 21 billion by the year 2110, and, in another thousand years, perhaps *60 million billion* people.[8] Incidentally, that number looks like this:

60,000,000,000,000,000

For comparison, approximate world population in 1990 looks like this:

5,300,000,000

2. *This population explosion is heavily centered in the LDCs.* In contrast to what one might have expected from Malthusianism, modern population growth is much more rapid in poor countries than in rich ones. Already by 1985, the LDCs had come to comprise three-quarters of the world's population. By some projections, they would reach 82 percent of the world's population by the year 2010, and close to 90 percent by the end of the next century.

3. *The pattern of population growth in the LDCs has been strikingly different from the historic experience of the West.* Essentially, the poor countries of the modern world have imported a public health revolution from the industrial world. This has made possible drastic drops in their death rates while birth rates remained relatively high—and all this in advance of major economic, social, and political development. In the West, the in-

crease in population in the modern era was part of a larger process of social, economic, and technological advance. Could it be that this premature population explosion would inhibit that larger process in the LDCs? And if it did, would that mean that population would keep expanding until, as Dr. Ehrlich predicted, hundreds of millions of people starved to death—that is, until the death rate, lowered by medicine, began to rise again through malnutrition and starvation?

### The Baby Boom in the Early Postwar Period

This alarming situation in the LDCs was given added weight by an extraordinary occurrence in the United States and, to a lesser degree, in other industrial nations. In contrast to the 1930s and early 1940s, when many scholars were worried about slackening population growth and the possibilities of economic "stagnation," in the 1950s we found ourselves in the midst of a **Baby Boom.** As the veterans returned from World War II, it seemed that almost everyone wanted to get married, apparently the younger the better; people everywhere seemed to want a house in suburbia, where, amid lawns, trees, and flowers, they would raise a large, happy family. The birth rate soared—so much so that one commentator wondered if, because of our affluence, we had entered a whole new stage of society. Instead of spending our vast new postwar wealth on more appliances and other material possessions, perhaps we would spend it on raising children, a large family being our great new "consumption good."[9]

Although the industrialized nations still were not matching the LDCs in terms of rates of population increase during the first two or three postwar decades, nevertheless it could be argued that population growth in the developed world had, *from an ecological point of view,* far more serious repercussions than even the higher rates of growth in the LDCs.

The reason, of course, was that our production per person (per capita GNP)

was so much higher. This high GNP led to (1) a much greater per capita consumption of nonrenewable natural resources (fossil fuels like oil, coal, and natural gas being the most obvious examples), and (2) a much greater per capita production of pollutants and toxic wastes.

Did this mean that population growth in the West was, on balance, more or less of a threat than population growth in the LDCs? Dr. Ehrlich thought it was more of a threat—*far* more, particularly in the case of the United States. Measured by the degree of "assault" on the environment, he concluded, "the birth of an average American baby is about twice the disaster for the Earth as the birth of an average English baby, and some 57 times the disaster of the birth of an average Indian baby!"[10] Clearly, this fifty-seven-fold disaster ratio far exceeded any differences in the U.S. versus Indian population growth rates, particularly during our Baby Boom.

Meanwhile, a new danger for the United States was being discovered. In 1985 the former governor of Colorado, Richard D. Lamm, and his colleague Gary Imhoff published *The Immigration Time Bomb,* in which they argued for severely restricting immigration to the United States on what appeared to be strictly Malthusian grounds: "What has been true for most of human history . . . is that human populations have been limited by the resources available to them."[11]

Thus, as it appeared to many in the 1960s and early 1970s and even today, the population problems of the world, though different in different contexts, were essentially universal. Humanity was outproducing in terms of numbers of people and quantities of goods the carrying capacity of the planet. No longer should we pride ourselves on our wonderful ability to fill up all the empty spaces of the world. No longer should we brag about how big our families were, how fast our town was growing. Henceforth, small was better.

Everywhere.

## HAVE WE OVERSHOT THE MARK?

But are we sure about all this? Is it possible that we are about to enter another historic watershed—so soon, in fact, that we have barely had time to adjust to the previous one?

In 1987 a best-selling book on population issues was *The Birth Dearth* by Ben J. Wattenberg, a senior fellow of the American Enterprise Institute. And this book was sounding the alarums not about population "bombs" but about population decline. The author was seriously urging Americans to bring forth *more* of those fifty-seven-fold disasters—the average American baby!

In light of what we have just said about the worldwide population explosion, how could such a view possibly be defended?

One should note immediately that there are few if any scholars urging a pro-natalist policy in the case of the LDCs. There is almost universal agreement that a lowering of birth rates and a slowing of population growth in the vast majority of these countries would be beneficial to the countries themselves and to the world. The youthful age structures of the LDCs are in themselves enough to ensure that these nations will have substantially increasing populations in the future even though the numbers of children *per mother* were to decline drastically.[12]

From the point of view of our study, of course, the question of desirable population size is focused on the industrialized world and the United States in particular. Has anything happened in this quarter to bring about another sea-change in attitudes?

Part of the answer clearly lies in the fact that the last quarter of a century has seen a sharp reversal of our immediate post–World War II experience as far as having babies is concerned. As already mentioned, we went from our unexpected Baby Boom to an equally unexpected Baby Bust with unprecedented rapidity. Nor is there any evidence that the sharp reduction in the size of our families is merely temporary. As the

title of Wattenberg's book phrased it, we have entered the era of the birth dearth.

What was causing Wattenberg's concern? The subtitle of the book was *What Happens When People in Free Countries Don't Have Enough Babies?* Clearly, he was worried about the size of the U.S. population (and of the Free World generally) relative to that of other countries. But this was not his only concern. The book was a far-reaching plea for increasing the U.S. birth rate on a variety of grounds.

Briefly, Wattenberg argued that a continuation of our low birth rate will lead to the following:

• *Economic problems:* We may not have enough young workers to support our increasing numbers of elderly persons; our national market may shrink; we may face collapsing investment opportunities as in the "stagnationist" theories of the 1930s.

• *Geopolitical problems:* The United States and the Free World will have declining power and influence as our populations plummet relative to those of the Communist bloc and the LDCs; with soon-to-be-falling populations, the Western world is committing geopolitical suicide.

• *Personal and social problems:* Life without children is less meaningful; the institution of the family is under siege; numerous social and cultural problems arise if we try to substitute large-scale immigration—particularly from poverty-stricken, less well educated societies—for the children we are not having.

In short, for Ben Wattenberg, the birth of an American baby, far from being a fifty-seven-fold disaster, is at least a triple (economic, geopolitical, and personal) blessing.

Indeed, he is not alone in this position. Although the dramatic decline and/or abandonment of the Communist regimes of eastern Europe has altered the world's geopolitical situation in ways no one, including Wattenberg, could have imagined even a few years earlier, some of his other concerns about low birth rates and declining population are clearly shared by others. In 1990, for example, the prime minister of Japan (where the birth dearth is even more evident than in the United States) warned about the possibility of worker shortages, overburdened welfare systems for the elderly, and general inflation if the extremely low rates of childbearing continued. Throughout the industrial world in general, there is a growing awareness that, instead of forecasting the *rate of advance* of our populations, we may soon be in the position of estimating their *rate of decline*.

Like Malthus and Ricardo, who envisaged "subsistence wages" for the future just when the great breakthrough of the Industrial Revolution was occurring, have we been discovering the "population bomb" just at the moment when our real problem is going to be our failure to "replace" ourselves?

## THE TASK BEFORE US

How difficult it is to answer this question may be indicated by Figure 1-3, which shows projections of the U.S. population until the year 2080 developed by the U.S. Bureau of the Census in 1989. Actually, these projections represent only 3 out of the 30 the

Census Bureau makes, each using different assumptions. As all Census Bureau demographers are quick to inform us, projections of this kind are not to be confused with forecasts. The former simply show the mathematical results of making certain assumptions. (As a practical matter, the middle series is often thought to be the most likely, and is sometimes used as the equivalent of a forecast.)

Leaving technicalities aside,[13] one cannot look at this graph without being impressed by the *range* of future outcomes that are at least considered possible. These go from a U.S. population in 2080 of *501.5 million* (highest series), more than double our population when the projections were prepared, to one of *184.6 million* (lowest series), a reduction of almost 25 percent.

Doubling—or reduced by a quarter! Population bomb—or birth dearth! Which will it be? Obviously, we will not be able to answer this question definitively in this book. What we can do is provide a framework of fact and analysis that will enable us to approach population problems in an intelligent way.

Our plan of attack is as follows:

*Part I:* In the remainder of this first part of the book we will develop an understanding of the major factors that have

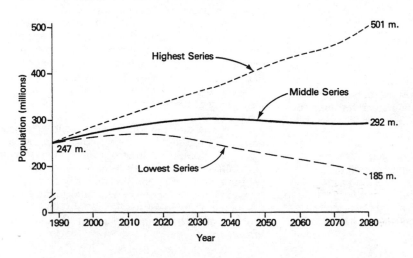

**FIGURE 1–3: Projections of U.S. Population, 1988–2080**

*Source:* "Population Estimates and Projections, 1989," *Current Population Reports,* Series P-25, No. 1018, U.S. Department of Commerce, Bureau of the Census, pp. 29–31.

influenced population change in the United States. Our emphasis will be heavily historical.

• *Parts II–V:* In the large middle section of the book, we shall show how these historical factors have affected the different age generations of our society, including also the generations of immigrants. Besides considering the specific factors that have shaped these groups, we will also study the major current issues that each generation poses, both in itself and in relation to other generations.

• *Part VI:* In our final part, we will look forward into the future, fully aware of all the difficulties involved, but also now armed with a considerable knowledge of how past and present demographic change does occur. Incidentally, we shall not hesitate to be speculative in this last section, and for a very good reason. Given the rapidity of modern change, and particularly in areas like biogenetics that could have truly revolutionary consequences for our future population, to be cautious is virtually to *guarantee* serious error.

Thus, we will travel the long route from past to posterity, with (we trust) sufficient scenery along the way to make the journey an inviting one.

## SUMMARY

1. The study of population is important because: (a) populations often change in complex, unexpected ways; (b) our decisions deeply affect these changes; and (c) the consequences of population change on our social, cultural, political and economic life are so profound.

2. During most of the world's history, large and increasing populations were usually favored. The world's population in the premodern period was quite small (by 1650, it was only around 500 million), and highly vulnerable to war, plague, drought, and other disasters. Also, larger populations could mean greater national political strength.

3. In the late eighteenth and early nineteenth centuries, Thomas Robert Malthus and his political economist friend David Ricardo punctured this favorable view with their "dismal science" projections. A geometrically growing population, they said, would run into land and natural resource constraints, bringing "diminishing returns" and keeping most of society at a subsistence level.

4. The Malthus-Ricardo pessimism had little resonance for the United States during most of our history because we had abundant and increasing land resources, and because a growing population brought the efficiencies of a large national market and (as some believed) helped us stave off economic stagnation.

5. After World War II, however, as Americans became aware of the exceptionally rapid rates of population growth in the LDCs and began to experience their own Baby Boom, attitudes changed sharply. Many argued that Malthusian dangers lay ahead; at a minimum, our rapid population growth, particularly in countries like the United States with high per capita gross national product (GNP), seemed clearly to be endangering the ecology of our planet.

6. No sooner had ZPG become the fashionable goal, however, than voices were raised encouraging American women to have more babies. The Baby Bust, beginning in the mid-1960s, raised the prospect of an aging society, with too few young people to support the elderly. Fears of economic stagnation were raised again, as were alarms about the decline of U.S. geopolitical influence and the weakening of the American family.

7. The difficulty of deciding what views are correct is suggested by the enormous range of possible U.S. population futures, from a high of over 500 million people in the year 2080 to a low of well under 200 million. This difficulty also underlines the importance of a careful study of the factors (including our own personal decisions) that will influence our changing population in the years ahead.

## KEY CONCEPTS FOR REVIEW

Decisions affecting population change: private; public; mixed

Smallness and vulnerability of premodern populations

Malthusian ratios: geometric; arithmetic

Advantages of U.S. population growth: national market; investment opportunities; immigration and diversity

Population explosion in the LDCs

Baby Boom

Baby Bust

Zero Population Growth (ZPG)

Effects of the "birth dearth": economic; geopolitical; social

Projections versus forecasts

Wide range of U.S. population projections for the year 2080

## QUESTIONS FOR DISCUSSION

1.  Describe a number of ways in which you feel that your decisions, both personally and through voting and/or participating in organized group activities, will have an impact on our population future. What meaning would you give to the statement: "Population change used to be largely a product of traditional or external forces; now it is largely subject to conscious human control."

2.  What are the main factors explaining the historic desire of most countries and peoples to expand their numbers?

3.  Explain the Malthusian ratios and show how Ricardo was able to treat population growth in a supply-and-demand analysis. Why did these early theories have little relevance to the American experience through most of our history?

4.  "Although the LDCs have far higher rates of population growth than industrialized nations like the United States, population growth in the latter is actually a far more serious danger from a global point of view." Discuss this statement, giving the arguments pro and con.

5.  What is meant by the "birth dearth"? Do you feel that whether American women have few or many babies will have a serious effect on our future (a) economy, (b) world influence, (c) family institutions? Some effect? Virtually no effect?

6.  Anticipating what lies ahead in this book, what would you imagine to be the main factors that would explain the very wide range of Census Bureau projections for the year 2080 (see p. 15)? Rank these factors according to what you believe to be their relative importance in explaining the huge difference between the highest and lowest projections. (After finishing Part I of the text, come back to these answers and see if you would change the factors and their ranking.)

## NOTES

1.  The best known of these pessimistic forecasts are contained in Jay Forrester's *World Dynamics* (Cambridge, Mass.: Wright-Allen Press, 1971); the Club of Rome's *Limits to Growth* (New York: Universe Books, 1972); and "A Blueprint for Survival" from the *Ecologist* (Tom Stacey Ltd. and Penguin Books, 1972). Most scholars today feel that these models made an inadequate allowance for the adjustments that human institutions and societies could and would make to the problems that they anticipated.

2.  Even very slow rates of expansion can, however, lead to fairly large population increases over very long periods of time. Thus the United Nations' "conjectures" for world population from 7000–6000 B.C. to A.D. 1 are from 5–10 million to 200–400 million. From A.D. 1 to A.D. 1650, the increase is from 200–400 million to 470–545 million. During this latter period the annual *rate* of increase is listed at 0.0 percent—*less than one-tenth of one percent.* See United Nations, *The Determinants and Con-*

*sequences of Population Trends,* Population Studies, No. 50, 1973, p. 10.

3. It is ironic that, whereas Malthus himself urged "moral restraint" and was opposed to contraception, the birth control movement that developed in England later in the nineteenth century is usually called *neo-Malthusianism.* What these later advocates had in common with Malthus was their alarm about the population problem, not its likely solution.

4. The "dismal science" title was given to economics by the British essayist Thomas Carlyle. The designation was a bit unfair in that Malthus's theory became somewhat more flexible and optimistic in subsequent editions of his *Essay.* Also, we might note in passing, even in Ricardo's rather grim world not everyone is worse off because of population growth. If you happened to own land (which becomes increasingly scarce as the number of people grows), you would do quite well. Land rents can be expected to rise persistently as population increases. Ricardo felt, however, that landlords contributed little to economic progress.

5. For further discussion of the demographic fate of the Native American population, and sources for further reading, see Chapter 2, pp. 30–31, 35, and Chapter 3, p. 55.

6. The most famous proponent of this view was Professor Alvin Hansen of Harvard University. See especially his presidential address to the American Economic Association, December 28, 1938, "Economic Progress and Declining Population Growth," *American Economic Review, 29*(1), Part I, March, 1939. It should be noted that while Hansen and his followers feared "stagnation," they also believed that the problem was solvable with appropriately Keynesian fiscal and monetary policies.

7. Paul R. Ehrlich, *The Population Bomb,* rev. ed. (New York: Ballantine Books, 1978), pp. xi, 24–25, 224.

8. For these calculations, see Pranay Gupte, *The Crowded Earth: People and the Politics of Population* (New York: W. W. Norton, 1984), p. 20.

9. This possibility was mentioned in W. W. Rostow's best-selling book *The Stages of Economic Growth* (Cambridge: Cambridge University Press, 1960), pp. 10–11, 91–92.

10. Ehrlich, *The Population Bomb,* pp. 202–203.

11. Richard D. Lamm and Gary Imhoff, *The Immigration Time Bomb* (New York: E. P. Dutton, 1985), pp. 6–7.

12. We shall return to the question of the LDCs in Chapter 25. We simply note here that there are some grounds for hope that population problems in these countries, however serious, may ultimately prove to be transient. This is because of dramatic declines in the birth rates in some (though definitely not all) of the LDCs. Thus, for example, between 1960 and 1980 the birth rate fell in South Korea by 44 percent, in Taiwan by 48 percent, in Thailand by 32 percent, in Malaysia by 31 percent, in Brazil by 30 percent, in Turkey by 26 percent, and in Indonesia by 24 percent. The largest LDC, China, has with variable success instituted a rather severe one-child-per-family policy in the cities. Among the many useful discussions of population and development prospects in the LDCs, the reader might consult Just Faaland, ed., *Population and the World Economy in the 21st Century,* Norwegian Nobel Institute (New York: St. Martin's Press, 1982); Gerald M. Meier, *Emerging from Poverty* (New York: Oxford University Press, 1984); and Lloyd G. Reynolds, *Economic Growth in the Third World, 1850–1980* (New Haven: Yale University Press, 1985). See also our further discussion on pp. 449–451.

13. We shall discuss these projections further in the next chapter. Also, for readers who wish a more technical analysis of the way demographers go about their work, including the making of projections, see Appendix at the end of the book.

# 2

# Our Historic War Against Mortality

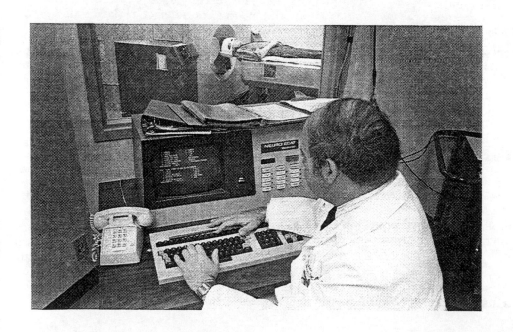

*argument;
deductive reasoning*

The classic example of a syllogism goes like this:

> All men are mortal;
> Socrates is a man; therefore,
> Socrates is mortal.

Like Socrates, we too are mortal. Nothing that has happened in the interval since the ancient Greeks has changed that monumental fact. But virtually everything else about our mortality *has* changed. Some years ago, archaeologists unearthed a Native American burial ground, the Libben site, in Ottawa County, Ohio. The remains were of a "pre-European-contact" tribe. Of the 1,289 skeletons found, 40 percent were of children age 5 or under, only 3 percent were of adults over 46, and the oldest was judged to be that of a man of 55.[1] The old had a very hard time in ancient times, and very few survived. But the young were just as badly off. In primitive societies, fewer than half the babies born would live long enough to have babies themselves.

The achievement of longer and longer life expectancy has been considered by some to be the single greatest accomplishment of the modern era.

## THREE BASIC COMPONENTS OF POPULATION CHANGE

The extension of life expectancy has, moreover, had an important effect on the changing size and structure of the world's populations, including the U.S. population. Reductions in mortality rates (and the associated increases in life expectancy) represent one of the three basic components that determine population change, past and future.

A simple equation showing how population has changed in a given period is the following:

Change in population =
    Births − Deaths + Net immigration

Or, in terms of symbols:

$$\Delta P = B - D + (I - E)$$

where $\Delta P$ is the change in total population in a given year, $B$ is the number of births, $D$ is the number of deaths, $I$ is the number of immigrants, and $E$ is the number of emigrants in that year.

In Chapter 1 we noted that the U.S. Bureau of the Census has made various projections of U.S. population to the year 2080. The differences between the highest, middle, and lowest series (see Figure 1-3) can be summarized in terms of differing assumptions about future trends in deaths, births, and immigration. The technical terms most frequently used are *mortality*, *fertility*, and *net immigration*. We shall have more to say about the definition of these three terms as we go along. For the moment, we shall use them roughly as follows:

• A "low" **mortality rate** will be considered equivalent to a "high" **life expectancy at birth**—the expected number of years to be lived on average by a person born in a given year.

• The **fertility rate** will be measured by the average number of children an American woman will have during her lifetime.

• Yearly **net immigration** will be considered to be the total influx of immigrants to the United States, including illegal immigrants and refugees, minus the outflow of emigrants to other countries.

Table 2-1 presents the low, high, and middle assumptions about mortality, fertility, and net immigration made in the projections (1989) of the Census Bureau.

To give some sense of the magnitude of the changes involved in these assumptions, we can note that U.S. life expectancy at birth in 1989 was estimated to be around 75 years. Thus the gains projected over the next 90 years range from 13 years on the high assumption to around 3 years on the low assumption. ("high" life expectancy

**TABLE 2-1: Principal Mortality, Fertility, and Net Immigration Assumptions**

| Subject | Low Assumption | Middle Assumption | High Assumption |
| --- | --- | --- | --- |
| Life expectancy at birth in 2080 | 77.9 | 81.2 | 88.0 |
| Ultimate lifetime births per woman | 1.5 | 1.8 | 2.2 |
| Yearly net immigration, thousands | 300 | 500 | 800 |

*Source:* Gregory Spencer, U.S. Bureau of the Census, "Projections of the Population of the United States by Age, Sex, and Race: 1988 to 2080," *Current Population Reports*, Series P-25, No. 1018, Table A, U.S. Department of Commerce, U.S. Bureau of the Census, p. 1.

refers, of course, to "low" mortality, and vice versa.)

In the case of fertility, the middle assumption approximates actual total fertility rates at the end of the 1980s, when the projection was made. The low and high assumptions involve apparently small, but actually quite significant, departures from recent childbearing patterns.

In the case of net immigration, the middle assumption assumes some ultimate reduction in recent estimated levels of immigration.

To transform these numbers into population projections, we have to combine them in different ways. The middle series, leading to a projected 2080 U.S. population of around 292 million, uses the three middle assumptions for mortality, fertility, and net immigration. Similarly, the lowest series, leading to a projected 2080 U.S. population of 185 million, uses the low assumptions; and the highest series, leading to a projected 2080 U.S. population of 501 million, uses the three high assumptions.

Looked at individually, none of these alternative assumptions seems either wholly unrealistic or in any way outside the range of possibilities. Certainly life expectancies could easily increase by 13 years, perhaps even more, during the next century. Changes in our fertility rates in the range of 1.5 to 2.2 are nothing spectacular and, in fact, do not compare with some of the *really* rapid changes we have experienced in the post–World War II period. Similarly, immigration, both historically and in some

recent periods, has varied well beyond the 300,000–800,000 range. So what has to strike us forcibly from this analysis is the enormous impact that even relatively small, and in no way unreasonable, changes may have on our population future, transforming us from relative stability to possible decline or quite massive growth.

## THE IMPORTANCE OF DECLINING MORTALITY

How important is the study of falling mortality, and hence rising life expectancy, to the student of population change? The answer is in some ways obvious, in others more indirect. Three points should be noticed:

1. The extension of life expectancy has without question been one of the most deeply prized goals of human endeavor. Between the founding of the Republic in 1789 and the present day, U.S. life expectancy at birth has increased from an estimated 35 years to 75.2 years in 1989 (Table 2-2). During the past hundred years alone, life expectancies in the industrialized nations of the world have increased more than in the entire previous history of the human race!

2. Declining mortality rates have contributed to the increase in the U.S. population, although their direct contribution has been less than that of changes in fertility rates. Declining mortality means that, in any given year, there will be fewer deaths than the previous year,

**TABLE 2-2: Life Expectancy at Birth, United States, 1789–1989**

| Year | Life Expectancy at Birth | Year | Life Expectancy at Birth |
|---|---|---|---|
| 1789[a] | 35 | 1950 | 68.2 |
| 1850[b] | 39.4 | 1960 | 69.7 |
| 1878–1882[b] | 42.6 | 1970 | 70.8 |
| 1890[b] | 43.5 | 1975 | 72.6 |
| 1900–1902 | 49.2 | 1980 | 73.7 |
| 1909–1911 | 51.5 | 1982 | 74.5 |
| 1919–1921 | 56.4 | 1984 | 74.7 |
| 1929–1931 | 59.2 | 1986 | 74.8 |
| 1939–1941 | 63.6 | 1989 | 75.2 |

[a] Parts of New Hampshire and Massachusetts only.

[b] Massachusetts only.

*Source:* U.S. Bureau of the Census, *People of the United States in the 20th Century*, by Conrad Taeuber and Irene B. Taeuber (Washington, D.C.: U.S. Government Printing Office, 1971); *Monthly Vital Statistics Reports* (National Center for Health Statistics).

and therefore the increase in population will be greater, other things being equal. Historically speaking, fertility changes have had more impact on our changing population growth than has the persistent decline in mortality. If, however, fertility behavior should remain relatively constant in the future, then mortality improvements—which are almost certain to occur—could have a greater proportional effect than in the past.

3. *Historically, mortality changes have had a great effect on fertility changes and thus a great indirect effect on population changes in the United States.* Falling mortality has been a major factor in the long-run decline in our fertility rate over time. Why have U.S. women been having fewer and fewer babies over the course of the past two centuries? One reason, almost certainly, is that more and more of these babies have been able to survive to adulthood over this historical span. Thus, to a degree, fertility effects on population growth reflect prior changes in mortality.

# THE THEORY OF DEMOGRAPHIC TRANSITION

This last point is worth emphasizing, for it leads to what has been called "one of the best documented generalizations in the social sciences"[2]: the **theory of demographic transition.** This theory was first suggested in 1929 by demographer Warren Thompson. It was developed more fully by another demographer, Frank Notestein, in 1945, and has been subject to many critiques, revisions, and reinterpretations since.[3]

In its simplest form, the notion of demographic transition is more a description of trends than a full-scale theory of why these trends are occurring. In general, industrial societies were said to go through three stages in their development:

*Stage 1:* Both birth and death rates are high; population growth is slow, although the potential for more rapid growth exists.

*Stage 2:* The death rate declines in advance of a decline in the birth rate; population growth is rapid.

*Stage 3:* The birth rate has declined to parity or near parity with the low death rate; in this stage of low birth and death rates, population growth is once again slow (or even negative).

Stage 2 is obviously the *transition* stage, where birth rates far exceed death rates and where population growth of the modern variety can be expected to occur. How this pattern might look graphically is shown in Figure 2-1.

This description becomes a theory only when we explain why birth and death rates should usually behave in this particular way. In the remainder of this chapter, we shall be examining the mortality side of the picture in the United States' experience; in the next chapter, we shall look at the fertility side.

For the moment, however, we wish only to note one fairly obvious implication of this

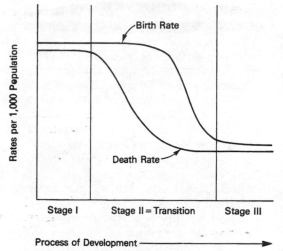

FIGURE 2–1:   The Theory of Demographic Transition

way of looking at population change. The decline in the death rate is seen to be occurring *before* the decline in the birth rate and to be a major factor in *producing* the declining birth rate. Indeed, in the early versions of the theory, changes on the mortality side were seen as wholly determining what happened on the fertility side. *Because* mortality was so high in the preindustrial society, fertility *had* to be high just to ensure the survival of a sufficient number of children to "replace" their parents in the population. Then, when mortality fell (for reasons we will explore in a moment), fertility fell in response, but with a lag because it involved complex changes in elaborate social customs, traditions, habits, and the like. Scholars have since demonstrated that the matter is much more complicated than this and that the factors affecting fertility are quite difficult to pin down. However, it is almost certain that *one* of the factors that inclines people to have fewer children is declining infant and child mortality. As the late Nobel prize winner for economics, Simon Kuznets, put it not long ago, the Western world's "long-term decline in fertility" was at least in part "a free and rational

response of would-be parents to higher survival rates of children."[4] What happens on the mortality side is thus important not only in and of itself but also because of its possible indirect effect on our attitudes toward family size.

## WHERE ARE THE KILLERS OF YESTERYEAR?

By any and all theories of modern population change in the developed world, declining mortality rates have been a universal factor during the past two centuries. One way of visualizing the enormous changes that have occurred is in terms of particular diseases. In Table 2-3, we present the **leading causes of death** in the United States in three different years: 1860, 1900, and 1988. Our progress can be put in a nutshell by a simple statement: *By 1988, eight of the ten leading causes of death of 1860 had completely disappeared from the list of leading killers.* Moreover, in the course of this development, both the means of battling mortality and the character of the battle have changed.

### The General Course of U.S. Death Rates

One measure of mortality that is frequently used is the **crude death rate.**[5] This is defined as the number of deaths in a given year per 1,000 persons in the midyear population. Since we would expect deaths to vary depending on the characteristics of the population, such as its age (and also sex and race) structure, there are times when more specific mortality measures are needed. However, even a general measure like the crude death rate is difficult to calculate before the end of the nineteenth century because of lack of reliable data.

Given this limitation, most (but not all) commentators would agree on the following generalizations:

*The death rate in the colonies and later in the early days of the new Republic was relatively low,*

**TABLE 2-3: Leading Causes of Death, United States, 1860, 1900, and 1989**

| Rank | Percentage of Total Deaths |
|---|---|
| **1860** | |
| 1 Tuberculosis | 19.8 |
| 2 Diarrhea and enteritis | 15.0 |
| 3 Cholera | 6.4 |
| 4 Pneumonia-influenza-bronchitis | 6.1 |
| 5 Infantile convulsions | 5.9 |
| 6 Stroke | 2.7 |
| 7 Diphtheria and croup | 2.7 |
| 8 Dysentery | 2.7 |
| 9 Scarlet fever | 2.5 |
| 10 Nephritis | 2.4 |
| **1900** | |
| 1 Pneumonia-influenza-bronchitis | 14.4 |
| 2 Tuberculosis | 11.3 |
| 3 Diarrhea and enteritis | 8.1 |
| 4 Heart disease | 8.0 |
| 5 Nephritis | 4.7 |
| 6 Accidents | 4.5 |
| 7 Stroke | 4.2 |
| 8 Diseases of early infancy | 4.2 |
| 9 Cancer | 3.7 |
| 10 Diphtheria | 2.3 |
| **1989** | |
| 1 Heart disease | 34.1 |
| 2 Cancer (malignant neoplasms) | 23.1 |
| 2 Stroke (cerebrovascular diseases) | 6.8 |
| 4 Accidents | 4.4 |
| 5 Chronic obstructive pulmonary diseases | 3.9 |
| 6 Pneumonia and influenza | 3.5 |
| 7 Diabetes | 2.2 |
| 8 Suicide | 1.4 |
| 9 Chronic liver disease and cirrhosis | 1.2 |
| 10 Homicide | 1.1 |

*Source:* For 1860 and 1900, Roy Walford, *Maximum Life Span* (New York: W. W. Norton, 1983), Table 1-1, p. 8; for 1989, adapted from National Center for Health Statistics, "Annual Summary of Births, Marriages, Divorces, and Deaths: United States, 1989," *Monthly Vital Statistics Report,* 38(13), August 30, 1990, Table H.

even compared with the economically advanced European countries like England and France. This is not universally accepted,[6] but such evidence as there is suggests that after the very harsh early struggles for survival, particularly in the Chesapeake Bay colony in Virginia, the colonists did quite well in the New World. There are many possible reasons for this: the temperate climate; the abundance of agricultural resources; the youthful age of our population, which, through younger marriages and ages of childbearing, led to higher survival rates for children; the vigor of people who were self-selected in terms of their willingness to endure the hardships of the New World; and the dispersion of the population in rural and agricultural settings, which tended somewhat to diminish the severity of epidemics. By any estimate, our death rate was far below our very high birth rate during the early days of the nation, and thus our population increased rapidly.

There is very little evidence of any decline in the U.S. death rate during the eighteenth century and even well into the nineteenth century. While historians have often believed that American mortality was declining over much of the course of our history, and certainly during most of the nineteenth century, a recent study by Peter D. McClelland and Richard J. Zeckhauser argues that there was no discernible trend in our death rate during the years 1800 to 1860. They suggest that the improvements in our living standards during this period, which would have been favorable to lower mortality, may have been offset by increased urbanization, with the resulting susceptibility to epidemic and contagion.[7] Figure 2-2, showing the estimated death rate in New York City from 1800 to 1910, makes clear that there was no downward trend in the first part of the nineteenth century, only extreme fluctuations as one or another epidemic struck the growing metropolis.

*From the late nineteenth century and to the*

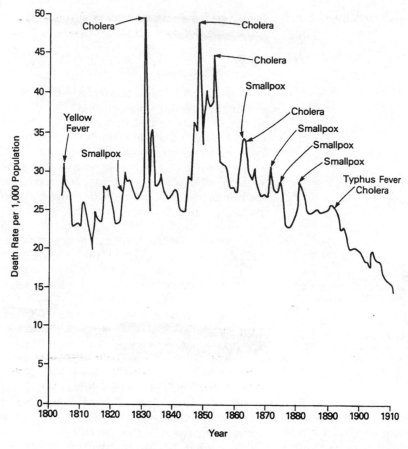

**FIGURE 2–2: Death Rate, New York City, 1800–1910**

*Source:* Reprinted by permission of the publishers from *Introduction to Demography* by Mortimer Spiegelman (Cambridge, Mass.: Harvard University Press, 1968), p. 88. Copyright © 1955 and 1968 by the President and Fellows of Harvard College.

*present day, there have been massive and historically unprecedented declines in our death rate.* Figure 2-2 indicates that, beginning around 1880, and despite the fact that there was another typhus-cholera epidemic, the death rate in New York City started to fall decisively. This fall continued in the twentieth century not just in New York but throughout the nation. Table 2-4 shows that the crude death rate was roughly halved between 1900 and 1989. Since our population was getting older during this period, the meaningful lowering of our mortality was even greater than this. In the second column of the table we present a second measure:

the **age-adjusted death rate.** This is basically what the crude death rate would have been had there been no change in the age structure of the population during these 90 years. This rate falls even faster than the unadjusted rate.

*As we move from the nineteenth century to the twentieth century, there is a persistent change in the forces making for lowered U.S. mortality: from general economic improvements and public health measures to much more specific advances in medical and biological science.* As we have already indicated, our favorable economic conditions probably contributed to our low mortality rate from the very beginning.

**TABLE 2-4:  U.S. Death Rates, 1900–1989 (per 1,000 population)**

| Year | Crude Death Rate | Age-adjusted Death Rate |
|------|------------------|-------------------------|
| 1900 | 17.2 | 17.8 |
| 1910 | 14.7 | 15.8 |
| 1920 | 13.0 | 14.2 |
| 1930 | 11.3 | 12.5 |
| 1940 | 10.8 | 10.8 |
| 1950 | 9.6 | 8.4 |
| 1955 | 9.3 | 7.6 |
| 1960 | 9.5 | 7.6 |
| 1965 | 9.4 | 7.4 |
| 1970 | 9.5 | 7.1 |
| 1975 | 8.8 | 6.3 |
| 1980 | 8.8 | 5.9 |
| 1985 | 8.7 | 5.5 |
| 1989 | 8.7 | 5.2 |

*Source:* Conrad Taeuber and Irene B. Taeuber, *People of the United States in the 20th Century* (Washington, D.C.: U.S. Government Printing Office, 1971), p. 500; for 1970–1989, National Center for Health Statistics, "Annual Summary of Births, Marriages, Divorces, and Deaths: United States, 1989," *Monthly Vital Statistics Report, 38*(13), August 30, 1990, Table 5.

Improved food, housing, and clothing throughout the nineteenth century continued to be factors favoring lower mortality. In the course of that century, these factors were increasingly supplemented by public health measures: isolation and quarantining, garbage and waste removal, the draining of marshes, and the building of community water and sewage systems. Often, however, these public health measures, while effective, were based on what we would judge today to be completely unscientific medical theories.[8] Thus, it was really only at the end of the nineteenth century and more especially during the twentieth century that modern medical knowledge played a large role in the lowering of U.S. mortality rates. The results then were often spectacular. For example, during the period when antibiotics and other "**wonder drugs**" were introduced, from 1937 to 1954, the U.S. mortality rate (age-adjusted death rate) fell at the astonishing average rate of 2.3 percent per year.

## Tuberculosis: A Case Study

In the year 1860, nearly one-fifth of all Americans died of tuberculosis. The disease was also rampant in Europe. Who has ever attended an Italian or French opera without hearing the heroine, usually a soprano, give that fateful little cough—a clue to the "consumption" that will, a number of arias later, do her in? In the seventeenth century, John Bunyan called tuberculosis "the captain of the men of death." Today it has disappeared from the list of the leading causes of death in the United States. In following the course of this disappearing act, we can actually capture much of the history of mortality decline in the United States.

*The first point to make is that actual scientific progress in the understanding and treatment of the disease was rather slow.* Although there is evidence of the existence of tuberculosis extending back at least to 3000 B.C., it was not until 1865 that a Frenchman, Jean Antoine Villemin, determined scientifically that the cause was a living agent. Seventeen years later, the great German bacteriologist Robert Koch, having discovered the curved rod of the tubercle bacillus, announced that he had found the cause of tuberculosis. Two years later, however, when he further announced that he had found the cure for the disease in a substance called "tuberculin," he was completely mistaken. Although many sufferers adopted Koch's treatment and although it continued to be used sporadically in the United States well into the twentieth century, the fact is that the remedy had no curative power whatsoever and in some cases actually worsened the condition. Thus, it was not really until the "wonder drug" era of the mid-twentieth century, with the development of streptomycin, isoniazid, ethambutol, and numerous other effective antibiotics and chemicals, that a fully scientific treatment of tuberculosis became possible.

*But if the first point is that scientific progress in this area was slow until relatively recently, the second point is that progress in the reduction of deaths due to tuberculosis was taking place well before the proper treatment, or even the cause, of the disease was understood.* This supports what we said earlier: that the declining death rate in the United States in the late nineteenth century derived more from general causes than from precise medical knowledge. Thus, we see in Table 2-2 that tuberculosis accounted for only 11.3 percent of U.S. deaths in 1900, as compared with 19.8 percent in 1860. Figures for Massachusetts show that deaths from respiratory tuberculosis fell from 365 per 100,000 population in 1861 to 190 in 1900, and then again— and still before antibiotic treatments had been generally applied—to 37 in 1945. Why?

The main answer seems to lie in a combination of improved living standards— better housing, nutrition, sanitation—*plus* various public health measures including education of the public about factors affecting the spread of the disease, *plus* a gradual growth of empirical, quasi-scientific knowledge of measures that seemed to aggravate and those that seemed to alleviate the conditions of patients suffering from the disease. Simple discoveries, such as that starvation diets, a recommended early-nineteenth-century treatment, were harmful and that good, nutritious food had positive effects, were quite important. One such discovery was that rest rather than vigorous exercise helped promote recovery. Dr. Harry F. Dowling reports on the case of the physician Edward Livingston Trudeau and the sanitarium he founded:

> The most famous sanitarium in the United States was founded by Trudeau at Saranac Lake in the Adirondacks Mountains of New York in 1884. Among the measures that had been in vogue for over a century was exercise in the open air, especially horseback riding, and at first exercise was an important part of the treatment in these sanitariums. Trudeau, who was himself a victim of the disease,

began to treat himself by vigorous hiking, riding, and hunting. After he nearly killed himself with strenuous exercise and was forced to rest for several months, his condition improved remarkably. Consequently, he made rest the mainstay of treatment for himself and his patients.

Meanwhile, public health efforts to educate the public about the disease, to improve its detection, and to control its chain of infection also contributed to the decline of the tuberculosis death rate in the early twentieth century. The National Tuberculosis Association was established officially in 1904. Efforts were made to diagnose the disease in larger populations, to register cases, and to isolate the infected from the well.

By 1989, as a result of this combination of economic progress, public health measures, and, finally, scientific medical treatment (and despite some rise in its incidence in part because of the spread of AIDS),[9] tuberculosis had not only disappeared from the list of the ten leading causes of death in this country but was responsible for only 0.7 deaths per 100,000 of our population. The history of this disease thus exemplifies the general pattern by which infectious diseases were eliminated or drastically reduced over the past century and a half.

## NEW KILLERS, NEW AGE GROUPS

Of course, the removal of a disease from the list of leading causes of death does not mean that the list itself disappears. Until that unlikely day when mortality ceases to be part of the human condition, there will always be a list of leading causes of death.

Indeed, what is particularly striking about Table 2-3 is the *changing character* of the leading causes of U.S. death and, by inference, their *changing impact by age group*.

## Infectious Diseases Give Way to Chronic Diseases

When we compare the three leading killers of 1988—heart disease, cancer, and stroke—with the leading killers of 1860, we notice that whereas the latter were **infectious** diseases, none of the former is. Looking at the lists as a whole, we find that in 1860 many of the leading killers were acute in nature, producing death in a short period of time. By contrast, the 1988 list is generally characterized by **chronic, degenerative diseases,** some of which produce long, lingering deaths. If chronic conditions, such as Alzheimer's disease or arthritis, which often disable their sufferers for years on end, were taken into account, we would have a pronounced picture of chronic, degenerative ailments.

This shift in our leading causes of death has made many observers wonder whether, in extending our life expectancies, we may have increased the number of years during which Americans suffer from ill health (technically called *morbidity*). As we go on in our study, we shall find that this issue of the *quantity* versus the *quality* of life is one of the major questions (and controversies) emerging as a result of our changing population.

But there is also a question concerning the changing character of our illnesses that is of immediate interest to us now. How amenable are these chronic, degenerative ailments to medical treatment? We had enormous success, particularly in the wonder drug era, in getting rid of acute, infectious diseases. Will we be able to match this achievement with the new problems we face? Will our mortality rates continue to fall, or will we face a period of slower decline, stabilization, or conceivably even increasing mortality rates?

At the end of the wonder drug period, there is no doubt that most observers believed that these chronic illnesses would be far more difficult to cure. This belief was, moreover, almost immediately verified (as

it seemed) by a sharp fall in the rate of decline of the U.S. death rate. While the rate had fallen by the remarkable 2.3 percent per year during 1937–1954, as already noted, the rate for 1954–1968 fell by a barely perceptible 0.1 percent. During this period, the death rate for males actually rose slightly. Consequently, virtually all predictions in the late 1960s and early 1970s were that we were reaching a plateau in the matter of declining death rates and increasing life expectancies. It was said that future progress would be uncertain and slow.

This forecast proved to be far too pessimistic. In the next period—1968 to 1980—the decline in our death rate (1.8 percent per year) was quite substantial. The gains here were largely attributable to improvements in death rates from heart disease and other cardiovascular ailments. These gains came partly from direct improvements in medical treatments, but they also derived from life-style changes involving diet, exercise, and reduced smoking. These life-style changes were themselves partly a result of our increased medical understanding of the diseases in question.

At the moment, there is a kind of standoff between those who feel that major improvements in American life expectancies lie ahead of us and those who feel that we are approaching a limit in which change is bound to decelerate. In later chapters in this book (especially chapters 8 and 22), we will be taking up this question at some length.

## Life Expectancies at Different Ages

Our medical progress and the changing character of our leading diseases has also had an impact on mortality by age group. In addition to the overall mortality rate, we can also measure **age-specific mortality rates.** A frequently used category is the **infant mortality rate,** which measures the number of deaths of infants (under 1 year of age) per 1,000 live births in a given year. We could also measure the number of deaths of children under age 5, or under 28 days (*neonatal mortality*), or, at the other end of the scale, mortality rates for those aged 65 and above, or 85, or even older.

Similarly, we can use various measures of life expectancy to show what is happening at different age levels. *Life expectancy at birth* is the most commonly used overall measure, but we can also ask about life expectancies at age 5, say, or age 20, or 60, or even 90. In general, of course, the *added* number of years of life expectancy will decline as we increase the age from which we are measuring.

As we might expect, virtually all of these mortality and life expectancies measures have shown gains over the course of this century. Mortality rates are lower and life expectancies are longer no matter from what age we measure them. But there are two generalizations that reflect the changing character of our medical progress that are important to keep in mind.

*Early in this century, and indeed before that, much of our advance in the area of mortality improved the chances of survival of infants and young people.* This is to say that much of our increased life expectancy at birth in the first decades of this century came about because of decreased mortality at young ages. Figure 2-3 shows the sharp decline in U.S. infant mortality from 1915 to 1989, when it fell

almost tenfold, from 95.7 to 9.9. We can note further that about three-quarters of this fall had taken place by 1950. As the infant mortality numbers fell to lower and lower levels, the percentage decrease has tended to become smaller. Similar, though somewhat less dramatic results for the earlier decades of this century would be found for young people of all ages. A major reason for this disproportionate advance in life expectancies at early ages was that our greatest progress was in the control of infectious diseases, and these diseases were the primary cause of death among young people.

By contrast, there was relatively little progress in extending life expectancies of Americans in the older age groups, because the major causes of death in late maturity and old age were not subject to the same kind of control as those for younger age groups. But this is now changing.

*In recent decades, as our attention has turned to chronic, degenerative diseases, we are now making much greater progress in extending life expectancies of the elderly,* and especially the very elderly. If we compare the 1900–1940 period with the 1940–1980 period, we find that the remaining years of life of white males at age 65 increased nearly four times as much in the later period as in the earlier; for white females at age 65 the gain was over three and a half times as great; the

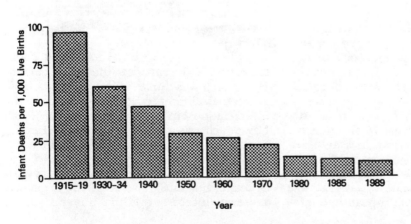

**FIGURE 2–3:  Declining U.S. Infant Mortality (Death Rates, Infants Under One Year)**

*Source:* Conrad Taeuber & Irene B. Taeuber, *People of the United States in the Twentieth Century* (Washington, D.C.: U.S. Government Printing Office, 1971), p. 511; for 1970–1989, National Center for Health Statistics, "Annual Summary of Births, Marriages, Divorces, and Deaths: United States, 1989," *Monthly Vital Statistics Report, 38* (13).

figures for nonwhite males and females at age 65 are somewhat less certain, but females in the nonwhite category also showed definite gains in the later period. It is notable, too, that in the 1968–1978 period, the greatest declines in mortality among elderly Americans were for the oldest old, those 85 and older. For the first time in our history, the reductions in mortality for the elderly have been as great or greater than those for many of our younger age groups.

In short, as public health and medical efforts have become focused on the chronic diseases of the elderly, we are getting unprecedented improvements in life expectancies for our older citizens. This is *a recent fact*, and one with large implications for our overall study.

## HAVE WE REALLY DONE ALL THAT WELL?

The foregoing discussion represents a generally favorable view of the American past as far as mortality is concerned. It suggests, indeed, an optimistic view of the future. As one disease after another has threatened our lives, we have attacked it and, with our increasing medical knowledge, secured major victories. Although this view is generally valid, there are some important qualifications that should now be addressed.

### The American Indian "Holocaust"

From a historical point of view, there is little doubt that the main exception to our general tale of declining mortality in this country has to do with our Indian population. A 1987 book by Russell Thornton, professor of sociology at the University of Minnesota, uses the term *holocaust* in its title, and the "holocaust" refers to the massive increase in Native American mortality following the arrival of whites from 1492 on.

Whether that term is appropriate or not depends on one's estimate of *how* massive the negative impact of European immigra-

tion on the American Indian was. As we mentioned in Chapter 1 (p. 10), we do not know how large the Native American population was at the time of Columbus's arrival. Thornton estimates that population in the area of the conterminous United States before "contact" at 5.65 million, which is about midway between other estimates, ranging from 720,000 to 12 million or more. A 1980 census monograph, published in 1989, cites a range of 2 to 5 million but notes that recent demographic studies may push estimates above the top of that range.[10]

What is certain is that this population was reduced during the course of the sixteenth through nineteenth centuries. The U.S. Census Bureau and the Commissioner of Indian Affairs estimated a Native American population of around 250,000 in the period 1890–1900. This could represent either a very substantial reduction of the Indian population—by about two-thirds or three-quarters—or a genuine "holocaust"— a reduction to 5 percent or even 2 or 3 percent of its original size.

Meanwhile, the Native American population has been growing since the beginning of the twentieth century, recently much more rapidly than U.S. population in general. By 1980 the Census Bureau estimated our Indian population at just under 1.5 million.[11] Thus, another way of looking at the 'holocaust' issue is to say that, depending on which estimates one believes, today's American Indian population in the United States has either (a) doubled, or (b) declined anywhere from 70 to 90 percent since Columbus.

There are also numerous issues about the causes of the early decline that occurred: How much was due to rising mortality, how much to declining fertility, how much to the interrelationship between the two? Also, how much was a direct or indirect effect of contact with Europeans, and how much was due to other causes?

Suffice it to say here that a major part of the decline must have been due to massive mortality increases and that a major part of these increases must have been due to the impact of the European newcomers. The latter brought smallpox, measles, the bubonic plague, scarlet fever, whooping cough, cholera, typhoid, and numerous other diseases for which the Indians had no immunity or resistance. Some tribes were wiped out completely in the course of a succession of epidemics. Others were reduced by half or more at a stroke. Further, the Europeans brought other causes of death—war, murder, displacement, the slaughter of the buffalo who were the mainstay of life for many tribes, and alcohol and alcoholism.

Despite all the uncertainties involved, it is no longer possible (as many pre–World War II studies of U.S. population did) to overlook the early demographic tragedy of the American Indian or to relegate it to a footnote. If the experience of most Americans since colonial days was one of originally low and ultimately sharply falling mortality, then this was decidedly not true of one very important group—those original immigrants from Asia who played host to the much later arriving immigrants from Europe.

### The Variety of Mortality Histories

It was not only the Native American whose mortality history differed from that of the generality of the American population. Indeed, that "generality" is itself rather suspect in that there was great variety in the histories of a number of different groups within the larger population.

We have already mentioned the varying experiences of different age groups as the character of disease and medical science altered over the course of our history. In chapters to come, we shall also be noticing two other major variations on the "standard" U.S. mortality history.

The first has to do with **race-specific mortality.** Besides the American Indians just discussed, the main category of racial

differences to attract our attention will be that of black Americans. This category is of considerable interest in the present day because black infant mortality is so much higher than that of whites, in the late 1980s roughly twice as high (17.9 per 1,000 black live births in 1987 as compared to 8.6 per 1,000 white live births). Black life expectancy is also in general lower than that of whites, although this would seem not to be true at very old ages. The fact that black death rates at ages 85 and above appear to be lower than those of whites has been called the "mortality crossover." Although it is not certain how much of this "crossover" simply reflects measurement difficulties, it may be that those blacks who survive to advanced ages have especially strong constitutions.

Although the comments just made suggest, accurately, that American blacks are disadvantaged compared to whites with respect to mortality, this is not the only way in which black mortality can be described. As we shall see later on (especially in Chapter 12), one could also emphasize the enormous improvements in black mortality and life expectancy that have occurred over the past century. Since 1900 black life expectancies have increased even more rapidly than those of the U.S. white population.

The second major mortality difference we will be discussing is **sex-specific mortality** or, more simply, male versus female death rates. The mortality experience of the sexes is quite different in a number of respects. More boy babies than girl babies are born, but boy babies have higher mortality rates than girl babies. An especially intriguing development is that the general mortality advantage of women over men has been increasing during the course of the twentieth century. In 1900–1902, there was a 2.0 year difference in female versus male life expectancy at birth: 48.3 years for women, 46.3 for men. By 1975 this advantage had increased to 7.8 years (76.6 versus 68.8). In the 1980s the differential narrowed somewhat, but in 1988 it was still nearly 7 years (78.3 versus 71.4).

Particularly notable over the course of the twentieth century was the increasing advantage of *older* women over *older* men. In 1900–1902, white males of 65 could expect to live an additional 11.5 years, while white females of the same age could expect to live 12.2 years—just over eight *months* longer. By 1987 this small advantage had increased over fivefold, to 3.9 *years*. Nonwhite females at 65 also increased their life expectancy advantage over nonwhite males during this period.

To what degree this differential is genetic, hormonal, or socioenvironmental has not yet been fully determined. There is some evidence that the greater prevalence of alcohol consumption and especially smoking among males (a difference that recently has diminished) may have been a major element in the widening of the differential over this century. Historically, men have had higher occupational mortality than women, and higher suicide, homicide, accident, and (in the case of war) combat death rates than women. Women, of course, have historically had high maternal mortality rates. Over this century, female mortality has fallen as these maternal death rates have been greatly reduced. The increasing safety of many male occupations has undoubtedly helped lower male mortality in very recent years and contributed to the slight narrowing of the sex differential since the 1970s.

To what degree the differential will continue to narrow or will expand still further in the future will obviously depend on the specific factors that change and how significant these changes are. If women's life-styles, including alcohol consumption and especially smoking, approach still more closely those of men, then we might expect the differential to narrow further. On the other hand, the effect of **AIDS,** with its heavy incidence in young men, could cause still further widening of the female advantage. Under any circumstances, however, the present gap already guarantees a changing sex structure in our population as we enter the Aging Society (see Chapter 5).

## Deficiencies and Uncertainties

Finally, we should note that any overall evaluation of our mortality history during the past two centuries must take into account the fact that progress has not always been smooth and, indeed, has sometimes not even lived up to our reasonable expectations.

Take the matter of infant mortality again. We have already noted the fact that black infant mortality is currently twice as high as that of whites. We could also mention the fact that the United States, as compared with other developed countries in Europe and with Japan, ranks rather poorly in its infant mortality rate, placing anywhere from fifteenth to eighteenth depending on the measures used. Only part of this is a result of the higher infant mortality rates of minority groups. Even in states like New Hampshire or Vermont, with very small minority populations, the rates would still be worse than those of Sweden, Finland, or Japan, and, in fact, would rank the United States only in tenth place overall. Although there is much controversy about how "good" or "bad" U.S. infant mortality performance is, there is little doubt that there is still room for improvement in this area.

Not only is our progress deficient in specific areas like infant mortality, but it also remains vulnerable to new challenges, the conquest of which can never be considered a given. Although we have recounted the mortality history of the United States in terms of the victories over various diseases, we could as easily have told the story in terms of tragedies and near misses. There was the great influenza epidemic of 1918 (which took more lives worldwide than World War I), the rampant polio epidemics of the early decades of the century, the 1957 flu that put almost half the nation to bed, the outbreak of Legionnaire's disease, the sudden emergence in Connecticut of Lyme disease in the 1980s. And, of course, overshadowing all, there is the mysterious appearance and rapid spread of the AIDS virus during the past decade.

The fact is that health, disease, and mortality rates are not fixed but *evolving* concepts. We change, our environment changes, our treatments change, and—both spontaneously and in response to those changes—the bacteria and viruses that threaten us also change. And all this, of course, is *in addition* to the much greater incidence of those chronic ailments of aging, like **Alzheimer's disease,** that are virtually guaranteed to confront us in the years that lie ahead.

So we had best think of our past accomplishments—which remain substantial—as markers along a very long race course rather than finish lines that we have already passed. The history of American mortality in the past century has almost uniformly been one of improvement. Maintaining that record into the future will be not so much a matter of winning any particular races as of sustaining ourselves indefinitely through a contest of unlimited duration.

## SUMMARY

1.   The three basic components responsible for changes in our population over time are mortality, fertility, and net immigration. Population increase (or decrease) = Births − Deaths + Net immigration.

2.   Mortality improvements, leading to increases in life expectancies, are important in and of themselves. Also, they may affect the future course of population change, and, historically, they have had a major indirect effect in causing reductions in fertility. The theory of demographic transition suggests that a pattern of falling death rates, followed later by falling birth rates, is characteristic of modern socioeconomic development.

3.   In the United States, death rates were, most observers believe, relatively low in the early days of our nation. What is certain is that they began falling sharply in the later nineteenth and twentieth centuries. Over the past 200 years, our life expectancy at birth has increased from an estimated 35 years to our current 75 years.

4.   In the course of this war against mortality, early advances were largely due to general economic development and public health measures, with scientific medicine playing a major role primarily in the twentieth century. Thus, taking tuberculosis as an example, we find that progress in fighting this dread disease occurred well before modern treatments were developed and even before the cause of the disease was fully understood.

5.   Over time, the character of our leading causes of death has changed from acute, infectious diseases to chronic, degenerative diseases. Meanwhile, progress against mortality, once largely confined to young people, is now increasingly allowing older people to live longer.

6.   Although overall an unprecedented achievement, our victories against mortality are marred by the enormous exception of the Native Americans, whose mortality rate increased sharply with the arrival of the Europeans and until the end of the nineteenth century. Also, the differential mortality rates of blacks versus whites, men versus women, and the United States versus other advanced industrial nations suggests a record that can still be improved on.

7.   The continuous arrival of new, threatening diseases (like AIDS) and the special battles against afflictions of the elderly (like Alzheimer's disease) remind us that the war against mortality is never won, only continued indefinitely to the next arena of battle.

## KEY CONCEPTS FOR REVIEW

Mortality rate
  crude death rate
  age-adjusted death rate
  age-specific mortality
  infant mortality

Life expectancy
  at birth
  at other ages

Fertility rate

Net immigration

Theory of demographic transition

Leading causes of death

"Wonder drugs"

Infectious versus chronic diseases

American Indian "holocaust"

Race-specific mortality: differential black versus white mortality

Sex-specific mortality: differential female versus male mortality

AIDS, Alzheimer's disease, and other new challenges

The war against mortality as changing, unending

## QUESTIONS FOR DISCUSSION

1.  Many people claim that the lengthening of life expectancies in the United States and other modern industrial nations represents one of the greatest, if not *the* greatest, of human achievements. Do you agree? How would you rank extending the quantity of human life versus improving the quality of human life?

2.  Explain the general principles of the "theory of demographic transition." Can you see any reasons that the experiences of today's poor countries (the LDCs) might differ from the historic experience of the United States and other developed nations? Give arguments to show that their birth rates may come down: (a) much more slowly or (b) much more rapidly than was the case in the Western world.

3.  Describe the historical evolution of the American war against mortality in terms of (a) the varying impact of economic, public health, scientific, and life-style factors in different periods; (b) the changing impact on different age groups; and (c) the differential effects on women versus men.

4.  Explain why historians and demographers can no longer ignore the mortality history of the American Indian. Do you personally feel that this demographic tragedy has been treated adequately in the reading you have done in American history?

5.  Explain why the mortality experience of black Americans can be both a source of pride and a source of great concern to Americans generally.

6.  Consider these two statements:

    The main effect of modern medical progress has simply been to substitute a new, and often more painful and protracted, set of diseases for the killers of the past.

    As new threats to human life occur, modern science will focus attention on them and— if the past is any guide—achieve major conquests over them.

    Does either statement seem wholly correct to you? partially correct? completely in error? Discuss.

## NOTES

1. Sherwood L. Washburn, "Longevity in Primates," in James G. March, James L. McGaugh, and Sara B. Kiesler, eds., *Aging: Biology and Behavior* (New York: Academic Press, 1981), p. 25.

2. William Peterson, *Population*, 3rd ed. (New York: Macmillan, 1975), p. 10.

3. For early formulations of the substance of the demographic transition approach, see Warren Thompson, "Population," *American Journal of Sociology, 34*(6), 1929, and Frank W. Notestein, "Population—The Long View," in T. W. Schultz, ed., *Food for the World* (Chicago: University of Chicago Press, 1945). For more recent versions and revisions of the theory, see Scott W. Menard and Elizabeth Moen, eds., *Perspectives on Population: An Introduction to Concepts and Issues* (New York: Oxford University Press, 1987), especially Kingsley Davis, "The Theory of Change and Response in Modern Demographic History," and John C. Caldwell, "Toward a Restatement of Demographic Transition Theory."

4. Simon Kuznets, "Notes on Demographic Change," in Martin Feldstein, ed., *The American Economy in Transition* (Chicago: University of Chicago Press, 1980), p. 335.

5. In more advanced demographic studies, a distinction is made between measures of the *frequency* of deaths (e.g., number of deaths per 1,000 of a given population during a certain period), and the *risk* of dying (the probable number of deaths per 1,000 of a given population during a given period). We mention this distinction, but we will largely ignore it in this textbook.

6. Thus, while demographers Conrad and Irene Taeuber state that "the mortality of the early American populations was low in comparison with that in many areas of the world at that time" (Conrad Taeuber and Irene B. Taeuber, *People of the United States in the 20th Century* [Washington, D.C.: U.S. Government Printing Office, 1971], p. 495), a more recent study finds that whether early American death rates were low, especially in comparison to those of Europe, "remains unclear" (Peter D. McClelland and Richard J. Zeckhauser, *Demographic Dimensions of the New Republic* [Cambridge: Cambridge University Press, 1982], p. 15). With admittedly insufficient evidence, we lean toward the view that mortality rates were lower in the colonies (after the first few years) than in characteristic European countries of the time.

7. McClelland and Zeckhauser, *Demographic Dimensions*, pp. 10–12.

8. Thus, many doctors in the mid-nineteenth century believed in the "miasmic theory," which attributed epidemics to changes in the atmosphere. Because these changes were believed to be due to poor sanitary conditions, policies prompted by this faulty theory were, in fact, often beneficial. See Harry F. Dowling, *Fighting Infection: Conquests of the Twentieth Century* (Cambridge, Mass.: Harvard University Press, 1977), p. 7. Our account of the treatment of tuberculosis is heavily indebted to Dr. Dowling's analysis in this book, especially pp. 70–81.

9. In some cities, tuberculosis is, in fact, spreading fairly rapidly. In 1991, the New York City health commissioner reported 3,520 cases in 1990, a 38 percent increase over the previous year.

10. The important census monograph is C. Matthew Snipp, *American Indians: The First of this Land* (New York: Russell Sage Foundation, 1989). Briefly summarized, estimates of the precontact American Indian population (in the conterminous United States) have been as follows: The lowest estimate was that of anthropologist Alfred Kroeber in 1939: 720,000. The highest estimates have come more recently from another anthropologist, Henry Dobyns, who in 1966 and in 1983 gave ranges for North America of as high as 10 to 12 million or above. Fifteen different estimates within this enormous range are presented in the Thornton book (Russell Thornton, *American Indian Holocaust and Survival: A Population History since 1492* [Norman: University of Oklahoma Press, 1987], pp. 22–33). See also William M. Devenan, ed., *The Native Population of the Americas in 1492* (Madison: University of Wisconsin Press, 1976), and Douglas H. Ubelaker, "Prehistoric New World Population Size: Historical Review and Current Appraisal of North American Estimate," *American Journal of Physical Anthropology, 45,* 1976. Although there remains basic disagreement about the numbers involved, the general tendency in recent years has been to revise them upward (making the ensuing demographic losses all the more serious). See Robert V. Wells, *Uncle Sam's Family* (Albany: State University of New York Press, 1985), pp. 62–65.

11. It should be pointed out that even today's figures on our Indian population are very difficult to assess. Thus, in 1980, while only 1.5 million people identified themselves as Indian by race, almost 7 million claimed some Indian ancestry. This is important to note because it suggests that large numbers of Indians have, in fact, passed into the general American population.

# 3

# *The Flight*
# *from Fertility*

*I*t is hard to imagine any fact of greater significance about a society than the number of its children. While mortality retains its hold on the human race, children serve as our small claims to something approaching immortality. The Old Testament spoke of children as "arrows in the hand of a mighty man": "Happy is that man that hath his quiver full of them" (Psalms 127: 4–5).

If this is true, then the United States may be laying the groundwork for a rather unhappy future. Once, in colonial times, our quivers were very full indeed. Although never reaching the absolute biological maximum, American women in the seventeenth and eighteenth centuries were producing, on the average, nearly 8 live births per married woman. By the late 1970s the number had fallen to less than 1.8, and in 1990 it was still below what we shall refer to in a moment as the **replacement rate.**

In this chapter, we begin discussion of one of the major themes of this book and, indeed, of the American experience: the flight from fertility.

## FERTILITY AND FECUNDITY

In common speech, the word *fertility* is used in a number of different senses, and it is worthwhile spending a moment on definitions.

### Fecundity versus Fertility

We begin with what is probably the cause of the most common misunderstanding of the term: failure to distinguish between the number of children a woman is capable of having and the number she actually has. At least since the 1930s, demographers have distinguished **fecundity,** the physiological capacity to produce children, from **fertility,** which measures the actual number of children produced. That these two terms refer to different characteristics is indicated by the fact that they can move in opposite directions over time and, in fact,

have characteristically done so in the course of U.S. history.

As this last comment suggests, the fecundity of a population, though physiologically determined, is not fixed but can change as historical circumstances change. It was once thought, for example, that the reason women were having fewer babies in the modern era was that their physiological capacity to produce offspring was being damaged by the hazards of an urban-industrial society. Actually, the main effect of the industrialization process has been to raise the income and nutritional levels of mothers (and fathers) and hence to increase their fecundity.

Examples of increased fecundity include the lowering of the age of **menarche** (first menstruation), the age at which conception becomes possible. In Norway, over the past century, the age of menarche has fallen approximately 4 years (from roughly age 17 to 13). At the other end of the scale, better living conditions also permit more women in a population to live throughout the whole of their childbearing years—that is, until **menopause** (cessation of menstruation). In both these ways, the improvement of living standards in the United States and other developed countries has increased the number of potential childbearing years and contributed to the increasing fecundity of their populations.

There also may be social practices that affect the physiological capacity to have children. One of the most important examples, historically, has been the prevalence of extended breast feeding. Prolonged breast feeding diminishes a woman's capacity to conceive and hence her fecundity over her childbearing years. A recent example of some importance is **sterilization.** Actually, for older men and women in the United States, sterilization has become *the most prevalent* form of birth control. In this case, fertility (the actual number of children produced) is being lowered by eliminating fecundity (the physical capacity for producing them).

A second general point of some importance is that, as far as one can judge, human societies have always operated at well below their maximum levels of fecundity. These levels are extremely high. In individual cases, where multiple births can occur, the levels are truly mind-boggling. According to the Guinness *1990 Book of World Records,* the world's most prolific mother is Leontina Albina of San Antonio, Chile, who had her fifty-fifth child in 1981 (included were five sets of triplets). Even she, however, does not match up to the reputed all-time record-holder, the first wife of the Russian Feodor Vassilyev, who in 1765 gave birth to her *sixty-ninth* child (including seven sets of triplets and four sets of quadruplets). Catherine the Great was reported to have evinced "wonderment."[1]

For a population group, the highest fertility actually observed is probably that of the Hutterites, a fundamentalist sect who live in North and South Dakota and in Canada and who practice no birth control. They are said to average as high as 11 or more children per couple. Even in the Hutterite case, however, fertility levels are still somewhat below the biological maximum, meaning that in all observed societies, there are invariably some practices and traditions that, consciously or unconsciously, limit the number of actual births.

## Measures of Fertility

Like mortality, fertility can be measured in a number of ways. Three of the more common measures are:

*Annual Number of Births.*   At the beginning of all fertility calculations are estimates of the number of live births occurring each year. In Figure 3-1, we present a graph of such estimates for the United States from 1800 to 1989. As we would expect, the **annual number of births** has grown historically as the size of the nation has grown. Less predictable are the ups and downs in the number of births during the past 50 or 60 years, matters we shall come to in a few pages.

*Crude Birth Rate.*   We learn more about actual childbearing behavior in the society by correcting the number of births for the size of the population. Does an annual birth of, say, 4 million babies indicate that couples are having a great many children, or rather few? The answer would clearly depend to

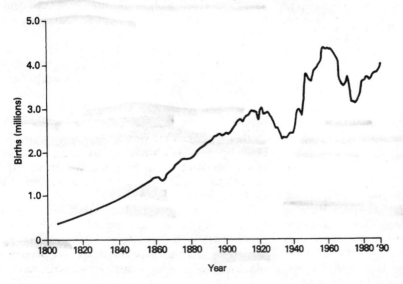

**FIGURE 3–1:   Annual Births in the United States, 1800–1989**

*Source:*   Prior to 1917, Ansley Coale and Melvin Zelnik, *New Estimates of Fertility and Population in the United States* (Princeton: Princeton University Press, 1963); 1917 to 1960, *Vital Statistics of the U.S.,* 1977, Table 1-2; 1960 to 1989, National Center for Health Statistics, *Monthly Vital Statistics Report,* 39 (4), August 15, 1990.

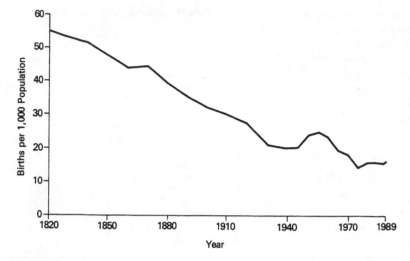

**FIGURE 3–2:   U.S. Crude Birth Rate, 1820–1989**

*Source:*   Charles F. Westoff, "Fertility in the United States," *Science,* 234, October 31, 1986, p. 555; from 1985 to 1988, National Center for Health Statistics, *Monthly Vital Statistics Reports,* 39 (4), August 15, 1990; and *Monthly Vital Statistics Reports,* 38 (13), August 30, 1990.

some degree on the overall size of the population involved. In China, with over 1 billion inhabitants, this would be a very small number of births; in France, with a population of 55 million, it would represent a huge number. The **crude birth rate** corrects for population size by measuring the number of live births in a given year per 1,000 persons in the midyear population.

In 1989, for example, the number of annual births in the United States was provisionally reported as 4,021,000. Our population in 1989 was 248,777,000. The crude birth rate in any given year is measured as follows:

$$\text{Crude birth rate} = \frac{\text{Annual number of births}}{\text{Population in thousands}}$$

For 1989, we have:

$$\text{Crude birth rate} = \frac{4,021,000}{248,777} = 16.2$$

Figure 3-2 traces the historical pattern of the U.S. crude birth rate.

Although this measure gets us closer to childbearing behavior in a society, its numerical value also depends on the age–sex composition of the society. Confusion arises when people interpret a rise in the crude birth rate to mean an increased propensity

to have children when, in fact, it may only reflect an increased proportion of the female population in the childbearing age groups.

Still, this is a useful measure because it is one for which data are usually available. Also, it gives us a direct way for measuring the **rate of natural increase** of a given population. If we subtract the crude death rate from the crude birth rate, we will measure the rate at which our population is increasing from natural causes—that is, apart from immigration. Thus, at a birth rate of 40 per 1,000 and a death rate of 20 per 1,000, the natural increase of our population would be 20 per 1,000, or 2 percent per year. If such rates maintained themselves over time and there was no immigration, then our population would, in fact, grow at 2 percent per year, doubling every 35 years.[2]

*Total Fertility Rate.*   **Total fertility rate** (TFR) is independent of the age structure of the society and tells us the number of children 1,000 women will bear during the whole of their lifetimes. We shall most often use this term on a "per woman" basis. A total fertility rate of 2,000 for 1,000 women would then be 2.0 on a per woman basis.

The total fertility rate is a more accurate measure of people's decisions about having children than the crude birth rate, but its measurement involves certain assumptions. The total fertility rate states the number of births 1,000 women would have over their childbearing years *if* they experience the *same* birth rates that women of specific ages (**age-specific birth rates**) actually had in a given year. Thus we have this complex definition:

*A total fertility rate of 1,932 in the United States in 1988 means that if a hypothetical group of 1,000 women had the same birth rates at each age (usually five-year age groups) as were observed in the United States in 1988, they would have a total of 1,932 children (approximately 1.9 per woman) by the end of their childbearing years, assuming that all of the women survived to that age.*

In Table 3-1, we present the estimated age-specific birth rates for U.S. women in 1988. The table is to be read as follows: 1.3 babies were born per 1,000 U.S. women in the 10- to 14-year age group in 1988; 53.6 babies were born per 1,000 women in the 15- to 19-year age group in 1988; and so on.

In order to get the total fertility rate from these numbers, we sum them (= 386.4) and multiply them by 5 (barring death, each woman will spend 5 years in each age group). The result is:

$$386.4 \times 5 = 1{,}932$$

**TABLE 3-1:   Age-specific Birth Rates, United States, 1988**

| Age | Age-Specific Birth Rates |
| --- | --- |
| 10–14 | 1.3 |
| 15–19 | 53.6 |
| 20–24 | 111.5 |
| 25–29 | 113.4 |
| 30–34 | 73.7 |
| 35–39 | 27.9 |
| 40–44 | 4.8 |
| 45–49 | 0.2 |

*Source:* National Center for Health Statistics, *Monthly Vital Statistics Report*, *39*(4), Suppl., August 15, 1990.

**TABLE 3-2:   Total Fertility Rate, United States, 1800–1989**

| Year | Total Fertility Rate | Year | Total Fertility Rate |
| --- | --- | --- | --- |
| 1800 | 7.0 | 1900 | 3.6 |
| 1810 | 6.9 | 1910 | 3.4 |
| 1820 | 6.7 | 1920 | 3.2 |
| 1830 | 6.6 | 1930 | 2.5 |
| 1840 | 6.1 | 1940 | 2.2 |
| 1850 | 5.4 | 1950 | 3.0 |
| 1860 | 5.2 | 1960 | 3.5 |
| 1870 | 4.6 | 1970 | 2.5 |
| 1880 | 4.2 | 1980 | 1.8 |
| 1890 | 3.9 | 1989 | 2.0[a] |

[a] Provisional estimate.

*Sources:* Prior to 1917: Ansley Coale and Melvin Zelnik, *New Estimates of Fertility and Population in the United States* (Princeton: Princeton University Press, 1963); 1917 to 1989: National Center for Health Statistics, *Vital and Health Statistics*, Series 21, No. 28, and *Monthly Vital Statistics Reports.*

Or, on a per woman basis:

$$\text{TFR} = \frac{1{,}932}{1{,}000} = 1.9$$

Table 3-2 and Figure 3-3 present estimates of the historical course of U.S. fertility rates since 1800.

The problem with this measure of fertility is that we actually know the completed fertility of a group of women only at the conclusion of their childbearing years. Thus, when we speak of a total fertility rate in 1988 of 1.9, we are forced to make an estimate of the completed fertility of women who have not yet finished, and in many cases are just beginning, their reproductive lives. If, for example, women decide to *postpone* their childbearing until later in life on the average, then the total fertility measure will tend to underestimate the completed fertility of these women.

Subject to these limitations, the total fertility rate also gives us a measure of what is called the *replacement rate*. This is the total fertility rate that a society with a stable age

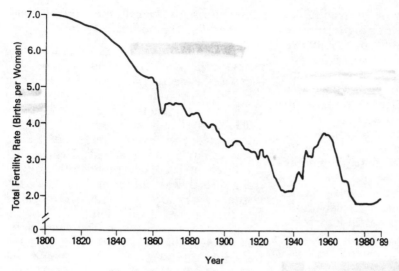

**FIGURE 3–3: Total Fertility Rate for the United States: White Population, 1800–1916; Total Population 1917–1989**

*Source:* Prior to 1917, Ansley Coale and Melvin Zelnik, *New Estimates of Fertility and Population in the United States* (Princeton: Princeton University Press, 1963); 1917 to 1989: National Center for Health Statistics, *Vital and Health Statistics,* Series 21, No. 28, and *Monthly Vital Statistics Reports.*

structure over time and without net immigration must maintain to replace itself. Any lower rate will lead under these circumstances to a declining population; any higher rate, to a growing population. One might suspect that the replacement rate would be 2 (2 children per woman, meaning that couples are exactly reproducing themselves), but in fact, in the developed world today, it is slightly higher than that—2.1. The higher number reflects an allowance for the fact that more boy babies are born than girls and that infant and child mortality prevents some girls from ever entering their childbearing years.[3]

## A BRIEF SURVEY OF U.S. FERTILITY HISTORY

The historic experience of the United States to some degree exemplifies the general theory of the demographic transition discussed in the last chapter. But it also has some special features. We will first sketch the broad outlines of our national fertility history, and then, in the next section, relate this experience to the demographic transition theory.

Four striking features characterize that history: (1) our very high fertility in the early days; (2) the massive decline of our fertility rate beginning quite early in the nineteenth century and continuing on through the 1930s; (3) the post–World War II **Baby Boom;** and (4) the post–Baby Boom **Baby Bust.**

*1. Initially High Fertility.* Although there is some disagreement about whether our death rate was exceptionally low in the early days of the Republic, there is little doubt that our birth rate from colonial times to the beginning of the nineteenth century was extremely high. At the time of the first census in 1790, our crude birth rate was estimated to be 55 per 1,000 population. This is almost certainly higher than the rate in many European countries of the time, which may have been in the neighborhood of 35 per 1,000. It is, indeed, higher than that found even in the so-called population explosions of most of today's LDCs. The total fertility rate implied by this number has been estimated at 7.7.

Although this rate is, as we know, below the theoretical maximum, it nevertheless suggests a strong bias toward early marriages and large families, with relatively little effort, either consciously or by traditional practices, to limit births. Using a guesstimate of our 1790 death rate of 28 per 1,000, we find that the birth rate figure of 55 per 1,000 would give us a rate of natural increase of 27 per 1,000, or 2.7 percent per year. Thus, quite apart from immigration (actually, a rather small percentage of the total in the late eighteenth century), we had a population that would double every 25 years. Had such a rate been sustained for the two centuries after 1790, our 1990 population would have been 256 times that in 1790, going from 3.9 million to just under a billion—and this from natural increase alone!

### 2. The Massive Long-run Decline in U.S. Fertility.

This explosive population growth obviously did not happen. It did not happen despite the fact that there was substantial net immigration during the nineteenth century and despite the fact that, at least from the late nineteenth century on, our death rate fell sharply.

Counterbalancing both these factors and producing a substantial slowing down of our rate of population growth over this period, there was a massive decline in U.S. fertility. In terms of total fertility rates, by 1940 the decline had reached 2.2. This was still above the replacement rate, but was less than one-third of our total fertility rate at the end of the eighteenth century (Table 3-2).

This decline in American fertility began at different times in different parts of the country, starting in the Northeast and then gradually spreading to the Midwest and the South. For the country as a whole, however, the remarkable thing is how *early* the process began. Every indication is that our fertility was declining from at least 1810 on. This was before our death rates were showing any conclusively verifiable decline, before the Industrial Revolution had had any substantial impact in the New World, and well before most European countries were experiencing falling birth rates. This has led some historians to call the United States "the world's first modern nation."

### 3. The Baby Boom.

As we entered the post–World War II period (Figure 3-3), there was a sharp reversal in the decline of the U.S. birth rate. From roughly 2.5 in 1945, the rate rose to a maximum of 3.8 in 1957. This change was almost completely unexpected and, even though our Boom-level fertility never reached anything like the levels of the early nineteenth century, the reversal was sharp enough to affect virtually every aspect of the United States' current population situation.

Analysts differ about the reasons for this sudden change in behavior, a matter we will discuss on pp. 47–49 and will return to often in later chapters. Superficially, however, we can note that many things were happening simultaneously: We had just emerged from two of the greater traumas of our history, the Great Depression and World War II; our veterans had returned home; for many of them, the GI Bill made marriage possible while going to college; the economy was vigorous; some couples who had deferred having babies during the Depression years had them now; and the automobile was making the concept of a happy home in the suburbs, surrounded by grass, dogs, and children, a real option.

At the time, it did not seem inconceivable that, at our very advanced stage of economic and social development, the century-and-a-half trend toward lower fertility was being permanently reversed. Since the United States was far and away the richest country in the world after the war, it was only to be expected that we would lead the way into the future. And, indeed, our Baby Boom was much more pronounced than the similar booms experienced in Europe at that time.

### 4. The Baby Bust.

In point of fact, however, the period of the Baby Boom was followed by what must be one of the sharpest fertility declines in human history. Between 1957 and 1976, less than two decades, the

U.S. total fertility rate fell from 3.8 to 1.7, or by more than 50 percent! As we have mentioned before, the severity of this drop was as unexpected as the sharpness of the Baby Boom that preceded it. Indeed, in the absence of any major traumas of the magnitude of the Great Depression or World War II to help explain this sudden reversal of direction, one must begin with a certain sense of awe at what took place.

For although everyone can point to certain developments during those years that undoubtedly affected the outcome—everything from the Pill and the legalization of abortion to the increase in the number of working women and the spread of new attitudes toward women in general—the fact is that a fall in fertility of this magnitude involves scarcely credible changes in virtually all aspects of our personal and social lives. Going from almost four children per couple on the average to less than two suggests that men and especially women were going through revolutionary changes not only in their attitudes but in the day-to-day management of their lives.

Was it possible, in this age of rapid mass communication, that wrenching social changes of this magnitude might become the order of the day? This possibility remains before us, although it must be said that there was also another possibility: namely, that the Baby Bust really does not need a special explanation—that it represents nothing more than the return of the United States to its long-run low-fertility trend. According to this view, the Baby Boom would be the real aberration and the only phenomenon in need of serious explanation.

## U.S. FERTILITY AND THE DEMOGRAPHIC TRANSITION

Under any circumstances, from a historical point of view it is the long-term downward trend in U.S. fertility that requires our major analysis. Recall that, even at the height of the Baby Boom, our fertility was still well below levels that were commonplace in the nineteenth century.

One explanation of population change that clearly does *not* help us is the Malthus-Ricardo analysis we developed briefly in Chapter 1 (pp. 9–10). We have already noted that this analysis was ill suited to our historic national experience in that natural resource shortages and diminishing returns were, at least until very recent years, irrelevant in the U.S. context. But the coup de grace to this analysis really comes from our fertility record. There is simply no way in which we can regard the U.S. population as responding positively to increasing living standards (real wages) over time. As we have become richer and richer, we have decided to curtail the numbers of our children, and dramatically. Even within our society, higher incomes are almost universally associated with fewer, rather than more, children per family.

Of much greater relevance is the **theory of the demographic transition,** for this approach, in any form, does posit a long-run decline in the birth rate in the course of a nation's modernization and economic development (see Figure 2-1). It also suggests that, after the transition, a country would enter a stage of low but relatively stable birth (and death) rates. We could, in fact, be in such a stage now. Population growth would be expected to be much slower than during the transition (as ours is now) and could even turn negative.

### Death Rates and Lowered Fertility

In the simple statement of the demographic transition theory, lowered death rates in the course of a country's economic development tend to lead, and to be a major factor in causing, the subsequent fall in the country's birth rate. With more children surviving, a rational response might simply be to have fewer children in the first place.

This version would seem to need modifying in the case of the United States. If we accept the admittedly uncertain evidence that there was no pronounced downward trend in the U.S. death rate during the eighteenth and the first several decades of the nineteenth century, then it would appear that our declining birth rate, beginning at least as early as 1810, *preceded rather than followed* the decline in the death rate. Only in the later nineteenth and twentieth centuries, with the precipitous declines in mortality that occurred then, can we perhaps explain the further declines in our fertility as a response to our improved survivability.

Some of the spirit of this simple approach may, however, be saved if we recall, first, that, after a difficult beginning, particularly in the Chesapeake Bay area, our mortality rate was quite low even in the early days because of our generally favorable living conditions, and, second, that our fertility rate in those early days was exceptionally high by the standards of the European countries from which we had emigrated. Thus, in effect, we did not begin our national experience from Stage I (high birth rate–high death rate; low rate of population increase) of the demographic transition. On the contrary, we were, from the seventeenth century on, right in the middle of the transition stage, or Stage II (birth rates greatly exceeding death rates; rapid population growth), with our population doubling every 25 years from natural increase alone.

According to this view, the things that would require explanation would be our initial conditions: our relatively low mortality rates, and especially our unexpectedly high fertility rates. These, in turn, might well be considered to have been natural results of the favorable but extremely underpopulated New World environment. As population then grew explosively, a similarly natural response, very much in the spirit of the theory of demographic transition, would have been to start limiting fertility. Thus, the early decline in U.S. fertility would reflect mainly the special starting conditions that America faced.

Although there is undoubtedly some truth in this view, this version of the theory of demographic transition is too simple to account for population change in the United States, or elsewhere for that matter. During the past century or two, it was not just low or falling mortality rates that characterized the developed world. Many other changes were also occurring, and these changes often affected birth and death rates in highly complex ways.

### From Rural-Agricultural to Urban-Industrial

Clearly, one of these factors was the great transformation that all developed countries, including the United States, have undergone, from a **rural-agricultural society** to a largely **urban-industrial society.**[4] At the beginning of the nineteenth century, probably 80 percent of our population was engaged primarily in agriculture, and 90 percent or more lived in rural areas. By the end of that century, the percentage of the U.S. labor force in agriculture had fallen to 39 percent (and today, of course, is down to 2 or 3 percent), and the percentage living in urban areas had risen to 40 percent. Thus, our declining fertility was accompanied by a massive movement from farm to industry and from country to city.

This movement undoubtedly had a profound effect on our desire to have children (our "demand" for children, as economists might put it). One fairly obvious reason is that, whereas children can be and were helpful workers on a farm from the very earliest ages, this is much less true in an urban environment. The Industrial Revolution, it has been said, caused "the sharpest ecological and physical cleavages ever experienced between workplace and domicile."[5] Although children were widely employed in the early factories, and although it was not until the beginning of the twentieth century that child labor was uniformly prohibited, the move from agriculture to industry generally made it more difficult to

→ kids financial asset on farm to financial burden in the city.

secure economic advantages from having additional children. Children may also have been more expensive to rear in urban environments, where food had to be bought rather than produced at home. Furthermore, living conditions in urban settings tend to be more crowded than those in the countryside, another factor favoring family limitation.

It should be stressed, however, that urban living was not the only factor contributing to our declining fertility. It is significant that both urban *and* rural fertility were separately in decline during the nineteenth and early twentieth centuries. One estimate is that the *shift* from rural to urban settings accounted for only 20 percent of the total fertility decline from 1810 to 1940.[6]

### Pervasive Technological Change

The aforementioned agricultural–industrial transformation was, of course, part of a general transformation in the Western world marked by the rapid advance of scientific knowledge and technological knowhow. The great breakthroughs associated initially with the British Industrial Revolution had begun to have a major impact on the United States by the 1840s and dominated much of our social and economic life in the remainder of the nineteenth and twentieth centuries.

The general effect of this great development was almost certainly to encourage efforts at family limitation. As we have already mentioned, part of this effect came indirectly through the lowering of infant and child mortality. But there were also more direct effects. In a technologically oriented society, higher levels of education in the work force are required, making it more expensive to raise and prepare children for entry into the outside world. Thus children not only contribute less to the family's economic well-being, but also represent significant added costs.

Technological progress also provides vast quantities of attractive new commodities, which offer alternatives to using the family budget for child rearing. It is also a major factor in creating strong possibilities for upward mobility. In a technologically advancing society, the chances of bettering one's status in life are vastly improved as compared to the much more slowly changing societies of the premodern era. But in this effort to get ahead, children can easily seem a major drawback. Later marriage, fewer children, a single-minded concentration on advancing one's career and social standing—such an approach, first analyzed with respect to declining birth rates in England,[7] obviously could have much relevance to the United States, with our characteristic admiration for "success."

Technology also can have a direct effect on family limitation by lowering the costs of birth control. In our own period, with the example of the Pill in mind and, indeed, with numerous future birth control technologies on the horizon, we may be inclined to overemphasize this factor. The truth is that, although the condom was developed in the eighteenth century and the diaphragm in the 1880s, the two main contraceptive practices in the United States as late as the 1930s were coitus interruptus (withdrawal) and the douche, with the condom coming in third and all other methods (including the diaphragm) adding up to a rather small fraction. Thus, although improved birth control technology may ultimately facilitate family limitation, it was not as crucial a factor in our historical fertility decline as some have supposed.

### The Changing Role of Women

As part of this large scientific-technological-industrial transformation of our society, there was also a major and ongoing transformation of the role of women in America. A number of factors made it increasingly possible and desirable for women to work outside the home:

• Fewer goods were produced in the

home and thus more things had to be bought with money income.

• Over time, jobs in the white-collar, service sector of the economy grew rapidly relatively to the blue-collar, physically demanding jobs of the goods-producing sector, increasing the number of desirable opportunities for women.

• As in the case of men, the increased socioeconomic mobility, the possibilities of getting ahead, and the abundance of new and desirable commodities to be purchased all gave money-earning careers a high priority.

• There has been a gradual change in the status of women from household drudge and/or household ornament to something approaching "equality" with men, suggesting that careers outside the home had become an expected and not in the least unnatural path for women to take.

We shall be discussing these various factors at greater length, especially in Chapter 11. For the moment, we emphasize only the major point that *virtually all these changes in the role of women in the course of a modernizing America suggest reasons for declining fertility.* In technical terms, it may be said that all these changes have tended to raise the **opportunity costs of having children.** The more opportunities women have to use money for desirable purchases and to earn money through relatively desirable jobs and ultimately full-fledged careers, the more it costs them to have children. A reasonable response to these higher opportunity costs could be, and almost certainly has been, to have fewer offspring.

## THE FERTILITY DECISION: HOW RATIONAL IS IT?

As one discusses the various factors that appear to have affected our long-run fertility decline, the question arises: Is there

some systematic theory that can relate this decline to the general processes of modernization and development of which it has been a part?

### Fertility as a Conscious Decision

Any such systematic theory would probably begin as an analysis of **fertility choice.** Individuals and couples are having fewer babies in the United States today than they had a century ago, not because they can't have them (fecundity problems), but because they *consciously choose* not to have them.

Already, this statement poses an issue to be explained. Historically, although no observed society (even the Hutterites) has operated at the level of maximum possible fertility, the practices by which its fertility was restricted tended to be adopted for other reasons (e.g., prolonged breast-feeding for the nutritional well-being of the child, or sexual taboos for religious reasons). How, then, did modern couples come to regard the fertility decision largely as one subject to their rational, personal choices?

The answer that most sociologists and historians give is that a characteristic feature of the Western world as it developed in the modern period was an increasing sense of freedom from other-worldly powers and a growing sense of mastery over one's environment and personal destiny. Historian David Landes, writing of Europe on the eve of the Industrial Revolution, notes "the high value placed on the rational manipulation of the environment." This feature, which is sometimes called **modernization,** sometimes **secularization,** he decomposes into two elements: "rationality, and what we may call a Faustian sense of mastery over man and nature."

Landes's main example of the workings of this new attitude is precisely the fact of European population control before industrialization occurred: "This is evidence presumably of self-restraint—an effort to restrict commitments to means—and as such is an excellent example of rationality in a particularly crucial and sensitive area of life." Similarly, sociologist Alex Inkeles has noted that a central characteristic of modern man and woman is their "openness to new experience, both with people and with new ways of doing things such as attempting to control births." Some observers go so far as to argue that this change in the *nature* of fertility control (from traditional means to conscious decisions) was even more significant in the long run than the fact of fertility decline itself.[8]

In any event, in the background of our discussion, we must always remember the crucial social and intellectual developments that permitted modern individuals to consider fertility as a proper object of their control. Even today there is nothing like perfect agreement on this matter, as the deep debates over abortion and the lingering restrictions (for example, among some Catholics) on the use of contraceptives remind us.

### Calculations of the Demand for Children

Within this framework of choice, many scholars have attempted to explain fertility decline in terms of calculations of the value of children to their parents. Perhaps the best known attempt to analyze the **"demand" for children in economic terms** is that of University of Chicago economist Gary Becker. Becker's analysis is formulated in terms of parents as consumers trying to maximize their utilities (satisfactions) as they use their incomes to "purchase" children as well as other goods. Although children are not bought on a market, they do have an effective price, which would include such things as expenditures on delivery, expenses of rearing and maintaining the child, and— very significantly—the time that must be diverted from other activities such as employment for the mother to take care of the child.

In Becker's formulation, parents derive satisfaction not only from the number of children they have but also from the *quality* of those children. In general, he finds that there is a strong negative relationship between the quantity and the quality of children demanded. Rising incomes in the course of modernization might lead us to expect that people would "purchase" greater numbers of children, but the fact is that they tend to purchase higher quality children and smaller numbers of them. Among other reasons, the rates of return on investment in the education of children tend to increase in the course of economic development. Thus, instead of purchasing more children, one purchases more years of college for each child, perhaps a graduate degree or two.

Within this framework, of course, all the factors we have been mentioning—the increasing cost of children in an urban as opposed to a rural environment, the reduced cost of birth control, the increasing income-earning opportunities of women, the availability of wonderful new consumer goods, and so on—can be included. All can be interpreted in relation to the changes in income and relative prices that face these modern utility-maximizing individuals.[9]

### Analysis of the Baby Boom and Bust

But are we really all that rational and calculating about the fertility decision? As we have mentioned several times, our Baby Boom was largely unexpected, as was the sharpness of the Baby Bust that followed. In point of fact, however, there have also been serious attempts to provide a systematic analysis of our Boom/Bust experience, again with a heavy emphasis on the economic factors involved. The most notable of these attempts is that of Richard A. Easterlin of the University of Southern California, with his so-called **relative income hypothesis**.[10]

Decisions about family formation, according to this theory, depend on young

*Cycle → low economy → ~~bus book~~ less babies → high economy*
*Boom grows up*
*BUST Bust grows up*
*More babies Boom*

people's assessments of their future prospects and the possibility of achieving the kind of life-styles to which they aspire. The brighter these prospects, the sooner they will tend to get married and the more children they are likely to have. These prospects are not judged by *absolute* incomes but by *relative* incomes—that is, incomes relative to what they have come to expect.

What young people have come to expect in the way of income is largely determined by their past income experience—namely, the past incomes of their parents. If one looks only at the male side of the picture (which Easterlin occasionally does, but only as an approximation), one could say that the relative income of a family can be expressed as the ratio of the recent earnings of young men to the past earnings of their fathers. The higher this relative income, other things being equal, the higher will be the fertility rate.

According to this view, the Baby Boom is explained primarily by the huge jump in relative income of the cohorts of young people forming families after World War II.[11] Their parents, as we know, were raising these young people as children during the Great Depression and then during the war. Parental real incomes during these two large national traumas were far below the earning opportunities facing young men during the great American growth spree of the late 1940s and 1950s. Hence young people felt exceptionally well off and could easily afford marriage and babies.

When the Baby Boomers grew older, however (the theory goes on), they all tried to enter the work force, creating pressure on limited job opportunities. For this group, their relative incomes were quite unsatisfactory. They were brought up to expect high and rapidly growing incomes. Instead, at least in part because of their own exceptionally large numbers, they faced a competitive job market and a relatively stagnant economy. Relative income was, therefore, low, and the Baby Bust ensued.

Indeed, on this theory one can see the possibility of a regular cycle of Booms and Busts. The small generation of Depression babies had splendid opportunities when it entered the job market. This group produced masses of babies. These babies, however, soon entered the job market in a great flood, producing much less satisfactory earning prospects, lowered relative income, and very few babies. When *these* babies grow up, however, they will be much sought after and will face an excellent job market. This group again will produce masses of babies. And so on, more or less indefinitely.

Two questions arise about this theory: *First,* how well does it apply to the pre-1940 experience? Easterlin's answer is that the situation then was different because general unemployment often dwarfed the relative income effects,[12] and because immigration tended to be high when demand for labor was high, thus wiping out the advantages of being part of a small cohort of young people. In short, things were different earlier in our history, and the theory has little application prior to 1940.

*Second,* how well does it apply to the post-1980 experience? As of 1990, the answer would appear to be—not too precisely. Easterlin had, in effect, predicted a rising fertility rate for the 1980s, and although there had perhaps been some very small increase by the end of the decade—the total fertility rate for 1989 was provisionally estimated at 2.0—the fundamental fact about U.S. fertility since the mid-1970s is that it has remained consistently low.

This fact does not necessarily negate the spirit of the Easterlin hypothesis. Birth rates could possibly turn up in the 1990s. More significantly, the relative income effects could be working in one direction while other factors might be operating in an opposite direction—for example, increasingly general acceptance of the idea that women should have careers of exactly the same scope, depth, and power as men have had. Without the relative income effect, it could be that U.S. fertility would have not remained constant but would have *fallen even further* during recent years. Thus, although current evidence is not very promising, the Easterlin hypothesis cannot be wholly dismissed at this point.

## VARIATIONS IN AMERICAN FERTILITY

Perhaps the main lesson to be derived from the foregoing discussion is that attempts to explain fertility changes through any single factor are likely to miss a great part of the story. Indeed, any attempt to explain our fertility history in terms of purely *rational* decision making is also likely to miss much of the story. For there are all sorts of social-cultural-political-religious-historical factors that determine the world views within which our rationality functions. These factors change over time and also vary among different groups of people at any given moment of time. Indeed, although we have been speaking of the United States' fertility history as though it were a single story, in point of fact, as in the case of mortality, there has been a great deal of variation in fertility *among different groups in our society.*

Since we will be discussing many of these variations in detail later in this book, let us now simply list some of the factors that can give rise to different fertility outcomes:

• *Religion:* In the United States, one of the most common notions historically (but still heard today) is that Catholics, with their official opposition to most contraceptive methods, are outreproducing Protestants, Jews, and other religious groups. Although early in our history there was some truth to this allegation, the major fact of the past two decades has been the convergence of Catholic and non-Catholic fertility rates. Although still somewhat above Protestant fertility rates (and rather more above the quite low Jewish rate), Catholic fertility has fallen sharply and in recent years has tended to linger below the replacement rate.[13]

• *Race and Ethnicity:* Black fertility rates

are higher than those of whites. During the Baby Bust, rates for both blacks and whites fell sharply, but as Figure 3-4 indicates, blacks still have higher fertility than whites. As the same figure indicates, Hispanics have higher fertility than either whites or blacks. Among major minority groups, Asian Americans generally have the lowest rates. The danger of placing people in such broad groups, however, is indicated by several facts: (1) whereas most Asian groups have low fertility, some (like the Hmong and the Cambodians) are well above the national average; (2) whereas most Hispanics exhibit high fertility, some (like the Cubans) are below the national average; and (3) whereas blacks and Hispanics on average have higher fertility than whites in general, the growing class of educated black and His-

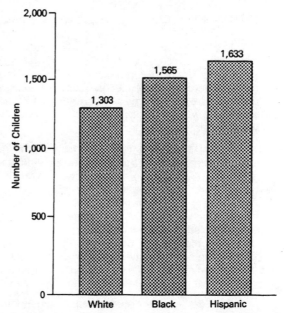

**FIGURE 3–4:  Fertility by Race and Ethnicity, 1988**
This chart measures the number of children ever born per 1,000 women aged 18 to 44 in 1988 in different racial or ethnic groups.

*Source: Current Population Reports,* U.S. Series P-20, No. 436, May, 1989, Table 1, pp. 15–16.

panic women have relatively low fertility rates.

• *Education:* A common fear in the 1930s, when the U.S. birth rate had fallen to what were then historically low levels, was that the heart of the decline was in the educated classes. That educated Americans do have fewer children than the less educated is beyond doubt. In 1988, women in the 18–44 age group who had had four years of college or more had 63.3 births per 1,000 women, whereas those who had not finished high school had 86.9 births, or 37 percent more. Incidentally, this factor explains a good part, but not all, of the difference between the fertility rates of different ethnic groups in the United States.

• *Income levels:* Another factor that ex-plains part (but not all) of ethnic fertility differences is income level. The effect of income level on fertility is quite striking. In 1988, for example, women whose annual family incomes were above $50,000 had only half the fertility rate of women with annual family incomes under $10,000.[14]

When we put these substantial fertility differences among different groups in our population *at a given moment in time* together with the substantial variation in U.S. fertility rates *over time*, we can understand why it has proved difficult to provide any simple, reliable theory of fertility behavior in this country, and even more difficult to predict that behavior in the future. We can also understand why it will be necessary to return to this intriguing subject often in the pages that follow.

## SUMMARY

1. *Fecundity* measures the physiological capacity to produce children, while *fertility* refers to the number of children produced. In the course of modern development, the fecundity of women often rises because of improved nutrition and living standards, while their fertility rates, measured in various ways, tend to decline.

2. In the United States, we began with initially very high fertility (a total fertility rate estimated as high as 7.7 in 1790), and then went through a massive fertility decline continuing on through the Great Depression of the 1930s. After World War II, this decline was interrupted by the Baby Boom, when the fertility rate reached a height of 3.8 in 1957, but then was resumed with the great Baby Bust beginning in the mid-1960s. In the late 1980s, our fertility rate was lingering around the below-replacement rate of 1.8–2.0.

3. The massive decline in U.S. fertility over the past two centuries shows some resemblance to the more general theory of demographic transition. We must keep in mind, however, that we really began in Stage II (rapid population growth) and not in Stage I. A full accounting of our experience, moreover, requires bringing many factors into consideration: the rural-agricultural to urban-industrial transformation, the many effects of technological and economic progress, and the changing role of women.

4. Attempts have been made to provide systematic theories of fertility choice, recognizing that the exercise of conscious choice in this area of life is to some extent a product of the modernization process. Economists have tried to analyze the demand for children, whether for quantity of children or quality of children, as a product of rational decision making by utility-maximizing individuals.

5. Efforts have also been made to explain the Baby Boom and the Baby Bust in economic terms, as in the relative income hypothesis of Richard Easterlin.

6. Our general failure to predict future fertility trends accurately suggests, however, that there are many social-cultural-historical factors involved besides those incorporated in our systematic theories. Also, we have to be aware that there is no single fertility story in our society at any given moment of time. Fertility can vary among groups for a variety of religious, racial, ethnic, educational, and income reasons. Thus, although there is no indication of any sharp forthcoming rise in the U.S. fertility rate, caution must be used in projecting such rates too far into the future.

## KEY CONCEPTS FOR REVIEW

Fecundity

Fertility

 annual number of births
 crude birth rate
 age-specific birth rate
 total fertility rate
 replacement rate

Menarche, menopause, and sterilization

Replacement rate

Rate of natural increase

Secular decline in U.S. fertility

Baby Boom

Baby Bust

Modernization and fertility choice

Theory of demographic transition

Rural-agricultural to urban-industrial change

Pervasive technological change

Changing role of women

Opportunity costs of having children

"Demand" for children in economic terms

Relative income hypothesis

Differential fertility by religion, race, education, and income class

## QUESTIONS FOR DISCUSSION

1. Distinguish *fecundity* from *fertility*. Why is it often the case in industrial countries like the United States that measures of fecundity and those of fertility will move in opposite directions?

2. Looking back at Figure 2-1, explain why the rate of *natural increase* in a society at any given time can be measured by the vertical distance between the two curves. Explain also why we say that the United States, from the earliest days, was really in Stage II of the transition, rather than Stage I.

3. We have described the fertility history of the United States in terms of four phases. What are these phases? In what respects was the U.S. experience special, and in what respects did it display features common to most industrial nations?

4. Since it is illegal to buy and sell children, in

what sense can it possibly be said that the quantity of children couples "demand" may be affected by the "price" or "cost" of children? What are some of the major factors that may have increased the relative price of children? Is the concept of *opportunity cost* important to this analysis?

5. From what you know of young people today, would you say that the number of children they wish to have is: (a) greater than, (b) equal to, or (c) less than the number their own parents had? Have you seen any change in direction in the number of children "demanded" in recent years? Would the *relative income hypothesis* be helpful in understanding your own observations?

6. "Decisions about marriage and having children may be partly rational but they certainly also involve important irrational elements as well." Discuss.

## NOTES

1. *1990 Guinness Book of World Records* (New York: Sterling Publishing Company, 1990), p. 14.
2. The reader will note that we say that a population growing at 2 percent per year doubles in 35 years,

not in 50 years. This is because we are dealing with "compound interest" growth. Thus, if we started with 100 million people in year 1, we would have 102 million people in year 2 at a 2 percent rate of increase. In year 3, however, we would not have just 2 million more people (for a total of 104 million), but $1.02 \times 102$ million ($= 104.04$ million), adding 2.04 million more. The general rule for the doubling of a population is called the "rule of 70" (based on the natural logarithm of 2). This rule states that to find the approximate number of years it takes a population to double, divide 70 by the growth rate (in percent). At 2 percent the doubling time is 70/2, or 35. At 1 percent, it is 70 years; at 5 percent, 14 years.

3. In addition to the total fertility rate, demographers sometimes measure the *general fertility rate,* or the number of births in a year divided by the number of women in the childbearing ages (usually, 15 to 44) in that year. This is like the crude birth rate, except that it is measured with respect not to the whole population but only to those bearing children in that year. Two other measures are the *gross reproduction rate,* a special case of the total fertility rate which measures the number of daughters a cohort of women will have ($=$ TFR $\times$ Female births/All births), and the *net reproduction rate,* which corrects the gross reproduction rate for the fact that all females do not live through the whole of their reproductive years. In principle, a net reproduction rate of 1 leads to a stable population. However, stability may be a long time in actually coming, depending on the age structure of the current population and also, of course, on whether or not there is net immigration. In 1986 the U.S. net reproduction rate was about 0.88, but our population continues to grow because of our age structure and immigration.

4. As we shall have many occasions to point out in later pages, this urban-industrial society is itself going through a continuing transformation. These changes affect both the kind of work we do (shifting from manufacturing to service industries) and where we live (from centralized cities to very complex suburban and exurban sites). Many years ago, sociologist Daniel Bell labeled this new phase the *postindustrial society.* The present chapter, however, is mainly concerned with historical developments and thus our use of the term *urban-industrial society* is simply a rather loose description of a major past transformation.

5. John Scanzoni, *Shaping Tomorrow's Families: Theory and Policy for the 21st Century* (Beverly Hills, Calif.: Sage Publications, 1983), p. 33.

6. See Conrad Taeuber and Irene Taeuber, *People of the United States in the 20th Century* (Washington, D.C.: U.S. Government Printing Office, 1971), p. 357. Also see W. Grabill, C. Kiser, and P. Whelpton, *The Fertility of American Women* (New York: Wiley, 1958). It should be noticed that as the character of farming has changed in modern times, becoming more mechanized and complex,

the rural–urban differences in fertility rates have narrowed and in some countries rural fertility is now slightly lower than urban fertility. See Gary Becker, *A Treatise on the Family* (Cambridge, Mass.: Harvard University Press, 1981), p. 97.

7. The standard reference here is to J. A. Banks, *Prosperity and Parenthood: A Study of Family Planning among the Victorian Middle Classes* (London: Routledge & Kegan Paul, 1954). It should be noticed that the effects of technology in creating new opportunities can easily be combined with its effects on lowering mortality in the explanation of long-run fertility decline. Thus, the eminent demographer Kingsley Davis concluded: "Under a prolonged drop in mortality with industrialization, people in northwest Europe and Japan found that their accustomed demographic behavior was handicapping them in their effort to take advantage of the opportunities being provided by the emerging economy.... Faced with a persistent high rate of natural increase resulting from past successes in controlling mortality, families tended to use every demographic means possible to maximize their new opportunities and to avoid relative loss of status." Kingsley Davis, "The Theory of Change and Response in Modern Demographic History" (1963), reprinted in S. W. Menard and E. W. Moen, *Perspectives on Population: An Introduction to Concepts and Issues* (Oxford: Oxford University Press, 1987), p. 40.

8. See David S. Landes, *The Unbound Prometheus: Technological Change and Industrial Development in Western Europe from 1750 to the Present* (Cambridge: Cambridge University Press, 1969), pp. 21–22. Also, Alex Inkeles, "Making Men Modern: On the Causes and Consequences of Individual Change in Six Developing Countries," *American Journal of Sociology,* 75(2), September 1969. Economist Richard Easterlin and sociologist Eileen Crimmins also note the importance of this change from "natural fertility" to "deliberate control by individual households." In this connection, they quote the French demographer Bourgeois-Pichat: "One of the main features of the so-called demographic revolution has been precisely to change not only the level of fertility but also change its nature. Having a child has been becoming more and more the result of free decision of the couple. And this change in the nature of fertility may be more important than the change in its magnitude." Easterlin and Crimmins, it should be added, also feel that the change in magnitude is itself "of major consequence." See R. Easterlin and E. Crimmins, *The Fertility Revolution: A Supply and Demand Analysis* (Chicago: University of Chicago Press, 1985), pp. 4–6.

9. Gary S. Becker, *Treatise on the Family,* especially Chapter 5.

10. For a comprehensive statement of the relative

income theory, see Richard A. Easterlin,, *Birth and Fortune: The Impact of Number on Personal Welfare* (New York: Basic Books, 1980).

11. The word *cohort,* as used in this paragraph, is a term frequently employed by demographers. In its most common sense, as a *birth cohort,* it refers to all persons born during a certain year or other period of time. Thus, as opposed to analyzing all people living at a certain moment of time, cohort analysis would typicaly follow those born at the same time over the course of their lifetimes. See Appendix, p. 474.

12. R. A. Easterlin, "American Population since 1940," in M. Feldstein, ed., *The American Economy in Transition* (Chicago: University of Chicago Press, 1980), pp. 294–295. This is a somewhat complicated point. Essentially, it is being said that, in the old days, the ups and downs of unemployment during the business cycle meant that even though you might be in a small cohort of young workers entering the labor market, you might not be facing particularly advantageous conditions. Thus, in the 1930s, even though the birth rate had been falling earlier in the century, the workers entering the labor market faced extremely bad conditions (the Great Depression). Only when, through modern fiscal-monetary policies, the government guarantees high employment does the small-cohort effect really work. The assumption here is, of course, that modern fiscal-monetary policies really do substantially moderate the ups and downs of the business cycle—probably a reasonable assumption.

13. Interestingly, it was estimated that, in 1989, the country in the world with the *lowest* total fertility rate—1.3—may be predominantly Catholic Italy.

14. For a brief but authoritative statement of the sources of differential fertility, see Charles F. Westhoff, "Fertility in the United States," *Science,* *234,* October 31, 1986.

# 4

# *America on the Move*

*M*ortality and fertility, we have seen, are fundamental influences shaping the growth of populations. Here we examine a third important variable—migration. America has been populated by immigrants from other lands and their descendants. Well over 50 million people have arrived on these shores since the first British settlements in North America nearly four centuries ago, much the largest long-distance population movement in history. Migration to America is one central thread in our history. Migration within America—from the East to the West, from the country to the city, from the inner city to the suburb, from the "Snowbelt" to the "Sunbelt"—is another equally significant one. Both of these processes need to be understood to grasp who we are and how we live today.

## THE PEOPLING OF COLONIAL AMERICA

The first Americans—the indigenous peoples of the New World whom Columbus called "Indians" as a result of his delusion that his ship had landed on the edge of Asia rather than the Bahamas—were immigrants. No evidence has survived to allow a detailed historical account of the first Indian settlers, but scholars agree that small bands of them from the Siberian plains crossed the Bering Straits to Alaska some 30,000 to 40,000 years ago. Some remained there, but others moved south in search of a more hospitable environment and eventually spread across North, Central, and South America. After the arrival of the European settlers of North America, the native population shrank drastically as a result of warfare and the spread of diseases to which they had no immunities. They were easily pushed into the interior by whites who wanted their land. By the time of the American Revolution the number of Indians in British North America had dropped to perhaps half a million.[1]

## The Population Explosion in Colonial America

Over the course of the seventeenth and eighteenth centuries, Britain planted 13 colonies in what became the territory of the United States of America, starting with the settlement at Jamestown, Virginia, in 1607. The population of these colonies grew at a spectacular rate, far more rapidly than in the French settlements in Canada or the Spanish and Portuguese colonies in Central and South America. There were fewer than 5,000 British subjects in North America in 1630. By 1650 there were ten times as many, about 50,000. Over the next half century the population grew fivefold, to a quarter of a million. By 1780 it stood at 2.8 million, a more than tenfold increase. This growth rate was staggering by comparison with that of the mother country. In 1650 the people of England outnumbered their brethren in North America by 100 to 1. In 1700 the ratio was down to 20 to 1, and by the time of the American Revolution (1775–1783) it was a mere 3 to 1. (By 1840 the population of the United States exceeded that of Great Britain.)

Much of this population growth was attributable to the very high birth rates and low death rates that prevailed in colonial America, matters considered in detail in preceding chapters. But the population expanded much more rapidly than was possible through natural increase alone. The other source of growth, one that gave American society a distinctive shape, was the large-scale immigration of newcomers who followed in the footsteps of the first white Englishmen.

### Slavery

One large and rapidly growing element of the population of British North America consisted of people who were not "immigrants" of the usual sort, who chose to come to the New World in search of greater opportunity. They were involuntary immigrants, African blacks who were captured in their homeland by members of rival tribes, sold to a European slave-trader by an African chieftain, and shipped across the ocean. Although there were Africans in Virginia as early as 1619, at first their numbers were tiny and their status somewhat ambiguous. In the closing decades of the seventeenth century, however, the English white indentured servants who had made up most of the labor force in the southern colonies were no longer willing to tolerate the miseries of life in the tobacco fields. The vacuum they left was filled by large numbers of Africans brought in through the international slave trade. By the time of the Revolution, slaves made up one-sixth of the population of British North America and one-third of that of the colonies south of Delaware.[2]

Although slaves were ruthlessly exploited and denied elemental rights, they were encouraged to form families and reproduced at a pace that gave them a rate of natural increase of 18 percent a decade, only slightly below that of southern whites. Between 1700 and 1780, a quarter of a million Africans were imported into the North American colonies. But the black population increased by almost twice that (by 448,000).[3] Slave-owners elsewhere in the Americas—in Cuba and Brazil, for example—worked their slaves to death at an early age, and simply bought more to replace them. American planters were distinctive in caring for their human property well enough to reap the profit from the slaves' natural increase.

### Colonial Immigration

The involuntary movement of Africans into British North America was exceeded by waves of immigration on the part of newcomers who did have a choice in the matter and saw the prospects for a better life in America. Many were English, like the first settlers, but toward the end of the seventeenth century and in the eighteenth century, increasing numbers were not.

North America drew waves not only of English settlers but of others as well. The Spanish, French, and Portuguese governments of the day took great pains to keep outsiders out of their overseas colonies in the Western Hemisphere. They did not trust strangers and barred them from entry. The British, by contrast, tolerated newcomers regardless of their national origin or religion, in the belief that the most rapid possible population growth would provide a source of raw materials for the home country and an ever-increasing export market for English goods. North America had an abundance of unsettled land, a tradition of tolerating dissenting religious groups quickly developed, and the law provided easy terms of naturalization for alien newcomers. The largest non-English immigrant groups to arrive were Germans and the three Celtic peoples of Great Britain—the Welsh, the Scots, and the so-called Scotch-Irish, Scottish Presbyterians who had moved to Ireland early in the seventeenth century and moved on to North America from the 1720s onward in search of economic opportunity and religious freedom. Pennsylvania, founded in 1681 with William Penn's promise of rich land on generous terms and full religious freedom, was a particularly strong magnet for these newcomers, but large numbers went to other British colonies as well.

English law governed the colonies, and English traditions of self-government took firm root. But the emerging culture was not a carbon copy of that in the mother country. Non-English-speaking immigrants preserved their native tongues, although their children seldom did so and their grandchildren almost never. It was a melting pot society long before the Revolution and the Constitution, with a degree of ethnic and religious diversity tolerated nowhere else in the world at that time in history. An English traveler who dined in a tavern in Philadelphia in 1744 reported that the two dozen men at the table were "a very mixed company of different nations and religions."

There were "Scots, English, Dutch, Germans, and Irish; there were Roman Catholics, Presbyterians, Quakers, Methodists, Seventh-Day men [Adventists], Moravians, Anabaptists, and one Jew."[4] By the time of the Revolution, one scholar has concluded, only about half of the inhabitants of the colonies had English blood in their veins.[5]

### Westward Movement

The first settlements in British North America were naturally on the Atlantic seaboard—Jamestown, Boston, New York, Baltimore, Charleston, Philadelphia. From the beginning, however, the lure of "free land" in the interior to the west exerted an overwhelming magnetic force. "The most persistent theme in American history," one historian has declared, "is the persistent westward march of the American people," and that march began almost immediately.[6] Visitors from the Old World sounded the theme again and again. The people of British North America had no roots. They were restless, always ready to hit the road. Compared with their brethren back home, said an English observer, they "acquire no attachment to Place. . . . Wandering about Seems engrafted in their Nature; and it is a weakness incident to it, that they should forever imagine that the Lands further off, are still better than those on which they have already Settled."[7] "From an early moment in their cultural history," an astute historian has noted, the people of the United States "looked inward to the creation of a new cultural space for themselves," because they had "a geographical opportunity" to occupy "a continental interior that was developable and habitable on a large scale by a new population."[8]

By the time of the Revolution, the land from the Atlantic coast to the Appalachian barrier was fully taken up, and colonists were casting covetous eyes on the millions of fertile and untilled acres west of the Appalachian chain. Anti-British sentiment that led to the drive for independence was provoked in part by King George III's Proclamation of 1763, which barred white settlement beyond the Appalachians to minimize conflict between the colonists and the Indians, and by the imperial government's attempt to incorporate what became the American Midwest into Canada via the Quebec Act of 1774.

## THE MASS IMMIGRATION OF THE NINETEENTH AND TWENTIETH CENTURIES

Over the course of the eighteenth century, down to the first census of the United States in 1790, the American population grew at an average of 36 percent per decade, doubling every quarter of a century. From 1790 to the election of Abraham Lincoln to the presidency in 1860, it continued to expand at almost precisely the same dizzying pace, averaging 35.5 percent each ten years over those seven decades. In his second annual message to Congress, in 1862, Abraham Lincoln took these figures as evidence of an "inflexible" and "reliable law of increase" that meant that by 1930 the U.S. population would exceed 250 million, double what it turned out to be.[9]

The continuity in the growth rate that led Lincoln to speak of a "reliable law of increase" was real. However, it masked two very important demographic changes in the antebellum period, changes that worked in opposite directions and cancelled each other out almost exactly. The first was a marked decline in the nation's rate of natural increase, the result of a sharp fall in fertility without any offsetting decline in the mortality rate (see Chapters 2 and 3). Almost exactly balancing the numbers lost through falling fertility was a massive rise in immigration from overseas that further reduced the proportion of settlers who derived from English stock.

### The Old Immigration

By the end of the nineteenth century, the newcomers from northern and western Europe who poured into the United States before 1890 had come to be known as the **"old" immigrants,** to distinguish them from those then arriving from eastern and southern Europe, the **"new" immigrants.** No reliable figures on immigration are available before 1820, when the U.S. government first began to record systematically all entering newcomers. But in the giant surge of immigration in the 15 years before the outbreak of the Revolution, no more than 10,000 people entered per year, and it is doubtful that the number exceeded that at any time before 1820. By the 1820s, when accurate data first become available, the volume of immigration was modestly above that, averaging about 14,000 a year. In the next decade, the 1830s, it quadrupled, to about 60,000 per year. In the 1840s it rose to about 170,000 per year, and in the decade preceding the Civil War it climbed again to an average of a quarter million people annually, twenty-five times higher than the prerevolutionary peak. Between 1790 and the Civil War, more than 5 million immigrants entered the United States, a number larger than the total population of the country in 1790 (Table 4-1).

After 1860 the continuing fertility decline began to drag down the overall population growth rate, despite continuing immigration on a quite large scale. Lincoln's prophecy was quickly proved false. Although both the Civil War and the prolonged business depression that began in 1873 deterred newcomers temporarily, immigration in the 1860s and 1870s continued at roughly its prewar pace of about a quarter of a million a year, and in the 1880s it surged to a new high of over half a million a year. Total population growth for the years 1860 to 1890, however, was down to little more than 25 percent per decade, fully a third below the prewar level.

How important was immigration to the development of American society in this

**TABLE 4-1: Immigrants Admitted and Immigration Rate per 1,000 Residents per Decade, 1820–1988**

|  | Immigrants (thousands) | Rate |
|---|---|---|
| 1821–1830 | 152 | 1.2 |
| 1831–1840 | 599 | 3.9 |
| 1841–1850 | 1,713 | 8.4 |
| 1851–1860 | 2,598 | 9.3 |
| 1861–1870 | 2,315 | 6.4 |
| 1871–1880 | 2,812 | 6.2 |
| 1881–1890 | 5,247 | 9.1 |
| 1891–1900 | 3,688 | 5.3 |
| 1901–1910 | 8,795 | 10.4 |
| 1911–1920 | 5,736 | 5.7 |
| 1921–1930 | 4,107 | 3.5 |
| 1931–1940 | 528 | 0.4 |
| 1941–1950 | 1,035 | 0.7 |
| 1951–1960 | 2,515 | 1.6 |
| 1961–1970 | 3,322 | 1.7 |
| 1971–1980 | 4,493 | 2.1 |
| 1981–1988 | 4,711 | 2.5 |
| Total | 54,367 | 3.3 |

*Source: Statistical Abstract of the United States: 1990* (Washington, D.C.: U.S. Government Printing Office, 1990), p. 9.

period? By one measure—the share of total population growth attributable to the influx of people from abroad—it was of considerable and sharply rising importance. In the 1820s, less than 4 percent of the nation's population increase was the result of immigration; by the 1850s it accounted for almost a third of the increase (31.6 percent); in the 1880s the influx from abroad was responsible for nearly 40 percent of total population growth.

Another way of judging the significance of immigration to a society is to ask what proportion of its population at any one time consisted of people born abroad. We cannot be sure of the size of the immigrant bloc before 1850, when the census first enumerated the place of birth of all U.S. residents (see Table 4-2). But had the question been asked, earlier censuses doubtless would have found a much smaller fraction of newcom-

*wouldn't it be 1st generation*

**TABLE 4-2: Percentage of U.S. Population Foreign-Born or of Foreign Stock**

| | Foreign-Born | Native-Born of Foreign Parentage | Foreign Stock |
|---|---|---|---|
| 1850 | 9.7 | NA | NA |
| 1860 | 12.8 | NA | NA |
| 1870 | 14.4 | 13.3 | 19.8 |
| 1890 | 14.7 | 18.3 | 33.0 |
| 1900 | 13.7 | 20.6 | 34.0 |
| 1910 | 14.8 | 20.5 | 35.3 |
| 1920 | 13.2 | 21.5 | 34.7 |
| 1930 | 11.6 | 21.1 | 32.7 |
| 1940 | 8.8 | 17.6 | 26.4 |
| 1950 | 6.9 | 15.6 | 22.5 |
| 1960 | 5.4 | 13.2 | 18.6 |
| 1970 | 4.7 | 11.4 | 16.1 |
| 1980 | 6.2 | 10.9 | 17.1 |

*Source: Historical Statistics of the United States, p. 19. The 1980 census regrettably dropped the question about parental nativity. The 10.9 figure is from the 1979 Current Population Survey, as given in Current Population Reports: Special Studies, Series P-23, No. 116, March 1982.*

ers than was discovered in 1850, when almost one of ten Americans—9.7 percent—was an immigrant. By 1870 the rising tide of immigration brought this figure up to 14.4 percent, one American in seven; by 1890 the proportion of foreigners in the land was still higher, 14.7 percent.

Immigrants, furthermore, had children themselves—**second-generation Americans**—people born in the United States of parents who were born elsewhere. The census-takers did not enumerate the second generation until 1870, but by then they made up 13.3 percent of the population. Immigrants and their native-born children together—known as the **foreign stock**—thus accounted for over one-quarter (27.7 percent) of the total population just after the Civil War, and by 1890 one American in three either was an immigrant or had grown up in an immigrant household. The proportion was even higher in urban centers, especially the largest ones, where immigrants disproportionately clustered. In New York City in 1890, people of foreign stock made up 77 percent of the population; in Chicago and Detroit this figure was 78 percent, in Cleveland 75 percent, in Boston and St. Louis 68 percent. [10]

The main source countries in the period of the old immigration were the British Isles, including Ireland, plus Germany and Scandinavia (see Table 4-3). Between 1820 and 1890 more than three out of four (77 percent) of the 15 million entering immigrants originated there. Germans made up the largest single element (30 percent), followed closely by the Irish (23 percent) and the British (18 percent), with the much smaller movement of Swedes, Norwegians, and

**TABLE 4-3: Country of Origin of Immigrants, 1820–1889**

| | Total (thousands) | Percentage from | | | | |
|---|---|---|---|---|---|---|
| | | Britain | Ireland | Germany | Scandinavia | Other |
| 1820–1829 | 128 | 19.5 | 40.2 | 4.5 | 0.2 | 35.6 |
| 1830–1839 | 538 | 13.8 | 31.7 | 23.2 | 0.4 | 30.9 |
| 1840–1849 | 1,427 | 15.3 | 46.0 | 27.0 | 0.9 | 10.8 |
| 1850–1859 | 2,795 | 13.5 | 36.9 | 34.8 | 0.9 | 13.9 |
| 1860–1869 | 2,082 | 14.9 | 24.4 | 35.2 | 5.5 | 20.0 |
| 1870–1879 | 2,742 | 21.1 | 15.4 | 27.4 | 7.6 | 28.5 |
| 1880–1889 | 5,249 | 15.5 | 12.8 | 27.5 | 12.7 | 31.5 |
| Total | 14,961 | 18.0 | 22.9 | 29.6 | 6.7 | 22.8 |

*Source: U.S. Bureau of the Census, U.S. Department of Commerce, Historical Statistics of the United States from Colonial Times to 1970 (Washington, D.C.: U.S. Government Printing Office, 1975), p. 105.*

Danes making up another 7 percent of the total. Each of these countries was experiencing explosive population growth and unsettling economic change that created a surplus of people who needed work desperately enough to cross the ocean to find it.

### The New Immigrants

The "new immigration" that began around 1890 was called "new" partly because it was on a considerably larger scale then ever before, but chiefly because it came from very different sources, from eastern and southern rather than northern and western Europe, and involved peoples whom many natives regarded as profoundly different from their predecessors. The "old" immigrants, most Americans came to think, fitted smoothly into their society and became valuable citizens. The "new" immigrants, by contrast, were allegedly inferior and unassimilable. This fear proved unfounded, as it turned out, but it became dominant after World War I. The result was the adoption of restrictive legislation that both cut back on the number of newcomers allowed into the country and imposed quotas that sharply discriminated against Italians, Greeks, Poles, east European Jews, and other "new" immigrant groups.[11]

The "new" immigration certainly was new by the test of sheer numbers. Before 1890 the peak year for immigrant entries was 1882, when some 779,000 newcomers entered the country. That number was exceeded in all but one year between 1903 and 1914. Almost 12 million immigrants arrived in the span of a mere dozen years, at a time at which the total U.S. population was well under 100 million (76 million in 1900, 92 million in 1910). Not only did the foreign stock far outnumber native-born Americans of native parentage in the country's great cities but in the entire northeastern region of the United States, immigrants and their children had a 52 to 48 majority over Americans of native stock in 1900, 56 to 44 in 1910, and 57 to 43 in 1920.[12] This immense demographic change fueled the natives' fears that they were being swamped by an invasion of alien beings.

As Table 4-4 indicates, after 1890 British, Irish, German, and Scandinavian newcomers continued to arrive in rather substantial numbers—more than 4 million over the next three decades. But the economies of their homelands had by then developed enough to offer satisfactory employment opportunities to most people who had earlier felt heavy pressure to leave. Similar pressures forcing emigration overseas were now being felt throughout eastern and southern Europe. One-fifth of the 18 million immigrants to the United States in the 1890–1920 period came from the Austro-Hungarian empire, another fifth from Italy, and close to as many (17 percent) from the Russian empire, a total of more than 10 million people. Although almost 6 out of 10

**TABLE 4-4: Country of Origin of Immigrants, 1890–1919**

| | | | Percentage from | | | |
|---|---|---|---|---|---|---|
| | Total (thousands) | "Old" Immigration | Russia | Austria-Hungary | Italy | Other |
| 1890–1899 | 3,695 | 46.1 | 12.2 | 14.5 | 16.3 | 10.9 |
| 1900–1909 | 8,202 | 19.8 | 18.3 | 24.4 | 23.5 | 14.0 |
| 1910–1919 | 6,348 | 14.9 | 17.4 | 18.2 | 19.4 | 30.1 |
| Total | 18,245 | 23.34 | 17.4 | 20.2 | 20.6 | 28.4 |

Source: *Historical Statistics of the United States*, p. 107.

immigrants in these years came from those three leading countries, both the Russian and Austro-Hungarian empires were made up of many different national groups with different languages and customs. There were Bulgarians and Belorussians, Czechs and Croatians, Latvians and Lithuanians, Magyars and Macedonians, Rumanians and Russyns, Slovaks, Serbs, Sicilians, and Slovenians. Nativists who feared that the new immigrants represented such radically different cultures that they could never find a place in America were wrong. But the incredible variety of peoples who made up the eastern and southern European immigration stream did make the task of absorbing them into the life of the nation a daunting one.

On the other hand, one feature of the new immigration that was frequently commented on by critics of the time might have been a source of some assurance. A growing number of newcomers were "birds of passage"—males of working age who came to the United States to toil and save for a brief period and then returned home, which means that the figures on total arrivals—**gross immigration**—give an inflated impression of the number of immigrants who actually settled and made a life for themselves in the United States. **Net immigration**—the number arriving minus the number returning—in 1901–1910 was only 72 percent of the number of total arrivals.[13] In many groups—Italians, Greeks, Poles, and other Slavs—a majority of immigrants went back home. That is the major reason why, despite the unprecedentedly huge million-a-year influxes, the proportion of residents of the United States who were foreign-born in 1910, 14.8 percent, was not much above what it had been in 1890 (see Table 4-2). There were more arrivals than ever before, but also more departures. Critics claimed that these "birds of passage" were ripping off the United States by taking the money and running. It is not clear, though, why this was bad for the economy or the society, and it diminished the strains of absorbing so many newcomers on a long-term basis. Such temporary immigrants were not prospective citizens but really "guest workers" like those found throughout western Europe today.

## Immigration since the 1920s

A series of increasingly tough laws designed to limit immigration in general and that of the new immigrants in particular were passed in 1917, 1921, and 1924. The first two of these were not very stringent, so that as many as 805,000 immigrants entered in 1921 and another 707,000 in 1924. The bite of the 1924 legislation was much stronger, however, and by 1928 the number of new arrivals had fallen to a little over 300,000. Because of the discriminatory quotas, few of these were the eastern and southern Europeans who had been pouring in in such large numbers; entries by new immigrants plunged to a mere 3 percent of their prewar level. Arrivals now were either from the "old" immigrant countries or from Canada or Mexico. It appeared that the United States had turned its back on the world, that the Golden Door had been permanently slammed shut.

The Great Depression that began in 1929 made entry into an America of breadlines and soup kitchens far less attractive. Only half a million immigrants arrived in the entire decade of the 1930s, and slightly more than that number returned home. Net immigration in the Depression decade did not contribute to population growth; it actually reduced it a bit.

After World War II, however, immigration resumed on an increasingly large scale. Although the restrictive quota system remained in force, special exemptions for refugees and displaced persons following the war allowed the immigration of over a million people in the 1940s, almost all of them after 1945. Special acts opened the doors to Hungarians, Cubans, and Czechs fleeing oppressive Communist regimes. And then, in 1965, a radically new immigration law increased the ceiling on new-comers and discarded the discriminatory national origins quotas. Entrants rose from one million in the 1940s to 2.5 million in the 1950s, 3.3 million in the 1960s, 4.5 million in the 1970s, and about 6 million in the 1980s (Table 4-1). (These figures leave out the unknown but undoubtedly quite large numbers of illegal immigrants; see the discussion in Chapter 20.)

In absolute numbers these figures are extremely high. The 1980s saw the entry of more immigrants than any decade in American history except the first one of this century. But considered as an **immigration rate** relative to the receiving population, recent levels of immigration have been fairly low by historic standards. The 1981–1988 immigration rate of 2.5 per 1,000 residents was less than a third of the rate in the two decades before the Civil War, and not even a quarter of the rate for 1901–1910.[14] Although the absolute numbers are very large, the size of the receiving population is much greater than earlier.

The size of current immigration flows may be looked at from a third vantage point as well. The absolute numbers are large. The rate is fairly low. A third way of assessing the magnitude of the phenomenon is global. How many of the world's immigrants are coming to the United States as compared to other countries? In the nineteenth century era of mass immigration, about two-thirds of the world's immigrants made the United States their destination. It is striking that this is still the case today. No other country in the contemporary world rivals the United States in its attractiveness to newcomers and its willingness to accept a great many of them. The era of completely unrestricted immigration is long over, but something of the old American confidence in our society's capacity to absorb and benefit from the presence of people born in other lands has been restored.

The character of immigration to the United States has shifted dramatically as a result of the 1965 law. The hostility toward Asian newcomers that had marked U.S. immigration law since the Chinese Exclusion Act of 1882 at last came to an end in 1965. Since then over 3 million Asians, 41 percent of total immigration, have entered the country, with the Philippines, China, Korea, and Vietnam the principal countries of origin (Table 4-5). As large a group, another 41 percent of the total, have come from Latin America. Mexico alone has sent over one million legal immigrants in the past 15 years, as well as an uncounted number of illegal ones.[15]

In terms of their educational and occupational backgrounds, recent immigrants fall into two classes. Most Asians are well educated, with 73 percent of them high school graduates and over a third (36 percent) having college degrees. Many move into professional or managerial occupations; there are currently 20,000 physicians from India practicing medicine in the United States, for example. Newcomers from Latin America, especially Mexico and Central America, more closely resemble typical immigrants to the United States before

**TABLE 4-5: Sources of Immigration, 1971–1988**

Total entrants (thousands)  9,204

Percentage from:
  Europe:  14.3
  Asia:  41.3
  Canada:  2.2
  Latin America:  41.2
  Other:  1.0

Leading countries (thousands):
  Mexico:  1,206
  Philippines:  735
  China:  589[a]
  Korea:  544
  Vietnam:  495
  Cuba:  415
  India:  377
  Dominican Republic:  331
  Jamaica:  306

[a] Includes Taiwan and Hong Kong.

*Source: Statistical Abstract of the United States: 1990*, p. 10.

_Model minority myth_

World War I, lacking education and skills. Some 77 percent of immigrants from Mexico have less than a high school education, and only 3 percent are college graduates. For entrants from the Dominican Republic the figures are 70 and 4 percent, respectively; for those from El Salvador, Nicaragua, Guatemala, and Panama, 74 and 4 percent.[16] Whether they still play the positive role their predecessors did, in an economy radically different from that of an earlier America, is a controversial issue that will be taken up in Chapters 20 and 21.

## PATTERNS OF INTERNAL MIGRATION

The first European settlers in British North America, and the successive waves of immigrants who followed in their footsteps, were restless people who refused to settle for the constricted opportunities open to them in the lands in which they were born. They were confident that the grass was greener elsewhere, that a better life was available to them across the ocean. The impulse to move on did not wither away once they had made their way safely to the New World. Instead, it became a national tradition. "The will to move that brought, at considerable risk to themselves, masses of migrants across three thousand miles of ocean also sent, at considerable risk to themselves, masses of migrants across three thousand miles of the North American continent."[17] Subsequent generations of Americans were like the pioneers, unsettled, restless, footloose, people always on the move and on the make.

### People in Motion—A Constant

The American propensity to move seems to have been strikingly constant over time, despite all the enormous changes in most aspects of our life in the two hundred years of our national existence. We have no systematic evidence on this point before 1850, but since then the Census Bureau has

**TABLE 4-6:** **Percentage of Native-Born Population Residing Outside Their State of Birth, 1850–1980**

| | |
|---|---|
| 1850: | 23.3 |
| 1900: | 21.8 |
| 1950: | 26.5 |
| 1980: | 30.8 |

_Source: Historical Statistics of the United States, p. 89; Statistical Abstract of the United States: 1988, p. 38._

provided a useful measure of internal migration by recording how many native-born Americans reside in a state other than the one in which they were born. In the middle of the nineteenth century, almost a quarter (23.3 percent) of the population had moved from where they had been born across at least one state boundary by the time the census-taker reached them (Table 4-6). (Some of these movers had lived in three or even more states, of course.) By the turn of the century the fraction had dropped a bit, to 21.8 percent, but in the twentieth century it has edged upward again. By 1950 it was 26.5 percent, a shade above the figure of a century before. It rose further over the next three decades, and in 1980 stood at 30.8 percent.[18]

This modest increase in mobility within the United States may be a function of the fact that average life spans have increased considerably. A century ago the people who are now retiring to Florida or Arizona would have been dead by retirement age. Allowing for that difference in the number of years in which one is alive and capable of changing residence, these data suggest a fairly constant migration propensity over the past century and a half.

Movement across state lines, of course, is only a fraction of all residential mobility. Many people move short distances, and in some states it is possible to move quite long ones, without leaving the state. The systematic evidence we have about this is confined to the post–World War II period. Since then, however, about one-sixth of the population has moved from one house to another each year. Over a five-year period, nearly half of the population changes houses (49.4 percent for 1955–1960, 44.1 percent for 1965–1970, 48.5 percent for 1970–1975, and 47.0 percent for 1975–1980). About half of those moves are within the same county; one-quarter are to other counties within the same state, and one-quarter are to another state.[19] This means that the typical American will live at no less than *fourteen* different addresses over the course of his or her lifetime, four as a dependent child moving with his or her parents and ten more as an adult! The scattered historical evidence available on this point suggests that a similar pattern prevailed in earlier periods as well.[20]

Although the rate at which restless Americans shift about from place to place appears to have been more or less constant, the prevailing direction of movement has altered over time. Four major waves of internal migration may be distinguished—movement from the settled east to the open frontier in the west, movement from the countryside to the city, movement from the inner city to the suburb, and movement from the **Snowbelt** or **Rustbelt** to the **Sunbelt.** Although the timing of these phases overlapped somewhat, especially that of the last two, they unfolded in rough chronological order.

### Westward Expansion and Settlement

The peace treaty with Britain that ended the revolutionary war gave the new-born United States a vast national territory that extended all the way to the Mississippi River, a land area of almost 900,000 square miles. But the spectacular growth rate of the population of British North America over the preceding two centuries made it plain that still more land would be required before long if the United States was to remain a land of independent farmers in accord with Thomas Jefferson's dream.

The next several decades saw a phenomenal geographical expansion of the young

republic. While the population expanded tenfold in the first 80 years under the government established by the Constitution (1790–1870), the density of the population—the number of inhabitants per square mile—increased only two and a half times, because the national domain quadrupled in those years.[21] Jefferson's purchase of the Louisiana Territory from France in 1803 added to the United States all of the present states of Arkansas, Missouri, Iowa, Nebraska, and South Dakota, and large portions of Louisiana, Oklahoma, Kansas, Colorado, Wyoming, Montana, North Dakota, and Minnesota. The purchase of "Florida" (which included not only the state of Florida but also chunks of Alabama, Mississippi, and Louisiana) from Spain in 1819, the annexation of Texas in 1845, the acquisition of the "Oregon" territory (Washington, Idaho, and part of Montana) through negotiations with Britain in 1846, the purchase of the Southwest from Mexico in 1848 after the Mexican War, and the purchase of Alaska from Russia in 1867 rounded out the boundaries of the continental United States, a territory of 3.5 million square miles.

Settlers surged into these new lands in the West at a dizzying pace. At the time of the first census, in 1790, only half a million Americans, 13 percent of the total, lived in the territories west of the original 13 seaboard states. By the time of the Civil War no less than 16 million people, 55 percent of the entire population, had moved into the interior. The framers of the Constitution were well aware of the expansive vitality of their society, and they took pains to provide for the easy entry of new states into the Union on an equal basis. Migrants to the West could thus be assured that they would not be held in permanent colonial subjugation to the original 13 states. As a result, a new state was added to the Union an average of once every three years in this period, bringing the total to 34 by 1860.

The course of the westward movement of the population is nicely rendered in visual form in the Census Bureau's map of the

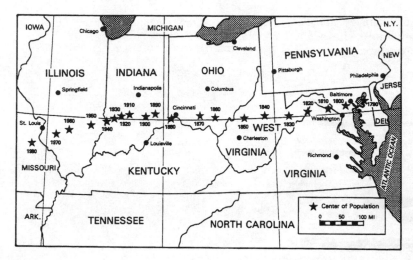

**FIGURE 4–1: Shifting Geographical Center of the U.S. Population, 1790–1980**

Source: *Statistical Abstract of the United States.*

shifting location of the **geographical center of the population** of the United States, the point at which there are equal numbers of people living to the north, south, east, and west (see Figure 4-1). At the time of the first census, in 1790, the geographical center of the population was 23 miles east of Baltimore, Maryland. On the eve of the Civil War, in 1860, it had moved 400 miles west and was in south central Ohio. By the turn of the century it was in southeastern Indiana. Since then it has edged across the rest of Indiana and Illinois and is now in Missouri, a bit south and west of St. Louis.

In a famous essay on "The Significance of the Frontier in American History" (1893), the great historian of the frontier experience, Frederick Jackson Turner, argued that the presence of vast amounts of unsettled land beckoning in the West was the fundamental force shaping the American character, the prime source of our national optimism. "The existence of an area of free land," he declared, "its continuous recession, and the advance of American settlement westward, explain American development."[22] Accordingly, he contended that a momentous watershed in U.S. history had been reached in 1890, when the Census Bureau declared that the frontier had vanished, that the East and West were no longer separated by an unbroken belt of counties settled at a density of less than two persons per square mile. One could no longer draw on a map a line from Canada to Mexico, west of which there was unsettled land there for the taking.[23]

Turner was right that the continuous westward thrust of the population down to his own day had given substance to the Jeffersonian myth of America as the land of the independent yeoman farmer. From the beginning to the end of the nineteenth century there was abundant "free land" to be had on the frontier, whether in western Massachusetts, Pennsylvania, and Virginia; in Ohio and Kentucky; in Illinois and Alabama; or in the Dakotas and Texas. No fewer than 3 million new farms were started in the West in the last great phase of agricultural settlement in the closing decades of the nineteenth century. But Turner focused too narrowly on agricultural expansion as the key to American values. He was right to say that "America has been another name for opportunity . . . [and] movement has been its dominant fact."[24] But mobility and opportunity, and the optimism they breed, have not disappeared with the closing of the farming frontier. Instead, they have been kept alive by an expanding, urban-based, industrial economy whose character Turner was unable to appreciate.

### The Urban Frontier

Long before the Census Bureau announced the end of the agricultural frontier, another profoundly important population shift was well underway—the rise of the city. At the time of the first U.S. Census, in 1790, only one American in 20 lived in a community of 2,500 or more, the census definition of an urban place. In every decade but one thereafter (1810–1820), the urban population grew more rapidly than the rural population, usually much more rapidly (see Table 4-7). By the time of the Civil War city dwellers were one-fifth of the population; by the opening of this century the figure was up to 40 percent. The 1920 census was the first to report an urban majority, and today almost three out of four Americans (74 percent) live in cities.

The urban frontier deserves as much attention as the rural frontier. Much of the westward thrust of the American people described here was a move not into open countryside but into burgeoning urban communities. The amazing growth of population in the nineteenth-century Midwest was brought about not only by farmers spreading across the prairie but also by people moving into Chicago, Cleveland, St. Louis, and hundreds of smaller urban centers that sprang up around them. Likewise, the boom in the Mountain and Pacific states in the twentieth century is not primarily the result of agricultural expansion but has come from the growth of "instant cities" like Los Angeles, San Diego, Portland, Seattle, Denver, and Phoenix, which were little more than small towns a century ago.

The soaring size of the urban population was in part due to the fact that immigrants from abroad flocked toward cities because the industries that offered them jobs—the steel factories of Pittsburgh, the garment shops of New York, the meat-

**TABLE 4-7:   Growth of the Urban and Rural Population, 1790–1980**

| | Percentage Urban | Percentage Change in Decade | |
| --- | --- | --- | --- |
| | | Urban | Rural |
| 1790 | 5 | — | — |
| 1800 | 6 | 60 | 34 |
| 1810 | 7 | 63 | 35 |
| 1820 | 7 | 32 | 33 |
| 1830 | 9 | 63 | 31 |
| 1840 | 11 | 64 | 30 |
| 1850 | 15 | 92 | 29 |
| 1860 | 20 | 75 | 28 |
| 1870 | 26 | 59 | 14 |
| 1880 | 28 | 42 | 26 |
| 1890 | 35 | 57 | 13 |
| 1900 | 40 | 37 | 12 |
| 1910 | 46 | 39 | 9 |
| 1920 | 51 | 29 | 3 |
| 1930 | 56 | 28 | 4 |
| 1940 | 57 | 8 | 6 |
| 1950 | 64 | 21 | 7 |
| 1960 | 70 | 29 | −1 |
| 1970 | 74 | 20 | −1 |
| 1980 | 74 | 12 | 11 |

*Note:* A new census definition of *urban* accounts for some of the increase in the urban population between 1940 and 1950.

*Source:* Adapted with permission of the Free Press, a Division of Macmillan, Inc., from Donald J. Bogue, *The Population of the United States: Historical Trends and Future Projections.* Copyright © 1985 by the Free Press.

packing plants of Chicago, the automobile factories of Detroit—were located in urban centers. What is often forgotten is that the city was a powerful magnet that pulled native-born Americans out of the countryside as well as attracting immigrants. The available figures on internal migration from the country to the city are much scantier than those on immigration, but the tidal waves of internal migration cityward seem to have been about as large as those bringing newcomers across the ocean in the years of mass immigration, and considerably larger in the period from the mid-1920s to the mid-1960s, when entry into the United States was severely restricted by law. The movement of southern blacks to northern cities, which began during World War I— to fill the jobs left vacant because immigration was disrupted by the war—is known as the Great Migration, a key turning point in African American history. The migration of whites from the farm to the city in these years was on an even larger scale. The question posed in the once-popular song, "How You Gonna Keep Them Down on the Farm after They've Seen Paree [Paris]?" applied equally to young people who had only seen Omaha, Akron, or Battle Creek. The heroes of Horatio Alger's endless series of rags-to-riches children's novels were usually farm lads who came to the city to seek their fortune. In reality, not many who made the journey found a fortune, but urban wages were much higher than those in the country, and the freedom and excitement of the city seemed preferable to the monotony and drudgery of farm work.

*Industrialization = urbanization*

### Suburbs and Inner Cities in the Automobile Age

Urbanization has been going on at a more or less steady pace since the birth of the republic. The past half century, however, has seen a profound transformation in the character of urban development. Before then, urban growth was strongly focused on the city center. The railroad was the key mode of transportation, and railroads centralized activity, bringing people and goods to terminals downtown. In recent decades the railroad has given way to the automobile and truck, and the areas of high growth have shifted from the old urban core to the periphery—the suburbs. The population of suburban communities on the outskirts of cities has grown spectacularly, and so too has the number of jobs located there. At the same time, the population of most central cities has stagnated or declined. Middle-class and relatively prosperous working-class Americans have fled to the suburbs, leaving the inner cities largely to the poor, especially the minority poor.

At the close of the Great Depression, in 1940, just over half (51 percent) of the U.S. population lived in **metropolitan areas**— that is, in cities of 50,000 or more or in the suburban communities that surrounded them (Table 4-8). The other 49 percent lived in smaller cities, towns, or rural areas. Residents of the central cities of metropolitan America outnumbered those in the suburbs by close to two to one (32 to 19 percent). Only one American in five had a home in suburbia.

The postwar years brought a remarkable population explosion in the suburbs. Nine million people moved to suburbia in the decade after the war, and the pace continued unabated thereafter. In the 1950s New York City's population declined by 2 percent, while its suburbs grew by 58 percent. By 1960, almost one-third (31 percent) of the U.S. population lived in suburban parts of metropolitan areas; in 1980 no less than 9 out of 20 did.

In part this immense shift in population was due simply to rising levels of affluence, and the normal desire of people to escape the noise, dirt, crowding, and crime that city dwellers must tolerate. That the first phase of the flight to the suburbs coincided with the postwar Baby Boom is hardly surprising. It seemed obvious that a single-family home on a tree-lined suburban street, not far from a spanking new school, was a

**TABLE 4-8:  Percentage of the Population Residing in Central Cities, Suburbs, and Nonmetropolitan Areas, 1940–1980**

|      | Central City | Suburb | Nonmetropolitan |
|------|------|------|------|
| 1940 | 32 | 19 | 49 |
| 1950 | 32 | 24 | 44 |
| 1960 | 33 | 31 | 36 |
| 1970 | 31 | 38 | 31 |
| 1980 | 30 | 45 | 25 |

*Source:* Adapted with permission of the Free Press, a Division of Macmillan, Inc., from Donald J. Bogue, *The Population of the United States: Historical Trends and Future Projections.* Copyright © 1985 by the Free Press.

better place for kids than a cramped apartment—and the average couple planned on having four kids. Thus, the Baby Boom triggered a great building boom on the vacant tracts along the metropolitan fringe, where land costs were far lower than in the city. Levittown, on Long Island, New York, was the pioneer mass production suburban development, which had a thousand imitators. In 1947 one could buy a four-room house in Levittown, with an attic convertible into two bedrooms, for under $10,000, with appliances included. Between 1940 and 1980 the proportion of American families owning their own homes rose from 44 to 65 percent, and most of those newly purchased dwellings were erected as a result of the postwar suburban building boom.[25]

The automobile took on a new significance in the suburban age. Americans have long been infatuated with their cars. As early as 1929, remarkably, there was one car on the road for every five residents of the country. But as of 1989 there are more than 176 million motor vehicles registered, one for every American of driving age![26] The staggering proliferation of automobile ownership was the sine qua non of suburban growth. Suburbanites must drive to get to work, or even to pick up a quart of milk. The suburban shopping mall, with its acres of free parking, is as important a symbol of our era as the great downtown department stores—Macy's, Filene's, Marshall Field, J. L. Hudson—were earlier in the century, or as the huge downtown railroad stations not far from them. Even more so, perhaps, because a much larger fraction of the population lives within easy reach of a shopping mall.

Public policy encouraged suburban growth in a variety of ways. Home ownership was subsidized by exempting the interest paid on home mortgages from income tax. The Federal Housing Authority (FHA) and the Veteran's Administration (VA) offered generous credit terms to home buyers. The benefits went disproportionately to suburbanites because most of the nation's stock of new homes was in the suburbs. Likewise, the vast expenditure on new highways brought about by the Interstate Highway Act of 1955 and similar decisions by state and local authorities were what made it possible to live dozens of miles from one's workplace and drive there in a reasonable time. Suburban dwellers who believe that the urban poor should "pull themselves up by their own bootstraps" as they themselves supposedly have done might note the importance of these public subsidies in making their own comfortable way of life possible.

The rise of the suburb went hand in hand with a decline of the central city. Since World War II no fewer than 18 of the nation's 25 largest cities have seen their populations shrink, not just relative to the U.S. population but in absolute numbers as well. St. Louis, for example, was home to over 800,000 people in 1950, when the flight to the suburbs had just begun; by 1980 the number had plunged to barely half that, back to about what it had been in 1890. Cleveland's 44 percent loss was only the most extreme example of a general pattern. In those same three decades of the suburban boom, the population dropped 39 percent in Minneapolis, 38 percent in Cleveland and Buffalo, 37 percent in Pittsburgh, 35 percent in Detroit, and 30 percent in Boston.[27]

The rise of suburbia and the decline of the central city has brought about growing segregation of Americans along social class and racial lines. As a result of the flight of middle-class people from the inner city and the movement of the better paying jobs as well, by 1959 the income of the average city dweller was 11 percent below that of the average suburbanite; by 1983 it was no less than 28 percent below. That same year 17 percent of the residents of the entire Detroit metropolitan area had incomes below the official poverty line; the figure for the city of Detroit itself was twice that (36 percent).[28]

As the inner cities became increasingly poor, they also became increasingly black and Hispanic. In 1980 blacks made up only 20 percent of the population of the Detroit metropolitan area, but 63 percent of the population of Detroit itself. In St. Louis the figure was 17 percent for the metropolitan area and 46 percent for the city proper.

The growth of a black middle class in recent years has brought a significant black influx into suburbia. The proportion of blacks residing in suburbia rose from 16 to 24 percent in the 1970s and increased further in the 1980s.[29] Nevertheless, there is a clear and growing division between affluent, largely white suburbs and poor, largely black inner cities. By now nonwhites outnumber whites in Chicago, Philadelphia, Detroit, Baltimore, Atlanta, St. Louis, Washington, New Orleans, Oakland, and many other cities, and the list is destined to grow. Without some major new public policy initiatives, the bleak job prospects for this new inner-city majority will make it difficult for them to believe in America as a land of opportunity.[30]

### Growth of the Sunbelt

In the nineteenth century and the early decades of the twentieth century, migrants—whether from abroad or the American countryside—headed for the cities of the Northeast and Midwest. Some of that traditional movement has continued in the past half century, particularly the migration of southern blacks to places like Chicago, Cleveland, and Detroit. However, the main thrust of the population has been away from the cities of the Snowbelt or Rustbelt (so named because of the rust accumulating on its closed factories) toward the Sunbelt. All but one of the country's 10 largest cities in 1940 lost population over the next four decades. The one exception—Los Angeles—was the only one of them in the Sunbelt, and it almost doubled in size. Of the 10 largest cities in 1980, Los Angeles was joined by four newcomers (Houston, Dallas, San Diego, and San Antonio), all in the Sunbelt. Their populations were three to four times what they had been in 1940. The largest cities of the old industrial heartland

lost nearly 3 million residents in those years, while the five largest Sunbelt cities gained 5.5 million. During the 1980s the population of the West grew by 21 percent and that of the South by 15 percent. The Northeast grew by a mere 4 percent in the decade, and the Midwest by less than 2 percent.[31]

Another indicator of this huge population shift—and one with vital political implications—is the declining weight of Snowbelt states in Congress and the Electoral College and the rising power of the Sunbelt. Between 1940 and 1990 New York and Pennsylvania together lost 27 congressional seats because of population change, Illinois 7, and Massachusetts and Ohio 5 each. The big gainers were California, with 32; Florida, with 17; and Texas, with 9.[32]

Blacks as well as whites, it should be noted, have been drawn into the booming Sunbelt area. The great historic flight of black people from the South reached a peak in 1970, when the proportion living there had fallen to 52 percent, down dramatically from 77 percent in 1940. Since then the trend has been reversed. The concentration of blacks in the Rustbelt states of the Northeast and Midwest has fallen off. The fraction in the West has grown from an insignificant 1.4 percent in 1940 to an estimated 8.5 percent in 1988.[33] And in 1988 the black population of the South had grown by over 3 million since 1980, a rise from 52 to 56 percent of the total.[34]

The growth of the Sunbelt is closely tied to the decentralizing forces that led to the suburban boom and the relative decline of the inner city. As automobiles and trucks became the dominant form of transportation, industry was freed from its dependence on downtown locations close to rail terminals, and was able to move out where land was cheaper. Land was cheaper in suburbia; it was less expensive, too, in the Sunbelt than in the more densely populated Snowbelt. In addition, labor costs were lower in the Sunbelt, where the trade union movement has traditionally been weak. The development of effective and economical air conditioning was crucial to making habitable places where summer temperatures easily reach 105 degrees. Political decisions to award defense contracts during and after World War II to firms outside the industrial heartland also played an important role.

These trends could possibly be reversed by unexpected developments, such as an acute oil shortage that might radically increase the cost of automotive transportation and air conditioning and give competitive advantages to the denser urban agglomerations of the Northeast and Midwest, whose decaying mass transit facilities might be restored. A stiff increase in the federal gasoline tax might provide a push in that direction. As yet, though, no developments of a magnitude to alter this fundamental pattern have taken place.

Whatever the future may bring, the historical record suggests that Americans are likely to continue to display the flexibility and adaptability, the optimism and opportunism, that are part of our heritage as a people in motion with an eye always on the horizon.

## SUMMARY

1.   Mobility from place to place is very much in the American grain and has been for almost four centuries. The American continent was peopled by newcomers from around the globe, and the influx of people seeking a new and better life here continues today. The vast majority of settlers chose to come to America, in search of greater economic opportunity and political and religious freedom. (The major exceptions were the blacks, forcibly brought to North America as slaves, and the American Indians already here, who were deprived of their lands and shouldered aside by the rapidly expanding population of white settlers.)

2.   In the first half of American history, from the first British settlements at the beginning of the seventeenth century to the Revolution near the end of the eighteenth century, immigration to North America was dominated by English, Irish, Scottish, and Welsh settlers, although there were significant numbers of Germans, Dutch, French, and others (as well as involuntary immigrants from Africa). Immigration on a vastly larger scale picked up steam in the early decades of the nineteenth century. The key sources of the "old immigration" were the British Isles, Germany, and the other countries of northern and western Europe. Toward the end of the century immigration fever subsided in those countries but spread into eastern and southern Europe, the countries of the "new immigration."

3.   Blaming the allegedly inferior newcomers for the mounting social problems of a rapidly urbanizing and industrializing America, in the 1920s the United States erected a legislative wall to bar the further entry of southern and eastern Europeans. However, the national quota origins system was relaxed after World War II and repealed altogether in 1965, opening the way to what may be called the "new new immigration" of our time. The main sources of newcomers now are Asia and Latin America.

4.   Movement from one place to another within the United States—internal migration—has been a central theme of American history as well. When the first census was conducted in 1790, the population was still strongly concentrated along the eastern seaboard of the country. In most places the frontier was within a few days' walk of the ocean. Thereafter, Americans surged across the Appalachian barrier into the rich plains of the interior, and eventually reached the Pacific.

5.   The rate at which Americans move around seems to have been surprisingly constant since the first accurate measurements became available in 1850. However, the dominant direction of movement shifted as the economy was transformed from an agricultural to an industrial one. By the end of the nineteenth century, the prospect of starting a new farm in South Dakota was less of a magnet than taking a job in a Pittsburgh mill or a Chicago meatpacking plant.

6.   In the years since World War II another great shift has taken place. Americans have been moving from the inner cities to the suburbs, and from the Rustbelt or Snowbelt to the Sunbelt.

## KEY CONCEPTS FOR REVIEW

"Old" versus "new" immigrants
Second-generation Americans
Foreign stock
Net versus gross immigration

Immigration rate
Geographical center of the population
Metropolitan area
Rustbelt or Snowbelt versus Sunbelt

## QUESTIONS FOR DISCUSSION

1. In what ways has the United States' special character as a giant magnet for immigrants shaped other distinctive features of our national life?

2. It has been said that ethnic conflict is to America what class conflict is to Europe. What are the pros and cons on this proposition? Should the fact that we are all, in some sense, immigrants make for national harmony? Might not importing huge numbers of people from dozens and dozens of antagonistic nations around the world instead have made U.S. history a story of unending civil war? Why didn't it?

3. Where was the frontier in 1790? 1860? 1890? Does the concept still have any application in today's United States?

4. What has been the role of technological changes in the shifting about of the U.S. population in recent decades?

5. The rise of suburbia and the decline of the inner cities, with their increasingly minority population, have been due in part to public policies. Is there thus some societal obligation to mount new programs aimed at ameliorating urban problems generated by past policies?

## NOTES

1. C. Matthew Snipp, *American Indians: The First of This Land* (New York: Russell Sage Foundation, 1989), p. 14.

2. U.S. Department of Commerce, U.S. Bureau of the Census, *Historical Statistics of the United States from Colonial Times to 1970* (Washington, D.C.: U.S. Government Printing Office, 1975), p. 1168.

3. Robert W. Fogel and Stanley Engerman, *Time on the Cross: The Economics of American Negro Slavery* (Boston: Little Brown, 1975), p. 29.

4. Stephan Thernstrom, *A History of the American People*, rev. ed. (New York: Harcourt Brace Jovanovich, 1988), p. 95.

5. Gary B. Nash, *Red, White and Black: The Peoples of Early America*, 2nd ed. (Englewood Cliffs, N.J.: Prentice-Hall, 1982), p. 200. Estimates suggesting a much greater predominance of people of English stock were developed in the 1920s and still have unfortunately widespread currency, having been reproduced in the generally authoritative *Historical Statistics of the United States*. They have been subjected to a devastating critique by Forrest and Ellen MacDonald in "The Ethnic Origins of the American People," *William and Mary Quarterly*, 3rd series, *37* (1980), 179–199, and a series of related papers in the same journal, *41* (1984), 85–135.

6. George W. Pierson, *The Moving American* (New York: Knopf, 1972), p. 7.

7. Pierson, *The Moving American*, p. 5.

8. John H. McElroy, *Finding Freedom: America's Distinctive Cultural Formation* (Carbondale, Ill: Southern Illinois University Press, 1989), p. 7.

9. Roy Basler, ed., *The Collected Works of Abraham Lincoln* (New Brunswick, N.J.: Rutgers University Press, 1953), Vol. V, p. 533.

10. Stephan Thernstrom, *The Other Bostonians: Poverty and Progress in the American Metropolis, 1880–1970* (Cambridge, Mass.: Harvard University Press, 1973), p. 114.

11. John Higham, *Strangers in the Land: Patterns of American Nativism, 1850–1925* (New York: Atheneum, 1963).

12. *Historical Statistics of the United States*, p. 23.

13. This explains the discrepancy between the net immigration figures given in Donald J. Bogue, *The Population of the United States: Historical Trends and Future Projections* (New York: Free Press, 1985), p. 17, and those on total arrivals in Table 4-1. The former are much lower than the latter in this period as a result of the very high return rate. For a detailed discussion of return migration rates, see Charles Price, "Methods of Estimating

the Size of Groups," in Stephan Thernstrom, ed., *Harvard Encyclopedia of American Ethnic Groups*, (Cambridge, Mass.: Harvard University Press, 1980), pp. 1036–1039.

14. U.S. Bureau of the Census, *Statistical Abstract of the United States: 1988* (Washington, D.C.: U.S. Government Printing Office, 1987), p. 10.

15. The extremely high figures for Mexicans, averaging 65,000 per year over these 16 years, may puzzle those who know that the 1965 law set a limit of 20,000 immigrants per year from any one country. The explanation is that the law makes very generous allowance for the entrance of close relatives of U.S. citizens, and that these entries do not count against the 20,000 quota. Of the 601,708 legal immigrants admitted in 1986, for example, over one-third (216,821) were exempted from the quota because they were relatives of citizens; *Statistical Abstract*, p. 11. The large resident population of Mexicans currently in the United States is thus able to bring in many relatives without regard to the 20,000 annual ceiling. Of those immigrants who do come in under the quota, furthermore, about 80 percent are selected because they are more remote relatives of immigrants already here. Those with occupational skills in short supply in the United States amount to less than 12 percent of the total. Some critics argue that much greater priority should be given to the admission of immigrants with needed skills and less to people whose only qualification is that they are related to people already here. For this view, see George Borjas, *Friends or Strangers: The Economic Impact of Immigration* (New York: Basic Books, 1990).

16. *Statistical Abstract*, p. 38.

17. McElroy, *Finding Freedom*, p. 129.

18. *Historical Statistics of the United States*, p. 89; *Statistical Abstract*, p. 38.

19. Bogue, *Population of the United States*, pp. 326–329.

20. Howard Chudacoff's study, *Mobile Americans: Residential and Social Mobility in Omaha, 1880–1920* (Chicago: University of Chicago Press, 1972) is the fullest examination of this question. Its findings fit nicely with the national data for the post–World War II United States.

21. The population density figures cited here do not include the 600,000 square miles in Alaska, since it was virtually unpopulated long after its purchase in 1867. Including Alaska in the density figures for 1870 would reduce them still further.

22. Frederick Jackson Turner, *The Frontier in American History*, (New York: Henry Holt and Co., 1920), p. 1.

23. Walter Nugent, *Structures of American Social History* (Bloomington: Indiana University Press, 1981), p. 14.

24. Turner, *The Frontier*, p. 37.

25. *Statistical Abstract*, p. 690.

26. *Statistical Abstract*, pp. 13, 576.

27. Bogue, *Population of the United States*, p. 120.

28. Kenneth T. Jackson, *The Crabgrass Frontier: The Suburbanization of the United States* (New York: Oxford University Press, 1985), p. 8; W. J. Wilson, *The Truly Disadvantaged: The Inner City, the Underclass, and Public Policy* (Chicago: University of Chicago Press, 1987), Chap. 2.

29. Bogue, *Population of the United States*, p. 136.

30. Wilson, *The Truly Disadvantaged*.

31. *Wall Street Journal Report*, "Census '90," March 9, 1990, p. R12.

32. *Wall Street Journal Report*, p. R10.

33. *Statistical Abstract*, p. 18.

34. *Boston Globe*, January 10, 1990, p. 3.

# Part II
# *THE OLDER GENERATION*

**5**

# The Aging Society

$A$merica is aging. Before the improvements in mortality and the flight from fertility described in Chapters 2 and 3, the United States, like most premodern countries, had an extremely *young* population. Our average life expectancy at birth in the colonial period, though varying in different colonies, was probably around 35 years. The total fertility rate averaged between 7 and 8. Children were everywhere. There were elderly individuals, sometimes very elderly, but they were few in number. Our **median age**— the age at which half the population is older, half younger—was around 16 years.

One way of describing the Aging of America is simply to say that over the past two centuries, our median age has more than doubled, to 32.7 years (Table 5-1), and to add that it is still rising and could conceivably, by the year 2050, reach a level nearly three times what it was in colonial days.

A new nation two hundred years ago, we were also a very young one. Today, our not-so-new nation is also a much older one—and growing older by leaps and bounds.

## THE POPULATION PYRAMID

The increase in the median age of populations is a very general phenomenon in the modern era, especially pronounced in the more economically advanced nations. The Japanese actually outlive us in terms of average life expectancies. The Swedes have a higher proportion of elderly in their population than we do.

This comment about the "proportion of elderly" is a significant one, because the term *Aging Society* often refers to a society in which the proportion of elderly persons is increasing. So viewed, the Aging of America may seem more dramatic than when framed in terms of median age:

• The number of Americans 65 and over has doubled during the past 30 years (while our total population was increasing by less than half).

• The number of Americans 85 and over has more than tripled during this period.

• Meanwhile, the fastest growing group at the moment has become the centenarians: The number of Americans 100 years or older is expected to quadruple in the next 15 years or less!

When we make this shift of focus from our median age to more specific questions about what is happening to the numbers and proportions of different age groups, we are introducing an important demographic tool: the **population pyramid.**

Figure 5-1 represents a population pyramid of a certain stylized shape. We measure age groups in 10-year intervals along the vertical axis and the percentages of people in each age group along the horizontal axis. As is conventional, we divide the pyramid down the center by sex, males to the left and females to the right.

Certain features of such a population pyramid are worthy of note.

*The Height of the Pyramid.* As we have drawn this hypothetical pyramid, the highest age category represented is 100–109 years. We do know that people have sometimes lived longer than 109 years—there

**TABLE 5-1: Median Age, United States, 1800–1989**

| Year | Median Age | Year | Median Age |
|------|-----------|------|-----------|
| 1800 | 16.0[a] | 1940 | 29.0 |
| 1840 | 17.8 | 1950 | 30.2 |
| 1860 | 19.4 | 1960 | 29.4 |
| 1880 | 20.9 | 1970 | 27.9 |
| 1900 | 22.9 | 1980 | 30.0 |
| 1920 | 25.3 | 1989 | 32.7 |

[a] Data for whites only.

*Sources:* U.S. Bureau of the Census, *Current Population Reports*, Series P-25, Nos. 1022, 1057.

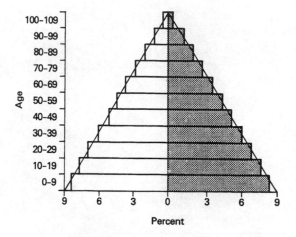

**FIGURE 5–1:   The Population Pyramid**
This population pyramid shows the percentages of a hypothetical population in different ten-year age groups. Sometimes five-year age groups are used. Also, the pyramid is sometimes drawn showing absolute numbers of people rather than percentages.

are authenticated cases of Americans having done so, as well as Japanese and other nationalities—but the number is minuscule, and thus the loss in generality here is very small.[1] Of course, we could have avoided the problem altogether by simply making our highest category 100 and over (100 + ). This customary solution to the problem would, however, give us no information about what the common **maximum human life span** is. This term (in contrast to **average life expectancy**) refers to the oldest age that individual members of a population have attained. As far as has been determined to date, this maximum age has not changed over the course of recorded history. The oldest individuals in ancient times—although there were very few of them—lived about as long as the oldest individuals surviving today. The aging of societies, historically speaking, has occurred through changes in the *shape* of the pyramid of a *given* height.

We wish to emphasize this historical point as a possible contrast to the *future* aging of our society, which may conceivably involve increases in maximum human life span—that is, a rise in the height of the pyramid (see Chapters 22 and 26). For the moment, we simply note that, were we to make our top category 100 +, we could not

show explicitly the possibility of an increase in maximum human life span.

*Aging as Changing Proportions of Young and Old.* As we have just stated, the aging of societies has taken place historically through changes in the shape of the pyramid. The wider the base, others things being equal, the younger the society. The wider the top, other things equal, the older the society.

Thus, if we compare Figure 5-2a with our original pyramid, we notice that the new pyramid has (1) a greater percentage of people in the older age brackets, and (2) a smaller percentage of people in the younger age brackets. These surpluses and deficits are shown in Figure 5-2b, where the two pyramids are superimposed.

One reason for emphasizing these rather obvious points is that they bring out an underlying principle that is often overlooked. Many people tend to think of the aging of a society simply in terms of longer and longer average life expectancies. But it is not just a question of more old people, but also one of fewer young people. Indeed, as we shall show in a moment, longer life expectancies at birth can actually be associated with the society growing "younger" rather than "older"—this because of their

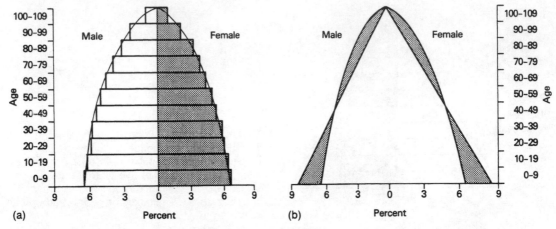

**FIGURE 5–2:   Different Proportions of Young and Old**

effect on the numbers of surviving young people.

Also, we should notice that, as we move from Figure 5-1 to Figure 5-2a, we begin to lose the perfectly pyramidal structure of our population diagram. Carried far enough, our population pyramid could in fact approach a rectangle, or even a top-heavy, inverted pyramid.

*Expanding, Stable, and Contracting Populations.*   We know from Part I of this book that whether a country's population expands or contracts over time will be determined by the three underlying factors: mortality, fertility, and migration. At any given moment of time, however, whether the population expands or not will also be significantly affected by its **age structure.** If there are a great many young people either in or entering the prime childbearing ages, then, for any *given* levels of age-specific mortality and fertility rates and of net immigration, the society will tend to expand more rapidly. If there are few people in these age brackets, then expansion will be slower or even negative.

In Figure 5-3, we compare age structures of two different population pyramids. In the case of the expanding population, there are large numbers of young people

either in or entering the childbearing years. In the case of the contracting population, there are more adults above the childbear-

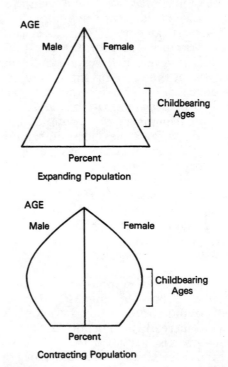

**FIGURE 5–3:   Expanding versus Contracting Populations**

ing ages and an insufficient number of children growing up to replace these young parents.

Of course, the matter is somewhat more complicated than this in that the age structure (shape of the pyramid) is itself determined by past fertility, mortality, and immigration rates. If we neglect migration and concentrate solely on fertility and mortality, we would find that, if these factors are unchanged, then, in the long run, not only the rate of population increase (or decrease) but also the age structure of the population will be stable over time.[2]

Since fertility and mortality rates (as well as immigration) are always changing, however, in most cases we will want to give very explicit attention to the age structure of a country's population. Thus, for example, the young age structures in today's less developed countries (LDCs) tend to mean that their populations will continue to expand quite rapidly, even though, in some cases, their fertility rates may be falling sharply.

## WHY AMERICA HAS BEEN AGING

All of these general comments will help us understand the complicated, and indeed often unexpected, features of the Aging of America to date.

### Aging in the Nineteenth and Early Twentieth Centuries

Between the year 1830 (the first year for which we have sufficient data to estimate a population pyramid for the United States) and 1945, the median age of the U.S. population increased from around 17 years to 29 years. The changing proportions of young and elderly are shown by the different shapes of the pyramids in Figure 5-4.

We have already suggested that the main factor causing these changing proportions of young and elderly was our **long-run decline in fertility.** The simple explanation of the Aging of America over this historic span is that American women were having fewer and fewer babies.

But what about the increase in life expectancy over these decades? Didn't that also make *some* contribution to rendering us an older society?

In terms of our simple explanation, the answer is no. During most of this period, the decline in mortality was particularly sharp among infants and young people. Consequently, the main effect of these advances was to increase the proportions of

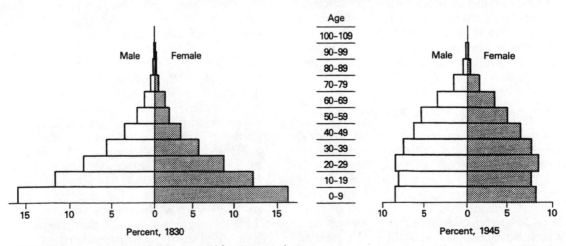

**FIGURE 5–4:   U.S. Population Pyramids, 1830 and 1945**

young people—widen the base—of our pyramid. A decrease in infant mortality is virtually equivalent to a rise in the birth rate. In point of fact, our declining fertility had to *outweigh* the tendency for more babies to survive in order to produce the aging of our society that did occur.

This is the simple explanation. A more complex view takes into account our discussion from Chapters 2 and 3, pointing out that the declining fertility was, in itself, to some degree a *response* to declining mortality and especially declining infant and child mortality.

The story on immigration in relation to the Aging of America is also somewhat complex. During the nineteenth century, the average age of our immigrants is estimated to have been around 24. This was above the median age of our population, which was still below 23 at the end of the century. In this direct sense, then, immigrants may be said to have contributed very slightly to the aging of our society during the nineteenth century.

Again, however, there are secondary effects to be taken into account, particularly the tendency of first-generation immigrants to have higher fertility rates than the rest of the population. Thus, we note that, in order to produce an Aging America, our general decline in fertility had to outweigh not only increasing infant survival rates but also the fact that immigrant groups in the nineteenth and early twentieth centuries brought temporarily higher fertility rates with them.

### Baby Boom and Baby Bust

And then, of course, at the end of World War II, Americans suddenly began to increase the numbers of their children. If declining fertility is the basic explanation of the Aging of America to 1945, then the Baby Boom must have had a sharp impact in making the United States younger. And it did. Between 1950 and 1970, our median age fell by 2.3 years—from 30.2 to 27.9.

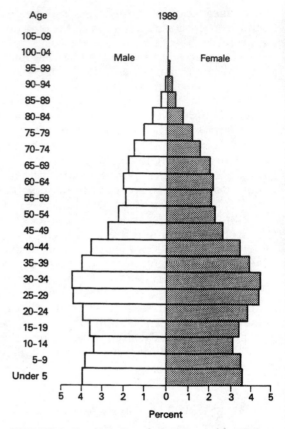

**FIGURE 5–5: U.S. Population Pyramid, 1989**

But then, with the great Baby Bust beginning in the mid-1960s and continuing on into the 1980s, the entire situation was reversed. Our median age began to rise again, and our population pyramid began to take on a rather peculiar shape. As Figure 5-5 shows, the U.S. population pyramid for 1989 has a clear bulge around its middle: these are the "Boomers" in the process of growing older. Immediately beneath them are the "Busters," producing a narrowing of the lower age groups. Mind you, for the *lowest* age groups (0–4, 5–9), the narrowing would be sharper except that the Boomers in 1989 were *all* in the childbearing ages. This means that although their fertility *rate* was still below the replacement level, the *absolute number* of children they produced was fairly high. This phenomenon—more children due to the numbers of Baby Boom parents even though individual parents produced relatively few children—is usually called the **echo boom.**

### Increased Life Expectancies at Older Ages

There was also another change occurring in the dynamics of the Aging of America in this recent period. As we discussed in Chapter 2, medical progress and changes in life-styles during the 1970s and 1980s produced substantial declines in mortality rates and increasing life expectancies *among our older age groups.* These changes have no effect in increasing the numbers of children in the country because women in the older age groups are beyond their childbearing years. At the same time, they directly affect the numbers of elderly and especially very elderly in the population.

It is, therefore, no longer appropriate to say, even in a simplified way, that the Aging of America is wholly due to our declining fertility. Medical and life-style changes are making it possible for the elderly to live much longer, and this is a direct contribution to our aging process. Furthermore, medical and life-style advances will almost certainly continue to contribute to the Aging of America in the future, for the simple reason that infant and child mortality is already sufficiently low that future medical progress is unlikely to have much direct effect in increasing the numbers of young people around.[3] At older ages, however, substantial opportunities remain for both medical and life-style changes to increase our life expectancies during our "golden years." It is no accident that the fastest growing age groups in the United States now are the oldest old.

## FROM PYRAMIDS TO RECTANGLES

One of the great symbols of the ancient world was the Egyptian pyramid. One of the great symbols of the modern world is the skyscraper. From pyramids to skyscrapers. From triangles to rectangles. From our population past to our population future. In these words and images we can, in fact, summarize what has been happening and what is going to happen to the U.S. population and, indeed, to the populations of all industrial nations in the modern world.

Not all of that story is known, of course. Here, however, are three sign-posts that point to the probable future of an aging America:

• *The Aging of the Boomers.* The Baby Boomers are growing older. When they arrived on the scene, they made the United States younger. By the late 1980s, they were truly "average" Americans in that their median age and the median age of the nation was about the same. And now, slowly but steadily and surely, they are making America older. One of the great socioeconomic concerns of our time is precisely this fear of what may happen when the Boomers begin to retire, around the year 2010.

• *The Persistence of the Baby Bust.* As we indicated in Chapter 3, the course of future U.S. fertility rates is very difficult to predict. At the moment, however, we should not be misled by the echo boom into thinking that another fertility revival is on the way. It may be—we noted the slight uptick in U.S. fertility in 1989 and 1990—but so far the *major* development of the last three decades has been the return of our fertility rate to its long-run declining trend and its subsequent persistence at a below-replacement rate. Low fertility will in all likelihood continue to contribute to the future Aging of America.

• *Life Expectancies at Older Ages.* To this we can also add our conclusion that future increases in life expectancies are likely to have the greatest impact on the older age groups. More old people will live to be very old, thus contributing directly to our societal aging process.

What might the net effect of these various factors be on the shape of our population pyramid some 30 or 40 years down the road? Figure 5-6 represents one attempt to estimate how our age structure might look in the year 2030.[4] We have juxtaposed it with our earlier population pyramid for the year 1830. Except for the elongated triangle at the top, representing the "oldest old," the new structure isn't a pyramid at all. It's basically a rectangle.

As it is sometimes put, we in the United States (and throughout the developed world) are busily engaged in "squaring" our population pyramid. Geometrically speaking, this is what the Aging Society is all about.

## SOME CHARACTERISTICS OF AN AGING AMERICA

In this book, of course, we are ultimately not interested in geometry but in people. What are some of the salient characteristics of an aging America in social, economic, political, and personal terms? Can we do anything to slow down this societal aging process? Would we want to?

### The Possible Dependency Burden of the Elderly

The characteristic of an aging America that has attracted the most attention is a result of the changing proportions of elderly relative to the U.S. labor force. If one takes the view that the elderly of each generation are basically provided for by the income produced by the working-age generation, then the elderly as a group—like young children—can be thought of as society's dependents.

We hasten to add that such a view is a very incomplete one because, as we all know, elderly persons typically *save* for their old age. They do this by accumulating assets such as stocks, bonds, savings accounts, and equity in their homes. They also save through a variety of private pension plans. Insofar as the elderly live off these past savings, they are no more dependent on society than are individuals in the prime

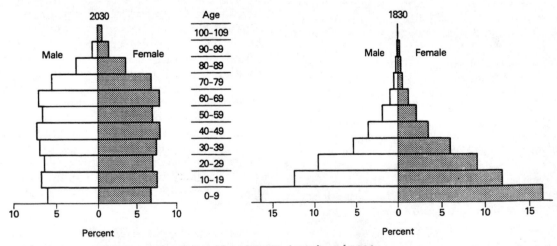

**FIGURE 5–6:   U.S. Population Pyramids, 2030 (Projected) and 1830**
The "squaring" of the population pyramid in an aging society is clearly shown in this contrast between the U.S. pyramid in 1830 (actual) and that for 2030 (projected).

THE AGING SOCIETY **83**

working-age groups. Furthermore, elderly persons also "save" through the taxes they pay for public programs like Social Security. These are matters we will be discussing in some detail in the next chapter.

It is also true, however, that elderly persons are often economically dependent to some degree on the working-age generation. A term sometimes used in this connection is the **elderly dependency ratio,** sometimes referred to as the *aged* or *gerontic* dependency ratio.[5] It is measured by the number of persons in the population 65 and older for each 100 persons in the prime working ages, 20 to 64 (sometimes 18 to 64). Thus, if we have 10 elderly for each 100 of working age, the ratio is 10; if we have 50 elderly for each 100 of working age, it is 50; and so on.

Now there is no question but that this elderly dependency ratio has been rising in our aging America and will continue to do so. In 1950 it was 14—roughly one elderly person for each 7 of working age. By 1987 it had risen to 21, an increase of 50 percent. By the year 2030, it could reach 39 or 40— one elderly person for every 2.5 persons of working age.[6]

Is this a cause for alarm? Some commentators think it is, and for a variety of reasons:

• In the early 1980s, when the elderly dependency ratio was relatively favorable, we already faced a crisis in our Social Security system. The Baby Boom generation was literally flooding into the work force at this time. Also, the percentage of women in the work force was increasing rapidly. If we faced a crisis then, what will happen when all the Boomers reach old age and our work force is weakened by the meager supply of Busters?

• One of the reasons for this early crisis was a rapid increase in Social Security benefits to retirees. In an aging America, the elderly will form a larger and larger potential voting bloc. With such political power

in their hands, will the elderly be likely to demand—and get—still greater benefits in the future?

• Moreover, the elderly dependency ratio overlooks an important factor that can worsen the ratio of actual retirees to actual workers in the United States. The effective dependency of the elderly will be determined in part by the average age at which older workers retire from the work force. In recent decades, there has been a significant lowering of the age at which Americans have been retiring. This trend toward earlier retirement, *combined* with the longer life expectancies at older ages, suggests historically unprecedented lengths of time in retirement—again increasing the potential dependency burden.

• The elderly require, on average, far more medical attention than the young. As science develops more and more elaborate medical technologies, such medical costs tend to rise in any event. How expensive will it be to sustain the lives of so many elderly with such elaborate technologies?

As we shall see, there is much to be said in rebuttal on each of these points.[7] Still, there is no question that an aging America will face an increased burden of supporting the elderly and could even face considerable intergenerational strife as a consequence.

### Changing Proportions of Men and Women

There are other characteristics of an aging America beyond the obvious changes in the proportions of different age groups. One of the more important is a change in our **sex structure.** We have already noted in Chapter 2 that life expectancy at birth for U.S. women is higher than that of U.S. men, that this difference is much greater than it was at the beginning of this century, and that there has been a dramatic increase in the female advantage in life expectancy at the older ages. Whether these differentials will narrow in the future (for example, as the proportion of female to male smokers increases) is not yet certain.

What is certain is that women now vastly outnumber men in the older age groups, and especially in the oldest age groups. In Figure 5-7, we show the different proportions of men and women in the older age groups in the United States in 1989. In the 80-and-over age group, women outnumber men by more than two to one. This imbalance between the number of women and men in an aging America has many personal and social consequences.

Because there are so many more older women than older men, because the general tendency is for men to marry women younger than themselves, and because widowers are more apt to remarry than widows, there is an increasing explosion of unmarried widows in all aging societies. For the United States and the developed countries in general, roughly three-quarters of women 80 years and older are widows. By

contrast, the number of elderly American men who are married exceeds the number of widowers.

The large number of elderly women living alone (primarily through widowhood, but also to an increasing degree through divorce and separation) raises a number of special problems for an aging America. Whether loneliness is one of these problems is subject to some dispute. Some studies indicate that elderly women, even those fairly recently widowed, adjust quite well socially and emotionally to their single state. The age group in which loneliness is the most severe problem may be much younger, the teenage years in particular.[8]

Still, there is no doubt that for many widows, and for those widowers who do not remarry, old age can be a rather desolate experience. This is particularly true where income is lacking to sustain an accustomed or satisfactory life-style.

In this regard, there is no question but that elderly women, and especially elderly black and other minority women, are often likely to find themselves with incomes near or below the poverty level. Pensions for elderly women have historically not been commensurate with those of men. Lack of adequate life insurance on the part of the deceased husband is another common problem. Thus, studies in the mid-1980s found that, among the aged as a whole, widows and other women who live alone are the groups most likely to be in poverty.[9] If those elderly women happen also to be black, the chance that their incomes will be below the poverty line rises to two out of three.

There also may well be a change in the nature of medical problems in the Aging Society because of the preponderance of older women. Although older women have longer life expectancies (lower mortality rates) than older men, they tend to suffer from more chronic ailments than men. Studies in East Boston, New Haven, and Iowa generally found that in each of three older age groups (65–74, 75–84, and 85+) women reported substantially more "disa-

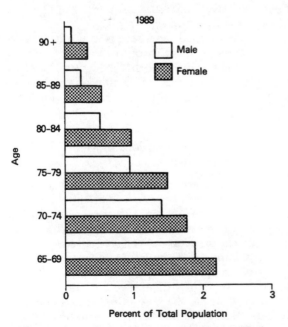

**FIGURE 5–7:   U.S. Elderly Population, 1989, by Sex**

bility" than did men.[10] Dr. Lois M. Verbrugge, a prominent expert in this field, writes:

> Comparing the mortality and physical health data, we find that older women often have worse health status than older men, yet they live longer.... Daily life for women has many aches and pains that are bothersome but not life-threatening. Ultimately, the "killer" conditions of heart disease, cancer, and stroke do manifest themselves and lead to death. In contrast, older men tend to be more bothered in daily life by precisely the problems (circulatory and respiratory) that often cause their deaths.[11]

It is thus possible that one of the policy issues in the Aging Society may involve how much money and research time to give to chronic ailments (like arthritis) that affect women disproportionately, and how much to give to terminal diseases (like heart disease and stroke) that strike earlier in the case of men. The general issue of *quality* versus *quantity* of life is thus subtly affected by the sex distribution of our elderly population.

### Minorities and the Young

But it is not just the older age groups that are changing in an aging America. Equally significant changes are taking place in the composition of the young people who will, in due course, be entering the work force and helping to sustain the elderly.

In Chapter 3, we indicated that the fertility of certain large minority groups—especially Hispanics and blacks—is above that of the general U.S. population. This in itself would suggest that minority groups would be more heavily represented than the majority group among the young people of an Aging America. But this is only part of the story. There are two other factors that will probably increase this representation even further:

1. For any given fertility pattern, the number of babies that a group will produce will be determined by its age structure. If the average age of a given group is younger than that of the majority population, it will be feeding proportionately more young people into the childbearing ages, and hence producing more young than the fertility rate itself might suggest. In the United States, both black and Hispanic populations are younger than the non-Hispanic white population. In 1986, while the median age of non-Hispanic white Americans was 33, the median age of black Americans was 27, and that of Hispanic Americans was under 25.

2. While during the nineteenth century, the median age of immigrants to the United States was around or above the median age of our population in general, the median age of today's legal immigrants is under 28, below the median American age of around 33. Furthermore, some of these immigrants bring cultural patterns that result in higher fertility rates. Thus, the relatively high fertility of currently resident Hispanics could be augmented by the even higher fertility of young newcomers, like those from Mexico and Central America.

The upshot of these considerations is that while the elderly in our aging America are heavily weighted toward non-Hispanic whites, the young are becoming relatively more weighted toward blacks and Hispanics. It has been estimated that in 1990, there were only two white Americans under 20 for each white American 65 or older, but over 4 young black Americans for each elderly black, and very nearly 7 young Hispanics for each elderly Hispanic. Thus, the U.S. labor force of the future is certain to have a very substantial black and Hispanic component.

Because these minorities are, on average, less well educated than the non-Hispanic white population, the challenge facing the U.S. educational system in the coming decades will be an imposing one. A highly productive labor force will be particularly important in the decades when the Baby Boomers begin to retire. Also, as we shall indicate in Chapter 17, many observers feel that the U.S. educational system is already failing to meet the needs of our increasingly technologically sophisticated civilization. New educational initiatives may be required.

## THE AGING SOCIETY— BETTER THAN THE ALTERNATIVES?

There is an old joke about aging that goes like this:

*Question:* "How do you feel about growing old?"

*Answer:* "Great . . . considering the alternative."

Suppose we ask that same question, not about ourselves as individuals but about ourselves as a *society.* How do we feel about *the United States* growing old? All things being equal, would we prefer to be a young society again—say, with a median age of 16, the way it was when our nation was new? Of course, in the joke, it is the alternative to aging that makes growing old seem so desirable to an individual. So we have to ask if there are, in fact, any alternatives in the case of the aging of a whole society?

Theoretically, there are three possible routes we might take if we were trying to keep the United States "younger" than it might otherwise be.

### Route 1: Rationing Medical Care for the Elderly

We know that one of the factors now making for the aging of America is the extension of life expectancies for the elderly and the very elderly. Many observers believe further that these extensions of life have led in many cases to an increase in the number of years in which older persons have suffered from infirmity and disability. We have extended the quantity of life, some say, at the expense of its quality. Examples of elderly individuals, kept alive by highly expensive life support systems beyond the stage at which any useful or even conscious existence is possible, are to be found daily in our hospitals and in media reports. Such circumstances—unfair it would seem *both* to the patients who endure these technological insults to their minds and bodies *and* to the society that must pay for the elaborate support systems—have prompted some observers to believe that the time has come to change our focus from extending the years of life, to improving the quality of life. Some have also suggested that it is now time to renew an ancient concept, that of a "natural life span" (as in the Biblical "three score years and ten"). Beyond this natural life span, the elderly, according to former Colorado Governor Richard Lamm, may sometimes have "a duty to die." Dr. Daniel Callahan, a medical ethicist from the Hastings Center, has suggested that, once such a span is completed, "medical care should no longer be oriented to resisting death."[12]

Essentially, this approach involves some form of *rationing* of medical care *on the basis of age.* It also would encourage a shift in research efforts away from life extension per se toward improving the *quality* of life for people of all ages—years of health, as it were, rather than years of life.

We shall talk about these issues again on many occasions, including a hard-nosed look at the question of just how great a saving of our medical resources could be achieved by any reasonable application of this approach. For the moment, however, we have to note that, as a way of keeping our society "younger," such an approach is a virtual irrelevance. Unless there were a truly *massive* change in our views about our elderly citizens—as in those old tales of Eskimos whose elderly float off on ice floes into the wintry night—we would not even scratch the surface of our aging problems by this route. This is because, although continued life extension for the elderly is *a* factor in our Aging Society, it is still a very *small* factor compared to the dominating influence of low fertility rates.[13]

Thus, apart from the significant moral issues involved in deciding when a life has run its "natural" course, and apart from a serious question as to whether we could even save much money by such an approach, we have to conclude that curtailing medical attention to the elderly is likely to have only a minuscule effect in retarding the aging of our society.

To achieve that end, we would need, in one way or another, to work at the other end of the scale—increasing the number of babies and young people.

### Route 2: Return to the Baby Boom?

So why not do it then? Have more babies again! Bring on a new wave of Boomers! Some people have predicted such a new wave. Some have urged it.[14] Why not?

There are two difficulties with this particular alternative. The *first* is that there is no evidence that young couples have any interest in bringing back a Baby Boom even approaching the level of the 1940s and 1950s. To reach such levels would require virtually a doubling of the nation's current fertility rate. Even those who urge a pronatalist policy would not expect, or even hope for, such a radical change in behavior. Realistically, and particularly given the massive entry of young women into the work force (and the slim likelihood that this trend will be significantly reversed), only very small increases in our fertility rates would be the most that could be expected in the coming decades. Like the rationing of medical care to the elderly, such small changes would have only a modest effect in slowing down the aging of our society.

And this leads directly to a *second* point, which is that the changes in fertility behavior

that would be required to keep America from aging further—say, keeping our median age at its 1989 level of 32.7—would involve truly massive changes in the *overall size* of our population. Suppose, say, that we wished to keep this median age through the year 2050. If we make "middle-series" mortality and immigration assumptions, this would require an increase in our fertility level from 1.9 (1989) to over 3, and an increase in our population in the year 2050 from the 1990 level of 250 million to around 600 million! And, of course, our population would continue to expand thereafter as well!

Most Americans are likely to feel that such a massive expansion of our numbers would be completely unsatisfactory from an ecological and environmental point of view. Even if our lands could support such numbers, the sheer crowding of people (with still more crowding promised for the future) would rule out such a "solution" in the minds of many of us.

Thus, on the Baby Boom front, the answer would seem to be that we don't really want to make the huge behavioral changes that would be required to make much difference and that, if we did, we would be very likely to regret the consequences in terms of sheer numbers of future Americans.

### Route 3: Increased Immigration

The final alternative would be to attempt to retard the Aging of America through the immigration route.

One of the great appeals of increased immigration in the Aging Society is that it provides a direct way of countering a major potential problem of such a society: the rising elderly dependency ratio. By admitting more young workers into the country, one not only lowers the rate of aging of the nation but also provides new recruits for what could be a badly depleted future work force. If the Baby Busters are not available in sufficient numbers to support the elderly retirees, why not then increase the work force. not through raising new babies to adulthood, but by importing young workers directly from abroad? The potential supply of such workers from Latin America—indeed, from Mexico alone—is very great. As we shall see in Part V, there are many parties both in the United States and in Latin America who have a strong interest in promoting such a solution.

But is it a solution?

The truth is that, on the scale that would be required to retard the Aging of America in any significant way, this "solution" really works no better than the others discussed earlier. Like the Baby Boom alternative, the immigration alternative suffers from the fatal flaw that it would require a similarly large expansion of our total population. Indeed, some of that expansion would come by the high-fertility route. We would have a version of a new Baby Boom through the increased proportion of our population in the high-fertility, prime childbearing age group. The only difference would be that the greater numbers of children to fill out the base of our pyramid would be increasingly from immigrant families.

In any event, most Americans would be likely to reject this approach on the simple ground of numbers. Whether by higher fertility or increased immigration, any attempt to counterbalance the increased numbers of elderly that are guaranteed to be with us in the next century with a proportional increase in the numbers of middle-aged people, young adults, and children of necessity involves *very large increases* in our total population.

Does the United States really want that?

## THE WINDOW OF OPPORTUNITY

Thus, even at the societal level, it seems that the alternatives to an aging America are impractical or unacceptable in one way or another. Furthermore, subsequent chapters will show that many of the problems of the Aging Society are far less overwhelming than they might seem at first encounter. Do we have an increased dependency burden in such a society because of the increased numbers of elderly? Well, then, what about the *reduced* dependency burden in that same society because we have fewer children to raise? Do elderly people have more chronic illnesses? But if modern medicine *focuses* on such illnesses, may they not go the same route to elimination as the acute infections of the recent past?

No one denies that the Aging Society will face serious problems, but in most cases there are countervailing forces that may make these problems at least reasonably manageable. This is particularly likely to be so if we try to analyze the problems carefully in advance so that we are able to anticipate them before they reach crisis proportions.

Fortunately, we will almost certainly have the time to do so. The present period—the last decade of the twentieth century and the first decade of the twenty-first—has been described as offering us a **window of opportunity** to prepare for any problems an aging America may bring forward. During this period, our work force, still including the Baby Boomers and perhaps further augmented by women and immigrants, will be a large and healthy one. In these two decades, if we are wise, we should be able to set our course in such a way that when the Baby Boomers begin flooding into the retirement ages, we will be able to manage the transition with relative ease.

Doing so will, of course, depend on the clarity of our understanding of the problems that may arise in that future period. To a careful study of such problems, therefore, we now turn our attention.

## SUMMARY

1. A population pyramid shows the percentages of the population in different age groups. When the base of the pyramid is broad, with large numbers of young people entering the childbearing years, the population will tend to expand. When the base is narrow, with too few young people to replace their parents, the population will tend to contract.

2. Since 1800, the United States has aged considerably, with our median age rising from 16.0 to 32.7 years, and with the proportions of old (65 and over) and very old (85 and over) age groups growing rapidly. By some projections, our median age in 2050 could be nearly three times what it was in colonial days.

3. This Aging of America has been affected by changes in our fertility, mortality, and migration rates. From 1830 to 1945 the major factor was not the increase in our life expectancies (which, in fact, allowed more *young* people to survive), but the decline in our fertility rate, which reduced the proportions of young people in the population and increased our median age.

4. For a short period after World War II (the Baby Boom), the United States actually became "younger" because of a sharp increase in fertility. The aging process soon resumed, however, as a result of: (a) the aging of the Baby Boomers, (b) the sharp decline in fertility during the post–Baby Boom period (the Baby Bust), and (c) the substantial increases in life expectancies at older ages due to medical and life-style changes.

5. Some commentators are worried about the Aging Society because of the increase in the elderly dependency ratio that will become particularly severe when the Baby Boomers begin to reach retirement age. Others note that there are important offsets to this burden, one example being the accompanying reduction in the numbers of children and young dependents.

6. Other changes that can be expected in an aging America are an increase in the numbers of elderly women, because women live substantially longer than men, and an increase in the proportions of minorities among our younger age groups.

7. None of the alternatives to an aging America seems attractive or, indeed, feasible. Rationing health care by age would have very little effect on our societal aging, while solutions depending on a perpetual Baby Boom or heavy immigration would involve (in addition to other possible problems) increases in our future population size beyond what most Americans would find acceptable.

8. Recognizing that the aging of America is inevitable does not mean, however, that we have cause to despair. With the available window of opportunity of the next two decades, we should have ample time to prepare for any problems that such a society may bring.

## KEY CONCEPTS FOR REVIEW

Median age

Average life expectancy versus maximum human life span

Population pyramid
    age structure
    sex structure
    ethnic structure

Squaring the pyramid

Long-run decline in fertility and societal aging

Echo boom

Elderly (aged, gerontic) dependency ratio

Alternatives to the Aging Society

Window of opportunity

## QUESTIONS FOR DISCUSSION

1. When people think of the aging of a society, they often think primarily of increases in average life expectancies. Explain why this view is very misleading as an account of America's aging in the nineteenth and early twentieth centuries. Explain also why, in recent years, increases in our life expectancies have had a different role in the aging of America from what they had historically.

2. The U.S. population pyramid for 1989 is neither a triangle nor a rectangle, but an irregular mixture of shapes. Explain the peculiarities of the shape of this particular pyramid. Can you relate this picture to an image frequently used to describe post–World War II U.S. demographics: a python swallowing a pig?

3. Describe how our elderly dependency ratio has changed in recent decades and how it is likely to change in the future. Why does the projected change in this ratio cause so much alarm for many observers? Do you share this alarm? If so, why? If not, why not?

4. Explain why poverty among the elderly and health care costs in the Aging Society might be affected by the proportions of older women to older men.

5. Immigration today has a somewhat different effect on the aging of America than it did during the nineteenth century. Why? Present arguments to support the two opposite views:

   a. Increased immigration is the natural solution to the problems of an Aging America.

   b. Increased immigration will only intensify the problems of an Aging America.

6. If modern biogenetics were to succeed in unlocking the secrets of aging, making possible a massive increase in *maximum* human life spans, would you be inclined to applaud, or to lock up the laboratories as fast as you could? Discuss the further information you might need before coming to a decision on this matter. Relate your arguments to the issue of the *quality* versus the *quantity* of life.

## NOTES

1. It should be said that, historically speaking, many more individuals have *claimed* to live to very advanced ages than have actually done so. For a discussion of these exaggerated claims, see Roy Walford, *Maximum Life Span* (New York: W. W. Norton, 1983), pp. 12–15. However, there are some reasonably authenticated cases of individuals living to 110 and beyond. *The Guinness Book of World Records* (New York: Sterling, 1991) states that the oldest human who ever lived was Shige-chiyo Isumi of Japan, who died in 1986 at the age of 120 years, 237 days. The oldest living American in 1990 was reported to be Carrie C. White, born in Florida on November 18, 1874.

2. Ignoring migration, the shape of the population pyramid, or age distribution of a population, will be determined by a complicated mathematical function including a mortality factor (the probability of surviving from birth to any given age) and a fertility factor (female births per head of population at each given age). If these two factors remain constant over a long period of time, then the age structure of the population will remain constant over time. If this constant structure has a wide base, the population will be growing at a

constant rate; if the base is narrower, the population will be stable; if narrower still, the population will be contracting. For those interested in the mathematics of this subject, see Mortimer Spiegelman, *Introduction to Demography*, rev. ed., 6th printing (Cambridge, Mass.: Harvard University Press, 1980), Chap. 9, esp. pp. 288–292.

3. This is not to say that the U.S. infant mortality record is perfect. As we know (see pp. ), the United States does not rank at the top of the world in terms of infant mortality: our record can clearly be improved. However, the rate (at below 10 per 1,000) is sufficiently low that even major improvements would not have the *quantitative* impact that we may get from extending life expectancies at older ages.

4. The pyramid for the year 2030 is taken from Gregory Spencer, "Projections of the Population of the United States, by Age, Sex and Race: 1988 to 2080," Current Population Reports, *Population Estimates and Projections*, Series P-25, No. 1018, p. 5. It is based on the middle-series census projections (1989). The reader should note that the areas of the 1830 pyramid and the 2030 rectangle are equal—both adding up to 100 percent. In

*absolute numbers,* of course, our 2030 population will be much larger than that of 1830.

5. Because there are many elderly persons who are not dependent (as we have just noted), and because some observers consider the word *dependent* pejorative, there is currently a move afoot to change the term *elderly dependency ratio* to *elderly support ratio.* For the moment, however, the former term (which we employ) is still in general use.

6. See Jacob S. Siegel and Cynthia M. Taeuber, "Demographic Dimensions of an Aging Society," in Alan Pifer and Lydia Bronte, eds., *Our Aging Society: Paradox and Promise* (New York: W. W. Norton, 1986), pp. 83–84.

7. We shall have many occasions to note that focusing—as so many popular articles do—*solely* on elderly dependency is to give a very misleading picture of our future burdens. As we know, a *major* factor in our societal aging has been our declining fertility. That is to say, if we have and will have a great many elderly to support, then we also have and will have relatively few children to support. Balancing our high elderly dependency ratio will be a low *youth* dependency ratio (ratio of children to the working-age population). See Chapter 6 for details.

8. Polls supporting this view can be found in Louis Harris and Associates, *Myth and Reality of Aging in America* (Washington, D.C.: National Council on Aging, 1974), and Louis Harris and Associates, *Aging in the Eighties: America in Transition* (Washington, D.C.: National Council on Aging, 1981).

9. See Ira Rosenwaike, with the assistance of Barbara Logue, *The Extreme Aged in America: A Portrait of an Expanding Population* (Westport, Conn.: Greenwood Press, 1985), p. 88.

10. See J. C. Cornoi-Huntley, S. J. Foley, L. R. White, R. Suzman, L. F. Berkman, D. A. Evans, and R. B. Wallace, "Epidemiology of Disability in the Oldest Old: Methodologic Issues and Preliminary Findings," in D. P. Willis, ed., "Health and Society," *Milbank Memorial Fund Quarterly, 63*(2), Spring 1985, pp. 350–376.

11. Lois M. Verbrugge, "A Health Profile of Older Women with Comparisons to Older Men," *Research on Aging, 6*(3), September 1984, pp. 292, 311.

12. Daniel Callahan, *Setting Limits: Medical Goals in an Aging Society* (New York: Simon & Schuster, 1987), p. 171.

13. Thus, for example, in the Census Bureau's 1989 projections, if we go from the lowest fertility rate assumption (1.5) to the highest (2.2), while holding life expectancy and immigration constant at the middle level, our projected population for the year 2080 goes from 219 million to 421 million, or a difference of *92 percent.* By contrast, going from the bureau's lowest to its highest life expectancy assumptions would alter the projected 2080 population by only *14 percent.*

14. The scholar who most clearly predicted something like a new Baby Boom is Richard A. Easterlin, author of *Birth and Fortune: The Impact of Numbers on Personal Welfare* (New York: Basic Books, 1980). The writer most closely associated with the call for more babies is Ben J. Wattenberg, in his bestseller, *The Birth Dearth* (New York: Pharos Books, 1987).

# 6

# Is There a Crisis in Social Security?

$A$merica's Social Security system[1] is without question one of the most successful programs the federal government has ever created. It has achieved major goals in terms of reducing poverty, raising incomes, and providing a sense of security and protection for our elderly citizens. Polls have shown that the system is enormously popular, not only with the elderly but also with the young who will, in theory, benefit from it themselves as they approach retirement. So popular is the program that politicians are constantly assuring the public that, no matter how large the public debt, no matter how high the priorities given other objectives—defense, the war on drugs, improving our national educational system—the *one* thing they will never reduce is their commitment to those sacred Social Security benefits.

But, of course, those benefits are not completely sacred—certain aspects of the program were trimmed during the "crisis" of 1983—and some observers feel that they may have to be trimmed again in the future. Along with the enormous popularity of the program there has grown up an increasing skepticism as to whether Social Security can survive the striking changes in our population described in the last chapter. Is the **U.S. Social Security program** viable in the Aging Society? The Baby Boomers are particularly concerned. "I doubt that it'll even be there when *we* retire!" is a sentiment frequently and openly expressed.

This sentiment is often accompanied by a suspicion that perhaps the present generation of elderly has been voting itself a particularly good deal at the expense of other important national objectives, and specifically at the expense of the working generation of Boomers. Thus, the question of whether our Social Security system can continue to flourish over the next 50 or 75 years has a bearing not only on a specific government program but also on the relationships between generations in the Aging Society.[2]

## A CAPSULE HISTORY OF SOCIAL SECURITY IN THE UNITED STATES

Oddly enough, the institution of a major social insurance system in the Western world did not occur in the leader of the Industrial Revolution, Great Britain, but in Germany, a country that had achieved full unification only in 1871. A decade later, in 1881, a social insurance program—which, in due course, was to include accident, disability, and pension insurance—was launched under the leadership of the famous German Chancellor Otto von Bismarck. Bismarck's motives were not confined to sympathy for the elderly and infirm; he was also well aware of the need to combat the threat of the rising socialist movement in Europe and to strengthen working-class allegiance to the nascent state. In general, too, German economists in the late nineteenth century tended to favor state action to foster development as compared with the more laissez faire approach in Britain and the United States.

### Social Security and the Great Depression

Comparatively speaking, then, our national social insurance program came rather late in time. The triggering event was without question the Great Depression of the 1930s.

Prior to this period, old-age dependency had been handled primarily by the family. A relatively small number of older people had accumulated enough property and savings so that they could support themselves without external help. Public pension plans helped out in the case of firefighters, police, and (beginning in 1920) federal civil service workers. By 1930 private pension plans, particularly for workers in large firms in steel, railroads, and heavy machinery industries, covered about 15 percent of U.S. employees (but not usually their spouses or dependents). Where neither family, past savings, nor pensions were available or adequate, there was always the "poorhouse" and various modest forms of public relief or private charity.

Also, it must be remembered that in 1930, 54 percent of men 65 and over were still in the labor force. Thus, a majority of elderly household heads worked, and, where they didn't, a patchwork of family support, past savings, small pensions, veterans' benefits, and public and private charity made old age survivable.

Then came the Crash of 1929 and the Great Depression of the 1930s, and suddenly all the components of this support system were jeopardized. The stock market plummeted, banks failed, agriculture collapsed, industry was devastated, and unemployment grew to historically unprecedented proportions. With 25 percent of the labor force unemployed by 1933,[3] where were the jobs by which the elderly who wanted to work could support themselves? Where also were the jobs for the young and middle-aged workers who were now called upon to support the frequently idled elderly? Where also were the stocks, bonds, and savings accounts that the most careful and prudent of Americans had set aside to prepare for their retirements? For that matter, where was the community support system at a time when many local governments were going into default and could not pay even their regular employees?

Perhaps the most significant aspect of this great national trauma was the sense that individuals, however careful and prudent, could be subjected to impersonal economic forces beyond their control. The elderly were by no means alone in their vulnerability to these forces, yet because of their age and often their increased infirmity, they stood out as requiring special assistance. Such assistance also, of course, could be indirectly helpful to the prime working-age groups in that, by making retirement more viable, it could reduce job competition from the elderly.

Paradoxically, the old-age insurance provisions set up by the Social Security Act of 1935 may have had a somewhat negative effect on the Depression that was still in progress. For although workers and their employers began paying taxes on January 1, 1937 (1 percent of of the employee's wage up to $3,000, matched by a 1 percent employer contribution), eligibility for retirement benefits was not to begin until 1942. Although the eligibility date was later changed to 1940, it can be argued, and was feared by some at the time, that building up a surplus in the **Social Security Trust Fund** when the economy was still mired in the Depression was bad economic policy. The issue of surpluses, in a different form, is still alive today, as we shall see in a moment.

Still, once the system began making payments, that early generation of covered retirees did quite well, particularly after the system was liberalized in 1939. The reason was that they were able to receive full benefits even though they had been contributing to Social Security only for a short period of time. Ida M. Fuller of Vermont, the first American to receive a Social Security check, retired in 1940 having contributed a total of $44 in payroll taxes. As it turned out, she lived to be 100 and received in return $20,884.52 in Social Security payments. Although this was an extreme case, virtually all the elderly retirees in the first decades of the program, and to some degree even today, have done very well if we measure specifically by the ratio of benefits received to contributions made.

How could the system pay out more to recipients than they had paid in? Actually, in the first few decades of Social Security there was no problem at all. In 1940, taxes were being paid by the entire covered work force of the nation, while benefits were being paid only to a relative handful of retirees. This start-up advantage of the program was perpetuated, moreover, throughout the early history of the program by the addition of new categories of workers who began paying taxes but were not eligible for benefits until later.

## Rediscovery of Poverty and the Great Society

Although the covered retirees of the 1940s and 1950s were doing nicely as measured by the rate of return on their Social Security contributions, and although that post–World War II period was generally characterized by expansion and prosperity, we must not conclude that all was well with the U.S. economy, and the elderly in particular. In the late 1950s, beginning with John Kenneth Galbraith's *Affluent Society,* and more particularly in 1962 with the publication of Michael Harrington's book *The Other America,* there occurred a phenomenon usually called the **rediscovery of poverty.** We had no Great Depression, but we still had poor people. Poverty, in the midst of our general "affluence," Galbraith told us, was a national "disgrace."

And those in poverty in the 1960s included many elderly people, particularly those who were living alone. Of those elderly persons living alone, some 40 percent of the men and two-thirds of the women had incomes below the poverty line. Furthermore, it had become apparent that many elderly people were facing one problem that literally could be insurmountable with the reduced incomes available to them: medical costs. At the personal level, a serious illness could be as financially catastrophic for a retiree as the collapse of the stock market and banking system had been in the 1930s.

What happened in response to these perceived needs was a major expansion of the Social Security program from the mid-1960s to the mid-1970s, beginning with the so-called Great Society legislation under President Lyndon Johnson. A veritable social revolution, not unlike that of the New Deal era, took place at this time. From the point of view of the elderly, there were two crucial developments:

1. *Medicare and Medicaid.* These two programs, instituted to alleviate the medical cost burdens of the elderly and poor, were enacted in 1965. **Medicare** was specifically designed for the elderly, while **Medicaid** applied to the poor of all ages, including the elderly poor. Medicare consisted of two programs, a hospital insurance (HI) plan for Social Security beneficiaries aged 65 and older and a supplementary medical insurance (SMI) plan to cover payments to physicians and surgeons, various in-hospital services, and certain other fees. Medicaid was a *means-tested* program; at present, over one-third of Medicaid expenditures go to persons aged 65 and older.

Taken together with earlier disability insurance (DI) legislation, the Medicare and Medicaid programs represented a major commitment of the U.S. government to address one of the central causes of outright poverty among our elderly.[4]

2. *Improved Social Security Benefits.* There was also during this period a direct attempt to protect elderly recipients from the ravages of inflation, and to increase their benefits in real (inflation-adjusted) terms. Congress increased Social Security benefits in 1968, 1970, 1971, and 1972. These benefit increases far exceeded the rate of inflation during this period. Furthermore, in 1972, when a **cost-of-living adjustment (COLA)** was introduced to make automatic benefit changes in response to rising prices, an inappropriate formula was used, resulting in a "double-indexing" of benefits. A measure sometimes referred to in this connection is the **replacement ratio:** the proportion of a wage-earner's prior earnings "replaced" by the earner's Social Security benefit. Prior to 1972, Social Security replaced 38 percent of preretirement income for an average worker retiring at the age of 65. The error of 1972 increased the replacement ratio to 55 percent for the same worker. Although the mistake was corrected in 1977, real benefits in general continued to rise throughout this period.

Thus, benefits were increasing and substantial new benefits, particularly in the area of health care, were being added. With the great expansion in the numbers of the elderly actually covered by these programs, Social Security was coming close to fulfilling not only the expectations but even the more improbable dreams of its founders.

### The Impact on the Well-Being of the Elderly

Partly as a result of the growth of the Social Security system, Americans 65 and older have made great strides economically during the post–World War II period. Once a clearly disadvantaged group, and still containing certain disadvantaged subgroups, this country's elderly are now, in many respects, better off than the rest of the population. In the case of poverty, the improvement has been dramatic. Figure 6-1 shows that the poverty rate of Americans 65 or over declined sharply from 29 percent in 1966, at the start of the Great Society advances, to 11 percent in 1989. From having a poverty rate nearly double that of the general population, the elderly now have a smaller percentage in poverty than the country as a whole.

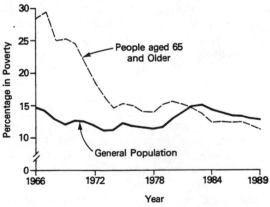

**FIGURE 6–1:   Poverty Rates in the United States, 1966–1989**

*Source:*   U.S. Bureau of the Census, *Current Population Reports,* Series P-60, No. 168, Tables 19, 20.

Meanwhile the average (mean) real incomes of the elderly have also been rising sharply in recent decades, both absolutely and relative to the average real incomes of working-age individuals. Although in some categories (e.g., individuals living alone), the elderly do less well than their younger counterparts, in other categories (e.g., per capita incomes in families), the elderly do better than certain working-age groups, especially the 25- to 34-year-old age group.

Furthermore, many of the numbers used to compare the elderly with other groups do not take into account the *in-kind* (noncash) benefits that both groups receive. Through Medicare, Medicaid, and even housing subsidies, the elderly receive more in-kind benefits than the general population. Thus official figures tend to understate the relative well-being of the elderly and to overstate their poverty levels. Also, full account is usually not taken of the fact that the elderly, particularly in the 65–74 age group, have higher asset holdings (savings accounts, certificates of deposit, stocks, and equity in their homes) than do younger groups.

On all these various dimensions, then, there is no question that the overall economic well-being of the U.S. elderly has improved enormously over the past few decades. The crucial role of Social Security in this achievement is underlined by the fact that there were two important reasons since the 1960s to expect that elderly incomes might *fall:* (1) the average age of the elderly was rising, and the "old old" are usually less well off than the "young old"; and (2) older Americans were retiring earlier and earlier, reducing the contribution of their own earnings to their incomes.

Thus, the improved benefits of Social Security, combined with the newer in-kind, and especially medical, benefits introduced during the 1960s, were a major factor in making possible the increasing ease of life for America's elderly. By 1986, 57 percent of elderly households were receiving over half their total incomes from Social Security.

## DUAL GOALS AND METHODS

Still, many younger Americans, particularly among the Baby Boomers, have become concerned about the Social Security system. One good reason for this concern, as we have noted earlier, was the "crisis" that developed—and under highly *favorable* demographic conditions—in the early 1980s. This crisis demonstrated that the program was more complex than at first met the eye. In particular, the program was revealed to contain a certain *dualism* of both *goals* and *methods*.

### Equity versus Adequacy

Students of the Social Security literature will frequently come upon two terms when the goals of the program are being described: *equity* and *adequacy*. By **equity,** we mean the fairness of the system in terms of providing a reasonable return to participants on the basis of their past contributions. By **adequacy,** we mean the capacity of the system to provide reasonable support to those elderly persons in need of such support.

These concepts in turn are at the heart of an important distinction between Social Security as a **social insurance** program and as a **welfare** program. Most people like to think of Social Security primarily as an insurance program. When they receive benefits in their old age, they often refer to them specifically as payments they have "earned" by their past contributions. No handout is involved; the government is simply honoring a past commitment to which the individual is "entitled." Hence also the frequent use of the term *entitlements* to refer to Social Security, Medicare, and other similar programs.

The fact, however, is that this insurance principle has been frequently and consciously compromised from the beginning. The decision to permit *early* benefits (that is, before their contributions would warrant) for the first generations of Social Security recipients is a case in point, as already noted.

But there are many other cases in point, and, indeed, the tension between equity and adequacy runs through the entire system. From the beginning, low-income recipients have received a higher return on their contributions than have high-income recipients. The replacement ratio of low-income workers is about twice that of high-income workers. There are many examples of tensions between the two principles in the effective treatment of women and men, minorities, and even specific age groups among the retiring elderly.[5]

Furthermore, there is a fundamental issue foreseeable in the future, deriving from the fact that, under almost any conceivable scenario, the present working-age generation will receive a substantially lower return on their Social Security contributions than has the present generation of retirees. This would seem to violate the equity/insurance features of the system. On the other hand, if tomorrow's retirees have reasonably high real incomes, then there may be no adequacy/welfare problem at all.

### Funding versus Pay-as-You-Go

Related to the dualism of objectives, but not exactly the same issue, is a dualism of *methods.* How is Social Security to be financed? Until the early 1980s, when the general public discovered otherwise, the popular view was that each worker paid contributions into a general trust fund and that benefits would in due course be paid out of this same fund. This financing of Social Security through prior **funding** suggests a life-cycle approach to retirement needs. During one's working years, one saves up privately (through savings accounts, stocks, home equity, and other accumulated assets) and also publicly (through payroll taxes) in order to accumulate sufficient funds to permit a comfortable old age. In this approach, the viability of the system is judged by the projected size of the Trust Fund in relation to projected liabilities.

A quite different view is suggested by a

**pay-as-you-go** method of financing. In principle, in this case, there is no fund at all (though one might wish for a small fund to cover occasional short-term drains on the system). Essentially, one taxes today's workers to provide income to today's retirees. Today's workers presumably agree to such an arrangement because of the implicit social contract that guarantees them similar treatment in their retirement years. According to this view, the viability of the system tends to be judged by the projected future incomes of tomorrow's workers from which the taxes to support tomorrow's retirees will have to be taken.

In the first approach, each generation takes care of its needs largely by its own efforts. In the second approach, each older generation is vitally dependent on the younger generation, and particularly on the willingness of the latter to honor the commitments on which the continuation of the system is based.

## THE CRISIS OF THE EARLY 1980S

These dualisms help explain why the **Social Security "crisis" of the early 1980s** came as such a shock to so many people. Most Americans *thought* we were operating an insurance program based on a trust fund method of finance. What we *discovered* was that virtually all the future liabilities of the system were *unfunded*. We were on a completely pay-as-you-go system—in fact, even less than that. *At the end of 1981, the Social Security Trust Fund was within 45 days of being completely exhausted. By November 1982 its cash reserves were exhausted, and $17.5 billion had to be borrowed from the Disability and Hospital Insurance trust funds.*

### Causes of the Crisis

This dramatic drawing down of the Trust Fund clearly represented an imbalance between the growth of total benefits and the growth of total contributions during the preceding years. Several underlying factors contributed to the growth of benefits during this prior period. We have noticed that, in the 1960s and early 1970s, the United States became aware of the relative poverty of elderly Americans and decided to do something to remedy this condition. The numerous benefit increases in Social Security during this period were voted enthusiastically by Congress on what was essentially an "adequacy" principle: the elderly were in special need; the Social Security program was an obvious (and temporarily easy) way to compensate for that need.

Even then, these benefit increases might have been handled except for the failure of the economy to cooperate properly. From a *labor force* point of view, the U.S. economy should have been in very good shape as we entered the 1980s. Virtually all the Baby Boomers had entered the prime working age group by that time. Also, we had an enormous influx of women into the labor force. Between 1970 and 1982 the U.S. labor force rose by 33 percent, the same percentage by which the number of Americans 65 and older was increasing.

When we look at actual *employment*, however, we find a different story. In no small part due to the two OPEC-engineered oil crises of 1973–1974 and 1979–1980, the mid-1970s through early-1980s in the United States was an era of "stagflation" (stagnation + inflation). Although our labor force was growing rapidly, so also was our unemployment rate, going from 4.9 percent in 1970 to 9.7 percent in 1982. This meant a corresponding reduction in payroll taxes flowing into the Trust Fund (and also some increase in benefits, as some discouraged older workers retired earlier).

Meanwhile, on the benefit side, the forces of inflation, now built into the Social Security system through COLAs (and, for a time, mistakenly overindexed into the system), were vastly increasing the monetary value of benefits. In those 12 years between 1970 and 1982, U.S. consumer prices went up *two and a half times,* causing an explosive drain on the resources of the Trust Fund.

In short, we had emphasized adequacy above equity in our Social Security goals and pay-as-you-go above funding in our Social Security financing, and, in the process, had made ourselves vulnerable to the winds of economic fortune. By 1983, the time for reform and retrenchment was at hand.

### The 1983 Social Security Reform

On April 20, 1983, President Reagan signed into law a series of Social Security amendments designed to solve the temporary crisis and to bring the system into long-run (75-year) actuarial balance. Essentially, these revisions move the system away from the pay-as-you-go principle and toward a funding principle of finance. To what degree this change, in itself, solves the long-run Social Security problem we will consider in a moment.

Briefly, the **1983 amendments** achieved their ends by: (1) increasing Social Security taxes and (2) reducing certain Social Security benefits. Table 6-1 shows how employer–employee and self-employed worker tax rates increased from 1982 (before the legislation) to 1989. These new rates in-

volved moving up certain tax rate increases scheduled for later years. The other major tax change of the 1983 legislation was to subject up to half of a recipient's Social Security benefits (when the recipient's income exceeds certain levels) to the federal income tax.

The benefit reductions included a delay in the July 1983 COLA until January 1984, and also certain adjustments in the way COLAs are calculated; the trimming of certain "windfall" benefits; and, perhaps most significantly, a gradual increase in the age at which full retirement benefits become payable. Historically, this age was set at 65; by the new legislation it was gradually increased to 66 by the year 2005 and 67 by the year 2022. Also, the benefits one can receive from retirement at age 62 are to be reduced.

One other change affecting retirees was a benefit increase, rather than a reduction. It involved a relaxation of the so-called earnings test, allowing recipients aged 65 to 69 to keep two-thirds rather than only half of their earned income above an annually adjusted exempt amount. As is fairly obvious, this change, like the changed retirement provisions, is designed to encourage older workers to remain active in the work

**TABLE 6-1:  Social Security Tax Rates**

| | | Contributions Applying to Old Age and Survivors' Insurance (OASI) Only: | | |
| | | Contribution (%) | | |
| Year | Annual Maximum Taxable Earnings | Employer | Employee | Self-employed |
|---|---|---|---|---|
| 1982 | $32,400 | 4.575 | 4.575 | 6.8125 |
| 1989 | $48,000[a] | 5.53 | 5.53 | 11.06 |
| | | *Contributions Including Disability Insurance (DI) Hospital Insurance (HI):* | | |
| *1982* | *$32,400* | *6.7* | *6.7* | *9.35* |
| *1989* | *$48,000[a]* | *7.51[b]* | *7.51[b]* | *15.02[b]* |

[a] This will rise annually by an automatic adjustment in proportion to increase in average earnings level.

[b] These rates are scheduled for the year 2000 and thereafter to rise to 7.65 percent each for employer and employee and 15.3 percent for self-employed persons.

*Source: Social Security Bulletin, Annual Statistical Supplement,* 1988, Table 2.A1.

force, in this case even when they are already on Social Security.

The total effect of these various changes is expected to promote an enormous increase in the Social Security Trust Fund during the next several decades, followed by a rapid decrease in the size of this fund over the subsequent decades. Figure 6-2 presents a 1989 Social Security Board of Trustees' projection of annual surpluses and deficits until the year 2046, and the accumulated size of the Trust Fund (OASI plus DI) over the course of those years. Other projections reach different results depending on a wide variety of possible assumptions, not only as to the changes in our population, but also as to the future state of our economy. Still, the main thrust is clear:

• Annual income to the Trust Fund (in current dollars) will exceed annual outgo until around the year 2030.

• In certain years, these annual surpluses will be as high as $500 billion.

• In or around the year 2030, the accumulated Trust Fund could reach a total of $11.9 trillion in current dollars. (In constant dollars, adjusted for expected inflation, the

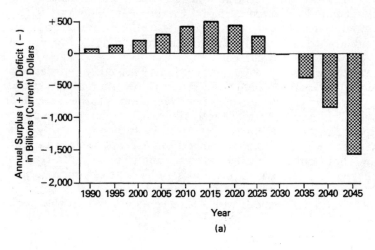

FIGURE 6–2a: Projected
Annual Social Security (OASDI)
Surpluses (+) or Deficits (−),
Selected Years

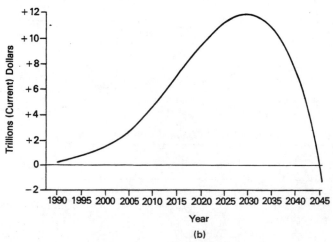

FIGURE 6–2b: Projected Social
Security (OASDI) Trust Fund, 1990–
2046
These projections are based on the
Social Security Administration's
Intermediate (Alternative II-B)
projections. Notice that Figure 6–2b
is expressed in *trillions* of dollars.

*Source:* 1989 Annual Report of the
Board of Trustees of the OASDI, House
Document 101-56, Table F-3, p. 132.

fund would reach a maximum of around $2.8 trillion. Incidentally, this sum is larger than the entire federal debt held by the public in 1989.)

• Immediately thereafter, the fund begins to diminish sharply, and by the year 2046 it will (on this projection) be completely exhausted. Annual outgo in the previous year (2045) will exceed income by over $1.5 trillion in current dollars.

These are startling numbers. In total, they probably tell us more about the way our population is changing than any other numbers we might cite. The huge buildup of the Trust Fund in the next few decades reflects the enormous impact of the Baby Boomers on the labor force, including the much higher employment rates of the women of the Baby Boom. It also reflects the fact that, although our society is aging during these years, the impact on Social Security is reduced because workers retiring during the late 1990s and early 2000s are from the very low birth rate generation of the Depression. A person born in 1930 reaches 65 in 1995. 1930 to 1945 were years of very low fertility, meaning that until 2010 at least, we have a relatively small cohort reaching retirement age. This gives us the "window of opportunity" referred to in the previous chapter.

What we see through that "window," in Figure 6-2, is the enormous buildup of a Trust Fund to meet our forseeable future obligations.

And then the window starts to close. The shift to annual deficits (actually beginning around 2020 in terms of inflation-adjusted constant dollars) reflects the enormous impact of the Boomers again, but this time in drawing down the fund. Here we have the huge retirement bulge, made all the more serious by the relatively small Baby Bust cohorts who will now be in the prime working ages.

What happens in the year 2046, when the fund is completely drawn down again?

Will we then face *another* 1983-style crisis? Some commentators have worried about this possibility, but the trustees of the fund, noting the difficulties of such long-range projections, "do not recommend that any legislative action be taken at this time [1989] to resolve the long-run deficit." Given our inability to predict changes in either our population or our economy over such extensive periods of time, this does seem a reasonable position, although, of course, the country must be ready for change as that future draws nearer.

## FACTORS FAVORING THE VIABILITY OF SOCIAL SECURITY

Given this limitation on our knowledge, we can still ask whether the reforms of 1983 have set up a system that, taking a number of probable developments into account, is likely to prove viable over the next several decades, including the retirement years of the Baby Boomers.

First, we note some important factors that suggest that the system will indeed be maintainable over this period:

*1. The Boomers will, in principle, be paying for their own Social Security pensions.* As far as one can judge, the present tax benefit arrangements for Social Security are such that the Baby Boom generation will be paying fully for the pensions they will be receiving. As the well-respected student of Social Security, Henry J. Aaron, has put it:

> The Baby-Boom generation will impose no burden on future workers for the benefits it will receive. The taxes it pays during its working life are projected under current law to exceed current Social Security costs, generate a reserve, and thereby add to national saving, the capital stock, and the productive capacity of the nation. This addition to productive capacity almost exactly equals the additional Social Security pension costs that result because the baby-boom generation is larger than those before it.[6]

Aaron notes that this statement is true only on the assumption that "other fiscal policy is given," a matter we will turn to in a moment. The point here is simply that we are no longer following an explicit policy whereby retirees gain far more from the program than what they contribute. Estimates vary, but the return that Boomers get will certainly be low, conceivably even negative. While this raises an important "equity" issue (and has, indeed, caused some observers to wish to privatize all, or at least part, of the present system), it strongly suggests that the system is viable—or at least that we are not inevitably headed toward some huge catastrophe when the Boomers retire.

**2. The bearable total dependency burden.** When considering the Social Security (and other) burdens that the Boomers and the aging of the society are likely to impose in the years ahead, we should really examine what is happening to the burdens imposed by other age groups. In the last chapter, we mentioned that offsetting an increased elderly dependency ratio, we were likely to have a substantially reduced **youth** (or "neontic") **dependency ratio.** While the elderly ratio measures the number of persons age 65 and above per 100 persons of working age, 18 to 64 (sometimes given as 20 to 64), the youth dependency ratio measures the number of persons under age 18 (or 20) per 100 of working age. Figure 6-3 shows what has been happening and what

is expected to happen to these two ratios, and to the sum of both of them (the **total dependency ratio**) over a 90-year period.

Now, it should be obvious that, as one cannot add apples and oranges, we cannot add young dependents and old dependents together as though their costs to society were equivalent.[7] Still, one has to be impressed by the fact that the total dependency ratio is quite low at present. More significantly, even after the Boomers have flooded into the 65-and-older age groups, the ratio remains well below what it was in the 1960s and even the early 1970s.

This point is doubly significant. *First,* it suggests that, as far as the total burden on the future working-age generation is concerned, it is by no means unsustainable under a wide variety of Social Security arrangements.

Second, it suggests that the "equity" issue vis-à-vis the Baby Boom generation is a bit more complex than might first appear. Although it is true that the Boomers are and will be paying something extra for their Social Security benefits (i.e., sustaining their own benefits through the buildup of reserves, while also paying a bonus to earlier retirees who did not fully sustain *their* benefits), it is also true that they have had many fewer children to support on the average. The *parents* of the Boomers may be getting a very good deal in their retirement, but, on the other hand, *they had twice as many children to support!* It is by no means clear

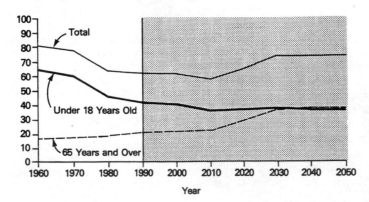

**FIGURE 6–3:  Number of Dependents per 100 Persons 18 to 64 Years Old: Estimates, 1960–1980; Projections, 1990–2050**

*Source:*  U.S. Bureau of the Census, *Current Population Reports,* Series P-25, No. 952, Table 6.

who has, or will have had, the better deal overall.

**3. The role of economic growth.** Furthermore, unless there is a radical change in our historical experience, American per capita real incomes will continue to rise over the next 70 years, very much increasing the size of the pool from which the benefits for all classes of dependents can be drawn.

Figure 6-4 shows the trend of increasing U.S. per capita real income (disposable personal income) over the past half century. A not unreasonable guess would be that our per capita incomes could increase at the rate of 1 percent per year over the next 70 years. This rate is well below our average historic rate of over 1.5 percent. If such a 1 percent rate were maintained, real income per person in the United States would *double over the next 70 years.* Even if the somewhat slower U.S. growth rate of worker productivity in recent years is all that the economy can sustain, estimates are that net real wages *would still rise substantially—for example, by one estimate, up 44 percent by the year 2040.*[8]

Economic growth has a clear bearing on

the Social Security issue considered from the point of view of either "equity" or "adequacy." Since the real incomes of the Baby Boomers are likely to be substantially higher than those of their parents over their entire life spans, it would not appear that they are being unfairly treated as a generation in any general sense. By the same token, the adequacy of Social Security benefits—if measured in terms of current absolute standards of comfort or of poverty—should be relatively easy to maintain in a growing economy.

Thus, our newly funded Social Security system, made feasible by the reduction in the number of our young dependents and by the rising incomes available through economic growth, is arguably a "safe bet" for the Boomer generation. It may even prove to be a good deal after all.

## SOME UNDERLYING QUESTIONS

Still, this conclusion seems a bit too pat. After all, we frequently heard reassurances about the viability of the system in the 1960s and 1970s—and there was no great flood of retirees to be worried about then—and yet we still managed to produce the "crisis" of 1983. Have we perhaps skirted over some underlying issues that should be faced more directly? The answer is yes, and in the next two chapters and also in later chapters we shall be considering some of these underlying issues in depth. For the moment, let us simply suggest two areas of potential problems that the foregoing arguments have not adequately taken into account.

### Issues Involving the Social Security Trust Fund

Will that Social Security Trust Fund depicted in Figure 6-2 be permitted to rise to such stratospheric levels? Even if it is permitted to rise to such levels, does it really tell us anything about the real resources available for sustaining Social Security pensions when the Boomers begin to retire?

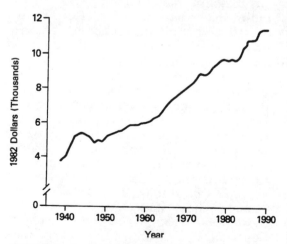

**FIGURE 6–4: U.S. Real Per Capita Disposable Personal Income, 1929–1989 (in Constant 1982 Dollars)**

*Source:* U.S. Department of Commerce.

The truth of the matter is that, although the Trust Fund *may*, as Aaron suggests, contribute to the resources available to pay the Baby Boomer pensions, it also *may not*. It depends.

In particular, it depends on whether or not the building up of the fund has actually contributed to a higher level of national income and capital stock when it comes time to draw down those reserves. The fundamental truth is this:

*Our ability to "afford" adequate (or equitable) pensions for the Baby Boom generation will depend on the size of our real national income and capital stock at the time the Boomers retire. Other things equal, the size of our future national income and capital stock will depend on the nation's rate of technological progress and its willingness to save and invest in added productive capacity.*

Where do the *real* resources come from to sustain our retirees at any given moment of time? Essentially, they come from current production *or* from the drawing down of past accumulations of capital. (The latter, for example, could involve people living in houses that they had bought earlier in life and which they allow to depreciate without repairing them.) Basically, there *are no other real resources available for this purpose.*

In principle, what the Trust Fund *should* do is to increase our country's total saving and investment so that we have a greater productive capacity and hence a higher future national income and capital stock available when the Boomers retire. This will *not* happen, however, if the fund is essentially used to finance other current consumption expenditures by the government.

But, surely, one might say, such behavior would be unthinkable on the part of the president and the Congress. Obviously, if you are going to save with one hand and overspend with the other, you have made no *net progress* whatever. In fact, however, we were operating in the 1980s as though this obvious truth did not hold or, at least, had no bearing on the future of the Social

Security system. The federal government, while running surpluses in its Social Security account, was running substantial deficits in its overall budget. These deficits, in total, more than matched the Social Security surpluses, leaving, for example, a *net overall federal deficit* in 1989 of $152 billion. It was partly to expose this fiscal sleight-of-hand that Senator Daniel Patrick Moynihan proposed that Social Security taxes be cut immediately and that the attempt to build up surpluses be abandoned.[9]

Of course, in the absence of Social Security surpluses, the federal deficit might have been even worse, in which case the Trust Fund could be said to have helped us prepare for our future pension obligations. Also, there is some controversy as to the true interpretation of the 1980s federal deficits, and how to measure them accurately.[10]

Still, our recent experience with government spending does somewhat shake one's confidence in the significance of the Trust Fund, and all the more since one has already heard people offering *serious reasons* that we should not just let it sit there accumulating, but should start spending it. *One* such serious reason is that federal government surpluses might have negative effects on the overall health of the economy. We mentioned earlier the worry some observers had during the Great Depression that the buildup (a very small buildup by today's standards) of the Trust Fund in advance of pension payouts may have been a negative factor as far as the overall health of the economy was concerned. But suppose we face a serious recession? Would we want the government accumulating surpluses at such times? Economists differ on this matter, and yet one can readily imagine that if the economy should falter (as, for example, it did in 1981–1982), Trust Fund accumulations might stop, and other expenditures might be increased sharply.

A *second* serious reason for raiding the Trust Fund might be that there were other specific expenditures the government wished to undertake but felt it was politically impossible or economically treacherous (because of the effects on incentives) to raise taxes to pay for them. Here the health care issue comes immediately to the fore. We shall be discussing this issue at length in Chapter 8, but suffice it to say here that one thing the Social Security reforms of 1983 definitely did *not* do was to put our national health care system on the same kind of financial footing as the old-age pension component of the system. At a minimum, further reforms in the Medicare and Medicaid elements of the system will have to be undertaken to guarantee their financial soundness.

### Will Economic Growth Solve Everything?

Even given that the Trust Fund may be unreliable, can't we still rely on economic growth to render most of our choices in the Aging Society quite painless?

Many observers believe so, although it must be said that this is another issue that is more complicated than appears at first glance. Besides the matters of saving and investment, economic growth is a complex process involving attitudes, entrepreneurship, technological progress, and the quantity and quality of the country's labor force.

Some commentators have felt that the Aging Society may produce a decline in those attitudes toward mobility, creativity, and change that are required to promote innovation and growth. Others have worried about the changing character of industrial enterprise in an advanced economy. We are moving more and more toward a service-producing as opposed to a goods-producing economy. Is it possible that technological progress will be less rapid in the service industries than it was in agriculture and manufacturing? Is a serious slowdown in our rate of productivity increase an inevitable feature of our long-run prospects?[11]

Is it possible, furthermore, that the shift from youth dependency to elderly dependency may work in subtle ways to depress our national rate of growth? The argument here is that while the total dependency burden may not be increasing in our Aging Society, nevertheless the shift from youth to elderly dependency will involve a *shift of expenditure from the private to the public sector*. *Public* expenditures on the elderly are estimated to run around three times those on children, which are largely for education, though also including certain welfare expenditures.

So the Aging Society may have an intrinsic tendency to shift our national expenditure balance from the private to the public sphere, ultimately requiring higher taxation. And although, in principle, economic growth will provide us with higher incomes to pay those taxes, we face two possible snags:

1. As our incomes rise, our desire for higher levels of consumption also tend to rise; we may resist the necessary tax increases even though, in principle, we could easily afford them.

2. Any shift to higher levels of public expenditure and taxation could act negatively on the private incentives which, historically, have played such a central role in the growth process. Taxed too heavily, will our talent for entrepreneurship wither and fade away?

Moreover, there are also serious questions about the quantity and quality of the labor force that will be available to us in the future. In the next chapter, we will be taking up one of the major developments of our era: the tendency toward earlier and earlier retirement on the part of our older and not-so-old age groups. Such early retirement affects the Social Security issue in two ways, both by increasing the number of years in which benefits have to be paid out and by decreasing the years during which contributions are paid in.

We also have very serious questions arising about the quality of the work force that will be providing not only the labor, but also the management and innovational capacity necessary for our continued economic growth. A 1989 study found that the educational system of the United States was demonstrably weak compared to those of a number of other countries, and especially in the critical areas of mathematics and science. In Chapter 17 we will consider this issue in some detail. Because immigrants entering this country are, in many cases, less well educated than the native-born, this question will also come up in Part V, where we discuss the character and future of immigration to the United States.

In short, while there is little doubt that robust economic growth in the future would ease many of the resource burdens of our Aging Society, such robust growth cannot simply be assumed to occur. It may need careful attention and nurturing. Otherwise, we may find that a prolonged downturn in our economic fortunes might confront us with another Social Security "crisis"—and this time in earnest!

## SUMMARY

1. The U.S. Social Security system was born in the Great Depression of the 1930s and is one of the most successful and popular programs of the federal government.

2. As expanded during the course of its history, and especially with the increase in medical and other benefits during the Great Society days of the 1960s and early 1970s, the program has contributed to a sharp reduction in poverty and a general improvement in living standards among the elderly.

3. Still, there is much skepticism among the Baby Boomers as to whether the program will be adequate when they retire. This skepticism was increased by the "crisis" of 1983, when the Trust Fund nearly ran out. Social Security was revealed then to have a certain dualism of goals (equity insofar as it is a social "insurance" system versus adequacy insofar as it is a social "welfare" system) and methods (funding versus pay-as-you-go). The crisis revealed that the equity/insurance principle had been greatly compromised and that the future liabilities of the system were largely unfunded.

4. The reforms of 1983 put Social Security on a much sounder actuarial basis by various measures that increased taxes and reduced benefits. These reforms lead in principle to a huge buildup of the Social Security Trust Fund into the next century, until it is drawn down to finance the needs of the retiring Baby Boomers.

5. Whether these reforms are adequate to the needs of our aging population will depend on a balance of positive and negative factors.

Positive factors are: (a) the buildup of the Trust Fund, which should ideally increase national savings and investment for the future; (b) the relatively low total dependency ratio even when the Baby Boomers reach their sixties and seventies; and (c) the prospect that economic growth, even though somewhat below our historic rate, may make both equity and adequacy goals achievable for the Boomers.

Negatively, we have: (a) the possibility that the Trust Fund may not lead to net additional accumulations of capital, being either raided for other uses (as, for example, health care programs), or offset by large deficit expenditures elsewhere in the budget (stimulated perhaps by an economic recession), and (b) the possibility that economic growth may be much weaker in the future for a variety of reasons, including the aging of the society, low-productivity growth in service industries, increased public-sector taxation, and both quantitative and qualitative (especially educational) weaknesses in our future labor force.

6. How this balance works out may largely determine not only the future of Social Security but whether we run the risk of intergenerational conflict in the decades ahead.

## KEY CONCEPTS FOR REVIEW

U.S. Social Security program

Social Security Trust Fund

Rediscovery of poverty

Medicare and Medicaid

Cost-of-living adjustment (COLA)

Replacement ratio

Changes in elderly poverty

Social Security "crisis" of the early 1980s

1983 amendments

Equity versus adequacy principles

Social insurance versus welfare program

Funding versus pay-as-you-go

Future fund accumulation

Youth dependency ratio

Total dependency ratio

Economic factors: U.S. saving and investment; future rate of growth

## QUESTIONS FOR DISCUSSION

1. Describe how elderly Americans managed to keep afloat in the days before Social Security. How did the Great Depression of the 1930s demonstrate the inadequacy of the previous elderly support system?

2. Describe the expansion of the Social Security system from the 1930s onward. What evidence suggests that this program has had a massive effect on the economic and psychological well-being of the United States' elderly?

3. What do we mean when we say that there is a *dualism* of goals and methods in our Social Security program? Would you favor emphasizing one goal or method above the others? What would be some of the issues involved in making your decision?

4. Explain why the accumulation of a large Social Security Trust Fund over the next few decades may: (a) guarantee that we will be able to sustain the system when the Baby Boomers retire or (b) have no real effect on the resources available for supporting the retired Boomers. Which outcome do you consider more likely and/or desirable?

5. In Chapter 5, the aging of today's America was attributed to three factors: (a) the aging of the Baby Boomers, (b) the continuing Baby Bust, and (c) the extension of life expectancies for older Americans. Relate each of these factors to the possible future viability of our Social Security system.

6. "The real future of Social Security will be determined not in Washington, D.C., but in the farms, factories, and offices of our nation. What we really need is more economic growth and more saving and investment to sustain the burdens of tomorrow's elderly." Discuss.

## NOTES

1. In this chapter we shall be referring mainly, though not exclusively, to the the old-age pension provisions of our Social Security system, entitled OASI, for Old Age and Survivors' Insurance. But the full title of the program is OASDHI, including also Disability Insurance (DI) and Hospital Insurance (HI), plus Supplementary Medical Insurance (SMI). There are also several other programs under the term *social security* used in a looser sense—as, for example, Medicaid—to which we shall be referring from time to time.

2. Concern about the burdens a large older generation may place on the working-age generation is by no means confined to the United States. It is a universal concern throughout western Europe and especially in Japan, where a very low fertility rate (1.57 in 1989) and the world's highest average life expectancy (81.8 for women and 75.9 for men in 1989) mean growing numbers of old people and a shortage of young workers to support the old-age welfare system.

3. In some respects, unemployment was even more desperate than the official statistics suggest. The rate in the nonagricultural work force actually reached 37.6 percent for January–March 1933. In the agricultural sector, unemployment is often

disguised: People return to the farms in very hard times but make little or no contribution to actual production.

4. Although we will refer to these programs occasionally in this chapter, our major discussion of their impact on the Aging Society will be in Chapter 8.

5. An obvious example of a conflict between the two principles was the 1939 provision that made the wife of an insured worker who had retired eligible for 50 percent of her husband's benefit when she reached age 65. From an "adequacy" point of view, a couple would presumably need more income than a single retiree. On the other hand, from an "equity" point of view, two workers (one, say, a bachelor, one a married man) who had each made the same contributions would be receiving very different rates of return in total. In the case of minorities, although there is no intention to treat them in a differential way, it can be argued that blacks, say, with lower incomes on the average, receive more than is appropriate by a purely equity calculation, but it can *also* be argued that, because their life expectancy is less than that of whites, they receive benefits for fewer years, thus getting *less* than they should by a purely equity calculation. Examples of such complications abound in the Social Security literature.

6. Henry J. Aaron, "Silver Threads . . . Pension and Health Policy for an Aging Society," mimeographed, November 30, 1988, pp. 17–18.

7. There has not been sufficient research to determine the average cost to society of a young as opposed to an elderly "dependent." A guesstimate is that the cost, including both public and private expenditures, may be roughly equal for young and old people, but that the public expenditures on each elderly person are higher, perhaps by a factor of three.

8. Aaron, "Silver Threads," p. 26.

9. Besides calling attention to the need for discipline in the federal budget process, Senator Moynihan was also criticizing the Social Security payroll tax as weighing too heavily on the poor—that is, being a regressive tax. Opponents of the Moynihan proposal—which included most economists—pointed out that, taking benefits into account, the total Social Security system was progressive rather than regressive. But the main criticism was that in abolishing the buildup of the Trust Fund, Moynihan would effectively be reducing national saving, and national saving is required to meet future retirement needs.

10. Economists differ as to whether the federal deficits of the 1980s were properly or improperly measured. Most economists viewed the size of the deficits with some alarm, but there were a few—notably Professor Robert Eisner, past president of the American Economic Association—who argued that failure to take into account inflation, government capital accumulation, and offsetting state and local government surpluses led to exaggerated fears about the magnitude of the deficit. Eisner even argued that the measured federal deficit of $155 billion in 1988 was actually an overall governmental *surplus* of $42 billion. Most economists, however, did not accept this judgment.

11. The fear here is that, while labor-saving inventions have greatly increased productivity in agriculture and manufacturing, there may be many service industries that depend primarily on labor time expended—nurses, teachers, police, and the like. Thus, productivity growth in those industries might be much slower than in the historically predominant goods-producing sectors. This idea is sometimes called "the cost disease of the service sector" by its advocates. See, for example, W. J. Baumol and A. S. Blinder, *Economics: Principles and Policy*, 4th ed. (New York: Harcourt Brace Jovanovich, 1988), pp. 640–643.

# 7

# *To Work or to Retire?*

On the surface, the issue of work versus retirement in the Aging Society seems a rather simple one:

- America's workers, we are told, are living longer and longer but retiring earlier and earlier.

- By and large, these workers are retiring early as a matter of choice—a choice made possible by our increasing real incomes and our rising retirement benefits, both public and private.

- But with the increase in the number of elderly and the added life expectancies projected for the future, we must now encourage elderly citizens to retire at later ages, or at least we must remove any incentives or requirements for early retirement. Hence, we had the 1983 reforms of Social Security, raising the "normal" retirement age in the next century, and also federal legislation (1986) effectively abolishing mandatory retirement ages throughout our economy.

This is the simple story, and there is a good deal of truth in it, although there is also considerable disagreement about each of the above points, including even the direction our future policies should take. Where agreement *does* exist is on the need for our society to become more flexible in the options it offers to our older citizens— this for the benefit both of the elderly and of U.S. society in general.

## THE COMPLICATED TREND TOWARD EARLIER RETIREMENTS

The first part of the story involves what appears to be a massive departure of our older workers from the U.S. labor force, and this despite substantial increases in life expectancies, especially among those older age groups (Table 7-1). As we investigate further, however, we find that the facts are a bit more complicated than this.

**TABLE 7-1. Life Expectancy at Age 65, U.S. Male and Female, Actual and Projected (In Years)**

| Year | Male | Female |
|------|------|--------|
| 1900 | 11.3 | 12.0 |
| 1910 | 11.4 | 12.1 |
| 1920 | 11.8 | 12.3 |
| 1930 | 11.4 | 12.9 |
| 1940 | 11.9 | 13.4 |
| 1950 | 12.8 | 15.1 |
| 1960 | 12.9 | 15.9 |
| 1970 | 13.1 | 17.1 |
| 1980 | 14.0 | 18.4 |
| Projected: | | |
| 1990 | 14.9 | 19.2 |
| 2000 | 15.6 | 20.1 |
| 2010 | 16.0 | 20.6 |
| 2020 | 16.3 | 21.0 |
| 2030 | 16.7 | 21.5 |
| 2040 | 17.0 | 21.9 |
| 2050 | 17.4 | 22.4 |
| 2060 | 17.7 | 22.8 |
| 2070 | 18.1 | 23.3 |
| 2080 | 18.5 | 23.7 |

*Source: Social Security Bulletin, 51*(2), February 1988, Table 14.

### Declining Labor Force Participation of Elderly Males

By **labor force participation rate,** we mean the percentage of workers in any given category of age or sex who are either working or consider themselves to be actively seeking work. If one is seeking work but not employed, then one is considered *unemployed.* If, on the other hand, one is not employed but is not seeking work, then one is considered to be out of the labor force, and one is not included in the participation figures. Although the concepts are clear enough, there are many borderline cases of so-called **discouraged workers**—that is, workers who would like to be in the labor force but who, because they cannot find jobs, stop looking for them and drop out of the labor force. Such behavior, as we shall note in a moment, is much more common among older than younger workers.

*Official Estimates.* In Figure 7-1 we present estimates of labor force participation rates for U.S. males 65 and over from 1890 to 1988. In 1890, according to these estimates, more than two-thirds (68.3 percent) of males 65 and older were in the labor force. As late as 1930, over half (54.0 percent) were still participants. By 1988, the percentage had fallen to 16.5 percent. *From over two-thirds of men 65 and older working to one in six in a single century!*

The **trend to earlier retirement** was also apparently spreading to younger and younger workers as well. In 1948, 89.5 percent of the male 55–64 age group were labor force participants; by 1988, the number had declined to 67 percent. Declines can also be found in the 45–54 age group and even to some degree in still younger age groups. Labor force participation of U.S. males has declined overall in the post–World War II period, and the median age of retirement has fallen to 62 or less, well under the "normal" retirement age of 65.

**FIGURE 7–1: U.S. Male Labor Force Participation Rates, Age 65 +**

*Sources:* Roger L. Ransom and Richard Sutch, "The Labor of Older Americans: Retirement of Men On and Off the Job, 1870–1937," *Journal of Economic History*, 46(1), March 1986, Table 2; U.S. Bureau of the Census.

On the face of it, we are dealing with what might be called a "retirement revolution" here. If the trend toward earlier retirements should continue along with anticipated increases in life expectancy at older ages (Table 7-1), then retirement—once something of a curiosity—could come to occupy 20 years or more, *well over a quarter of the average worker's life!* From a personal point of view, this would represent as major a change in the life course of the typical American male as any we will be discussing in this book.

***But Are the Historical Figures Accurate?***
This strong conclusion may, however, have to be modified somewhat if recent studies prove to be validated by subsequent research. One important study concerns the *timing* of the trend toward earlier retirement in the United States. According to Professor Roger L. Ransom of the University of California (Riverside) and Professor Richard Sutch of the University of California (Berkeley), the picture presented here understates the amount of retirement among male workers occurring in the United States in the late nineteenth and early twentieth centuries. In an article in the *Journal of Economic History* (March 1986), they suggest that full retirement from the labor force was fairly common in this early period, that the trend until the 1930s among nonagricultural workers was actually toward *later* retirement, and that it is only from the 1930s on that the current trend to earlier retirement manifests itself.[1]

The picture that these scholars present in terms of labor force participation for U.S. males 60 and over is shown in Figure 7-2. It is evident that there is no downward trend in these rates until 1930. Furthermore, the lower curve, labeled "Adjusted for Shift Away from Agriculture," is rising until the 1930s. The meaning is this: During these 60 years, there was a substantial shift of American workers from agriculture to industry. Agricultural workers tend to retire later in life than industrial workers. There-

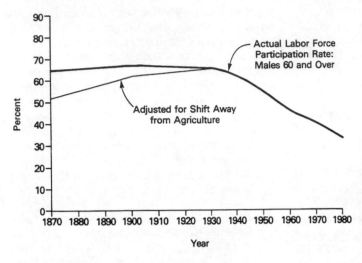

**FIGURE 7-2:   U.S. Male Labor Participation Rates, Age 60 and Over**

*Source:*   Roger L. Ransom and Richard S... "The Labor of Older Americans: Retireme... Men On and Off the Job, 1870-1937," *Journal of Economic History,* 46(1), March 1988, Figure 3, p. 19.

fore, this shift should have brought a *decrease* in the overall labor force participation rate. But that rate (the top curve) was essentially constant. This means that there must have been an upward shift in labor force participation by workers in industry to compensate for the shift in the agriculture/industry balance in the country as a whole. The bottom curve shows what this upward shift would have been assuming *no* change in the balance between the two sectors. This upward shift, Ransom and Sutch suspect, may have involved older workers moving into less demanding jobs late in life.[2] Thus, the trend toward earlier retirement may be of much more recent vintage than previously thought—a phenomenon of the last 50 or 60 years only.

***How Much Less Are Older Males Working Today?***   A second question is whether labor force participation rates really tell us what we want to know about the work life patterns of our older citizens. According to researchers Mark D. Hayward of the University of Southern California and William R. Grady and Steven D. McLaughlin of the Battelle Memorial Institute in Seattle, these rates do not take adequate account of mobility in and out of the labor force by older workers. They devise a method for estimating these

multiple labor force exits and entrances, and divide an older worker's life expectancy into two parts: (1) **work life expectancy,** and (2) **nonworking life expectancy.** Over an admittedly brief period (1972–1980), they find that for American males 55 years of age, their total remaining life expectancy increased from 19.44 years to 20.95 years, their work life expectancy decreased from 8.14 to 7.99 years, and their nonworking life expectancy increased from 11.30 years to 12.96 years.

The main point they make is that there was virtually no change (only 0.15 years) in work life expectancy. What really happened was that nonworking life expectancy simply soaked up the increase in overall life expectancy. "Clearly," they write, "the major contributing factor to the increases in nonworking life expectancy during the period was the decline in mortality among older males—not changes in labor force behavior."[3] In a word, these workers were not retiring very much earlier; their retirements were getting longer primarily because they were living longer.

Although it is doubtful that this conclusion could be applied to the strong overall trend to earlier retirement, nevertheless this research does suggest that some caution must be used in interpreting our labor force participation figures. In general, we can conclude that American men are undoubtedly both living longer *and* retiring earlier, but the magnitude of the latter change is difficult to assess accurately.

### Labor Force Participation of Elderly Females

A further complication in judging the overall impact of American retirement changes is that the numbers for women look quite different from those for men. In Figure 7-3, we show the measured labor force participation rates for U.S. females for various older age groups during the post–World War II period. Unlike those of men, the labor force participation rates of most women rose during this period. The one exception is the 65+ group, which fell slightly from the early 1960s on, and which is a very small group in any event.

Clearly, these curves reflect in great part the massive postwar entry of women into the U.S. work force that we have often

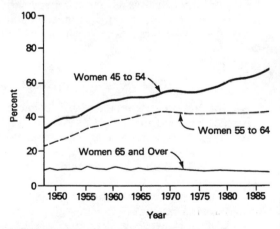

**FIGURE 7–3: U.S. Female Labor Force Participation Rates, 1948–1987**

*Source:* Henry J. Aaron, "Silver Threads . . . Pension and Health Policy for an Aging Society," *Fulfilling America's Promise: Social Policies for the 1990s.* Edited for The Center for Humanities and Social Sciences, Williams College, by Joseph A. Pechman with the assistance of Michael S. McPherson. Forthcoming from Cornell University Press. Used by permission of the publisher.

referred to and will be studying in some detail in Chapter 11. Because these rates are still well below those of men, it may be that they will continue to increase in the years ahead. This would tend to make men's and women's participation in the labor force somewhat more similar, and would also offset some of the losses in labor supply if the trend toward earlier retirement among American men continues.

In general, we can conclude that any tendency for women to want to retire earlier is currently being counterbalanced by the overall movement of women into the work force. We thus have increased female labor force participation at the younger ages and something of a stand-off at the older ages. As in the case of men, of course, the effect of increased life expectancy at the older ages is to increase the average number of years in retirement.

## RETIREMENT AND THE AMERICAN DREAM

During the Baby Boom era, the image that most caught the spirit of America was the single-family house in suburbia, with a commuting husband, a cheerful homemaker wife, a pleasant lawn, and lots of children.

What would be the symbol of the Aging Society? It, too, might be a single-family house, with a nice lawn and a cheerful wife, but there would not be any children around (except grandchildren for occasional visits), and the husband would not be commuting any more. He and his wife would be enjoying an early, comfortable, and lengthy retirement. According to this view, the trend toward earlier and longer retirements simply reflects the fulfillment of one more part of the American Dream.

### Surveys Suggest Americans Want to Retire Early

One of the rather striking discoveries of recent years has been that the raising and then the effective abolition of the mandatory retirement age in this country had little or no effect on the trend toward earlier retirement. The number of workers who were being literally *forced* to leave the work force at age 65 or 70 was apparently very small. Workers were evidently leaving the work force for the same reason that, historically, they had fought for shorter work weeks and longer vacations—they prefer leisure to work!

Numerous studies confirm that such an attitude is widespread. Thus, one study of retirement among American men reaches this conclusion: "If one is compelled to make a single generalization about retirement, perhaps the most valid would be that it is generally entered into voluntarily, found to be pleasant and not regretted even after many years."[4] Similarly, in a study of retirement of men and women from lower level jobs, scholars found that "for the most part they retired early of their own free will and, what is more, most of them are convinced, in retrospect, that they had made the right decision."[5]

Thus, "leisure," along with better food, clothing, housing, and appliances, is considered by most Americans to be a desirable "good," and, as our incomes rise, we wish to have more of it. Early retirement in this sense is to be understood in the same way as the fact that we purchase, say, more elaborate home entertainment—TVs, stereos, VCRs—as our standard of living rises.

### The Affordability of Retirement

By this same logic, a main question for workers about when to retire is whether or not they feel they can afford to retire. And there is little doubt that a major factor in enabling Americans to retire earlier has been the increase in Social Security benefits as well as in private pension benefits during the past half-century. Social Security benefits are now received by 90 percent of elderly Americans. Private employer pension plans, very limited in extent earlier in this century, now cover large numbers of wage and salary workers. Also, there are government pen-

sions for civilian workers, military pensions, and pensions from unions. In total, two-thirds of U.S. wage and salary workers are covered by private and public pensions.

Social Security pension benefits plus these private and public pensions "replace" about 44 percent of the average American's preretirement income and account for about 50 percent of the retirees' average family income. Furthermore, other Social Security benefits, notably disability insurance, have made it affordable for many injured or health-limited workers to retire earlier than was the case in the past.

Thus, the same surveys mentioned earlier find that most retirees, although worried about such hazards as inflation, generally feel that they are doing all right economically. For example, 93 percent of retired married men in a 1967–1979 survey believed that they had enough to "get by"; nearly two-thirds claimed to have money left over or, at least, enough for "a little extra sometimes."[6] In a questionnaire given to lower level workers who had retired early, the reason most frequently mentioned for having stopped work was because "I could afford to."[7]

### Personal Satisfactions of Retirement

Nor has the experience of retirement proved disappointing to most retirees. Again, there is a great deal of evidence to suggest that the average early retiree does not regret his decision. Very close to the "I could afford to retire" response among lower level workers was the response "I had worked long enough," and also "The pressures of work were getting too great." In general, the thing that retirees like *most* about their retirement is the simple fact that they don't have to work any more.

Of course, the activities and attitudes of retirees vary widely. Some who are officially "retired"—as defined, say, by receipt of Social Security pension benefits—continue to work for wages to a greater or lesser degree to supplement their public (and/or private) pension benefits. Some move. Some travel. Some engage in volunteer work. A goodly number find time for increased reading, pursuit of hobbies, such exercise as health permits, and visiting with children and friends. Lest too cheerful a picture be given of these activities, however, it should be mentioned that the single leisure-time occupation that fills most hours for most retirees is watching television. On average, it may account for something like 40 percent of the time retirees spend on leisure activities in general.

How one views the way retirees spend their time may depend on one's overall conception of what old age and retirement signify in a person's life. Some argue that the later years should be a time for a graceful "disengagement" from the pressure and rush of ordinary daily life; others believe that it is highly important that the "activity level" in a person's life be maintained through hobbies, exercise, and volunteer and other work well past any official retirement age. The latter view has become increasingly common in recent years as studies have shown the beneficial effects of challenging activities on the physical and especially the mental faculties of elderly persons (see Chapter 22, pp. 397–398).

From the point of view of the retirees themselves, however, and despite numerous specific problems with health, finances, and occasionally boredom, the general attitude toward retirement is favorable. If the "**work ethic**" dominated our Puritan past, the "**retirement ethic**" seems very much alive in the United States today. At least, that is the story being told by the majority of retirees, many of whom, indeed, find retirement even better than they had expected it to be.

## VOLUNTARY, INVOLUNTARY, AND SEMIVOLUNTARY RETIREMENTS

The foregoing description conveys an important truth, but again we must pause to note that the simple story is not quite the whole story. Our view of early retirement as a matter of personal, self-fulfilling choice has to be qualified in a number of ways.

1.   *There is a definite group of elderly persons, both men and women, who intend "never" to retire and who, indeed, keep working hard often to the end of their lives.* Although this group is fairly small, it does include a number of highly productive individuals. Its existence suggests, moreover, that one's view of the benefits or drawbacks of retirement may be very much influenced by one's view of the drawbacks or benefits of work. If labor in the marketplace were more interesting, if its demands were less stressful, if, especially, the schedules of such work could be more flexibly arranged, would there, in fact, be many more people who would change their minds and choose work over retirement, or at least over early retirement? In short, attitudes toward retirement reflect not only the quality of retirement itself but also the quality of the work that is being offered.

2.   *Some surveys reveal that there are significant numbers of retirees, particularly at the younger ages, who consider that their retirements were "involuntary."* Much of this evidence is summarized in Malcolm H. Morrison and Cynthia Taeuber, "Labor Force Participation of America's Older Population." They write:

> Although retirement satisfaction is high, significant numbers of retirees (one-third to one-half) say they would prefer to work, especially part-time (National Council on Aging, 1975 and 1981). . . . Hausman and Paquette (1987) used the Retirement History Survey to determine that about 75 percent of men aged 55 and younger who retired, did so involuntarily because of health, age discrimination, or unemployment; 61 percent of those aged 55–59 retired involuntarily as did 41 percent of those aged 60 or 61, and 27 percent of those aged 62, the age at which men qualify for early Social Security benefits.[8]

Thus, although there is an apparently clear majority of men who retired in their sixties for "**voluntary**" reasons, there is a substantial minority of such men who did so for "**involuntary**" reasons. In the younger age groups, this minority becomes in fact a clear majority.

3. *So-called discouraged workers often retire only because the employment opportunities available to them are felt to be inadequate.* We have put "voluntary" and "involuntary" in quotes in the preceding paragraph because the truth is that these two categories are often difficult to distinguish. This is clearly the case with discouraged workers, a category we mentioned earlier. When young workers lose their jobs, they seldom wish, or can afford, to withdraw from the labor force. Also, the jobs available to them are more likely to be in line with their previous work experience. When older workers lose their jobs, however, they often find it extremely difficult to obtain work that is in any way comparable to the jobs they previously held. Thus, although there may be jobs available in the economy in a general sense, these older workers may find that retirement is preferable to the jobs *actually available to them personally.* Over one-third of men aged 60 to 64 who lose their jobs fail to find another and choose instead to retire.[9]

4. *The analysis of retirements because of health and/or disability is particularly complex.* On almost all surveys of reasons for retirement, one of the reasons given for retirement is poor health. We can see immediately that there are obvious definitional problems here. Except in the fairly rare cases of clearcut and total disability, poor health can occur in all sorts of degrees, preventing one from carrying out certain jobs (say, lifting heavy construction materials), but not others (say, being an office receptionist). It may also lead to withdrawal from the labor force under certain circumstances (say, if one has plenty of money and few responsibilities) and not in other circumstances (say, if one has little money and large responsibilities).

Again, the voluntary/involuntary retirement distinction becomes fuzzy at best.

But this is only the beginning of this particular problem. It may seem odd that the number of health-related retirements has been rising at a time when our life expectancies have been increasing, including specifically our life expectancies at the older ages. Actually, as we shall see in our next chapter, there is no necessary contradiction between these two developments, particularly if our lengthened life expectancies primarily allow disabled or health-impaired persons who would otherwise have died to survive. Still, it is difficult to believe that an increase in ill health among the elderly could account for a major part of the increase in early retirements that has occurred in recent years. And this is particularly so since *the increase in retirements because of ill health went along with major changes in the availability of disability benefits under our Social Security program.* In the decades of the 1960s and 1970s, **disability benefits** rose sharply, the wage replacement rate for a disabled worker with a wife and child reaching 68 percent in 1978. At the same time, the number of beneficiaries was rising some sevenfold.

Does this mean that it was not poorer health but increased benefits (leading to increased reports of poor health) that caused the upsurge in health-related early retirements? Scholars agree that this effect was present, but disagree as to how important it was quantitatively.[10] In either case, it once again becomes very difficult to sort out the voluntary as opposed to involuntary element in these health-related early retirements.

5. *Pension plans and other employer incentives for promoting early retirement.* Finally, the voluntary/involuntary distinction is also blurred when we come to consider various incentive systems that may be set up to encourage early retirement when, under more ordinary circumstances, the worker might actually have preferred to remain in

the labor force. In general, it was still true for the majority of workers in the late 1980s that they faced a reduction in the lifetime value of their pensions if they did not retire early, and even if they continued part-time work on their jobs.

Also, our newspapers in the 1980s were filled with accounts of corporations trying to *induce* older workers to retire. In their attempt to "downsize" and achieve greater efficiency in an internationally competitive environment, these firms often set up elaborate incentive systems to get older workers, often including high-level management, to retire before schedule. A whole new terminology was introduced to describe what was going on. "**Golden handshake**" was the phrase most often used: Retiring was made so financially attractive to the worker or executive that it became literally "an offer you can't refuse." When the negative side of the incentive offer was being emphasized (that is, the *dis*incentive to staying on), the phrase "**golden boot**" was sometimes used.

Meanwhile, corporations were trying to retain the services of some of their younger workers. To continue the metallic metaphor, "**golden chains**" were sometimes employed to make it disadvantageous for young workers to discontinue their employment with the firm. Pension and other benefits could be set up so as to make it (a) costly to leave the firm while young, and (b) costly to remain with the firm when old. It should be added, too, that until the 1983 Social Security reforms, older workers fared better actuarially by retiring before, rather than at, the age of 65.

Why would firms want to get rid of their older workers? And how important a factor was this in terms of the trend toward early retirements? There could, of course, be many reasons that firms might prefer younger to older workers. One general reason might be put this way: Because of seniority systems and other arrangements designed to retain workers (and to give them a sense of advancement in their working lives), older workers may effectively be paid more than their productive contributions to the firm, while young workers are characteristically paid less. Under such circumstances, top management would have a clear economic incentive to replace older with younger workers.

This factor, according to one account, may have been particularly important during the years when the Baby Boomers began entering the labor market. Between 1965 and 1980, the percentage of the labor force under 35 increased from 38 percent to 51 percent. Abundant in supply, younger men became less expensive. This led to a substantial increase in the earnings differential between men in the 45–54 age group as compared to all younger men. With younger men cheaper to hire, many firms—particularly those engaged in "downsizing"—had a special reason for encouraging their more senior workers to retire.[11]

Were such retirements, when they did occur, "voluntary" or "involuntary"? Perhaps it is better to think of them as in between, or "semivoluntary." Many individuals would have preferred that such offers, often of a take-it-or-leave-it variety, had never been made. Once the offers were made, however, it became either too advantageous to retire or too disadvantageous to remain on, so they were accepted.

"I *chose* to retire," many golden handshake recipients might well say, "but I would have preferred not to have *had* to choose."[12]

## SHOULD AN AGING SOCIETY PROMOTE LATER RETIREMENT?

During the dark days of the Great Depression of the 1930s, one of the arguments for the Social Security system was that, by encouraging earlier retirements, it would make room in the labor force for younger workers who were having such difficulty finding jobs.

Are we now entering a new phase of our national life where we will soon be facing shortages of younger workers and where our policy should be to encourage later retirements from our older workers? The 1983 Social Security reforms moved us a step in this direction by raising the "normal" (full-benefit) retirement age to 67 by the year 2027. Is this the way we should be heading?

### View I: We Must Encourage Later Retirements

The argument for promoting later retirements—or, at least, fighting off the trend to earlier retirements—is two-pronged:

1. Many of our elderly are retiring involuntarily today or at least only semi-voluntarily. As life expectancies for the elderly increase still further in the next century, the prospects of longer and longer retirements will become more unattractive, and we must alter public and private policies to make sure that there are good, satisfying jobs in the marketplace for older workers. However "golden" the handshake, discarding workers in their early sixties and even their fifties and late forties must cease.

2. We simply cannot afford the dependency burden that is doubly increased by early retirement—that is, more older dependents and fewer older workers in the labor force to support them. All the arguments that have made some observers dubious about the future viability of Social Security are relevant here. We are not accumulating investment capital for the future; our productivity growth is slowing down; the quantity and quality of our future labor force are likely to be inadequate; the shift to elderly dependency from young dependency is likely to increase the public sector, bring higher taxation, diminish incentives for growth; and so on. To which list we shall add in our next chapter: that our future health care burdens, particularly for the rapidly growing group of *older* old people, will intensify all these problems greatly.

The need for more older workers in our future labor force can be illustrated by Figure 7-4. During the post–World War II period, it is argued, we were "saved" from the problems of an Aging Society by the fact that there was an *enormous expansion* in the percentage of our population participating in our labor force. This trend is likely to continue, but at a decelerating rate until the end of this century, at which time it will be sharply reversed. Looking at the right hand side of Figure 7-4, we can see the curve sloping down and then settling in at a level well below our 1990 level of participation.

The reasons for the earlier expansion were, of course, the entry of the Baby Boomers into the labor force and the massive postwar increase in female participation

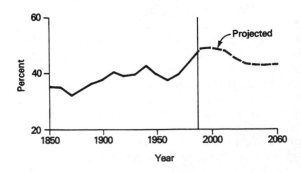

**FIGURE 7–4:  U.S. Labor Force As a Percentage of Total Population, 1850–2060**

*Source:* Henry J. Aaron, "Silver Threads . . . Pension and Health Policy for an Aging Society," *Fulfilling America's Promise: Social Policies for the 1990s.* Edited for The Center for Humanities and Social Sciences, Williams College, by Joseph A. Pechman with the assistance of Michael S. McPherson. Forthcoming from Cornell University Press. Used by permission of the publisher.

in the labor market. Similarly, the reasons for future decline will be the replacement of the Baby Boomers by the Baby Busters and the inevitable slowing down of the rate of increase of female participation. Under these circumstances, it is claimed, we will absolutely *need* older workers to remain in the labor force much longer than at present.

### View II: Early Retirement Is an Affordable Blessing

The opposing argument is also two-pronged:

1. The fact that the majority of early retirements appear to be both voluntary and enjoyed by the retirees is stressed. If older workers *choose* to depart from the labor force, and if there is no evidence that they later *regret* that choice, then why should we try to set up elaborate schemes to distort those choices?

2. Economic growth, combined with the decreased number of youthful dependents, should make it easily possible for us to maintain our elderly retired population at a reasonable standard of living even if still earlier retirements occur in the future. If per capita incomes increase at 1 percent a year for the next 70 years, they will have *doubled* in real terms by the year 2060. Thus, the elderly will be quite able to choose to take some of this increased income in the form of increased "leisure" if that is their pleasure.

As far as the *need* for older workers in the labor force is concerned, the adherents of view II could also refer to Figure 7-4. Instead of emphasizing the right-hand side of the figure, however, they would emphasize the left-hand side. Despite the projected decrease in the labor force/population ratio in the twenty-first century, we still end up in the year 2060 with *a far higher ratio than at any time in our history up until World War II.*

In short, the elderly want to retire early.

We can afford the early retirements. Let nature take its course and stop worrying about the matter.

## OF PYRAMIDS AND RECTANGLES AGAIN

Most of us are likely to feel that neither of these two points of view is fully satisfactory. There is obviously great uncertainty about the future rate of economic growth. There is the difficulty of determining how "voluntary" or "involuntary" retirements are. Also, it is not clear that we should give such high priority to the views of the retirees themselves. After all, one of the fundamental rationales for having a *compulsory* Social Security system is that, left to their own devices, individuals will not make correct decisions about their own futures. They will spend too much today, and be caught short tomorrow when they are old and infirm. Similarly, it may be the case (or it can be argued) that people, individually, may find it in their own interest to retire early, but that in doing so they will place burdens on other workers that they do not fully take into account.

Indeed, it may well be that the implications of retirement policy for younger workers extend well beyond the question of the resource burden of supporting the retirees. In particular, the choices made in this area may substantially affect the *advancement opportunities* of those younger workers.

In Figure 7-5, we return to our old friends from geometry, pyramids and rectangles, once again. Our population "pyramid," as we know, is becoming increasingly "squared" and, in the next century, will be virtually a perfect rectangle.

The pyramid shown in Figure 7-5a is not, then, a population pyramid but what we will call a **job pyramid.** It is based on the not unreasonable notion that there are fewer management and highly skilled jobs available than jobs requiring lesser skills. The perfect example for such a hierarchical

Work Classification

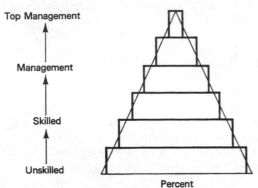

FIGURE 7–5a:  Stylized Job Pyramid

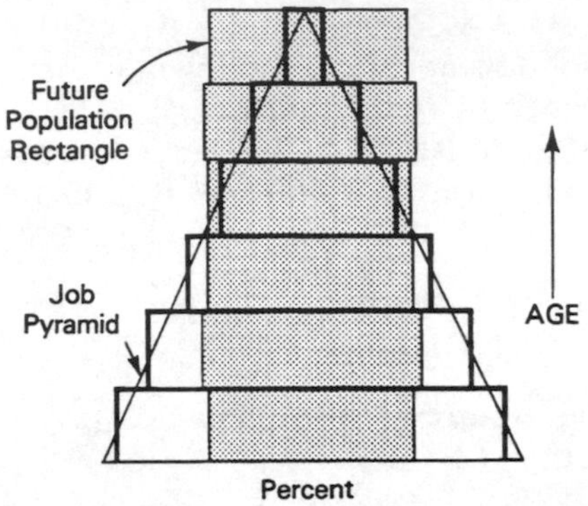

FIGURE 7–5b:  Population Rectangle and Job Pyramid

structure would, of course, be the armed services, where there are more privates than corporals, than sergeants, than lieutenants, than colonels, than generals, and so on up to the single commander-in-chief.

Our job pyramid is drawn in a perfectly stylized fashion and would probably fit no real-world industry even in its main outlines. However, it does convey an important element of truth, and, in particular, it enables us to bring out certain of the complexities of retirement policy.

In Figure 7-5b we have superimposed a stylized population rectangle for the working age groups over the job pyramid. For illustrative purposes, we assume that the number of people who want to work is roughly equal to the number of jobs available. Our interest is in the effects of the different *shapes* of the two structures.

Now, if older workers were all to remain in the labor force, then we would obviously not have enough higher level jobs to offer them. What might the solution to such a problem be?

Two solutions suggest themselves. One would involve the excess of older workers moving down to lower level jobs as they are displaced at the higher reaches of the job pyramid. Ransom and Sutch, we recall, suggest that during the nineteenth century,

many older workers did just this—moving to less demanding jobs late in life.

The other main solution would involve older workers crowding into the job pyramid at the highest level they can achieve. This would mean that it would be extremely difficult for young workers to rise very far in the job scale over time. As compared to a situation where the population structure was pyramidal (rather than rectangular), the average worker would have to spend more time at lower level jobs. Also, each worker's chances of rising to the "top" would be considerably diminished.

This is a very simplified picture, of course. Indeed, the job structure itself, if measured in terms of relative wages, would not remain fixed under these pressures. It has often been pointed out that with the relative shortage of young people to fill entry-level jobs, the wage rates for those jobs might be expected to rise. This would reduce the wage differential between older and younger workers, which might in turn increase the relative demand for older workers.

Still, there is a potential conflict of objectives here that we should not minimize. From the point of view of supporting a large population of elderly persons, we will likely want to keep older workers in the labor force as long as possible. But from the point of view of making room for the advancement of younger workers, we may very well want to encourage early retirements, particularly as the proportion of elderly in the population keeps increasing.

The conflict is not just theoretical. We have already seen it in the explosion of "golden handshakes" and "golden boots" that occurred in the corporate world during the last decade.

## EXPLORING NEW OPTIONS

The conflict we have just mentioned is not, of course, an inevitable one. It becomes severe only if we take a very rigid view of the job structure of our society and of the characteristic career paths of individuals over their lifetimes.

One partial "solution" to the problem, as already mentioned, is for older workers, as in the past, to accept less demanding, lower level jobs at the ends as well as at the beginnings of their careers. Since heavy physical work is becoming less common, and since virtually all new job creation in the U.S. economy is in the service sector, there should be fewer tangible obstacles to such a solution than in the past. With the relative shortage of available younger workers, conditions of work in entry-level positions may well improve so as to be somewhat more attractive to older workers.

Very probably, this part of the solution will work only if there is a general increase in **part-time employment.** Many elderly persons who would not want to take on service sector work on a full-time basis might be willing to do so if hours could be adjusted to a more limited basis. In general, an increase in part-time job options, including also work that can be done at home, may make possible an increased labor force participation of older workers without involving any diminution of opportunities for the younger cohorts coming along to take their places.

There is also, however, another route that we might call the **multiple-career lifestyle.** By pursuing more than one, and conceivably even three or four, career paths during one's lifetime, an individual might be able to accomplish a number of objectives appropriate to the Aging Society.

For one thing, one could avoid the problem of boredom implicit in a world where people are living very long lives and where the single-career path, even when the career is interesting, is likely to become mind-numbing if pursued for 50, 60, conceivably even 70 or 80, years. Also, such a pattern could help solve the pyramid versus rectangle problem. That problem requires that people in general spend more time at entry- or low-level as opposed to advanced or high-level positions. And, of course, when one starts off on a new career, this, indeed, is what one has to do: take a step backward for a time in order to explore new avenues.

Not that such moves will be easy for individuals to make or for society to accept. How many individuals would really be willing to accept cuts to entry-level salaries twice, or even three or four times, in their lives? Apart from the important attitudinal changes required, there is a clear need for society to provide opportunities for education, training, and *re*training for individuals late in their lives. It is quite possible that the dual- or multiple-career pattern could work only if we change our whole concept of when and how education is to take place in our lives. Until now, we have always tended to think of "schooling" as occurring in the early years of our lives, ending with high school, college, or a professional degree. One of the major changes that may be required to make the Aging Society viable, or at least fulfilling, may be to view **education as a lifelong process,** or a process that may be returned to in a serious way again, or even a number of times, later in life.[13]

There do exist some programs for older students that are currently attempting to meet such needs.[14] Their impact so far has been rather minimal, but they could expand enormously in the decades ahead. What is certain, both from the point of view of the individual older person and from that of the Aging Society as a whole, is that a new flexibility in terms of job structures and professional and technical education will be required if our transition to the rectangular populations of the future is to be a smooth one.

Without such flexibility, options for both old *and* young in the Aging Society may be less fulfilling than one might wish.

## SUMMARY

1. According to standard estimates, there has been a massive decline in U.S. labor force participation rates for males 65 and over during the past century: from 68.3 percent in 1890 to 16.5 percent today. Declines are also shown for men in the middle age groups.

2. While declining participation and earlier retirement are clearly occurring, there is some dispute about (a) when this withdrawal from the labor force began occurring (Ransom and Sutch argue it did not begin until the 1930s) and (b) to what degree it is offset by reentry into the labor force after retirement (Hayward, Grady, and McLaughlin argue that there is substantial mobility back to work for the elderly). Also, the pattern of labor force participation for women is different from that of men, increasing retirement for older women being mostly offset by the increasing tendency of women of all ages to join the work force.

3. Under any circumstances, earlier retirement plus increasing life expectancies for the elderly means that most older Americans now face unprecedented numbers of retirement years. There is considerable evidence that, given the benefits available through Social Security, private pensions, and other programs, most retirees are happy to retire early and do not regret the decision after the fact. They are simply fulfilling one of the cherished aspects of the American Dream.

4. However, retirement decisions are not always voluntary, and, indeed, the distinction between "voluntary" and "involuntary" decisions is complicated in the case of "discouraged workers," workers who retire because of "health," and those who are enticed or pressured into early retirement by "golden handshakes," "golden boots," or wage-and-pension patterns that discourage remaining on the job after certain ages.

5. Some observers say that we must now encourage later retirements because (a) many older workers would really prefer to continue working and (b) we need them to support the burdens of elderly dependency in the next century with the weak labor force growth anticipated. Other observers say that we should let the elderly retire when they want because (a) most early retirees do not regret their decision and (b) economic growth will make their early retirements easily sustainable.

6. Disproportions between *job pyramids* and *population rectangles* in the Aging Society suggest a potential conflict between the goal of augmenting the labor force with elderly workers and the goal of keeping advancement opportunities open for younger workers. Institutional and personal flexibility, as in the case of more part-time employment, lifelong educational opportunities, and multiple-career life-styles may be necessary to resolve this dilemma.

## KEY CONCEPTS FOR REVIEW

Labor force participation rate
    male
    female

Discouraged workers

Trend to earlier retirement

Work life expectancy versus nonworking life expectancy

"Work ethic" versus "retirement ethic"

"Voluntary" versus "involuntary" retirement

Disability benefits

Golden handshake, golden boot, golden chains

Productivity of older versus younger workers

Job pyramid versus population rectangle

Part-time employment

Multiple-career life-style

Education as a lifelong process

## QUESTIONS FOR DISCUSSION

1. Describe the general trend to earlier retirement by U.S. males during the past century. What are the main issues in question about (a) the timing of this trend and (b) the magnitude of the trend in recent years? Contrast the labor force participation of U.S. females in the past 40 years with that of U.S. males.

2. Economists sometimes speak of any good that we buy more of as our income rises as a "normal" good. Would you consider leisure time to be a "normal" good? Does your answer have any possible bearing on early retirement decisions by U.S. workers?

3. Most sociological surveys suggest that early retirees made their decision willingly and do not regret it after the fact. Do you think the testimony of the retirees themselves can be trusted in all circumstances? Is it possible that some might want to put a good face on their situations even though they were privately dissatisfied? What if many say they retired because of health reasons? Could we infer from this that the objective health status of older Americans is deteriorating these days? Even if the testimony of the retirees were accepted as accurate, what other considerations might you take into account in, say, formulating a public retirement policy?

4. Debate the pros and cons of the following proposition: "We must reverse the trend toward earlier and earlier retirement by the next century, not because it would be nice to but because we have no alternative!"

5. What is meant by the statement that the job structure and the population structure of the Aging Society may be out of alignment? Discuss the possible implications of this misalignment in terms of pyramids and rectangles.

6. Do you personally feel that longer and longer life expectancies and earlier and earlier retirements are compatible or incompatible? What new options would you suggest to make it more attractive for older workers to remain longer in the work force of the future?

## NOTES

1. The procedures by which Ransom and Sutch arrive at this unconventional conclusion are detailed in their article, Roger L. Ransom and Richard Sutch, "The Labor of Older Americans: Retirement On and Off the Job, 1870–1937," *Journal of Economic History*, 46(1), March 1986, pp. 1–30. Because historical data are seldom fully accurate and often not comparable to more modern data, differences of opinion on their exact interpretation are unavoidable.

2. They call this a form of "on-the-job-retirement," which was accomplished "by a move down the occupational ladder from a skilled or semiskilled industrial job to a less skilled industrial job or to a service-sector occupation. An elderly glass blower, for example, might become a bottle packer, a floor sweeper, or a doorman. Such a change late in the work life reduced the demands placed upon the worker while maintaining a flow of wage income, albeit a reduced stream, to his household." Ransom and Sutch, "Labor of Older Americans," p. 2. Whether a similar form of reduced labor force participation for the elderly may be viable in the Aging Society is an interesting question. We discuss it briefly later in this chapter.

3. Mark D. Hayward, William R. Grady, and Steven D. McLaughlin, "Recent Changes in Mortality and Labor Force Behavior among Older Americans: Consequences for Nonworking Life Expectancy," *Journal of Gerontology: Social Sciences*, Vol. 43(6), 1988, p. S196.

4. Herbert S. Parnes, "Conclusion," in Herbert S. Parnes, et al., *Retirement among American Men* (Lexington, Mass.: D. C. Heath, 1985), p. 218.

5. Dean W. Morse, Anna B. Dutka, and Susan H. Gray, *Life after Early Retirement* (Totowa, N.J.: Rowman and Allanheld, 1983), p. xii.

6. Herbert S. Parnes and Lawrence J. Less, "Economic Well-Being in Retirement, in Parnes et al., *Retirement among American Men*, Figure 5-3, p. 114.

7. Morse et al., *Life after Early Retirement*, p. 17.

8. Malcolm H. Morrison and Cynthia M. Taeuber, "Future Labor Force Participation of America's Older Population," mimeographed, pp. 94, 120–121. See also Jerry A. Hausman and Lynn Paquette, "Involuntary Early Retirement and Consumption," in Gary Burtless, ed., *Work, Health and Income among the Elderly* (Washington, D.C.: Brookings Institution, 1987), pp. 151–181.

9. Henry J. Aaron and Gary Burtless, "Introduction

and Summary," in Aaron and Burtless, eds., *Retirement and Economic Behavior* (Washington, D.C.: Brookings Institution, 1984), p. 8. They also note that the average length of unemployment for workers who do finally take jobs is especially long for the elderly and infirm.

10. See Donald O. Parsons, "The Decline in Male Labor Force Participation," *Journal of Political Economy, 88,* February 1980, pp. 117–134; Robert H. Haveman, Barbara L. Wolfe, and Jennifer L. Warlick, "Disability Transfers, Early Retirement and Retrenchment" in Aaron and Burtless, eds., *Retirement and Economic Behavior,* pp. 65–93; and the ensuing "Comment" by Joseph P. Newhouse, pp. 93–96. Briefly, Parsons considers the increased benefits to have been the major cause of declining male labor force participation in the 1960s and 1970s. On the other hand, the study by Haveman, Wolfe, and Warlick suggests that these effects, while "statistically significant," are "quantitatively small." About this study, however, J. P. Newhouse concludes that "the amount of uncertainty is greater than the authors imply." In short, the issue is still up in the air.

11. See Rachel Floersheim Boaz, "Labor Market Behavior of Older Workers Approaching Retirement: A Summary of Evidence from the 1970s," in Charles W. Meyer, ed., *Social Security: A Critique of Radical Reform Proposals* (Lexington, Mass.: D. C. Heath, 1987).

12. Two recent summaries of the complex literature on why male workers have been retiring early are: Christopher J. Ruhm, "Why Older Americans Stop Working," *The Gerontologist, 29*(3), 1989, and Michael D. Hurd, "Research on the Elderly: Economic Status, Retirement, and Consumption and Saving," *Journal of Economic Literature, 28*(2), June 1990. esp. pp. 589–606.

13. Even apart from multiple-career possibilities, lifelong education may be very important for tomorrow's elderly to avoid job obsolescence. Concludes a Senate study: "It is extremely important to encourage the maintenance of skills and lifelong education to prevent older worker obsolescence and to provide individuals with skills to compete on a fair basis for jobs within or outside of their companies. Up-to-date skills are more important than any age-related capabilities in human resource cost and older worker productivity." "Developments in Aging: 1987," Vol. I, Report 100-291; Report of Special Committee on Aging, U.S. Senate, February 1988, p. 137.

14. One good example is the Center for Creative Retirement sponsored by the University of North Carolina at Asheville. Said the acting director, Alf Canon: "We're looking for people in their third quarter [50 to 75]. We hear from people who are 65, or maybe as young as 50, who have decided to move into a secondary career, or have decided they want to volunteer. They're shifting gears, but they often have 20 or 30 years of activity in front of them." Quoted in the *Fort Lauderdale Sun-Sentinel,* November 9, 1987, p. 3D. For further discussion of this issue, particularly if there is a future increase in maximum life spans, see Chapter 22, pp. 402–403.

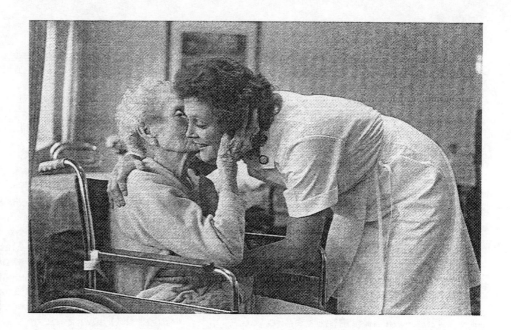

**8**

# Health Care
# and the Elderly

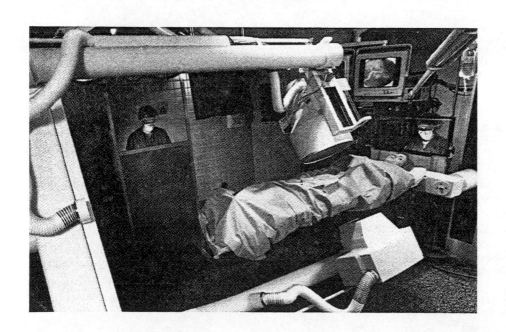

*T*echnological progress confers many benefits. But it also causes problems, and sometimes the problems are a direct consequence of the benefits. Expensive new medical technologies both save lives and impose heavy new costs. Older individuals preserved from the ravages of an acute life-threatening illness may become prone to chronic infirmities.

Suppose we found a treatment for cancer that was both a guaranteed cure *and* enormously expensive. Would we hold a national holiday for rejoicing? Or would we, like a prominent British observer, "wake up screaming at the prospect"? How in general do we weigh the benefits of expenditures on health care against their costs in terms of other desirable objectives?

This issue is not confined to the Aging Society. Cancer sometimes strikes the young as well as the old. Very large medical costs today are spent on infants, premature babies for example. Still, there is little doubt that the Aging of America has been an element in the vast expansion of medical costs we have witnessed in recent years and may be an even more significant element in the future.

## THE REVOLUTION IN HEALTH CARE EXPENDITURES

Figure 8-1a shows the growth of per capita health care expenditures in the United States since 1929. In current dollars, annual health expenditures per capita increased over this period from $29 in 1929 to $2,354 in 1989. Of course, much of this increase must be attributed to general inflation. However, even when we rule out the effects of general inflation by measuring in constant dollars, we still get a massive increase in both per capita and aggregate health care expenditures. Between 1929 and 1989, health expenditures in the United States rose from 3.5 percent of gross national product to 11.6 percent. These expenditures, moreover, still outpace general inflation, and are projected to rise to 15 percent of GNP by the year 2000 (Figure 8-1b).

What is behind this virtual revolution in the way Americans spend their national income? First, let us list the factors that have contributed to the rise in our health care costs quite apart from the aging of our society:

1. *The development of expensive new technologies:* Modern medicine has graduated far beyond the "take an aspirin and get a good night's sleep" stage. Many of today's miracles require extremely expensive equipment. Diagnosis has been revolutionized by such techniques as computerized tomography (CT scanning), magnetic resonance imaging (MRI), and positron emission tomography (PET). Kidney dialysis, megavolt radiation therapy, and intensive care units all require elaborate equipment to be used in what are often life-saving treatments. Other new technologies, such as heart and kidney transplants, again often life-saving, are also extremely costly.

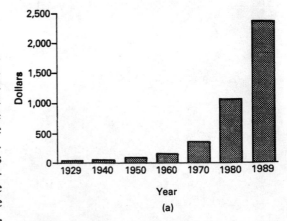

**FIGURE 8–1a: Per Capita Health Care Expenditures, United States, 1929–1989 (in current dollars)**

*Source:* Health Care Financing Administration.

126

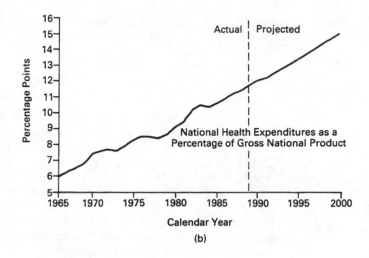

**FIGURE 8–1b: U.S. Health Expenditures as a Percentage of GNP, Actual and Projected, 1965–2000**

2. *Medicine as a labor-intensive service:* Relatively speaking, however, equipment costs are a small percentage of U.S. health-care costs, as indeed are drugs.[1] Medicine is intrinsically a *labor-intensive* occupation, which, as many commentators have noticed, is another factor tending to raise medical costs. In general, industries where labor is not easily replaced by machinery tend to have rising prices relative to those that can be automated. Industrial societies easily mass produce shirts and shoes, but around-the-clock nursing still takes 24 hours of labor time no matter how technologically advanced the society is.

3. *In medicine, supply sometimes creates its own demand:* A special feature of medicine as an industry is that the suppliers of the service (the physicians) can have large effects on the demand of the consumers of the service (the patients). Particularly when dealing with less urgent forms of elective treatment, the patient's decision to go ahead with a given procedure may be heavily influenced by, if not wholly determined by, the advice of the doctor involved. Stanford University scholar Victor R. Fuchs writes: "Where surgeons are more numerous, the demand for operations increases. Other things being equal, a 10 percent higher surgeon/population ratio results in about a

3 percent increase in the number of operations and an *increase* in price."[2]

4. *Malpractice suits:* Ask any *doctor* why his or her fees are so high and you are likely to get a lecture on the evils of U.S. tort law, jury awards, and the avarice of lawyers. Fear of malpractice suits causes doctors to order many additional tests and treatments, and in some cases to change their specializations.

5. *Rising general incomes:* In a relatively poor, agricultural society, most of the labor force must be devoted to producing the necessities of life—food, clothing, and shelter. It has been argued that, as the society progresses, consumer demand tends to direct itself increasingly to nonagricultural goods (manufactures), and ultimately to service industries, health care being a notable example. In the United States, as we have lived longer and longer and become, by some measures, healthier and healthier, some observers feel that our interest in "good health" has become almost obsessive.[3]

6. *Health insurance, private and public:* Without question, a *major* factor in the increase in health care expenditures in the United States has been our private and public health insurance programs. We have

really witnessed two separate "revolutions" here:

The first revolution involved the great growth of private health insurance in the years following World War II. The spread of private insurance was given a large boost in the 1940s and 1950s by the IRS ruling that employer health insurance contributions were to be excluded from the wage base for tax purposes. By 1988, 77.5 percent of Americans had some form of private health insurance, and 81.4 percent of this insurance was employment-related.

The second revolution, of course, occurred with the introduction of Medicare and Medicaid in 1965 as part of the expansion of our Social Security system. Interestingly, when they were passed, the cost of these public programs was not expected to be great. In point of fact, Medicare expenditures have increased rapidly (Table 8-1), as have those under the Medicaid program. Already by 1983, public expenditures had increased to some 41 percent of all U.S. health and medical care expenditures.

The significance of these two revolutions was that they expanded the principle of **third-party payments** in our national health care system. This greatly reduced the incentives for either physicians or patients to practice restraint in the quantity, quality, or price of services rendered and received.

**TABLE 8-1. Federal Outlays on Medicare, 1967–1990 (billions of dollars)**

| Year | Outlay | Year | Outlay |
|------|--------|------|--------|
| 1967 | $ 4.5 | 1984 | 57.5 |
| 1970 | 7.1 | 1986 | 70.2 |
| 1975 | 15.6 | 1988 | 78.9 |
| 1980 | 35.7 | 1989 | 85.0 |
| 1982 | 39.1 | 1990[a] | 96.7 |

[a] Estimate.

Source: U.S. Health Care Financing Administration, *Economic Report of the President, 1990.*

Healthy individuals might prefer a less expensive system, but, when ill, those same individuals might demand every conceivable treatment, no matter what the cost to society. With insurance coverage, physicians might be all too willing to oblige.

7. *From family to public responsibilities.* Related to the increase in government expenditures for health care in the economy has been a decline in family responsibility for individuals who cannot cope for themselves. Some of the caregiving that used to be given free of charge at home is now provided in the marketplace by professionals. To a degree, therefore, the measured increase in health care expenditures in the United States in recent years overstates the actual increase in services provided, being simply a substitution of measured services for unmeasured private services. As the number of people who may require extensive long-term care grows, this substitution could increase in the years ahead.

## HEALTH CARE IN THE AGING SOCIETY

This last comment brings us to the aspect of the problem of most direct interest to us namely, the effect of the Aging of America on our health care revolution. From what we have said so far, it is obvious that health care expenditures in the United States would have been rising sharply in recent decades even in the absence of major changes in the age structure of our population. It is *also* true, however, that those age changes have been an important factor in our increasing medical costs and, indeed are likely to affect those costs even more significantly in the future.

### The Health Care Needs of the Elderly

Much of the underlying story can be summed up in three simple points:

1. *Health care costs are higher for elderly than for nonelderly individuals.* Health care

expenditures in the United States on elderly individuals (65 and over) were estimated in 1984 to be four times as much per capita as for the rest of the population.

2. *The number of Americans 65 and over will increase dramatically in the years ahead.* It is projected that the percentage of Americans 65 and over will nearly double between 1990 and 2050 (from 12.6 percent to 22.9 percent). If the factor of four times as much per capita health care expenditure for this group (compared to the general population) were to remain constant, this in itself would imply a rise from *around one-third of all national health care expenditures to well over half of all such expenditures* going to the elderly in the year 2050.

3. *The age composition of the elderly is likely to make their health care costs rise even more rapidly.* Within the 65-and-older group, those 85 and older—the "oldest old" in contrast to the "young old"—will be growing most rapidly. Figure 8-2 shows the historic growth in numbers of Americans 85 and above and the expected growth of this group to the year 2050. From 1990 to 2050, this group is expected to increase from 3.3 to 15.3 million, or nearly fivefold. In percentage terms, the oldest old would go up from 10 percent to 22 percent of the 65-and-over age group. Since health expenditures generally increase with age, there will be a tendency for expenditures on the elderly to rise even more rapidly than the numbers of 65-and-over Americans would suggest.

Thus, it is apparent that the Aging of America will be a major factor in the future course of our health care costs.

### A Medicare Crisis Looming?

But this is only part of the story. While these health care expenditures have been rising, there has also been a long-term shifting of the burden of health care to the public as opposed to the private sector. Medicare, as we have said, was originally

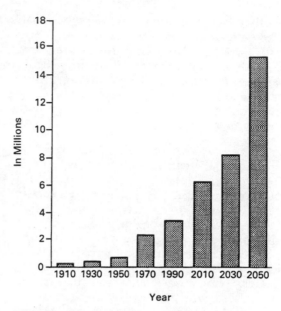

**FIGURE 8–2:  Population 85 Years and Over, Actual and Projected, 1910–2050**

*Source:*   U.S. Bureau of the Census, decennial censuses for specified years; and "Projections of the Population of the United States, by Age, Sex, and Race: 1988 to 2080," *Current Population Reports,* Series P-25, No. 1018.

expected to be a fairly small program; it has become huge (Table 8-1). If current trends are projected, Medicare expenditures would exceed all Social Security pension and survivors' benefits before the year 2010. By 2015, Medicare could conceivably overtake both Social Security *and* defense expenditures combined.

Moreover, unlike Social Security, as we mentioned in the last chapter, Medicare has not been put on a sound actuarial basis for the financing of expected future outlays. In 1988, an intermediate projection was that it would run out of cash by the year 2005. The potential demands on the public purse for Medicare must also be put in a context of the following:

• It is widely recognized that Medicare, even when supplemented by Medicaid, currently provides inadequate coverage for **catastrophic illnesses** and also for long-term and nursing home care for the elderly. Despite an unsuccessful effort in 1988 to improve catastrophic illness coverage, there is little doubt that further efforts will be made to increase Medicare outlays in both these categories.[4]

• There was also growing awareness that our national health care system in general had gaping holes in it, particularly for poorer Americans. It was estimated that in 1988, 32 million Americans had neither public nor private health insurance coverage. Medicaid, originally designed for the poor in general, has been forced to increase its expenditures for **long-term care** for the elderly poor. Since long-term care is extremely expensive, this has meant that the percentage of poor people covered by Medicaid fell from 65 percent in 1976 to under 40 percent in 1984.

• Meanwhile, legislation is regularly being introduced into Congress that would require employers to pick up larger and larger health care tabs for their employees. This is occurring in a context where, according to the *Wall Street Journal*, "companies that have toted up the long-term cost of their past health-care promises have been shocked at the result"; this may mean efforts to provide "much less generous benefits for current and future retirees."[5]

• Finally, as we also noted in our last chapter, these potential demands for expanded benefits and coverages were occurring at a time when the federal budget was already running a substantial deficit, even when the Social Security *surplus* is considered part of the overall budget.

Is this the Achilles' heel of the Aging Society? Are we on a collision course between the seemingly almost insatiable desire of that society for health care expenditures and virtually all other social requirements, including a rate of taxation that permits and encourages a respectable rate of growth?

## CONTAINING COSTS: A COUNTERREVOLUTION?

Public officials and scholars alike have not been unaware of these perils. This awareness has led both to practical action to try to restrain the explosive growth of health care costs, and to a theoretical debate about the wisdom (or unacceptability) of rationing health care by age.

### Cost Containment through DRGs

Probably the best known effort to fight rising health care costs under Medicare was the introduction of **diagnosis-related groups** (**DRGs**) in 1983. Essentially, the old system whereby patients' bills, and Medicare payments, were determined by the hospitals and the doctors, was replaced by one in which fees were set for some 468 different illness categories. The DRG approach does two things: It sets the fees in advance rather than after the fact, and it transfers the cost risks from the payer (for Medicare, the government) to the care provider. Thus, hospitals, in effect, are rewarded for quickly treating and discharging patients, and penalized when their costs are out of line.

Although not the only factor involved, the introduction of DRGs undoubtedly played a role in an almost immediate decline in the average length of hospital stays, and in the occupancy levels of hospitals during the 1980s. This new system, moreover, was only one of a variety of changes made by the government, private insurers, and health maintenance organizations (HMOs) to reduce incentives to overtreat patients and to stimulate productive efficiency in the delivery of health care.

Although there have been accomplishments in the area of cost containment and although the emphasis in the 1980s had clearly shifted away from the free-wheeling days of the 1960s and 1970s, it cannot be said that real solutions to our potential health care crisis have yet emerged. As already stated, health expenditures continue to rise more rapidly than our national income. It has been found that when the average length of hospital stays is reduced, average costs per patient-day often tend to rise. Also, there is the question of the effect of cost containment measures on the well-being of patients. Two years after the DRGs were introduced, two-thirds of surveyed doctors felt that the quality of U.S. hospital care had deteriorated since the introduction of the prospective payment system. In 1988, a controversial study in the *New England Journal of Medicine* found that states (like New York, Massachusetts, and Maryland) that attempted to regulate hospital costs strictly had higher inpatient mortality rates than hospitals where little attempt was made to cut hospital costs. Said the authors: "These findings raise serious concerns about the welfare of patients who are admitted to hospitals in highly regulated areas and those admitted to hospitals in relatively competitive markets."[6] In other words, according to the authors, the efforts to cut costs, not always but in some circumstances, can also cut care.

### Rationing Medical Care?

Which immediately raises the issue: Do we essentially *have* to cut care? Will the **rationing of medical care** in one form or another become a necessary feature of the Aging Society? There are really two questions here: (1) Will such rationing be necessary? (2) If so, should we ration primarily (or totally) on the basis of age?

*Pros and Cons of Rationing.* The basic argument for rationing is contained in the numbers we have already mentioned, showing a growth of health care expenditures which, if unchecked, could literally wipe out virtually every other desirable social objective. This is usually combined with the view, first, that efforts to contain costs, like DRGs,

HMOs, preferred providers, and the like, have barely scratched the surface of the problem; and, second, that medical research is capable of developing endless numbers of expensive new technologies if allowed to proceed without constraints of some kind. If every patient in the nation on every occasion were given what is considered the very best and latest treatment for the illness in question, costs would simply skyrocket out of sight. This position is sometimes supplemented by the view that, in many cases, these expensive new technologies, though often favored by doctors and eagerly sought by patients, sometimes have only marginal effects on the actual health of patients.[7]

The opposite argument is, first, that Americans do not want to accept restrictions on the quality and quantity of care they receive when they are ill; second, that there is still ample room for the development of further cost-reducing procedures, through, for example, the further spread of competitive HMOs; and, third, that there are many examples of new medical technologies that are not more but *less* expensive than old technologies. Thus, one can cite new preventive technologies that are less expensive than maintenance or curative technologies (e.g., polio vaccines versus the old iron lung technology), or cheaper alternative means of treatment (say, angioplasty to unclog blocked arteries versus open heart surgery.)

On this last point, the rationers argue that it is misguided to think that new technologies will ever reduce health care expenditures. A main reason is that these new technologies, even when they are cheaper (and often less invasive and traumatic for the patient), tend to be so widely used that total costs are raised even though the treatment on a per patient basis is substantially reduced.

*Rationing by Age?* Even among those who believe that some form of rationing is inevitable, there is a sharp dispute as to whether *age* should be the exclusive or even the primary criterion on which that rationing should be based. As we noted in Chapter 5, Dr. Daniel Callahan stirred up a national debate on this issue by proposing that, after an older person had lived a reasonably "full life," we should limit the number of heroic (and expensive) medical technologies devoted to extending that person's life.

Dr. Callahan's thesis involved two elements. In a negative sense, he argued that the trend of medical care costs, and especially their anticipated future trajectory, requires us to set limits somewhere. In a positive sense, he argued that the concept of a "natural life span" is ultimately more humanly satisfying than the obsessive search for longer and longer life expectancies no matter what the quality of those longer lives may be. He suggested that it is important philosophically that we accept death as a natural *part* of the life cycle, rather than as a *negation* of life.

This philosophical point, in turn, leads to many other issues that will concern us in this book. In a society where life is short, for example, children play an obviously crucial role in sustaining the species, but also, more personally, in giving their parents a sense of extension into the future. But as individuals live longer and longer and become more and more their own extensions into the future, do the concepts of life cycles, of the family unit, of children taking up where their parents leave off, of "passing the torch," as it were—do all these tend to break down?

In a sense, then, Callahan was trying to stress the mutuality and interdependence between generations. His concept of a "full life" or a "natural life span" really implies that, after we have taken our shot, we ought more or less to stand aside and let the next generation take over. Indeed, it becomes our obligation, as older citizens, to help the younger generation, not to appropriate the maximum of society's resources for ourselves.[8]

To what degree this philosophical position is viable in an age when "natural life spans" may conceivably be on the verge of major extensions, we will consider in later chapters. For the moment, however, we note mainly that Dr. Callahan's proposal, *conceived purely as a matter of cutting the growth of health care expenditures*, is on somewhat shaky ground. The main reasons are that, to make the idea of cutting off medical care to the elderly even partially acceptable to Americans, one has to (a) limit it to quite old individuals, say, in their late seventies or more probably their eighties; (b) restrict it to fairly elaborate procedures that are used in only a limited number of cases; (c) combine it with a considerable (and not inexpensive) amount of medical attention designed to keep these elderly comfortable during what can often be quite long terminal illnesses; and (d) make sure that such rationing that occurs is not effectively confined to poor people.

And the trouble with doing all this is that it means that the actual reduction of health care expenditures achievable by such rationing is likely to be small. Dr. William B. Schwartz and Henry J. Aaron, for example, estimate that denying all future medical progress to the elderly would slow the 5 percent annual growth of U.S. medical costs by less than one-half percent. Ezekiel J. Emmanuel of the Harvard Kennedy School suggests that by focusing on the *quality*, rather than the quantity, of life for the elderly, we could easily end up *increasing* medical costs. Since "one year in a quality nursing home can cost in excess of $25,000 for a single patient," Dr. Callahan's " 'cost cutting' proposals could be very, very costly."[9]

Thus, most critics conclude that, *if* rationing of medical care proves necessary, it is highly doubtful that age alone can be the primary criterion. Simple restriction of the availability of expensive technologies, independently of who gets to use them, may be required. Indeed, some of the philosophically questionable uses of elaborate medical technologies now occur at very young ages. Who should get to use our scarce resources: a person of 75 who is in full possession of his or her faculties and is still a happy and productive member of society, or a low-birth-weight, premature infant who may incur hundreds of thousands of dollars to survive for a few more years in a highly impaired, even semicomatose state?

The truth is that most of us do not want to have to make such choices. This, of course, is why medical rationing, easy to discuss in principle, becomes an extremely difficult and stressful subject to deal with in actual practice.

## MORTALITY AND MORBIDITY

So we return to the question of rising medical costs again, knowing that rationing on any criterion will be painful to put into effect, and wondering if there may not be some basis for a more hopeful outlook.

In fact, there is such a basis, although once more our investigation thrusts us into the middle of a serious controversy. In some respects, this controversy deals with the most basic issue of health care needs in the Aging Society. The issue may be framed as follows:

*As we continue to extend life expectancy for the elderly in the Aging Society, will we be increasing the number of healthy years that these people live or the number of unhealthy years? From a technical point of view, will the decreases in mortality we achieve in the future be accompanied by decreases or increases in morbidity?*

**Mortality** refers to death, **morbidity** to health status. What relationship can we see between these two apparently related, yet distinct, concepts?

### The Two Conflicting Trends

When we increase life expectancy (reduce the mortality rate), we will usually have two quite different effects on the general health of our population:

*Tendency 1.* When any illness is "conquered," either by medical advance or economic progress or life-style changes, the health of the individuals who might have suffered from that illness and been laid up by it clearly is improved. At age 60, say, a certain number of elderly persons used to be bedridden or in poor health because of strokes and heart ailments. As progress has been made in treating and avoiding such diseases, there are a number of 60-year-olds who no longer suffer from these particular disabilities. They will enjoy better health. Thus, the same progress that has extended their lives will also be permitting them to live a greater number of healthy years.

*Tendency 2.* At the same time that these medical and other advances are permitting some 60-year-olds to enjoy better health, they are also permitting certain 60-year-olds who would normally have died from these conditions to survive. In general, it can be argued that those whose lives are spared will be the weaker and the more infirm of that particular age group. These frail "marginal survivors," as they are often called, will add a number of 60-year-olds to the population who are in poorer, not better, health. This point is sometimes described by the statement that, whereas we used to die from sudden, acute diseases, now we are spared to live a life of chronic ailments.

Presumably, these surviving individuals consider themselves better off than they would have been before the "progress" took place (that is, insofar as being alive and ill is generally considered being "better off" than not being alive). Still, from the point of view of the average health of the elderly population, they represent a negative rather than a positive element.

So, many older individuals will be healthier, but many additional unhealthy individuals will survive. At a minimum, this strongly suggests that the *differences* between the healthiness of individuals at any given age are likely to become increasingly wide. From our point of view, however, the main question is the net balance between the two effects. Have recent reductions in mortality among the elderly been associated *in total* with reduced or increased morbidity?

Although the question would seem to permit a clear-cut answer, the fact is that the evidence so far is quite mixed. A 1987 study, for example, reached these ambiguous conclusions:

> We began this paper with the question "Are Americans living longer healthy lives as well as longer lives?" Our answer clearly depends on our definition of health. If the definition of health is an ability to participate fully in the normal activities of every day life, the answer is that Americans are not living longer healthy lives. Additions to life expectancy between 1970 and 1980 were concentrated in disabled years—primarily years of long term disability. On the other hand, if we limit our definition of ill health to days spent in bed, we conclude that, below age 85, most of the increase in life expectancy has been in non-disabled years, not years in bed. . . .

Thus, these measures

> . . . allow us to conclude that increases in life expectancy between 1970 and 1980 have been largely concentrated in years with a chronic disabling illness . . .

but

> . . . In spite of the increases in long term chronic disability, these findings allow us to discount the somewhat popular idea that advances in medical science are leaving us to spend increasing proportions of our lives as bed-ridden dependent persons.[10]

The apparent simplicity of the question disappears as soon as one recognizes the number of factors that can distort the statistics. Is reported disability the same as objective disability? We already know, as

discussed earlier (p. 116) that this is doubtful when federally financed disability programs enter the picture. Also, increased medical knowledge, or frequency of medical treatments, can increase the reports of ill health and disability. Long-term institutionalization may reflect chronic ill health, or it may reflect different societal living arrangements (for example, more elderly persons living away from their children, more childless elderly), or different socioeconomic and financial conditions (Are the elderly better able to afford nursing homes? Will Medicaid be paying?)

Perhaps the only thing that can be said so far is that there is no overwhelming evidence to support the dominance of either of the two trends above the other. Both are important and both are operative.

## Will Morbidity Ultimately Be "Compressed"?

But what about the future? If there is no obvious dominance of either trend at the moment, can we find any signposts for the future? In the early 1980s, a hopeful note on this issue was struck in a number of articles by J. F. Fries, arguing what is called the **compression of morbidity** thesis. Since those original articles, there have been numerous discussions and critiques of this particular notion.[11]

Both the thesis and its criticisms can be illustrated by Figure 8-3. We measure age on the horizontal axis and the probability of survival (expressed as a percentage) on the vertical axis. Our hypothetical mortality curve tells us that an individual's chance of surviving to, say, age 63 is 80 percent. By the same general logic, the hypothetical morbidity curve tells us an individual's chance of surviving to age 63 in good health—only 60 percent. The area between the two curves, area B, represents the amount of "poor health" in this hypothetical society, while area A tells us the number of healthy years in the society.

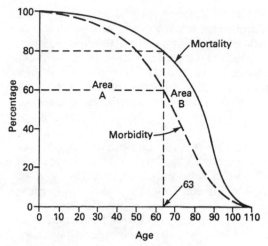

**FIGURE 8–3: Mortality and Morbidity**
These hypothetical "survival curves" tell us the percentage chances of an individual living to a certain age (mortality curve) or remaining in "good health" to a certain age (morbidity curve). In this figure, individuals have an 80 percent chance of living to be 63 and a 60 percent chance of remaining in good health to age 63.

A variety of future alternatives *could* lie before us:

1. *Compression of morbidity:* According to Fries, we are approaching the end of our ability to push out the mortality curve. That is, we are coming very close to our "natural life span" for almost everybody. This means that medical progress can be increasingly concentrated on reducing morbidity—producing good health during the now relatively fixed years of our life expectancy. Compression of morbidity occurs because the mortality curve is relatively fixed and the morbidity curve is moved outward, "compressing" area B.

2. *Growing morbidity:* The opposite view is that, in our efforts to extend life expectancies, we neglect to pay sufficient attention to reducing poor health and disability among the survivors. This would result in an expansion of area B as the mortality curve continues to move outward while the morbidity curve remains relatively fixed.

3. *Morbidity and mortality curves are interrelated:* An intermediate position suggests that the two curves are likely to move together, and usually in the same direction. Thus, improvements in treating poor health are usually likely to have at least some effects in extending life expectancies. As we move the morbidity curve outward, then, we would expect at least some favorable effect on the mortality curve. This position is more eclectic than the other two and, while in principle almost certainly more defensible, gives us little direct guidance as to which trend will dominate in the future.

Furthermore, there is a whole range of considerations into which we have not yet entered. Figure 8-3 is drawn, like our earlier population pyramids, with an effective maximum life span of around 110 years. But there is the possibility, which we shall take up in Chapter 22, that the mortality curve may be shifted far beyond the boundaries of this particular diagram. Some of those who expect this future possibility believe that the morbidity curve will also be dragged out with the mortality curve—vastly increasing area A, the amount of "good health" in the society. If, as has been argued, most of our ill health (and medical expense) is experienced in the last year or so of our lives, then when we extend our lives massively we will also massively reduce the proportion of unhealthy to healthy years in those longer lives.[12]

While deferring consideration of this highly speculative issue until later, we can nevertheless make one other point of a hopeful nature. *If it is true that the more pessimistic future threatens us, there is still a general reason for believing that there will be some light at the end of the tunnel.* If we get mortality reductions *without* morbidity reductions, then it is almost certain that *health* will become a dominating issue in our society and that both scientific research and life-style changes will increasingly be directed toward improving health. The health consciousness of the 1980s has already demonstrated this point to a degree. Given this interest and attention, there seems no reason to believe that health should be less amenable to improvement than life expectancy. As the problem changes, the search for solutions will also change. So far at least, the history of human progress suggests that, as new problems develop, we have been able to meet the new challenges effectively. The burden of proof, in short, would seem to lie with those who claim otherwise.

## ALZHEIMER'S DISEASE: SYMBOL OF HOPE OR DESPAIR?

There is probably no better way to symbolize the basic difficulties surrounding the issue of health care in the Aging Society than by looking briefly at one specific problem: **Alzheimer's disease.** Since the scientific study of this disease is currently very intensive, we cannot predict what its status will be ten years or even one or two years from this writing. The two main points we wish to make, however, are independent of the exact outcome for this or any other particular disease:

*1. Alzheimer's disease represents the potential health care burdens of the Aging Society in almost every dimension—personal, social, philosophical, and economic. It is a problem whose extent is crucially influenced by the numbers and proportions of old people in the society, and thus is a direct reflection of the changing U.S. population.*

Various congressional reports in the late 1980s have made clear just how enormous the present and potential burdens of Alzheimer's disease are in this country. It should be said immediately that, in an important sense, the economic burdens of the disease are by no means the worst part of it. Alzheimer's disease destroys memory gradually over a long period of time. This is reflected first in minor lapses (not turning off the stove, leaving doors unlocked, losing track of objects, forgetting familiar names), but gradually grows much worse, destroying awareness of intimate friends and family members, and reducing the victim to such helplessness that total nursing care, whether by a nursing home or by the family, is required.

All this represents a major tragedy not only for the victim but for all those around the victim who must mourn the loss of capacity in someone they love, who must bear the caretaking burden either personally or financially or often both, and who also, of course, share the increasing concern of all Americans that they, too, will one day fall victim to the disease.

The numbers involved are appalling and getting much worse. It was estimated that in the late 1980s about 1.5 million Americans were so afflicted by Alzheimer's disease that their impaired mental functions made it impossible for them to care for themselves. The cost of care and treatment annually is perhaps as high as $48 billion. To give one a sense of a magnitude here, this works out to about $750 per year for every family of four in the United States.

But since Alzheimer's is overwhelmingly a disease of the elderly, and especially the older elderly, these costs are expected to grow explosively as our society ages. (While the chance of contracting Alzheimer's at ages 65–74 is only 1 percent, the chances at ages over 85 are 20 to 30 percent.) Federal studies have concluded that the disease will soon be affecting one out of every three families in the United States and that, by the year 2040, in the absence of prevention or cure, there could be a fivefold increase in the incidence of serious affliction—from 1.5 million to 7.4 million persons. At today's prices, and allowing for a small increase in our overall population, this would lead to an annual average cost per U.S. family of four of $3,000 by the year 2040. Multiply this by the many other chronic ailments that afflict the elderly and you have a clear and simple statement of the health care problem in the Aging Society.

2. *As our awareness of the tragic implications of Alzheimer's disease has grown, there has been an expanded research effort investigating the causes of this and other forms of senile dementia. This research effort seems to be bearing fruit and, indeed, within recent years, has brought exciting breakthroughs in the understanding of Alzheimer's. It seems highly likely that, well before that fivefold increase in the incidence of the disease manifests itself, major advances in prevention, treatment, and even cure will have occurred.*

If the late 1980s brought forth the disturbing news just referred to, it also brought news of discoveries "more exciting than anything we've seen in the last 10 years of Alzheimer's research" (according to Boston researcher Dennis Selkoe). Indeed, during the years 1987 through 1990, not only scientific journals like *Nature, Science* and *The Lancet,* but daily newspapers throughout the country as well, were reporting significant leaps in the understanding of the mechanism of this extremely complex disease. Working on the problem were teams of scientists at countless universities and research institutes, not only in the United States but also in France, Japan, and other nations. Much of this research centered on the increased understanding of what is almost certainly an important genetic component in some forms of Alzheimer's disease. (Whether all forms of the disease are hereditary, or some are and some are not, is still under investigation.) Genetic markers have been found that can guide scientists in their effort to pinpoint the specific gene or genes that may be involved in causing the disease, or creating a predisposition to the disease that may then be triggered by other factors. Work has also been done on the genetic basis for the production of amyloid, a substance found in large quantities in the abnormal brain structures of Alzheimer's sufferers. This research seems to have dovetailed with research involving Down's syndrome, the victims of which often exhibit Alzheimer-like symptoms at relatively early ages and who may also suffer from excessive amyloid deposits.

No one—not even the scientists most intimately involved in this research—can predict when, or even if, these various leads will produce anything approaching a cure for Alzheimer's. In 1990, for example, new research suggested that Alzheimer's disease might be not one but a cluster of closely related disorders, a finding that might greatly complicate the search for a cure.[13] Still, given the revolutionary pace of medical and especially of genetic research in recent years, and given further the fruitful application of computer technology to this area of research, it seems unnecessarily pessimistic to believe that all this will lead nowhere.

If Alzheimer's disease stands as a clear symbol of the potentially desperate problems of an Aging Society, it also can stand as a clear symbol of the ways in which the forces of science and technology may generate ways around problems previously deemed to be desperate. Will a case study of Alzheimer's disease written 20 years from now resemble our case study of tuberculosis (pp. 26–27)? Might we then be reporting the vast diminution or even virtual disappearance of the disease? One cannot count on it, but one certainly cannot count the possibility out either.

## WHAT SHOULD BE DONE NOW

Since we do not know this particular outcome, since we do know that, under any circumstances, health care costs are bound to rise significantly in the Aging Society, and since we also know that we have not yet made proper financial provision for those rising future costs—for all these reasons, we now come to the same conclusion we did in the case of Social Security:

*We should do our best to use the present "window of opportunity" before the Baby Boomers retire to prepare for the almost certain dependency burdens we will face beginning in the second decade of the next century. This preparation will include those factors, like increased saving and investment, more general research and development, and renewed emphasis on education, that promote technological progress, capital accumulation, and economic growth. It will also specifically include increased research in areas (like Alzheimer's disease) that clearly affect the health status of the Aging Society.*

This conclusion is as easy to state as it is apparently difficult to put into practice. What it means, in essence, is that we should be giving the future a particularly high priority in our thinking at this stage of our national life. This is not a particularly good time for the nation to overspend, to postpone hard choices until tomorrow, to let down our guard with respect to education and research, both future-looking activities.

Prudence strongly suggests that it would be unwise for us, say, to plunder our Social Security surpluses to fund (directly or by more surreptitious mechanisms) our approaching Medicare and Medicaid deficits, or to expand those or any other current health care programs without, at the same time, making adequate financial provision for them. Ultimately, of course, the method of finance is far less significant than the real flows of resources occurring beneath the surface. Saving, investment, education, research, economic growth—these are what we need to make the Aging Society not only viable, but a social condition to be welcomed with open arms.

## SUMMARY

1. U.S. health care costs have risen from 3.5 percent of GNP in 1929 to 11.6 percent in 1989 and could well rise to 15 percent by the year 2000.

2. Apart from the Aging of America, factors causing this rise in costs include new technology, labor-intensive services, demand-creating supply, malpractice suits, rising general incomes, and especially third-party payments, both private and public.

3. The Aging of America will seriously affect future health care costs because: (a) per capita health care costs are four times higher for persons 65 and over than for the general population; (b) the percentage of Americans 65 and over is projected to increase from 12.6 percent of the population (1990) to 22.9 percent (2050); and (c) the "oldest old"—those 85 and older—are increasing more rapidly than the "young old," and their health care costs are higher still.

4. The looming crisis in public health care financing (Medicare and Medicaid) reflects the fact that these programs have not yet been placed on an actuarially sound basis. This has prompted cost containment measures (like diagnosis-related groups) and also a debate on the rationing of health care by age. Although rationing of some kind may ultimately be required, it is evident that it would be extremely difficult to reduce health care costs by age rationing.

5. A key underlying issue, still unresolved, is whether future medical progress will lead to a compression of morbidity, an increase in morbidity, or a difficult-to-predict interaction between mortality and morbidity advances. One hopeful suggestion is that, if mortality improves while morbidity lags behind, there will in all probability be an increased societal interest in investigating and promoting better health.

6. The tragedy of Alzheimer's disease stands as a useful symbol of the health problems of an Aging Society. Very large increases in costs from Alzheimer's emerge from the projection of current trends, yet increased scientific attention to this ailment suggests that treatment, cure, or prevention may possibly occur in the not-too-distant future.

7. Since future advances are always uncertain, prudence suggests (as in the case of Social Security pensions) that the United States prepare now by building up its capital stock and educational and research capabilities so that future health care burdens may be sustainable.

## KEY CONCEPTS FOR REVIEW

Revolution in health care costs

Third-party payments

Health care in the Aging Society

Looming Medicare crisis

Catastrophic illness

Long-term care

Diagnosis-related groups (DRGs)

Rationing of medical care

Mortality and morbidity

Compression of morbidity

Alzheimer's disease

Preparing for future health care burdens

## QUESTIONS FOR DISCUSSION

1. Apart from the changing age structure of our society, what main factors have been responsible for the rising percentage of U.S. GNP devoted to health care in recent decades? If, as projected, this percentage rises to 15 percent in the year 2000, would you consider this too high, too low, or about right? Make an imaginary list of other priorities·you might have—food, housing, education, defense, environmental protection, and so on. Where would health care rank on this list in terms of percentage of GNP? Is there any percentage devoted to health care that you would consider clearly too high?

2. Why will the Aging of America lead to further increases in health care costs?

3. Is it possible that people, when well, can feel that society is paying much too much for medical care, but then, when ill, can insist that the very latest and most expensive technologies be used in their treatment? Does the existence of third-party payers (whether private insurance companies or the government) have anything to do with this apparent inconsistency?

4. "Increases in life expectancy must lead to better average health in the population because modern medicine is curing the diseases that lead to death." Discuss the reasons for this position, and indicate why it is an incomplete and possibly erroneous statement.

5. If rationing of medical care must be instituted, would you prefer to do it strictly on the basis of age, or (as, for example, sometimes happens in countries like Great Britain) by a variety of means, such as having long waiting lists for certain operations, avoiding very expensive technologies, limiting the equipment available in certain areas of the country, and so on? What criteria would you prefer?

6. Since Social Security pensions have been set up on a presumably sound actuarial basis and Medicare has not (as of 1990), why do we still say that the basic solution to both programs in the future is essentially the same? Describe that solution.

## NOTES

1. One estimate (for 1981) was that medical equipment costs were only 0.5 percent of total U.S. health expenditures, and drug expenditures were about the same 0.5 percent. See H. David Banta and Annetine Gelijns, "Health Care Costs: Technology and Policy," in C. J. Schramm, ed., *Health Care and Its Costs* (New York: Norton, 1987), p. 260.

2. Victor R. Fuchs, *The Health Economy* (Cambridge, Mass.: Harvard University Press, 1986), p. 147.

The word *increase* is italicized because, in the normal case, a greater supply of any product or service would be expected to *lower* its price.

3. This excessive concern with the state of our health has been stressed by Dr. Arthur J. Barsky, a psychiatrist at Harvard Medical School and Massachusetts General Hospital. He writes: "[The] medico-media hype, promulgated by media people, advertisers, public relations experts, manufacturers and even some members of the health

professions, induces a cultural climate of alarm and hypochondria, undermining feelings of well-being.... Feelings of ill health and disability are amplified when every ache is thought to merit medical attention, every twinge may be the prodrome of malignant disease, when we are told that every mole and wrinkle deserves surgery." This is one of several reasons Dr. Barsky offers to explain "the paradox of health": namely, that we are objectively healthier, but feel subjectively less healthy now than in the past. Arthur J. Barsky, "The Paradox of Health," *New England Journal of Medicine, 318*(17), February 18, 1988, pp. 416–417.

4.  In 1988, a program to expand Medicare to cover catastrophic illnesses was actually passed into law. However, the program was designed to be financed by the elderly themselves on the basis of a surcharge on their federal income taxes. By 1993 this surcharge was scheduled to rise to 28 percent, and a maximum of $2,100 for a married couple. This increase in taxes brought a huge outcry from the elderly and, despite the previous support of the American Association of Retired Persons (AARP), the legislation was quickly rescinded. Although no one· can be sure of the significance of this protest, it would seem clear that elderly were opposed not to the new coverage but to its method of financing.

5.  Amanda Bennett, "Firms Stunned by Retiree Health Costs," *Wall Street Journal*, May 24, 1988, p. 41. Although the article suggests that businesses may try to cut back on their health care commitments, it also points out that such retrenchments are "likely to meet determined opposition."

6.  See Stephen M. Shortell and Edward F. X. Hughes, "The Effects of Regulation, Competition and Ownership on Mortality Rates among Hospital Inpatients," *New England Journal of Medicine, 318*(17), April 28, 1988. The authors conclude: "We found significant associations between higher mortality rates among inpatients and the stringency of state programs to review hospital rates.... It is important to incorporate quality-assurance procedures and systems to monitor patients' outcomes into public and private programs designed to contain costs or promote competition, or both" (p. 1100).

7.  Thus, Henry J. Aaron and William B. Schwartz, in their comparison of the British and American health care systems, note that although the United States pays at least twice as much on a per capita basis, the evidence shows "that the large differences in per capita average medical expenditures between the two countries are not associated with large differences in life expectancy." Aaron and Schwartz, *The Painful Prescription: Rationing Hospital Care* (Washington, D.C.: Brookings Institution, 1984) pp. 12–13. Victor Fuchs also reports his "basic finding"—that is, "when the state of

medical science and other health-determining variables are held constant, the marginal contribution of medical care to health is very small in modern nations." Fuchs, *The Health Economy*, p. 274.

8.  Dr. Callahan emphasizes the role of moral obligations throughout his book. Indeed, one of his criteria for a "tolerable death" is that "one's moral obligations to those for whom one has had responsibility have been discharged." Here he has in mind especially the obligations of parents to their children. This sense of the interdependence of generations is a major theme in his work. D. Callahan, *Setting Limits: Medical Goals in an Aging Society* (New York: Simon & Schuster, 1987), pp. 66–67.

9.  Interestingly, Aaron and Schwartz, although they feel that rationing medical care by age would have only marginal effects on health care costs, nevertheless argue that some form of rationing will be necessary, largely because of the expensiveness of new medical technologies. See Aaron and Schwartz, *The Painful Prescription*, p. 135.

10. Eileen M. Crimmins and Yasuhiko Saito, "Changes in Life Expectancy and Disability Free Life Expectancy in the U.S.: 1970–1980" (Andrus Gerontology Center, University of Southern California, mimeographed, September 1987), pp. 19, 24.

11. For the "compression of morbidity" position, see J. F. Fries, "Aging, Natural Death and the Compression of Morbidity," *New England Journal of Medicine, 303,* 1980, and "The Compression of Morbidity," *Milbank Memorial Fund Quarterly/ Health and Society, 61*(3), 1983. For articles bearing on this thesis, see Jacob A. Brody, "Prospects for an Ageing Population," *Nature, 315* June 6, 1985; Lois M. Verbrugge, "Longer Life but Worsening Health? Trends in Health and Mortality of Middle-Aged and Older Persons," *Milbank Memorial Fund Quarterly/Health and Society, 62*(3), 1984; M. W. Riley and K. Bond, "Beyond Ageism: Postponing the Onset of Disability," in M. W. Riley, B. B. Hess, and K. Bond, eds., *Aging in Society: Selected Views of Recent Research* (Hillsdale, N.J.: Lawrence Erlbaum Associates, 1983); and K. G. Manton and B. J. Soldo, "Dynamics of Health Changes in the Oldest Old: New Perspectives and Evidence," *Milbank Memorial Fund Quarterly/Health and Society, 63*(2), 1985. Our Figure 8-3 is an adaptation of the model used in the Manton/Soldo article, p. 210.

12. This position has been taken in one form or another by such scholars as B. L. Strehler, R. L. Walford, and V. R. Fuchs, the last emphasizing the number of years until death as opposed to the number of years from birth in assessing our health care needs. We take up this issue in more detail in Chapter 22.

13. P. St. George-Hyslop et al., *Nature, 347,* September 13, 1990, pp 194–197.

# Part III
# *ADULTS: YOUNG AND MIDDLE-AGED*

**9**

# The "Traditional" American Family

*P*art II ended with a discussion of the ways in which a generation that is growing older may impose health care and other burdens on the working-age generation. In Part III, we now focus on adults, both the young and the middle-aged. This group is clearly a bridge between the very young and older generations. Through its labor force participation, it provides crucial support for the elderly generation on the one hand, while through this same participation and the formation of families and the raising of children, it provides for the generation to follow. Important changes in the U.S. labor force and especially in the American family will be our concern in the next five chapters.

In this chapter, we take a bird's-eye view of the history of the American family from colonial times through the immediate post–World War II period. We shall find that what we think of as the "traditional" American family was not as universal and certainly not as fixed in time as we may like to imagine. This point will be made even more dramatically in Chapter 10, where we consider the striking changes in American families that have occurred in just two postwar generations.

Following this discussion, we will focus more specifically on family and labor force changes as they affect women (Chapter 11), men (Chapter 12), and black Americans (Chapter 13). Other large minority groups, especially Hispanics and Asian Americans, will be our main focus in later chapters, particularly in Part V.

## FUNDAMENTAL CHARACTERISTICS OF FAMILY LIFE

Toward the end of this book, when we come to consider the future of "**the family**," we shall find that great disagreement exists today as to what definition it is proper to use (see pp. 408–410). For the moment, let us distinguish two senses in which we might employ the term: (1) as representing **a virtually universal institution** by which human beings historically and even prehistorically have organized the succession of the generations, and (2) as the more specific institution memorialized by such popular artists as Norman Rockwell and sometimes considered **the "traditional" American family.** We begin with the more general definition.

In his historical survey of the changing American family, Carl N. Degler cites five characteristics that he believes are to be found in family life in virtually all known cultures.[1] Briefly, these are as follows:

1. "A family begins with a ritual between a woman and a man, a ceremony that we call marriage, and which implies long duration, if not permanence, for the relationship."

2. "The partners have duties and rights of parenthood that are also socially recognized and defined."

3. "Husband, wife, and children live in a common place."

4. "There are reciprocal economic obligations between husband and wife—that is, they both work for the family, even though the amount and kind of labor or production may be far from equal."

5. "The family also serves as a means of sexual satisfaction for the partners though not necessarily as an exclusive one."

It is fairly obvious that some of these characteristics are less universal than others. The least universal probably is the requirement of common residence, in that there are known cultures where husbands and wives do not live together; indeed, even in Western history, we have instances—as, for example, in the case of the families of seafaring men—where time spent living under a single roof was the exception rather than the rule. Also, there is obviously a great deal of latitude required in our understanding of the term *partners* since **polygyny** (marriage of one man to more than one woman) and **polyandry** (marriage of one woman to more than one man) have existed in various cultures, although **monogamy** (marriage of one woman to one man) remains the most common marital arrangement even where other forms are permitted.

In general, however, these characteristics do describe an institution that, *in the past,* was common and accepted in virtually all societies. Nineteenth-century theorists, like Karl Marx's collaborator Friedrich Engels, posited the existence of group marriage among primitive peoples, but their views have not been confirmed by subsequent research. Writes Kathleen Gough:

> All known hunters and gatherers live in families, not in communal sexual arrangements. Most hunters even live in nuclear families rather than in large extended kin groups. Mating is individualized, although one man may occasionally have two wives, or (very rarely) a woman may have two husbands. Economic life is built primarily around the division of labor and partnership between individual men and women.[2]

Our first conclusion then, is that, historically speaking—we come to the present and future later in our study—there is such an institution as "the family" that has very deep roots in human experience and that, though variable, is definable in a reasonably definite way.

## THE "TRADITIONAL" AMERICAN FAMILY

Our second conclusion, however, must be that the "traditional" American family, though consistent with the preceding general definition, involves a much more specific family form, and one that is far less universal even within the particular experience of our own society.

What characteristics would we have to add to those already mentioned to approximate what would have been considered during most of this century as the typical American family form? Roughly, we should have to expand the above five points to include the following:

1. Marriage is essentially by the choice of the partners involved and is based on romantic love. The "traditional" American family, in song and story, is founded on love, not on crass economic motives, and certainly not on a system of selection governed by the parents or families of the young couple-to-be. This characteristic is different from, but related to, another important feature of that family: the centrality of the ties between husband, wife, and children, as opposed to other kinship ties. The "traditional" family is a **nuclear family,** wherein the husband–wife–children nexus takes precedence over the blood ties of wife or husband to their other relatives. This is sometimes called a **conjugal family,** in contrast to a **consanguine** (of the same blood) or **extended family,** where there is great emphasis on grandparents, uncles, aunts, cousins, and so on. The prevailing family ethic in the United States over most of this century has been that, once married, you owe your deepest allegiance to your spouse and children, not to your parents.

2. The marriage partners not only have general duties and rights with respect to parenthood, but the children in very important ways "come first." This need not imply a permissive home—discipline can often be required and sincerely exercised for the child's welfare—but it does imply that the well-being and future happiness of the children loom very large in the psychology of the parents and in the goals of the family.

3. Although husband, wife, and children usually live together in the same place (with the exception of sea captains, traveling salesmen, and the like), the home is physically occupied during daytime hours by the mother and small children only. Except on weekends, the father is off at work, often a commuter, and the older children are off

at school. A standard image of the "traditional" American family is that of a wife at the door of a pleasant single-family home, holding a small baby, waving goodbye to her husband and an older child or two, who are going off to work and school, respectively.

4. The reciprocal economic obligations of wife and husband are that the husband brings in the money and the wife provides numerous household and child-rearing services and is often the one who spends the money that the husband brings in. The husband is the producer, the **sole provider,** while the wife is the homemaker and the organizer of consumption. In relation to the external market, the household is a unit of consumption rather than production, although many of the services the wife provides (like doing the laundry) are effectively equivalent to market-provided services. This sexual division of labor is characteristic of every "traditional" family to a degree, but particularly when the children are small.

5. The family is, in principle, the *only* place where sexual satisfaction is to be sought and achieved, but it is also meant to provide much deeper satisfactions as well. It is, in the phrase made famous by historian Christopher Lasch, a **"haven in a heartless world."**[3] It is a shelter for both husband and children, with the wife-mother serving as an "angel of consolation." It is essentially a private world, set apart from the public world and giving meaning to private lives, which are judged to be deeper and more significant in some sense than typical public lives, which are led in the hurried, unreflective arenas of industry and commerce.

When these several characteristics are added to the more universal features of families—including the relative permanence of family relationships—it will be a rare reader who does not realize that such "traditional" families are far from characteristic in the United States of the 1990s.

One may indeed wonder whether they even exist today. This is a matter to which we will give considerable attention later on. For the moment, our questions have to do with the past. Was this "traditional" family typical through all or most of our history? If not, how did it come into being? And how universal has it been among different groups in our society?

## THE COLONIAL FAMILY

The simple answers to the foregoing questions are: No, the "traditional" American family as we have described it was not characteristic of our entire history. It developed in response to a variety of large socioeconomic and demographic developments in the course of the nineteenth century, and it never, even in its heyday in the late nineteenth and early twentieth centuries, was equally characteristic of all ethnic and racial groups.

If we go back to colonial days, we find a number of differences that mark off American families from the "traditional" model (though not from the more universal model we first described). Admitting the wide range of practices depending on the region of the country and the national and racial backgrounds of the people involved, we would qualify the five special characteristics just discussed as follows:

*1. Parental approval and other factors besides romantic love played a role in colonial marriages.* In general, parental approval was required in all the colonies before a particular courtship could begin; parental consent was also a prerequisite to marriage. In this sense, and also in two other senses—that economic factors may have played a fairly large role in marriage decisions, and that, at least among the Puritans, love was often expected to grow within the marriage rather than to precede it—the role of romantic love in courtship and marriage was somewhat less in the colonies than in our vision of the "traditional" American family.

Still, romance was never wholly lacking; parental consent was seldom withheld; in the Southern colonies, romantic love probably ranked somewhat higher in the hierarchy of values than in the more puritanical North;[4] furthermore, even where economic considerations were involved, as in gifts of property from both sets of parents, the gifts were often set up in such a way as to guarantee the independence of the young couple.[5] This last point is worth emphasizing because it suggests an important way in which the colonial family was very much like our so-called "traditional" family: It was essentially a nuclear family, not an extended family. Modern research strongly suggests that the nuclear family in England and the colonies antedated the Industrial Revolution of the eighteenth and nineteenth centuries; conceivably, it was even a precondition for the rapid economic development that ensued (see pp. 282–283). In any event, if only for demographic reasons—the very small number of grandparents relative to parents and grandchildren because of high mortality and high fertility—it is clear that the three-generation household was the exception rather than the rule in the colonial period and, indeed, ever since.

*2. Children were not children for very long.* Although colonial parents, like all parents, were concerned with the well-being of their children, this concern, particularly among the Puritans, was often expressed through an upbringing that would seem very disciplined, if not harsh, today. Perhaps the most striking thing about the colonial family was that children were thought of *as* children for such a short period of time. At the ages of 6 or 7, they were considered old enough to take their place in the economic enterprises of the family, or to be boarded out as servants or apprentices to other families. We shall consider the changing worlds of childhood in America in more detail in Chapter 14.

*3. The father's place of work was characteristically at home, or very nearby.* The charac-

teristic occupation of 90 percent of colonial men was farming. Even when men engaged in other crafts and trades, they also often spent at least some time in the fields. Because there was little formal schooling outside the home, and because children were "little workers" from an early age, they too worked in or near the home (or as servants or apprentices in nearby homes). The family was, in fact, the major unit of economic production during this period. Besides farming, the husband was a builder, carpenter, sometimes leather-worker, shoemaker, iron forger, general repairman. In the economically self-sufficient units that were the colonial homes, the wives, assisted by their daughters, did the cooking and preserving, the sewing, ironing, and mending. They gardened, made candles, and nursed the ill. A major difference between the colonial family and our "traditional" family concept is precisely this central role of the colonial family as a **productive unit,** as opposed to a unit largely isolated from the world of production and markets.

*4. Although the husband was considered the head of the family and although there was a sexual division of labor in terms of kinds of work, the sharp division between provider-husband and homemaker-wife did not exist.* Since the family was a unit of production, it was impossible in colonial times to make so sharp a demarcation between the home and the workplace and between the work of women and the work of men as would occur later on. It is only a small exaggeration to say that while men were the farmers, women were the manufacturers in this early American society. Even as late as 1810, Secretary of the Treasury Albert Gallatin could note that "two-thirds of the clothing, including hosiery and of the house and table linen worn and used by the inhabitants of the United States, who do not reside in cities, is the product of family manufactures." He estimated this at ten times the value of what was produced outside the home.[6] These important manufactures were largely the work of American women. Thus, the delineation of a "work" sphere for men and a "domestic" sphere for women has little relevance to the country at this time.

Still, it should not be thought that women in the colonial period enjoyed a high degree of equality with men. Men were still the rulers of the roost within the family, and the proper posture for a woman was considered to be submission to her husband's wishes and commands. Formal education, such as it was, was largely denied to women, and in some colonies they could use the schools only in summertime, when the boys were not occupying the classroom. Modern research suggests, indeed, that the majority of New England women at this time were illiterate.[7] In the South, where there was more of a tradition of chivalry, it is possible that women were more gently treated, although even there the family was strongly patriarchal in nature. In short, the fact that women shared very similar (though usually not the same) kinds of productive work as men in the colonial period says little about their general status at this time.

5. *The colonial family, far from being a retreat from the real world, performed numerous functions of what later would be considered a public or social nature.* Because production was centered in and around the home, clearly there was little sense in which the colonial family could be considered a shelter or haven from the outside world: It was a key unit in the business of that larger world. In his study of the Plymouth Colony, John Demos, besides calling attention to the "business" side of family life, notes that the colonial family was also

• A "school": Most education, before the rise of the common schools, was carried out in the home.

• A "vocational institute": It was in the domestic setting that the young learned farming, spinning, weaving, and carpentry.

• A "church": Although formal churches clearly were important, daily "family worship" was usually considered indispensable.

• A "house of correction": Criminals were sometimes sentenced to become servants in the houses of citizens who could help discipline and reform them.

• A "welfare institution": In the absence of other external institutions to handle such matters, the family household became at various times a "hospital," an "orphanage," an "old people's home," and a "poor house."[8]

There was, in short, no significant aspect of community life, whether economic, political, or social, in which the family unit was not in one way or another engaged. The *privacy* of the "traditional" family had very little analogue in the colonial family. Indeed, considering the relatively small size of the early colonial houses and the large size of their families, the concept of privacy even *within* the colonial family is of doubtful relevance.

## THE EMERGENCE OF THE "TRADITIONAL" FAMILY

What we have shown so far is that, although family life was obviously of towering importance in our early history, the institution in that period differed in a number of ways from the so-called "traditional" model. Since we shall be showing later on that the American family has always encompassed considerable variety, and has also always been in a process of change, the reader may wonder if, in fact, the "traditional" concept is purely mythical—that is, of no actual reality in our national past.

Some students of the subject do come to this conclusion, although this seems extreme and can hardly explain the central place that this concept maintained in our national consciousness until fairly recently. In any event, what is clear is that a number of changes occurred, beginning in the late eighteenth or early nineteenth centuries and extending well into our own century, that sharply altered the colonial family we have just described and moved a great many middle-class American families in the direction of the "traditional" model. A bird's-eye view of these great trends would have to include at least the following factors.

### Industrialization and Urbanization

In most accounts of the changing family scene, pride of place is usually given to the process of industrialization and urbanization that transformed the United States from a land of small farmers living in small towns and rural settings to a nation of factories and offices, many associated with business firms of national or international scope, with production often centralized in densely populated urban areas. A brief graphical description (Figure 9-1) shows changes in two dimensions of this process over most of the nineteenth and early twentieth centuries. During this period, the fraction of our labor force engaged in agriculture decreased from nearly three-quarters to under one-quarter, and the percentage of our population living in urban areas increased by nearly eightfold.

The direct relevance of this massive development for the American family is twofold: First, it drastically reduced the central role of the family as a producing unit in the economy. As we suggested in an earlier discussion (p. 44), it has been said that the Industrial Revolution caused the greatest break between domicile and workplace in human history. Not only was agricultural production reduced to an increasingly minor place in the hierarchy of national industries, but manufacturing production increasingly moved away from the home and small craft shop into larger, and physically removed, business firms.

Second, as a direct consequence of this development, the work of the husband was also removed from home and shop. In itself, this displacement did not ordain that the

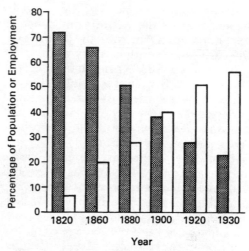

**FIGURE 9–1:  Agriculture and Urban Living, 1820–1930**
The transformation of America from an agricultural to an urban society had deep effects on the American family.

*Source:*  U.S. Bureau of the Census, *Historical Statistics of the United States, Colonial Times to 1970,* Bicentennial edition, Washington, D.C., 1975, Tables A 6-8, A 57-72, D 75-84.

husband become a sole provider, as described in the "traditional" model. However, it did lay the groundwork for this transition, and, furthermore, it also meant the increasing physical removal of the man of the family from the home and from constant daily contact with his children. Among other things, he would no longer be teaching his sons how to farm, build, make shoes, or, for that matter, read the Bible.

### Women's Work

In principle—particularly in view of the reduced areas of responsibility of the family that we will come to in a moment—women's work could also have been removed physically from the domestic hearth. Indeed, the role of American women in the early industrialization of the nation should not be underestimated. Over half the labor force in the early-nineteenth-century cotton mills was female. In 1850, one-quarter of the labor force in U.S. manufacturing industries was female. In a sense, this was only natural considering the primary role women had had in manufacturing pursuits when these were carried out in the home.

Meanwhile, although the main single employment for women in the nineteenth century was domestic service, women also began entering the various professions, although entry here was often extremely difficult and a very high percentage of professional women were in one career, teaching. Nevertheless, as the century wore on, women's participation in the labor force did increase somewhat, a development that continued on into the early twentieth century with occasional ups and downs (Figure 9-2).

Throughout this period, however, the participation rates for women remained far below those for men. For example, in the early decades of the twentieth century, male labor force participation averaged around 80 percent, whereas female participation was only a little above 20 percent. Even more significantly from our immediate point of view, female labor force participation was radically different in terms of age structure. As Figure 9-3 indicates, in 1900, women's employment is heaviest in the early age groups and then falls off sharply after age 24. By contrast, male participation reaches its highest level in the 25-to-44 age group. What this fact signifies is that, at least among white women, the overwhelming majority of working women in the nineteenth and early twentieth centuries were young and single. Married white women had a very low participation rate, married white *mothers* even lower. The general pattern is clear: These women worked until they got married and then, by and large, left the labor force to attend to what were considered to be their primary responsibilities.

## Reduced Fertility

These "primary responsibilities" were, of course, taking care of the domestic side of family life: housekeeping and child rearing. Interestingly, from a certain point of view, it would seem the case that these responsibilities were declining throughout the period in question. One major way in

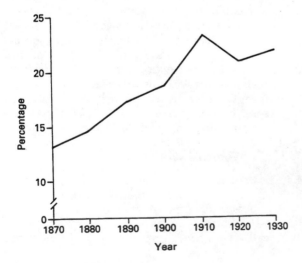

**FIGURE 9–2: Labor Force Participation Rates, U.S. Women, 1870–1930, By Decade**

*Source:* U.S. Bureau of the Census, *Historical Statistics of the United States, Colonial Times to 1970,* Bicentennial edition, Washington, D.C., 1975, Table D 11-25.

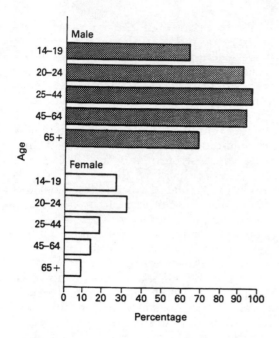

**FIGURE 9–3:   Labor Force Participation Rates By Sex and Age, 1990**
In 1900, U.S. male labor force participation reaches its peak in the 25-to-44 age group, whereas female participation falls off after ages 20–24, as most women married and became homemakers.

*Source:*   Donald J. Bogue, *The Population of the United States: Historical Trends and Future Projections* (Glencoe, Ill.: Free Press, 1959) Table 16-2, p. 426. Copyright © 1985 by The Free Press.

which they were declining we need only mention here, as it has been discussed extensively throughout this book: the extraordinary decline in fertility throughout the nineteenth century and into our own. Over the period from 1800 to the 1930s, we moved from families that averaged seven or eight children apiece to those that averaged around two. In quantitative terms (which, of course, are not the only relevant terms), the tasks of child rearing were being reduced at the same time that the economic functions of the family were also being reduced.

### Reduction of Certain Other Family Functions

Furthermore, a number of other functions connected with the family in colonial times were also being siphoned away from the family sphere. A major case in point is formal education. Again, we will not spend time on this subject here—in this case, because we discuss it at length later (see Chapter 14 and, especially, Chapter 17). Suffice

it to say now that the nineteenth and early twentieth centuries saw a massive expansion in our public and private school systems, including instruction at advanced as well as elementary levels, and that the role of the home in providing either general education or vocational training to the young was very much reduced relative to that of extrafamily institutions.

But a similar development also occurred with respect to those other functions John Demos described in connection with families in the Plymouth Colony. The family no longer needed to provide hospital, jail, old people's home, or general welfare facilities for the community, because there were now specific public institutions for handling all such problems. This is obvious today. Babies used to be born at home; now they are characteristically born in hospitals. Indeed, a significant number of American babies today are born by Caesarean operations, which suggests not only that the locale of births has changed but that the character of the delivery has become professionalized. In general, instead of relying on the all-purpose family for a multitude of tasks, the modernization of our society has involved an increasingly specialized division of labor, which has taken not only economic production and educational training out of the home, but also many of the social functions that the family once performed as a matter of course.

### The Cult of Domesticity

With the call of the marketplace increasingly insistent as the great processes of industrialization rolled forward, and with professional practitioners and institutions taking over many previously familial functions, what was there left to do for all those women who stopped working, or had never worked, when they married and agreed, happily or unhappily as the case may be, to confine themselves to domestic life? There was nothing new about the slogan "woman's place is in the home." What was new was that the home had changed. How was the woman to spend her days?

The simple answer is: She was to spend her time helping to create the "traditional" American family. Indeed, her role was central to that family in that the functions it was now called upon to perform, which were increasingly of an affectional, nurturing, consoling, comforting, supportive nature, were functions in which it was believed women excelled. Whether one believes that the confinement of married women to such domestic tasks was equivalent to their imprisonment or, quite the contrary, the beginning of a recognition of their extraordinary virtues, the fact is that those who exulted in the "traditional" family—women as well as men—did, in fact, argue that women were morally superior to men. For this reason, they could be entrusted with the nurturing and rearing of children, who, though now fewer in number, had come to be prized and cherished in a way that would have been difficult in a harsher environment and age. Quality in children had taken the place of quantity, and the nurturer of quality was the mother.

Partly because of the importance attached to this task, and also perhaps because of the feeling that women should be intelligent and helpful companions to their husbands as they returned home battle-weary from factory or office, women's education did expand substantially over this century or more. Often illiterate in early times, by the mid-nineteenth century women had made great strides, and by 1870, when statistics were first kept, the number of girls who were graduated from high school was greater than the number of boys.[9]

Furthermore, although confined to the home as far as participation in the economy was concerned, nineteenth-century women were by no means confined to the home as far as large social issues were concerned. When it came to charitable and especially moral matters (like alcohol consumption), the virtues that women were believed to possess, and which especially fitted them for domestic life, also had clear applications to U.S. society in general. The campaigns of the Women's Christian Temperance Union (1874), the Prohibition Party (1872), and the Anti-Saloon League (1896), as well as the activities of Jane Addams and others in settlement house work toward the end of the nineteenth century, indicate an extension of the domestic sphere to the public arena.

Still, there is little doubt that the deepest responsibility of a woman in this period was that of wife and mother in the privacy of a home whose economic foundation was secured by her husband.

## VARIETIES OF AMERICAN FAMILIES

We have seen, then, that something like the "traditional" family did exist in nineteenth- and early-twentieth-century America, not only as myth or ideal but as a substantial reality. We should not, however, make the opposite mistake of believing that it was the only reality. Far from it. Although we shall be discussing immigrant and black families in later chapters, we must at least note here that they departed in certain ways from the "traditional" model.

### Immigrant Families

Given the enormous variety of ethnic backgrounds represented by the floods of immigrants who entered the United States in the nineteenth and early twentieth centuries, it would be surprising if their family structures did not show considerable differences from the "traditional" American model and, indeed, great heterogeneity within the several immigrant groups. Ethnic values have always been retained to an appreciable degree within the overall American culture: Immigrants tended to join their native groups first, settling in certain cultural enclaves; they tended to be more urban than the already resident American population; in the first and sometimes the second generation they had higher fertility rates; and so on. Over longer periods, perhaps the most remarkable part of the historic immigrant experience was that the "melting pot" had a certain reality: By the third generation most of these groups were behaving, in their family lives as well as in their individual lives, in ways little distinguishable from those of their fellow "Americans."

Still, at any given time in the late nineteenth and early twentieth century, a considerable proportion of our population were recent immigrants, with the foreign-born averaging around 14 or 15 percent of our population in those decades. These groups were often unskilled and frequently quite poor, and this poverty did affect their family lives in many instances. As compared to the "traditional" family, immigrants often had lower marriage rates, had a higher percentage of women in the labor force, and made a much greater use of child labor as compared to the child-protective middle-class American family that had emerged so powerfully at this time. Indeed, much of the outrage of the progressive era reformers who wished to banish child labor was occasioned by what they felt to be abuses with respect to immigrant children.

Also, it should be noted that male immigrants substantially outnumbered female immigrants, the proportion rising as high as 70 percent in the 1901–1910 decade. Thus, at any given time, there were great numbers of unattached single males who did not live in an ordinary family setting. In general, families in the late nineteenth century often took in boarders; it is estimated that in 1900 perhaps one-quarter of all American households contained at least one boarder. But in the case of immigrant men the percentage was much higher, a frequent arrangement being a boardinghouse with several single men from a particular ethnic group (say, Slovenians) living with a married couple of the same group, with the wife and other women in the family running the boardinghouse to make ends meet.

### Black Families

The family life of blacks was affected more drastically by economic change than was true for the families of European immigrants. Both immigrants and blacks were exploited and excluded from certain work. All started out at the bottom. Race, however, meant that the bottom was not the same for all groups. Blacks, as indentured servants and slaves, were *forced* to be part of America, unlike European immigrants who came by choice. The severe discrimination and political control that blacks faced must be considered in viewing the history of their family life.

Historians and social commentators disagree about the important question of the effects of slavery and economic conditions on the evolution of the black family in America. The theme of family disorganization as a result of slavery and urbanization was developed by the black scholar E. Franklin Frazier in his classic 1939 study, *The Negro Family in the United States.*[10] Later, a somewhat similar theme was advanced in a controversial government report written by now-Senator Daniel Patrick Moynihan (see pp. 226–227).

In Frazier's view, it was slavery and economic factors, not cultural factors, that determined the structure of families among blacks. Slavery affected black families through the absence of legal marriage, the use of black women as sexual partners for the slave masters,[11] and the greater number of black men than black women, which encouraged casual sexual contact among black men and women. The most important bonds became those between a mother and her children. Frazier wrote that, by contrast, the family system of *free* blacks was relatively stable. He noted that, after the Civil War, black men, no longer bound to a plantation, moved about and changed partners frequently. Illegitimacy was common and carried no stigma.

Frazier showed that variation did exist in black family life and there were certainly some two-parent families, especially among blacks who aspired to middle-class status. He found, however, that the matriarchal family form was the dominant type of black family, a result of slavery but also later of economic conditions. In the 1890s the boll weevil wiped out many sharecroppers and tenant farmers, who headed North to industrial jobs. Some of the migrants were single men who were not interested in marriage. Others were men from stable families who intended to have their families with them but found it difficult to do so. Housing for blacks was scarce, expensive, and in the worst parts of town. During World War I, jobs were plentiful for blacks, but afterwards they were difficult to come by, particularly when the Depression hit. These conditions inevitably led to broken families, said Frazier, and increased the disorganization of many urban black families.

Beginning in the mid-1970s, many historians began to disagree with the Frazier study. These critics revised their view of the slave family and portrayed the black family not as "disrupted," but as adaptive and enduring despite the extreme stress of slavery, discrimination, mass migration to Northern cities from a rural culture, and urban poverty. Herbert Gutman's 1976 book, *The Black Family in Slavery and Freedom*,[12] emphasized not only adjustments to the disorganizing influences of slavery and urbanization, but also success in maintaining culture and stable family systems in spite of everything.

Gutman used plantation records, records from manuscripts held by the Freedman's Bureau, and census data to "prove" that two-parent households prevailed during and after slavery and that a strong kinship system was formed that helped to retain the integrity of the family. Census data in particular were used to show the predominance of two-parent families. But Gutman's own work indicates that a significant minority, about one-third of households, were run by single parents. Additionally, Paul J. Lammermeier's 1973 study indicated that 40 percent of black families in the Ohio River Valley Basin between 1850 and 1880 were headed by single women.[13]

In short, black family experience has differed significantly from the "traditional" model, not only in today's world, but historically to a greater or lesser degree. From what *perspective* this experience should be viewed is a subject we will take up later (pp. 226–228).

## DEPRESSION, WAR, BABY BOOM

As we have noted in earlier chapters, the 35 years from the crash of 1929 to the end of the Baby Boom in 1964 were very curious ones in American history. We went through the greatest economic collapse in our history, participated in the largest war in the world's history, and then plunged into not another depression (as widely anticipated) but a great boom period—both economically and in terms of marriages and babies.

What of the fate of the "traditional"

family during this period? Was it prospering or languishing in decline?

On the surface, it would seem that, at least as far as the national consciousness was concerned, the immediate postwar period saw a resurgence in traditional family values. The popular television shows of the period—"Ozzie and Harriet," "Leave It to Beaver," "Father Knows Best"—all seemed to celebrate such values, and the American dream of the period seemed fairly clearly defined as a single-family house in the suburbs, with the wife at home, taking care now of three or four children as opposed to the two of the Depression era, and the husband-father even farther removed from the family during the week as improved means of transportation, and especially the automobile, made the commuter's life feasible.

In point of fact, although in some respects the immediate postwar period did involve a nostalgic return to prewar and even pre-Depression values, in other respects it saw a continuation of trends that, in the next generation, were to bring the "traditional" family to a universally recognized state of crisis. The complexity of change over these three-plus decades can be seen in four variables:

1. *Age at Marriage.* In one respect, these decades provided a continuation of a past trend, which, if anything, could be taken to signify the growing importance of marriage to young Americans. As Figure 9-4 shows, the median **age at first marriage** for both men and women was basically falling between 1890 and the end of the Baby Boom. Men married at 26, on average, in 1890, but at 22 or 23 in the 1950s; women's ages at first marriages correspondingly fell from 22 to 20. If there was any reversal of the trend during this period, it was briefly during the Great Depression, when economic circumstances forced many young couples to postpone marriage. In general, however, this variable suggests a *continuity of trend* over the 75 years from the late nineteenth century on.

2. *Number of Babies.* In direct contrast, the **fertility** rate, as we know from earlier discussions, changed abruptly during the course of these decades. Since the overall trend in U.S. fertility has been downward since at least the early nineteenth century, the distinct fall in this measure during the Great Depression could be regarded as basically a continuation, or slight intensifica-

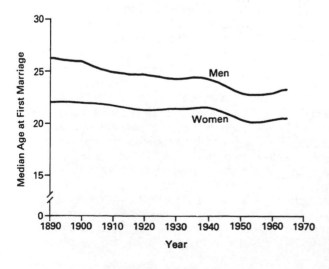

**FIGURE 9–4:  Median Age at First Marriage, By Sex, 1890–1964**

*Source:*  Arlene F. Saluter, "Changes in American Family Life," U.S. Bureau of the Census, *Current Population Reports, 1989,* Series P-23, No. 163, Adapted from Figure 3, p. 5.

tion, of prior trends. But no such interpretation is possible for the postwar Baby Boom. At this time, and unlike the case of marriage age, there is a sharp break in the historic downward trend in fertility. What is complex here is interpreting this break. As far as the traditional family is concerned, did this departure from trend represent a rejection of the past or a desire to return to the past? This is to say that we can view the Baby Boom either as a *break in trend*—an exceptional, aberrant period of no larger significance—or as a *restoration of the past*—a period when fertility was restored to levels prevailing early in the century. Perhaps even both interpretations contain an element of truth (see pp. 47–49).

3.   *Women in the Work Force.* Here again, complexity is the rule. If, for example, we look at census years only, we find no real discontinuities at all during the period we are discussing. **Labor force participation rates** for women were clearly trending upward throughout:[14]

|  | 1930 | 1940 | 1950 | 1960 |
|---|---|---|---|---|
| Female labor force participation rate: | 22.0% | 25.4% | 30.9% | 34.9% |

However, this simple description is a bit too simple. It leaves out, for example, the strong impetus that World War II gave to women's employment outside the home. With millions of otherwise employable young men in the service and with the huge pressure on our productive capacity occasioned by the war, "Rosie the Riveter" became a key figure in the popular culture. Given the demands of the war effort, it was all right if Rosie was married, or even a mother.

These broad figures also fail to disclose the important fact that there was a surprising break in trend during this period. In particular, between 1940 and 1960, participation rates actually *declined* for women under 35—the mothers of the Baby Boom. The increased percentage of overall female participation was due to the very rapid expansion of employment of women above 35.[15] Those younger mothers, then, represent in terms of labor force participation—as in terms of the number of their children—a temporary break in the twentieth-century trend and a return to behavior somewhat reminiscent of an earlier period in the century.

4.   *Divorce.* Something similar can also be said about the stability of marriage during this period. Actually, if we look at crude figures on divorce rates from, say, 1920 to 1970 (Figure 9-5a), we see striking fluctuations around a generally ascending trend. From 1920 to 1933 the **divorce** rate was actually falling. During the Depression, married couples simply couldn't afford to get divorced. Then, when the war was over, all those dissatisfied couples made up for lost time, and the divorce rate soared.

A more instructive story is told by Figure 9-5b, developed by sociologist Andrew Cherlin. Here, we extend the divorce record back to 1870, and, instead of measuring the crude divorce rate, we are measuring, for each year, the proportion of marriages that will end in divorce before one of the spouses dies. For the later years, these proportions obviously have to be based on projections, since many of these marriages still exist and are intact.

Two things are of interest to us in this formulation: (1) the overall trend (like that of female labor force participation) is clearly and unequivocally upward over time, as shown by the path of the smooth curve; and (2) there are certain deviations from this trend on a year-to-year basis. In particular, the period of the 1940s and 1950s (when the Baby Boom parents were getting married) generally lies below the curve, whereas the period of the 1920s and 1930s, and again the period of the 1960s, generally lie above the curve.

Thus, again, we have a strong overall trend—in this case toward increased divorce—and something of a break in the trend during the Baby Boom period. As

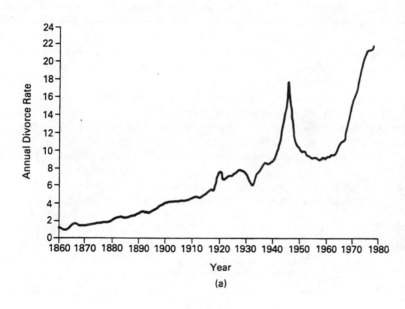

Year

(a)

**FIGURE 9–5a:  Annual Divorce Rates, United States, for 1920–1978: Divorces per 1,000 Married Women Aged 15 and Over; for 1860–1920, Divorces per 1,000 Existing Marriages**

*Sources:*  1860–1920, Paul H. Jacobson, *American Marriage and Divorce* (New York: Rinehart, 1959), Table 42; 1920–1967, U.S. National Center for Health Statistics, Vital and Health Statistics, Series 21, No. 24, *100 Years of Marriage and Divorce Statistics* (1973), Table 4; 1968–1978, U.S. National Center for Health Statistics, Vital Statistics Report, Advance Report, Vol. 29, No. 4, Supplement, *Final Divorce Statistics 1978*, Table 2. Taken from Andrew Cherlin, *Marriage, Divorce, Remarriage* (Cambridge, Mass.: Harvard University Press, 1981), Figure 1-4. Copyright © 1981 by the President and Fellows of Harvard College. Reprinted by permission of the publishers.

Year Marriage Was Begun

(b)

**FIGURE 9–5b:  Proportion of Marriages Begun in Each Year That Will End in Divorce, 1867–1973.**

*Source:*  Taken from Andrew Cherlin, *Marriage, Divorce, Remarriage*, Figure 1-5. Copyright © 1981 by the President and Fellows of Harvard College. Reprinted by permission of the publishers.

Cherlin puts it, "Those who married in the decade or so following the war were the only cohorts in the last hundred years to show a substantial, sustained shortfall in their lifetime levels of divorce."[16]

Overall, then, the Baby Boom period would seem to represent a break in long-run trends that were moving the United States away from the "traditional" family. The emphasis on children, the return of young mothers to the home and away from the workplace, and the temporary lull in the otherwise inexorably rising tendency for marriages to end in divorce—all these would seem to represent a move back in the direction of earlier values enshrined in that institution. Even the one case in which young couples in the 1950s were in line with historic trends—the falling age at first marriage—would seem to be consistent with a growing dedication to the family. Thus, it is quite possible that those family-oriented television shows of the early postwar period did in fact reflect an important national consensus. It is perhaps no accident that, even after the war and Rosie the Riveter, a 1945 *Fortune* poll showed that 63 percent of Americans felt that a woman should not work if her husband was able to support her.

However that may be, one thing is quite certain: the experience of the Baby Boom period, being out of line with most twentieth-century trends, made the developments *after* the Boom seem even more dramatic than they might otherwise have appeared. What might have looked like a simple continuation of the past in the quarter century after the Baby Boom appears instead like a virtual *revolution* in our way of life, and particularly our family life. To this revolutionary contrast, our next chapter is devoted.

## SUMMARY

1.   In general terms, the institution of the family has been virtually universal in all known societies. These general terms, according to Degler, involve marriage rites implying a relatively permanent union, parental responsibilities, common residence, reciprocal economic obligations between husband and wife, and a locus for sexual satisfaction.

2.   Our concept of the "traditional" American family adds a number of elements to this: nuclearity and the importance of romantic love; the cherishing of children; a division of labor in which the husband goes off and earns the income, the older children go to school, and the wife remains at home with the younger children and homemaking responsibilities; and the notion of the home as a haven of privacy and consolation away from the harsh world of business and commerce.

3.   The colonial family, though varying over the years and in different colonies, exhibited some of the traits of this "traditional" family, like nuclearity, but differed from it in significant ways: possibly somewhat less emphasis on romantic love; the shortness of the period of childhood before children became "little workers"; the father usually working at or near the home; the mother engaged in home manufactures and other work while the husband farmed; and the family fulfilling many public functions (school, church, jail, welfare provider) rather than being a private haven apart from the outside world.

4.   The emergence of the "traditional" family in the nineteenth and early twentieth centuries was thus a historically conditioned phenomenon resulting from many different developments, including industrialization and urbanization, changing attitudes toward women and women's work, reduced fertility, the development of public institutions replacing certain colonial family functions, and the spread of the cult of domesticity.

5.   Not all families shared equally in this development; immigrant families and especially black families never fully conformed to the "traditional" pattern even in its heyday around the turn of the century.

6.   In the 35 years from the crash of 1929 to the end of the Baby Boom in 1964, the fortunes of

the "traditional" family shifted in complicated ways. In general, as measured by such variables as age at first marriage, fertility, percentage of women in the work force, and divorce rates, many of the trends seemed to be working against the "tradi-tional" pattern until World War II and its immediate aftermath. At that time, there was a break in many trends and a return to older values and behavior patterns—a development that was soon to be sharply reversed.

## KEY CONCEPTS FOR REVIEW

The family as a historically universal institution

The "traditional" American family

Monogamy

Polygyny

Polyandry

Nuclear family (conjugal family)

Extended family (consanguine family)

The colonial family

Family as a unit of production

Family as a unit of consumption

Sole-provider husband

Cult of domesticity

Public functions of the family

"Haven in a heartless world"

Varieties of families
    immigrant families
    black families

Effects of urbanization and industrialization

Mid-twentieth-century trends
    age at first marriage
    women in the work force
    fertility
    divorce

## QUESTIONS FOR DISCUSSION

1.  Describe the characteristics of the institution of the family that seem to be fairly universal throughout human history. How many of these characteristics would you say apply to your own personal experience of family life? To the family lives of your friends and neighbors?

2.  Answer question 1 again, this time with respect to what has been called the "traditional" American family.

3.  "From early colonial days to the end of the nineteenth century, the American family was continually losing key functions, yet paradox-ically it was a more cherished institution at the end of that period than at the beginning." Dis-cuss.

4.  It has been argued that the Industrial Revolu-tion, by separating men's work from the home and thus underlining even further the already existing sexual division of labor, caused a dimi-nution in the status of women in all Western societies, and in America in particular. Do you agree or disagree? Were women also making important gains in the United States during the nineteenth and early twentieth centuries—in education, work force, social issues, suffrage, respect for motherhood, women's "superior" morality, and the like? Do these gains seem trivial to you or, on the contrary, more than enough to offset women's losses during this era?

5.  What are some of the important trends affecting the American family that were apparent in the middle decades of the twentieth century? Why is it often said that the immediate postwar pe-riod represented an aberration in terms of our longer run history?

6.  It has been said that the American family does not exist—only families exist. How well does this point of view apply to the U.S. experience of the nineteenth and early twentieth centuries?

## NOTES

1. Carl N. Degler, *At Odds: Women and the Family in America from the Revolution to the Present* (New York: Oxford University Press, 1980), pp. 3–4.

2. Kathleen Gough, "The Origin of the Family," in Arlene S. Skolnick and Jerome H. Skolnick, eds., *Family in Transition*, 5th ed. (Boston: Little, Brown, 1985), p. 32.

3. Christopher Lasch, *Haven in a Heartless World: The Family Besieged* (New York: Basic Books, 1977). Also see his interesting book, *The Culture of Narcissism: American Life in an Age of Diminishing Expectations* (New York: Norton, 1978).

4. Thus, historian Edmund Morgan describes a proposal of marriage to a southern belle in dramatic terms: "The lady must be approached with fear and trembling as a kind of saint, the lover prostrating himself either literally or figuratively before her, while she betrayed great surprise and distress at the whole idea." But he also notes that there was a more prosaic side to southern marriages at this time, with "money so proper a consideration in the choice of a mate that newspapers, in announcing weddings, sometimes stated the sums of money involved." Edmund Morgan, *Virginians at Home* (Charlottesville: University of Virginia Press, 1963), pp. 31–39.

5. John Demos, *A Little Commonwealth: Family Life in Plymouth Colony* (New York: Oxford University Press, 1970), p. 182.

6. Degler, *At Odds*, p. 367.

7. William M. Kephart, *The Family, Society, and the Individual*, 4th ed. (Boston: Houghton Mifflin, 1977), p. 83.

8. Demos, *A Little Commonwealth*, pp. 183–184.

9. Degler, *At Odds*, p. 309.

10. E. Franklin Frazier, *The Negro Family in the United States* (Chicago: University of Chicago Press, 1966), originally published in 1939.

11. In 1860, 13 percent of the black population (about 600,000 people) were counted in the census as "mulattoes," which suggests that interracial sex was not uncommon. See U.S. Bureau of the Census, *Negro Population in the United States: 1790–1915*, pp. 207–208.

12. Herbert G. Gutman, *The Black Family in Slavery and Freedom, 1750–1925* (New York: Vintage Books, 1976).

13. Paul J. Lammermeier, "The Urban Black Family of the Nineteenth Century: A Study of Black Family Structure in the Ohio Valley, 1850–1880," *Journal of Marriage and the Family, 35*, August 1973, pp. 440–456.

14. Source of numbers is U.S. Bureau of the Census, *Historical Statistics of the United States, Colonial Times to 1970*, Part 2 (Washington, D.C., 1875), Table D11–E25, pp. 127–128.

15. James P. Smith and Michael P. Ward, "Women's Wages and Work in the Twentieth Century," prepared for the National Institute of Child Health and Human Development, R-3119-NICHD, October 1984, p. xvi.

16. Andrew Cherlin, *Marriage, Divorce, Remarriage* (Cambridge, Mass.: Harvard University Press, 1981), quoted in Skolnick and Skolnick, *Family in Transition*, p. 87.

# 10

# A Tale
## of Two Generations

Over the last two generations, the United States has been on a demographic roller coaster. In the last chapter, we described some of the changes that occurred in the structure of America's families from colonial times through the immediate post–World War II period. In this chapter, we concentrate on a comparison of just two generations—those who were parents (or of parental age) during the Baby Boom of 1946–1964, and their children as adults and parents in the 1970s and 1980s. For convenience, we will refer to them loosely as *parents-of-the-Boomers* and *Boomers-as-adults*.

The justification for focusing on this particular comparison is that demographic changes during the past half century have in most respects been more rapid than at any time in our previous history. Figure 10-1, showing the change in fertility rates with which we are already familiar, suggests the revolutionary nature of the difference between the two generations at a very basic level. But this tremendous upswing and then downswing in having babies is only one part of the story and, indeed, can be viewed as simply reflective of attitudinal changes with respect to sex, marriage, divorce and other family issues that have affected every aspect of adult life.[1] Are such changes permanent, temporary, possibly cyclical? This large question we defer to the end of our study, particularly Chapter 23 ("Does the Family Have a Future?"). For the moment, we simply catalog the remarkable transformations that have occurred in three main areas of adult life: (1) having and raising children, (2) marriage, and (3) labor force participation.

## HAVING AND RAISING CHILDREN

The sharp rise of **fertility rates** to 3.8 children per woman in 1957, followed by its sharp decline to below 2 for most of the 1970s and 1980s, provides a major component of our "tale of two generations," but, as we have said, it is by no means the whole

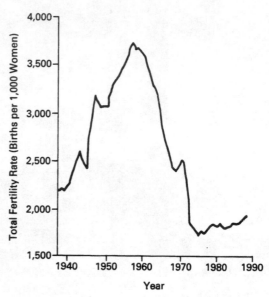

**FIGURE 10–1: U.S. Fertility Change 1938–1989**
A major factor underlying our "tale of two generations" is the rapid fertility change over the last half century.

*Source:* Adapted from Arlene F. Saluter, "Changes in American Family Life," U.S. Bureau of the Census, *Current Population Reports*, Series P-23, No. 163, August 1989, Figure 6.

of the story. There have been changes also in the numbers of childless women and the length of time women remain childless, in the percentages of out-of-wedlock births, in the number and percentage of abortions, and in the parental context in which children are raised.

### Childlessness

If we compare women born in the 1930s (in the parents-of-the-Boomers generation) with women born in the 1950s (the Boomers), we find a sharp increase in the rate of **childlessness.** For the older cohort, approximately 9 percent have never had children; for the latter, it is expected that around 16 percent will remain childless. It is true that, among adult Baby Boomer women, only about 1 in 10 say that they expect to remain childless. However, it is probable that they are being overly optimistic. At the end of the 1980s, 4 in 10 women aged 25 to 29 had not had children yet. Furthermore, as women delay marriage and then delay childbearing into their thirties, more will be unable to have the children they want despite the intensive attention medical scientists are directing toward infertility problems. Recent evidence suggests that more women will remain childless than these women themselves expect, and that those who have children will have fewer than they expect. As age increases, so does the probability of health problems and infertility, and also the difficulty of finding an eligible husband. In 1990, the parents-of-the-Boomers, hoping to become grandparents, frequently dropped hints that "the time has come," and their adult-Boomer children replied that they would get around to it "eventually." But the biological clock continues to tick, and some at least will find that the time is past before "eventually" arrives.

### Nonmarital Childbearing

In 1957, at the height of the Baby Boom, the parents-of-the-Boomers gave birth to just under 202,000 babies out of wedlock. Thirty years later, the Boomers-as-adults gave birth to over 930,000 babies out of wedlock.

Roughly speaking, the parents-of-the-Boomers preserved something approximating traditional attitudes toward nonmarital childbearing. That attitude was that children were to be born to, and raised by, married couples. The few teenagers who did get pregnant were often sent away to out-of-town relatives or maternity homes for unwed mothers, where they could quietly have their babies and put them up for adoption. In the case of white women, the ratio of nonmarital to total births at the beginning of the Baby Boom in 1946 was 21 per 1,000. This was not very different

from the ratio of 15 per 1,000 for all races in 1920, a quarter of a century before. Although this ratio did rise somewhat during the Boom period, reaching 34 per 1,000 in 1964, it remained true in the case of white parents-of-the-Boomers that an out-of-wedlock birth was a very unusual event and one that most young women were eager to avoid.

The Boomers-as-adults have behaved quite differently. The bottom curve of Figure 10-2 shows the dramatic increase in nonmarital births to white women that occurred in the next generation. In 1988, there were 177 out-of-wedlock births per 1,000 births to white women, an increase of over eightfold since the height of the Baby Boom in 1957. An out-of-wedlock birth is no longer that unusual an event among white mothers and, among many men and women, is regarded as a perfectly acceptable choice, or at least deserving of no particular social opprobrium.

If **nonmarital childbearing** is no longer that unusual for white women, it has actually become majority behavior for blacks over these two generations. Historically, black women have had more children out of wedlock than white women, and going back to 1920, it is estimated that women other than white (primarily black) showed a ratio of nonmarital to total births of 125 per 1,000. As just mentioned, this compares with 15 per 1,000 for all women in 1920. During the early postwar period, black parents-of-the-Boomers had more out-of-wedlock children than whites, but marital births were still more common. The ratio rose from around 170 per 1,000 in 1946 to 245 per 1,000 at the end of the Boom in 1964. Then, as Figure 10-2 shows, the ratio began to skyrocket, reaching 635 out-of-wedlock births per 1,000 total births in 1988. By the end of the 1980s, only about one-third of black babies were being born to married couples.

People are often confused by the fact that whereas the ratio of nonmarital to total births is far higher for blacks than for

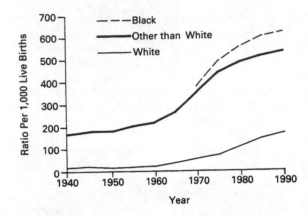

**FIGURE 10–2: Births to Unmarried Women, Ratio per 1,000 Live Births, 1940–1988**

*Source:* National Center for Health Statistics.

whites, birth *rates* of unmarried black women have fallen somewhat for the Boomers-as-adults generation, while those of comparable white women have been rising. For example, the number of births per 1,000 unmarried black women aged 15 to 44 fell from 96 in 1970 to 82 in 1987, while during the same period the number for white women *rose* from 14 to 25.

What this means in the case of blacks is that it is (a) the decreased proportion of women who are marrying and (b) the reduced fertility of married couples that explains the increase in the proportion of children born out of wedlock in the last 20 years, *not* an increase in the birth rate for unmarried women. For both blacks and whites, one of the consequences of declining and delayed marriage (of which we will speak in a moment) is increased nonmarital fertility because of more years of exposure to the risk of an out-of-wedlock birth.

### Abortion

As attitudes toward **premarital sex** and nonmarital childbearing have become more liberal from the earlier to the later generation, much the same can be said of attitudes toward **abortion.** In none of these cases, however, can it be said that the more liberal attitude has been universally accepted, and, in the specific case of abortion, the 1980s saw a major conflict between the proponents of freely available abortions (the so-called *pro-choice* group) and those who would restrict abortion rights in various ways (the so-called *pro-life* group). In 1989 the Supreme Court appeared to have handed certain powers of limiting abortion back to the states, thus narrowing the scope of the famous 1973 *Roe* v. *Wade* decision, which had legalized abortion nationally. While this was considered a positive sign by the pro-lifers, there was evidence to suggest that pro-choicers had much popular support and that politicians who made restricting abortion part of their electoral strategy might run into problems.

Whatever the shift in attitudes may have been, there is no doubt that abortion, once legalized, was far more widely practiced by the Boomers-as-adults generation than by their parents. Accurate data are lacking before *Roe* v. *Wade* because abortion was still illegal in many states. Legal abortions are estimated to have increased from 184 per 1,000 live births in 1972 to 422 per 1,000 live births in 1985. Specific estimates for young women under age 20 suggest nearly a doubling of the number of pregnancies terminated by abortion in the single decade between 1973 and 1983. The teenage abortion rate in the latter year was running well over 40 percent. Between abortion and miscarriage, it is probable that less than half of teenage pregnancies now result in live births. This represents a major behavioral change between the two generations.

### Living Arrangements of Young Children

Television sometimes reflects important changes in our family patterns. The situation comedies of the parents-of-the-Boomers generation, such as "Ozzie and Harriet," "Father Knows Best," "I Love Lucy," and "Leave it to Beaver," all showed biological parents guiding their children along. Today's programs show children being guided not only by the traditional two biological parents (as in "The Cosby Show") but also by the more complex arrangements of multiple "fathers," single mothers and their "friends," stepparents (with stepsiblings), grandparents, adoptive parents, and so on.

The proportion of children living with two parents fell drastically between the two generations (Figure 10-3), particularly for black children. Overall, between 1960 and 1988 the proportion of children under 18 living with just one parent rose from around 1 out of 11 to 1 out of 4. Actually, the proportion of children who are expected to experience a single-parent living arrangement at some time in their childhood is much higher—perhaps as high as 60 percent for children born in the late 1980s.[2]

Furthermore, of children living with two parents, not all are living with their natural parents. In a Census Bureau study,[3] Arlene Saluter showed that, in 1985, 58 percent of children lived with both their natural parents; 16 percent lived with two parents, one of whom was a stepparent; 21 percent lived with their mother only; and about 5 percent lived with their father only, or in foster homes or other situations. The legal system is now starting to address the rights and responsibilities of stepparents, and a few states have even declared official "Stepparent Days." Needless to say, the charts of genealogists are becoming increasingly complex.

One other noteworthy change between

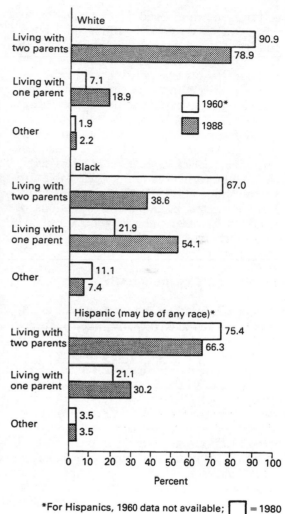

*For Hispanics, 1960 data not available; ☐ = 1980

**FIGURE 10–3: Living Arrangements of Children under 18 Years, 1960 and 1988**

*Source:* Arlene F. Saluter, "Changes in American Family Life," U.S. Bureau of the Census, *Current Population Reports*, Series P-23, No. 163, August 1989, Figure 12.

the two generations is a sharp increase in the percentage of children in one-parent homes whose parent was never married (as opposed to being divorced or separated). As suggested earlier, this phenomenon is more pronounced among black than white families. Thus, despite the fact that white children outnumbered black children by more than five to one in 1988, more black children (2.7 million) than white children (1.5 million) lived with a never-married mother. It should be noted that the reported increase in children living with a **never-married parent** may, to some degree, reflect improved data collection as well as the increased willingness of parents to admit being "never-married." Also, it is a fact that unmarried black teenagers are less likely than white teenagers to put their babies up for adoption. Still, the broad changes we have indicated in the family situations of children between the two generations are beyond doubt.

## IN AND OUT OF MARRIAGE

A woman in her fifties, a veteran of 30 years of marriage, recently asked jokingly: "Who could ever have imagined that 'until death do us part' would take so long?" The two generations have had radically different experiences in the proportion of life spent in marriage. There has been a sharp reduction in marital stability. Marriage occupies a less central place in the life of the Boomers-as-adults than it did for their parents. A study by Professor Thomas Espenshade of the data since World War II suggests that marriage in the United States has been declining as a social institution since at least 1960. In judging this, he uses the following criteria: postponement of marriage, a lower proportion getting married, a lesser proportion of life spent in wedlock, and a shorter duration of marriage.[4]

The shift away from marriage began for whites in the 1960s and for blacks in the 1950s. This shift has been more dramatic for blacks than for whites. In the early 1950s, white women spent 54 percent of their life expectancy at birth in the married state, compared with 43 percent by the late 1970s. For black women, the shift was from 45 percent to just 22 percent (about 16 years) over that same period. White males

are the only population group for whom marriage comprises more than half their life expectancy at birth (53 percent in the 1975–1980 period).[5]

### Age at First Marriage

In the previous chapter, we noted that the median **age at first marriage** in the United States was dropping slowly during most of the twentieth century, a decline interrupted to some degree by the Great Depression, but then accelerating sharply during the early years of the Baby Boom period. What Figure 10-4 shows is how dramatically this trend changed between the parents-of-the-Boomers generation and the Boomers-as-adults generation. From a low

**FIGURE 10–4:   Median Age at First Marriage, by Sex, 1940–1988**
Earlier marriages in one generation, and then postponing marriage in the next: This is part of our "tale of two generations."

*Source:*   Arlene F. Saluter, "Changes in American Family Life," U.S. Bureau of the Census, *Current Population Reports,* Series P-23, No. 163, August 1989, Figure 3.

of 20.1 years at the height of the Baby Boom, the median age at first marriage for U.S. women rose to 23.6 years in 1988. This is actually higher than the median age at first marriage for women way back in 1890 (22.0 years). In the case of men, a similar change is noted, with a fall to 22.5 years during the Boom, followed by a rise to 25.9 years in the late 1980s, this being just shy of the level in 1890 (26.1 years). An increasing postponement of marriage has thus been a characteristic feature of today's adult generation as opposed to that of their parents.

### The Never-Married

Sometimes marriage never comes. The proliferation of dating services, to an estimated 5,000 nationwide in 1990, is indicative of the substantial rise in the proportion of both men and women under age 35, the prime ages for marrying, who have not yet married for the first time. Figure 10-5 shows

the extent of the change for men and women by different age groups between 1960 and 1988. The percentage of never-married women has more than doubled in every age category under 35. For men, there is a similar increase, though somewhat smaller in percentage terms since men have always married somewhat later than women. For both sexes, much of the change has taken place since 1970.

Consumer studies show that young singles buy single-family homes, china, silver, and other domestic items much as married couples do. Since Prince or Princess Charming may never show up, both young women and young men are making the purchases that mark permanency and are traditionally associated with married life.

For some, deciding not to marry is a definite choice. But others vacillate, putting off the decision until the choice is virtually gone. Singleness becomes less of a choice and more of an unalterable fact of life. In the mid-1980s, there were some disputes

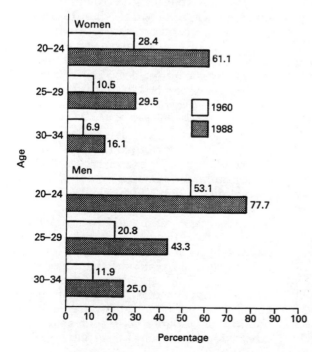

**FIGURE 10–5:  Persons Never Married, by Age and Sex, 1960, 1988**
The increasing percentage of single individuals is no illusion; it represents an important change from the previous generation.

*Source:* Arlene F. Saluter, "Changes in American Family Life," U.S. Bureau of the Census, *Current Population Reports,* Series P-23, No. 163, August 1989, Figure 4.

among demographers as to the chances of never-married women marrying as they entered their thirties and forties. Although early reports of the virtual impossibility of older women finding suitable mates were proved to be exaggerated, it is still estimated that some 10 percent of today's young women will never marry, compared with only 5 percent of older women.[6] In general, as we have already noted, the increase in singleness has contributed to increases in premarital births as women spend more of their childbearing years unmarried.

### Nonmarital Cohabitation

Much of the decline in marriage has been offset by increased living together outside of marriage. In the parents-of-the-Boomers generation, cohabitation of young unmarrieds was quite exceptional. Even as late as the birth cohort of 1940–1944, only 8 percent of men and 3 percent of women had cohabited before age 25. In contrast, in the birth cohort of 1960–1964 (Boomers), an estimated 33 percent of men and 37 percent of women had cohabited before age 25.[7]

The change became very apparent in the age of the "flower child"—the so-called Age of Aquarius in the late 1960s and early 1970s. Some young people, especially those away from home and in college, started living together. Initially, most kept this a secret from their parents. They gave each other phone numbers that parents could call that would seem acceptable. But in due course, most parents-of-the-Boomers came to accept "living together." Most have even stopped writing to ask advice columnists what to call the live-in mate. The Census Bureau solved the problem, in a fashion, by calling the couples "persons of the opposite sex in shared living quarters", and one reporter quickly penned a loving ode to his "POSSLQ."

By 1988, the number of unmarried-couple households had increased to 2.6 million, or 3 percent of all households. In a 1989 study, demographers Larry Bumpass and James Sweet found that almost half of persons in their thirties and half of the recently married have cohabited at some point. They also found that cohabitation usually ends within a few years either by marriage (about 60 percent of first cohabitations) or by the breakup of the couple.

### Marital Dissolution

Annual **divorce** rates have fluctuated with wars and the economy, but the upward drift over time has been unmistakable. Self-help books, feminist literature, and popular literature have delved deeply into the many aspects of divorce, from how to handle it financially to how to cope emotionally. The parents-of-the-Boomers said that they were not always happy in marriage, but the general expectation for the period was that they should "stay together for the sake of the children." In 1940–1945, the probability for white females that a marriage would end in divorce was about 14 percent. For black females, it was somewhat higher, 18 percent. By 1960, percentages for both white and black females had increased (to 20 and 30 percent, respectively), but the great majority of marriages continued to remain intact.

For the Boomers-as-adults, the experience with divorce has changed sharply. Boomers generally say that, as far as the children are concerned, it is better for them to live with a divorce than to suffer through the tribulations of a bad marriage. By 1984 demographers estimated that the rate of marital dissolution had reached 56 percent. More recently still, Teresa Martin and Larry Bumpass have estimated that, if current trends persist, two out of three first marriages will have ended in divorce or separation over a 40-year time span. According to them, "The duration of this trend strongly suggests that the roots of current patterns of marital instability are deep, and not just a response to recent changes in other domains such as fertility, sex-role attitudes, female employment, or divorce laws."[8]

With such an increase in marital dissolution, it will come as no surprise that the average **duration of marriage** has fallen between our two generations, and this despite increases in life expectancies over this same period. In 1940–1945, the average duration of marriage for white women was 32 years, whereas in 1975–1980 it had fallen to 23 years. For black women, marriage duration has always been much shorter, but it too has been falling, from 23 years in 1940–1945 to less than 15 years by 1975–1980.

By some measures, the divorce rate was declining in the 1980s, but this decline was affected by shifts in age at first marriage and also by the age structure of the population due to the prior Baby Boom. Martin and Bumpass doubt that declines in the crude divorce rate signal any reversal of long-term trends:

> Increases in divorce since 1965, as well as declines in marriage and fertility rates, are best seen as a continuation of the long-term reduction of family functions that has occurred in conjunction with the transformation of our economy and an increasing cultural emphasis on individualism. When viewed from this perspective, we must ask whether the underlying changes have run their course.[9]

This position, which suggests a possible further decline in the future role of the family, is subject to much debate, as we shall see later in Chapter 23. It is, however, appropriate to note here that the increase in marital disruption of the last generation is widespread, affecting all social, economic, age, and racial subgroups in U.S. society, and in many European countries as well.[10]

### Remarriage

Because of the increase in divorces, the absolute number of **remarriages** has been rising between the two generations. So also has the proportion of all marriages that are remarriages. In fact, the majority of persons who divorce after their first marriage will remarry within three or four years. At the present time, about one out of every three persons marrying has been married previously and, for about half of all marriages, at least one of the partners has been previously married.

In one respect, however, there has been a decline in the remarriage rate between the two generations. In 1963 the remarriage rate for women aged 25 to 44 was 179 per 1,000 divorced women in that age group. By 1986 the rate was down to 111. The fall was especially sharp for black women. In other words, although the absolute number of remarriages and the proportion of all marriages that are remarriages have been rising, the percentage of divorcees who remarry has been on the decline, and quite substantially so.

Finally, it should be noted that the average duration of remarriages, like that of first marriages, has been on the decline. This, too, has contributed to the overall shorter duration of marriages and the lesser proportion of life spent in wedlock noted by Professor Espenshade (see p. 166).

### Household Composition and Family Type

Changes in marriage and childbearing, as already noted, have led to increases in single-parent families and families with stepparents, smaller households, and more households without children. Children used to have a variety of special names for their grandparents. Now many children have to use their imaginations to name all the substitute parents in their lives. For example, one child didn't want to call her new stepmother "Mom," nor did she want to call her by her first name. She finally settled on "Sommy," her condensed version of "Stepmom."

In 1960 about half of all households were either families with no children or nonfamily households (that is, people who live alone or exclusively with persons un-related to the householder). By 1988 this number had risen to two-thirds (Figure 10-6). The proportion of households composed of a married couple and their own children under 18—what many think of as the "tra-ditional" family of the previous chapter—dropped from 44 percent of households in 1960 to 27 percent in 1988. This decrease was true regardless of the householder's age (Figure 10-7).

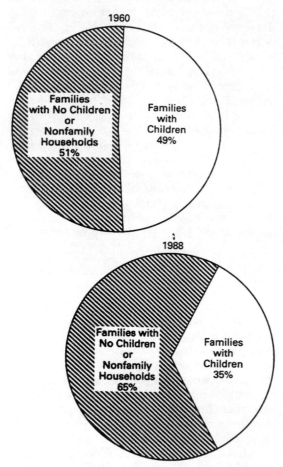

**FIGURE 10–6:    Composition of Households, 1960 and 1988**

*Source:*  Arlene F. Saluter, "Changes in American Family Life," U.S. Bureau of the Census, *Current Population Reports,* Series P-23, No. 163, August 1989, Figure 8.

At the same time, the percentage of "other families" with children was doubling between 1960 and 1988, from 4 percent to 8 percent. "Other families" include both those with female householder and no hus-band present, and those with male house-holder and no wife present. Both types of "other families" have increased between the parents-of-the-Boomers and the Boomers-as-adults generations, although by far the more important group statistically is the mother–child group. By 1988, single-parent families of the mother–child variety *made up 24 percent of all family groups with children.* Despite the popular movie *Kramer versus Kramer,* with its strong suggestion that the mother could leave the family and the father could be the one to take care of the children, father–child families remain rare. Although up sharply from the immediate postwar period, such father–child families still rep-resented less than 4 percent of all family groups in 1988.

This increase in single-parent families has been experienced by all major groups in U.S. society. In 1988 over half of all black families with children were maintained by women alone, up from about one-third as recently as 1970. For Hispanics and whites, the 1988 proportions are much lower (29 percent and 18 percent, respectively), but both groups have experienced significant increases over the years.

Based on the patterns established by the Boomers-as-adults, it appears that 6 of 10 of today's children will live for some length of time with a single parent. Living with one parent was in 1988 the situation of about one-quarter of all U.S. children, up sharply from 9 percent in 1960 while the Baby Boom was in progress. Note further that the reasons for single parenthood have changed between these two generations. In 1960, more than one-quarter of the children living with a single parent lived with a widowed parent. In 1988 widowhood was involved in only 6 percent of the cases.

Thus, single-parent families in the pres-ent generation of parents are almost exclu-

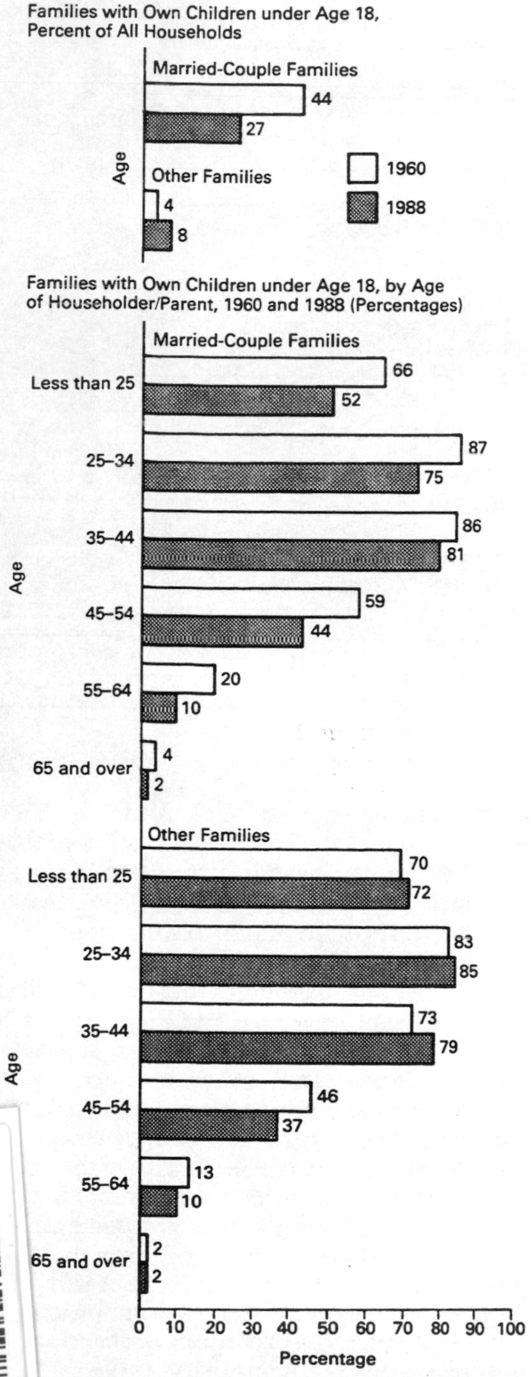

Families with Own Children under Age 18,
Percent of All Households

Married-Couple Families

Age

| Married-Couple Families | |
|---|---|
| 44 | 1960 |
| 27 | 1988 |

Other Families

| | |
|---|---|
| 4 | 1960 |
| 8 | 1988 |

Families with Own Children under Age 18, by Age
of Householder/Parent, 1960 and 1988 (Percentages)

Married-Couple Families

Age

| Less than 25 | 66 / 52 |
|---|---|
| 25–34 | 87 / 75 |
| 35–44 | 86 / 81 |
| 45–54 | 59 / 44 |
| 55–64 | 20 / 10 |
| 65 and over | 4 / 2 |

Other Families

Age

| Less than 25 | 70 / 72 |
|---|---|
| 25–34 | 83 / 85 |
| 35–44 | 73 / 79 |
| 45–54 | 46 / 37 |
| 55–64 | 13 / 10 |
| 65 and over | 2 / 2 |

Percentage (0 10 20 30 40 50 60 70 80 90 100)

**FIGURE 10—7: Composition of Families with Children, 1960 and 1988**

sively a product of divorce or unmarried parenthood. The growth in this category will be of continuing interest to us throughout our study, since the single-parent family, especially those with a female householder and no husband present, are overwhelmingly poorer than married-couple families. Furthermore, the gap in income between the two kinds of families has increased as we move from the parents-of-the-Boomers generation to that of the Boomers-as-adults. Real median income of married-couple families more than doubled between 1947 and 1988, while that of families maintained by women alone rose by only about one-third.

## REVOLUTION IN THE WORK FORCE

Julia Child, the famous chef, has noted that times have changed since her first cookbook was written in the 1960s. She laments that the young women of today don't know the principles of good cooking, and she proposes to solve their lack of basic knowledge with her book, *The Way to Cook*. Child's book may become a history book as a much as a cookbook—a last reminder of a time when there were enough hours in the day for practicing the domestic arts. As more and more married women spend more and more time on the job, they have fewer hours to do personally all that is necessary to meet Child's admonition to "never lose sight of a beautifully conceived meal."[11] Food marketers are always planning ways to help working women with time problems; for the 1990s, they are planning more food that can be grabbed, zapped, and gulped. Supermarkets, too, are increasingly geared to people who rarely cook from scratch. We can expect to see more frozen foods and more prepared foods that need only be microwaved. In fact, those who design su-

*Source:* Arlene F. Saluter, "Changes in American Family Life," U.S. Bureau of the Census, *Current Population Reports,* Series P-23, No. 163, August 1989, Figure 10; adapted by the authors.

permarkets predict that commodities for home food preparation (such as baking supplies) eventually will all but disappear and that such items will be found only in specialty stores.

As is obvious, the main reason for these and many other changes in life patterns between the parents-of-the-Boomers and their adult children is the massive increase in the labor force participation of women over the two generations, and especially the rapid increase of such participation by mothers of young children. We will devote the next chapter to an analysis of this revolutionary development, specifically as it relates to working wives and mothers. Here we briefly summarize only a few general characteristics of the changes in the U.S. work force between the two generations.

### Labor Force Participation of Men

Obviously, the most striking changes over the past three decades have taken place with respect to the labor force participation of women, not of men. Indeed, total male labor force participation over this period has run counter to the trend among women. Figure 10-8 shows that the labor force participation rate of American women rose sharply from 1959 to 1989. The total male participation rate, however, actually fell during this time—from 84 to 76 percent. The rate fell for both white and black males, a major factor being the reduced participation among older men, which we discussed in Chapter 7. In the prime family formation ages of 25 to 34, virtually all married men are in the labor force, and this has not changed between the two generations. There has, however, been a change with respect to teenage (age 16 to 19) employment. In the case of white males, labor force participation of 16- to 19-year-olds increased from 56 percent to 61 percent between 1959 and 1989, while in the case of black teenage males there has been declining participation—from 56 to 45 percent. This problem of the employment of

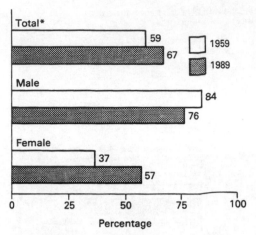

**FIGURE 10–8: Labor Force Participation Rates (Percentages), by Sex, 1959 and 1989**
Between our two generations, total labor force participation rates rose despite a fall in male participation. Reason: the rapid entry of American women into the labor force.

[a]Civilian labor force only; data relate to persons 16 years of age and older.
*Source: Economic Report of the President,* February 1990, Table C-36.

young black males we shall return to later (see pp. 264–266). Here we simply note that reduced teenage labor force participation of black males helps explain the greater overall decline in such participation for black as opposed to white males.

Although the changes just noted are less dramatic than those we shall mention with respect to women, there are two senses— one objective, the other subjective—in which the male labor force role has changed substantially between the two generations. Objectively, there is the fact that the husband's role as a sole provider of family income in married-couple families has changed drastically. Already, over half of all married-couple families have a working wife to go along with the working husband. The role of sole-provider husband now occupies a distinctly minority status. Subjectively, there is the acknowledged fact that men in the adult-Boomers generation are far more willing to accept working wives and mothers than were the men of their parents' generation. We shall develop these points at greater length in Chapter 12, noting then the ambiguities in male roles that have developed in recent years.

### Labor Force Participation of Women

Women have joined the labor force in record numbers, and never before in our history have they shown such a strong commitment to continuous employment in the labor force. Figure 10-8 shows that, while male labor force participation was falling between 1959 and 1989, that of females was rising—from around 37 percent to 57 percent.

Actually, general figures like these understate the extent of women's recent entry into the labor market, as they include women older than those in the Baby Boom cohort. If we restrict ourselves to that cohort—to women born between 1946 and 1964, who would be in the age group 25 to 43 in 1989—then about 7 in 10 of these women are in the U.S. labor force.

Furthermore, the most striking aspect of the change is the increased labor force participation of wives, and especially that of young mothers. As late as 1970, just 4 out of 10 married mothers with children under 18 were in the labor force. By the late 1980s, more than two-thirds of wives with children were in the labor force. The sharpest increase was for wives with very young children. Just in the 18 years between 1970 and 1988, the labor force participation of wives with infants (children 1 year and under) more than doubled—from 24 percent to 52 percent.

Up until the early 1960s, married women with no children had higher labor force participation rates than wives with children. This was primarily because of the low rate of participation of women with children under age 6. This long-standing pattern began to change in the 1970s and has now been reversed. We shall be discussing the complex of economic and noneconomic factors behind this change in Chapter 11.

Historically, black women have had higher overall labor force participation than white women, even when married. But now that divorce and later marriage is a more prominent factor in the lives of white women, the gap between the labor force participation rates of black and white women is narrowing.

Working women are not casual participants in the labor market, and wives are increasingly taking jobs that require year-round, full-time commitment. The average number of hours worked has increased over the last few decades, although the average is still not as high as the average for men. The increase in full-time commitment affects women's seniority and is related to progression within an occupation and to eventual lifetime earnings.

### Education and Occupations of Women

If the tale of the two generations of women is one of increasing labor force participation, it is also one of **increasing education for women.** In 1946, at the beginning of the Baby Boom, only about one-third of women 25 and older had completed four years of high school or more. By the 1980s this number had increased to 70 percent and above. Figure 10-9 shows the increasing percentages of college and advanced degrees earned by women between 1965 and 1985. In specific professions, advances have been by leaps and bounds. Between 1960 and 1982, for example, the percentage of law degrees conferred on women rose from 2.5 to 33.4; medical degrees from 5.5 to 25.0; even engineering (a stereotypical male profession) witnessed an increase in women's degrees from a minuscule 0.4 percent to 10.8 percent.

As far as the occupations in which women are engaged, there was also change. Here, however, there is considerable dis-

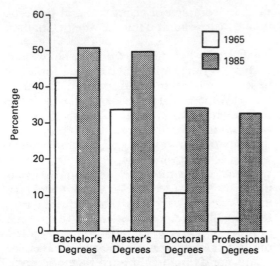

**FIGURE 10–9: Percentage of Earned Degrees Received by Women, 1965 and 1985.**

*Source: Economic Report of the President,* January 1987, Chart 7-2.

agreement as to the true extent of the change and as to the role that gender discrimination played in denying women access to certain kinds and levels of employment. Similarly, there is disagreement as to the underlying reasons for the continuing lag of women's earnings behind those of men.[12]

As far as our specific purpose in this chapter (a comparison of two generations) is concerned, however, there is little doubt about the *direction* of change, certainly with respect to women's range of occupations. Paul Ryscavage of the Census Bureau notes that the 1970s were a pivotal decade because occupational sex discrimination declined, albeit modestly.[13] He showed that during this decade almost half the net employment

growth of women took place in occupations in which women held less than 40 percent of the jobs in 1970. By 1980 occupational sex segregation had declined by about 9 percentage points; that is, about 59 percent of employed women would have had to change occupations to attain the same occupational distribution as men, whereas in 1970 the comparable figure was 68 percent—a large drop relative to past decades.

Ryscavage found that the most significant changes in major occupational groups were in managerial and professional specialty occupations and in service occupations. However, the majority of women in the managerial and professional fields remained in predominantly female occupations such as teachers and registered nurses. Also, most employment for women in the technical, sales, and administrative support occupations remained in the traditionally female jobs of secretary, office clerk, and cashier. Service occupations became more integrated, especially among janitors and cleaners, bartenders, and guards, but most female service workers continued tradition by working as nursing aides, child care workers, and waitresses.

Thus, despite the increase in female doctors, lawyers, and even carpenters, many stereotypes about the nature of "women's work" remain. Women have made progress in entering traditionally male occupations, especially managerial and professional specialty occupations But the majority of women are still in traditional female occupations. And the actual number of women in the higher paying jobs is relatively small. These are points we shall want to return to again.

## SUMMARY

1. In this chapter we have focused attention on two generations: the parents-of-the-Boomers and the Boomers-as-adults. The reason for this focus is that there have been major changes in attitudes and behavior between these two generations. Among other things, these changes have affected:

(a) the having and raising of children, (b) marriage, and (c) labor force participation.

2. With respect to the having and raising of children, a major underlying change is, of course, the sharp rise in fertility when the parents-of-the-

Boomers were having their children and the sharp decline in fertility as the Boomers themselves came of age. But there were a number of other changes as well, including:

a. Increasing childlessness

b. An increase in the ratio of out-of-wedlock births to total births, especially for blacks but also quite sharply for whites

c. A major increase in the abortion rate

d. An increase in the variety of family arrangements under which children are raised, including a striking increase in the number of children living in a single-parent, especially mother-only household

3. With respect to marriage, there is much evidence to support the view that this institution has been on the decline between the two generations. This evidence includes:

a. A later marriage age, as the adult Boomers tend to postpone marriage as compared with their parents

b. An increase in the percentage of never-married men and women in all age groups

c. A changed attitude toward premarital sex and a higher rate of nonmarital cohabitation

d. A very substantial increase in the likelihood of divorce, with an informed estimate being that two out of three recent first marriages (and also remarriages) will eventually end in dissolution

e. A declining remarriage rate for divorcees, and a declining average duration for remarriages

f. An increase in single-parent households largely because of divorce, separation, and never-married mothers, the last having special weight in the case of black single-parent families

4. With respect to the labor force, there has been a virtual revolution in the relative roles of men and women between the two generations. Labor force changes include:

a. A general increase in the overall labor force participation rate over the past 30 years

b. A decline in the male labor force participation rate as American men have retired earlier (plus some decline in black teenage participation), and a growing acceptance by men of the fact that they are no longer characteristically the sole providers for their families

c. A very substantial increase in women's labor force participation, with around 7 in 10 of adult-Boomer women now in the labor force, and with a striking increase in the number of mothers with very young children currently in the work force

d. An increase in women's educational levels and in the range of employment open to them as compared with the generation of their parents, although it should be added that the majority of women still remain in relatively low paying occupations that are predominantly female

## KEY CONCEPTS FOR REVIEW

Fertility rate

Childlessness

Nonmarital childbearing

Premarital sex

Abortion

Household arrangements involving children
    both natural parents
    one natural parent, one stepparent
    mother only
    father only
    foster care and other

Never-married parents

Age at first marriage

Divorce and remarriage

Duration of marriages, remarriages

Economic conditions of mother-only families

Labor force participation rate
    males, older males, black teenagers
    women, adult Boomer women, mothers of infants

Educational advances of women

Mixed labor market conditions for women

## QUESTIONS FOR DISCUSSION

1. How do your own views differ from those of people you know in other generations (e.g., your parents and their friends, grandparents, or younger generations, as the case may be) on these subjects:

   (a) Premarital sex

   (b) Abortion

   (c) Divorce

   (d) Out-of-wedlock childbearing

   (e) Single-parent families

   (f) Mothers of infants working

   (g) Sex discrimination in the job market

2. Continuing from question 1, over the past decade, have you:

   (a) noticed any change in your parents' (or other generations') views on these issues?

   (b) experienced any change in your own views on these issues? If yes, explain why.

3. It has been said that marriage is a declining institution and has been for the past 30 years.

What statistical evidence can be assembled in support of this proposition? Can you reconcile these findings with the fact that a Harris poll indicates that by a margin of 65 percent to 18 percent Americans believe that married people are happier than singles?

4. Describe the major changes in the sex composition of the U.S. labor force that have occurred between the two generations considered in this chapter. Do you feel that these changes are essentially irreversible, or do they simply represent another swing of the social pendulum?

5. Federal, state, and local governments, and the courts, have played an increasing role in American life over the past 50 years. Can you think of any ways that government actions have affected the trends described in this chapter? Are there policies affecting the future of these trends that you feel the government should be taking, either legislatively or through the courts? Specify.

## NOTES

1. These attitudinal changes clearly affect teenage life as well as adult life. No better example can be given than changes in attitudes toward teenage premarital sex. Once frowned upon, such premarital sex during adolescence is now widely accepted. In less than two decades between 1970 and 1988, the proportion of adolescent women who reported having had premarital sexual intercourse rose from 28.6 percent to 51.8 percent. See William Pratt, "Premarital Sexual Experience among Adolescent Women—United States, 1970–1988," *Morbidity and Mortality Weekly Report*, Centers for Disease Control, *39*(51–52), January 4, 1991, p. 929–932.

2. Arthur J. Norton and Paul C. Glick, "One-Parent Families: Social and Economic Profile," *Family Relations, 35*, 1986, pp. 9–17.

3. Arlene F. Saluter, "Marital Status and Living Arrangements: March 1988," U.S. Bureau of the Census, *Current Population Reports*, Series P-20, n. 433 (Washington, D.C.: U.S. Government Printing Office, January 1989). In this chapter, we have drawn heavily on data from Saluter's work in this article and also in Arlene F. Saluter, "Changes in American Family Life," U.S. Bureau of the Census, *Current Population Reports*, Series P-23, No. 163, August, 1989.

4. Thomas J. Espenshade, "Illegitimacy and Public Policy," *Population and Development Review, 11* (2), June 1985.

5. Ibid., pp. 201–203, 238.

6. Arthur J. Norton and Jeanne E. Moorman, "Current Trends in Marriage and Divorce among American Women," *Journal of Marriage and the Family, 49*, February 1987, pp. 4–5.

7. Larry L. Bumpass and James A. Sweet, "National Estimates of Cohabitation," *Demography, 26* (4), November 1989, pp. 615–625.

8. Teresa C. Martin and Larry L. Bumpass, "Recent Trends in Marital Disruption," *Demography, 26* (1), February 1989, p. 44.

9. Ibid., p. 37.

10. J. Sardon, "Evolution de la nuptialité et de la divortialité en Europe depuis la fin des années 1960," *Population, 41*, pp. 463–482.

11. Julia Child, *The Way to Cook* (New York: Knopf, 1989), p. xi.

12. Few, if any, serious scholars would doubt that one of the reasons for the continuing lag of women's wages behind those of men has been sex discrim-

ination in the labor market. Where disagreement arises, it is in determining how big a factor discrimination has been compared to other factors, and whether serious discrimination still exists today. For two different interpretations of the evidence, see Barbara R. Bergmann, *The Economic Emergence of Woman* (New York: Basic Books, 1986), especially Chapters 4–7, where Bergmann argues that discrimination is at the root of "occupational segregation," which in turn is at the root of "women's poor position in the labor mar-

ket" (p. 86). Then see Claudia Goldin, "Understanding the Gender Gap," *New Perspectives,* Fall 1985, pp. 9–13, where Goldin argues that it was not because of discrimination but "precisely because the participation rate of women increased so markedly in the post–World War II period that the gender gap failed to narrow" (p. 13). See also pp. 191–192.

13.  Paul Ryscavage, Bureau of the Census, "Changes in Occupational Sex Segregation During the 1970s," unpublished manuscript.

# 11

# *Working Wives and Mothers*

*I*n the last two chapters, we have concerned ourselves with general changes in American family life, marriage and work, both historically and in the post–World War II period. In this chapter and the next, we will look at these changes specifically from a *gender* point of view. In this chapter we will consider some of the major developments that have affected women's lives in recent years; in Chapter 12 we turn our focus to men's lives.

The two subjects are, of course, very much intertwined. A major development affecting *both* women and men has been the massive increase in the labor force participation of women, especially wives and young mothers, during recent decades. An analysis of the factors behind this large development will be the main focus of the present chapter.

Before getting into this question, however, let us say a word about the nature of the gender distinction we are making in this and the next chapter.

## DISTINCTION BETWEEN SEX AND GENDER

We begin by noticing a distinction that is increasingly being made between **sex** as a biological concept, and **gender** as a construct that is socially and historically determined.

Divided on a sexual basis, the male and female of the human species have a number of obviously differentiating characteristics. Women can have babies, men cannot. Underlying the overt anatomical differences, there is the determining difference in sex chromosomes: the normal male has one X and one Y chromosome; the normal female two X chromosomes. Differences associated with biological sex are widespread and varied, including hormonal differences (e.g., relative amounts of the female sex hormone estrogen as opposed to the male sex hormone testosterone), organ structures (e.g., possible differences in the *corpus callosum*

and the lateralization of the brain), physiological differences (e.g., female menstruation), and underlying genetics (e.g., relative susceptibility to various diseases with a genetic component).

Sometimes it is difficult to sort out the biological from the environmental component of sex differences. We have already noticed that the fact that women live longer than men probably has a genetic basis, but that life expectancy is also influenced by environmental factors (see above, pp. 29–30). At the same time, recent research suggests that male–female differences may be apparent at the very deepest level. For example, it is now believed that, for the same gene, the genetic inheritance of a child may be somewhat different depending on whether that gene is inherited from the mother or the father.[1]

In contrast to sex, *gender* refers to the complex of attitudes, roles, behaviors, and expectations by which what a society considers to be **masculine** is differentiated from what it considers to be **feminine.** The distinction is an obvious one. Women are more likely to wear dresses than men. When men do wear dresses, for example, in theater productions such as the Hasty Pudding shows at Harvard where female roles are taken by men, audiences have no difficulty in recognizing that biological men are taking on many of the gender attributes of women. In the world of opera, there is the important category of "pants roles" (e.g., Cherubino in Mozart's *Marriage of Figaro*), where biological women take on the roles of men. Of course, women currently wear pants every day, a thoroughly acceptable part of being "feminine" today, although in an earlier era it would have been considered a violation of the feminine gender role.

We have used the example of dramatic roles above because it raises the question of the degree to which gender categorizations in a society are essentially no more than social and historical constructions, that is, roles we are taught to play from the cradle by the expectations of society. Wearing dresses as opposed to pants is obviously socially determined behavior, which can change—and has changed—radically over time. In earlier centuries, men's clothing was in fact often far more lacy and dandified than women's.

But is this also true of deeper attributes of behavior? To what degree is it simply a socially constructed, historically conditioned attitude that finds most men to be more competitive, aggressive, and emotionally less expressive than women, whereas women are likely to be more emotional, supportive, and nurturant than men? Is there anything special in the mother–child relationship, or is it simply a social artifact that binds the two together? Why do men tend to prefer and do better in mathematics than women? Why do women generally have a stronger interest in art and culture and less interest in Sunday afternoon football than most men? To put the question generally: To what degree are differences in gender separable from differences in sex? Is anatomy "destiny," as the Freudians once claimed? Or are history, economics, power, sexual politics, and other socially conditioned factors at the heart of the matter?

Without trying to answer these deep questions, one can certainly notice that there has been a profound change in the way most scholars look at the matter today as compared with earlier in this century. Broadly speaking, earlier analyses tended to find the basis for gender roles largely in sex differences, including primarily the need for women to bear and nurse children. A characteristic evolutionary view goes roughly like this:

> Bipedalism, or walking upright, had many evolutionary advantages for the human species, as did the development of larger brains. But walking upright, which makes possible the free use of the hands for gathering food and using tools and weapons, required a smaller pelvis than the larger-brained offspring needed for passage through the birth canal. Hence, human babies were born at an earlier stage of development than previ-

ously, and were characterized by prolonged dependence on their mothers. The role of women, then, was to stay home taking care of their largely helpless infants, while men roved over forest and savannah to bring home animals slaughtered in the hunt. Man, the "provider" or "breadwinner," and woman, the "mother" and "homemaker," are thus seen to be roles deeply sanctioned by the evolutionary process.[2]

From such a viewpoint, it is easy to deduce other aspects of the gender roles of both men and women, such as the allegedly active, aggressive, independent, dominant nature of men, as opposed to the supposedly passive, supportive, nurturing, and dependent nature of women.

In recent years, there has been a sharp shift in emphasis away from this approach, with many scholars in both "women's" and "men's" studies stressing the fact that gender roles are much more historically and socially determined than was previously believed.

In the last two chapters, we saw the rapidity of change in family, marriage, and work roles assigned to men and women in recent decades. And if any further proof is needed, the following more detailed analysis of the changing role of women in the American workplace should demonstrate the point beyond question. There is obviously far more variability in gender construction than a simple biological, sex-role model implies. Indeed, this very variability poses us with social and personal questions of enormous importance.

## WIVES AND MOTHERS AT WORK

In the last chapter, we noticed the increased labor force participation of U.S. women since World War II, and especially that of women of the Baby Boom generation. Of course, women have always been in the labor force to some degree. Single women, widows, women who were divorced or separated—all these have often had to fend for themselves in the marketplace even in the era of the male "breadwinner." In recent years, there has been a marked increase in the category of women who, lacking a husband, have had to take responsibility for their own economic well-being. What is most striking about modern women, however, is the enormous growth in labor force participation of wives and mothers in intact families. As we noted in the last chapter, the greatest increase in female labor force activity has been for married women with infant children. Historically, this group did *not* enter the labor force to any significant degree (although this was less true of black mothers than white mothers, as we point out later). Why did this happen?

First, a few facts:

### The Dual-Earner Family

In Figure 11-1, we focus not on men and women in general but specifically on

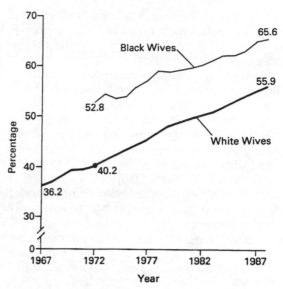

**FIGURE 11–2: Percentage of Married Women (Spouse Present) in Civilian Labor Force, by Race, 1967–1988**

*Source:* Bureau of Labor Statistics, *Handbook of Labor Statistics*, Bulletin 2340, August 1989, Table 6, pp. 34, 36.

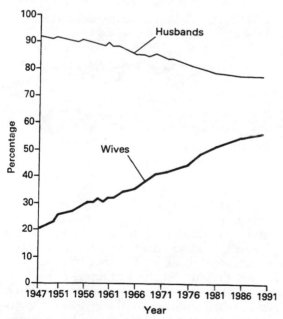

**FIGURE 11–1: Labor Force Participation Rates of Husbands and Wives**

*Source:* U.S. Department of Labor, Bureau of Labor Statistics, *Handbook of Labor Statistics*, Bulletin 2340, August 1989, Table 6.

husbands and wives in married couple families where the spouse is present. At the beginning of the post–World War II era, roughly 80 percent of married-couple families received no earned income from the wife. By 1988, only 43 percent of such families had nonearning wives. Except for the relatively small number (around 4 percent) of married-couple families where the wife is the sole breadwinner, the 57 percent of families where the wife is working are **dual-earner families.**

Thus, we can now say that the "typical"—that is, the majority—American married-couple family is a dual-earner family. This is especially true of black families, where, even at the beginning of the century, substantial percentages of wives in intact families were in the labor force, mostly in domestic service as maids, cleaning women, laundresses, and the like (see Chapter 13, p. 219). But, as Figure 11-2 indicates, it is also true of white wives, whose participation rate increased by a remarkable 20 percentage points (from 36 to 56 percent) in the short period from 1967 to 1988.

Actually, these numbers, dramatic as they are, probably understate the real impact of working wives as far as the *working-age* generation is concerned, because they also include elderly married couples where women's labor force participation has been basically constant over the past two decades. Among working-age families, the truth is that the husband-sole-breadwinner model is now not only marginally but substantially in the minority.

And this fact has had a considerable impact on the economic situations of married-couple families. Initially, the impact of the wife working was less because most married women worked only part time or for only part of the year. In 1960, only 7 percent of wives contributed more than half of total family earnings. However, women's contributions have been increasing; by 1980, 12 percent were contributing more than their husbands.[3] Since 1986, moreover, a majority of married women have begun to work full time and year round.

Figure 11-3 shows the large and widening difference between median family incomes in dual-earner families and those where the husband is sole earner. By 1987 the gap had risen to over $9,600. Clearly, as we shall discuss in a moment, the economic advantage of dual earners was not irrelevant to the expansion of the numbers of working wives in recent years. The relatively *dis*advantaged position of wives as sole earners, as shown by the lowest curve, is also something that will be discussed.

### Working Mothers

If it was unusual for wives in intact families—especially white families—to be in the labor force at the beginning of the twentieth century, it was even more unusual for mothers to be so engaged, and almost unthinkable for mothers of very young chil-

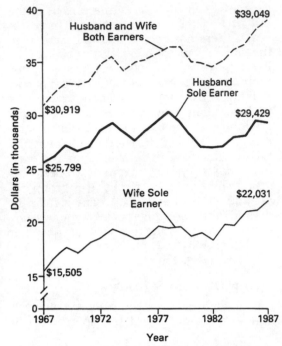

**FIGURE 11–3: Median Family Income (in 1987 Dollars) by Number of Earners, 1967–1987**

*Source:* Bureau of Labor Statistics, *Handbook of Labor Statistics,* Bulletin 2340, August, 1989, Table 61, p. 256.

dren to work outside the home. When many observers now speak of a "revolution" in the labor force, it is often with respect to the entry en masse of young mothers into jobs outside the home.

Figures 11-4a and 11-4b show a breakdown of the changes in the percentages of married women in the labor force by the presence of children and by their ages. These are all intact families, with the husband present. At the beginning of the century, we would have been talking about no more than 5 percent of these young mothers in the labor force. Even in 1960, fewer than 19 percent of mothers with children under 6 were working outside the home. What is striking is the enormous *rapidity* of the changes that have occurred. Just as the

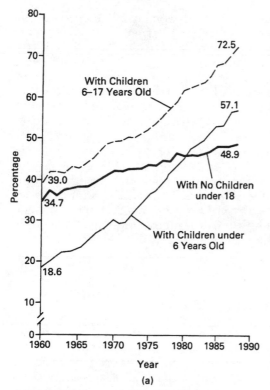

**FIGURE 11–4a:** **Percentage of Married Women (Spouse Present) in Civilian Labor Force, by Presence and Age of Children, 1960–1988**

*Source:* Bureau of Labor Statistics, *Handbook of Labor Statistics,* Bulletin 2340, August 1989, Table 57, pp. 242–243.

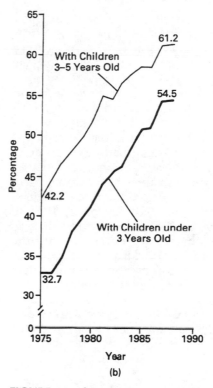

**FIGURE 11–4b:** **Percentage of Married Women (Spouse Present) with Children under 6 Years in Civilian Labor Force, by Age of Children, 1975–1988**

*Source:* Bureau of Labor Statistics, *Handbook of Labor Statistics,* Bulletin 2340, August 1989, Table 57, p. 244.

"typical" working-age family is now a dual-earner family, so the "typical" mother of children, including very young children, is now in the labor force.

Interestingly, the lowest category of participation and the one showing the slowest growth is that of married women with no children under 18. This, however, is not as surprising as it might seem, since this category includes many older women, whose labor force participation, as we have mentioned before, is low and has not been rising significantly.

### Women's Earnings

There are basically two ways of describing the earnings of the women who have flooded into the labor force in recent decades. Both of them are suggested by Figure 11-3. The first way emphasizes the gains that women have made in recent years and is suggested by the steeper *slope* of the sole-earner wife's curve as compared to that of sole-earner husbands. Between 1967 and 1987, sole-earner wives' median family income rose from around 60 percent to well over 70 percent of sole-earner husbands' median family income. The second way emphasizes the *position* of the sole-earner wife's curve, which is very far below the sole-earner husband's curve.

Of course, sole earners are the exceptions now for both men and women. However, the general story for working women is similar to what we have just described—it has both a positive and a negative side to it. Figure 11-5 shows that women have made substantial gains in their real annual earnings in recent decades, rising from a median level of under $11,000 a year in 1955 to over $16,500 in 1989, as measured in 1985 dollars (i.e., in real terms, excluding the effects of inflation). This is a substantial gain, and it is, moreover, more rapid than the growth of annual real earnings for men during this period.

On the other hand, the gain with respect to men's superior incomes has been uncertain and slow. It has been estimated that

fully employed women made 60 cents for every dollar men earned in 1959, 62 cents in 1980, and 68 cents in 1989. Recent statistics indicate that between 1979 and 1987, the wage gap between the sexes fell an average of 0.9 percent per year. At the rate the gap is closing, women would not achieve wage parity with men until the year 2020. Furthermore, considering the *total* economic situation of women, including the amount of leisure available to them, the proportion not married, and those with added financial responsibilities for children, Victor R. Fuchs doubts that the economic condition of women improved at all over the past quarter century.[4]

## WHY ARE WIVES AND MOTHERS IN THE WORK FORCE?

The rapid entry of wives and mothers into the labor force is such a profoundly important development that there is virtually no aspect of our national life that is not relevant to it. Furthermore, all the factors that we will discuss—demographic, technological, economic, social, and political—are deeply interwined. We will first list these factors and then take up the overall question: Are more women working now because they "need to," or because they "choose to"—or is this distinction so blurred as to be almost useless?

Important factors in the increased labor force participation of wives and mothers are as follows.

### Demographic Factors

The fact that women have fewer children to take care of today is invariably cited as a major factor in the increased labor force participation of women, including women who are mothers. Having one or two children implies very different demands on parental time than having four or five or (way back in our history) seven or eight. Furthermore, women now have increased

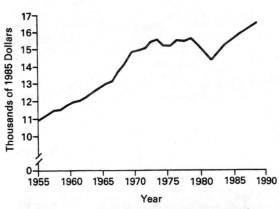

**FIGURE 11–5: Women's Annual Wage and Salary Income (1985 Dollars), 1955–1989**

Note: Data are median wage or salary income of year-round, full-time, civilian workers (14 years and over through 1978 and 15 years and over after 1978). Self-employed persons are excluded. Data beginning 1975 are not strictly comparable with earlier figures. Data are converted to 1985 dollars using the consumer price index for all urban consumers.
*Sources:* U.S. Department of Commerce, U.S. Department of Labor, and Council of Economic Advisers; authors.

control over conception and can better determine the timing of births. This means that women have the opportunity to increase their educational attainment and experience in the labor force before the birth of their first child. Labor force commitments begun early in this fashion can often continue after the birth of the first or later children. Furthermore, the increased life expectancies of women mean that there is far more time in a total life span apart from the period when dependent children must be raised. In both respects—reduced fertility and increased longevity—women have more years of life free of the responsibility of child rearing than women did earlier in history, even allowing for the special need for nurturing and caring for children in an increasingly complex world.

Although demographic factors are undoubtedly important, they can be somewhat overemphasized. For one thing, these factors are themselves products of other developments of a complicated socioeconomic and technical nature. (See especially the discussion of fertility reduction in Chapter 3.) More important perhaps is the fact that, although the trend toward increasing labor force participation by U.S. women generally goes along with the twentieth-century trend toward reduced fertility, the correspondence is by no means perfect. For example, women born between 1931 and 1935 (the parents-of-the-Boomers generation) had more children (3.2) over their lifetimes than did women born between 1871 and 1895 (2.9), yet twice as many of them worked on the average. Noting this fact, James Smith and Michael Ward suggest that "childbearing can easily be overrated as a cause of the long-run increase in women's work."[5]

### Technological Factors

As demographic factors overlap with other factors, so do technological developments, particularly with economic factors, which we list next. Ignoring this unavoidable overlap, we can specify at least three main technological changes that have contributed in some measure to the increased labor force participation of wives and mothers:

1. *Reduced housework:* Curves plotted over recent decades showing the increased percentages of households with various appliances—vacuum cleaners, washing machines, refrigerators, electric mixers, clothes dryers, dishwashers, and most recently microwaves—almost all point ever upward as the modern house or apartment becomes a miniature replica of a power-driven commercial factory. Add to this the vast number of fully prepared items—food, clothing, hardware—that can be bought in stores (as opposed to being produced at home), and you have a major reduction in the time required to keep house at any given level of homemaking quality. In principle, these advantages could be used to *increase* the quality of housekeeping, but most indications are that women find low-to-moderate levels of housekeeping quite acceptable today, and devote fewer hours to child care and housework than in the past.[6]

2. *Changes in the technology of production:* Changes in agricultural technology have made it possible to reduce the percentage of the U.S. labor force involved in agriculture to a nearly trivial 2 or 3 percent. Although women worked hard on the farms, their work was not usually counted as commercial production and they were not listed as members of the paid labor force. As the family farm declined over time, more women entered the "official" labor force.[7] In some respects even more significant has been the *general* shift of productive work from heavy manual labor (including agriculture, but also mining, construction, and much manufacturing) to service-sector industries. The very rapid increase of white-collar versus blue-collar employment has made a far greater number of jobs easily available to women.

3. *New products:* Technology not only makes new methods of production available

but also creates new products for consumers to demand and use. The interplay of technology and economics here is, of course, virtually complete. However classified, the abundance of new consumer goods continually acts to shift the accepted standard of living upward, providing both a pressure and an incentive for families to earn more income. The average level of real income per capita in the United States has probably risen over four times since the beginning of the twentieth century, but with the variety of new goods available for purchase, many families—even solidly middle-class families—may feel as much pressure to bring in additional dollars as did their much "poorer" forebears. And, as we have seen in Figure 11-3, dual-earner families do much better these days than single-earner families.

### Economic Factors

The new technologies of production and consumption just discussed can be thought of as part and parcel of a general process of economic growth that has characterized the U.S. economy since at least the mid-nineteenth century and has brought increasing abundance to the majority of our citizens. But why should increased abundance lead to greater labor force participation on the part of women? Shouldn't it work the other way?

In point of fact, greater abundance, when associated with an increase in the *husband's* real income, could lead to a decrease in women's labor force participation (but see the later discussion on pp. 189–190). Indeed, one of the factors used to explain the great increase in the number of working wives and mothers since the early 1970s was the fact that the real earnings of husbands were stagnant during this period, actually falling by around 10 percent between 1973 and 1981. But *women's* incomes are a different matter. Figure 11-5 shows a pattern of considerable real gains in women's earnings since 1955 (a pattern that basically extends back into the nineteenth

century), and most studies suggest that this has been the most important single factor in the growth of female employment. In 1987 the President's Council of Economic Advisers estimated that over half the growth of female employment between 1950 and 1980 was in response to real increases in women's wages. Smith and Ward calculate that a one percent increase in women's wages will increase their labor supply by eight-tenths of one percent.[8]

The strong impact of higher wages on women's labor force participation is believed to derive from two main factors: (1) directly, because higher wages make working in the marketplace more rewarding and attractive, and (2) indirectly, because higher wages have an equally important indirect effect on reducing fertility as the "opportunity cost" of raising children has increased (see Chapter 3, pp. 42–44).

There is, indeed, another indirect effect that could be added. Insofar as the chances of divorce and separation are increased by the financial independence of women, then increasing employment opportunities for women at reasonably good wages make it more likely that marital dissolutions will occur. To prepare for the *possibility* of such dissolutions, most women will feel it highly advisable to have careers, or at least some kinds of jobs, that they can turn to. In general, as University of Michigan researcher Gregory Duncan has shown, women have a greater chance than men of experiencing an event that will dramatically reduce their economic well-being.[9] Thus, the increased earnings of women, insofar as they make traumatic events like divorce more likely, also—and rather paradoxically—create a greater need for women to accumulate experience in the labor force.

Economics, then, plays a major role in the increasing employment of wives and mothers, both directly and indirectly. The question of whether we should primarily think of economic factors as creating new "options" for women or as intensifying their "need" to work, we defer for a moment.

## Social Factors

The issue of divorce, just mentioned, may have an important economic component, but that is certainly not its only, or perhaps even primary, component. In the last chapter, we spent considerable time discussing changes in attitudes and behavior that have occurred over a wide range of areas in recent decades. One of the most important areas of such change has been in attitudes toward the presence of wives and mothers in the labor force. At the beginning of this century, married women in the work force were at a tremendous disadvantage as compared not only to men but even to single women. Comparably qualified married women earned nearly one-third less income than single women. In the Depression of the 1930s, married women were often denied jobs because, in principle, they had husbands to depend on, and jobs were extremely scarce.

The post–World War II era has seen a major attitudinal change in this respect. Beginning with the publication in the United States in 1953 of *The Second Sex* by the French writer Simone de Beauvoir and, even more significantly, with the publication in 1963 of *The Feminine Mystique* by Betty Friedan, there was an outpouring of so-called **feminist** literature in this country. A central theme of this literature is that women had too long been confined to the home, and to second-class status in general, and that only by moving fully into the world of work on a basis of equality with men could women fulfill their full potentialities. Although subsequently there has been some pulling back from the stronger feminist positions, there was clearly a period when, for many women, to define themselves primarily as a "mother" or "homemaker" was considered a form of sexual treason. This was, in effect, a 180-degree reversal from the old position that "woman's place is in the home."

One place where this attitudinal change clearly had a major effect was in the area of education. In the previous chapter we noted the strong gains that women have made educationally during the postwar era. These gains, in themselves, are a definite factor in the increasing labor force participation of women given that, other things being equal, higher levels of education and labor force participation have always gone together. In addition to this quantitative factor, however, there has also been a qualitative change in educational objectives for women. Mary Lyon, the founder of Mount Holyoke College for women, said upon its opening in the nineteenth century, "Oh, how immensely important is the preparation of the Daughters of the land to be good mothers."[10] Today's education for women has moved light years away from such a concept, and basically is now considered in much the same perspective as education for men—as an investment, a way to make a better living and to improve the overall quality of their lives.

## Political Factors

These changes in social attitudes have also had effects on the political and institutional setting in which women seek employment in today's United States. Not every goal of the feminists has been achieved. The Equal Rights Amendment (ERA), a major goal of organizations like the National Organization for Women (NOW), despite its passage by Congress in 1972 and despite majority support for it by both men and women in public opinion polls, failed to secure ratification by the necessary number of state legislatures. Much of the opposition to ERA came, in fact, from women who argued that the amendment might reduce certain privileges women enjoyed, including the legal right to support from their husbands.

Nevertheless, both legislation and actions by the courts have gone at least part of the way toward reducing discrimination against women, and especially wives and mothers, in the workplace. The basic charter for antidiscrimination legislation in the United States in matters of both race and sex, is the Civil Rights Act of 1964. Title VII of this act states:

> It shall be an unlawful employment practice for an employer—(1) to fail or refuse to hire or to discharge any individual, or otherwise to discriminate against any individual with respect to his compensation, terms, conditions, or privileges of employment, because of such individual's race, color, religion, sex, or national origin; or (2) to limit, segregate, or classify his employees or applicants for employment in any way which would deprive or tend to deprive any individual of employment opportunities or otherwise adversely affect his status as employee, because of such individual's race, color, religion, sex, or national origin.

This and other antidiscrimination measures have made it more costly for employers to discriminate against women, and case studies show that the laws did have important effects in some occupations. (To take a small example, in the bartending trade, unions had excluded women on the grounds that serving drinks would corrupt them; with the enactment of antidiscrimination laws, women were free to become bartenders, and a number have done so.) Indeed, the basic premise of court action in many cases moved from discrimination against women to what some opponents considered discrimination *in favor of* women—that is, **affirmative action.** Such favorable discrimination has been justified on the grounds that given past and continuing discrimination against women, affirmative action is not only fair but also "promotes the hiring of the more competent and prevents the hiring of the less competent."[11]

Whether or not one accepts this argument, there is little question that the legal climate, along with general social attitudes, has changed in a way favorable to wives and mothers working as compared to times past. This, too, has contributed in some degree to women's increased labor force partici-

pation, at a minimum ratifying legally changes that were already beginning to occur for other reasons noted earlier.

## NECESSITY, OPTION, OR BOTH?

Betty Friedan, one of the originators of modern feminism, once explained women's working very simply. Women work "out of sheer economic necessity . . . because they must to survive." Is this a fruitful way of looking at the dramatic increase in the percentages of working women in recent years?

Certainly there is a good deal of anecdotal evidence to suggest that the dual-earner family, once considered a luxury, has become required by the conditions of modern American life. Having two incomes, it is said, has become a key factor in whether a family can afford to buy a home. In 1987 four out of five home buyers were two-income families, compared with half in 1976. Real interest rates have tended to be high in recent years. The percentage of income spent on gross rent increased significantly between 1960 and 1987 (from 19 to 28 percent). Meanwhile, the costs of educating children have skyrocketed, with college tuitions and other expenses rising far more rapidly than the general rate of inflation. This factor makes it especially important that families with children have a second earner.

There is also a certain amount of statistical evidence to support the **work-as-sheer-economic-necessity viewpoint.** We have mentioned the decline in the real earnings of men during the 1970s. During the 1980s, educational attainment declined among men aged 25 to 34, with serious implications for earnings, job stability, and job prospects. Between 1980 and 1987, the percentage of young men in this age group with only a high school education increased from 35 to 40 percent, while the number with a college degree decreased from 28 to 25 percent. Over this same period, the average real wages of 25- to 34-year-old men with a high school education declined from $21,000 to $19,700, a reflection in part of declining demand for their low-level skills. Frank Levy has calculated that, at current rates of productivity growth, today's 30-year-old man with only a high school diploma will reach a peak lifetime income of $26,300, which is $3,200 less than his father's peak income.[12]

Do low incomes for husbands mean that wives and mothers are more likely to be in the work force? The answer is complicated, as Table 11-1 and Figure 11-6 suggest. We will return to these numbers in a moment, but as far as the "sheer necessity" case is concerned, we can note that, in general, wives with children who are in the upper half of the income distribution (as calculated by their husband's incomes), are somewhat

less likely to be in the work force than wives in the lower half of the income distribution.

Finally, there is the previously mentioned **vulnerability of women** to events that may radically lower their economic position—widowhood and, especially, divorce and separation. Over the long run, it is argued, the risks undertaken by a woman who does not develop her skills and experience can be severe. It is a necessity to work today, because tomorrow she may be on her own, and if she has not worked in the past her earning power may be so limited as to reduce her to absolute poverty.

Although these arguments carry some weight, it is very doubtful that "sheer necessity"—interpreted in any way that implies basic needs for food, clothing, and

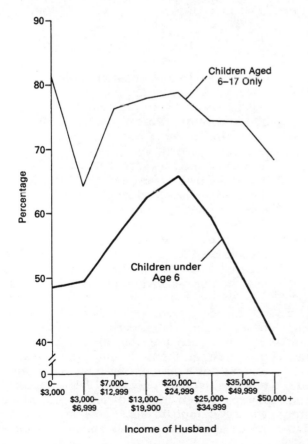

**FIGURE 11–6: Percentage of Wives Aged 16 to 34 with Children Who Are in the Labor Force, by Income of Husband, March 1988**

*Source:* Bureau of Labor Statistics, *Current Population Survey,* March 1988, unpublished tabulations.

**TABLE 11-1. Labor Force Participation Rates of Wives Under 35 with Children, by Their Husband's Income Position, 1960, 1977, 1988 (Percent)**

| | | Husband's Income Position: | | | |
| | Total | Bottom Quartile | Second Quartile | Third Quartile | Top Quartile |
| --- | --- | --- | --- | --- | --- |
| With Children under 6: | | | | | |
| 1960 | 18.1 | 25.1 | 21.2 | 16.9 | 10.7 |
| 1977 | 39.7 | 46.0 | 44.4 | 38.8 | 28.7 |
| 1988 | 56.8 | 53.7 | 64.2 | 55.7 | 40.1 |
| Relative percentage increase, 1960–1988 | 213.8 | 113.9 | 202.8 | 229.6 | 274.8 |
| With Children 6–17: | | | | | |
| 1960 | 41.5 | 49.6 | 51.9 | 39.3 | 28.7 |
| 1977 | 60.3 | 62.3 | 65.3 | 60.2 | 54.2 |
| 1988 | 75.6 | 74.9 | 78.5 | 74.4 | 68.5 |
| Relative percentage increase, 1960–1988 | 82.2 | 51.0 | 51.3 | 89.3 | 138.7 |

*Source:* Paul Ryscavage, Bureau of Labor Statistics, "More Working Wives Have Husbands with 'Above-Average' Incomes," *Monthly Labor Review, 102*(6), June 1979, Table 3, p. 41. Data for 1988 are from unpublished tabulations of the *Current Population Survey*, March 1988.

shelter (as suggested, for example, by Friedan's reference to survival)—is really helpful in explaining the dramatic movement of wives and mothers into the work force in recent years. There is the fundamental fact of historic rising real incomes to cope with. Families with the husband as the sole earner are today far richer in terms of real income than they were at the beginning of this century, and yet the percentage of wives now working has increased by a factor of 10 or more. If basic necessities were at stake, the trend should be a reverse of what it has actually been.

But even in recent years, the economic necessity argument tends to break down rather badly. Table 11-1 and Figure 11-6 certainly do not suggest any overwhelming tendency for wives with children to enter the work force because of the low incomes of their husbands. Indeed, the *increase* in labor force participation rates over the 1960–1988 period is much stronger for women with high-income husbands than for those with low-income husbands. This fact is confirmed by a recent study by Penn State researchers David Eggebeen and Alan Hawkins, who divide white married mothers into two groups: those whose husbands have "adequate" incomes (defined as more than twice the poverty level) and those whose husbands' incomes are below that level. They found that, between 1960 and 1980, there was a much greater increase in the percentages of working married mothers in the first group than in the second. They concluded: "Whereas providing basic necessities used to be the dominant motive for married mothers' labor-force participation, now standard-of-living preferences dominate."[13]

Indeed, when we consider the list of factors we discussed earlier as influencing women to enter the labor force, it is evident that most of them fit much more easily under a "**new options**" heading than under one of economic "necessity." Higher wages, fewer children, reduced housework, more attractive kinds of jobs, floods of new consumer goods, as well as an emphasis on women's equality, self-fulfillment, and so on—all these suggest the opening up of new opportunities for women far more than the harsh pressures of necessity and survival. Even the increased vulnerability of women to untoward events like divorce and separation has an element of "new options" in it. Without women's growing financial independence, it is at least doubtful that the modern trends toward increased marital dissolution, especially among white women, could long have been sustained.

Does this mean, then, that the "new options" view wins the debate hands down?

Hardly. In fact, this second view is, in many ways, as superficial as the first. It does not account for the fact that many working wives and mothers genuinely feel that it *is* necessary for them to work and that *not* working is not a realistic choice open to them. For one thing, when one looks at the basic demographics involved, the distinction between options and necessities becomes extremely cloudy. One of the reasons wives and mothers work today is that they have many fewer children than they had in the past. Now, although the decisions of women (and men) to reduce the numbers of their children may seem a simple exercise of a personal option, there is a deeper sense in which it represents objective necessity. Maintaining the fertility rates of the nineteenth century or even the recent Baby Boom period would very quickly prove untenable from a societal point of view. The U.S. population increased over sixtyfold in the last two centuries, mainly from natural increase; there is simply no way that such rates could be sustained over a future of any substantial length.

Given this reduced fertility, the alleviation of the burdens of housework, and also the enormous increase in women's life expectancies, it can be argued that the old option—devoting one's life to home, husband, and children—has essentially been destroyed. It is almost a case of being technologically unemployed. Women have been displaced from the career of homemaker-motherhood in much the same way as, say, farmers have been displaced from agriculture by labor-saving farm technologies. There is simply not a sufficient demand for the services that women almost exclusively used to provide. The new "necessity," psychologically speaking, is for women to enter the labor force and build lifetime careers.

This underlying psychological necessity is buttressed, of course, by the dangers of being left on one's own through divorce and separation, and also by the well-documented rise in consumer demands as real incomes rise over time. These increased needs do not have to be purely materialistic and selfish ones like brie, BMWs, and VCRs, but can also reflect a desire for one's children to have the best of everything, including, especially, very expensive college and even graduate educations.

In short, in a psychological if not a brute physical sense, "options" very quickly can become "needs," and both sides can well claim a partial victory in the debate.

## AREAS OF CONCERN

Although the foregoing analysis has a rather genial tone—it seems that everyone is essentially correct—it must not be thought that the vastly increased labor force participation of wives and mothers is without controversy. Three issues about working women stand out, each bringing forth radically different opinions and analyses:

### The Gender Gap

Why do women earn less than men, and what, if anything, should be done about it? If women have made advances in terms of wages and choices of occupation during recent decades, as they almost certainly have, why is it that occupational choices seem still to follow sexually segregated lines in many cases, and why do fully employed women still earn only about 68 percent of what their male counterparts earn? Many observers find it ironic that today's husbands by and large say that they approve of their wives working, and yet somehow women end up by and large with lower incomes than their approving husbands. Some have urged strong moves to alter this situation, as, for example, adopting so-called **comparable worth policies**—that is, evaluating a given job not in terms of what the marketplace determines but in terms of the nature of the demands of the job and of the qualifications and training needed to fulfill it.

How one feels about such policies, or about the affirmative action approach mentioned earlier, is likely to depend on one's analysis of the reasons for the **gender gap** in wages and occupations. As we have already suggested in passing, there is much disagreement on the analysis. Three broad approaches have been offered to explain the gender gap in recent years.

*First,* it has been argued that the gap primarily reflects the relative lack of education and labor force experience of women as compared to men. The increased labor force participation of women in recent decades had the effect of bringing many inexperienced and relatively less educated workers into the labor force, and this has prevented the average level of experience and education of working women from rising relatively to that of men. This analysis is basically hopeful in that, as more and more women enter the work force, there will come a time when women's work force experience will approach very closely that of men. Also, women's gains in education are already becoming a positive element in the picture. According to this view, held for example by Claudia Goldin of the University of Pennsylvania, even in the absence of any special government policies we should expect to see a substantial narrowing of the gender gap in the future.[14]

A *second,* and almost diametrically opposed, view is that of Barbara Bergmann of American University. Professor Bergmann argues that attributing the "wage gap to the fact that women have fewer years of expe-

rience than men" leaves "a great deal of the gap unaccounted for." She finds that the real difficulty is in sex segregation on the job. "Many jobs are considered 'men's jobs' or 'women's jobs,' " she writes, "and that is the key to women's poor position in the labor market." Because sex discrimination is at the heart of the matter, Bergmann has little faith that market forces will largely resolve the problem over time. She urges a twelve-point policy agenda, including measures to ensure that wage rates are based on "comparable duties."[15]

A *third* view is that the problem ultimately reflects the different family responsibilities of men and women. Victor R. Fuchs, writing in *Science,* states that "virtually everyone agrees" that "as long as parents are responsible for children and this responsibility is borne disproportionately by women, sex differences in the labor market are likely to persist."[16] This view is made explicit in analyses that deal with the so-called "mommy track"—a concept we shall consider later (see pp. 418–419). As far as closing the gender gap is concerned, this may be the most pessimistic analysis of all, unless, of course, the raising of children comes to be more proportionately shared between fathers and mothers. But are we, in fact, moving in that direction?

### Are Our Children Being Cared For Properly?

The last question here touches on two remaining areas of great concern. The first is the impact of the changing roles of mothers in the labor force on the rearing of the next generation. Of course, working mothers are only part of the picture here. As we have noted, there has also been a vast increase in the number of single-parent families as divorce, separation, and never-married mothers swell the ranks of children who must depend on only one of their two parents. If that single parent (whether father or mother, though most commonly the mother) also is in the labor force, the question of **child rearing** and child care becomes particularly intense. But even where the family is intact, the impact of mothers of young children, especially infants, taking on part-time and increasingly full-time work, on the well-being of their children is a major area of interest for us. For some observers, it is also a major area of concern for the future of our changing population. We will be devoting a large segment of Part IV of this book precisely to this question.

### How Are Men Adjusting to the New Roles of Women?

The other remaining question has to do with the impact of all these changes on American men. On the surface, the attitude of the American male to wives and mothers working has altered sharply over the past generation. The dual-earner household is an accepted fact of life, even when very young children are involved. To say this, however, is not to describe in any detailed way the role of the husband in that household—if, in fact, he is even *in* that household any more. Clearly, the previous question about the well-being of our children is no longer, if it ever was, exclusively a question about maternal child rearing. As women more and more enter the labor force, the role of the husband and father in the home automatically becomes an increasingly significant issue.

To this and other questions about the new roles of the American male, we will turn in our next chapter.

## SUMMARY

1. A distinction is increasingly made today between *sex* as a biological concept and *gender* as a construct that is socially and historically determined. Deep questions remain about the degree to which sexual factors (hormonal, structural, physiological, genetic) underlie gender roles (attitudes, behaviors, and expectations regarding masculinity and femininity), but the tendency today is to emphasize the importance of historical, social, and cultural factors in this interrelationship.

2. The changing gender role of women is nowhere more clearly seen than in the increased participation of wives and mothers in the U.S. labor force in recent decades. The dual-earner family is now more common than the husband-sole-provider family, and the majority of mothers of children, including very young children, are now in the labor force. Change in this area has been extremely rapid and represents a radical departure from the gender roles common earlier in this century.

3. Wives now make a substantial contribution to the total incomes of dual-earner families, although sole-earner wives clearly lag behind sole-earner husbands.

4. There are countless interrelated reasons for wives and mothers to be entering the work force in such large numbers. They include such factors as:

a. *Demographic:* Increased longevity and especially reduced fertility free women's time and energies for labor force participation as compared to times past.

b. *Technological:* Gadgetry and appliances that reduce housework, changes in the technology of production that lead to reduced employment in farming and manual labor and to increased service and white-collar employment, and the invention and introduction of countless new and desirable consumer goods all combine to make working outside the home easier and more desirable for women.

c. *Economic:* The increase in women's real wages over time may explain half or more of women's increased labor force participation, by making market work more attractive and also by raising the opportunity cost of having children.

d. *Social:* Changing attitudes about "women's place," including the growth of feminism and new views about women's education, have encouraged many women to give more importance to careers than in the past.

e. *Political:* Antidiscrimination measures have reduced at least some of the obstacles women face in their attempt to achieve parity with men in the labor market.

5. Evidence sometimes cited to show that wives and mothers are now working out of "sheer economic necessity" (e.g., stagnation in husbands' earnings in recent years, the high cost of housing and educating one's children, the economic vulnerability of women through divorce and separation), stands up rather weakly in the face of the great general economic gains over this century, which have made most families richer by any crude material standard. There is, however, a deep psychological need for women to work as the role of mother-homemaker has declined in lifetime importance, and as the rising standard of living and also the special economic vulnerability of women make added earnings and employment experience highly desired by many women.

6. Concerns about wives and mothers in the labor force include dissatisfaction about the gender gap in wages (due to women's work inexperience? discrimination? maternal responsibilities?) and worries about the way we are now raising our children and about the roles of husbands and fathers in our changing society.

## KEY CONCEPTS FOR REVIEW

Sex versus gender distinction

Masculine versus feminine roles

Husband–sole provider

Dual-earner families

Increase in employment of mothers of young children

Employment of black versus white wives

Increased earnings of women

Gender gap

Feminism

Reasons for women working
  demographic
  technological
  economic
  social
  political

"Necessity" to work versus "new options" (or both?)

Economic vulnerability of women

Affirmative action, comparable worth

Concerns about child rearing

## QUESTIONS FOR DISCUSSION

1. Historically, married women without children have always tended to have a higher labor force participation rate than married women with children. But this is no longer true. Explain when this change occurred and why it may have occurred.

2. It is said that our society needs women in the labor force in ever-increasing numbers because otherwise we will face serious future labor shortages. Why might such labor shortages develop in the future? Are there any sources of added labor, besides women, on whom the United States might draw in the future? Do you see any reason to feel concern about these anticipated shortages?

3. "Women have always been in the labor force—it's just that they never got paid for their work before." Discuss this statement. Insofar as you feel it to be true, what bearing does this have on the net impact of women's market work on the true value of total U.S. production?

4. Defend each of these propositions: Wives and mothers work today:

   (a) Out of sheer economic necessity

   (b) Largely because it is fulfilling materially and personally to have a career

   (c) Because the alternative of being a full-time homemaker for life is, for most women, no longer sufficiently satisfying

5. If there were an alternative (d) in question 4 in which you expressed a summary of your own view on the matter, how would you phrase that alternative?

6. Although most observers believe that, in one form or another, the dual-earner family is here to stay, almost everyone also believes that there is something unsatisfactory about the present arrangements for working wives and mothers. Discuss what some of these unsatisfactory things might be.

## NOTES

1. What new research suggests is that the sex of the parent who provides a gene makes a difference in the pattern of the inheritance of some diseases, as well as in fetal and adult development. See "First Impressions," *Scientific American*, October 1989, p. 34; "Prader Lacks Fader; Angelman Misses Mom?" *Science News*, 136, November 18, 1989, p. 324; and "New Evidence Supports Genomic Imprinting," *Science News, 139,* April 6, 1991, p. 213.

2. For background reading on the evolutionary view of the basis for gender roles, see Claire M. Renzetti and Daniel J. Curran, *Women, Men, and Society: The Sociology of Gender* (Boston: Allyn and Bacon, 1989).

3. Suzanne M. Bianchi and Daphne Spain, *American Women in Transition*, a Census Monograph Series (New York: Russell Sage Foundation, 1986), pp. 200–202.

4. Comparing 1959 with 1983, Victor Fuchs writes: "The women to men ratio of money income almost doubled, but women had less leisure while men had more, an increase in the proportion of women not married made more women dependent on their own income, and women's share of financial responsibility for children rose. The net result for women's access to goods, services, and leisure in comparison with that of men ranged from a decrease of 15 percent to an increase of 4 percent, depending on assumptions about income sharing within households." Victor R. Fuchs, "Sex Differences in Economic Well-Being," *Science, 232,* April 25, 1986, p. 459.

5. James P. Smith and Michael P. Ward, *Women's Wages and Work in the Twentieth Century*, report prepared for the National Institute of Child Health and Human Development, R-3119-NICHD (Santa Monica, Calif.: Rand Corporation, 1984), p. xix.

6. Research by John P. Robinson (see pp. 204–206), indicates that women do twice as much around the house as men, or about an additional 10 hours per week. To put this in historical context: 10 years ago, they did three times as much as men, and 20 years ago six times as much.

7. Smith and Ward, *Women's Wages*, p. xix.

8. *Economic Report of the President*, January 1987, p. 214; Smith and Ward, *Women's Wages*, p. xxi. This estimate by Smith and Ward includes the effect of higher wages for women in reducing family size.

9. Greg J. Duncan, "The Volatility of Family Income Over the Life Course," unpublished manuscript, April 1987.

10. Joellen Watson, "Higher Education for Women in the United States: A Historical Perspective," *Educational Studies, 8,* Summer 1977, pp. 133–146.

11. Barbara Bergmann, *The Economic Emergence of Women* (New York: Basic Books, 1986), p. 163. This conclusion follows from her contention that "discrimination is still very much a factor in current personnel decisions." In this case, affirmative action simply cancels out *dis*advantages women would otherwise face.

12. Frank Levy, "Incomes, Families, and Living Standards," in R. Litan, R. Lawrence, and C. Schultze, eds., *American Living Standards: Threats and Challenges*, Chap. 4 (Washington, D.C.: Brookings Institution, 1989).

13. Eggebeen and Hawkins are quoted in "White Married Mothers, Working for Better Life," *Wall Street Journal*, March 15, 1990.

14. Claudia Goldin, "Understanding the Gender Gap," *New Perspectives*, Fall 1985, pp. 9–13.

15. Bergmann, *Economic Emergence of Women*, p. 87, pp. 302–309.

16. Fuchs, "Sex Differences in Economic Well-Being," p. 464. For a further discussion of the economics of the gender gap, see "Symposium on Women in the Labor Market," *Journal of Economic Perspectives, 3* (1), Winter 1989, pp. 3–75.

# 12

# *The American Male— Liberated or on the Run?*

In discussing the gender division of our changing population in the last chapter, we noted that many scholars now emphasize the fact that gender roles are much more historically and socially conditioned than was previously believed. The sharp change in the role of women in the labor force during recent decades proves the point rather decisively. Women now are engaged in numerous occupations that were once thought to be the exclusive province of men. The very concept of married women, and especially married women with children, having "careers" (as opposed to the odd job here and there) is a new one, a product clearly of sociohistorical, not biological, change.

But what of American men? What do we see in the way of role changes in the male half (or nearly half) of our population? Are the changes as dramatic as in the case of American women?

The question is actually quite difficult to answer, if only for the reason that American men seem to be taking divergent paths at the present time. We find clear-cut evidence that, in response to the dramatic demographic changes of recent decades, some men have become more open-minded, caring, and responsive where women and children are concerned, while others have virtually abandoned ship, avoiding traditional commitments whenever possible.

Actually, the matter is even more complicated than this, since there is evidence that many American men feel a sharp ambivalence *within themselves* about the changes that have been occurring, particularly with respect to the role of women in the society. Nor can we take it for granted that the attitudes of American men have been shaped purely and simply in response to changes on the part of American women. It has been argued that a masculine revolt against the traditional male role in society may have occurred prior to the women's liberation movement, or at least simultaneously with it, and with an independent momentum of its own. What does it mean

to be "masculine" in the last decade of the twentieth century? An apparently easy question to answer in the days, say, of John Wayne, the matter is now surrounded by ambiguity and controversy.

We will only scratch the surface of these issues in the following pages since, if "women's studies" is a relatively young field, **"men's studies"** is a real newborn, hardly able to stand on its own feet yet.[1] Still, the questions raised here are of great importance and are likely to be with us increasingly in the decades ahead.

## HISTORICAL OVERVIEW OF MEN'S ROLES

If we start back with our colonial past, we can find a number of ways in which the masculine role in American society has been changing over time. We briefly note changes with respect to three aspects of that role: (1) nature of men's work, (2) relationships with women, and (3) fatherhood.

### Changing Nature of Men's Work

If the "Man the Hunter" view, mentioned in the previous chapter, was ever an accurate description of man's economic role in our evolutionary past, it would seem to have little relevance to most of American history. In colonial days, men did not typically wander far and wide over forest and savannah in search of game, but for the most part worked in agriculture or craft occupations in the vicinity of their homes, doing work that was usually distinguished from, but not very different from, work done by their wives (or, for that matter, their young children; see pp. 237–238).

With industrialization, men's work roles did become more sharply distinguishable from women's as the former moved from farm to factory, from rural area to city, and from home-centered to market-centered occupations, while the latter became, if anything, even more fully home-centered, raising children, cooking, preserving, washing, ironing, mending, and doing or supervising countless other household chores. In the course of the twentieth century, as we know, this distinction between men's and women's work roles became increasingly blurred. Like men before them, and especially during the past thirty years, women, too, took on jobs and in many cases developed substantial careers outside the home.

Meanwhile, the nature of men's work was also undergoing substantial transformation. If Man the Farmer was already substantially different from Man the Hunter, then Man the Factory Worker was even more different, and Man the Stockbroker or Computer Programmer or File Clerk was even further removed from his presumed ancestor. Except on our ever-receding frontier, the work that American men did during most of our history was becoming less physical, more sedentary, more indoors, less heroic, more intellectual, and often more routine than what was typically considered masculine work in our nation's past.

Traditional "masculinity" was preserved in the highly competitive nature of some occupations—stockbrokers do, in fact, describe the world around them as a "jungle"—but in large, faceless, bureaucratic organizations, whether private or public, male derring-do became increasingly irrelevant or even counterproductive. Only in the military, in sports, and, yes, in John Wayne's movies of the Old West did the heroic element survive—for the most part vicariously.

The realm of men's work has, in short, become **demasculinized**—not only because women have entered virtually all areas of men's work to some degree, but because the work itself has changed in character. Vicarious masculinity, as in the case of watching Sunday afternoon football, is, in essence, not a participation in, but an escape from, the world of work.

## Men's Relationships with Women

Whether men have always tended to dominate women in terms of political and social power and prestige is an interesting anthropological question. Were women more "equal" to men in primitive societies than in more developed societies? Did the Industrial Revolution tend to increase social and political discrimination against women (e.g., by separating off the market-oriented work of men more sharply from the domestic work of women), or was it really the beginning of an improvement in the status of women (e.g., note the increasing contributions of women to literature, art, and science from the nineteenth century on)?

Scholars differ on these deep issues,[2] but there can be little question that male attitudes toward women have altered sharply over the course of the United States' relatively brief history as a nation. The case of the woman suffrage movement is quite sufficient to prove the point. At the beginning of this century, only four states had granted women the right to vote. Incidentally, these states—Wyoming, Utah, Idaho, and Colorado—were all ones in which men greatly outnumbered women. In other states, women's interests were apparently to be expressed *for* them by their husbands, fathers, and brothers.[3]

Not that women were held in general disrespect by men at this time. Although the Nineteenth Amendment guaranteeing women the vote was not passed until 1920, the U.S. Congress had already, in 1914, gone on record affirming that "the service rendered the United States by the American mother is the greatest source of the country's strength and inspiration." Thus, although not yet considered worthy of, or having any real need for, the vote, women certainly deserved to have a special celebration (**Mother's Day**) in their honor.[4]

That there was a certain ambiguity in the attitude of American men toward women at this time should not surprise us. The truth is that although enormous changes in attitude have taken place in recent years, the degree of ambivalence of American men in their relationships with women may well have increased. On the one hand, there is no question that the vast majority of American men now believe that women should have political, social, and economic opportunities on a basis of equality with men. Undoubtedly gender discrimination still exists, but, as far as explicit policy is concerned, the cutting issue at the end of the 1980s was not equal versus unequal opportunity, but equal opportunity versus affirmative action. The whole battleground had shifted from denial of rights and opportunities to the possibility of making up for past discrimination by favoring women over men, at least in certain contexts.

On the other hand, it can be argued that the respect given women in earlier days has actually been on the wane. The increasingly explicit depiction of women as sex objects through the once rather shocking but now seemingly bland pages of *Playboy*, followed by more lurid publications, X-rated films, and other forms of pornography, has not suggested any growing appreciation of the human qualities of women. From Mother's Day to **Playmate of the Month** was hardly an elevation of women and, by many, was considered a degradation of their status.

At the same time, the new sexual freedom was putting great stress on men's concepts of themselves. Whether the more forthright, initiative-taking attitude of women was a factor in the apparent growth of male (and female) homosexuality is a matter of dispute.[5] What is more demonstrable is that men were now put on notice that their sexual behavior was to be judged rather coolly in performance terms. Intimate relations between the sexes could, for men, become a kind of physical and psychological stress test.

This threat to the male's sense of his own masculinity may, in turn, have led some men to put excessive emphasis on a *macho* approach to life. As is often noted, there was an extraordinary increase in violence, and especially in the explicit description of violence, in movies and television in the last two decades. This increase in explicit *machismo* took place at the same time that it became increasingly accepted that men should be allowed to show a tender—even tearful!—reaction to emotional events both on and off screen. The simultaneous appeal of Rambo and sensitive Ted Kramer in *Kramer versus Kramer* indicates the ambiguity of the concept of masculinity in the present-day United States. We shall return to this point in a moment.

### Men's Role as Fathers

If men's roles in the workplace and in relation to women have been changing over the past two centuries, so also has their role in relation to children. Sociologist Joseph H. Pleck has described three distinct phases in the characteristic American conception of fatherhood over this period.

*Phase 1: Eighteenth and Early Nineteenth Century—Father as Moral Overseer.* Although colonial mothers did most of the actual caretaking of their children, colonial fathers were believed to have more influence on the young, particularly with respect to moral upbringing. An early-nineteenth-century poem suggests the order of things:

> The father gives his kind command,
> The mother joins, approves;
> The children all attentive stand,
> Then each obedient moves.

At this time, then, it is the father, more than the mother, who is the teacher of the young and who is considered to have major responsibilities for their character development, for preparing sons for their occupations, and for approving or disapproving the courtships and marriages of their daughters. During this period, the father's work most often kept him in or near the home, so that he could fulfill these responsibilities. Even when children left home, most of their letters were written to their fathers rather than their mothers.

***Phase 2: Early Nineteenth to Mid-Twentieth Centuries—Father as Distant Breadwinner.*** During this time, according to Pleck, "a gradual and steady shift toward a greater role for the mother, and a decreased and more indirect role for the father is clear and unmistakable." Whereas earlier men were considered to have superior reasoning powers compared to women (and thus to be preferable guides for the young), now the increasingly common view was that women, because of their greater "purity" and unselfish natures, were the more desirable influence, particularly for the very young. At this time—again in contrast to the earlier period when fathers were often awarded child custody in the few divorce cases that occurred—the presumption came to be that children should remain with their mothers when husband and wife separated. This, of course, was the time when the father's work took him increasingly away from the home. He had a duty to "support" the family, but his direct contact with his children, his knowledge of what was actually going on in the family, and his authority within the domestic sphere were all substantially attenuated.

***Phase 3: 1940–1965—Father as a Sex-Role Model.*** Although the distant breadwinner model of fatherhood persisted during this next period (and remains definitely alive even today), in the period during and after World War II, there was a concern both (a) that maternal influences on children had become excessive and (b) that the absence of the father—a common occurrence, of course, during the war itself—could have deleterious effects on children. Boys, particularly, were seen as endangered by "momworship" or "smotherhood"; they

needed a father so as to have a role model for developing a proper male identity. Girls were also believed to need the father's instruction. The father, indeed, was believed to be the primary transmitter of sex roles for both sons and daughters. In this period, the father was still largely absent from the home except on weekends, but his example was considered to be important, and a somewhat greater involvement with his children was generally encouraged.

***Present Implications.*** What about the quarter century since 1965? Pleck suggests that although the father-breadwinner model was still dominant in the 1980s, the other models—moral overseer and sex-role model—were present as well and, indeed, were being greatly extended. One possibility is the much talked about "**new father**"—"he is present at birth; he is involved with his children as infants, not just when they are older; he participates in the actual day-to-day work of child care, and not just play; he is involved with his daughters as much as his sons."[6]

This description makes it clear that the ambiguities we noticed with respect to the roles of American men today are by no means confined to the workplace or to relationships with women. Indeed, it may be in the area of fatherhood that the greatest ambiguity of all has emerged. For if the foregoing is an accurate description of what Americans increasingly believe the role of the father to be, what are we to make of the fact that the late twentieth century has seen, through separation, divorce, and female-headed families, an almost unprecedented separation of fathers from their natural children? In many households, the role of the father is all too clear. He is not there!

## WHO IS LIBERATING WHOM?

In focusing on the state of affairs at the end of the 1980s, we face two obvious facts: that important changes in our concepts of masculinity have been taking place, but that there is a great ambiguity in all these new concepts. We also face an interesting question: *Why* have men been changing during recent decades?

Even here, there are two different theories. The more commonly accepted theory is that insofar as our concept of "masculinity" has been freed from its traditional moorings, it is a direct consequence of changes in the roles, behavior, and attitudes of women. If men have become "liberated," it is, in fact, because women's liberation produced this reaction. Sociologist Michael S. Kimmel puts it this way:

> Research suggests that although both masculinity and femininity are socially constructed within a historical context of gender relations, definitions of masculinity are historically reactive to changing definitions of femininity.

Changing definitions of femininity may, in turn, be related to underlying demographic changes. Because of lowered fertility, for example, women may be able to take a more active participation in the labor force and in the public sphere generally. As they do this, they develop a new ideology (say, feminism) which justifies these changes and which then prompts necessary adjustments on the part of men.

This view also suggests that men generally are reluctant to make these necessary adjustments. Kimmel goes on:

> Masculine "reactivity" has a political component as well, not unnoticed by feminist scholars; in a society based upon the institutional power of men over women, men benefit from inherited definitions of masculinity and femininity and would be unlikely to call them into question.

In other words, not only do changes in men's concepts of themselves occur largely in reaction to developments on the part of women, but these changes are accepted only grudgingly. This is for the simple reason that men have characteristically held the upper hand in the "power relations" between the sexes and are reluctant to yield their historic advantages.[7]

A quite different approach is suggested by the feminist writer Barbara Ehrenreich. She suggests that changes in men's attitudes in the post–World War II period were, at least initially, generated by a *male* rebellion against the traditional roles assigned to men by modern society. There was the critique of the "organization man," of the dehumanizing aspects of work in an impersonal, bureaucratic economy. There was the critique of monogamy celebrated from the first issue of *Playboy* (1953), through the Beat Generation of the late 1950s and early 1960s, and on to the communal living arrangements of the rebellious youth of the late 1960s. Writes Ehrenreich:

> The gray flannel rebel resented his job. The playboy resisted marriage. The short-lived apotheosis of the male rebellion, the Beat, rejected both job and marriage. In the Beat, the two strands of male protest—one directed against the white collar work world and the other against the suburbanized family life that work was supposed to support—come together in the first all-out critique of American consumer culture.

Although the Beat writers and their beatnik and hippie successors soon lost popularity, the male rebellion continued, according to Ehrenreich, with new concerns about the damage the traditional male breadwinner role was doing to men—to their hearts in particular. Men were dying much younger than women, many from coronary heart disease. Stress was obviously an important factor. Men with "type A" personalities who were excessively devoted to achievement, competition, and aggression, who were always under pressure, always feeling their responsibilities keenly—who possessed the whole catalogue of what had traditionally been considered "masculine" values—were particularly at risk. Excessive masculinity was apparently not only burdensome for women to bear, but a direct hazard to men's health.

Add to this a growing sense that masculine virtues—for example, heroism in war—seemed much less appropriate in the nuclear age, and that men (as well as women) should be free to realize their own personal potentialities even if it meant abandoning responsibilities to others—and you have the basis for a *male* rejection of the traditional masculine roles of breadwinner, husband, and father. That the feminist movement ratified this male role rejection—essentially, by redefining femininity to include a much greater independence of men than in the past—could be interpreted then as simply giving momentum to a drive already well underway. Indeed, *anti*feminist women, like those who led the fight against the Equal Rights Amendment (ERA), made the major argument that ERA would allow men to escape their responsibilities to women, an escape that many men were already far too willing to take advantage of.[8]

Thus, underlying the ambiguities in today's concept of masculinity in the United States we have this tantalizing question: Have American men been changing because the new roles of women as equal partners in work and play have stimulated, or effectively forced, such changes upon them, leading them to be more sensitive, responsive, and fair-minded than in their historic roles? *or* Have American men been all too ready to abandon their historic responsibilities, secretly welcoming women's liberation as providing an opportunity to relax and enjoy life and let women have the stress (and coronaries) if that is what they seem to want?

## HOW MUCH HAS CHANGED IN PRACTICE?

Each view undoubtedly contains at least a small kernel of truth. But how small, or large? The only real hints we can get to an answer lie not in broad sociological generalizations but in practical changes in the way men are now conducting their day-to-day lives. There are some obvious indicators: changes in the character and quantity of work men do on the job; changes in their attitudes toward "feminine" tasks like housework and child care; changes in their sense of family obligations, and to their children in particular. How big have the actual changes been?

### Changes on the Job Front

Obviously, in one clear sense, the traditional breadwinner role of the American male has changed: he is no longer characteristically the *sole* breadwinner. It is also clear that, when asked, the characteristic American male approves of married women working outside the home. The change in attitude as reflected in polls over the last half century is summarized in the January 1987 Report of the President's Council of Economic Advisers:

> Questions concerning women appeared in at least six polls in the 1930s, and fewer than 20% of the respondents in any of the polls approved of married women working outside the home. In a 1960 national survey, slightly more than one-third of husbands had either favorable or qualifiedly favorable attitudes towards their wives working. By the 1980s, however, the overwhelming proportion—nearly two-thirds—of both men and women reported that it is less important for a wife to help her husband's career than to have one of her own.[9]

To this picture of male adjustment to changing times, we must, however, add a number of complicating considerations:

1. If men have adjusted to being less than the sole breadwinner, they appear to have adjusted much less well to being less than the *primary* breadwinner. Where women earn more than their husbands do, serious marital problems often arise. "It's a fact that the higher the woman's earnings,

the higher the chance of divorce," according to Harvard University economist David E. Bloom. "We don't know exactly why."[10] Although some of this increase in marital disruption almost certainly reflects the changed attitudes of the higher earning wives—they are much less economically dependent on their husbands than are women with low or no incomes—still, it is widely believed that many men find the loss of authority and prestige they suffer from their lesser economic status hard to accept.

2. There is at least some evidence that, quite apart from the size of the wife's earnings, married men suffer a certain amount of emotional damage when their wives enter the work force. Ronald C. Kessler and James A. McRae, Jr., of the University of Michigan conclude on the basis of a large national survey that there is "a significant positive relationship between spouse's employment and psychological distress among married men in this country." (They also find that the mental health of married women is *improved* when they are employed outside the home.) Although they admit that this finding may alter over time, these researchers conclude that, in the early 1980s, many men were suffering psychologically in consequence of their wives' employment, and that much of the effect was due to the violation of traditional sex-role orientations.[11]

3. Although the matter is complicated by the tendency of men to retire earlier in their lives (see Chapter 7), there is fairly clear evidence that, as women have been devoting increasing numbers of hours to work outside the home, men have been devoting less to such work. Between 1959 and 1983, it is estimated that the average number of hours an American male in the 25-to-64 age group spent each year in gainful employment fell from 1,875 to 1,667, or by about 11 percent. Meanwhile, the number of hours women were devoting to gainful employment rose from 572 to 979, or by over 70 percent.[12] Do men approve of

their wives working simply because it has made life easier for them? We will return to this question in a moment.

4. The de facto segregation of types of jobs by gender—which Barbara Bergmann of American University calls "the key to women's poor position in the labor force"—has changed much more for women in recent decades than for men. That is to say, women have, in general, found it desirable to enter stereotypically "male occupations," while men have been more reluctant to enter "female occupations."

In an interesting study, sociologist Christine L. Williams of the University of Texas compared women in the Marines (a classic "male" occupation) with men in nursing (a similarly classic "female" occupation). She found that, although the men were in many ways more "welcome" in nursing than women were in the Marines (Recall their slogan—"We are looking for a few good *men!*"), nevertheless the male nurses were very worried about establishing their "masculinity" in this uncharacteristic occupation. By contrast, the women in the Marines were quite unconcerned about proving that they were still "feminine":

> Male nurses go to great lengths to carve a special niche for themselves within nursing that they then define as masculine; preserving their masculinity *requires* them distancing themselves from women. Women in the Marine Corps feel they could maintain their femininity even in a foxhole alongside the male "grunts." For the women I interviewed, femininity was not "role defined" in the way that masculinity was for the male nurses.[13]

Williams suggests that this difference between the sexes derives from the fact that infant boys and girls are both primarily brought up by their mothers. Thus, girls have little difficulty establishing gender identification, whereas for boys and adult men there is a need to renounce and separate themselves from this early feminine identification. Proving that they are "masculine" becomes for men an important, difficult, and in many ways lifelong occupation.

Whether this theory is correct or not, the finding that men may have considerable difficulty in adjusting to what they consider "feminine" occupations is an important one. It bears directly on our next question: What has been happening in the domestic sphere, where gender distinctions traditionally have been very strong?

## Male Participation in Housework

Women are spending more hours in the work force, men somewhat fewer hours. Does this mean that men are now spending more time in relieving women of their traditional duties of housework and child care? This question is easier to ask than to answer, as the following studies show.

In the same study in which he noted the decline in men's labor force hours (market work), Victor R. Fuchs calculated changes in men's and women's contributions to housework and child care. These calculations, based on computer tapes of the Censuses of Population and Current Population Surveys, are shown in Table 12-1.

These numbers suggest that during this 24-year period, women's total hours of work (market and home) increased by about 5 percent, whereas men's total hours of work fell by about 8 percent. Since, according to these numbers, men worked more than women in the earlier period, this change brought the sexes to approximate parity in

the early 1980s. From our immediate point of view, however, the interesting thing to note is that although the hours women devoted to housework plus child care fell substantially (by 14 percent), the hours men devoted to housework plus child care remained virtually unchanged, increasing by only *one hour* per year.

In connection with her own survey, sociologist Arlie Hochschild summarized a number of previous studies of the housework and child care contributions of men and women.[14] Although early studies found that husbands of working wives did little more at home than husbands of homemaking housewives, studies during the late 1970s and 1980s showed "mixed findings." A 1977 study from the University of Michigan found that women were averaging 2.2 hours more of total work per week than men. A 1985 Boston University study found that working married mothers averaged 85 hours of total work a week, compared to married fathers' average of 66 hours—a leisure gap of 19 hours a week. A variety of further studies found little or no added contribution to housework or child care by husbands when their wives went to work. On the other hand, a later University of Michigan study found that "women work only a tiny bit longer than men each day." Men were not doing more in the home; it was simply that women were doing less.

Hochschild's own research made her dubious of this last finding. Her results, based on interviews with 50 two-job couples, indicate that the working wives were putting

**TABLE 12-1.    Hours of Work, Ages 24 to 64, by Sex, 1959 and 1983**

|  | *1959* | | *1983* | | *Women/Men Ratio* | |
|---|---|---|---|---|---|---|
|  | *Women* | *Men* | *Women* | *Men* | *1959* | *1983* |
| Hours of work (annual) |  |  |  |  |  |  |
| Market | 572 | 1,875 | 929 | 1,667 | 0.30 | 0.56 |
| Housework | 1,423 | 542 | 1,252 | 560 | 2.62 | 2.24 |
| Child care | 266 | 76 | 201 | 59 | 3.52 | 3.41 |
| Total | 2,261 | 2,493 | 2,383 | 2,287 | 0.91 | 1.04 |

*Source:* Victor R. Fuchs, "Sex Differences in Economic Well-Being," *Science* 232, April 25, 1986, p. 460. Reprinted by permission.

in substantially more total work time than their husbands. Using the phrase "second shift" to refer to the job of homemaking which is added on to a first shift of regular employment, she concluded:

> We found that 18 percent of men shared the second shift in the sense of doing half of the [domestic] tasks. . . . These 18 percent didn't necessarily do half of the *same* tasks as their wives did; they did half of the tasks in each category overall (these 18 percent did 45 to 55 percent; none did more); 21 percent did a moderate amount (between 30 and 45 percent); and 61 percent did little (between 30 percent and none).[15]

The reference to the fact that men didn't do the same domestic work as women is in line with a frequent complaint of feminist writers that when men *do* do things around the house, they usually choose the pleasant ones (say, playing with the baby rather than vacuuming or changing diapers or, most difficult, managing and planning domestic activities). Hochschild also suggests that when women earn more than their husbands, they often work particularly hard at home, in effect "making up" to their husbands for doing "too well" in their outside employment.

A survey based on diary reporting from a representative sample of Americans gives quite different results from those of Hochschild.[16] Table 12-2 and Figure 12-1 describe a picture in which American women in all age groups in the 18-to-64 range *gained* in leisure time between 1965 and 1985. Men also gained on the average, although vir-

**TABLE 12-2.  Free Time Per Week By Selected Demographic Characteristics**

|  | Men | | | Women | | |
|---|---|---|---|---|---|---|
|  | 1985 | 1975 | 1965 | 1985 | 1975 | 1965 |
| All, 18–64 | 40 | 38 | 40 | 39 | 38 | 34 |
| Age: |  |  |  |  |  |  |
|   18–35 | 43 | 42 | 43 | 39 | 40 | 36 |
|   36–50 | 34 | 33 | 34 | 35 | 34 | 32 |
|   51–64 | 44 | 40 | 36 | 44 | 39 | 35 |
| Marital Status: |  |  |  |  |  |  |
|   Married | 37 | 37 | 37 | 37 | 37 | 35 |
|   Not married | 48 | 48 | 45 | 43 | 42 | 32 |
| Children at home: |  |  |  |  |  |  |
|   None | 43 | 42 | 43 | 41 | 40 | 35 |
|   One or more aged 5 or older | 39 | 33 | 35 | 38 | 35 | 33 |
|   One or more under age 5 | 31 | 41 | 35 | 34 | 38 | 34 |
| Employed |  |  |  |  |  |  |
|   No | 56 | 55 | 63 | 47 | 44 | 40 |
|   Yes (10+ hours per week) | 36 | 36 | 33 | 34 | 31 | 27 |
| Day of the week: |  |  |  |  |  |  |
|   Monday | 4.9 | 5.4 | 4.6 | 5.1 | 5.5 | 3.4 |
|   Tuesday | 5.0 | 4.8 | 5.0 | 5.0 | 5.3 | 4.2 |
|   Wednesday | 5.3 | 4.8 | 5.2 | 5.3 | 4.4 | 4.3 |
|   Thursday | 5.0 | 4.1 | 5.3 | 5.1 | 5.4 | 4.7 |
|   Friday | 5.0 | 4.7 | 5.1 | 5.0 | 4.8 | 4.4 |
|   Saturday | 7.0 | 6.2 | 6.4 | 6.3 | 5.6 | 5.9 |
|   Sunday | 8.0 | 8.4 | 8.6 | 7.4 | 6.9 | 7.3 |

*Source:* Americans' Use of Time Project, Survey Research Center, University of Maryland, 1985 as reported in John P. Robinson "Time's Up," *American Demographics*, July 1989. Copyright American Demographics 1989. Reprinted by permission.

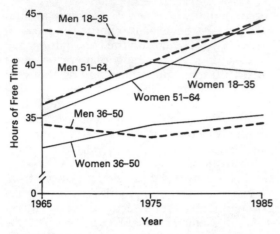

**FIGURE 12–1: Hours of Free Time Per Week, By Sex and Age, 1965, 1975, and 1985**

*Source:* This chart is based on data presented in Table 12-2.

tually all this gain was in the 51-to-64 age group, reflecting the tendency toward earlier retirement noted in previous chapters. The reasons for the *general* increase in leisure time are a shorter work week for most employed persons, fewer children and fewer households with any children, and people spending more of their lives unmarried. Looking specifically at women with one or more children under age 5 at home as compared with men in the same situation, this study finds that there was no change between 1965 and 1985 in the hours of leisure such women enjoyed (34 hours a week), but that the fathers involved experienced a *decrease* in leisure time over this period and in 1985 actually had *three fewer hours* (31 hours) of leisure per week than their female counterparts. Taking all age groups together, men were judged to have 40 hours of free time a week, compared with 39 hours for women.

Clearly, only modest conclusions can be drawn from these conflicting studies. It is certain that women are now giving less time to home and child care than in the past and that men are working less outside the home

than previously. It is also fairly certain that such added time, if any, men are giving to home and child care is less than the reduced time given by women to these occupations. Whether working mothers of young children are, on average, working many more hours than their husbands or, conceivably, slightly fewer hours, cannot at this point be satisfactorily determined.

## Men's Discharge of Paternal Responsibilities

The confusion of statistics we face in trying to apportion men's versus women's contributions to domestic responsibilities also unavoidably affects our judgment about late-twentieth-century American men in their role as fathers. There are, however, other statistics we can turn to which are very revealing about current paternal attitudes. These statistics strongly suggest that the "new father"—the present-at-birth, diaper-changing, bath-giving, lover-equally-of-both-daughters-and-sons, emotionally expressive, model-and-guide father—is certainly not universal in the United States of the late twentieth century.

We have already discussed the growing phenomenon of female-headed households in recent decades (pp. 170–171). In Table 12-3, we present estimates of the percentages of families with children under 18 that are maintained by the mother only. In this

**TABLE 12-3. One-Parent Family Groups Maintained by Mother (Excluding Widows), 1970–1988**

| *Percentage of All Families with Children under 18* | | | |
|---|---|---|---|
| | *1970* | *1980* | *1988* |
| Total | 9.2 | 17.2 | 22.2 |
| Never married | 0.8 | 3.3 | 7.9 |
| Spouse absent | 4.6 | 5.4 | 5.2 |
| Separated | 3.2 | 4.6 | 4.4 |
| Divorced | 3.7 | 8.5 | 9.1 |

*Source:* U.S. Bureau of the Census. *Current Population Reports,* Series P-20, No. 433, Table 9.

particular table we exclude widows so that the percentages bear more particularly on changes in men's attitudes toward family responsibilities. We see how, through the increase in divorce, separation, and never-married mothers, the percentages of families with only the biological mother present increased by nearly two and a half times between 1970 and 1988.

In Table 12-4, we examine the distribution of children among different types of households and how it has changed between 1981 and 1988. Here we divide the distribution of children into two main categories: (1) those brought up in households where the biological father is present and (2) those brought up in households where he is absent. What is striking here is the degree to which biological fathers have been separating themselves from their natural children. *In 1988, 34 percent of American children, or slightly over one third, were being brought up in homes without their natural fathers present.* This was up from the already very high number of 30 percent in 1981.

These estimates do not imply, of course, that stepfathering or other forms of fathering are necessarily or even usually inferior to fathering by a biological parent. They do reflect seriously, however, on the attitudes that many American men today bring to the responsibility of fatherhood. Whoever happened to be the initiator of the divorce, separation, or conception "without benefit of clergy," many of today's fathers are physically separated from their children and have little opportunity to practice the "new fatherhood" that some sociologists and psychologists suggest is today's ideal.

Furthermore, there is additional evidence to suggest that, in at least a good number of these cases of physical separation, the absent father is reluctant to sustain the financial and/or emotional commitments that his children would seem to warrant. A Census Bureau study found that in 1987, 59 percent of mothers with children present were awarded child support by the courts from the absent fathers. Of those due pay-

**TABLE 12-4. Distribution of U.S. Children Under 18 By Family Living Arrangements, 1981 and 1988**

|  | 1981 | 1988 |
|---|---|---|
| Household where biological father is present: | | |
| Total (percentage) | 71% | 66% |
|   Both biological parents | 67 | 60 |
|   Father only | 2 | 3 |
|   Father-stepmother | 2 | 3 |
| Household where biological father is absent: | | |
| Total (percentage) | 30% | 34% |
|   Mother only | 18 | 21 |
|   Mother-stepfather | 7 | 8 |
|   Adoptive parents | 2 | 2 |
|   Grandparents or other relatives | 2 | 2 |
|   Foster parents, other nonrelatives or in group quarters | 1 | 1 |

Percentage distribution may not total 100 due to rounding.

*Source:* Report 101-356, Select Committee on Children, Youth, and Families, U.S. House of Representatives, p. 51; adapted by the authors.

ment in 1987, only half the women received the full amount due, one-quarter received less, and one-quarter (24 percent) received nothing at all. The average (mean) amount of annual child support by those who actually received anything was $2,710 in 1987 dollars. In total, including payments due 1.1 million women who received nothing, actual child support payments amounted to 68.5 percent of the total due. In the case of never-married women, the award rate was very low (20 percent) and the poverty rate was very high. Indeed, for the group of families with absent fathers as a whole, the poverty rate was a high 34 percent.[17]

This failure of many absent fathers to meet even the minimum financial requirements of their children has been called the nation's "greatest form of lawlessness." It should be noted, however, that these Census Bureau estimates have not been universally accepted. Critics like Sanford Braver of Arizona State University and Charlene Depner, director of the Child Custody Study at Stanford University, point out that these estimates were based on interviews with the mothers involved. Interviews with absent fathers produce much higher estimates of payments made. Many such fathers, indeed, feel that the courts are highly prejudiced against men in child support cases. Groups like Concerned Fathers and FERICS (Fair and Equal Responsibilities in Child Support Laws) have been formed to protest what they conceive to be the gender bias favoring women and impoverishing men.

There is little doubt, however, that so-called "deadbeat Dads" do exist. In 1989 the state of Florida actually began publishing the names of the worst offenders in the newspapers and circulating their pictures to the general public. Other states have passed laws to garnishee wages of nonpaying fathers, and in 1989 Congress considered legislation to require all states to develop similar laws.

Furthermore—although again the extent of the neglect is hard to determine—there is little question that many of these absent fathers show very little interest in the emotional needs of their children. Studies indicate that nearly half the children in mother-headed households have not seen their fathers during the year preceding the study. As the separation persists, contact tends to become less and less frequent. University of Pennsylvania sociologist Frank Furstenberg suggests that the country is developing a dual pattern in which "good dads" and "bad dads" are both on the increase. In an Urban Institute study on the changing American family, he contrasts the "vogue" of fatherhood (fathers attending childbirth classes, being in the delivery room, reading fathers' "self-help" books, and the like) with the unwillingness of many young men to marry girls who are pregnant with their children, the poor performance of absent fathers on child support payments, and the failure of some fathers to contact their children for weeks, months, even years on end. At the same time that the United

States seems to be discovering the importance of fatherhood, the number of men (including the growing number of single men who choose not to marry at all) fleeing from a serious commitment to fatherhood is on the increase.

A coincidental development? Not according to Furstenberg, who writes: "The simultaneous appearance of the good father and the bad father are two sides of the same cultural complex." Both are due to the "the breakdown of the good-provider role for men." And this raises the ominous possibility that the "bifurcation of fatherhood could continue unabated" into the future.[18]

## CAN DIVERGENT PATHS CONVERGE?

In a broad sense, gender roles in the United States have been changing in what can be described as two contrasting ways. From one point of view, it can be stressed that we have moved a long way (though obviously not completely) from a rigid sexual division of labor in the society, in which women were the dependent and unequal members, to one in which sex and gender have become far less determinant with respect to role, opportunity, and power, and in which men and women are viewed as equals and considered more in *human* than in purely sexual terms.

From a quite different point of view, it can be argued that what has happened is a transformation of an essentially *complementary* relationship between men and women, each having his or her role to fulfill, each supporting the other though in different ways, into an essentially *competitive* relationship, with both sexes trying to fill the same socioeconomic and psychological space, and with resulting antagonism, hostility, and flight from commitment afflicting both sexes.

For those who wish to carry the present changes still further, the ideal future is often represented in terms of a kind of generalized **androgyny.** Gender roles disappear;

men and women equally have careers; there is no sex stratification in the labor market, nor is there any at home, where housework and child care are shared equally on the average; in many cases, where the wife's career is the more serious, the husband does far more of the domestic work, or, of course, vice versa. In such a world men often cry, and women frequently show themselves to be stoic. Because of the feminization of men, violence abates in personal lives, on the city streets, and in the relations of nations. Because of the masculinization of women, sports are the province of women quite as much as men; indeed, coed sports (as in mixed doubles in tennis) become by far the most common athletic activity. Homosexual, lesbian, and bisexual relationships are fully accepted by all as a matter of *human* sexual preference. Children are often brought up in nonheterosexual households, with "fathering"—whether by a natural father, a stepfather, a surrogate father, or a lesbian "father"—being considered a natural and highly important vocation.

For those who fear the extension of present trends into such an androgynous future, many of the developments just described would be considered anathema. Furthermore, they will argue that such a future is unlikely to occur. For the move in such a direction would, they claim, be accompanied by a simultaneous rejection of what was happening, a backlash that is already highly visible and could be expected to become much worse. Men would refuse to accept the docile, compliant roles assigned to them. Women are already increasingly critical of men. A 1990 Roper Organization poll found a substantial increase over the past 20 years in the percentage of women who considered men "basically selfish and self-centered."[19] The ancient "war of the sexes," ameliorated historically by the need of each sex for the other—their basic complementarity—would intensify. Marriages would collapse even more than at present. Men would go off by themselves—some to homosexual unions, some to highly macho patterns of life,

fostering the abuse and degradation of women. Children would be frequently abandoned and forgotten. Forcible rape would increase. Men's inherent tendencies toward competitiveness, aggression, and violence, freed from the restraints of the gentler, civilizing influence of women, would be a greater problem than ever. The *attempt* to promote androgyny would, it would be argued, create the widest division between the sexes the race has ever known.

Two paths in the woods—neither totally satisfactory, it would seem, to most present-day Americans. Does a third path exist? If it does, it might be one along which American men and women could travel neither in an undifferentiated fashion, nor in a "separate but equal" fashion (a path already discarded in the area of racial discrimination), but in an **"equal but different"** fashion.

No one knows if such a path is really possible. To be workable, it would most likely have to fulfill three important objectives:

1. Men agree not only in principle but in practice that women shall have equal opportunity to exploit the full range of career possibilities open to men. The demographic factors we have been discussing in this book—longer life expectancies and historically low fertility rates—make any other arrangement for women untenable.

2. Women agree that there is no need to merge all masculine and feminine gender traits into one androgynous unity. Unisex might ultimately prove to be quite boring, and, in any event, most men (and indeed very probably most women) are likely to rebel against such a merger.

3. Both men and women agree that parents have a serious and fundamental obligation for the care, support, nurture, and education of their children. The two-career family, a basic assumption of our third path, must not lead to the neglect of the future generation.

In some respects, indeed, this last point is the most important. A group that has often been lost sight of as adults of the two genders try to straighten out their complex relationships is the children. Since these often neglected children represent our future, we will devote Part IV explicitly to a study of issues affecting them. First, however, we must give some attention to important ethnic and racial differences among adults in "our changing population."

## SUMMARY

1.   Over the course of our history, the roles of American men have changed in a variety of ways:

a.   *Nature of work:* The economic division of labor between men and women has seen first a sharper differentiation of men's work with the Industrial Revolution and then, more recently, a narrowing of the gap between the genders; also, men's work has increasingly been "demasculinized" over time.

b.   *Relationships with women:* Men's relationships with women, always filled with ambiguities, have become perhaps even more ambiguous in modern times; in earlier days, men revered women as mothers and denied them the vote; today, men acknowledge that women should be treated as equals but sometimes show them disrespect, hostility, and even violence.

c.   *Role as fathers:* From moral overseer to distant breadwinner to sex-role model to the hypothetical "new father" of today, American men have seen the role of father in constant evolution; but, again, ambiguity is the rule, with the new, caring, expressive father standing side by side with the neglectful, absent father.

2.   Some scholars believe that the evolution of men's roles has been a response, often reluctant, to changes in the roles of women. Others argue that men, rejecting much of the stress and pressure of modern society as well as the stricter bonds of monogamy, have also initiated change on their own.

3.   How much change there has been in practice is difficult to determine:

a.   *On the job front:* Men overwhelmingly and publicly approve of wives' working but are uneasy when their wives outearn them. They feel some stress with the loss of their sole breadwinner role and are quite reluctant to enter what are considered "women's" professions. Also, as their wives work more in the marketplace, men in general work somewhat less;

b.   *On the housework and child care front:* While women on the average have definitely reduced their hours of work on the domestic front, and men have reduced theirs in the marketplace, it is unclear who works more hours in general and it is also unclear by how much men are increasing their participation in household duties. On the last point, most studies suggest that the answer is "not very much."

c.   *Paternal responsibilities:* The caring "new father" does exist; yet many children—in 1988, over one-third of all U.S. children—do not live with their natural fathers, and some of these absent fathers give little time, attention, or money to their offspring.

4.   Neither a wholly androgynous future nor a future in which many men harbor strong hostilities toward women appeals to most Americans. Whether an "equal but different" path to the future is achievable remains to be seen.

## KEY CONCEPTS FOR REVIEW

Men's studies

Ambiguity of gender roles

Man as
   hunter
   farmer

factory worker
organization man

Demasculinization of men's work

Denial of women's rights

Mother's Day

Support for women's rights

Playmate of the Month

Father's roles
  moral overseer
  distant breadwinner
  sex-role model

The "new father"

Sources of "men's liberation"

Statistics on
  men's/women's market work
  men's household work
  absent versus present fathers

Androgyny

"Equal but different"

## QUESTIONS FOR DISCUSSION

1. What do we mean by the concept *vicarious masculinity?* Does this concept seem to you to have any relevance to the life patterns of today's American men? If so, can you relate it to changes in the nature of "men's" work over the past two centuries?

2. When Congress spoke of women as the "greatest source of the country's strength and inspiration" at a time when women did not have a constitutional right to vote, were the congressmen simply being hypocritical? Or is it possible to hold both views sincerely? Do we have any such instances of men's ambivalence toward women in today's America?

3. Trace the roles of American men as fathers until the mid-1960s as outlined by Joseph Pleck in this chapter. Of the three roles he describes, what, if anything, would you say remains of each today?

4. Take sides and defend this statement: "One of the great (advantages/disadvantages) of the women's liberation movement was that it did much to promote the liberation of men."

5. Looking into the future, how likely or unlikely do you think it that American men

   will be increasingly content to take on what were historically considered "women's" occupations?

   will participate more and more fully in housework and child care?

   will cry more often at movies and watch less football on weekends?

   will be there when their children need them?

   will be there when (if) their wives need them?

6. Does "equal but different" strike you as: (a) a hypocritical ideal, (b) an impractical ideal, (c) an undesirable ideal, (d) a desirable ideal whose time has come? Give your reasons.

## NOTES

1. Sociologist Michael S. Kimmel describes the various reactions he encountered when he introduced a course in men's studies at Rutgers in 1985. A characteristic reaction was, "Why do you need a separate course on men? Aren't all courses that don't have the word 'woman' in the title implicitly about men?" He explains his answer in his essay "Teaching a Course on Men," in Michael S. Kimmel, ed., *Changing Men: New Directions in Research on Men and Masculinity* (Beverly Hills, Calif.: Sage Publications, 1987).

2. Controversies over the degree of equality or inequality between the sexes in primitive, preliterate societies are summarized in L. D. Scanzoni and J. Scanzoni, *Men, Women, and Change*, 2nd ed. (New York: McGraw-Hill, 1981), pp. 45–53. For strikingly opposing views on the subject of the historical development of *patriarchy* (defined, in the widest sense, as a male-dominant society), see Gerda Lerner, *The Creation of Patriarchy* (New York: Oxford University Press, 1986) and Steven Goldberg, *The Inevitability of Patriarchy* (New York: William Morrow, 1974).

3. Such views were sometimes expressed not only by men but also by women at this time. See Peter G. Filene, *Him/Her/Self—Sex Roles in Modern America*, 2nd ed. (Baltimore: Johns Hopkins University Press, 1986), pp. 34–35.

4. Ibid., p. 40.

5. One has to say "apparent" growth of homosexual behavior because it is not known whether the greater publicity given homosexuality in recent

years reflects an actual increased incidence or simply increased openness about sexual preferences in the society. A similar problem occurs when we attempt to measure the amount of violence against women. Television specials and other media accounts often speak of an "epidemic" of rape and other violence towards women. However, a recent U.S. Department of Justice study finds that violent victimizations of women have remained at a relatively constant rate between 1973 and 1987, and that the rate of rape has gone down sharply—from 1.9 (1973) to 1.3 (1987) rapes per thousand women age 12 or older. In this case, there has been an increase in media attention but an apparent drop in this kind of criminal behavior. (See Caroline Wolf Harlow, "Female Victims of Crime," U.S. Department of Justice, January 1991, NCJ-126826.)

6. The foregoing discussion of men's roles as fathers is largely based on Joseph H. Pleck, "American Fathering in Historical Perspective," in Kimmel, *Changing Men*, pp. 83–97. Pleck, in turn, expresses his indebtedness to the scholarship of A. Rotundo and J. Demos.

7. Kimmel, *Changing Men*, p. 14.

8. For her general view on the importance of the male rebellion against traditional masculine values, see Barbara Ehrenreich, *The Hearts of Men: American Dreams and the Flight from Commitment* (Garden City, N.Y.: Anchor Press/Doubleday, 1983). Ehrenreich notes that the antifeminist opponents of ERA often stressed women's vulnerability and the danger that husbands would simply renege on their obligations to defend and support them. She quotes famous ERA opponent, Phyllis Schlafly: "Even though love may go out the window, the obligation should remain. ERA would eliminate that obligation." (p. 148).

9. *Annual Report of the Council of Economic Advisers,* January 1987, p. 215.

10. David E. Bloom is quoted in Laurie Hays, "Pay Problems: How Couples React When Wives Out-Earn Husbands," *Wall Street Journal,* June 19, 1987. The increased divorce rate in families where the wife's occupational status is higher than the husband's is also noted in Uma Sekaran, *Dual-Career Families: Contemporary Organizational and Counseling Issues* (San Francisco: Jossey-Bass, 1986), p. 33.

11. Ronald C. Kessler and James A. McRae, Jr., "The Effect of Wives' Employment on the Mental Health of Married Men and Women," *American Sociological Review,* 47, April 1982, pp. 216–227.

12. Victor R. Fuchs. "Sex Differences in Economic Well-Being," *Science, 232,* April 25, 1986, pp. 459–464.

13. Christine L. Williams, *Gender Differences at Work: Women and Men in Nontraditional Occupations* (Berkeley: University of California Press, 1989), p. 14.

14. See "Appendix: Research on Who Does the Housework and Childcare," in Arlie Hochschild, with Anne Machung, *The Second Shift: Working Parents and the Revolution at Home* (New York: Viking, 1989), pp. 271–278.

15. Ibid., p. 276.

16. John P. Robinson, "Time's Up," *American Demographics,* July 1989, pp. 32–35. Professor Robinson is director of the Americans' Use of Time Project, Survey Research Center, University of Maryland. Robinson also undertook a collaborative study with Jonathan Gershuny of the University of Bath, England of the comparative records of the United States and the United Kingdom in the matter of the household division of labor. Their general conclusion was: "We conclude that in the two countries, women in the 1980s do substantially less housework than those in equivalent circumstances in the 1960s, and that men do a little more than they did (although still much less than women). These changes correspond closely to developments in four other countries (Canada, Holland, Denmark, and Norway) for which historical time-budget evidence is available." Jonathan Gershuny and John P. Robinson, "Historical Changes in the Household Division of Labor," *Demography, 25* (4), November 1988, p. 537.

17. U.S. Bureau of the Census, "Child Support and Alimony: 1987," *Current Population Reports,* Series P-23, No. 167.

18. Frank F. Furstenberg, Jr., "Good Dads—Bad Dads: Two Faces of Fatherhood," in A. Cherlin, ed. *The Changing American Family and Public Policy* (Washington, D.C.: Urban Institute Press, 1988), pp. 193–194, 215.

19. Associated Press, "Junk Males," *Fort Lauderdale Sun-Sentinel,* April 26, 1990. According to the Associated Press report, the Roper Organization Poll of 3,000 women found that whereas 32 percent of women in 1970 found that "most men are basically selfish and self-centered," by 1990 the percentage had increased to 42 percent. Also, the percentage who were annoyed by pictures of nude women in men's magazines had increased (from 43 to 61 percent), and the percentage who felt that men "are basically kind, gentle and thoughtful" had decreased (from 67 to 51 percent). Oddly enough, the poll also found that, despite this grim picture of men, more than nine out of ten women said that marriage was better than living alone.

# 13

# *Black America— Two Steps Forward*

As the title of this chapter suggests, black Americans have made substantial progress during the course of their long and difficult history on these shores. The first great step forward was the abolition of slavery and the passage of civil rights laws and three constitutional amendments during the early years of Reconstruction after the Civil War. Emancipation was clearly a crucial step forward for blacks and a sine qua non for all future progress.

The second great forward step has taken place in our own time. The history of black America during the late nineteenth and early twentieth centuries, though an improvement over the worst years of slavery, was nevertheless brutalizing and demoralizing in its own right. Beginning in the days of the New Deal in the 1930s, growing during World War II, and then blossoming into a full-fledged national campaign during the 1950s and 1960s, a Civil Rights Revolution rocked the United States. There was an assault on the countless discriminatory laws and practices that had mocked previous professions of "equality." The achievements of this revolution will be underestimated only by those unfamiliar with U.S. history.

But those achievements should not be overestimated, either. "Two steps forward" implies something less than a totally successful advance. Worse, it lends itself to the added phrase ". . . and one step backward."

Has such progress as there has been, insufficient at best, altogether failed to reach certain segments of the black community? Has there, in fact, been retrogression in some quarters, growing disorganization, despair?

We cannot hope to answer such large questions here. What we shall try to do is to gain an overall view of the demographics of blacks, starting back in colonial times. A historical sense of changes in our black population provides an indispensable background for the study of many current issues facing black America.

## POPULATION PERCENTAGES: DECLINE AND RISE

Just as most Americans are unacquainted with the population history (and tragedy) of the American Indian, so many of us have little idea of how the numbers of black Americans have changed over time. In particular, because black population growth now exceeds that of whites, many people have the impression that this has always been so and that blacks as a *percentage* of our national population have been rising since the earliest times.

The actual facts of the matter, however, are quite different:

*From the first census of the United States (in 1790) until the 1930s, the percentage of Americans who were black fell by half. Since that time, this percentage has risen but remains far below what it was at the founding of the Republic. Even looking as far ahead as the year 2080, it is probable that the percentage of Americans who are black will still be below what it was three centuries previously.*

Let us develop these points a bit further.

### Black Population Trends

Unlike some immigrant groups, blacks were among the earliest settlers of colonial America, arriving at the Jamestown settlement in 1619, one year before the Pilgrims landed at Plymouth Rock. They were settled in the colonies before the institution of slavery existed, often being held in the status of indentured servants, a classification very common among early white immigrants as well.[1] The first official recognition of slavery in the colonies was in Virginia in 1661. In 1700 there were probably around 28,000 Africans and their descendants living in the colonies, nearly 60 percent in Virginia alone. By the time of the War of Independence their numbers had increased greatly, with particularly heavy importation of Africans between 1740 and 1780. Black slavery had by then become thoroughly institutionalized. At the time of our first census in 1790, our black population was estimated at 757,000, of whom 92 percent were slaves.

In 1990, two centuries later, the estimated U.S. black population had risen to over 31 million. This is a very large increase, and yet, as we have already suggested, it represents a substantial *percentage decrease* in relation to our total population. Figure 13-1 shows what has happened to that percentage over time. From a height of 19.3 percent, or nearly one-fifth of the U.S. population, in 1790, the percentage fell steadily to 9.7 percent in 1930, or almost exactly half what it had been 140 years earlier. Since the 1930s, the percentage has been increasing slowly, rising to an estimated 12.4 percent in 1990. Middle-Series Census Bureau projections place the percentage at 16.3 in the year 2080. It could be higher or lower, of course. But the best guess is that it will still be below the percentage in the late eighteenth and early nineteenth centuries.

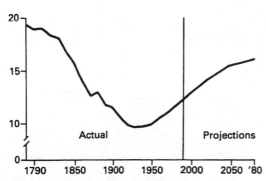

**FIGURE 13–1: Black Population as a Percentage of Total U.S. Population, Actual and Projected, 1790–2080**

*Source:* Projections are Middle-Series Projections from Gregory Spencer, "Projections of the Population of the United States by Age, Sex, and Race: 1988 to 2080," U.S. Bureau of the Census, *Current Population Reports*, Series P-25, No. 1018, p. 10.

## From 1790 to 1930: Why the Sharp Decline?

There are two major factors which explain the percentage decline of black Americans from 1790 to 1930:

*1. The slave trade was ended in the early nineteenth century, while the immigration of other nationalities continued to add to U.S. population growth.* The major period of forced migration from Africa to North America was the mid- to late eighteenth century. There had been some reactions against the **slave trade** from the beginning, and it was officially abolished by Congress in 1808. An illegal slave trade continued after this time, and in 1820 Congress passed an additional law defining the slave trade as piracy. Although some further slave trading may have occurred, it is estimated that by 1860 there were very few foreign-born blacks in the United States, slave or free.

Meanwhile, **immigration from Europe** continued to swell the nation's white population. From 1870 to 1930, over 20 million immigrants settled in this country, accounting for about a quarter of our net population increase during that period.[2] At the height of this flood in the early 1900s, foreign-born residents made up nearly 15 percent of our total population. These new immigrants, many from southern and eastern Europe, were an important source of labor for northern employers, a fact of some significance in terms of the opportunities available to the relatively recently emancipated slaves and their descendants. In terms of our present discussion, this large-scale immigration helps explain the declining percentage of blacks in the total U.S. population.

*2. A high death rate limited the rate of natural increase of the black population.* In the British Caribbean islands, slave populations failed to perpetuate themselves and were constantly augmented by importations from Africa. This may also have been true in the very early days in North America because of a **high death rate** among the slaves and an unbalanced sex ratio in favor of men. From the early eighteenth century on, however, the U.S. slave population was more than reproducing itself and, indeed, the substantial growth of our black population in absolute numbers in the nineteenth and early twentieth centuries was essentially due to a positive rate of natural increase.

The rate of natural increase was somewhat limited, however, by the relatively high death rates of black Americans. Average life expectancy at birth in 1900 for blacks and races other than white is estimated at 33 years, compared to 48 years for white Americans. This is actually below the estimated life expectancy of white Americans in 1790, and conceivably may have represented a *decline* in black life expectancy from the middle of the nineteenth century.[3] As late as the decade 1921–1930, the crude death rate per 1,000 for blacks and races other than white averaged between 16 and 17, half again as high as that for whites at around 11. These relatively high mortality rates restrained the rate of black population growth and thus contributed to the declining percentages of black Americans.

### From 1930 to 1990: Why the Increase?

A reversal in the factors making for the earlier declining percentages is, as one would expect, responsible for their rise during the past 60 years. Immigration to the United States fell off sharply from the mid-1920s onward, and, although there has been an increase in immigration since the mid-1960s, it is smaller in percentage terms than the great influxes of the early part of this century. Also, it should be noted that the proportion of legal immigrants who are black is increasing, from under 4 percent in 1960 to an estimated 12 percent in 1988. Even more dramatic is the change in black mortality rates. We indicated in Chapter 2 that black mortality rates are still higher than those of white Americans. What needs to be emphasized in our present context, however, is the stunning **increase in black life expectancy** over this century. This is shown in Figure 13-2. In 1900, as we have said, black life expectancy at birth is estimated at no more than 33 years. By 1988 it had risen to 69.5 years, or a gain of around 111 percent. The gain in white life expectancy over this period—from 48 to 75.5 years—was also dramatic but less so. What this has meant is an increase in the rate of natural increase of the black population relative to that of the white population. Comparatively speaking, black death rates have fallen more relative to black birth rates than white death rates have fallen relative to white birth rates. The result: an increasing proportion of blacks in the U.S. population.

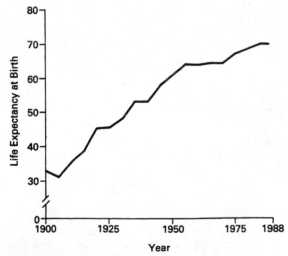

**FIGURE 13–2: Black Life Expectancy, at Birth, 1900–1988**
Note: Figures for 1900–1970 are for black and races other than white; 1970–1988 figures are for blacks only.

*Sources:* U.S. Bureau of the Census, *Historical Statistics of the United States: Colonial Times to 1970* (1975), 107–115, p. 53; *Statistical Abstract*, 1989, 1990.

## Projections to 2080

This increase is expected to continue in the years ahead, as shown in Figure 13-1. Of course, projections always depend on the assumptions behind them, which may be wrong. In the Middle Series projection we have used, it is assumed that there is a convergence of black and white life expectancies at birth at 81.2 years in 2080. It is also assumed that there is a convergence of black and white fertility rates at 1.8 live births per woman in 2080. This would basically represent a continuation of recent white fertility rates (estimated at 1.8 in 1987) and a fairly substantial decline in black fertility (estimated at 2.3 in 1987). On immigration, the assumption is that legal immigration (net) is 500,000 a year and that something under 11 percent of this will be black.

Given these admittedly precarious assumptions, the percentage of U.S. population that is black will rise from 12.4 percent (1990) to 16.3 percent (2080), still below the 19.3 percent achieved in 1790.[4]

## OF MIGRATIONS—PEOPLE AND JOBS

In studying our changing black population, it is also necessary to consider its geographical, residential, and occupational redistributions over time. The dislocations involved in this history are difficult for white Americans—even though they themselves have also been a highly mobile population—to appreciate fully.

### Forced Migrations

At the beginning, of course, was the original forced **migration** of Africans to America via the slave trade. This meant the disruption of family, kinship, village, tribal, cultural, and other ties that had characterized and made life viable in the African homeland.

But the original passage from Africa to North America was by no means the only forced migration American blacks were to endure. At the individual level, there was always the possibility of sale and/or the physical removal of a slave from his or her place of birth and family relations. This forcible breakup of families affected not only children, usually teenagers and young adults, but also spouses. Historians differ as to the extent of the destruction of the black family during slavery. Some have suggested that it was very much in the slaveowners' self-interest to keep the slave family together (and also reasonably well fed and clothed) so that slave reproduction rates could be sustained. Others have suggested that forced sales of family members were common, causing the destruction of perhaps one in every six or seven slave marriages. In either case, substantial numbers of slaves were forcibly removed from their places of birth according to the dictates of others (slaveowners), rather than by their own decisions.[5]

This was particularly true in the decades before the Civil War, which saw a forced migration of blacks from the tobacco plantations of the Upper South (states like Virginia and North Carolina) to the cotton plantations of the Lower South (states like Alabama, Mississippi, and Louisiana). Between 1790 and 1860, the percentage of America's slaves residing in the Lower South increased from 24 percent to 78 percent. Indeed, by the beginning of the Civil War, more than half the U.S. black population lived in states outside those formed from the original thirteen colonies.

### Three Great Migrations

The forced migrations of Africans and African Americans from the seventeenth century through the Civil War involved many hundreds of thousands of people. The migrations of blacks that have taken place in our own century have involved many millions of people. Partly they have been voluntary migrations; partly they have been required by fundamental socioeconomic forces. Certainly among the most rapid redistributions of a population in history, these migrations demand our attention if we are to understand the current situation of black Americans. They involved three dimensions: geographical, residential, and occupational.

*Geographical: Leaving the South.* On the eve of the Civil War, it is estimated that 92.2 percent of black Americans lived in the South. Beginning as a trickle in the 1870s and building up to a flood in the period from the beginning of World War II through the 1960s, black Americans went north and west. Table 13-1 shows the extent of this out-migration from the South (a trend now reversing itself, as we will note on p. 220). In the 30 years from 1940 to 1970, a net of 4.3 million blacks moved from the Southern states to those in the Northeast, the Midwest, and the West. It is important to stress the word *net* because the actual movement of blacks was much greater than this, given that there were also blacks moving to (or back to) the South, as well as between other regions. In "gross" terms, in

1965–1970, for example, black in-migration to the South was over 40 percent of out-migration. Thus, the actual **geographical** movement of black Americans was even more spectacular than the numbers in Table 13-1 suggest. In net terms, the percentage of black Americans living outside the South increased from 7.8 percent in 1870 to 47.0 percent in 1970. Of these, about 16 percent were living in the West, 41 percent in the Northeast, and 43 percent in the Midwest. This shift of population is all the more striking in that, by the late 1960s, there was a strong movement of white Americans *out of* the Northeast and Midwest *toward* the Sunbelt states of the South and West (see Chapter 4).

*Residential: From Country to City.* In the nineteenth century, blacks lived overwhelmingly in rural areas. As late as 1890, only 20 percent of the black population lived in urban areas. This was substantially below the general population, which had become increasingly urbanized with the great industrialization surge from the 1840s on. In the twentieth century, however, all

**TABLE 13.1.   Out-migration of Blacks from the South, 1870–1970**

| Decade | Black Population in South at Start of Decade (1000s) | Estimated Net Out-migration of Blacks (1000s) | Percentage Out-migrants of Mid-Decade Population |
|---|---|---|---|
| 1870–1880 | 4,421 | 71 | − 1.4 |
| 1880–1890 | 5,954 | 80 | − 1.3 |
| 1890–1900 | 6,761 | 174 | − 2.4 |
| 1900–1910 | 7,923 | 197 | − 2.4 |
| 1910–1920 | 8,749 | 525 | − 5.9 |
| 1920–1930 | 8,912 | 877 | − 9.6 |
| 1930–1940 | 9,362 | 398 | − 4.1 |
| 1940–1950 | 9,905 | 1,468 | −14.6 |
| 1950–1960 | 10,225 | 1,473 | −13.7 |
| 1960–1970 | 11,312 | 1,380 | −11.9 |

*Source:* Reynolds Farley and Walter R. Allen, *The Color Line and the Quality of Life in America.* Copyright © 1987 Russell Sage Foundation. Used with permission of the Russell Sage Foundation. Based on U.S. Bureau of the Census, *Historical Statistics of the United States: Colonial Times to 1970* (1975), series A-176; *Current Population Reports,* series P-23, no. 80, table 8; Everett S. Lee, et al., *Population Redistribution of Economic Growth: United States, 1870–1950,* vol. 1 (Philadelphia: American Philosophic Society), 1957.

this changed. Blacks flocked to the cities in huge numbers, passing whites in terms of the percentage urbanized in the mid-1950s and going on to extend that margin through the next three decades. In 1980, 81 percent of blacks lived in urban areas as compared to 73 percent of whites. These figures actually understate the degree to which black urbanization has come to exceed that of whites, for these "urban" figures include suburbs as well as central cities. In 1980, 58 percent of our black population lived in central cities, as compared to only 25 percent of our white population. Numerous central cities had come to have majority black populations—Newark, New Jersey (58.2 percent), Detroit (63.1 percent), Atlanta (66.6 percent), Washington, D.C. (70.3 percent), East St. Louis, Illinois (95.6 percent). The rapidity of this transformation from rural to urban living has no precedent among other ethnic groups in our nation's history.

*Occupational: Leaving Farming and Domestic Service.* During the nineteenth and twentieth centuries, the United States moved massively from a predominantly agricultural economy to a manufacturing and, more recently, high-tech service economy. In this process, black Americans lagged behind for numerous reasons, including competition for industrial jobs with immigrant groups and severe discrimination from employers and from labor unions as well. In 1890, 90 percent of black workers were still to be found in agricultural or domestic service occupations. As late as 1920, 49 percent of the nation's blacks lived on farms, and the great majority of employed black women were in domestic service. The subsequent change in black occupations is as striking as their changes in geographical and residential occupations. Between 1950 and 1980, for example, the percentage of black women engaged in household work fell from 40 percent to 5 percent. At the same time, the percentage

of black men engaged in farming fell from 26 percent to 3 percent.

Were these **occupational** changes "voluntary" or "involuntary"? Did blacks leave agriculture because they were "pushed" off the farm or because they were "pulled" to more attractive pursuits? Probably both factors were involved. The increasing mechanization of U.S. agriculture, particularly in the twentieth century, has meant a vast reduction in the quantity of labor required on our nation's farms. Since blacks were predominantly agricultural workers, the effect of these technological changes was especially felt by them. On the other hand, there were also "pull" factors since wages in the more industrialized sections of the country were higher than in the South, and also since immigrant competition for jobs in the North was substantially reduced by the restrictions placed on immigration from the mid-1920s until the mid-1960s.

In either event, the transition from an agrarian to a modern industrialized economy which occurred over a period of a century and a half for white Americans was concentrated for American blacks in less than half that time. Indeed, much of it has taken place within the last few decades.

### Recent Trends

Nor is that transition in any way complete. For example, a major trend in the case of white male employment has been in the direction of professional and other white-collar jobs. But whereas 43 percent of white males were employed in white-collar jobs in 1980, only 25 percent of black males were so employed. Furthermore, among the blue-collar workers, whereas whites were heavily represented among "Craftsmen and Precision Workers," blacks predominated in areas like "Transport Equipment Operators and Handlers," "Laborers," and so on.[6]

It should also be said that there have been certain recent trends that have departed from the massive geographical and residential shifts that dominated during the first several decades of this century. One of the less well known of these trends is the reverse movement of American blacks **back to the South.** Beginning in the early 1970s and gaining force later in that decade, there was a net out-migration from the Northeast and Midwest toward the South and the West. Indeed, the absolute increase in the black population in the South between 1970 and 1980 was the largest single increase by blacks in any decade, or region, in U.S. history.[7] Essentially, this flow reflected the decline of employment opportunities in the northern industrial cities and the expansion of such opportunities in the Sunbelt.

There has also been a substantial **movement of blacks into the suburbs** surrounding our large metropolitan areas. Between 1950 and 1980, the percentage of blacks in the suburbs rose from 11.5 percent to 23.3 percent. Although this latter percentage is still less than half the percentage of whites residing in suburbs (48.4 percent in 1980), it would appear to reflect the same kind of outward movement experienced by whites, though with the customary "lag." It cannot be said, however, that this movement of blacks to the suburbs gives evidence of the increasing residential integration of blacks within the larger American community. Racial segregation in the suburbs is characteristic and showed relatively little sign of improvement in recent years.

## TWO STEPS FORWARD

Two striking facts emerge from any survey of the United States' black population changes over the course of our nation's history: (1) How far behind the black population has been in terms of virtually every index that is customarily used to indicate personal well-being—whether health, life expectancy, education, occupation, income, available opportunities, or simple human freedom, and (2) how rapidly changes have been occurring within this population and in its relations to the larger society as it has emerged from enslavement and servitude.

We said earlier that black Americans have taken two very large steps forward in their history, the first via their emancipation from slavery, the second as a result of the Civil Rights Revolution of recent memory. We could also define these two steps forward in somewhat different terms, reflecting not so much different periods of time as different areas of black life. Two notable areas are (1) advances in political and civil rights and (2) advances in economic and material well-being.

### Political and Civil Rights

Without question, the political status of black Americans has improved dramatically in the little over a century and a quarter since the **Emancipation Proclamation.** In principle, the three Reconstruction amendments would appear to have resolved all central political questions as between whites and blacks in terms of "equality." The Thirteenth Amendment (1865) completed what the Emancipation Proclamation had started and abolished slavery within the United States. The Fourteenth Amendment (1868) prohibited any state from depriving "any person of life, liberty, or property, without due process of law" or denying "any person within its jurisdiction the equal protection of the laws." The Fifteenth Amendment (1870) stated specifically that the right to vote could not be "denied or abridged . . . on account of race, color, or previous condition of servitude."

In point of fact, of course, the acquisition of full political and civil rights by blacks did not follow immediately or without serious subsequent retrogression from these apparently clear declarations. In the Reconstruction period, there were many political advances for Southern blacks, including their election to state legislatures, the U.S. House of Representatives, and even the U.S. Senate. These advances were short-lived, however, and by the latter part of the nineteenth century, black–white segregation in the South was more intense than it had been under slavery. During the 1890s, blacks in the South lost the vote; the Supreme Court began to reverse much of the civil rights legislation passed during Reconstruction; in *Plessy* v. *Ferguson* (1896), the Court ruled that "separate but equal" facilities were constitutional, thus confirming the nearly universal pattern of Southern school segregation. Meanwhile, violence against blacks was increasing. It is estimated that there were 2,000 to 3,000 lynchings in the last decade and a half of the nineteenth century. In the early twentieth century, although lynchings declined, Jim Crow segregation became the order of the day. In 1915 the Ku Klux Klan, originally founded and then disbanded during Reconstruction, reemerged in Georgia. Although the new Klan had many targets—Catholics, Jews, atheists, adulterers, and the like—blacks remained subject to its harsh intimidations.

All of which is to say that when the Civil Rights Revolution of the post–World War II era burst upon the national scene, it confronted a nation deeply divided on the basis of race, and in which the key word in "separate but equal" was definitely "separate" and not "equal." In this context, the impact of this revolution has unquestionably been enormous. Blacks not only have the vote today but are a major voting force, particularly in our larger cities, many of which now have black mayors. In the crucial decision, *Brown* v. *Board of Education of Topeka* (1954), the Supreme Court overturned the "separate but equal" doctrine that had justified school segregation. In 1955 a black woman, Rosa Parks, refused to give up her bus seat to a white man, thus beginning the famous Montgomery, Alabama, bus boycott, a protest joined by a young minister, Dr. Martin Luther King, Jr. In the course of the next decade, Dr. King was at the center of numerous protest movements, dramatizing the second-class citizenship of black Americans, and helping secure passage of the Civil Rights Act of 1964, the most com-

prehensive civil rights bill in U.S. history, and the Voting Rights Act of 1965.

In that same year, 1965, violent riots began in the Watts district of Los Angeles, followed by race riots in other U.S. cities, most notably in Detroit in July 1967, where 43 people were killed, 14 square miles of the city were gutted by fire, and 15,000 troops had to be brought in. In 1967 an executive order of President Lyndon Johnson directed federal contractors to "take affirmative action to ensure that employees are treated during employment, without regard to their race, color, religion, sex or national origin." Thus began an era of "affirmative action" to redress wrongs due to *past* discrimination, a complex policy that is still evolving today.[8] Meanwhile, in 1968, the national Kerner Commission was describing the United States as a country divided by race, and Dr. King was assassinated. Fifteen years later, President Ronald Reagan signed a bill establishing a federal holiday in honor of Dr. King, the first national holiday named for a black American. New leaders emerged in the black community during this ongoing Revolution—some more aggressive than Dr. King, like Stokely Carmichael and Malcolm X. By the 1980s, however, the Reverend Jesse Jackson, operating within the American political system, had become the first black to run a serious campaign for the nation's presidency. In November 1989, New York City joined numerous other large U.S. cities in electing its first black Mayor, David N. Dinkins, while in Virginia, L. Douglas Wilder became the nation's first elected black governor.

That this civil rights revolution, taking up where emancipation and reconstruction had left off, did not accomplish *everything* for black Americans is obvious. Recently, indeed, there has been some backing away from certain past civil rights initiatives, particularly in the area of employment discrimination. A number of Supreme Court decisions in the late 1980s made it somewhat more difficult to prove racial discrimination in employment. In 1990 Congress passed a new civil rights bill that would have facilitated minority lawsuits alleging workplace bias. This legislation was, however, vetoed by President Bush on the grounds that the bill would have effectively enacted hiring "quotas." Although civil rights groups and Democratic legislators denied this allegation and were considering sending the President similar legislation again in 1991, most observers agreed that the preferential hiring of minorities, and certainly any form of racial "quotas," had become increasingly unpopular in the nation at large.

Despite this recent controversy, there is little doubt that in a strictly limited legal, civil, and political sense, the advances brought about by the civil rights revolution have been enormous. Considering the power of the one-person-one-vote character of a democracy, these political achievements are as important as they are clear-cut.

### Economic Progress and the Emerging Black Middle Class

If, even in the political sphere, the advances of black Americans have to be somewhat qualified, that qualification is far more necessary in the case of their socioeconomic "step forward." This large qualification will be the subject of the next section of this chapter. However, seeing that the glass is half empty should not blind us to the fact that it is also now half full, particularly when, in an earlier era, the glass was virtually dry.

In point of fact, there is overwhelming evidence that black Americans have moved forward in terms of their material well-being, not only since the days of slavery but since the end of World War II. To prove this central truth, we need do little more than to look at Figure 13-2 again, because there is probably no single measure of the level of living more important than life expectancy.[9] In effect, Figure 13-2 tells us that American blacks are far more favorably situated today in a general sense than they

were at the turn of the century. They still lag behind American whites in life expectancy, but the absolute improvement they have experienced is striking, and the gap between blacks and whites has definitely narrowed.

For recent decades, we can, of course, use far more specific measures to chart **black economic progress.** Indeed, the problem is which of several different measures to use. *Earnings* from wages and salaries, for example, are different from *income*, which includes interest, dividends, and other property income as well as transfer payments. Transfer payments themselves may be either *cash* benefits (usually included) or noncash, *in-kind* benefits (often excluded). Incomes for *families* may be different from incomes per *employed person*, which may, in turn, be different from incomes *per capita*. Also, there is the question of whether to use *median* or *mean* values when comparing average incomes or earnings over time, or between blacks and whites.[10]

Although they do not tell the whole story, Tables 13-2 and 13-3 give definite evidence of an important economic "step forward" by black Americans during the past half century. Postponing all qualifying remarks, we see that the median income of black males who received income rose from $3,400 in 1939 to $10,148 in 1987 in constant dollars, or about threefold in real terms. As a percentage of white male income, black income rose from 41 percent to 59 percent during this period. In the case of black women, their median income rose from 36 percent to 82 percent of that of white women over 1939–1987.

Table 13-3 is interesting not only because it uses a different measure (hourly wages) but also because it shows what has been happening to different age groups. Hourly wages for black males rose relative to those of white males for every age group from 1940 to 1980. However, in the youngest age group presented (25–34), black males were approaching fairly close to parity

**TABLE 13-2.  Median Income for Black and White Adults Who Received Income, 1939–1987 (in 1984 Dollars)**

| | 1939 | 1949 | 1959 | 1969 | 1979 | 1985 | 1987 |
|---|---|---|---|---|---|---|---|
| **Men:** | | | | | | | |
| Median income: | | | | | | | |
| Black | $3,400 | $5,200 | $7,100 | $11,200 | $11,100 | $10,400 | $10,148 |
| White | 8,300 | 10,800 | 15,000 | 19,200 | 17,600 | 16,500 | 17,233 |
| Racial gap | −4,900 | −5,600 | −7,900 | −8,000 | −6,500 | −6,100 | −7,085 |
| Black as percentage of white | 41% | 48% | 47% | 58% | 63% | 63% | 59% |
| Percentage with income: | | | | | | | |
| Black | N.A. | 85% | 88% | 86% | 87% | 87% | 87% |
| White | N.A. | 89% | 92% | 93% | 96% | 96% | 96% |
| **Women:** | | | | | | | |
| Median income: | | | | | | | |
| Black | $1,800 | $2,200 | $3,000 | $5,200 | $5,800 | $6,100 | $6,212 |
| White | 5,100 | 4,700 | 4,700 | 6,200 | 6,300 | 7,100 | 7,567 |
| Racial gap | −3,300 | −2,500 | −1,700 | −1,00 | −500 | −1,000 | −1,355 |
| Black as percentage of white | 36% | 46% | 62% | 84% | 92% | 85% | 82% |
| Percentage with income: | | | | | | | |
| Black | N.A. | 54% | 63% | 73% | 83% | 85% | 85% |
| White | N.A. | 46% | 52% | 65% | 90% | 91% | 91% |

Data for 1939 refer to wage and salary earnings only. Data from 1939 and 1949 were obtained from the decennial censuses. Data for subsequent years refer to all monetary income and were obtained from the Current Population Survey. Figures for 1939, 1949, and 1959 refer to whites and nonwhites; for later years, to whites and blacks. Through 1969, income questions were asked of persons aged 14 and over; since then, of persons aged 15 and over.

*Sources:* U.S. Bureau of the Census, *Census of Population: 1950*, P-C1, Table 137; *Current Population Reports*, Series P-60, Nos. 80, 90, 127, 132, and 154. Adapted by authors from Table 10-4, Reynolds Farley and Walter R. Allen, *The Color Line and the Quality of Life in America.* Copyright © 1987 Russell Sage Foundation. Used with permission of the Russell Sage Foundation.

with white males—that is, a black/white ratio of 84.3 percent. Theoretically, this should lead to a greater convergence of earnings in the future.

What all this means is that the common perception that the postwar era has seen a substantial expansion in the numbers of "middle-class" black Americans has much validity. By most average measures, whether of income and earnings, of occupational distribution, or even of life expectancy, blacks still lag behind whites. But the gap in living standards has definitely narrowed, and the possibility of ultimate "convergence" is certainly not out of the question. In the 1930s, one of the most popular radio shows was "Amos 'n' Andy," a presentation of black Americans in caricature (actually performed by white actors). "Blackface" minstrel shows were still being presented at that time. In the 1980s, one of the most popular television programs was the "Cosby Show," featuring two upper-income black professional parents. This show is no more characteristic of the "typical" black family today than "Amos 'n' Andy" accurately typified blacks in the 1930s. The *shift* in emphasis is, however, significant and undoubtedly does correspond to an important reality.

## . . . AND ONE STEP BACKWARD?

But not the only reality.

We will be discussing this further reality later in this book, when we deal with poverty among children (Chapter 15) and the possible future course of poverty in the United States (Chapter 24). For the moment, we note only that there is another common perception that also has much validity, namely, that an important segment of the black community is not moving forward at all, but is stalled at a very low level of socioeconomic and personal well-being. Why this group exists, and whether or not it should properly be called an "underclass," is a matter of dispute, as we shall note in a

**TABLE 13-3.   Black–White Hourly Wage and Salary Ratios: Men, by Age, 1940–1980**

|       | 1940 | 1950 | 1960 | 1970 | 1980 |
|-------|------|------|------|------|------|
| 25–34 | 48.9 | 68.4 | 67.2 | 76.1 | 84.3 |
| 35–44 | 43.0 | 62.6 | 63.6 | 67.2 | 75.9 |
| 45–54 | 40.2 | 57.7 | 59.7 | 64.2 | 72.7 |
| 55–64 | 40.6 | 56.3 | 57.6 | 62.6 | 68.6 |
| Total | 43.6 | 62.4 | 62.6 | 68.0 | 76.3 |

Calculated by dividing weekly earnings by hours worked during survey week.

*Source:* Census of Population, 1940–1980; Public Use Sample. Taken from U.S. Commission on Civil Rights, "The Economic Progress of Black Men in America," mimeographed, October 1986, Table 1-4, p. 13.

moment. That its existence signifies a flaw in the forward progress of black America, and may even represent a large "step backward," is beyond serious debate.

Briefly, we have:

*Unemployment.* Black unemployment rates have been rising throughout most of the postwar era, averaging a little over 8 percent in the 1950s and increasing to over 15 percent on average in the 1980s. White unemployment rates have also generally risen during this period, but not so rapidly, and in the 1980s were typically well under half of black rates. Furthermore, unemployment percentages fail to disclose significant differences between black and white labor force participation rates. In 1954, black labor force participation was substantially higher than that of whites; by the 1980s, it had fallen below that of whites. A particularly significant change took place in the case of young black males. In the 16-to-19 age group, black male labor force participation declined from 61.2 percent in 1954 to 40.6 percent in 1990, while the rate for white males in that age group was rising (from 57.6 percent to 59.4 percent). In 1990, over half of white males aged 16 to 19 were employed, whereas only 28 percent of comparable black males were employed. In general, from 1980 to 1990, the employment-to-population ratio for blacks was running around 8 percentage points below that of whites.

*Increase in Single-Parent Families.* There have been dramatic changes in the structure of black families over the past half century, including a major increase in the number of black one-parent family groups with children. Just in the years between 1970 and 1988, that number increased from 1.15 million to 3.0 million, and the percentage of all black families with children headed by a single parent rose from 35.7 percent to 59.4 percent. (White one-parent family groups with children were much less numerous in percentage terms, although the percentage was also rising: from 10.1 percent in 1970 to 21.7 percent in 1988.) Of the 3.0 million one-parent black family groups in 1988, 2.8 million, or 94 percent, were headed by the mother, and they included well over half of all black children under 18. Average family income for these mother-only black families was only 28 percent of that of two-parent black families with children.

*Poverty.* Compared with the years before World War II, there has been a sharp decline in poverty among blacks in the postwar decades. In the 15 years between 1959 and 1974 alone, the black poverty rate fell from 55.1 percent to 30.3 percent. *Since 1974,* however, there has been a sharp increase in black poverty in absolute numbers of persons and even a small increase in percentage terms. From 1974 to 1989, there was an increase of 2.1 million blacks living in poverty, representing an increase in the poverty rate from 30.3 to 30.7 percent. Because 1989 was a year of general prosperity, this was not merely a cyclical phenomenon. By the late 1980s, nearly half of all black children were living below the poverty level (see Chapter 15).

*Segregation.* Anyone who has visited the inner city of any of our large metropolitan areas knows that residential segregation remains a major fact of contemporary American life. This heavy concentration of blacks in our central cities is a reflection of the great cityward migration of blacks noted earlier in this chapter, but also of the heavy *out*-migration of whites, some of which may have been due to the black inflows.[11] The recent movement of blacks to the suburbs has not deeply changed the segregated nature of U.S. society, this migration representing in many cases an extension of the segregated city into its outlying districts. Indeed, the out-migration of middle-class blacks from the inner cities has, according to some observers, only deepened the isolation and social disorganization of the remaining ghetto residents.[12]

Perhaps the ultimate test of the separation or integration of ethnic groups in a society is the rate of intermarriage. *Endogamous* (within-group) marriages among blacks are exceptionally high and *exogamous* (black–white marriages) are very low compared to other ethnic groups. In 1988, out of over 47 million married couples in which the husband was white, only 69,000 (or less than 0.15 percent) of the wives were black; and out of 3.8 million couples where the husband was black, only 149,000 (or just under 4 percent) of the wives were white. There has undoubtedly been some increase in black–white marriages in recent years, but the levels are still very low, and there seems to be little difference between age groups in this respect. In 1980 the rates of endogamous marriages for blacks by age groups were as follows:

| | |
|---|---|
| *Under 25* | 97.77% |
| *25–34* | 98.58 |
| *35–44* | 99.08 |
| *45–54* | 99.01 |
| *55–64* | 98.57 |
| *65 and Over* | 98.66 |

Thus, blacks and whites remain largely separated not only residentially but also maritally.[13]

*Social Indicators: Crime, Homicide, Drugs, Disease.* Life in the ghettos is very different from life outside the ghettos in a number of ways. The social problems afflicting young black males have drawn much recent attention. Some have called these problems the **new morbidity,** citing such statistics as the following:

• The leading cause of death among black males aged 15 to 24 is homicide.

• While black males represent 6 percent of the U.S. population, they represent 40 percent of the prison population.

• Black drug use is higher than that of whites, perhaps by a factor of three.

• Twenty-three percent of all male AIDS cases between 1981 and 1986 were among black males.

• Black male dropout rates from school exceed those of whites and also those of black females.

• Young black men have the highest rate of unwed fatherhood and the lowest rate of marriage of any major ethnic group.

On top of this, of course, there is the problem, already mentioned, of high joblessness and low labor force participation among young black males.[14]

When we add to all this the exceptionally high poverty rates among black children and women in single-parent families, we can understand why the term *underclass* has come into common use. Is this large "step backward" to be a permanent problem in the America of the future?

## DIFFERENT PERSPECTIVES ON THE PROBLEMS OF BLACK AMERICA

As already mentioned, we shall be coming back to some of these problems in future chapters. Here we wish to note only that there are many different **perspectives** from which they can be viewed. In 1965 Daniel Patrick Moynihan wrote a report, *The Negro Family in America: The Case for National Action,* that caused sharp controversy at the time and ever since. In one respect, the report was prophetic: It called attention to changes in the black family that have become much more pronounced in the ensuing quarter century. In emphasizing the importance of family structure to the current plight of many poverty-stricken blacks, it also struck a chord that is still resonant today, perhaps more so than when the report was written.

The report, however, also spoke of the "pathology" of Negro family life, and the response from black scholars was immediate. According to Professor Harriette McAdoo of Howard University, the major criticisms of the report were that the existing literature on Negro families had not been consulted, that some research studies had been misinterpreted, and that the data for a few were generalized onto the total population. Some years later, the government determined to treat the racial issue with "benign neglect"; this decision was "unfortunate, and probably had a devastating impact upon families."[15]

As these comments suggest, there are many basically different ways in which the history and culture of black Americans can be viewed, and especially with respect to the evolution and current state of the black family. In 1978, sociologist W. R. Allen classified these different perspectives under three headings: (1) *cultural deviant,* (2) *cultural equivalent,* and (3) *cultural variant.*[16]

*Cultural Deviant.* In this view, the black family with its high rate of never-married mothers, absent fathers, and children raised in single-parent homes represents a "pathological" condition. Improving the lot of poor blacks requires that steps be taken to strengthen their family structures—that is, to bring them more into conformity with the conventional white family structure. Without such change, general socioeconomic developments and/or government policies intended to help black Americans will fail.

Why has the black family developed this "pathology"? Many different explanations are possible within the general framework of the "cultural deviant" point of view. One approach, emphasized by Moynihan in his report, though developed earlier by E. Franklin Frazier (pp. 153–154), emphasized the aftereffects of slavery, which purportedly destroyed the black family structure, leaving it too weak to handle the strains that adjustment to modern urban-industrial society required. Another, quite different approach—equally controversial—blames the collapse of the black family on government policies dating largely from the War on Poverty era of the 1960s. In his 1984 book, *Losing Ground: American Social Policy: 1950–1980,* Charles Murray developed this thesis at great length, attributing the growth of poverty among blacks and the increase in out-of-wedlock children and single-parent families largely to the expansion of a welfare system that weakened the family and encouraged dependence on the state.

*Cultural Equivalent.* This approach emphasizes the basic commonality of values between blacks and whites as far as families are concerned. Indeed, differences between the black experience and that of whites in general are attributed to broad socioeconomic forces that affected the two groups in different ways. With this approach, emphasis would be given to the massive disruptions in black life caused by the rapidity of their transformation from a rural, agricultural society to a highly urbanized, industrial society. Held captive in the South for much of their history, discriminated against in both North and South, subject to severe competition for jobs from immigrant groups who generally received preferential treatment, blacks were then required by large technological and socioeconomic forces to make a lightning-like transition to the modern high-tech world. As a further irony, their great postwar move to the Northern cities was still in progress when those Northern industrial centers began to suffer severe economic hardship and decline.

From this viewpoint, the black family has actually held up quite well in adapting to the extraordinary strains under which it has been placed. In a work referred to earlier (see p. 154), historian Herbert G. Gutman stressed this adaptive capacity even under the harsh regime of slavery. What is remarkable, he pointed out, is that the attachments of husbands and wives, and of parents to children, remained very deep in the slave culture even when families in many instances were forcibly separated by slaveowners by sale or physical removal. If the black family was having a difficult time in postwar America, Gutman asserted, it was largely because of the vast forced march out of agriculture ("a modern Enclosure Movement without parallel in the nation's history") and not because of any "pathology" in the black family.[17]

*Cultural Variant.* Unlike the foregoing two approaches, both of which essentially take the white middle-class family as a norm, this third approach emphasizes the different values that blacks have developed over time, either from their African heritage or from their special history and experience in America. Like the cultural deviant approach, and unlike the cultural equivalent approach, the cultural variant approach admits that black family values are different from those of whites. It emphasizes, however, that these values have an integrity and importance of their own, and that attempts to alter them to conform to white values are mistaken, and, in many cases, essentially "racist."

A frequent emphasis from this point of view is on the "extended family" of black history as opposed to the "nuclear family" of white history. In this connection, sociologist Niara Sudarkasa develops a contrast we have mentioned earlier (see p. 145) between families organized around "a consanguineal core group" (a large extended family based essentially on blood relationships), and those organized around the "conjugal pair" (families that are more limited in size and are based on the legal, as opposed to blood, connection between husband and wife). The latter has been dominant in European history, she contends, while the former was often dominant in African history.[18]

Those who favor this approach are unlikely to accept the concept of "underclass," with its subtle implication that the only desirable goal is to join the American mainstream with its essentially white middle-class values. The cultural variant approach does not, however, suggest that all is well with the black family in today's America. For today's black family may well be falling short by the values and standards of blacks themselves. Thus, for example, it may be that the accelerated rural–urban transformation that U.S. blacks have suffered would be particularly hard on the family structures on which blacks were dependent. Writes

Joyce A. Ladner, professor of social work at Howard University:

> The Black family has always relied heavily on the extended family to meet its obligations, particularly in child-rearing. When Black families migrate to an urban area, they find themselves faced with two major problems—unemployment and inadequate housing for multigenerational households. Thus, urbanization removes an important support for maintaining a cohesive family.[19]

This approach differs from the previous two in that, although it admits to serious problems in today's black population, it nevertheless insists that these ultimately must be judged (and should be corrected) taking black, rather than conventional white, values into account.

As we deal further with issues involving the changing black population in later chapters, the reader will want to examine our analyses with these three quite different perspectives in mind.

## SUMMARY

1.  Contrary to the impression many people have, the percentage of the U.S. population that is black was considerably lower in 1990 (12.4 percent) than it was two centuries before in 1790 (19.3 percent). As recently as 1930, this percentage was down to 9.7, or half what it had been at the beginning of the republic.

2.  The declining percentage of blacks from 1790 to 1930 was due in great part to the ending of the slave trade (while white European immigrants came in large numbers), and the high black death rate. The subsequent growth of our black population has been due to changes in immigration policy (i.e., immigrant numbers were lowered for a time; also, there are now considerable numbers of black immigrants) and sharply increasing black life expectancies (though still lagging behind white levels).

3.  Even after the ending of forced migration due to slavery, blacks have had a history of migrations in the United States. These have been: (a) geo-

graphical (leaving the South, especially from 1940 to 1970; more recently, returning to the South in fairly substantial numbers); (b) residential (from rural to urban, especially to central cities); and (c) occupational (from agriculture and domestic service to industry). These changes have been accomplished in a much shorter time period than is typical in this country.

4.  Blacks have made "two steps forward," as reflected in their emancipation from slavery and their civil rights gains since the 1950s and 1960s. Another way of classifying the forward progress of black Americans:

    a.  *Political and civil rights:* The 1989 election of a black mayor in New York City and a black governor in Virginia are only symbols of the unquestioned political and civil rights gains blacks have made since the dark days of slavery.

    b.  *Economic progress:* Though still lagging behind whites on most measures, black gains in income and earnings, occupational distribution, and overall life expectancy have been significant and support the general impression that the black middle class is growing appreciably.

5. Still, the possibility that there has also been "one step backward" is suggested by heavy unemployment, an increase in single-parent families, recent rises in poverty rates, continuing segregation, and the "new morbidity" (homicide, criminality, drug use, AIDS, school dropouts, out-of-wedlock childbearing) in certain segments of the black population.

6. In viewing black life in the United States, and especially black family life, three different perspectives, originally developed by W. R. Allen, are sometimes used:

a. *Cultural deviant:* The black family is in a "pathological condition" due to the aftereffects of slavery, or perhaps the unintended effects of modern welfare programs.

b. *Cultural equivalent:* Black families have adjusted fairly well considering the socioeconomic strains under which they have been placed (displacement from agriculture, rapid urbanization, etc.), and will approximate white middle-class values when conditions improve.

c. *Cultural variant:* Because of their total cultural history and background, blacks have different family values than whites, and these values have an integrity and importance of their own, making them worth preserving, although, of course, their expression can also run into problems at times.

## KEY CONCEPTS FOR REVIEW

Black population trends
    slave trade
    white European immigration
    death rate trends

Increases in black life expectancy at birth

Migrations under slavery
    to America
    within America

Twentieth-century migrations
    geographical
    residential
    occupational

Current migrations
    return to the South
    to the suburbs

"Two steps forward" (two interpretations)

Emancipation Proclamation

Modern civil rights advances

Recent economic progress

". . . and one step back"
    unemployment
    single-parent families
    poverty
    segregation
    the "new morbidity"

Three perspectives on the black family
    cultural deviant
    cultural equivalent
    cultural variant

## QUESTIONS FOR DISCUSSION

1. Explain how it was that the black population of the United States fell from over 19 percent of the total population in 1790 to under 10 percent in 1930. What accounted for its subsequent rise to over 12 percent in 1990? What major assumptions are employed in the Middle-Series Census projections of a 16.3 percentage by 2080?

2. "One of the problems of the great migrations of blacks in recent decades is that they have

been too fast for the people involved to make the necessary life adjustments." Discuss with respect to the main geographical, residential, and occupational movements of American blacks in the twentieth century.

3. Summarize the main political and civil rights gains blacks have made in the United States since 1860. Do you think a black man could be elected president of the United States in this century? What would his chances be com-

pared to those of a white woman, in your opinion?

4. Does the representation of black Americans on television programs and commercials today seem to you:

   (a) Disproportionately infrequent, disproportionately frequent, about right?

   (b) Basically fair-minded, condescending and superior, other?

   (c) Effective or largely ineffective in altering white attitudes toward blacks? black attitudes toward blacks? black attitudes toward whites?

5. It has been said that black Americans are following two diverging socioeconomic paths, with the gap between successful and unsuccessful blacks becoming wider every day. What hard evidence could you present to support such a view? Explain.

6. Using the different perspectives on black family life as a guide, why do you think that some people speak unequivocally of a largely black "underclass," while others reject the concept?

## NOTES

1. Historians have estimated that nearly half of the total white immigration to the 13 colonies came as "bound servants." See Herbert G. Gutman, *The Black Family in Slavery and Freedom, 1750–1925* (New York: Vintage Books, 1976), p. 337.

2. We refer here to "net" immigration. "Total" immigration, not deducting for "emigration," was, of course, substantially higher. See Chapter 4, p. 59.

3. Since no one can know precisely what mortality rates were for blacks in the mid-nineteenth century, it is uncertain whether, or by how much, they may have increased during the remainder of that century. Some of the factors that bear on this issue are the standard of living of blacks under slavery (particularly diet) as compared to the decades after Emancipation, and the prevalence of various diseases (like tuberculosis and venereal disease) in the late nineteenth century. It is quite possible that economic conditions for many rural blacks in the Deep South were worse after Emancipation than before, and that widespread disease brought definite reductions in life expectancies in the post–Civil War years. Disease may also have been a factor in reducing black fertility at this time. Although the total fertility rate for blacks was higher than that of whites throughout the post–Civil War era, it was falling throughout this period (until World War II, in fact). This reduction in fertility was, of course, another factor tending to limit the rate of natural increase of the black population in the period we are discussing. For a summary of evidence on early black mortality and fertility trends, see Reynolds Farley and Walter R. Allen, *The Color Line and the Quality of Life in America* (New York: Russell Sage Foundation, 1987), Chaps. 2–4. This book, a Census Monograph Series publication, is an invaluable source of information on black demography, and we refer to it frequently in this chapter.

4. The Middle Series Projections are taken from Gregory Spencer, pp. 1–27. The assumption of converging fertility rates (achieved in the Middle Series by the year 2050) is difficult to assess. We will return to this question in Chapter 24, pp. 435–437.

5. We discuss the effects of slavery on the black family very briefly on pp. 153–154. For discussion of some contending views, see Robert W. Fogel and Stanley L. Engerman, *Time on the Cross: The Economics of American Negro Slavery* (Boston: Little, Brown, 1974), and Paul A. David, Herbert G. Gutman, Richard Sutch, Peter Temin, and Gavin Wright, *Reckoning with Slavery: A Critical Study in the Quantitative History of American Negro Slavery* (Oxford: Oxford University Press, 1976).

6. See Frank Levy, *Dollars and Dreams: The Changing American Income Distribution* (New York: Russell Sage Foundation, 1987), Table 7–3, pp. 134–135.

7. See William P. O'Hare et al., *Blacks on the Move: A Decade of Demographic Change* (Washington, D.C.: Joint Center for Political Studies, 1982), p. 11. Of course, the large size of this increase in black population in the South in 1970–1980 (a little over 2 million) was more a reflection of natural increase than of net immigration.

8. The Supreme Court has dealt with many affirmative action cases and continues to deal with them in each session. Its decisions have left a somewhat unclear line between circumstances in which affirmative action—preference for blacks and others—is permitted, or can be required by the federal government of its contractors, or can be imposed by a court on public and private employers, and those where it is not. In general, preference may be required or accepted to resolve a past history of discrimination (the evidences for which are not always clear, and may themselves be disputed). Recent cases have dealt with the issue of how long such a preference may be

required; with when or whether seniority provisions in labor contracts may take precedence over affirmative action requirements; with whether a locality may require a certain fixed percentage of its contracts to be given to firms headed by minorities; and with other issues. Since the Bakke decision of 1978, it is clear that colleges and universities may give preference to black applicants, but they must not maintain a rigid quota. Affirmative action and discrimination law has blossomed into a major branch of labor relations law, and it is evolving steadily.

9. An example of the use of life expectancy at birth as a "reasonably good surrogate measure" of the standard of living of a group (when other measures are unavailable) is Stanley Lieberson's comparison of American blacks with people living in south, central, and eastern European nations in the late nineteenth and early twentieth centuries (a time when these nations were sending large numbers of immigrants to the United States). Lieberson found that American blacks had lower life expectancies than virtually all these groups over the period 1880–1920. From this he inferred that American blacks were in a disadvantaged position relative to these new immigrant groups arriving on our shores. See Stanley Lieberson, *A Piece of the Pie: Blacks and White Immigrants since 1880* (Berkeley, Calif.: University of California Press, 1980), pp. 372.–374.

10. The *mean* (or average) income statistics give a higher weight to very high incomes than do *median* income statistics, which simply separate the upper half from the lower half of the income distribution. Since white males tend to have more very high incomes than black males (or females of either race), mean income comparisons suggest a wider disparity between blacks and whites than do median figures. In 1985 median income figures for black and white males were, respectively, $10,400 and $16,500, a difference of $6,100. The comparable mean figures were $12,900 and $20,800, a difference of $7,900. Farley and Allen, *The Color Line,* p. 294. In general, great care must be used in knowing exactly what figures are being cited in these economic comparisons.

11. Thus, between 1950 and 1970, in 11 out of 12 U.S. cities with the largest black populations, white out-migration tended to account for more than half the increase in the black population percent-

age. Writes demographer Larry Long: "Of course, migration of the two groups may not be independent. . . . A high rate of immigration of blacks might encourage white outmovement to new homes and suburban schools, and a high rate of white outmigration from northern cities could encourage black inmigration by creating housing vacancies." Larry Long, *Migration and Residential Mobility in the United States* (New York: Russell Sage Foundation, 1988), p. 155.

12. This view is taken, for example, by Nicholas Lemann in two *Atlantic Monthly* articles on "The Origins of the Underclass," June–July 1986.

13. See Stanley Lieberson and Mary C. Waters, *From Many Strands: Ethnic and Racial Groups in Contemporary America* (New York: Russell Sage Foundation, 1988), Table 6-1, p. 199.

14. The term *new morbidity* and the statistics describing it in this paragraph are taken from National Health Policy Forum, Issue Brief No. 494, George Washington University, Washington, D.C., 1988. The "new morbidity" might, in some respects, be better called the "new mortality." In 1988, homicide was the leading cause of death not only of young blacks, but also of adult blacks aged 25 to 44. The effect of black homicides, combined with a tripling of AIDS cases among blacks over 13 years old from 1986 to 1989, has been to cause a small reduction in black life expectancies, thus temporarily reversing the entire century-old trend to longer black life expectancies noted earlier in the chapter.

15. Harriette McAdoo, "The Moynihan Report Revisited," unpublished manuscript, 1990.

16. Walter R. Allen, "The Search for Applicable Theories of Black Family Life," *Journal of Marriage and the Family,* February 1978, pp. 117–129.

17. Gutman, *The Black Family,* p. 466. Gutman also lays part (though a much smaller part) of the blame for the breakup of the black family on the U.S. welfare system, which he calls a "new Poor Law" (p. 468).

18. Niara Sudarkasa, "Interpreting the African Heritage in Afro-American Family Organization," in Harriette Pipes McAdoo, ed., *Black Families* (Newbury Park, Calif.: Sage Publications, 1988), pp. 27–43.

19. Joyce A. Ladner, "The Impact of Teenage Pregnancy and the Black Family: Policy Directions," in McAdoo, *Black Families,* p. 299.

ch.
or

# Part IV
# *THE CHILDREN*

383
236
147

# 14

# *The Changing Worlds of Childhood*

*N*ot too long ago, an influential book by the French historian Philippe Ariès put forth the proposition that the whole concept of **childhood** was essentially a modern invention that had no real counterpart, say, in medieval times.[1] Whether this hypothesis is wholly or partially accepted, there is little doubt that the serious *study* of childhood, and its past history, is a quite recent phenomenon. Nor is there much doubt about two main conclusions that can be drawn from this recent study:

1. There have been important historical changes in the way in which children have been brought up over the last few centuries, and in the roles children are expected to fulfill in the larger society. Just as we have seen that the "traditional" American family is not a fixed but an evolving concept, so we now understand that American children have been viewed very differently in different historical periods, both as to their basic nature and in their relationship to adults.

2. The present set of arrangements for bringing up our children—arrangements that of course, vary enormously from one family situation to another—is cause for considerable alarm. Almost no one, from radical to liberal to conservative to reactionary, seems pleased with the job that Americans are now doing in the matter of child rearing.

In Chapters 15–17, we shall be considering three of the major ways in which the problems of American children have attracted attention: poverty, parental and other sources of child care, and education. In this chapter, we shall consider how the world of children has been changing over the course of our national history, and why the present situation presents us with new, and rather imposing, challenges.

## CHILDHOOD IN PREINDUSTRIAL AMERICA

Because the historical study of childhood is relatively recent, it is difficult to make accurate generalizations about the way children were brought up in preindustrial America, say, from colonial times until the beginning of the nineteenth century. This difficulty is compounded by major differences in the experiences of children in at least three ways:

1. *Geographical differences:* The experiences of childhood were often very different depending on the area of the country we are talking about. An example of a major difference in the colonial period is that between the New England settlements and the Chesapeake colonies. Infant mortality, for example, was much higher in the latter region; also, parents often died at younger ages. Thus, comparing them with New England children, historian Ross W. Beales, Jr., concludes that Chesapeake children "were frequently orphaned; received poorer educations; might experience the tensions of living in ever-changing households containing an extraordinary range of relatives and strangers; were given earlier responsibilities in managing property; and had little parental guidance in choosing a spouse and in the timing of marriage."[2] Other geographic differences would be found between urban and rural child-rearing conditions and between those in settled communities and those on the frontier.

2. *Ethnic and racial differences:* Recent immigrants often had different child-rearing patterns from those of earlier settlers. Furthermore, immigration during the eighteenth century increasingly involved immigrants of non-English origins. By 1775 nearly 20 percent of America's population was black, and nine out of ten of these blacks were slaves. Thus, black children in

the eighteenth century experienced very different childhoods from those of whites: The mortality rate for black children under 4 years of age was double that of white children; also, black children, both boys and girls, most often began work in the fields at ages 7 to 10, frequently being sent away from home to other plantations or sold to other masters.

Another important difference was that of the childhood experience of Native Americans. Actually, this experience was itself highly varied because of differences in tribal practices. In general, however, it can be said there was a greater role of kinship, clan, and community in the rearing of Indian children.

3. *Socioeconomic class differences:* The well-to-do, the middle class, and the poor all faced different problems and found different solutions to the raising of children in preindustrial America. Differences in parental education were similarly important. Indeed, one of the interesting developments that was to occur as the United States grew and developed economically from the eighteenth century onward was the gradual spread of the standards of the educated middle class to other classes in our society.

Given all these factors, as well as many other sources of variation, it is clear that any generalizations about childhood in America before the great industrialization surge of the nineteenth century will be less than ironclad. Taking the broadest possible view, however, there is considerable agreement on the following:

• *The characteristic setting for American childhood during this period was the nuclear family.* It is probably accurate to say that the norm was that grandparents would live with their children and grandchildren. Because life expectancies were short, however, relatively few grandparents survived to reside with their grandchildren. Thus, in practical terms, most households consisted of a nuclear family of just two generations: parents and their children.

• *Death, particularly the death of infants and young children, was a common experience for virtually all families.* Despite variations between regions, all parts of the country experienced what we would today consider extremely high rates of infant and child mortality throughout the seventeenth and eighteenth centuries. In colonial times, almost every family could expect to lose two or three children in their early childhoods. In the eighteenth century, epidemics were still common, often wreaking severest havoc on the young, occasionally wiping out entire families. These losses were greater among blacks, city dwellers, and the poor.

One of the important questions raised by the frequency of early death is how it may have affected the emotional relationship of parents to children. Although there are some who question the idea, it has been argued that the frequent loss of children reduced or limited the degree of emotional involvement parents could invest in their children. It could be simply overwhelming to place all one's hopes and dreams in one's children and to find, not occasionally but as a matter of constant fact, that one or several of them would die in childhood.[3]

• *Children from an early age were involved in productive activities, usually in and around the home, but sometimes also outside the home.* One of the reasons for believing that "childhood," in our modern sense of the term, did not exist in preindustrial societies is that children went to work almost immediately after completing the stage of infant dependence.[4] At the beginning of the nineteenth century, we were still an overwhelmingly agricultural society, and much of such industry as we had was accomplished either in the home or in relatively small craft establishments. Boys went to work in the fields with their fathers as soon as they were physically capable of helping. Girls, meanwhile, worked in or around the home, helping with numerous chores and learning the skills of spinning, weaving, and mending clothing. In certain cases, boys would be apprenticed out to other homes or shops to learn specific crafts; girls sometimes went to other households to perform domestic services. Children of the poor were occasionally bound to a master by law. Between 1734 and 1805, under a Boston law, numerous children of the poor, half of them between the ages of 5 and 9, were bound out, the boys apprenticed to tradesmen and husbandry, the girls serving as housemaids.[5]

Because of the roles children assumed as "**little workers**" or "useful children," the period of childhood in preindustrial America was not as sharply marked off from later stages in life as it was to become subsequently. Children, like their fathers, were engaged in the economic enterprise which was a core feature of the family unit. In this respect, they were also like their mothers, whose work in the home provided many products that, today, we would purchase in the marketplace. There was, however, a sharp division of roles by sex, both for the little workers and for their parents. Contributing to economic production did not in any way imply equality of status between males and females, as indicated earlier in our discussion of the family (pp. 147–148).

It should also be noted that the usefulness of children extended well beyond their early years. There was, of course, no Social Security program or other regularized public provision for the elderly in the early days of the nation. The family was the prime source of support for the elderly, and children were seen as security against the potential infirmities and hardships of their parents' old age.

## CHILDHOOD IN AN INDUSTRIALIZING AMERICA

When we think of the Industrial Revolution in late-eighteenth- and early-nineteenth-century Great Britain, we often call to mind vividly brutal scenes of child labor, boys and girls being exploited in the early cotton mills, tiny chimney sweeps being forced up dark, cramped passages, occasionally with the threat of a fire being set beneath them. Such atrocities did occur, in America as well as in Britain. If, however, we focus our attention on the rising middle class, the class that largely carried forth the socioeconomic revolution that we call "modernization" or "development," and the class that set the standards to which, in the early twentieth century, the families of the poor would also aspire, we find a very different story.

That story involves the increasing removal of children from the world of work; the growth of sentiment attached to childhood, home, and motherhood; and a longer period of education for children both in the home and in the expanding schools of the nation.

### From Little Workers to a Protected Childhood

One of the most important and obvious differences between the childhood experiences of preindustrial America and those of the industrialized society of the later nineteenth and early twentieth centuries was the gradual removal of children from the world of work. Insofar as agriculture remained a numerically important pursuit even into the twentieth century, there were still many children in rural areas who participated in family chores much as in the old days. For the urban middle classes, however, childhood—and, in due course, **adolescence**—was set apart from the productive life of the family.[6] As it is sometimes put, the home ceased to be a unit of *pro-*

*duction* and became primarily a unit of *consumption.*

This change in the position of children clearly reflected a number of developments that we have already discussed in connection with the evolution of the American family. The basic economic factors were undoubtedly the increasingly sharp break between home and workplace that occurred following the Industrial Revolution, and also the lengthening of time needed to prepare children for entry into an increasingly complex modern industrial society. Furthermore, the separation of children (and their mothers) from the world of work was made possible by the rising standard of living that modernization produced.

This last factor helps explain why, during most of the nineteenth century, and indeed into the twentieth, the children of the poor remained active in the work force well after the departure of the middle-class young. Industrialization actually created many job opportunities for children. In the United States between 1870 and 1900, there was an increase of over a million child workers and, in the new Southern textile mills, one-third of the work force was between ages 10 and 13, or even younger.[7] In immigrant families, children characteristically were economically productive family workers. And of course, as mentioned, children remained active workers in the diminishing but still substantial agricultural sector.

However, the urban middle classes set the new tone on the matter of child labor, and this was soon reflected in strong local, state, and national campaigns against such labor. In the early twentieth century, reformers found inexcusable "the commercialization of child life." A New York clergyman argued that "a man who defends the child labor that violates the personalities of children is not a Christian. . . ." Others noted that "those who are fighting for the rights of children find their stoutest foes in the fathers and mothers, who coin shameful dollars from the bodies and souls of their own flesh and blood." Poor families might argue that their economic situation (unlike that of their prosperous middle-class critics) really did require productive contributions from their children, and even that work was good for children, or at least better than idleness.

Ultimately, however, the victory went to what has been called "the useless child."[8] By the late 1930s, both legally and by cultural consensus, the American child and even the early adolescent was largely debarred from the nation's productive enterprise.

### Increasing Sentiment toward Children

The battle against child labor reflected not only the increasing ease of the middle classes but also a new conception of what childhood ideally should be. The nineteenth century has actually been called "the century of the child," referring to the growth of a more affectionate, sentimental, protective attitude of Americans toward their children. Particularly important here is the new sense of the home as a haven from the world of work, and especially the changed role of women who, like children, were also increasingly physically separated from the working world. Thus, we have not only a growing sense of the sacredness of The Child, but also of The Home, and of The Mother in the Home. By the end of the century, the **Cult of Domesticity** was at its height. And within the domestic sphere, the role of women was supreme. As noted scholar, Carl Degler writes: "It is surely not accidental that the century of the child is also the century of the Cult of True Womanhood."[9]

To what degree the increased time, attention, and emotion directed toward children reflected the gradual decline in infant and child mortality over the later nineteenth and early twentieth centuries is unclear. (It could be, as one commentator has suggested, that, instead of lowered mortality being a cause of increased attention to children, it would have been a *result* of that increased attention to children; that is, children who were better taken care of tended to have better survival rates.[10]) It does seem fairly certain, however, that the status of both mothers and children was rising during this era, with women in some cases taking over functions previously reserved for men. Writes Professor Anne M. Boylan:

> Given the importance of the impressions children received from their environments, most childrearing theorists agreed that parents and not servants should take primary responsibility for children's upbringing. More to the point, mothers seemed best cut out, not only by opportunity but also by temperament, to rear children. Whereas earlier childrearing books had often been aimed at the father or had depicted him as the ultimate disciplinarian and final authority in families, the new works that poured from the popular press after 1820 portrayed the mother as having primary responsibility for children's socialization. Fathers had a place, to be sure, especially in training sons as they got older, but it was a distinctly secondary place.[11]

This heightened status of both motherhood and childhood can also be interpreted to reflect a new view of the future that accompanied the great success of the modernization process. In traditional, preindustrial societies, change is slow and improvements in living standards and the quality of life are uncertain at best. During the course of the nineteenth and early twentieth centuries, however, the United States was ablaze with economic and social advance, the **Idea of Progress** becoming, in some respects, our dominant philosophic concept. This idea crucially involves the future in our *present* satisfactions; that is to say, it is in *today's* imagination of the better future that lies ahead that we take such

great pride and pleasure. And, of course, the future is essentially the domain of our children and our children's children.

Thus, during the course of the nineteenth and early twentieth centuries, the "little workers" of our historic past were transformed into our **"best hope for the future."** To make sure that their children had a better life than their parents had had became an important goal for American families, a goal further sanctifying the preeminent nurturer of the young, the mother.

### The Crucial Role of Education

But it was not only the mother who was to be involved in this great nurturing project—it was also the school. During the course of the nineteenth century, the battle for universal, tax-supported **public education** in the United States was fought and won. There had been earlier advocates of such a system, of course, notably Thomas Jefferson, who in 1779 called for a program of three-year local schools that would be free for all white children between the ages of 7 and 10. However, Jefferson's proposal never materialized, and such education as there was for poor children took place either at home, in charity schools, or in church. Meanwhile, more well-to-do children were educated either in private schools or by tutors at home.

From the 1830s on, however, numerous milestones mark the nation's progress toward the ideal of free education for all. In the late 1830s, industrial states began adopting laws that required poor children working in factories to attend school three months a year. In 1852 Massachusetts adopted the nation's first universal compulsory education law. New York followed in 1853, and other states joined in until the last state—Mississippi—completed the roster in 1918. Meanwhile, compulsory education was also becoming "free" education, though not always without a fight. Thus,

New York State did not abolish all tuition rates until 1867, and Connecticut, Rhode Island, and Michigan did not do so until somewhat later.[12]

The expansion of public schools gradually came to include high schools as well as elementary schools. In 1827 Massachusetts required every town of 500 or more families to set up a public high school. But progress at the secondary level was slow. On the eve of the Civil War, there were only 300 or so public high schools in the nation. By the end of the nineteenth century, this number had grown to six thousand, but even then the average American had only about five years of schooling. The subsequently rapid growth of U.S. public education is shown graphically in Figure 14-1.

In some respects, this growth of public education was consistent with, and really an outgrowth of, the other developments we have just been discussing: the withdrawal of children from the work force and the increasing sentiment attached to the childhood years. What was involved was a further extension of the period of youthful dependence, reaching, as the twentieth century wore on, well into the years of adolescence and even early adulthood. This could be explained, in part, by the greater demand for literacy and computational ability in an advancing industrial society. It also could be explained, in part, by the increasing sentiment attached to children and especially to the psychological role children played as inheritors of a presumably ever-better future.

Indeed, the theme of the relationship of education to progress—technological, economic, social, political—was frequently sounded by the early pioneers in the field of universal public education. A leading scholar of the history of American education, Lawrence A. Cremin, describes the motivation of Horace Mann (1796–1859):

> The commanding figure of the early public-school movement, he had poured into his vision of universal education a boundless faith in the perfectibility of human life and institutions. Once public schools were established, no evil could resist their salutary influence. Universal education could be the "great equalizer" of human conditions, the "balance wheel of the social machinery," and the "creator of wealth undreamed of." Poverty would most assuredly disappear, and with it the rancorous discord between the "haves" and "have-nots" that had marked all of human history. Crime would diminish; sickness would abate; and life for the common man would be longer, better, and happier.[13]

Thus, the parental desire that their children should have better and happier lives than their own could find expression in the increased schooling of the children in very much the same way as it found expression in protecting children from the workaday world and in the emotional nurturing of those children in the bosom of the family.

In another respect, however, the trend toward more and more years of public education (and/or private education outside the home) was a movement away from the primacy of the family in the rearing of children.

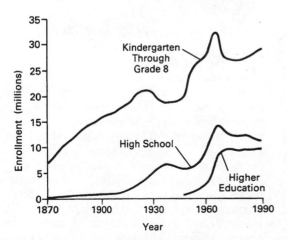

**FIGURE 14-1:  Enrollment in U.S. Public Education, 1870–1990**

*Source:*   National Center for Education Statistics.

While the home remained the main center of the affectional lives of American children, the preparation of children for their ultimate participation in the world of jobs, professions, and citizenship increasingly took place outside the family. To that degree, the development of public education represented a diminution of the role of the family *even compared to preindustrial America.* For in that earlier period, sons and daughters most often received their preparation for the workaday world from their fathers and mothers or from other close kin.

This movement away from the primacy of the family was also abetted by the increasing **professionalization** of the social sciences, and of child psychology in particular. Harvard's first doctorate in psychology went to Granville Stanley Hall in 1878. Hall went on to become president of Clark University in Worcester, Massachusetts, and, in 1904, to publish a massive two-volume work whose title alone suggests the weight and scope of the new disciplines: *Adolescence: Its Psychology and Its Relations to Physiology, Anthropology, Sociology, Sex, Crime, Religion, and Education.* The professional expert in education and child rearing had made an impressive entrance upon the American scene.

The combination of (1) increased public, extrafamily education and (2) the growing role of professionals in determining what was or was not best for one's children, though a natural outgrowth of parental interests, could also potentially undermine them. A possible paradox is suggested by sociologist Brigitte Berger, who notes that the values of the bourgeois (modern middle-class) family contained

within them the seeds of their own destruction. . . . Education would free itself of its family linkage and burgeon into powerful institutions with an anti-family animus, or at least with vested interests antagonistic to those of the family. The experts who started out as allies of the bourgeois family would develop interests and viewpoints of their own at odds with the family.[14]

Whether one agrees or disagrees with this particular paradox, there is little doubt that, during this great period of American modernization and industrialization, the forces that had so strengthened the child–home–family nexus in the late nineteenth and early twentieth centuries were also subtly working to weaken and possibly destroy it. Before describing these forces, however, we must pause—as we must in discussing virtually any aspect of American demography—to note some features of the period following World War II.

## STRANGE INTERLUDE

Two developments of that demographically curious period are relevant here: (1) the resurrection and, in some ways, intensification of the child-centered home pattern, and (2) the subsequent development of the so-called generation gap—the rebellion in the 1960s of many youths against home, family, school, and Western civilization generally.

### The Child-Centered Home Revitalized

Many of the trends that were subsequently to weaken both the "traditional" American family and the place of children within that family were either delayed or temporarily reversed in the two decades after World War II. We have already discussed these changes in earlier chapters: the sharp upturn in fertility during the Baby Boom, increasing suburbanization and the separation of the father's work even farther from the home, the temporary pause in the trend toward increased female labor force participation among the mothers of the Baby Boom generation. In general, the home and family, presided over by a present mother, a mostly absent father, and fairly numerous children became the ideal of middle-class Americans.

In some respects, moreover, this home was actually *more* **child-centered** than had been the home of the late-nineteenth-century Victorians. The single word that was universally used to describe the trend in child rearing after World War II was **permissiveness.** Children were to be allowed to develop relatively freely, to learn to express themselves, to find and realize their own natural talents and preferences.

Much of this mood was attributed to the enormous success of Dr. Benjamin M. Spock's manual, *Baby and Child Care,* which came out in 1946 and became one of the greatest best-sellers of all time. This may be unfair to Dr. Spock, whose main apparent emphasis was on common sense and whose opening sentence to parents was: "You know more than you think you do."[15] Also, the book went through changes in various editions, gradually admitting the possibility of replacing maternal care with that of the father, or even some form of day care institution. Nevertheless, in the early editions—those published during the Baby Boom period—there is no question but that the nurturing and raising of small children is considered an activity of paramount importance, that this activity is conceived to take place in a home largely isolated from the world of work, and that the key figure in this endeavor is the mother. "It was not sufficient for the mother to be present most of the time in early Spock," writes one commentator, "but mandatory that she be present all the time. For home is the school of infancy in this literature, the curriculum is articulated in a child-rearing text, and the teacher-trainer of choice is the mother." Thirty years later, in 1976, though now including men in his discussion, Dr. Spock still emphasized the primacy of the home in his hope that "there will always be men and women who feel that the care of children and home is at least as important and soul satisfying as any other activity, and that neither men nor women will feel the need to apologize for making that their main career."[16]

Thus, during the first two decades after World War II, the emphasis on children, domesticity, and the crucial role of the mother in child rearing was arguably as strong as it had ever been in our history.

## The Generation Gap

Which makes it all the more ironic that this generation of children (or, more accurately, some members of this generation of children), when they grew up in the 1960s, were quick to announce their dissatisfaction, disenchantment, and even hostility toward the world of their parents. "Never trust anyone over 30" was the motto of the era (a decidedly curious slogan in a century where life expectancies for the young had increased so materially). More explicitly than at any time in our nation's history, a "generation gap" had been proclaimed. A central characteristic of such a gap is that one's deeper allegiances go horizontally, by **age** or **peer group,** rather than vertically through time: to one's grandparents, parents, children, and so on.

Like the Baby Boom that preceded it, the era of **youthful rebellion** of the late 1960s and early 1970s has been subject to many analyses, none of which commands universal agreement. Did the "permissiveness" of the upbringing of these young people have anything to do with it? Was it the general "affluence" of the early postwar years? Could it have been the sheer numbers of young people in the teenage and pre- and post-teenage groups? Or was it possibly something more specific, like disillusion over the war in Vietnam, or concern about social issues like poverty, racism, and environmental degradation?

One theory suggested that what we were witnessing was the emergence of a new stage of developmental growth. Childhood had long since been set aside from the world of adults. So also had adolescence. Now, continuing the same extension of preadult life, we were to add another stage: what psychologist Kenneth Keniston called **postmod-**

**ern youth.** Thus, if adolescence is assumed to end at age eighteen, this new stage of pre-adulthood would occupy the years from eighteen to twenty-six.

Keniston explains the emergence of this new stage as deriving from many of the same forces that produced the stage we call adolescence:

> Just as making a later stage of adolescence available to large numbers of children was an achievement of industrial society, so a post-adolescent stage of youth is beginning to be made available by post-industrial society. In discussing the relationship of affluence and adolescence, I argued that industrial society had freed children from the need to work at the same time that it demanded skills teachable only through post-childhood education. These changes went hand in hand with new social attitudes that eventually made it seem desirable for most children to experience a post-childhood, preadult stage of continuing psychological growth.
>
> In the last third of the twentieth century, comparable changes in the economy, education and social attitudes are slowly permitting growing numbers of young men and women the possibility of a post-adolescent, preadult stage of psychological development. . . . What industrial society did for the years between twelve and eighteen, post-industrial society is beginning to do for the years between eighteen and twenty-six. For the most talented and privileged, deferred entry into the economic system because of continuing higher education is not only possible, but highly desirable.[17]

Although the new stage of youth is made possible by a further development of the same forces that "created" adolescence, there are important distinctions between the two stages in Keniston's view. For one thing, adolescence "is today a majority phenomenon, clearly recognized, sanctioned, and institutionalized in many variants of the "teen-age" culture. But the chance to have a youth is only available to the most-talented, well-educated, rich, sensitive, or lucky in our society." This may change, but so far we are dealing with a "minority of a minority," largely of the affluent.

More significantly, the stage of post-modern youth is *qualitatively* different from adolescence, and, indeed, occurs only after the typical struggles of adolescence have been resolved. Thus, the individual has already passed through the stage of rebelling against his parents, has established his emotional independence from his family, has come to terms with his sexuality and his own particular pattern of sexual adjustment, and has established an inner identity.

What then remains to be accomplished before adulthood? Essentially, the individual, having come to terms with him or herself, must now come to terms with society. "The focal issue of youth," writes Keniston, "is the issue of social role, of the *individual's relationship to the structures of the established society*" (emphasis in the original).

We can now understand the bearing of this analysis on the upheavals of the 1960s and, indeed, why this analysis appeared in a book entitled *Young Radicals: Notes on Committed Youth.* For, although one way of solving one's relationship to society—the "establishment"—is to adjust one's ideas and behavior to the going norms, and another is to withdraw from society altogether, there is also a further alternative. This alternative, widely practiced in the youthful rebellions of the 1960s, is to attack the establishment and to try to change it in radical ways.

Since Keniston's book was published in 1968, at the height of the student uprisings, much of the analysis has a rather archaic flavor today. What perhaps remains is the strong sense of *generational* identity that Keniston found in the young people of that time. He writes:

> Identification with a generational movement, rather than a cross-generation organization or non-generational ideology, distinguishes post-modern youth from its parents and from earlier generations. It also creates "generational" distinctions involving

five years and less. . . . Generations succeed each other quickly: whatever is to be done in and by youth must be done soon.

The concept of the **generation gap** or really "gaps" was a creation, then, of the youth of the Baby Boom generation. As we have already said, there is a deep irony in this considering the strong generational interests their parents had expressed through the medium of the child-centered home. But there are more than ironies in the separation of the generations. For the concept of such a separation, once accepted, can be applied to and/or against any and all generations. And in this generational division of society, there is little doubt as to which group is most likely to be hurt. It is the group that has no resources of its own and is most dependent—and, in our complex industrial society, increasingly depen-

dent—on the largesse of other generations. It is our children.

## THE EQUIVOCAL STATUS OF TODAY'S CHILDREN

We have briefly traced the changing worlds of American children from the earliest days through the youth of the Baby Boomers. We turn now to the children of today, the children of the continuing Baby Bust. Since we will be taking up specific aspects of the new generation in the next three chapters, we shall indicate here only a broad framework within which this subject may be studied.

Perhaps the key word in describing this framework is "equivocal." Equivocality shows up in both facts and attitudes. Figure 14-2, taken from the 1991 *Kids Count Data*

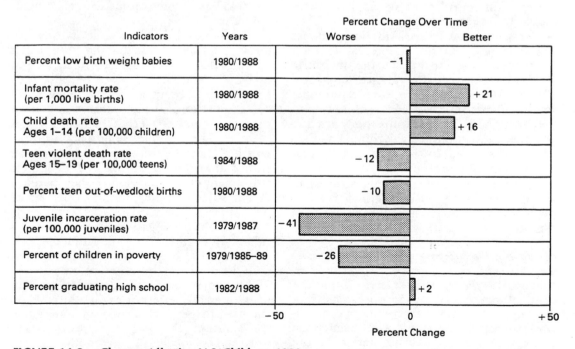

**FIGURE 14-2: Changes Affecting U.S. Children, 1980s**

*Source: Kids Count Data Book* (Washington, D.C.: The Center for the Study of Social Policy, 1991), p. 9.

*Book* of the Center for the Study of Social Policy, gives a bird's-eye account of the changing status of U.S. children during the 1980s, with minus items outnumbering the plus items.

As for attitudes toward children, we have author Germaine Greer writing about the "profound lack of desire for children which prevails in Western society"—a new phenomenon. "Historically, human societies have been pro-child; modern society is unique in that it is profoundly hostile to children."[18] On the other hand, in a June 1988 survey, the Census Bureau informed us that a total of 91 percent of American women in their late twenties had either had children or expected to have them one day. By one account, then, our attitudes toward children have changed sharply, and in a negative direction; by the other account, the traditional desire to bear children seems alive and healthy.

Perhaps most puzzling is that there should be any doubt about the matter. Even in harsh colonial times, Americans always had a strong emotional interest in their children, an interest that, during the course of the nineteenth century and certainly during the Baby Boom era, was paramount among all our interests. How could we possibly imagine that Americans today are hostile, neutral, or indeed anything less than totally committed to the care and nurture of the next generation?

Three major developments, all of which we have encountered before, will help explain why this unsettling question has to be raised.

*1. For the first time in our national history, we have reduced the number of children we are having below the replacement level.* Given that the prolonged fall in our fertility rate during the nineteenth and early twentieth centuries was associated with an increasing emotional commitment to the rearing and nurturing of our children, the further drop to **below the replacement level** does not necessarily mean that we are now reducing that emo-

tional commitment. There are, however, a number of indications suggesting that the role children play in fulfilling their parents' emotional lives may be less strong today than in the immediate postwar period.

Collectively, a society that does not have enough children to replace itself would seem to have lost the intensity of interest in the future that gave children such a special place in earlier decades. At the individual level, it appears that the extreme form of this loss of interest—purposeful **childlessness**—may be on the increase. Certainly the public advocacy of childlessness as an appropriate choice for a woman has increased. Research into the early-twentieth-century United States revealed not a single signed article defending childlessness. Today, numerous books and magazine articles justifying this option are to be found. The reason, according to Marian Faux, writer of one of these books, is simply that "childlessness has become an increasingly acceptable lifestyle."[19]

Clearly, this is still a minority opinion, but it could be the case that the attitude that accepts childlessness as a normal, and in many cases desirable, state of affairs, is simply an extreme form of a much more common attitude, which finds in one, or at most two, children all that the family wishes to raise. There is a sense in many of these writings that children exist in competition with, rather than as expressing the ultimate fulfillment of, the interests of their parents. It is possible that the intensity of the debate over abortion in the late 1980s and early 1990s also represents a conflict between this newer view and the more traditional view of children as beyond price, almost sacred. The increase in the **abortion** rate in the 1970s and 1980s is often defended in terms of the negative effect of having the child on the life prospects of the woman undergoing the abortion. *Pro-choice* refers to the woman's choice, obviously not to that of the fetus.

All of these points have comebacks. Childlessness is very probably not rising as rapidly as its advocates have suggested. Much of such increase as there is may reflect decisions to have children later in life, which then lead to fecundity problems resulting in inadvertent childlessness. Similarly, the desire to have only one or two children could reflect not a lack of interest in having children but a commitment to having "high-quality" children in an age when educational and other child-rearing costs are soaring. Also, abortion decisions, though made by the prospective mother, often can be defended with respect to the interests of the unborn child, particularly when the mother is poor, uneducated, and scarcely more than a child herself.

In short, the picture is mixed—yet hardly conveying a vision of children as our great hopes for the future.

*2. The weakening of the nuclear family threatens the institution that, historically, has taken primary responsibility for the rearing and nurturing of young children.* Since we have already discussed the changing American family structures at length (especially in Chapters 9 and 10), we need here only mention the direct impact of some of these changes on the young. Briefly, we have two major developments, growing illegitimacy and divorce rates.

The **illegitimacy** rate is rising to the point where, by the late 1980s, nearly a quarter of American children were being born out of wedlock; although many of these young mothers will marry in due course, some will not, and many of those who do will go through a period of great difficulty when their children are infants and most vulnerable.

**Divorce** rates have also risen sharply in recent decades, with the effect that at least 40 percent of American children will live through the divorce of their parents, and perhaps 20 percent of them will live through two divorces before reaching the age of eighteen.

The combination of these two factors has led to a doubling of the percentage of children living with just one parent—from 12 to 24 percent—between 1970 and 1988. It is estimated that 60 percent of children born at the end of the 1980s will spend at least part of their childhood in a single-parent home. Numerous others, of course, will be living in stepparent households.

Is this decline in the nuclear family, as traditionally understood, necessarily harmful to children? Sociologists and psychologists differ on this issue. Some emphasize that bad marriages can be as harmful, or more so, to children as separation or divorce. Others stress the wrenching effect of divorce itself, the sadness many of these children feel, their emotional problems, their difficulties in school, and also the economic problems that single-parent families face. Studies in 1990 and 1991 found that children in mother-only or mother-stepfather families had more than twice the rate of emotional and behavioral problems that children in intact mother-father families had, and that the departure of the father usually led to a doubling of the percentage of children in poverty.[20]

We will be discussing these issues in future chapters. For the moment, we simply ask whether these recent trends suggest anything about the attitudes of parents toward their children. Again, there can be disagreement on the answer to this question. Dissolving a bad marriage is sometimes undertaken mainly or even wholly with the interests of the children at heart. Fathers who are separated from their children often feel the loss keenly and make strenuous efforts to keep in touch with them and follow their schooling and general development.

Still, the story is again a mixed one. Young men who sire children and then abandon their mothers can hardly be said to have a deep interest in the well-being of those children. Nor can such interest be imputed to the numerous fathers who, after divorce or separation, fail to make child support payments, and often have little or no further contact with their children, even by telephone. Nor can we feel that couples who separate or divorce because of various personal incompatibilities always give first priority to the emotional stresses their children may suffer in consequence. In total, these developments at least bring into question the depth of our commitment to our offspring.

*3. The departure of the father from home to workplace during the nineteenth century is now being complemented by the increasing departure of mothers from home to workplace, leaving the care of adolescents, children, and even infants in very uncertain hands.* Not only is the nuclear family in disrepair, but even within the nuclear family there has been a major shift of emphasis as far as the role of the mother is concerned. As we discussed in Chapter 11, not only have more women been entering the labor force in the post–World War II era, but the greatest increase since 1975 has been in the labor force participation of mothers, and especially of mothers of young children. The increased labor force participation of mothers of young children is by no means limited to low-income, working-class families; in fact, the rate of increase in recent years has been greater for women with high-income husbands than for those with low-income husbands (see p. 190).

This situation, where a majority of mothers of young children have jobs outside the home, contrasts sharply with the situation at the beginning of the twentieth century when, in the case of married white women, only 2 percent were in the labor force. To put it another way, the cult of domesticity, which had counterbalanced the loss of economic functions of the household during industrialization, and which gave a central place to child rearing, had virtually disappeared by the 1980s.

What makes this situation disturbing to both liberals and conservatives (though for different reasons) is that this potential deficit with respect to child rearing was not accompanied by the emergence of other agents or institutions that could handle this task satisfactorily. In general, as we shall discuss in Chapter 16, day care and other extrafamily institutions were generally thought to be inadequate to the responsibilities quite suddenly thrust upon them. Furthermore, the public school was already itself in a state of crisis, and could hardly discharge yet another new function (see Chapter 17).

In short, a possible gap in our child care arrangements has been created without adequate provision for compensating solutions. This has led some observers to believe that, for the moment at least, the interests of the present younger generation are being sacrificed to other adult interests, which, for whatever reason, now have a higher priority.

## CONTINUITY OR COMPETITION?

American children have evolved from "little workers" to our "best hope for the future" to a present status that can only be called "equivocal." Underlying the specific problems we shall be taking up in the next three chapters is a quite general philosophical question. The question may be put in terms of "**continuity versus competition**" or an "intergenerational versus generational view" of society:

*When we approach social issues from the point of view of our own individual interests or those of our peer group or generation, it is very easy to look at other generations, including that of our children, as being in competition with ours. Children are expensive, they get into trouble, they take time. (Similarly, of course, at the other end of the spectrum, the elderly are expensive, impose burdens, require attention, and so on.) We would be able to live more comfortably, have more freedom of choice about our sexual partners, be better able to plan our careers and life-styles, and the like without children.*

*An alternative view is to think of the younger generation as an expression of the basic con-*

*tinuity of human life and society. These young people are not really in competition with us but are an extension of our interests into the future. Raising children carefully and well is not just an obligation but a deep expression of the present satisfaction we derive from imagining their lives and circumstances after our own departure from the scene. In this intergenerational view, children are not obstacles to, but a substantial part of, our adult fulfillment.*

Most readers will immediately conclude that both views are true in part; it is a matter of degree. The underlying question, then, is this: *To what degree has the American concept of children been shifting from the intergenerational, continuity-focused, future-oriented view so prominent a century ago, to the generational,* more self-centered, present-oriented view that finds its extreme expression in neglecting, abandoning, or simply not having children?

Have we become, as some critics claim, a "narcissistic" society in which individualism, self-realization, and affluence combine to elevate our own personal concerns above the demands of both past and future? Or does the continuing, strongly expressed interest of the overwhelming majority of young adults in marriage and having children suggest that the longer run, intergenerational view still has a deep appeal and will reassert itself in due course? Readers may wish to keep this question in mind as they go on to the more concrete problems facing the younger generation considered in the following chapters.

## SUMMARY

1. The study of "childhood" is a relatively recent phenomenon, but it brings out two important points: (a) that concepts of childhood change considerably over historical time, and (b) that there is much concern about our current child-rearing practices.

2. In preindustrial America, although there was great variety in the situations in which children were brought up (as there is today), most children were raised in nuclear families, were vulnerable to and acquainted with early death, and were characteristically "little workers" in or near the family farm or craft establishments.

3. During the nineteenth and early twentieth centuries, although poor children and immigrant children often continued to work, the children of the expanding middle class went from being little workers to a more protected childhood. There was a growing sentiment attached to children, and their education, whether at home or, increasingly, in public schools, became a matter of general concern. This was an age devoted to Progress, and children were the nation's "hope for the future."

4. In the mid-twentieth century, a strange interlude occurred featuring, *first,* an intensification of the child-centered home pattern, with "permis-siveness" (sometimes, but not quite accurately, attributed to the influence of Dr. Spock) the watchword for child rearing during the Baby Boom period, and, *second,* a rebellion in the 1960s of many young people against their parents and society in general. Some psychologists believed that a new stage of "postmodern youth" had emerged.

5. The children of the Baby Bust in the 1970s and 1980s have seemed to occupy an "equivocal" status. Young parents continue, by large majorities, to want to have children. Yet below-replacement-level families are common, purposeful childlessness is somewhat on the increase, abortion has grown sharply, divorce and separation along with never-married parents mean that many children are no longer raised in the traditional nuclear family, and both parents now frequently work outside the home with, so far, no generally accepted substitute plan of child rearing for replacing them.

6. A question to be explored further, then, is: Are we moving away from an intergenerational view of society, which stresses the continuity of grandparents, parents, and children over time, toward a generational view of society in which each generation (or peer group) sees its own interests as being essentially in competition with those of earlier (grandparents) and/or later (children) generations?

## KEY CONCEPTS FOR REVIEW

Changing concepts of childhood
    little workers
    best hope for the future
    equivocal status
Adolescence
Postmodern youth
Home as a unit of consumption versus production
Cult of Domesticity
Spread of public education
Professionalization of child care
Idea of Progress

"Permissiveness" and the child-centered home
Youth rebellion of the 1960s
Generation gap
Changing attitudes to
    below-replacement level families
    childlessness
    abortion
    divorce and separation
    illegitimacy
    parental care versus day care
Continuity versus competition among generations

## QUESTIONS FOR DISCUSSION

1.  It is often said that children are very valuable economically to their parents in an agrarian society. Does this view apply to colonial America? Discuss how changes in the stage of industrialization in the United States may have influenced our concepts of "childhood."

2.  "There were as many different 'childhoods' in colonial America as there were economic classes, races, ethnic groups, and regions of the country. Indeed, the same statement is still true today." Discuss.

3.  What is the relationship of the Idea of Progress to our views on children? Do you believe in the Idea of Progress? Yes? Somewhat? Not at all? In a poll in 1989, a majority (53 percent) of Americans said that they thought the future

would be less good than the present. Could this have any bearing on our attitudes toward having and rearing children?

4.  Why do we say that the youth rebellion of the 1960s was in many ways an "ironic" development?

5.  List any developments since the 1970s that might lead one to conclude that Americans are becoming "hostile to children" (Greer). In each case, suggest a possible counterargument.

6.  Which concept best expresses your view of the relationship of the several generations: "competition" or "continuity"? Do current trends seem to be heading toward or away from your preferred concept?

## NOTES

1.  Philippe Ariès, *Centuries of Childhood: A Social History of Family Life* (New York: Random House, 1962), first published in France in 1960. The idea, of course, is not that children did not exist, but that they were viewed at an early age as essentially small adults.
2.  Ross W. Beales, Jr., "The Child in Seventeenth Century America," in Joseph M. Hawes and N. Ray Hiner, eds., *American Childhood: A Research Guide and Historical Handbook* (Westport, Conn.: Greenwood Press, 1985), p. 41.
3.  For a discussion of the roles of death and bereavement in colonial American homes, see Peter G. Slater, "From the Cradle to the Coffin: Parental Bereavement and the Shadow of Infant Damnation in Puritan Society," and Daniel Blake Smith, "Autonomy and Affection: Parents and Children in Eighteenth Century Chesapeake Families" in N. Ray Hiner, and Joseph M. Hawes, eds., *Growing Up in America: Children in Historical Perspective* (Chicago: University of Illinois Press, 1985). Slater argues that, despite the presence of early death,

Puritan families did feel considerable love and affection for their children. This was somewhat complicated, however, by the doctrine of predestination and the possibility of infant damnation.

4. Another reason for believing that childhood was not set apart from adult life in premodern society was that children in medieval portraits tend to be dressed in the same kind of clothing as their elders—that is, as miniature adults. Also, there is some evidence that adults and children tended to share common games, as well as common work, in the medieval period. The view that childhood is a wholly modern invention is not, however, shared by all historians and sociologists.

5. Constance B. Schulz, "Children and Childhood in the Eighteenth Century," in Hawes and Hiner, *American Childhood*, p. 70.

6. For an interesting discussion of the historical evolution of the stages of preadulthood in a European (primarily English and German) context, see John R. Gillis, *Youth and History: Tradition and Change in European Age Relations, 1770–Present* (New York: Academic Press, 1981). Gillis argues that in preindustrial Europe there was typically a stage of "youth" that began at around age 7 or 8 and went on to the mid- to late twenties. This was a period of semi-independence during which many children would go off to other homes as apprentices, servants, or (if wealthy) to boarding schools. The period usually ended with marriage and the setting up of an independent household. There was in this arrangement no recognition of a separate period called "adolescence." The latter was a "creation" of the late nineteenth century and was associated with a longer period of dependence and also the newly drawn lines between primary and secondary education (see Gillis, esp. Chaps. 1 and 3).

7. Viviana A. Zelizer, *Pricing the Priceless Child: The Changing Social Value of Children* (New York: Basic Books, 1985), p. 70. The comments on child labor in this section of the text are taken from her Chapter 3: "From Useful to Useless: Moral Conflict over Child Labor."

8. Ibid., p. 74.

9. Carl Degler, *At Odds: Women and Family in America from the Revolution to the Present* (New York: Oxford University Press, 1980), p. 74.

10. This argument is made in Edward Shorter, *The Making of the Modern Family* (New York: Basic Books, 1975), on the grounds that, in Europe at least, the increased sentiment for children actually *preceded* the decline in infant and child mortality.

11. Anne M. Boylan, "Growing Up Female in America, 1800–1860," in Hawes and Hiner, *American Childhood*, p. 155.

12. Robert L. Church, *Education in the United States* (New York: Free Press, 1976), pp. 58–61.

13. Lawrence A. Cremin, *The Transformation of the School: Progressivism in American Education, 1876–1957* (New York: Vintage Books, 1964), pp. 8–9.

14. Brigitte Berger and Peter L. Berger, *The War over the Family: Capturing the Middle Ground* (Garden City, N.Y.: Anchor Press/Doubleday, 1983), p. 103.

15. It is interesting to note that Dr. Spock's views were in definite contrast to a preceding emphasis (influenced by behaviorism) on a rather rigid approach to child rearing. Mothers were told they knew very little; they must trust the experts and adhere to very rigid timetables in bringing up the young. In this context, Dr. Spock's approach came as a considerable relief and comfort to many young parents.

16. See Nancy Pottishman Weiss, "Mother, the Invention of Necessity: Dr. Benjamin Spock's *Baby and Child Care*" in Hiner and Hawes, *Growing Up in America*, p. 302. For further discussion of the impact of Dr. Spock, see Marie Winn, *Children without Childhood* (New York: Pantheon Books, 1983), esp. Chap. 6.

17. Kenneth Keniston, *Young Radicals: Notes on Committed Youth* (New York: Harcourt, Brace, 1968), pp. 264–265. All quotes from Keniston are from this book, Chapter 8, "Youth and History." Whether this period (age 18 to 26) represents a genuinely new stage or simply a prolongation of adolescence is, of course, a matter of dispute, particularly in those cases where the youths are still dependent financially on their parents. There is no question, however, that there was a rise in the age of marriage at this time, probably driven more by the desire to experience life, "find oneself," and the like than by any obvious economic need or shortfall.

18. Germaine Greer, *Sex and Destiny: The Politics of Human Fertility* (New York: Harper and Row, 1984), p. 2.

19. Marian Faux, *Childless by Choice: Choosing Childlessness in the '80s* (Garden City, N.Y.: Anchor Press/Doubleday, 1984), p. vii. Faux has conducted research on attitudes toward childlessness earlier in this century. While she has found an occasional *anonymous* article defending the decision to have no children, she notes that such an article is "as extraordinary as it is rare."

20. Nicholas Zill and Charlotte A. Schoenborn, "Developmental, Learning, and Emotional Problems: Health of Our Nation's Children, United States, 1988," advance data from *Vital and Health Statistics*, No. 190, National Center for Health Statistics, 1990; Suzanne Bianchi and Edith McArthur, "Family Disruption and Economic Hardship: The Short-Run Picture for Children," *Current Population Reports*, p. 70, No. 23, January, 1991. A study suggesting that many of the behavioral and other problems of children in divorced families may be due to conditions predating the divorce is A. J.

Cherlin, F. F. Furstenberg, P. L. Chase-Lansdale, K. E. Kiernan, P. K. Robins, D. R. Morrison, and J. O. Teitter, "Longitudinal Studies of Effects of Divorce on Children in Great Britain and the United States," *Science*, 252 (June 7, 1991), 1386–1389.

# 15

# *Children in Poverty*

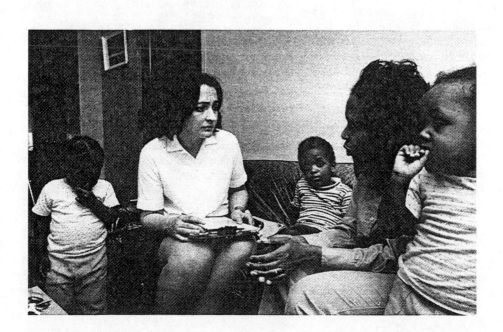

*I*n his presidential address to the Population Association of America in May 1984, Samuel H. Preston underlined a striking fact and posed an interesting question.[1] The fact was that the economic well-being of the nation's children, and especially of children in lower income families, had been deteriorating in recent years, while that of the nation's elderly had been improving substantially. By the early 1980s, the percentage of persons 65 and older below the official "poverty level" had fallen below the national average, while that of persons under 18 had risen well above that average.

The interesting question was whether population numbers had anything to do with these changes. One might have thought, Preston wrote, that demographic changes would have worked in the opposite direction. A striking feature of these years was the unexpectedly large growth of our elderly population. With so many more elderly people to support, one might have expected (thinking along Malthusian lines) that the resources available to support the elderly (everything from Social Security income to nursing home facilities) would have been stretched too far and that the economic condition of the elderly might have worsened. At the same time, the Baby Bust was producing fewer and fewer children. Shouldn't there have been more than ample national resources to raise all, or certainly most, of these young people above the poverty line?

But it went the other way. And without exactly blaming the elderly for the unhappy fate of our children ("their principal role here is instead that of a comparison group"), Preston does argue that the changing numbers in each group played an important role in the outcome.

## THE EXTENT OF CHILD POVERTY IN AMERICA

Before trying to explain why poverty among children has increased and what, if any-

thing, we can do about it, let us marshal a few facts on the subject.

### Measuring Poverty

The official **poverty index** is subject to many difficulties of interpretation. Fundamentally, the index is meant to measure the amount of income a family, or individual, would require to meet its essential costs of living. Since children are characteristically dependents, whether they are above or below the poverty line will depend on the incomes of their families.

The index was originally calculated at three times the cost of an economy food plan prepared by the Department of Agriculture; it is updated each year to reflect changes in the consumer price index. For a family of four in 1989, the average poverty threshold was $12,675. This figure is adjusted upward or downward depending on the size of the family.

Problems with the index arise because:

• It does not include **noncash public transfers,** like food stamps, school lunch programs, health benefits, and subsidized housing.

• It takes into account only income and not the capital assets (like houses) of families or individuals.

• It makes no allowance for unreported or underreported income.

• It is based on before-tax income and does not make allowance for the payment of income taxes or Social Security or certain other deductions.

Some of these adjustments would reduce measured poverty. For example, making an allowance for noncash public transfers reduces measured poverty by anywhere from 8 percent to 37 percent, depending on the way these "in-kind" benefits are evaluated. Other adjustments (like correcting for taxes) would increase measured poverty. Furthermore, there are some observers who feel that we should take into account not only *absolute* poverty (as is measured by the index) but also *relative* poverty—how well the poor are doing relative, say, to the median incomes of families and individuals in the country as a whole. They note, for example, that in 1959 the ratio of the poverty threshold to median income for an American family of four was 49 percent; by 1987, it had fallen to 32 percent.

Despite all difficulties of interpretation, the official poverty index remains a useful guide to the condition of our poorer citizens. Certainly any sustained increase in child poverty would be, and is, cause for concern.[2]

## Children versus Other Age Groups

In his Population Association address, Preston showed the deteriorating poverty position of children as compared to the elderly for the period 1970–1982. In Figure 15-1, we compare three age groups (0–17, 18–64, and 65 and above) for the somewhat longer period 1967–1989. We see that over these two decades, poverty rates fell sharply for seniors, remained relatively constant for adults of working age, and increased substantially for children. The pattern for adults below 65 is somewhat variable, with a decline in the poverty rate until 1978, followed by a rise until 1983, and then a subsequent decline. The early 1980s were, of course, a period of recession in the U.S. economy generally.

The curves for children and elderly persons also show some fluctuations, although the overall poverty trend for the former is up and for the latter is definitely down. Over these twenty-two years, the percentage of the elderly in poverty declined by over 60 percent, while for children the percentage rose by about 18 percent.

Further, it seems to be the case that, within the group of families with children, the poor were getting poorer and the rich richer during much of this period. Sheldon Danziger and Peter Gottschalk calculate that

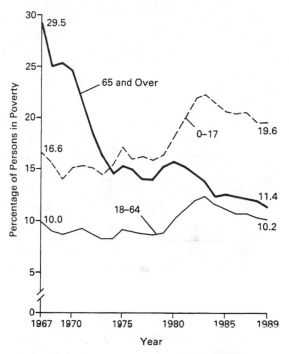

**FIGURE 15-1: Poverty by Age Groups, 1967–1989**

*Source:* Bureau of the Census, *Poverty in the United States, 1987, Current Population Reports,* Series P-60, No. 163, February, 1989.

the share of total income of families with children received by the bottom one-fifth (quintile) of such families fell from 6.59 percent in 1967 to 4.16 percent in 1984. Meanwhile, the share of the top quintile of such families was rising from 38.54 percent to 42.13 percent.[3]

Finally, *within* the age group of children, it is the youngest children who are poorest. In Figure 15-2, we show poverty rates for children aged 0 to 5 as compared to children 6 through 17. In 1988, a year of general prosperity, the poverty rate for the former was a shocking 22.6 percent. The youngest and most vulnerable, it would seem, are the hardest hit.

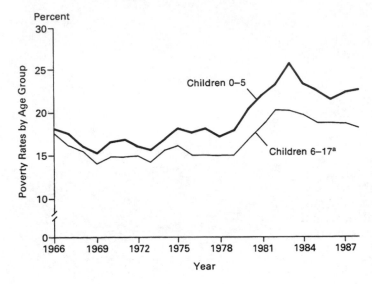

**FIGURE 15-2:  Poverty Rates of Children, by Age, 1966–1988**

*Note:*  Data are for all children for 1966–1974 and for 1988; data are for children related to the householder for 1975–1987.

[a] Data are for children aged 6–15 only for 1966–1974; for 1975–1988 data are for children aged 6–17.

*Source:*  U.S. Bureau of the Census, *Current Population Reports,* Series P-60 for relevant years.

## Poverty among Children by Family Type

The emphasis we have given to the increase of poverty among American children does not conflict with, but is in fact intimately related to, another emphasis that runs through the entire poverty literature: what is called the *feminization of poverty.* The linkage is provided by the fact that the proportion of our children in **female-headed households** has been rising dramatically in recent years.

The salient facts are these:

1.  *Poverty in female-headed households is far more common than in two-parent households.* In the late 1980s, the poverty rate in families with a female householder and no husband present was running at between *five and six times* the rate for married-couple families.

2.  *The real incomes of female-headed families with children have been falling relative to those of two-parent families with children.* Danziger and Gottschalk estimate that between 1967 and 1984, while the average family income of two-parent families grew by 14.1 percent, that of female-headed families fell by 6.5 percent.[4] There has also been some inching up of the official poverty rate for female-headed families with children in recent years, from a low of 39.6 percent in 1979 to 42.8 percent in the prosperous year 1989. (It actually rose to 47.8 percent in the recession year 1982.)

3.  *The number of female-headed families has been rising sharply in recent years.* Because of the increase in divorce and separation, and also in childbearing by single mothers, the number of female-headed families with children rose from 2.5 million in 1959 to 7.4 million in 1989. The percentage of all families with children that were female-headed more than doubled during these years, from 9.4 percent to 21.1 percent. (There was also an increase in the number of families with children headed by a male, with no wife present, but the numbers are smaller, going from 0.3 million in 1959 to 1.4 million in 1989.)

In recent decades, then, we have had a substantial growth in families with a female householder and no husband present. These female-headed families have poverty rates far exceeding those of married-couple families. Furthermore, the relative income disadvantage of these families has been increasing. The overwhelming result is this:

*The percentage of American children living in a female-headed household increased nearly two-and-a-half-fold between 1960 and 1989. More than half of all children born in the late 1980s could expect to spend some time in a mother-only family before reaching the age of 18. And over half of all poor children in the United States now live in female-headed households, compared to less than a quarter in 1960.*

It is thus clear that the phenomenon called the **feminization of poverty** could just as easily be termed the **impoverishment of children.**

### Child Poverty by Race and Ethnic Background

The majority of poor children in America are white, the percentage running around 60 percent in the late 1980s. The proportion of white children who are in poverty, however, is much lower than that of blacks or Hispanics. Figure 15-3 shows the trend of poverty percentages for whites, blacks, and Hispanics under 18 for the years 1974 to 1989. All these percentages rose during this period, but the continuing disparity—with the Hispanic child poverty rate over two times that of whites, and the black rate three times the white rate—makes it clear that minority group children have suffered disproportionately from economic deprivation.

It must be remembered, further, that there is a great difference between occasional "spells" of poverty—for example, after a divorce and before remarrying, or after losing a job and before getting a new one—and poverty sustained over long periods of time. Minorities, and particularly blacks, are more likely to be in the latter group than are whites. A study by Greg J.

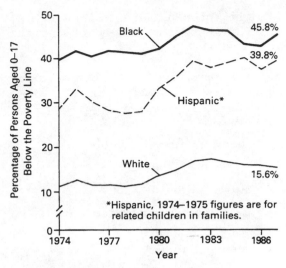

**FIGURE 15-3:  Poverty Among Children, by Race, 1974–1989**

[a] Hispanic, 1974–1975 figures are for related children in families.

*Source:*  U.S. Bureau of the Census, *Current Population Reports,* Series P-60 for relevant years.

Duncan and colleagues found that, in their sample survey conducted over the years 1969 through 1978, 62 percent of the "persistently poor" (below the poverty line for 8 or more years) were black. An Urban Institute study, using a definition of the "underclass" (see Chapter 12) in terms of behavior rather than income, found that, in 1980, 59 percent of this group was black and another 10 percent Hispanic. This total of nearly 70 percent contrasted with the overall population percentage of blacks and Hispanics of around 15 percent.[5]

Indeed, in thinking of the conditions actually facing many minority children, poverty percentages, though disheartening enough in themselves, hardly tell the whole story. We have in fact a constellation of problems that, viewed in totality, represent a generational tragedy that may well be the most serious social problem facing the United States in the years ahead.

In this broader context, we can do no better than quote the words of Marian

Wright Edelman, summarizing a study of the Children's Defense Fund, of which she is president:

Compared to white children, we found that black children are

*twice as likely to*

- die in the first year of life
- be born prematurely
- suffer low birthweight
- have mothers who received late or no prenatal care
- see a parent die
- live in substandard housing
- be suspended from school or suffer corporal punishment
- be unemployed as teenagers
- have no parent employed
- live in institutions;

*three times as likely to*

- be poor
- have their mothers die in childbirth
- live with a parent who has separated
- live in a female-headed household
- be placed in an educable mentally retarded class
- be murdered between five and nine years of age
- be in foster care
- die of known child abuse;

*four times as likely to*

- live with neither parent and be supervised by a child welfare agency
- be murdered before one year of age or as a teenager

- be incarcerated between fifteen and nineteen years of age;

*five times as likely to*

- be dependent on welfare; and

*twelve times as likely to*

- live with a parent who never married.[6]

These striking comparisons are not intended to belittle the problem of poverty among white children, or, certainly, the very extensive poverty among Hispanic children. (The latter group we will be considering again in Part V, especially Chapter 21.) What they do suggest, however, is that although we can to some degree speak of the growth of child poverty in general terms, we must also recognize that it is not a single problem, but actually many different problems with many different factors playing a part.

## WHAT HAPPENED TO THE WAR ON POVERTY?

In Samuel Preston's analysis, referred to at the beginning of this chapter, the reasons for the increase in child poverty relative to poverty among elderly persons in the last decade or so have to do with the family and the state. Because of declining family support, the United States' two classes of "dependents" (the young and the old) were both more vulnerable than in the past. In the case of the elderly, there was a vast increase in public support to make up the difference; in the case of the children, public support was much more meager. The reason for the difference in support levels was essentially political: The elderly, by their increased numbers, their greater financial assets, and their ability to mobilize for effective political action, could get the state to act vigorously on their behalf. The children could not—hence, reduced poverty for one group, increased poverty for the other.

But surely we cannot say that children were totally ignored by the state during this time. What about Aid to Families with Dependent Children (AFDC), food stamps, school lunch programs, Medicaid for poor families? For that matter, what about the **War on Poverty** in general? In 1962 the Survey Research Center of the University of Michigan asserted that "the elimination of poverty is well within the means of federal, state and local governments," and could be achieved "simply by the stroke of the pen." The whole enterprise, they judged, would cost no more than $10 billion a year.

We have, however, been spending far more than that (even in inflation-adjusted dollars) since the War on Poverty began in 1965. How, then, could we have what seems a worsening situation for our children, the age group that represents our collective future?

### The Uncooperative Economy

If we look back at Figure 15-1, we can see that the really sharp rise in the poverty rate for children took place between 1978 and 1983. Another, somewhat smaller rise took place between 1973 and 1975. It is no coincidence that in both these periods the U.S. economy was suffering from sharply increasing unemployment. Between 1973 and 1975, our unemployment rate went up from 4.8 percent to 8.3 percent. Between 1978 and 1983, it went up from 6.0 percent to 9.5 percent. Indeed, there were periods in the early 1980s when unemployment reached double-digit levels, the highest measured unemployment since the Great Depression of the 1930s.

Just as there are great difficulties in measuring poverty and/or family income, we should recognize that unemployment figures are also somewhat suspect. (For example, although the unemployment rate was very high in 1983, the employment-to-population ratio was actually better than it had been in 1965, when the War on Poverty

began.) Still, there is a great deal of evidence to suggest that the 1970s and early 1980s were a tough period in the U.S. economy generally. Labor productivity growth declined. Because of the oil crises engineered by the Organization of Petroleum Exporting Countries (OPEC) and many other factors, inflation rose even at a time when unemployment was rising. Then, at the beginning of the 1980s, when a serious (and successful) effort was mounted to curb accelerating inflation, a sharp recession ensued.

The point relevant to our discussion is this: Faced with what was, in many respects, a deteriorating economic situation, the government was operating under adverse conditions as far as poverty was concerned. **Pretransfer poverty**—poverty as estimated in the absence of all public assistance to the poor—was worsening, perhaps by 3 percentage points over the period 1965 to 1987.[7] Under these circumstances, just to hold one's own in the War on Poverty would have been a reasonable achievement, or so some social scientists have claimed.

### The Case for Renewing the War

Indeed, a number of observers go further than this. They argue that, as far as it went, the War on Poverty was successful. The problem was that it was cut back too severely in the late 1970s and early 1980s. These are some of their claims:

1. Poverty among children *before* the War on Poverty began was substantially higher than it was in the late 1980s. In 1959, for example, the poverty rate for persons 17 and under was 27.3 percent (compared with 19.6 percent in 1989.)

2. Measured poverty in both the pre–War on Poverty years and the late 1980s does not include noncash transfers. Since these in-kind benefits programs have grown since the mid-1960s, their inclusion would effectively reduce current child poverty rates relative to those before the War on

Poverty began. Various specific studies also show the nutritional, health, and other benefits for children in these programs.

3.   The main cash program for helping children, **Aid to Families with Dependent Children (AFDC)**, has been falling in real (inflation-adjusted) terms since the mid-1970s. This reduction of benefit levels, and also the tightening of eligibility requirements, meant that by 1988, real outlays had declined by 25 percent in comparison with 1975. During this period, while the number of children in female-headed households was rising substantially, the number of children receiving AFDC benefits declined by over 800,000. Thus, deteriorating family structures and difficult economic conditions were met with lower and lower levels of cash assistance.

4.   Although noncash benefits were rising in the 1960s and early 1970s, even they began to tail off in real terms from 1979 on. In terms of families, the average value (in 1986 dollars) of noncash benefits received by the poor fell from $4,221 in 1979 to $4,088 in 1986. Furthermore, an increasing percentage of those in-kind benefits were for medical care, the dollar value of which to the poor is hard to evaluate.[8]

In short, according to this view, poverty among children has been definitely alleviated by public transfer programs, though in a difficult period when many factors were operating to increase their level of poverty. In recent years, moreover, the failure of government programs to keep up with the obvious needs of families with children has been a major factor in the increase in child poverty.

### In the War on Poverty, Poverty Won

"Some years ago," President Reagan is quoted as having said, "the federal government declared war on poverty and poverty won." In contrast to the view just developed, a contrary opinion is that the War on Poverty not only failed, but in many ways worsened conditions for children in particular. Offsetting the points just made, adherents of this view make the following claims:

1.   The War on Poverty totally failed to live up to the promises of its promoters. Recall the estimate of $10 billion a year as all that was needed to solve the nation's poverty problem. In 1987, for persons with limited incomes, the value of noncash benefits *alone* had reached $116.2 billion. And as far as the small decrease in child poverty between 1959 and 1987 is concerned, we should have had a far greater decrease than this simply from the growth of the economy. This small decrease is not a tribute to, but an indictment of, the effectiveness of the War on Poverty.

2.   With respect to the sluggishness of the economy in the 1970s and early 1980s, the expansion of government activity during those years (of which the War on Poverty was a part) was at least one of the factors weighing the economy down. It helped foster inflation, caused higher tax rates, and diminished economic incentives. The cutting back of poverty programs and the tight-money recession of 1982–1983 were necessitated by the previous Great Society habit of expanding government expenditures to meet every conceivable social or individual need.

3.   These welfare expenditures not only burdened the economy in a general sense, but also tended to create welfare dependence on the part of young parents and, through their children, to create intergenerational welfare dependence. Instead of encouraging hard work and personal responsibility, these programs encourage reliance on the state for support. They promote the breakup of families by making economic survival easier after separation or divorce. Perhaps more significantly, they encourage women to have children out of wedlock because such children result in

increased payments to the young mothers involved. Where AFDC benefits have been conditional on the absence of the father of the children, the potential undermining of family structures is all too evident. Moreover, even where welfare subsidies are not biased in the direction of single parenthood, marital breakups may increase simply because of the higher incomes available to the families in question.[9]

In general, then, this second position is that, although it might appear that the state should take over family responsibilities for children when families have failed to do so, this very action tends to undermine the families that are supposed to be helped. In the extreme case, we get a vicious circle of welfare dependence in which young mothers have out-of-wedlock daughters who, like their mothers, become unwed mothers and go on welfare themselves. Thus, from this point of view, the overall failure of the War on Poverty is hardly surprising; welfare reform rather than welfare expansion is clearly called for.

## ROLE OF THE FAMILY

As is quite obvious, one of the crucial issues in the preceding debate concerns **family structures.** What is the effect on the viability of the family unit when the state plays an increased role in providing income, whether cash or noncash, to poor families with children? Few argue that the increased intervention of the state promotes stronger families. The general "liberal" position is simply that the negative effects are modest and are quite dwarfed by the positive effects of better food, health, and housing on the children involved. The "conservative" view, by contrast, is that the negative effects are substantial and that, in the effort to raise living standards for poor children through state action, one is undermining the family and ultimately creating more poor children.

It would be convenient if a clear-cut answer could be given to this question. However, as we indicated in Chapters 9 and 10, there are many different factors that have resulted in the breakdown of the "traditional" American family, and there is also much about this development that remains mysterious.

Indeed, disagreement in this area begins even with scholars questioning the impact of the growth of female-headed households on the increase in child poverty. One observer—Karl Zinsmeister of the American Enterprise Institute—claims that "within the past several years it has become generally accepted that family breakdown is now the primary force causing poverty in the United States." A similar theme appears in Charles A. Murray's controversial book (1984), *Losing Ground.*

On the other hand, Victor Fuchs of Stanford argues that the emphasis on **female-headed households** as a factor is overstated. He stresses the fact that child poverty is centered in households with larger numbers of children, and that children's welfare is highly dependent on labor income. (This is in contrast to the elderly, who are highly dependent on nonlabor income—pensions, interest, Social Security, and the like.) A major factor causing the increase in child poverty in recent years was the decrease of labor income while nonlabor income was growing. The impact of the increasing number of female-headed households was relatively minor by comparison.

Similarly, Mary Jo Bane of the Kennedy School of Government at Harvard finds that, overall, family structure changes have had relatively little effect on the U.S. poverty rate. Her admittedly "surprising" result is: "The poverty rate in 1979 would have been about 16 percent lower than it was had family composition remained as it was in 1959. Family composition changes contributed almost nothing to the increase in poverty between 1979 and 1983."[10]

Views on these issues also change over time. A few years ago, for example, it was widely argued in academic circles that there was little or no intergenerational transmission of poverty (a well-known concern of conservatives). More recent evidence, however, is that women raised in female-headed households are more likely to have premarital births, to form their own female-headed families, and to drop out of high school—all factors likely to keep them in poverty—than do children of two-parent families.[11]

When it comes to an explanation of *why* female-headed households have grown so rapidly, disagreement only increases further, and it is fair to say that there is no generally accepted explanation of this phenomenon. This is true even at the most basic level. For example, it has often been argued that a main reason for increased divorce and separation has been that women, through their own job opportunities or through welfare, are better able to maintain their independence than in a previous harsher era. We have discussed this point earlier (see Chapters 9 and 10).

In direct contrast, it has been argued that a main reason for divorce and separation, and also for the increase in the number of out-of-wedlock children, is *adverse* economic conditions. Economic pressures on young families, according to this view, increase the likelihood of marital conflict. Similarly, these unfavorable pressures make it less likely that early conceptions by teenagers will be legitimated by marriage.

This latter view is developed by Richard A. Easterlin, whose analysis of the effect of different cohort sizes we have met earlier in connection with our discussion of the Baby Boom and Baby Bust (pp. 47–49). It is part of his general explanation of the growth of child poverty in recent decades. Essentially, he argues that the adverse change in children's fortunes is due to a "severe deterioration in the wage and unemployment rates of adults in family forming ages." This, in turn, has resulted from general economic conditions ("a slackening of growth of aggregate demand"), and also from "a growth in supply of younger relative to older adults." The latter, of course, refers to the fact that our young parents during the 1970s and 1980s were from the huge Baby Boom generation.

His general conclusion is that this deterioration in wage and unemployment rates "has raised poverty rates of children and young adults directly via its impact on income within families of given types, especially married-couple families, and indirectly, via its impact on the demographic composition of young adults, especially through the rise of female-headed families due to increased divorce and nonmarital fertility rates." Furthermore, the poverty rate for children has risen even more rapidly than for young adults because "they are more adversely affected by the rise in female-headed families and do not have some income-preserving options available to young adults, namely, remaining single to avoid the economic sacrifices entailed by family status, or, if married, remaining childless."[12]

By Easterlin's hypothesis, both the increase in child poverty and the growth of female-headed households may prove to be transitory phenomena. The reason is that the new generation entering the labor market will be from the much smaller Baby Bust cohort. Their wages and employment conditions should improve, meaning, if he is correct, higher incomes for young parents, and less marital dissolution and nonmarital childbearing.

Interestingly, a corollary to this thesis would appear to be that welfare benefits, by raising poor family incomes, might tend to keep families together rather than to separate them.

Despite these many disagreements, there is one point on which virtually all commentators agree—namely, that minority children, and especially black children, suffer particularly deep consequences from poverty, and that this poverty has been gravely worsened by the changing black family structure. Because many of these families are "persistently poor," moreover, one wonders how transitory their poverty will prove to be even given the favoring conditions Easterlin posits. Let us now say a few preliminary words on this crucial subject.

## POVERTY AMONG BLACK FAMILIES WITH CHILDREN

Although there is some question about the general effect of changing family structures on poverty, there seems little doubt that, in the case of black children, this effect has been substantial. We know from our discussions in Chapter 12 that important segments of the black community have made large economic, social, and political strides during recent decades. During this same period, poorer black citizens, once possessed of a reasonably stable family structure and

community life, have seen the substantial breakup of that family structure and, in many cases, increasing disorganization in their community life.

The effect of these community, and especially family, changes has been most pronounced in the case of women and children. In Table 15-1, we bring together various statistics related to the family structure and poverty conditions of black families and children. It is apparent that, though subject to more strains than were white families in the early post–World War II period, black families were nevertheless largely intact. The percentage of female-headed households was small; the marriage rate was high; the percentage of children born to unmarried women was relatively low. During the subsequent 40 years, all this changed drastically, and during the past 10

**TABLE 15-1. Black Families, Women, Children**

| | Year | | | | |
|---|---|---|---|---|---|
| | 1950 | 1960 | 1970 | 1980 | 1988 |
| Female-headed families (percentage of all black families) | 17.6 | 21.7 | 28.3 | 40.2 | 42.8 |
| Percentage of women married by age group | | | | | |
| 14–24 | 30.9[a] | 25.7 | 21.3 | 13.1 | 9.6[b] |
| 25–44 | 67.2[a] | 64.9 | 62.0 | 44.7 | 39.9 |
| 45–64 | 57.6[a] | 52.8 | 54.1 | 46.0 | 41.9 |
| Births to unmarried women (percentage of all births) | 16.8[c] | 21.6[c] | 37.6 | 55.2 | 61.2[d] |
| Percentage of related children under 18 in female-headed families | na | 19.5[e] | 37.2 | 59.3 | 52.2 |
| Percentage of children under 18 in poverty | na | na | 39.8[f] | 42.3 | 45.8[g] |
| Percentage of poor children under 18 in female-headed families | na | 76.6 | 67.7 | 64.8 | 68.3 |

N.A. = Not available.

[a] Figure is for 1947.

[b] Ages 15–24.

[c] Figure for black and other nonwhite.

[d] Figure is for 1986.

[e] Figure is for 1959.

[f] Figure is for 1974.

[g] Figure is for 1987.

*Source:* U.S. Bureau of the Census; *Statistical Abstract of the United States, 1988.*

or 15 years, and despite public assistance programs, there has been an increase in already high levels of poverty for black children.

Not all the news, even on the child poverty front, is bad. Although exact figures are not available for all persons under 18 for the period before 1974, there is no doubt that poverty among black children was much higher in the early years after World War II (and higher still in the 1930s and before). The Census Bureau estimates that in 1959, considering only related children in families, the black poverty rate was 65.6 percent. Thus, the 45.8 percent of 1987, though an increase over the early 1970s, and though shockingly high in itself, in relation to our expectations and also to the comparable white rate (15.6 percent), nevertheless does represent substantial improvement over the even more disastrous rates afflicting black children historically.

Also, although the percentage of black out-of-wedlock births has increased substantially, this is not, as many reports seem to suggest, because of vast increases in the number of births to unwed teenage mothers. Actually, there has been a dramatic decline in the black teenage birth rate in recent years (from 147.7 in 1970 to 100.3 in 1987), and, more recently, there has even been a decline in the birth rate of unmarried black teenage mothers. The reason for the increased *percentage* of out-of-wedlock black births shown in Table 15-1 is that the percentage of black women who have not married has increased, and also that the fertility rate of *married* black women has been falling. The latter factor may account for well over one-third of the increased proportion of births accounted for by unmarried women.

If, as suggested earlier, the expansion of welfare programs cannot account for all, most, or possibly even any of this family breakup and recent increase in child poverty,[13] then how *do* we account for what is, without question, a dramatic change in the actual living conditions under which a ma-

jority of black children are now brought up?

Perhaps the most intriguing explanation to develop in the late 1980s was that the problem centers on the unavailability of suitable young black men for young black women to marry. The major factor behind this deficit is the high rate of joblessness among young black men. This high rate of joblessness, in turn, is a reflection of both high unemployment rates and low labor force participation rates for black males aged 16 through 19 and 20 through 24. In Table 15-2, we take into account both of these factors by measuring the employment-to-population ratio of young black males from 1954 to 1988, and comparing it with that of young white males in the same period.

The results are striking. In the 16-to-19 age group, the ratio of employment to population for blacks declined from 52.4 percent to 29.4 percent; in the 20-to-24 age group, there was also a decline, though less striking, from 75.9 percent to 63.9 percent. By contrast, the ratio for white males aged 16 to 19, was somewhat higher in 1988 (51.7 percent) than it was in 1954 (49.9 percent), and was over 75 percent higher than the comparable 1988 black rate. A similar, though smaller, difference is shown for the 20-to-24 age groups.

This joblessness, according to sociologists like William Julius Wilson of the University of Chicago, contributed heavily to marital instability among young black families and also to the increasing number of unmarried mothers. An unemployed male does not promise much, at least in a financial way, to a prospective marital union. In addition, the ranks of eligible young black males are further reduced by (1) their higher mortality rates, including homicide, and (2) their higher rates of imprisonment.[14]

What emerges from this analysis is the possibility that family breakdown among whites and blacks may have quite different

**TABLE 15-2. Male Employment/Population Ratio, by Age and Race, 1954–1988 (Civilian Noninstitutional Population)**

| Year | Black[a] Males Age 16–19 | Age 20–24 | White Males Age 16–19 | Age 20–24 | Year | Black[a] Males Age 16–19 | Age 20–24 | White Males Age 16–19 | Age 20–24 |
|---|---|---|---|---|---|---|---|---|---|
| 1954 | 52.4 | 75.9 | 49.9 | 77.9 | 1972[b] | 31.6 | 70.4 | 51.5 | 77.1 |
| 1955 | 52.7 | 78.4 | 52.0 | 80.4 | 1973[b] | 32.8 | 72.6 | 54.3 | 80.2 |
| 1956 | 52.2 | 78.1 | 54.1 | 82.3 | 1974 | 31.4 | 69.9 | 54.4 | 79.8 |
| 1957 | 48.0 | 78.8 | 52.4 | 80.5 | 1975 | 26.3 | 59.4 | 50.6 | 74.3 |
| 1958 | 42.0 | 71.4 | 47.6 | 76.6 | 1976 | 25.8 | 61.3 | 51.5 | 76.9 |
| 1959 | 41.4 | 75.9 | 48.1 | 80.8 | 1977 | 26.4 | 61.0 | 54.4 | 78.7 |
| 1960[b] | 43.8 | 78.4 | 48.1 | 80.5 | 1978[b] | 28.5 | 62.2 | 56.3 | 80.6 |
| 1961 | 41.0 | 75.6 | 45.9 | 78.8 | 1979 | 28.7 | 65.5 | 55.7 | 81.1 |
| 1962[b] | 41.7 | 76.3 | 46.4 | 79.6 | 1980 | 27.0 | 60.9 | 53.4 | 77.5 |
| 1963 | 37.4 | 74.9 | 44.7 | 79.1 | 1981 | 24.6 | 58.3 | 51.3 | 77.0 |
| 1964 | 37.8 | 78.1 | 45.0 | 79.3 | 1982 | 20.3 | 53.9 | 47.0 | 73.9 |
| 1965 | 39.4 | 81.6 | 47.1 | 80.2 | 1983 | 20.4 | 54.5 | 47.4 | 74.3 |
| 1966 | 40.5 | 82.9 | 50.1 | 81.0 | 1984 | 23.9 | 58.0 | 49.1 | 78.0 |
| 1967 | 38.8 | 80.3 | 50.2 | 80.5 | 1985 | 26.3 | 60.4 | 49.9 | 78.0 |
| 1968 | 38.7 | 78.0 | 50.3 | 78.6 | 1986[b] | 26.5 | 61.3 | 49.6 | 79.2 |
| 1969 | 39.0 | 77.3 | 51.1 | 78.7 | 1987 | 28.5 | 62.1 | 49.9 | 79.6 |
| 1970 | 35.5 | 72.9 | 49.6 | 76.8 | 1988 | 29.4 | 63.9 | 51.7 | 80.1 |
| 1971 | 31.8 | 68.2 | 49.2 | 75.4 | | | | | |

[a] Data for 1954 to 1971 are for blacks and races other than white.

[b] Not strictly comparable with data for prior years.

*Source:* Bureau of Labor Statistics Data for 16- to 19-year-olds are from *President's Economic Report, 1988*. Data for 20- to 24-year-olds: (a) Whites: 1954–1983, from *Handbook of Labor Statistics*, Bulletin 2217, June 1985, Table 16. 1984–1988, *Employment and Earnings*, January issue for indicated years, Table 3. (b) Blacks: 1972–1983, *Handbook of Labor Statistics*, Bulletin 2217, Table 16. 1984–1988, *Employment and Earnings*, January issue Table 3. 1957–1971, Labor force statistics derived from the *Current Population Survey*, 1948–1987, Bulletin 2307, Table B-4.

patterns of causation, reinforcing our earlier point about the difficulty of generalizing in this area. Wilson, and Kathryn M. Neckerman, also of the University of Chicago Sociology Department, put the contrast this way:

It seems likely that the chief cause of the rise of separation and divorce rates among whites is the increased economic independence of white women as indicated by their increasing employment and improving occupational status. . . . That the employment status of white males is not a major factor in white single motherhood or female-headed families can perhaps also be seen in

the higher rate of remarriage among white women and the significantly earlier age of first marriage. By contrast, the increasing delay of first marriage and the low rate of remarriage among black women seem to be directly tied to the increasing labor force problems of men.[15]

Thus, the high, and increasing, level of **poverty among black children,** which most scholars agree has been seriously affected by the deterioration of the black family structure, may—at least so this argument goes—be largely due to the extremely high level of **joblessness of young black males.**

Where unemployment is high, marriages easily break up and many marriages never take place at all. Family breakdown and poverty for women and children are the result.

Although this approach to the problem deserves, as Wilson and Neckerman suggest, "renewed scholarly and public policy attention," it unfortunately leaves us with almost as many unanswered questions as we began with. The largest of these questions, of course, is why the employment prospects of young black males should have deteriorated so sharply during the past two decades. Many explanations have been offered—the relocation of firms outside the central cities; decreased demand for agricultural labor; general economic slowdown and increasing unemployment percentages; decreasing demand for less skilled, less educated laborers; competition for entry-level jobs with large numbers of women entering the labor force; competition for such jobs with low-wage immigrants; the availability of welfare; expectations exceeding realities so that young blacks would not take jobs considered demeaning; the availability of crime as an important employment alternative; the growing acceptability of the culture of drugs, unemployment, and illegitimacy as opposed to settling down to career-building activities; the general isolation of the ghetto community from the larger society; and so on.

To date, however, most of these explanations have left a large part of the problem of young black male joblessness unexplained. In many instances, as Harry J. Holzer of Michigan State suggests, it is difficult even to distinguish "cause" from "effect." "For instance," Holzer asks, "do many young people engage in crime because of weak opportunities in the regular market, or do their illegal activities lower their interest in (by providing alternative income) and ability to obtain regular jobs?"[16] One can make guesses on such questions, but hard knowledge is extremely difficult to come by.

What one can say, conclusively, is that the problem of "persistent poverty" among children, so heavily centered in black and other minority populations, is likely to require a different analysis from the more intermittent poverty of majority whites.

## SOME HOPEFUL NOTES

We shall return to the problem of children in poverty, and of poverty in general, when we consider possible future trends in Chapter 24 ("Will the Poor Always Be with Us?"). At that time, we shall consider what ultimately may be the most serious demographic dilemma we face in this area: the fact that the poor, and especially the persistently poor, generally have higher fertility rates than do middle-class families. Does this mean that our present poverty problem—and the poverty problem of children in particular—is likely to *worsen* in the years ahead? Or are there ways around this dilemma?

For the moment, however, we should note that, by the end of the 1980s, there were a number of developments that provided some hope that the problems of poverty among American children might be ameliorated in the coming decade. We mention three points in particular.

1. *Insofar as labor force factors, particularly for young workers, are involved in causing child poverty (directly or indirectly), the situation should improve in the 1990s as opposed to the 1970s and early 1980s.* Several analysts we have mentioned—Easterlin, Fuchs, Wilson, Neckerman—attribute increased child poverty in one way or another to labor force problems, either for the entire cohort of Baby Boomers entering the labor market, or for young black males in particular. If poor employment prospects do tend both to lower incomes for married families and to increase marital instability, and if, further, this effect has been keenest and most devastating for young black males—admit-

tedly rather large "if's"—then the relative labor shortages to be expected as the Baby Bust generation trickles into the labor market could help to lower child poverty rates both in the country as a whole and in the ghetto in particular. Almost everyone agrees that this is a favorable factor for the future; *how* favorable depends on the analyst in question.

2.  *Despite disagreements about the effect of welfare on poverty, there is something close to general agreement that policies ought to be developed that discourage welfare dependence and encourage the self-sufficiency of welfare recipients as far as is feasible.* One has to say "close to general agreement," for there remain some observers who feel that any attempts to educate, train, or provide jobs for the poor are essentially unworkable, or at least too costly in relation to their prospective benefits. Sociologist John B. Williamson of Boston College and psychologist Michael Morris of the University of New Haven conclude their study of poverty policies with a reluctant rejection of self-sufficiency policies: "If the problem of poverty is defined such that the only way to solve it is through greatly increased self-sufficiency, we believe that there is no realistic solution to poverty in the United States." The only poverty policy that works, they feel, is direct assistance to the poor, plus, of course, general policies to stimulate economic growth.[17]

Still, the increasingly common view among experts is that direct aid to the poor is only a panacea and that the focus should be much more on training, education, and actual work experience. **Workfare** as opposed to **welfare,** once considered demeaning to the poor, is now widely regarded as the way out of poverty for those who otherwise might languish in a permanently dependent state with no realistic options available to them. Mind you, this is a solution that faces a host of difficulties when it comes to the poverty of children, our special concern in this chapter. For to make a serious

effort to bring young, unmarried mothers into the work force is to require that much of the care of their children be handled by public agencies. This question of child care is fraught with difficulties, as our next chapter will demonstrate in detail.

Still, at a minimum, it can be said that the easy optimism and sentimental analyses of the early days of the War on Poverty have now given way to much more careful and sophisticated studies of the problem. Developing self-sufficiency among the poor, though difficult to achieve, is nevertheless a much more desirable objective than simply, and temporarily, relieving income deficiencies. Some useful combination of the two goals can undoubtedly be worked out as our experience with various policies increases over time.

3.  *The growing awareness of the special problem of children in poverty is leading to policies framed specifically to assist children, policies that should do at least something to reverse the trends of the past two decades.* Despite the difficulties of the "workfare" approach for female-headed households, other steps can be taken that focus directly on the needs of the children in such households. Probably the most important of these steps is the effort, just recently getting underway in any serious sense, to enforce child support payments from absent fathers. This effort, too, has its problems—where the needs are greatest, the paternal resources for fulfilling them may be least—but the past failure of our society to assess adequate child support awards, and the failure of fathers to fulfill even the minimums required of them, present obvious opportunities for improvement. Wisconsin has, for some years, been engaged in a child support demonstration project whereby children in the families involved receive either benefits financed by taxes on absent fathers or a socially insured minimum where these benefits prove insufficient. In general, the focus on the needs of children, ultimately perhaps leading to

some universal form of child allowance system such as is prevalent in Europe, may help ameliorate this pressing socioeconomic problem.

If a society can, as some have suggested, be judged largely by the way it treats its children, then the need for reform in this area would seem to be compelling.

## SUMMARY

1. Poverty among American children has grown substantially over the past 20 years, and in 1989 was measured at a rate of 19.6 percent. This contrasted with poverty rates among elderly citizens of 11.4 percent and among working-age Americans of 10.2 percent.

2. The impoverishment of children has occurred at the same time that a "feminization of poverty" has taken place. Poverty is much greater in female-headed families than in married-couple families. Female-headed families have increased substantially in the past two decades, and, by the late 1980s, over half of all poor children in the United States were living in female-headed households.

3. The recent increases in child poverty have occurred despite the expenditures of billions of dollars in the War on Poverty, originally launched in 1965. Difficult economic conditions made poverty harder to overcome, at least in the 1970s and early 1980s. Also, beginning in the late 1970s, there were cutbacks in the real value of cash benefits to poor families with children under AFDC. Some observers attribute the increase in child poverty in significant measure to federal retrenchment in this area.

4. Other observers, noting the overall increase in welfare expenditures since the mid-1960s, including, until quite recently, very large increases in noncash benefits (food stamps, school lunches, housing assistance, Medicaid), believe that the War on Poverty has essentially been a failure. Indeed, they argue that by diminishing work incentives and weakening the institution of the family, these programs may have actually worsened the problem.

5. Scholars differ about the importance of family breakdown in causing the increase in child poverty, and also differ about the reasons for that breakdown—for example, whether increased income or increased poverty is more likely to encourage family dissolution and illegitimacy. Most scholars agree, however, that, in the difficult case of poverty among black children, family breakdown is a major factor to be considered.

6. Why black family formation has changed so dramatically over recent decades is also a matter of dispute, although one theory is that the changes are due to the increasing unavailability of employed, marriageable young black males.

7. Despite obvious problems with most suggested "solutions" to child poverty in the United States, hope for the future arises from possible improvements in labor markets for young adults, increased awareness of the need to supplement simple welfare with work and/or training alternatives, and a growing sense that child poverty *is* a major problem and that we need to focus our attention on it more sharply than in the past.

## KEY CONCEPTS FOR REVIEW

Poverty index (threshold)

Pretransfer poverty

Cash versus noncash benefits

Aid to Families with Dependent Children (AFDC)

Differences in poverty rates by
    age group
    family structure
    race/ethnicity

War on Poverty
    success or failure?
    effect of recent retrenchments
    impact on economic incentives
    and the institution of the family

Poverty among black children

Unemployment among young black males

Female-headed households

The feminization of poverty and the impoverishment of children

Welfare versus workfare
Increased focus on child poverty

## QUESTIONS FOR DISCUSSION

1. It has been said that the economic fate of the United States' two main groups of dependents (children and the elderly) has been very different during recent years. Describe this difference numerically. How would you account for the opposite trends in poverty rates affecting these two groups? Does it seem appropriate to you to compare these two groups, or does this comparison simply confuse matters?

2. Explain briefly why it is difficult to interpret the meaning of official poverty-level measurements. Can you see similar difficulties in making statements about other economic measurements, such as family incomes, unemployment percentages, and the like?

3. Why do we say that the phenomenon called the "feminization of poverty" could just as easily be called the "impoverishment of children"?

4. "Having low family incomes is only one of the characteristics that describe the situation of poor black children in present-day America. In fact, there are numerous other indices that suggest a condition approaching the genuinely tragic. These range from illiteracy to homicide." Discuss.

5. Did Poverty win the War on Poverty? List as many factors as you can that support this proposition, and make a similar list of those that seem to contradict it. Take into account the role of general economic factors, family structures, and changes in political outlook in Washington.

6. Relate what you have learned in this chapter to Chapter 14's discussion of the "equivocal" status of children in late-twentieth-century America.

## NOTES

1. Samuel H. Preston, "Children and the Elderly: Divergent Path's for America's Dependents," presidential address to the Population Association of America, published in *Demography, 21* (4), November 1984.
2. For a more detailed discussion of the various possible measures of poverty and their problems, see M. Morris and J. B. Williamson, *Poverty and Public Policy* (New York: Greenwood Press, 1986), esp. pp. 14–23.
3. Sheldon Danziger and Peter Gottschalk, "Families with Children have Fared Worst," *Challenge*, March–April 1986, Table 4, p. 43.
4. Ibid., Table 1, p. 41. It should be noted here that statistics on average family income are very difficult to interpret, for a variety of reasons. "Average" often refers to *mean* income, which can behave differently from *median* income. Family *size* may change over time, as indeed it has in the United States in recent years as family units have become smaller over time. Also, there are numerous different *income* concepts that can be used. Paul Ryscavage, a labor economist with the Census Bureau, distinguishes six separate income measures that the federal government used to measure

real income over the period 1973–1986. One measure increased 22 percent over this period, another measure less than 3 percent. Paul Ryscavage, "Understanding Real Income Trends: An Analysis of Conflicting Signals," *Business Economics*, January 1989, pp. 36–42. The moral is: Be sure you know exactly what is being measured in this area, and how this measurement relates to the specific problem you wish to solve.
5. Greg J. Duncan et al., *Years of Poverty, Years of Plenty* (Ann Arbor, Mich.: Institute for Social Research, 1984), p. 49. I. V. Sawhill, "Poverty and the Underclass", in I. V. Sawhill, ed., *Challenge to Leadership* (Washington, D.C.: Urban Institute Press, 1988), Table 7-3, p. 230.
6. M. W. Edelman, *Families in Peril* (Cambridge, Mass.: Harvard University Press, 1987), pp. 2–3.
7. For estimates of poverty with and without transfer payments, see S. Danziger, R. Haveman, and R. Plotnick, "Antipoverty Policy: Effects on the Poor and the Nonpoor," in S. Danziger and D. Weinberg, eds., *Fighting Poverty: What Works and What Doesn't* (Cambridge, Mass.: Harvard University Press, 1986), Table 3.1, p. 54.
8. After noting the decline in the average real value

of noncash benefits between 1979 and 1986, sociologist Mark S. Littman concludes as follows: "While the growth of noncash benefits was a factor in keeping down the growth in the average deficit of poor persons in the 1960's and 1970's, it is not a factor that can be used to explain away the growth in the deficit of poor persons in the 1980's." Mark S. Littman, "Poverty in the 1980's: Are the Poor Getting Poorer?" *Monthly Labor Review*, June 1989, p. 17.

9. See Chapter 24, pp. 439–440.

10. Mary Jo Bane, "Household Composition and Poverty", in Danziger and Weinberg, *Fighting Poverty*, p. 214.

11. One scholar who originally found that there were very few intergenerational effects was Frank Levy of the University of Maryland. He writes: "Recent studies suggest that the transmission of poverty across generations is growing. Sociologists Sara McLanahan and Larry Bumpass estimate that white women raised in a two-parent family have a .05 chance of premarital birth, but white women raised in a female-headed family double the chance to .10. For young black women, the chances are .35 and .57 respectively. . . . Other recent studies show that children raised in female-headed families have lower probabilities of completing high school and, for blacks, earlier initiation into sexual intercourse, both predictors of future poverty." Levy speculates that the difference between the earlier and later studies might reflect improved methodology, or, quite possibly, changing behavioral norms. Frank Levy, *Dollars and Dreams:*

*The Changing American Income Distribution* (New York: Russell Sage Foundation, 1987), pp. 211–212.

12. Richard A. Easterlin, "The New Age Structure of Poverty: Permanent or Transient?," mimeographed, 1987, p. 13.

13. Although many scholars believe that the effects of welfare programs on family structures have been overstated, few would argue that they have had no effect whatsoever. The effects may, however, be more subtle than one expects. For example, Mary Jo Bane, quoted earlier, while finding little effect of welfare on the fertility of young mothers, finds that it may affect their leaving home and setting up new households of their own. This act in itself can have roundabout implications for their poverty status.

14. In the 1980s, homicide was the leading cause of death of black men aged 15 to 34. In the 20-to-24 age group in 1980, 9.5 percent of black male high school dropouts were in jail. (The comparable figure for white male high school dropouts aged 20 to 24 was 2.5 percent.)

15. W. J. Wilson and K. M. Neckerman, "Poverty and Family Structure: The Widening Gap between Evidence and Public Policy Issues," in Danziger and Weinberg, *Fighting Poverty*, p. 256.

16. H. J. Holzer, "Can We Solve Black Youth Unemployment?," *Challenge*, November–December 1988, p. 48.

17. Morris and Williamson, *Poverty and Public Policy*, p. 172.

# 16

# Who's Watching
# the Children?

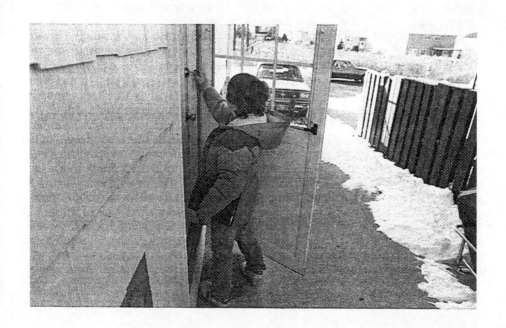

$A$s in the case of child poverty, the issue of child care in the United States today involves a paradox. With proportionately fewer children to support, we have larger percentages of children in poverty. And with fewer children to care for, we seem to have an increasing inability to provide them with adequate care. On the inadequacy of this care, observers on all sides of the political spectrum agree, but—again as in the case of differing views on the War on Poverty—the analysis of, and especially the "cure" for, this malady is a matter of deep controversy.

According to one view, the transfer of much of the care of young children, including infants, from the family to outside caregivers is an inescapable development, necessitated by largely irreversible trends toward increasing participation by women in the labor force, separation, divorce, single motherhood, and economic necessity. Under these circumstances, the social crime is not to have adequately funded and regulated day care centers or similar institutions to provide decent and healthful care for our children. The state is seen as neglecting its responsibilities to the next generation by its failure to give adequate financial support to these child care alternatives. A serious problem for this point of view is the possibility that better provision of these child-care alternatives may further undermine the already weakened institution of the family.

An opposing view, by contrast, while not necessarily denying the state an important role in solving the crisis that is developing on the child care front, emphasizes the importance of restoring care for children to the nuclear family, and, in most cases, the importance of the unique role of the mother within that family. State action, according to this view, should not be subsidizing parents who wish to put their children in extrafamily care institutions, but, if anything, should be subsidizing parents who wish to take care of their children in the home. The basic responsibility for raising young children should remain the family's, not the state's. A serious problem for this view occurs in the case of single mothers in poverty. How does one reconcile the view that women should stay home and raise their own children with the now widely held opinion that "workfare" should increasingly replace "welfare" in our poverty programs?

We shall not try to resolve the issue between these contrasting views here, but only to set out some of the relevant evidence that has been accumulated in recent years. First, however, let us sketch out how arrangements for child care in the United States have been changing.

## THE NEW CHILD CARE ARRANGEMENTS

All the changes in the American family that we have described in Chapters 9 and 10 have a clear bearing on the ways in which care for American children, from infants and toddlers to teenagers, has been transformed in the post–World War II era. The "Leave it to Beaver" image of a nonemployed mother staying at home with the children in an intact husband-wife family is increasingly remote from reality. Not only do we have the increase in single-parent families from 12.8 percent of families with children under 18 in 1970 to 27.3 percent in 1988, but we also have the rapid increase in working women in both single-mother and married-mother households. In 1988, 63 percent of mothers with children under the age of 14 were in the labor force, and there was no difference in participation rates between married and single mothers. Among mothers, moreover, the most rapid growth of participation in the labor force over recent years was in the case of mothers with infants under 1 year of age. This went from 35.7 percent in 1978 to 50.8 percent in 1988.

What child care arrangements were made for these children while their mothers were at their jobs?

## Primary Care Arrangements for Children of Employed Mothers

In 1990 the Bureau of the Census reported on a study of child care arrangements for children of employed mothers in 1986–1987.[1] **Primary care arrangement** refers to the way the child was usually cared for during most of the hours while the mother was working. **Secondary care arrangement,** as the name implies, refers to the second most frequently used arrangement while the child's mother was working.

In Figure 16-1, we show the primary care arrangements for children of employed mothers for two age groups, children under 5 and children 5 to 14. One obvious difference between these age groups, of course, is that school is the primary care arrangement for over 70 percent of the older children. As shown in the more detailed breakdown of Table 16-1, only 9.3 percent of children under 5 were in nursery school, preschool, or kindergarten while their mothers worked.

Perhaps the most striking feature of the arrangements for children under 5 is that less than one-third of their primary care (29.9 percent) took place in their own homes. The most common single arrange-

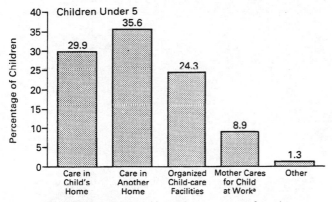

aIncludes women working at home or away from home.

(a)

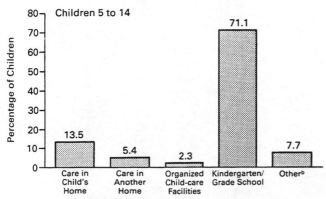

bIncludes child cares for self (4.1 percent) and mother cares for child at work (3.6 percent).

(b)

**FIGURE 16-1: Primary Care Arrangements for Children with Employed Mothers, Fall 1987**

*Source:* U.S. Bureau of the Census, "Who's Minding the Kids?," *Current Population Reports,* Series P-70, No. 20, July 1990.

**TABLE 16-1. Primary Care Arrangements for Children Under 5, by Mother's Employment and Marital Status, Fall 1987**

| Primary Child Care Arrangements Used by Employed Mothers for Children under 5 | All Mothers | | | Married Mothers, Husband Present | | | All Other Marital Statuses[a] | | |
|---|---|---|---|---|---|---|---|---|---|
| | Total | Employed Full Time | Employed Part Time | Total | Employed Full Time | Employed Part Time | Total | Employed Full Time | Employed Part Time |
| Number of children (thousands) | 9,124 | 5,677 | 3,447 | 7,474 | 4,507 | 2,967 | 1,650 | 1,171 | 480 |
| Percentage | 100.0 | 100.0 | 100.0 | 100.0 | 100.0 | 100.0 | 100.0 | 100.0 | 100.0 |
| Care in child's home | 29.9 | 24.2 | 39.2 | 30.0 | 24.2 | 38.9 | 29.2 | 24.3 | 41.2 |
| By father | 15.3 | 9.7 | 24.5 | 18.2 | 11.8 | 27.8 | 2.3 | 1.6 | 4.1 |
| By grandparent | 5.1 | 5.5 | 4.4 | 3.7 | 3.9 | 3.4 | 11.3 | 11.5 | 10.8 |
| By other relative | 3.3 | 2.9 | 3.9 | 2.2 | 2.2 | 2.3 | 8.1 | 5.7 | 13.8 |
| By nonrelative | 6.2 | 6.1 | 6.4 | 6.0 | 6.3 | 5.5 | 7.6 | 5.6 | 12.5 |
| Care in another home | 35.6 | 38.9 | 30.2 | 35.4 | 38.6 | 30.6 | 36.5 | 40.1 | 27.7 |
| By grandparent | 8.7 | 8.8 | 8.5 | 8.5 | 8.4 | 8.7 | 9.5 | 10.4 | 7.3 |
| By other relative | 4.6 | 5.0 | 4.1 | 4.7 | 4.8 | 4.4 | 4.7 | 5.8 | 2.2 |
| By nonrelative | 22.3 | 25.0 | 17.6 | 22.2 | 25.3 | 17.6 | 22.3 | 24.0 | 18.2 |
| Organized child care facilities | 24.4 | 28.4 | 17.6 | 23.4 | 28.1 | 16.5 | 28.3 | 29.7 | 24.8 |
| Day/group care center | 16.1 | 19.2 | 10.9 | 15.4 | 19.3 | 9.6 | 18.9 | 18.8 | 19.2 |
| Nursery/preschool | 8.3 | 9.2 | 6.7 | 8.0 | 8.8 | 6.9 | 9.4 | 10.9 | 5.6 |
| Kindergarten/grade school | 1.0 | 1.4 | 0.4 | 0.9 | 1.3 | 0.3 | 1.4 | 1.7 | 0.6 |
| Child cares for self | 0.3 | 0.4 | — | 0.1 | 0.1 | — | 1.1 | 1.6 | — |
| Mother cares for child at work | 8.9 | 6.7 | 12.6 | 10.1 | 7.8 | 13.7 | 3.4 | 2.5 | 5.8 |

[a] Includes married, husband-absent (including separated), widowed, divorced, and never-married women.

*Source:* U.S. Bureau of the Census, "Who's Minding the Kids?" *Current Population Reports,* Series P-70, No. 20, July 1990, Table 1, Part B.

ment (35.6 percent) was care in another home, while organized child care plus kindergarten provided care for just over one-quarter of the children (25.4 percent). The 8.9 percent of these children who were under their mother's care were attended by their mothers either at home or on the job. A common arrangement here was of a mother employed either as a private household worker or a child care worker herself. One of the jobs mothers of young children sometimes hold is taking in other children while taking care of their own children at home.

Further elaboration of these statistics for children under 5 is provided in Table 16-1, where the employment of mothers is broken down into full-time or part-time work and their marital status is broken down into married, husband-present and "all other" (see the note at the bottom of the table). As one would expect, many fewer preschool children of full-time working mothers were cared for in their own homes (24.2 percent) than was the case with those of part-time working mothers (39.2 percent). Full-time work for mothers was associated with less care from fathers as well (9.7 versus 24.5 percent). Because full-time working women often have the same nine-to-five schedules as their husbands, neither parent might be available during the mother's working hours. Part-time work, by contrast, can sometimes be arranged so that, while the mother is off at her job (say, in the evening), the father can sit with the children at home.

In the case of mothers without husbands present, as opposed to those in intact families, the percentage of children given primary care by their fathers naturally fell even more sharply (from 18.2 to 2.3 percent). This change, however, did not mean that more children in single-mother families were cared for outside the home. The slack was largely taken up by grandparents and other relatives, who accounted for 19.4 percent of primary care in mother-only households, but for only 5.9 percent of care in husband-present households.

Since the care of infants (children under one year of age) is a particularly sensitive issue in the changing character of the American family, it should be noted that almost the same percentage of children under one year were cared for outside their own homes (68.8 percent) as compared to 3- and 4-year-olds (73.4 percent) and a slightly higher percentage than that for toddlers of 1 and 2 (67.3 percent). The use of organized child care facilities does, however, rise with the age of children in the under-5 group.

## Secondary Child Care Arrangements

When the primary care arrangement for the day is concluded and when the mother is still working, children may be taken care of by someone else or they may take care of themselves. These secondary arrangements are much more common for school-age than younger children, applying to some 35 percent of 5- to 14-year-olds. What is typically involved here is after-school supervision. Table 16-2 provides a breakdown of the type of child care arrangements for those children 5 to 14 for whom a secondary care arrangement was utilized.

An interesting category here is "child cares for self." Here we are dealing with what are sometimes called **latchkey children**—children who typically return from school to an empty house. Table 16-2 gives this number as 1.3 million. This, however, is an underestimate of the number of children who return from school to a house without adults present. A 1987 Census Bureau study concluded that 2.1 million children aged 5 to 13 returned home to an adultless house in December 1984, and 7.1 million came home to a house where no parent was present.[2] Private polls and magazine surveys suggest that as many as 40 percent or more of parents leave their children on their own after school at least once

**TABLE 16-2.   Secondary Child Care Arrangements,
Children 5 to 14, Fall 1987**

| Type of Arrangement | Number (Thousands) | Percentage |
|---|---|---|
| Total | 5,997 | 100.0 |
| Care in child's home: | 2,263 | 37.7 |
| By father | 748 | 12.5 |
| By grandparent | 276 | 4.6 |
| By other relative | 969 | 16.2 |
| By nonrelative | 271 | 4.5 |
| Care in another home: | 1,499 | 25.0 |
| By grandparent | 493 | 8.2 |
| By other relative | 264 | 4.4 |
| By nonrelative | 742 | 12.4 |
| Organized child care facilities | 619 | 10.3 |
| Kindergarten/grade school | 83 | 1.4 |
| Child cares for self | 1,293 | 21.6 |
| Mother cares for child at work[a] | 239 | 4.0 |

[a] Includes women working at home or away from home

*Source:*   U.S. Bureau of the Census, "Who's Minding the Kids?,"
*Current Population Reports*, Series P-70, No. 20, July 1990, Table 6,
p. 19.

a week; nearly one-quarter may leave them alone every school day. Furthermore, Table 16-2 refers to the fall of 1987 and does not take into account the problem of children 5 to 14 during the summer months when school is out. Here the primary care arrangement disappears, and other arrangements must be made by full-time and even part-time working mothers. The percentage of school-age children who go unsupervised more than doubles in summer as opposed to the school year.

Another note on numbers should be mentioned. Although economic necessity is often behind, or felt to be behind, the drive of mothers of small children to enter the labor force, the matter is really much more complicated than that. A 1988 Census Bureau report found that almost three-fifths of all college-educated women with infants under one year of age were employed, compared with only 34 percent of those who

had not finished high school. Also, the proportion of unsupervised children would appear to be higher for whites than for blacks and to rise with income levels. For full-time working mothers in 1984, the proportion of children on their own after school was 10.0 percent where the family income was under $10,000 and 16.6 percent where the family income was $35,000 and over.

Finally, to conclude this section on statistics, it should be noted that the one unmistakable trend that the 1990 Census Bureau report points out is the increase in the use of organized child care facilities for preschool children of employed mothers. Between 1977 and 1987, the percentage of children for whom such care was the primary arrangement rose from 13 percent to over 24 percent, or nearly doubled. This increase was almost wholly at the expense of care by other relatives (or the mother at work), and thus represents a shift not only to group care, but also a further shift to extrafamily care.[3]

## THE INADEQUACIES OF PRESENT ARRANGEMENTS

As we indicated earlier, although deep differences of opinion exist about both causes and cures, there is almost universal agreement that the present substitutes for in-home parental (or other family member) child care are unsatisfactory. Of course, the list of grievances one might draw up against such substitutes would depend on the particular arrangement involved. The three basic types of primary care for young children are: (1) care in the home by a sitter or, more rarely, a professional "nanny"; (2) family day care outside the home; and (3) center day care.

The strengths and weaknesses of each arrangement differ. Infants and toddlers may generally do better in home or family day care, while preschoolers benefit more from center day care.[4] The weaknesses also may differ. Thus, while day care centers may often lack the more personalized involvement sometimes (but not always) found in sitter care or other family care, the latter characteristically employ untrained caregivers in settings of enormous variability. The arrangements in family care are also often unstable as the financial, marital, and other conditions of the caregivers alter. Truly professional care—as in the British nanny system—is extremely rare in the United States. Women who take in other children seldom do so for extended periods. They move on, take better jobs; their own children grow up; in general, such arrangements, though fine at their best, are frequently unsatisfactory and occasionally even perilous for the children involved.

Because family or sitter day care is so variable, it is difficult to make many generalizations about these kinds of care. Organized day care has been much more carefully studied than the more informal arrangements. Also, as already noted, organized care has expanded rapidly as a primary care arrangement in recent years. For these reasons, we will limit our comments primarily to center day care.

Such comments can begin with what is, in fact, an almost universally agreed-on proposition, namely, that the *quality* of center day care in the United States today is inadequate. Its inadequacy stems from at least three factors.

*1. Group Size and Staff-to-Child Ratios.* Most studies of center day care stress the importance of **staff-to-child ratios** and **group size,** particularly for younger children.[5] In general, these studies have found that the *maximum* group size to assure *minimum* quality was 6 to 8 children for infants, 12 children for toddlers, and 16 to 18 children for preschoolers. The maximum staff-to-child ratios are generally believed to be 1:3 for infants, 1:3 to 1:5 for toddlers, and 1:7 to 1:9 for preschoolers.

In Table 16-3, we compare these standards with state regulations of group size and staff-to-child ratios as they existed in the mid-1980s. Of course, these regulations change all the time, though not necessarily in a favorable direction. In view of the pressures created by inadequate center facilities and in order to reduce costs per parent, some states, for example, were easing, rather than stiffening, their staff-to-child ratios during the 1980s.

In general, it is evident that, in the great majority of states, limits on group size and staff-to-child ratios, where such limits even exist, are well below levels designed to give minimal quality care as judged by various studies of professionals in the child development field. Almost everyone agrees that where groups are too large and staffs too small, the children will suffer.

*2. Quality and Pay of Day Care Workers.* Another point on which virtually everyone agrees is that, considering the importance

**TABLE 16-3.   Group Size and Staff-to-child Ratios**

| Category of Children | Professional Guidelines | State Regulations |
|---|---|---|
| *A. Maximum group size allowed* | | |
| Infants | 6–8 | 6–8 (10 states) |
| | | 9–20 (8 states) |
| | | No limit (32 states) |
| Toddlers | 12 | 12 or under (10 states) |
| | | 14–16 (5 states) |
| | | 20 or above (4 states) |
| | | No limit (31 states) |
| Preschool | 16–18 | Under 20 (5 states) |
| | | 20–45 (12 states) |
| | | No limit (33 states) |
| *B. Staff-to-child ratios allowed* | | |
| Infants | 1:3 | 1:3 (3 states) |
| | | 1:4 (18 states) |
| | | 1:5–1:8 (21 states) |
| | | No limit (8 states) |
| Toddlers | 1:3–1:5 | 1:4–1:5 (13 states) |
| | | 1:6–1:7 (7 states) |
| | | 1:8–1:10 (21 states) |
| | | 1:12–1:15 (6 states) |
| | | No limit (3 states) |
| Preschool | 1:7–1:9 | Under 1:10 (4 states) |
| | | 1:10 (20 states) |
| | | 1:11–1:18 (22 states) |
| | | 1:20 or more (4 states) |

*Source:* Genevieve Clapp, *Child Study Research: Current Perspectives and Applications*, Tables 2-1 and 2-2. Copyright © 1988 by Genevieve Clapp. Adapted with permission of Lexington Books, an imprint of Macmillan, Inc.

and difficulty of their work, day care providers are extremely underpaid. Day care workers are often paid below-poverty-level wages and, as a group, fall in the bottom 5 or 10 percent of all wage earners. Their educational level is considerably higher than their wage level, placing them roughly in the middle percentiles of the nation. In general, day care workers, including head teachers in center facilities, earn far less than teachers in public schools, often as little as half as much.

Although hardly overqualified for their responsibilities, these center workers are clearly overqualified relative to their wages.

Of course, a standard argument can be made that if the market values their services in this niggardly fashion, then the proper recourse for day care workers should be to seek alternative employments. Unfortunately, this is exactly what they do do, thus creating a major problem. We are dealing with an occupation in which burnout and high rates of staff turnover are endemic. The task of looking after too many infants, toddlers, and preschoolers for long hours, day after day, places a very heavy psychological drain on day care staffs. When they feel that they are inadequately compensated financially, and when this undercompensation would seem to reflect society's low estimate of the value of their services, the temptation to leave and seek alternative employment often becomes irresistible.

The reason the **high turnover rate** is so important is that, particularly in the case of smaller children, continuity of caregivers may be a major factor in giving them a sense of emotional security. Changes in child care arrangements are frequent. A National Health Interview Survey on Child Health found that one-fourth of the children receiving child care in 1988 had changed child care arrangements at least once in the twelve months preceding the survey interview.[6] Even when center staffs remain constant during a child's stay at a given center, the child who is at the center full-time each day will be dealing with a great variety of teachers and caregivers at different times of the day (in obvious contrast to a family situation, where contact is heavily centered on parents and siblings, especially the mother). With changing child care arrangements and with multiple caregivers who also frequently change over the course of the year—indeed, with those who remain often being pressured and harassed because of their low wages and generally unfavorable economic situations—the chances that the child will experience a supportive, nurturing, and stable environment are obviously greatly reduced.

**3. Health Considerations in Center Day Care.** One of the great advantages of center day care, compared, say, to babysitters or care in another home, is the variety of programs, toys, and other facilities that the larger center can provide. One of the great *dis*advantages is the greater **spread of germs and infections.** Medical experts have sometimes described the transmission of illness through day care centers as "one of the whole nation's major health problems." Dr. Stanley Schuman of the Medical University of South Carolina, writing in the *Journal of the American Medical Association,* warned that "communities large and small are experiencing outbreaks of enteric illness—diarrheas, dysentery, giardasis and epidemic jaundice—reminiscent of the presanitation days of the 17th century."[7] Many of these diseases, are relatively minor, but in certain cases—as with haemophilus influenza type B (HIB), a major cause of bacterial meningitis—the diseases can be life-threatening.

There is disagreement as to how serious the center day care health threat really is. Perhaps, for some children, greater exposure to certain diseases will help build up immunities to protect them later in life. Perhaps, in any event, a few runny noses are a small enough price to pay for the other advantages of center care.

However, most observers consider the spread of day care diseases a serious problem. In some cases, repeated exposures to the diseases cause not less but more serious harm. Where infants are involved, it is doubtful that continuous exposure to germs and infections is anything but disadvantageous to their healthy development. Furthermore, the diseases engendered in the centers (and, to a lesser degree, in group care in homes) often spread to the caregivers, and also to the parents and siblings of day care children when they return to their homes. Finally, there seems little doubt that, *from the sick child's point of view,* center care is likely to be far inferior to that the child would receive from his or her mother or other family caregiver at home.

In principle, of course, parents do not bring sick children to the day care center. In point of fact, however, where the parents have their own working schedules and where it is often difficult to determine, in advance, whether the child is truly sick in the early morning hours, the benefit of doubt often goes to bringing the child in and hoping for the best. The difficulties of then reaching the parents and coping with a possibly seriously ill child at the center until help can arrive are manifold.

For all these reasons, there is almost universal agreement that, if day care centers are to fulfill their roles responsibly, every effort should be made to "clean up their act" and observe numerous well-established procedures to stem the tide of contagion. The *problem* is that most of these sanitary procedures require more staff time and attention, and in some cases better facilities, than currently exist in many centers. Thus, as with group size, staff-to-child ratios, and day care worker salaries, these needed improvements will cost more money than is currently available.

The bottom line appears to be this: Everyone agrees that, *if* day care centers are to be widely and effectively used, they should provide *quality* care. But quality care is expensive. At the end of the 1980s, small, inadequately paid, burned-out staffs in often unsanitary settings were trying to meet the needs of growing numbers of single and married parents who were opting for this form of child care. Dissatisfaction with these conditions was undoubtedly a major factor in the passage of a significant piece of federal child care legislation in 1990, a matter that we return to in a moment.

## IS DAY CARE THE WAY TO GO FOR YOUNG CHILDREN?

Present arrangements for taking care of America's children seem, then, to be unsatisfactory in many instances. But which way is the United States to go? Ruth Sidel, professor of sociology at Hunter College, believes we must expand the quantity and improve the quality of our day care facilities. Writing in 1986, she attacked the approach of the Reagan administration:

> Although one child-care specialist has recently stated, "Day care has become as American as apple pie and baseball," the facts do not confirm her optimistic statement. Not only have funds for day care been cut back over the past four years but, perhaps even more importantly, the rhetoric of the Reagan administration and its allies has undermined public perception of the need for day care by nostalgically recalling and mythologizing another era—perhaps the 1950s, more likely the 1920s—and longingly trying to recapture it.[8]

On the other hand, Burton White, head of the Harvard Preschool Project, is greatly concerned about the transfer of the responsibility for raising babies from the nuclear family to others:

> Today many people take it for granted that soon after a new child is born it is perfectly all right for the child-rearing responsibility to be assumed by other members of society paid for the task. This point of view alarms me—and not only me but also a fair number of other people who have taken a hard look at the situation.[9]

As we have said earlier, we shall not try to resolve this very deep dispute, but will simply suggest some of the research findings that are used to support each position. We concentrate primarily on the issue as it affects babies and younger children.

### View 1: Day Care Is Here to Stay and Must Be Expanded

In the foreground of this case there is usually a belief in the inevitability of the transfer of at least certain child-rearing responsibilities from parents, and mothers in particular, to outside caregivers or agencies. A stylized statement of the case could go as follows:

*1. The trends that are taking young mothers out of the home are deep-seated and will not be reversed.* We refer here to all those factors affecting the status of women in recent years, including divorce, separation, and single motherhood, but especially the rapid entry of young mothers into the work force. These trends are believed to be largely irreversible and, since fathers and grandparents are likely to take up only part of the slack (at best), the child care that these mothers otherwise would have given must be provided by someone else. There is simply no alternative.

*2. "Traditional" patterns of child rearing were often inadequate in the past, and may be particularly so today.* Dr. Sidel writes of "mythologizing" earlier family arrangements. Many supporters of expanded day care feel that the "traditional" family has been highly romanticized. Where we have more broken homes today, in earlier periods we had more bad marriages, with all the unfortunate consequences for children of marital conflict and stress. Similarly, the increasing number of working mothers today may mean less direct maternal care, but it provides a useful role model for children, especially daughters, and it also reduces the frustration levels of women who, in the past, kept virtual prisoners in the home, felt isolated, helpless, lacking in self-esteem—hardly the best atmosphere in which to raise young children. Furthermore, in the case of young, poorly educated mothers living in poverty, often in racial or ethnic ghettos, there is strong evidence that day care can improve on home care with respect to certain aspects of child rearing. Most studies suggest that day care (or at least quality day care) results in improvement in cognitive ability and test scores for economically disadvantaged children as compared to their home-raised counterparts. In sum, we should not compare day care to some idealized family child-rearing structure, but to the realities of what existed in the past, and especially of what exists today.

*3. The negative effects of day care on children are often overstated.* In general, it is argued, there is no evidence that day care is harmful when it is adequately provided. Thus psychiatrists Stella Chess and Alexander Thomas conclude in their review of maternal employment: "The data are abundant and the conclusion clearcut: The children of mothers working outside the home are not harmed if a satisfactory substitute caretaker (or caretakers) is provided."[10]

An interesting question is whether such conclusions can be applied to very young children, infants in particular. In this connection, there has been a shift in sentiment among some child development experts in recent years. Fortified by Freudian theory and several studies of institutionalized children in the 1940s and 1950s, many students of child development had concluded that the very early months and years of a child's life were of crucial importance in the development of the individual over his or her entire life span. Insofar as parental and especially maternal care was critical during this early period, day care could be assumed to have potentially deleterious long-run effects. What has happened in more recent decades is that some psychologists have concluded that while the early years are important, so also are later years—that is to say, the individual in later years is far more plastic than the crucial-early-experiences theorists had suggested. Good later experiences can counteract poor early ones. "It appears," writes psychologist Jerome Kagan, "that some problems observed during the first year continue for two or three years and then gradually vanish due, we suppose, to the therapeutic effect of new experiences."[11] Or, as Dr. Genevieve Clapp sums up her survey of this particular literature: "All stages of development appear to be important. It appears that good starts

can be lost and poor starts, with careful effort, can be remedied."[12]

At a minimum, those who accept these findings can take comfort in the notion that, if required to begin day care for their children at the very earliest ages—even at a few days or weeks old—they are not necessarily imposing some irreversible loss on the child. Possibly, of course, they are imposing no loss at all.

*4. Day care—again when adequately provided—has many positive features for the children involved.* As we have mentioned, some studies have suggested that intellectual development in the case of economically disadvantaged children is improved through center day care. Other studies suggest that, on a wide range of tests of intellectual development, center day care children do better than home-reared middle-class children as well. This applies only to high-quality day care, of course, and the advantage may be quite temporary.

As far as social development is concerned, the possible advantage of center day care depends to some degree on what it is being compared to. An article in the October 12, 1987, *Newsweek* recounts the isolation of many of today's children who are raised at home. Writes the mother, a part-time history teacher at William and Mary:

> There is little informal, neighborhood life left—even in a small town. . . . Keep a kid at home and he'll have no one to play with. While my son spends his solitary hour at the playground, I daydream as I watch him. Perhaps someday we will live someplace where it will be possible for him to play outside with other children without any prior planning. But right now, even on weekends and evenings when kids are back in their neighborhoods, they remain indoors. It is no longer safe to roam the neighborhood as I could when I was a child. Instead, they watch TV inside the temperature-controlled fortresses we call our homes. Safe but solitary, they are insulated from the weather and further isolated from contact with their peers.[13]

This lament is from a mother who very much wanted to raise her child largely at home. In its description of the child's isolation, it is reminiscent of the laments of many suburban women whose isolation, indeed, may have been a major factor in their desires to enter the work force. The day care center can become, in a certain sense, the child's equivalent of the mother's labor force participation. Instead of isolation, the child has frequent and daily contact with children of the same and/or different ages, and also, of course, with a number of adult caregivers. Most studies suggest that the effect of day care is to make children much more peer-oriented than those raised at home. They are also likely to be more aggressive, assertive, and in some cases independent. Compared to many home situations, this may be a definite improvement.

In short, given the realities of the U.S. economy and American family life, day care—providing always that it is *quality* care—may be not only our best bet, but a good bet as well.

### View 2: Parental Care Is Superior and Should be Encouraged in Every Way Possible

In the foreground of this case, there is usually the view that socioeconomic trends, including those that require parents to leave their children in the care of others, are by no means inevitable. Trends have changed direction in the past, and they can change direction in the future. A stylized statement of this case could go as follows:

*1. With fewer children to care for and longer life expectancies, there should be ample time and space for women (and men) both to achieve major careers and to raise their young children.* If we look at the *deepest* trends in our society, this argument goes, we find that they should make possible increased parental care for children. Instead of four, five, or even seven or eight children, we now average two or fewer per mother. Women now live to be 78 or 79 on the average; soon the average may be over 80, some day perhaps 90 or higher. Since most of the debate about child care focuses on the early, preschool years, we are talking about six or seven years out of a mother's life (or, for that matter, out of a father's life, if social mores move sufficiently in that direction), perhaps a 10-year maximum. During most of this period, moreover, part-time work, either at home, or combined with a modicum of outside day care, could easily be combined with child-rearing responsibilities. Once the *concept* of women having major careers is accepted and the business community has made the required minimal adjustments, the way should be open to a full professional life *and* devoted parental care. There are 60 years between the ages of 20 and 80; it should not be difficult to fit in 10 or 15 percent of this time for the purpose of raising one's own children.

*2. The roots of the "traditional" patterns of child rearing may go much deeper than contemporary critics suggest.* Dr. Sidel, we have noted, wants to "demythologize" traditional family arrangements. On the opposite side of the fence are those, like Brigitte and Peter Berger of Boston University, who note that much modern research suggests "that the demythologizers have themselves been demythologized." An important finding of this research, they write, is this: "The notion that the nuclear family is an exclusive product of modernity can itself be shown to have been a myth. This is all the more important in that . . . the alleged problems of the nuclear family . . . constitute the common empirical base for all the major participants in the current debate over the family." In other words, the concept that the characteristic married-couple-plus-children household is a very recent phenomenon—a largely passing phase during the industrialization process, and therefore expendable as we enter new phases—may be more mythological than the hypothesized romanticization of the "traditional" family.[14]

The Bergers believe that the nuclear family extended back into Western history well before the industrialization period and, indeed, may have been a percursor, or even a precondition, of the modernization process. It is also very possible that the family unit, including both extended and nuclear versions, is deeply embedded in the entire human evolutionary process and is related to such elemental developments as walking upright, brain size, and especially the prolonged period of dependence of human offspring compared to those of other species. "The family," writes ethologist Phon Hudkins, "is the only social institution that is present in every single village, tribe, or nation we know through history. It has a genetic base and is the rearing device for our species."[15] In short, the argument goes, when we tamper with such a deep-seated institution for raising our young as the family has been over modern Western history, and perhaps over the entire course of human history, we do so only at great risk to our children.

*3. Day care, even quality care, does have certain unavoidable disadvantages compared to parental care.* In a general sense, and on the average, parents have a far deeper and more personalized interest in their children than can even the most conscientious day care provider. The latter sees children in groups, the groups change, the care provider changes. Quite apart from any assumed genetic maternal or paternal feelings for the child, the sheer absence of continuity over time dooms the development of any *deep* personal attachments between provider and child. (Where day care is of poor quality and the turnover of staff rapid, of course, this problem assumes monumental importance.)

One problem is more specific than this, however, relating directly to those early months we discussed previously. The proposition that the first year or two of a child's life has no more or less importance than any other year or two is by no means universally accepted. Psychologist Jay Belsky of Pennsylvania State University, summarizing recent research at the ninety-fifth annual convention of the American Psychological Association in 1987, while finding no harm from quality day care for toddlers after the first year of life, was much concerned about placing children in day care during that first year, an increasingly common practice. In earlier writings, Belsky and his colleagues have stressed the importance of close infant–adult relationships:

> A primary social task for the infant is to establish a close emotional relationship with another human being. The individual with whom the child develops this first **attachment relationship** (emphasis in the original) is usually the mother, but always an individual who holds a special place in the baby's life. . . . [This attachment relationship gives the baby] a source of security so as to be able to move about the environment and freely explore.[16]

Earlier, Professor Belsky had been an important supporter of day care, but, beginning in 1985, he saw signs that infant insecurity, as measured by what is called the **Strange Situation Procedure**,[17] was high among infants in day care, particularly those exposed to such care for more than 20 hours a week. Insofar as this attachment relationship is important to the long-run development of the child, as Belsky and his colleagues clearly believe, then extensive day care during the first year of life could prove harmful in many cases. Needless to say, many child development specialists disagree with Belsky's conclusions. Perhaps the only general agreement here is that the long-run effects of extensive day care on the child's eventual adulthood are not really known. Given this lack of knowledge, however, many proponents of parental care suggest that we had best not risk a radical change from tradition-tried methods of child rearing.[18]

*4. Many of the so-called advantages of day care over parental care are dubious at best.* Finally, proponents of parental care are doubtful of many of the so-called advantages of day care for the child's intellectual and social development. Such gains on intellectual tests that children in very high quality centers achieve over home-reared children do not seem to confer lasting advantages. Furthermore, the presumed superior social ease the child gains with his or her peers is claimed to be of questionable value. Insofar as these peer relationships are achieved at the expense of deeper child–adult attachments, it is not certain that a net social gain has been accomplished. Further, the attitudes displayed by day care children are by no means wholly desirable in a social setting. "The gravest social development problem presented by the day care child," writes Fredelle Maynard, author of *The Child Care Crisis,* "is increased aggressiveness. On this point all investigators agree: day care children are more inclined to get what they want by hitting, threatening, kicking, punching, insulting and taking possessions without permission. . . . A recent report found day care children performed *fifteen* (emphasis in original) times as many aggressive acts as home-reared agemates."[19] Adds Marion Blum, educational director of the Wellesley College Child Study Center: "It is another irony about day care that ignoring the issue of aggression in day care may eventually impact on future aggregate costs to society."[20]

In sum, this second view holds that there is no basic demographic reason that requires parents to abandon large portions of the early care of their children to society at large. Parental (and perhaps especially, though not certainly, maternal) care has clear-cut advantages in most cases owing to the depth and continuity of the child–parent nexus. Since, at best, day care's long-run effects are uncertain, this is definitely *not* the option on which society should place its bet.

## THE 1990 CHILD CARE LEGISLATION

Given the depth of the disagreements suggested by the two views we have just presented, it is rather remarkable that an important federal child care bill was passed in 1990 with almost no fanfare whatsoever. This event was even more remarkable in that the bill was part of the total deficit reduction package worked out between Congress and the president, yet it involves the government in important new fiscal responsibilities. Although the initial expenditures are relatively modest, the potential for the program to expand in future years is obvious to both proponents and opponents of the legislation.[21]

Essentially, the legislation provides for closer regulation and inspection of day care facilities and for a program of federal grants to the states aimed at making child care more available and affordable for working families. The grant program would provide $2.5 billion over a three-year period to fund child care services for families with incomes lower than 75 percent of their state's median income. Also, 25 percent of these funds would be set aside for improving the quality of child care, including possibly increasing teacher salaries.

From our point of view, what is perhaps most interesting is that this legislation, which appears to be a major first step in increasing government responsibility, and reducing family responsibility, for the care of young children, was advertised as a *pro*-family initiative. The Conference Agreement between the House and Senate describes the purposes of the grant program as:

> . . . intended to build on and strengthen the role of the family by seeking to ensure that parents are not forced by the lack of available programs or financial resources to place a child in an unsafe or unhealthy child care arrangement; to promote the availability and diversity of quality child care services; to

expand child care options available to all families who need such services; to provide assistance to families whose financial resources are not sufficient to enable such families to pay the full cost of necessary child care; to improve the productivity of parents in the labor force by lessening the stresses related to the absence of adequate child care services; and . . . to improve the quality of, and coordination among, child care programs and early childhood development programs.[22]

There is very little question that this legislation is primarily designed to ease the circumstances of working parents who find it necessary and/or desirable to use day care in place of parental care. Because such programs must be funded by general tax revenues, they mean of necessity a redistribution of income from parents who raise their own children (who are taxed) to parents who use day care (who may also be taxed, but are subsidized as well). Thus, the 1990 legislation is in line with *View I* (above) and would be regarded by proponents of *View II* as undermining, rather than strengthening, the institution of the family. We will come back to this general issue again, especially in Chapter 23.

## THE "SLEEPER" ISSUES

Most of the discussion in this chapter has been concerned with the rearing of young children: infants, toddlers, and preschoolers. But, of course, the issue of raising the next generation also involves the fate of these children as they grow older, attend regular schools, become teenagers and ultimately adults. Indeed, one of the great difficulties of judging the issue of early care, as we have mentioned, is that we know so little about the long-run effects of this care.

These are the so-called sleeper questions: What may we be finding out 10 or 15 years from now about the effects of our present child-rearing practices on the teen-

agers and young adults who will then be emerging? Is it possible that we are already beginning to see some effects of parental and/or governmental neglect? And what of the direct effect on teenagers of the "latch-key" phenomenon we mentioned earlier? Or will those effects also appear only much later in life in ways that we find hard to anticipate?

These questions are extremely important, for if Americans are increasingly concerned about the inadequacy of our child care arrangements, they may be even more concerned about what is happening with our teenagers. Teenage pregnancy, abortion, drug and alcohol abuse, excessive television watching, poor academic achievement, violence, and gang warfare are among the worries that arise in any discussion of the current state of America's teenagers. Last but not least is the rise in the youth suicide rate: Between the mid-1950s and the mid-1980s, this rate tripled. It leveled off in the late 1980s, but at what most observers feel is a tragically high level.

At this point, no one can say with any confidence that these disturbing developments either are or are not related to our changing patterns of child rearing or, even more deeply, to the new attitudes toward children we discussed in Chapter 14. In 1986, an article by Peter Uhlenberg and David Eggebeen in *The Public Interest* attracted much attention. Entitled "The Declining Well-being of American Adolescents," the article attributed much of the recent decline in the well-being of 16- and 17-year-olds to the weakening of parental controls occasioned by the rising divorce rates and the increasing number of working mothers. Other commentators, however, like Frank Furstenberg, Jr., and Gretchen Condran, find the empirical evidence for this hypothesis unconvincing. While admitting that "the situation of youth today is far from ideal," Furstenberg and Condran suggest a more eclectic explanation, involving such factors as the size of the Baby Boom generation and the specific historical circumstances of the 1960s and 1970s, such as Vietnam and Watergate.[23]

Perhaps neither explanation is wholly satisfactory. We can only emphasize the urgency of more research in these areas: it is, after all, the future of the nation that is at stake.

In one particular respect, this future does seem clearly in jeopardy, and the future happiness and self-realization of the coming generation as well: the evident weakness and decline of the United States' educational system.

On this critical issue, we will focus our attention in the next chapter.

## SUMMARY

1.   Great changes in the care of children have taken place in recent years as single-parent families have become more common and there has been a rapid rise in the labor force participation of mothers of young children. In 1987, fewer than one-third of children under 5 of employed mothers were primarily cared for in their own homes while their mothers were at work. Latchkey children, older children who return home from school to an adultless house, now number in the millions.

2.   It is widely recognized, on all sides of the political spectrum, that the United States' current substitutes for parental care are inadequate. Commonly used care arrangements outside of family members include: (a) care in the home by a sitter, (b) family day care outside the home, and (c) center day care.

3.   The most rapidly growing and widely studied arrangement is center day care. Although this type of care has advantages over other forms of care, especially for preschoolers, it is also deficient in the eyes of most critics because:

a.   Group size and child-to-staff ratios are often too high.
b.   The quality and pay of day care workers are too low and their turnover rates too high.
c.   Center day care often plays host to rampant minor, and sometimes serious, contagious diseases.

4.   Although there is agreement on the deficiencies of current child care arrangements in the United States, there is sharp disagreement as to what our future policy should be. One view is that the quantity and quality of day care need to be improved through substantial public subsidies. This view argues that trends in the family and in women's labor force participation will not be reversed; that "traditional" patterns of child rearing were often unsatisfactory; that the negative effects of day care are very minor; and that, in fact, day care has many positive features, as, for example, in improving the cognitive development of many children.

5.   The opposite view states that basic demographic trends (fewer children to care for, longer life expectancies) make it easily possible for parents to care for their own children, that this pattern of parental care is firmly rooted in our historical and even our genetic past, that day care can never provide the continuous and deep personal attachments that parents can give to their children, and that such advantages as day care seems to confer, as, for example, in cognitive development, have proved to be very short-lived.

6.   In 1990, federal legislation was passed subsidizing extrafamily day care through a program of grants to the states.

7.   What needs more research, everyone agrees, is the long-run effect of our new patterns of child rearing, not only on teenagers, but also on the adulthoods of the children now being raised.

## KEY CONCEPTS FOR REVIEW

Primary care arrangements

Secondary care arrangements

Self-care and latchkey children

Types of nonrelative care
  sitter care in the home
  family care outside the home
  center day care

Center day care issues
  group size
  staff-to-child ratios
  quality of day care workers

staff turnover rate

spread of contagious diseases

"Mythologizing" traditional families

"Demythologizing" the "demythologizers"

Early years are crucial versus all stages of development are equally important

Attachment relationship

Strange Situation Procedure

Cognitive versus social development

1990 child care legislation

"Sleeper" issues

## QUESTIONS FOR DISCUSSION

1. "Underlying demographic changes, involving especially the increased participation of mothers in the labor force, mean that the demand for good day care is bound to increase in the United States in coming decades."

   "Underlying demographic changes, involving especially low fertility rates and increased life expectancies, mean that parents should easily be able to raise their own children and still have substantial careers."

   Discuss the conflict involved in these statements.

2. Describe the characteristics of child care arrangements for children under 5 in the United States in the late twentieth century. How do they differ from arrangements one might have found in the late nineteenth century? in the late eighteenth century?

3. Explain the term *latchkey children.* Do you know of such children in your own experience? Do you feel it is appropriate or inappropriate to regard the problems of some of today's adolescents (suicide rates, drug and alcohol abuse, poor schoolwork, etc.) as reflecting lack of parental interest and supervision?

4. Write an essay in which you discuss the advantages and disadvantages of center day care for children, making clear how these advantages or disadvantages may differ depending on the age of the children involved.

5. After writing this essay, develop what you would consider to be an ideal day care policy for the federal (or state or local) government to follow. Does the 1990 child care legislation move the country closer to or further away from your ideal policy?

## NOTES

1. U.S. Bureau of the Census, "Who's Minding the Kids? Child Care Arrangements: Winter 1986–87," *Current Population Reports*, Series P-70, No. 20 (Washington, D.C.: U.S. Government Printing Office, 1990).

2. U.S. Bureau of the Census, "After School Care of School-Age Children: December, 1984," Series P-23, No. 149 (Washington, D.C.: U.S. Government Printing Office, 1987). Estimates of the numbers of latchkey children in the mid-1980s have actually varied widely—from 1.4 million to 15 million

children. A detailed study of third graders in seven elementary schools in a suburban school district in Dallas, Texas, found that 23 percent of the children returned from school to a home without adult supervision. D. L. Vandell and M. A. Corasaniti, "The Relation Between Third Graders' After-school Care and Social, Academic, and Emotional Functioning," *Child Development* 59:1988; pp. 868–875.

3. U.S. Bureau of the Census, "Who's Minding the Kids?," pp. 4–5. The report notes that the decline

in the use of relatives as caregivers "may reflect the overall increase in the labor force participation of women outside the home, thus reducing the potential number of female relatives available for child care services."

4. Thus, Professor Sandra Scarr notes that her researches indicate that children "under three have a different set of needs from those over three years. The care typically provided in the centers was not entirely suitable for very young children but much more appropriate for older children." Sandra Scarr, "Child Care," Hearings before the Select Committee on Children, Youth and Families, U.S. House of Representatives, May 6, 1984, p. 654.

5. See Jay Belsky, Richard M. Lerner, and Graham B. Spanier, *The Child in the Family* (Reading, Mass.: Addison-Wesley, 1984), and the useful general surveys of the literature in Genevieve Clapp, *Child Study Research: Current Perspectives and Applications* (Lexington, Mass.: D. C. Heath, 1988), esp. pp. 41 ff., and C. D. Hayes, J. L. Palmer, and M. J. Zaslow, eds., *Who Cares for America's Children?* Panel on Child Care Policy, National Research Council (Washington, D.C.: National Academy Press, 1990), esp. Appendix B.

6. D. A. Dawson and V. S. Cain, "Child Care Arrangements: Health of Our Nation's Children, United States, 1988," advance data from *Vital and Health Statistics of the National Center for Health Statistics*, 187, October 1, 1990, p. 6.

7. Stanley Schuman, "Day-Care-Associated Infection: More Than Meets the Eye," *Journal of the American Medical Association*, 249(1), January 7, 1983, p. 76. See also Marian Blum, *The Day-Care Dilemma: Women and Children First* (Lexington, Mass.: D. C. Heath, 1983), p. 74, and Fredelle Maynard, *The Child Care Crisis* (New York: Viking Penguin, 1985), p. 166.

8. Ruth Sidel, *Women and Children Last* (New York: Viking Penguin, 1986), pp. 115–116. It should be noted that the quotation about "apple pie and baseball" comes from Blum, *The Day-Care Dilemma*, and is not really meant as an "optimistic statement." Blum is actually quite critical of current day care trends.

9. Burton L. White, "Foreword" to Maynard, *The Child Care Crisis*, p. xii.

10. Stella Chess and Alexander Thomas, eds., *Annual Progress in Child Psychiatry and Development* (New York: Brunner/Mazel, 1985), p. 223.

11. Jerome Kagan, "Family Experience and the Child's Development," *American Psychologist*, 34, October 1979, p. 888.

12. Clapp, *Child Study Research*, p. 23.

13. Phyllis A. Hall, "All Our Lonely Children," *Newsweek*, October 12, 1987, p. 12.

14. Brigitte Berger and Peter L. Berger, *The War Over the Family* (Garden City, N.Y.: Anchor Press/Doubleday, 1983), pp. 86–87.

15. Phon Hudkins is quoted in William Raspberry, "Bring Back the Family," *Washington Post*, July 17, 1989. See also Chapter 2, "The Evolutionary Basis of the Child in the Family," in Belsky, Lerner, and Spanier, *The Child in the Family*, pp. 7–16.

16. Belsky, Lerner, and Spanier, *The Child in the Family*, p. 48.

17. Sometimes called the Ainsworth Strange Situation Procedure, after its originator, Mary Ainsworth. Essentially, the test involves watching the child's reactions as he or she is subjected to a variety of stresses, including the mother's departure, the presence of strangers, reunion with the mother, and the like.

18. That Professor Belsky's views are not wholly shared in the profession was made clear in the late 1980s as the controversy spilled over into the popular press. Concerning the idea that day care might be harmful for infants, Tiffany Field, a professor of pediatrics and psychology at the University of Miami, said: "I think its bunkum." Sandra Scarr, whose researches we have noted earlier, said that Belsky's views represent a backlash against the women's movement: "The advice for women has always been to get out of the work force. This is just another way of saying the same thing." Perhaps the only agreed-upon statement in the whole controversy was that of Professor Edward Zigler, director of Yale's Bush Center in Child Development and Social Policy: "We aren't going to know the answers to these questions until these babies grow up and raise children of their own. Only then will we see how the bonding process has been affected." All quotes are taken from Thomas E. Ricks, "Day Care for Infants is Challenged by Research on Psychological Risks," *Wall Street Journal*, March 3, 1987, p. 35.

19. Maynard, *The Child Care Crisis*, p. 119.

20. Blum, *The Day-Care Dilemma*, p. 24.

21. Press reports suggested that advocates of the bill, like Representative Pat Schroeder of Colorado, saw the legislation as only the beginning of a much larger future program. This was exactly what opponents of the bill believed—and feared.

22. *Congressional Record—House*, October 26, 1990, p. H12681.

23. See Peter Uhlenberg and David Eggebeen, "The Declining Well-being of American Adolescents," *The Public Interest*, 82, 1986; and Frank F. Furstenberg, Jr., and Gretchen A. Condran, "Family Changes and Adolescent Well-Being: A Reexamination of U.S. Trends," in Andrew Cherlin, ed., *The Changing American Family and Public Policy* (Washington, D.C.: Urban Institute Press, 1988).

# 17

# *Educating the Next Generation*

In the 1988 presidential campaign, George Bush declared that he wished to become known as the "education president." In a certain sense, this declaration simply continued a long series of pronouncements about education in our nation's history dating back to Thomas Jefferson. In the nineteenth and early twentieth centuries, as we have noted in Chapter 14, public education in the United States came to play a larger and larger role in the process of transmission of skills, knowledge, and culture from one generation to the next.

In another sense, the renewed attention to education in recent years seems to have been a consequence of a rather striking break in the record of generational change. Just as child poverty has been rising rather than declining, just as the family unit has been weakening in its capacity to rear and nurture young children (with as yet no viable alternative institution in general existence), so the educational system of the country seems to be running in reverse, or at least in neutral, and this at a time when forward progress seems particularly vital.

In the somewhat overdramatic, but nevertheless attention-getting, phrases of the National Commission on Excellence in Education in *A Nation at Risk* (1983):

> If an unfriendly foreign power had attempted to impose on America the mediocre educational performance that exists today, we might well have viewed it as an act of war.... We have, in effect, been committing an act of unthinking, unilateral educational disarmament.[1]

With no real evidence of improvement in the U.S. educational performance in the ensuing years, on April 18, 1991 President Bush announced a sweeping proposal for "nothing less than a revolution" in the nation's public school system. In this chapter we will take up many of the underlying issues that emerged during the national debate that followed Bush's announcement.

## EDUCATION FOR OUR CHANGING POPULATION

We have just said that our educational system seems to be failing us at a time when educational progress seems especially vital. In *A Nation at Risk*, the particular importance of education to the United States these days is seen in relation to our international position. How well will an undereducated American be able to compete in the high-tech future with Japan, Europe, and the newly industrialized countries (NICs) of Asia like Taiwan, South Korea, and Singapore? This particular concern was given added weight more recently (1989) by a report of the Educational Testing Service in Princeton, New Jersey, which found that in a survey of six countries, 13-year-old U.S. students scored at the bottom in mathematics and next to the bottom in science. The countries included South Korea (an NIC), but not Japan, and included Ireland and Spain, neither particularly noted for achievements in science, as well as Canada and Britain. Only Ireland scored lower than the United States in science (469 to 479), and, at that, Ireland was substantially ahead of this country in mathematics (504 to 474). In terms of international competitiveness, the somewhat alarming fact was that South Korea was easily at the top in both categories.

While public concern about our international competitiveness is undoubtedly justified, our own interest in the U.S. educational system is focused more on its relationship to our changing population. To what degree are the trends that are shaping our present and future population being affected by, or causing new demands to be placed on, our national educational enterprise? How well is that enterprise responding to those demands?

A brief listing of some interrelationships between American population change and American education reveals how closely the two subjects are intertwined:

1. *Educating the next generation:* This is an obvious interconnection, giving us the title for this chapter. All populations change through the replacement of older by younger generations. In the most general sense, education, whether accomplished at home, at school, or on the job, is the means by which the next generation is prepared to take its place in this process of succession.

2. *Reeducating the older generation:* In the Aging Society, the need for the educational system to engage in a process of lifelong education and training is becoming increasingly apparent. As we have mentioned in early chapters and will stress again later (see especially Chapter 22), continuing education is no longer a luxury but a requirement in a society where potential working lives may extend for many decades and where technological change threatens obsolescence to those who lag behind. We will not consider this point further in the present chapter.

3. *The need for an educated labor force in the future:* The Aging of America does have direct implications for the educational needs of the upcoming generation in that (a) the low fertility of present-day parents does imply (other things being equal) slow, zero, or even negative labor force growth in the future, and (b) longer life expectancies for elderly Americans could mean a substantial increase in demands for Social Security, health care, and the like. In both respects, the productivity of the next generation is a matter of some concern, particularly since some observers believe that advanced technology will make particularly heavy demands on the educational qualifications of our future labor force. This relationship between education and productivity is clearly one to which we must return later in this chapter.

4. *Education and the changing family:* Education outside the home is related to the changing American family in at least two important ways. In the first place, the increasing expense of educating children, particularly at higher educational levels, is widely cited as a reason (a) that parents wish to have fewer children these days, and (b) that parents who do have children feel a need to become two-income families. Both factors undoubtedly have some effect in reducing (or keeping low) our national fertility rate. In real (constant-dollar) terms, educational costs in the United States have risen dramatically in recent years.

In the second place, changes in marital practices (never-married parents, divorce) and in child rearing in the home (both parents working) have created a widely expressed feeling that the schools should take over many of the functions traditionally handled by the family unit. This is not confined to publicly supported day care, preschool and kindergarten, but includes as well the possibility of using the schools as places for after-school activities for children of all ages who might otherwise return to parentless, and in some cases actually unsafe, homes.

5. *Education as a route to the American mainstream for immigrant, minority, and other disadvantaged groups:* Historically, education has been the mechanism by which different ethnic and racial groups have found ways to improve their lot and to enter into full participation in U.S. society. In this sense, there is nothing new about the demands being placed on our educational system today as compared with times past. At the same time, the situation of our urban schools, with their often heavy concentrations of blacks and Hispanics, is regarded by some commentators as approaching the disaster level. A 1988 report of the Carnegie Foundation for the Advancement of Teaching was called *An Imperiled Generation: Saving the Urban Schools.* It warned that "everyone's future is imperiled if disadvantaged young people are not economically and civically prepared" and called for a "comprehensive

federal program" to meet the urban school "crisis." The seriousness of this situation is compounded by many factors (a notable example being the widespread use of drugs in the inner city), and is clearly affected by the breakdown of viable family units in disadvantaged communities within our society. In this respect, then, our educational system is again being called upon to deal with problems that, in earlier times, tended to be handled within the family unit.

For all these reasons, our educational system, always an important part of the American dream and of our actual historic accomplishment, has achieved a particularly pivotal place in meeting the demands of today's changing population.

## ACHIEVEMENTS AND CRISES

Since all the talk in the late 1980s has been in terms of the "crisis" in American education, we should perhaps begin by noting that, during the past century, there has also been much in the way of progress. Figure 17-1 makes clear that the trend toward a **rising number of years of schooling,** which we have already observed for the nineteenth and early twentieth centuries, has continued in the mid- to late twentieth century. The percentage of Americans aged 25 to 29 who have spent 12 years in school more than doubled between 1940 and 1988. The percentage of Americans in that age group who had had four or more years of college almost quadrupled.

This progress was by no means confined to white, middle-class students. The median number of years of schooling completed by blacks 25 years or older increased from 9.8 years in 1970 to 12.4 years in 1988, while for Hispanics the increase was from 9.1 to 12.0 years. Minority college enrollments also increased. The percentage of blacks 25 and older who had completed four or more years of college increased from 4.4 percent in 1970 to 11.3 percent in 1988. The similar percentage increase for Hispanics was from 4.5 to 10.0 percent. These percentages represent strong gains for blacks and Hispanics, although, of course, they remain below the comparable number for white Americans, 20.9 percent of whom had completed four or more years of college in 1988.

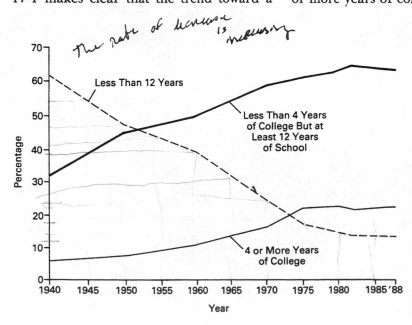

**FIGURE 17-1: Years of School Completed by Persons 25 to 29 Years of Age, 1940–1988**

*Source:* U.S. Department of Commerce, Bureau of the Census, *1960 Census of Population,* Vol. 1, Part 1; and *Current Population Reports,* Series P-20, "Educational Attainment in the United States"; *Statistical Abstract of the United States, 1990.* Adapted by the authors.

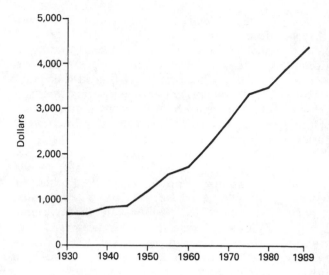

**FIGURE 17-2: Total Expenditure per Pupil, Public Elementary and Secondary Schools, 1930–1989 (Constant 1985–1986 Dollars)**

*Source:* Based on data from U.S. Department of Education, National Center for Education Statistics. *Statistics of State School Systems* and *Revenues and Expenditures for Public Elementary and Secondary Education;* and Center for Education Statistics, "Common Core of Data" survey and unpublished data; National Education Association, *Estimates of School Statistics.* 1986–87; *Statistical Abstract of the United States, 1990.* Estimates adapted by the authors.

*Note:* Expenditures for 1981–1989 are estimates.

Also, as Figure 17-2 indicates, there has been no apparent stinting of educational expenditures in the United States in recent decades, at least as compared to the distant past. Between 1930 and 1989, total expenditures per pupil in public elementary and secondary schools in the United States rose in real terms (constant dollars) from $687 to an estimated $4,388, or more than six times. This growth remained strong in the 1980s, with **per pupil expenditures** increasing by more than 25 percent in real terms from 1981 to 1989. This overall record suggests a definite determination to maintain educational quality and to expand the reach of our educational system to groups heretofore excluded.

Despite these apparently favorable numbers, the entire post–World War II period has witnessed a succession of **"crises" in our educational system**—a phenomenon that, we should say, is not completely new in our long-run historical experience. At least since 1892, when the National Education Association created a panel to examine the country's high school curriculum—the so-called Committee of Ten, under Harvard President Charles W. Eliot—we have been attempting as a nation to cope with trouble-some problems in our educational enterprise. Some of those early issues have been resolved—for example, no one seriously proposes that Greek and Latin should be restored to their earlier eminence in our curricula. Others still remain with us, usually in a somewhat different form—for example, what should be the balance between vocational and academic work in our schools? How much "tracking" of students by different curricula should be permitted? How much grouping by ability?

In more recent years, there have been three fairly distinct crisis periods in our schools:

1. *The post-Sputnik alarms:* In 1957, the Russians put the world's first satellite in orbit and created an immediate panic in the United States about the decline of our educational system. This event occurred after a period in which "progressive" education, with its emphasis on "life adjustment education" and "meeting the needs of the whole child," had been very much in vogue.[2] This approach (like its companion "permissiveness" in early child care) was already under criticism by many educators and ordinary citizens who preferred a return to a more

traditional academic approach. Sputnik delivered the coup de grace. It was one thing to talk about educational fads and fancies; it was a very different thing when national survival might be at stake. The result was a major push in the direction of more rigorous academic requirements; the development of innovative teaching techniques; and encouragement of the study of mathematics, science, and engineering.

2.  *Civil rights and the Great Society:* No sooner had rigor and academic "excellence" been installed as the goals of our schools than the country faced a quite different challenge to our educational system: its ability to welcome and incorporate on truly equal terms blacks and other minority groups. The key event here, occurring before Sputnik, was undoubtedly the 1954 Supreme Court decision in *Brown* v. *Board of Education of Topeka* repudiating the separate-but-equal doctrine under which school segregation had been previously justified. More generally, the civil rights movement, the Kennedy presidency, the Great Society programs of the Johnson administration, the student protest movements and the growth of the "counterculture" in the 1960s—all these taken together brought about a sharp shift in our national educational priorities. "The fifties movement for excellence," write the authors of *The Shopping Mall High School,* "thus had been replaced at the top of the national education agenda, only a decade after it began, by an even more intense movement for equality. . . . Educators turned their attention away from improving quality to extending equality. And public pressure for improved quality faded as politically active Americans turned to the problems of blacks and poor people."[3] The impact of this change in goals on the schools' curricula was to increase the range and variety of courses offered, including many remedial courses, and, according to most observers, to promote grade inflation and to lower course and graduation standards.

3.  *A Nation at Risk:* And then the pendulum swung back again. In the early and mid-1980s, a series of reports from various commissions, public and private, concluded that our schools were failing in their most important single goal—educating their students in English, history, mathematics, science—indeed, all academic subjects. The most startling and influential of these reports, as we have already suggested, was that commissioned by the U.S. secretary of education and published in 1983 under the full title: *A Nation at Risk: The Imperative for Educational Reform.* In the box that follows, we present the "indicators of risk" unearthed by this commission. As is obvious, they amount to a wholesale indictment of our educational system, particularly at the high school level, but also at the collegiate level and, by implication, at lower educational levels as well.

This indictment, supported by later indicators—like the international test of science and mathematics achievement mentioned earlier—produced a massive change in the rhetoric surrounding the issue of schooling in the United States. The key word, as, in a sense, it had been after Sputnik, was *excellence.* There were demands that grade inflation stop, that requirements for graduation be raised, that national competency tests be seriously considered, that teachers' salaries and professional qualifications be increased, and that the content of the high school curriculum be stiffened. Referred to by the commission as a "cafeteria" in which the "appetizers and desserts can easily be mistaken for the main courses," the curriculum must now be reformed so that each student takes a minimum of:

- Four years of English
- Three years of mathematics
- Three years of science
- Three years of social studies
- One-half year of computer science

## INDICATORS OF THE RISK

The educational dimensions of the risk before us have been amply documented in testimony received by the Commission. For example:

○ International comparisons of student achievement, completed a decade ago, reveal that on 19 academic tests American students were never first or second and, in comparison with other industrialized nations, were last seven times.

○ Some 23 million American adults are functionally illiterate by the simplest tests of everyday reading, writing, and comprehension.

○ About 13 percent of all 17-year-olds in the United States can be considered functionally illiterate. Functional illiteracy among minority youth may run as high as 40 percent.

○ Average achievement of high school students on most standardized tests is now lower than 26 years ago when Sputnik was launched.

○ Over half the population of gifted students do not match their tested ability with comparable achievement in school.

○ The College Board's Scholastic Aptitude Tests (SAT) demonstrate a virtually unbroken decline from 1963 to 1980. Average verbal scores fell over 50 points and average mathematics scores dropped nearly 40 points.

○ College Board achievement tests also reveal consistent declines in recent years in such subjects as physics and English.

○ Both the number and proportion of students demonstrating superior achievement on the SATs (i.e., those with scores of 650 or higher) have also dramatically declined.

○ Many 17-year-olds do not possess the "higher order" intellectual skills we should expect of them. Nearly 40 percent cannot draw inferences from written material; only one-fifth can write a persuasive essay; and only one-third can solve a mathematics problem requiring several steps.

○ There was a steady decline in science achievement scores of U.S. 17-year-olds as measured by national assessments of science in 1969, 1973, and 1977.

○ Between 1975 and 1980, remedial mathematics courses in public 4-year colleges increased by 72 percent and now constitute one-quarter of all mathematics courses taught in those institutions.

○ Average tested achievement of students graduating from college is also lower.

○ Business and military leaders complain that they are required to spend millions of dollars on costly remedial education and training programs in such basic skills as reading, writing, spelling, and computation. The Department of the Navy, for example, reported to the Commission that one-quarter of its recent recruits cannot read at the ninth grade level, the minimum needed simply to understand written safety instructions. Without remedial work they cannot even begin, much less complete, the sophisticated training essential in much of the modern military.

*Source:* National Commission on Excellence in Education, *A Nation at Risk: The Imperative for Educational Reform* (Washington, D.C.: U.S. Government Printing Office, 1983), pp. 8–9.

---

College-bound students would preferably add:

• Two years of foreign language

So "excellence" was back, and rigorous programming was to replace "cafeteria" or "shopping mall" curricula. During the 1980s, the new (or reborn) rhetoric swept the nation. Some observers felt that major changes were taking place. They could point to numerous examples of states and communities that had stiffened requirements for school graduation, college entrance, or teacher qualification. Furthermore, it could be argued that, at long last, the public was getting into the act, demanding seriously higher standards from their schools. In the September 3, 1989, *New York Times,* Chester E. Finn, Jr., professor of education at Vanderbilt University, wrote of "seismic changes in the ground rules of the education system." Noting the striking results of a 1989 Gallup poll, he pointed out that "in sharp contrast to a century-old practice, people say they want national educational standards, a national curriculum and national tests."[4]

One has to notice, however, that in the September 6, 1989, *New York Times* (three days after Finn's article appeared), there was an article by Joseph Berger entitled "Social Ills Pull Educators' Concern to New Issues." Its main theme was that "educators are turning their attention from issues like the curriculum to social problems, including crack, AIDS, child abuse and the growing number of splintered and troubled families." Was the country already beginning to backtrack on its commitment to curricular excellence?

## TESTING: CRITICISMS AND CONSEQUENCES

There are clear reasons that a simple resort to "excellence" usually proves difficult in practice, but before going into them let us ask two prior questions: (1) how *valid* is the claim that our educational system is being engulfed by "a rising tide of mediocrity"? (2) What measures might we use to judge the *consequences* of educational decline? Both these questions involve a judgment about the meaning of tests, like the SATs, that were used in *A Nation at Risk* and other reports to demonstrate the deterioration of our educational standards.

### "Weak Arguments, Poor Data, Simplistic Recommendations"

The above heading is the title of a critique of the various educational reports

published just a few months after *A Nation at Risk*. It was written by two policy analysts, Lawrence C. Stedman (University of Wisconsin) and Marshall S. Smith (Wisconsin Center for Research), and presents a wide-ranging attack on the methods and results of several of the education studies of the early 1980s. We list here a summary of their comments on the "indicators of risk" from *A Nation at Risk* (see box):

The international test comparisons used by the Commission are based on out-of-date information (accumulated in 1964–71) and, in any event, were generated from noncomparable student bodies. For example, in West Germany only 9 percent of the age cohort reached their last year of high school in the early 1970s while in the U.S. about 75 percent did.

The statements about "functional illiteracy" are, in some instances, based on controversial and, again, out-dated information. Also, the result for 1974 (13 percent of 17-year-olds being "functionally illiterate") is actually an improvement over earlier (1971) results.

The statement that "over half the population of gifted students do not match their tested ability with comparable achievement in school" sounds suspiciously like "over half of the sample scores below the median."

The Commission cites SAT score decline "with no indication that the population taking the tests has changed fairly dramatically during the same period." A major study of the SAT decline from 1964 to 1973 found that between two-thirds and three-fourths of the fall could be attributed to the changing social composition of the takers.

Some of the College Board test results are worrisome, but even here the Commission fails to note that the average (mean) grades on the College Board advanced placement tests in science and mathematics increased between 1969 and 1979, as did the number of students taking the tests.

The national science assessment test declines did occur, but they were small (4.7 percent over an 8-year period) and, in the case of reading performance, younger students were improving while teenagers were holding their own.[5]

To these specific criticisms can also be added more general criticisms which some educators have made with respect to SATs and other educational tests: that they test the wrong kinds of abilities; that the tests are racially or ethnically biased; most recently, that they are also biased by gender— female students in 1987 were lagging behind male students not only on the mathematical aptitude test (453 to 500), but also on the verbal test (425 to 435). The former has been a standard result in the history of the SATs; the latter is a newer phenomenon. In short, Stedman and Smith claim that the nature of our national data on school performance is "abominable." Although serious decline *may* have taken place, they admit, we are very far from being able to *prove* that it did.

## The Possible Consequences of Decline

Although there is undoubtedly some truth in these criticisms of the alarming reports of U.S. educational decline, very few observers feel that our standards have been satisfactorily maintained from the 1960s on. Frequent complaints have been coming in from industry that new job applicants are simply incapable of dealing even with rudimentary tasks, like reading instructions, let alone making any kind of complex mathematical computations. These complaints continued throughout the 1980s. Testing students in 1986–1988, the National Assessment of Educational Progress found that only 6 percent of 17-year-old students could solve multistep problems and use basic algebra; only 8 percent could draw conclusions and infer relationships on the basis of scientific knowledge; and only 5 percent could synthesize and learn from specialized readings.[6]

Furthermore, efforts to explain the decline in test scores from 1967 to 1980 on

the grounds that the school population was growing and changing in racial and ethnic composition simply are not borne out by the facts. The decline was larger for whites than for minorities, larger in the suburbs than in the central cities, evident in private as well as public schools, as large or possibly larger for more able students than for less able students, and particularly large for higher level skills in contrast to basic skills. There has been, for example, a very large decline in the number of students achieving above 700 on the verbal SAT. Also, when tests like the Iowa Test of Educational Development (ITED), which largely rule out the problem of the changing selectivity of the population, are used, the same pattern of declining scores from 1967 to 1980 is apparent.[7]

Nor does the slight improvement in test scores that has occurred in the 1980s adequately remove our concern about declining school achievement. In Table 17-1, we show what has happened to verbal and mathematical components of the SAT from 1967 to 1990. While some of the ground lost has been regained in the mathematical aptitude test, the verbal score in 1990 matched the nation's lowest scores ever (in 1980 and 1981). On the SATs at least, our college-bound students are still well below the levels achieved in the mid-1960s. Also, the improvement in the mathematical aptitude scores in the early 1980s, such as it was, appears to have come to a halt in the late 1980s.

Furthermore, even when tests, like the ITED, which effectively corrects for changing population selectivity, show a more substantial rebound in scores during the 1980s, they do not prove that the problem has now been solved. For the truth is that prior to the mid-1960s, most of these test scores tended to show major gains over time. Thus, a study by John Bishop of Cornell University argues that "the general intellectual achievement of high school seniors remains substantially . . . below the level that would have been reached if the trends of the 1940s,

**TABLE 17-1.** Scholastic Aptitude Test Scores of College-Bound Seniors, 1967–1990

|  | 1967 | 1970 | 1975 | 1980 | 1981 | 1982 | 1983 | 1984 | 1985 | 1986 | 1987 | 1988 | 1989 | 1990 |
|---|---|---|---|---|---|---|---|---|---|---|---|---|---|---|
| Verbal | 466 | 460 | 434 | 424 | 424 | 426 | 425 | 426 | 431 | 431 | 430 | 428 | 427 | 424 |
| Math | 492 | 488 | 472 | 466 | 466 | 467 | 468 | 471 | 475 | 475 | 476 | 476 | 476 | 476 |

1950s and early 1960s had continued, rather than reversing after 1966."[8]

Has this had consequences on the present and future **productivity of our labor force?** This question, which we raised earlier, obviously has enormous importance in terms of the ability of our labor force to sustain the not inconsequential burdens of a rapidly aging population. Bishop's conclusion is that these effects are substantial and that they will increase in the future. Using a complex econometric model, he finds that, because of the lowering of labor quality implied by the fall in the measured intellectual achievements of American young people, GNP in 1987 was $86 billion lower than it would have been had previous educational achievement trends been maintained.

More dramatic is his assessment of the long-run impact of the failure of educational achievement to advance as in decades past:

> Even with an assumption of big gains in academic achievement in the future, the forecast is for a 6.7 percent labor quality shortfall in the year 2010. The cumulative total social costs through 2010 of the test score decline have a present value (at a 6 percent real discount rate) of $3.2 trillion.[9]

The year 2010, we might note, is the year when we see the beginnings of the flood of Baby Boom retirees.

## THE GREAT SCHOOL DEBATE(S)

That there is *a* problem even report critics like Stedman and Smith agree. What is unclear is how serious the problem is, what its root causes are, and, above all, exactly what, if anything, can be done about it.

Following the publication of *A Nation at Risk*, Beatrice and Ronald Gross of Columbia University edited a book called *The Great School Debate*. More appropriately, the last word should be plural, reflecting the many different issues on which educators disagree. We group these disagreements into two major categories: (1) underlying problems and (2) school reforms.

### Underlying Problems

Why does the United States, which always placed such a high premium on schooling, suddenly seem to be having so much trouble in educating its younger generation? There are at least three questions here on which the experts disagree.

*Question 1: To what degree is the problem with the schools or with changes in the surrounding society?* Insofar as the decline in the test scores reflects a changing population of test-takers and school-attenders (obviously not the whole explanation), then we would be wrong to conclude that the problem is with our educational system. On the contrary, the problem would simply reflect the additional difficulties that a more broad-based school system must handle. These are really social rather than narrowly educational or curricular problems. And there are many other societal changes that could affect our school performances.

One of these is the increasing influence of television. Neil Postman has argued that television has the effect of diminishing the critical skills and abilities needed for our educational curriculum. He notes that the average length of a shot on a network show is 3.5 seconds: "This means that every 3.5 seconds, more or less, there is a new point of view or angle of vision and a new pictorial image to process." Postman also estimates that, by the age of 20, the average young American has been exposed to 700,000 commercials on television.[10] Is it conceivable that the vast exposure of our youth to television (and, of course, to other modern media—movies, VCRs, stereos, and Walkmen) has had substantial negative effects on standard academic progress? Some observers think so, although, interestingly, the subject of television is barely discussed in *The Great School Debate* and is not even mentioned in *A Nation at Risk*.

Another influence coming from outside the schools is the family. When we come to discussing the extraordinary scholastic achievements of Asian American students (Chapter 19), we shall make frequent reference to the importance of the family unit in providing motivation for children and an environment in which learning is encouraged. But surely if this is the case, then the relative breakdown of the American family in recent decades (single, absent, and/or working parents as well as teenage pregnancy among students themselves) might be expected to loom large in the failure of children to live up to our educational expectations. Yet the subject of the family is barely mentioned in *A Nation at Risk*, and, when it is, it is simply to tell parents that they must be a "living example" of what they expect their children to emulate.

There is also the question of student drug abuse—a subject again conspicuous by its absence from *A Nation at Risk* and even from *The Great School Debate*. A Gallup poll of the public's attitudes toward the "chief problems" facing the local public schools showed that in 1987 the problem most frequently mentioned was "use of drugs," followed next by "lack of discipline."[11] In some respects, the public's perception, which is that drug use is getting worse and worse ("use of drugs" was mentioned much less

frequently in the 1970 poll), may lag behind the reality. According to a survey by the U.S. Department of Health and Human Services, drug and alcohol use by high school seniors may have peaked with the class of 1980 or 1981. However, by past standards, such use remained high throughout the 1970s and 1980s. In 1975, 68.2 percent of high school seniors reported having used alcohol and 30.7 percent illicit drugs during the previous 30 days. In 1986 the percentages were 66.3 and 27.1 respectively, hardly a significant decline, particularly since, on the average, more harmful drugs may have been involved in the later year.[12]

Again, we would appear to have a major problem, which has a serious potential for affecting student performance, but which is a problem more of the larger society than of the schools per se.

***Question 2: To what degree is the goal of equality in our schools in competition with the goal of quality?*** In our description of the post–World War II "crises" in our schools, we seem to have gone from emphasizing quality ("**excellence**"), to emphasizing equality, back to emphasizing "excellence" again, with possible further swings of the pendulum still ahead of us. All of which suggests that each of these goals must be purchased at the expense of the other. But is this necessarily the case? Why cannot we both improve top standards in our schools and, at the same time, improve the achievement levels of the widest possible range of students?

Most of the educational reports in the early 1980s did, in fact, take this point of view, without, it must be said, much analysis to substantiate their positions. Here is the confident statement from *A Nation at Risk* (p. 13):

> We do not believe that a public commitment to excellence and educational reform must be made at the expense of a strong public commitment to the equitable treatment of our diverse population. The twin goals of

equity and high-quality schooling have profound and practical meaning for our economy and society, and we cannot permit one to yield to the other in principle or in practice. To do so would deny young people their chance to learn and live according to their aspirations and abilities. It also would lead to a generalized accommodation to mediocrity in our society on the one hand or the creation of an undemocratic elitism on the other.

But is the world of education so nicely arranged as this comforting paragraph suggests? Critics were quick to point out that many commission recommendations—as, for example, raising high school graduation standards—could easily also raise the number of school dropouts, a serious phenomenon already, and one particularly grave for minority and disadvantaged children.[13] Also, since the current "cafeteria" (or "smorgasbord") curriculum was, at least in part, an outcome of the attempt to accommodate different levels of student ability and background, how seriously can one begin to standardize and upgrade the curriculum without limiting avenues for the less well prepared—avenues that, though unsatisfactory in some respects, are at least better than nothing?

More generally, one critique puts the problem as follows:

Although people wish to avoid a choice between equity and excellence, there is no way to avoid choices in the allocation of resources. Consider three conditions of resource allocation. (1) If resources are directed primarily toward fast students, we are likely to cultivate instances of exceptional achievement, but to deprive slow students of opportunities for mastery. (2) If resources are distributed equally, slow students, still operating at a disadvantage compared to fast students, will have greater opportunities, and the level of excellence among the fast students will decline from the first condition. (3) If resources are directed primarily toward slow students, their opportunities to attain any given level of mastery would approach those of the fast students, but the level of excellence among fast students would be the lowest of the three conditions.[14]

With unlimited resources, perhaps everything is possible. But operating in the real world may be quite a different matter.

*Question 3: To what degree should the school be taking over responsibilities from other institutions in the society—most notably the family?* Before we turn to our next set of questions—having to do with school reform—we should ideally know what we are asking the schools of the country to accomplish. We essentially have two views on this issue. One states that the schools are overburdened, that their primary function has been lost in their attempt to handle all those **societal problems**—child poverty, broken homes, single parenting, teenage pregnancies, drug and alcohol abuse, violence, gang warfare—that essentially originate outside the school but impinge on the school's ability to educate the next generation. Let society handle these problems by other institutions—whether by strengthening the family unit or increasing the number of social workers or, in the last analysis, demanding harsher juvenile punishments in the courts—and let the schools concentrate on the one thing they know best: how to teach students to read, write, comprehend mathematics and science, and learn something of their Western heritage and of the larger world around them. So says one view.

The other view takes the opposite position—namely, that since the United States' other social institutions, and especially the family, are so weak, there is no alternative but to extend the functions of what, historically speaking, has been one of our most effective instruments for improving the lives of our children and the quality of our labor force: our school system. In 1989, one of the major television networks ran a program on a midwestern school system that had extended its functions to replace or supplement the family in terms of both the ages of the children for whom it takes responsibility and the number of hours a day that children of all ages can spend in the school building. For infants and tiny toddlers to teenage high school seniors, the school is there—open very early in the morning, and closing only in the evening, at an hour when the last of the working parents could return to pick up their young charges.

What a success this school was! the announcer intoned enthusiastically. And the final, and presumably wholly convincing, evidence of its success was that, at the end of what was sometimes a 10- or 11-hour day, many of the children did not want to go home. "My child would sooner stay here all the time," one mother said happily, indicating her approval of the varied, caring program the teachers, social workers, and others were providing her child while she and her husband were otherwise occupied. Some people might feel that this mother had a rather strange view of the proper role of the home in a child's life. Still, this opinion is quite widespread: We have already available to us an institution that can take up the slack for a society that is having problems in rearing the next generation. We would be foolish not to use it.

### School Reform

Given these divisions of opinion as to the basic analysis of the problem, and as to the goals our schools should be pursuing, it will come as no surprise that educators and other public officials differ sharply on the nature of the specific reforms that should be instituted to resolve our current "crisis." Even allowing that there has been a general tilting of interest in the direction of "excellence," we still have these difficult further questions:

*Question 4: Is the problem basically one of money (resources) or one of nonmonetary reforms (attitudes, school organization, greater efficiency)?* In discussing the possible conflict between quality and equality,

we quoted analysts who emphasized resource constraints: If you did such-and-such for the slower students, you'd have this much less for the faster students, and so on. The implication is that the conflict could be greatly lessened if you simply had more resources in general: greater school appropriations for more teachers, higher salaries, better facilities, more qualified principals and superintendents.

Unfortunately, there is little evidence that increasing school resources has any connection with the quality of the average American school's performance. We have already noted (Figure 17-2) the substantial rise in real per pupil school expenditures in the United States over the past half century. During the test decline years of the 1960s and 1970s, these per pupil expenditures approximately doubled in constant-dollar terms. More significantly, national studies show very little if any correlation between school performance and resource-determined factors such as school size, teacher/student ratios, minimum and maximum teacher salaries, or length of service (and seniority) of faculty and staff.[15]

What do we conclude from this? In 1989 then—Secretary of Education Lauro Cavazos argued that "increases in spending are not matched by improved performance. We are already spending more than our competitors, and yet our students consistently fall behind the competition in comparable scores." We need not more money, but "restructuring." To which Democratic Senator J. Robert Kerrey of Nebraska replied: "We all know that money alone will not solve the problems faced by our schools. However, to imply that increased spending is counterproductive is itself counterproductive. . . . We have the wallet. What we need is a willingness to act." He then outlined a program for the federal government on the principle that "it is time to put our money where our mouth is."

Is more money the solution, or a way of avoiding the harder issues that a true solution implies?[16]

*Question 5: Should we be moving in the direction of national standards, funding, and involvement or of strengthening local control and school autonomy?* When "excellence" becomes an important goal of our educational system, most reformers tend immediately to think in terms of national, or at least statewide, quality standards to ensure that high school diplomas actually mean something academically. Chester Finn, we noted earlier, spoke of the "seismic" change in attitudes as the public is now demanding national standards and tests. Usually, along with such demands comes the concomitant demand for more federal funding, as demonstrated by the remarks of Senator Kerrey.

There is, however, a potential problem here. The researches of John E. Chubb and Terry M. Moe suggest that a central difference between high-performing and low-performing schools is the degree of school **autonomy.** Chubb refers to a distinction between "teams" and "hierarchies." In the latter, when success is achieved, it tends to be through the use of rules and monitoring; in the former, even without many formal regulations, success results because the members share a strong interest in the goals of the organization. "Teams" are more "autonomous" in the sense that they function more from within and less as a response to external regulation.

The problem that Chubb and Moe see with the new wave of school reforms is that they may, in fact, further diminish school autonomy. Performance improves when a school's teachers, its principal, and, not least, the parents of the students are most active in decision making in the school. Nationwide, or statewide, educational standards tend to work in the opposite direction, setting up further rules, regulations, and guidelines, not to mention additional bureaucracies, which restrict the freedom of action of the local units. It is fairly obvious that both some autonomy and some regulation are needed. The question is: What is the right balance between them and, in particular, are current reforms moving us

closer to or further away from that correct balance?[17]

*Question 6: To what degree, if any, should parental choice, including choice of private versus public schools, be encouraged?* **Public schools** have been the glory of the education-for-all principle so highly prized in our nation's history. But polls in the 1980s showed that Americans were increasingly disenchanted with their local public schools. More serious perhaps is the evidence that, even when corrected for family income and other socioeconomic indices, students do better academically in private, and especially Catholic, schools than they do in the public schools.

This evidence has been developed by Professor James S. Coleman and his associates in two main books, *High School Achievement,* written with Thomas Hoffer and Sally Kilgore (1982), and *Public and Private High Schools,* co-authored by Thomas Hoffer (1987). In explaining the superior achievements of students in Catholic schools, they discuss three forms of capital: *human capital in the family* (roughly, educational level of the parents); *social capital in the family* (the actual presence of the parents in the home and their interest in their children's work); and *social capital in the surrounding community* (the degree to which, say, parents of the schoolchildren know each other and each other's children.) All forms of capital are important, but where the Catholic schools seem to have a special advantage is in the sense of community from which they spring and which they in turn stimulate. In an earlier epoch, when Americans often lived in small towns with close-knit neighborhoods and across-the-fence friends, this community also existed for students and their parents in the public school setting—but much less so today.

Interestingly, Coleman and his associates found that the advantages of Catholic schools were particularly strong for blacks, Hispanics, and others from lower socioeconomic groups. If students have backgrounds that are weak in the three forms of capital just noted, they are likely to find Catholic schools (or sometimes private boarding schools) optimal in terms of academic achievement.

Does this mean that the nation's historic romance with public schools is turning sour and that we should now use our tax monies, not to foster public schools, but to give parents vouchers that they can use in one way or another to select schools of their choice for their children?[18] Some observers feel that way, noting among other things the possibly beneficial effects that a stronger private school sector (now around 12 percent of U.S. school enrollments) might have by creating more competition for the public schools. On the other hand, withdrawing students with educationally motivated parents from a given public school setting might simply worsen conditions for the remaining students. Middle-class white flight from many of our inner city schools has undoubtedly already played a part in creating the "imperiled" urban generation of which Ernest Boyer of the Carnegie Foundation has written. Thus, even though, in principle, many disadvantaged children might do better in Catholic or other private schools, in practice a retreat from our historic public school tradition could conceivably leave the majority of such children in more desperate straits than at present.

## THE CHALLENGE REMAINS

Many of the issues just discussed were prominent in the national debate that followed the presentation of the educational reform proposals by President Bush and his Secretary of Education, Lamar Alexander, in the Spring of 1991. The administration's program urged (and was criticized for urging) experimentation with vouchers and parental choice between different public schools and even between public and private schools. Similarly, the proposals suggested (and were criticized for suggesting) volun-

tary nationwide exams, school performance report cards, and new experimental schools in each congressional district. As always, the issue of money came up, with the administration taking the position that U.S. schools were already generously funded compared to those of other nations, while critics argued that states and local districts, currently burdened with growing deficits, and facing potential teacher and salary cutbacks, could not give effect to any serious educational innovations without added federal support.

In stressing these disagreements on educational issues, we should not, however, overlook the abundant knowledge that is being accumulated relevant to the future of our schools:

• *Demographic knowledge,* such as we are developing in this book, tells us why education will play such a pivotal role in the nation's future, particularly as our society continues to age.

• *Economic knowledge* tells us why education is so important to the future productivity of our labor force. Certainly one of the most important discoveries in the field of economic growth analysis in the post–World War II period has been determining the crucial role of human capital in increasing a nation's economic growth and standard of living. Years ago, it was assumed that the major factor causing growth was physical capital—dams, tractors, factories, machinery. But we know now that technological progress based heavily on research and development and on the skills and education of our labor force is more important. Schools, colleges, postgraduate work, and advanced research—these are not individual luxuries but social necessities.

• *Sociological knowledge* has taught us that the results of formal schooling depend on many factors outside the school: family background, the depth of contact of generations within families, the community surrounding the family and the school. It has also taught us that what happens *within* the school is determined only in part, if at all, by the physical and monetary resources available to the school's bureaucracy. Much more significant may be the spirit that pervades the school, the freedom teachers have to innovate and inspire, the degree to which students feel that the goals of the school are not imposed on them, but are, in fact, their own goals, and, of course—going back to the family again—the degree to which parents take an active and concerned interest

in the well-being and progress of their children.

Perhaps the most hopeful note of all is that the United States is now making a truly serious effort to mobilize this accumulating knowledge in the form of useful proposals to reshape the nation's school system. Whatever the fate of President Bush's program, or other alternatives that may be developed in the years ahead, this focusing of attention on a clearcut and pressing national need should eventually bear significant fruit.

## SUMMARY

1. Education is an important subject for those studying our changing population because it involves the preparation of the next generation to take over from those that precede it. It is particularly important today because of: the need for a highly educated future labor force; weaknesses in the institution of the family; and the need to provide routes for immigrants and disadvantaged minority groups into the American mainstream. Also, as mentioned in earlier chapters, lifelong education is of special importance in an Aging Society.

2. Despite very considerable resources devoted to it, the U.S. educational system has suffered a number of crises over the past century, including the post-Sputnik alarms, and the special demands placed upon the system by the Civil Rights Revolution. The present crisis, which involves declining achievement levels and the U.S. falling behind many other nations on comparative tests, is regarded by many as the most serious the country has ever faced.

3. Although there are critics who believe our testing system is inadequate, there is much general evidence, including reports from industry, that our students are often incapable of handling demands like reading instructions or making simple computations. The loss in national output alone from

these inadequacies may run into the billions or even trillions of dollars over time.

4. Given this concern, there are several debates as to the nature of the underlying problems:

a. Is the problem largely with the schools or with the society at large (television, lack of parental attention, drugs)?

b. Are the goals of equality and quality in competition?

c. How far should the schools take over from other institutions, notably the family?

5. There are also debates about the desirable nature of school reform:

a. Do we need more money or changes in attitudes and organization?

b. Should we set national standards or strengthen local autonomy?

c. Should we increase parental choice among schools or concentrate on strengthening the public schools?

6. Demography, economics, and sociology all have roles to play as we attempt to resolve these dilemmas, whether through President Bush's dramatic 1991 reform proposals or through other alternatives that may emerge.

## KEY CONCEPTS FOR REVIEW

Rising number of years of schooling

Rising per pupil expenditures

Crises in U.S. education
    post-Sputnik
    civil rights and integration
    falling achievement levels

*A Nation at Risk*

*The Shopping Mall High School*

Education and labor force productivity

Excellence as a goal

Possible negative factors
    television
    inadequate family supervision
    drugs

School versus societal problems

Equality versus quality

School versus family responsibilities

Money versus reorganization

National standards versus autonomy

Public schools versus choice

## QUESTIONS FOR DISCUSSION

1. What do you feel are the major achievements of the U.S. public education system over our past history? How will the tasks facing this system in the future be affected by our changing population? How will they be affected by socioeconomic changes now going on in U.S. society?

2. Summarize the evidence that suggests that the United States has become, educationally, a "nation at risk." Is this evidence convincing to you? Discuss the possible costs to U.S. society of declining educational standards.

3. Professor Chester Finn writes of "seismic changes" occurring in American education in recent years. What does he mean? As a student, have you felt any "shock waves" from these supposedly seismic changes?

throwing money at the educational system for years and standards have only kept falling."

"It's ultimately a resources problem. If you want more equality, you have to give up quality. If you want more quality, you have to give up equality. There just aren't enough dollars in the system to do both."

Discuss these apparently conflicting views.

5. Some say that the schools are the solution to the family's problems; others say that the family is the solution to the school's problems. If both statements are true to some degree, how would this affect your priorities in reshaping our public school system?

6. "Free choice is the basis of our economic and political systems; free choice of schools should also be the basis for our educational system."

Debate the pros and cons of this assertion.

## NOTES

1. National Commission on Excellence in Education, *A Nation at Risk: The Imperative for Educational Reform* (Washington, D.C.: U.S. Government Printing Office, 1983), p. 5.
2. For the shift from progressive education to more rigorous academic standards after Sputnik, see Diane Ravitch, *The Schools We Deserve* (New York: Basic Books, 1985), esp. Chapter 5, "American Education: Has the Pendulum Swung Once Too Often?" For a more general history of progressiv-

ism in schools see Lawrence A. Cremin, *The Transformation of the School: Progressivism in American Education, 1876–1957* (New York: Knopf, 1961), and his more recent *American Education: The Metropolitan Experience, 1876–1980* (New York: Harper & Row, 1988). For an account that places more emphasis on social class in the history of our schools, see Michael B. Katz, *Reconstructing American Education* (Cambridge, Mass.: Harvard University Press, 1987).

3. A. G. Powell, E. Farrar, and D. K. Cohen, *The Shopping Mall High School* (Boston: Houghton Mifflin, 1985). This quotation is taken from Chapter 5, "Origins" (pp. 292–293), written by D. K. Cohen, professor at the Harvard Graduate School of Education.

4. Chester E. Finn, Jr., "A Seismic Shock for Education," *New York Times*, September 3, 1989. Finn reports on the Gallup poll results showing, for example, that the public prefers the introduction of national achievement standards for schools (70 percent to 19 percent), a standardized national curriculum (69 percent to 21 percent), and standardized national testing (77 percent to 14 percent). That such nationalized standards may involve certain problems, we will discuss on p. 302.

5. This summary is based on L. C. Stedman and M. S. Smith, "Weak Arguments, Poor Data, Simplistic Recommendations: Putting the Reports under the Microscope," in B. Gross and R. Gross, *The Great School Debate*, Chapter 4, pp. 83–105 (New York: Simon and Schuster, 1985). The paper originally appeared as "Recent Reform Proposals for American Education," *Contemporary Education Review*, 2 (2), Fall 1983.

6. Council of Economic Advisers, *Economic Report of the President* (Washington, D.C.: U.S. Government Printing Office, 1991), p. 122.

7. See John H. Bishop, "Is the Test Score Decline Responsible for the Productivity Growth Decline?" *American Economic Review*, 79 (1), March 1989, esp. p. 194. For those unfamiliar with the term, the phrase "6 percent real discount rate" is inserted here in recognition of the fact that dollars lost or gained in a future year are not worth as much as dollars lost or gained today. $100 lost next year is less of a loss than $100 today because money earns interest. At 6 percent, I could take $100 today, have $106 next year, pay off next year's $100 loss and still have $6 left over. Thus the need to "discount" future losses.

A further note here is that it should be mentioned that, in general, the changing populations taking these standardized tests do make some difference to the outcome, sometimes rather oddly. For example, in 1989 national SAT scores declined slightly, even though the scores of non-Hispanic white students and all major minority groups either were constant or were up a point or two. Reason: There was a higher proportion of minority students (whose scores are below the national average) taking the test.

8. Ibid., p. 195.

9. Ibid., p. 179. The basic reasons that the future effects are so large in the Bishop model are: (a) the large size of the test decline between 1967 and 1980 (estimated to be the equivalent of 1.25 grade levels; (b) the fact that it represents a break from a historic *upward* trend in our educational achievement levels; and (c) the fact that the graduates of this down period will remain in the labor force for the next 50 years.

10. Neil Postman, *Conscientious Objections: Stirring up Trouble about Language, Technology and Education* (New York: Knopf, 1988), pp. 154–155.

11. "The Nineteenth Annual Gallup Poll of the Public's Attitudes towards the Public Schools," *Phi Delta Kappan*, September 1987, cited in National Center for Education Statistics, *Digest of Education Statistics, 1988*, U.S. Department of Education, Table 20, p. 27.

12. Digest of Education Statistics, 1988, Table 101, p. 117.

13. Thus, "Doc" Howe, President Johnson's commissioner of education, writes: "Ideas about solutions for the 25 percent dropout rate from American high schools, and particularly for the 40 to 50 percent rate found in major cities, are scarce in the recent reports . . . and some recommendations are likely to increase dropouts." He finds it "absolutely astounding . . . that so many intelligent people could look for so long at American schools and say so little about this problem." Harold Howe II, "Giving Equity a Chance in the Excellence Game," in Gross and Gross, *The Great School Debate*, pp. 285–286.

14. F. M. Newmann and T. E. Kelly, " 'Excellence' and the Dignity of Students," in Gross and Gross, *The Great School Debate*, p. 226.

15. See John E. Chubb, "Why the Current Wave of School Reform Will Fail," *The Public Interest*, 9, Winter 1988, p. 32.

16. The Cavazos and Kerrey quotes are taken from J. Robert Kerrey, "Education: Restructuring Isn't Enough," *The Washington Post*, June 27, 1989. It should be added that there is a debate, not only about the effect of money on educational quality, but also about how to measure how much the United States actually spends on education per student. The Department of Education tends to use a measure of constant dollars per student, while a liberal think tank, the Economic Policy Institute, argues that we should measure such expenditures as a percent of national income. Such a measure would place the United States near the bottom rather than near the very top of industrial nations in educational expenditures. See "Is U.S. Education Underfunded?" *The Washington Post*, January 17, 1990, and "Education: Money Isn't Everything," *The Wall Street Journal*, February 9, 1990.

17. For a summary of the Chubb and Moe views, see Chubb, "Why the Current Wave of School Reform Will Fail," pp. 28–49. An interesting experiment in increasing school autonomy, called by some the boldest and most radical experiment in U.S. educational history, was launched in Chicago in the fall of 1989. Power was being shifted from the board of education of the third-largest school system in the country to parent- and community-

led councils at each of the city's 600 schools. These schools have 70 percent of their students below the poverty line, and have a dropout rate of 45 percent and test scores at the very bottom of the nation's percentiles. Whether this sharp move from bureaucracy and centralization to local control will be successful remains to be seen.

18. It should be noted that Coleman and his colleagues, although many of their investigations suggest advantages to private and/or religious education, are cautious in drawing conclusions on this matter. "The evidence," Coleman and Hoffer write, "does not point unequivocally to widespread benefits of policies that would increase freedom of choice in education, such as vouchers that could be used in any public or private school." J. S. Coleman and T. Hoffer, *Public and Private High Schools: The Impact of Communities* (New York: Basic Books, 1987), p. 242.

# Part V
# THE NEWCOMERS

# 18

# *Immigration:*
# *Old and New*

*T*he central role of immigration in its history inspired a scholar to describe the United States as "the permanently unfinished country." Some aspects of the story have been examined briefly in Chapter 4. Here we look at the question in more depth.

## THE SOURCES OF AMERICAN IMMIGRATION

In American history, four immense waves of immigration have arrived to reshape society. To know why immigrants came, we have to understand the conditions in the home societies that caused the departures and the conditions in the receiving communities that attracted newcomers. The combination of "push" and "pull" forces generated immigration. Similar **push and pull factors** affected areas of the world experiencing mass exodus. International migrants were thus united through a common underlying relation with the process of global development.

### European Immigration in the Agrarian Era

In the seventeenth century, the English drive for trans-Atlantic empire produced the push and pull forces bringing the first wave of immigrants to America. The commercialization of the English rural economy displaced many farmers into the ranks of the unemployed. These were recruited to work the farms and resources of the New World colonies who could supply raw materials to the mother country and consume its manufactured goods. By 1700, nearly all colonies employed some combination of advertising, land grants, labor incentives, arranged transportation, and easy legal requirements to increase the flow of immigrants.

Through the seventeenth century, the vast majority were drawn from England. In New England, the migrants came in families and were independent farmers. They were Puritans seeking a religious haven. In the southern colonies, most were indentured servants, single laborers pushed overseas by economic hardship. Like a giant magnet, the colonies drew farmers and laborers, and some artisans as well, who had been dislodged from their moorings by the changing English economy.

In the eighteenth century, newcomers began to arrive from Scotland, Ireland, and the European continent. The two most important new sources of immigration were Germany and Ireland. Before 1776, 100,000 Germans migrated to the colonies. Most came from the Rhineland of Germany, where religious persecution of Protestants and war-caused stringencies encouraged people to leave. Northern Ireland sent 250,000 Scotch-Irish emigrants to British North America by 1776. They, too, had been driven abroad by religious persecution and economic setbacks. Generous rights for aliens and easy naturalization quickly made land and occupations legally available to non-English newcomers.[1]

The tide of immigration crested in the decade before the American Revolution. Most of the newcomers came from the British Isles. They included a wave of immigrants from central and northern England who migrated in family units and were middling farmers. They were driven by the hope for more opportunity rather than the desperation of extreme poverty. The pull factor of good land was more important in their decision to migrate than the push factors. For these English farmers, immigration to America was an opportunity rather than a kind of economic or religious exile, as was common with many immigrants in the seventeenth century.[2]

### European Immigration in the Industrial Era

Patterns of immigration in the nineteenth century changed so radically from the colonial era that it constituted a separate regime of immigration. The yearly volume of migration increased by over twentyfold in the nineteenth century. An average of 10,000 immigrants arrived annually in the eighteenth century; in the nineteenth century an average of 200,000 immigrants a year came. Annual totals rose steadily toward several hundred thousand arrivals a year (Table 18-1). The numbers from Ireland and Germany mounted highest. Two million Irish Catholic immigrants and 1.5 million German immigrants arrived in the three decades before the Civil War. They comprised two-thirds of all immigrants who arrived from 1830 to 1860. The cultural distance between immigrants and natives widened as European continental immigration increased. By 1860, 10 percent of the U.S. population was Catholic, with even a higher proportion in the cities. Whereas in the colonial era immigrants settled in the countryside to take up agricultural occupations, nineteenth-century immigrants

concentrated in the cities. They filled the demand for labor in the early stages of the industrial economy.[3]

After 1880 American immigration was fed increasingly by streams originating from southern and eastern Europe. The arrivals from this formerly unrepresented area were called the "new immigrants" to distinguish them from the "old immigrants" from northern and western Europe. The largest groups were, in order of numbers, the Italians, the Slavs, and the Jews. They came chiefly from three countries: Italy, Austria-Hungary, and Russia. In Italy, the southern provinces produced 80 percent of the emigration. From 1899 to 1924, 3.8 million Italians immigrated. People speaking one of the several Slavic languages formed the second largest group in the new immigration: 3.4 million Slavs entered from 1899 to 1924. From 1899 to 1924, among the eastern Slavs, Russians, Ruthenians, and Ukrainians were most numerous. Among the western Slavs, Poles, Czechs, and Slovakians were the largest groups. And among the southern Slavs, Slovenians and Croatians predominated. Jews from eastern Europe constituted the third major element of the new immigration, comprising 1.8 million arrivals from 1899 to 1924. Three out of four Jewish immigrants in the United States came from Russian territory. One out of four eastern European Jews came from Austria-Hungary (Galicia, Bukovina, and Hungary) and the independent state of Romania.[4]

Although Italians, Slavs, and Jews predominated in the early twentieth century, other groups such as Greeks, Hungarians, and Finns contributed substantial numbers. Five hundred thousand Greeks, 500,000 Hungarians, and 300,000 Finns entered the United States from 1899 to 1924, when the new immigration from southern and eastern Europe was curbed by the imposition of restrictive immigration quotas. Policymakers, holding that these newcomers were proving difficult to assimilate, sharply reduced the numbers of admissions of these immigrants.

**TABLE 18-1.    Net Immigrant Arrivals per Decade, 1810–1970**

| Decade | Net Arrivals (in 1,000s) |
|---|---|
| 1811–1820 | 71 |
| 1821–1830 | 123 |
| 1831–1840 | 493 |
| 1841–1850 | 1,420 |
| 1851–1860 | 2,593 |
| 1861–1870 | 2,102 |
| 1871–1880 | 2,622 |
| 1881–1890 | 4,966 |
| 1891–1900 | 3,711 |
| 1901–1910 | 6,294 |
| 1911–1920 | 2,484 |
| 1921–1930 | 3,187 |
| 1931–1940 | −85 |
| 1941–1950 | 1,362 |
| 1951–1960 | 3,180 |
| 1961–1970 | 4,018 |

*Source:* Richard A. Easterlin, "Economic and Social Characteristics of Immigration," in Stephan Thernstrom, ed., *Harvard Encyclopedia of American Ethnic Groups, 1980.* Reprinted by permission of Harvard University Press.

### Early Immigration from Asia and Latin America

The influx from these regions constituted a small fraction of total immigration in the late nineteenth and early twentieth centuries—somewhat less than 5 percent. Nevertheless, Asian immigration was the first important intercontinental mass migration to the United States from outside Europe. The sequential arrival of the Chinese, Japanese, Koreans, East Indians, and Filipinos formed the first wave of newcomers from East Asia. Over a million came to the United States and Hawaii, mostly to Hawaii, which became an American possession in 1898. Asian migration was periodic and shifted from one sending country to another over time. American lawmakers placed restrictions on various categories of immigrants from Asian countries, such as male laborers, at successive times. (Chapter 19 will provide a closer examination of the patterns of immigration from Asia.)

Immigration from Mexico, Puerto Rico, and the West Indies became a major new force in the early twentieth century. Unlike immigration from East Asia, the flow from the New World was not numerically limited. Puerto Ricans faced no restrictions, for they were American citizens and Congress decided not to impose quotas or annual ceilings on Western Hemisphere nations until 1965. From 1901 to 1940, by far the largest group from the Western Hemisphere came from Mexico, a total of 750,000. Over 320,000 immigrants arrived from the West Indies, and about 90,000 Puerto Ricans also came. They eased the shortage of labor caused by the restriction of European and Asian immigration.

### Postindustrial Immigration: The Rise of Third World Migrants

Immigration slumped as a result of the combined effects of restrictionism, the Great Depression, and World War II, but it began to rebound at the end of the war through the admission of refugees and war brides.

The gates of mass immigration were reopened through the passage of the Hart-Cellar Act of 1965, which raised the annual ceiling on admissions from 150,000 to 290,000 and provided for equal admissions from countries formerly disadvantaged by discriminatory quotas. A new era of immigration began, in which Third World arrivals surpassed those from Europe. At the turn of the century, European immigration accounted for 97 percent of annual admissions; in 1975, however, Asia and the other Americas sent 77 percent, while immigrants from Europe made up only 19 percent.

The annual volume of immigration surged after 1965 toward the levels of the peak years of the late nineteenth and early twentieth century. These official yearly totals, however, were misleading underestimates. This was because the flow of undocumented immigrants (those who entered the country illegally or overstayed their visas) mounted in the 1960s. Public attention was focused chiefly on those from Mexico, but thousands more came from the Caribbean islands and parts of Central and South America. Illegal immigration from Europe grew as well.

Refugee immigration became a major factor in the middle of the twentieth century. The historic conception of America as an asylum for the oppressed of the world had moved Congress to admit limited numbers fleeing Nazi persecution, persons displaced by war, and war brides. After 1960, the flow of refugees grew fastest not from Europe but from Asia, Africa, and Latin America. By the 1980s, 100,000 refugees from these regions entered the country each year.

## THE CAUSES OF IMMIGRATION

Why was such a great exodus to the United States unleashed? Current scholarship has revised older, impressionistic answers to this question. Catastrophe was rarely involved in triggering immigration. A long series of gradually worsening conditions usually caused uprooting. Moreover, immigration was not a blind, panicky flight. It was a rationally planned and structured response to change. The United States was not an all-powerful magnet. The pull of American opportunity could not have produced immigration without concurrent displacing factors. Furthermore, attractive alternatives to the United States existed in the peripheral regions of Latin America, Africa, and Australia.[5]

### Push and Pull Factors in the Industrial Era

In the industrial era, the most basic push factor was the abatement of what the English economist Thomas Malthus identified as the ancient checks on population increase—famine and disease. Economic reorganization led to a sharp drop in death rates while birth rates remained high. This **demographic transition** produced a steady rise in natural increase, the excess of births over deaths. In eighteenth-century western Europe, mortality declined through improvement of the food supply. Farmers installed more efficient marketing arrangements and productive techniques like crop diversification. The quality of nutrition improved as New World corn, rice, and green vegetables were imported. Concurrently, fertility rose to new levels.[6]

New economic opportunities such as cottage industry permitted earlier marriage and thus more childbearing years. Improved nutrition extended the life spans of fertile parents and promoted higher survival rates for babies. When the demographic transition struck southern and eastern Europe in the late nineteenth century, it produced the highest rates of natural increase in the world. In East Asia, Mexico, and the Caribbean the demographic transition also began in the late nineteenth century, as nutrition and health care improved.

How was this population explosion related to migration? After all, rapid population growth did not itself guarantee a high rate of migration. The key link between population growth and migration was pressure on resources that created a **surplus population,** a pool of people economically squeezed to become available for emigration. The pressure of population on land was vitally important. In western Europe, when this pressure became acute in the early nineteenth century, the unemployed and underemployed in rural areas began to emigrate. It was an area with embryonic industrialization, heavily dependent on agriculture for subsistence and for commercial profit. Southern and eastern Europe in the late nineteenth century resembled western Europe earlier in the century. Southern China, southern Japan, Korea, the Philippines, northern Mexico, and the insular Caribbean were also agrarian areas whose economies could not absorb the surplus population. In all these regions, the supply of land was not sufficient to support the burgeoning population. Farms became minutely subdivided or morselized; masses of the peasantry were forced into tenantry.

Other causes of the growth of surplus population with poor economic prospects were not foreseen by Malthus, but were analyzed by Karl Marx. Early industrial capitalism displaced artisans by creating the factory system of production. For example, German weavers were thrown out of work by competition with factory-made British textiles. Cottage industry could not compete with manufacturing.[7] In southern China, British manufactured imports undermined household manufacturing. Also, the emerging capitalist economy grew by boom and bust cycles. The pressure of temporary worsening was placed on farmers in the form of fluctuating crop prices and on workers by slack times. As the economies of Asia, Latin America, and the Caribbean were drawn within a global market, peasants and laborers became more vulnerable to economic vicissitudes.[8] War, conquest and political upheaval—symptoms of political centralization—occasionally aggravated economic troubles to further encourage immigration. An exodus from Germany occurred in the years after the abortive revolution of 1848. Chinese immigration was spurred by the great civil war known as the Taiping Rebellion (1851–1864). Korean immigration was stimulated by Japanese invasion and conquest in the first decade of the twentieth century. Mexicans displaced by the Revolution of 1911 crossed to the United States to rebuild their lives. The wave of Jewish immigrants from Russia and Armenian immigrants from Turkey were driven away by organized violence and massacre.

Not to be underestimated in the promotion of emigration was the liberalization of status in the nineteenth century. In eastern Europe, the abolition of serfdom legally released the masses of Slavic peasantry to leave the landlord domains. In China and Japan, centuries-old bans on emigration were lifted.

What were the pull factors with which these push factors interacted? The principal pull factor causally related to immigration is what economists call the **demand pull for labor.**[9] The differential between Europe and the United States in the demand for labor created a net pressure to emigrate to America. Skilled labor was more valuable in the United States, so British artisans went there to get higher wages. The American economy generated an immense number of new occupational slots that could be filled only by recruitment of immigrant labor. In the nineteenth century, the United States was the greatest job-producing nation in the world. From 1850 to 1900, 3 million new farms were established. From 1800 to 1900, 35 million industrial jobs were created.

Capital-intensive industrialization in late-nineteenth-century America attracted transient immigrant labor, workers who could be fired in slack time and, in boom time, could be quickly pooled into a work force. **Transient labor migration** was made possible by faster, cheaper, and safer transportation. In Europe, railroads and canals speeded travel to ports of embarkation. In Mexico railroads brought immigrants from remote rural areas to the U.S. border. In East Asia, new transoceanic carriers like the ships of the Pacific Mail Steamship Company transported immigrants with unprecedented speed. Vessels carrying immigrants across the Atlantic grew to 5,000, 10,000, and even 20,000 tons, allowing as many as 1,000 passengers to be carried on one voyage. Moreover, transoceanic travel became routine and rapid, taking a week to 10 days across the Atlantic and slightly longer across the Pacific.

Increasing knowledge of American opportunity also promoted a greater willingness to emigrate. This was due to higher educational levels, the output of the power printing press, and the subsequent dissemination of travel literature about the United States. Fifty travel books on America were published in nineteenth-century Germany. Two hundred were published in England in the quarter century before the Civil War. American state governments, territorial governments, land companies, and railroad companies also published immigrant guidebooks in foreign languages.

The spread of communications facilitated the organization of immigration in a process called **chain migration.** Chain migration was a universal device for reshuffling immigrants to all points of the globe. According to John S. MacDonald and Leatrice D. MacDonald, *chain migration* is "that movement in which prospective migrants learn of opportunities, are provided with transportation, and have initial accommodations and employment arranged *by means of primary social relationship with previous migrants.*[10] The "America letter" from immigrants informing prospective migrants in the home society was a key link in chain migration.

### Push and Pull Factors in the Postindustrial Era

The acceleration of the demographic transition in the Third World created a new crisis of surplus population in the late twentieth century. This became a powerful engine driving newcomers from the most impoverished areas of Latin America and the Caribbean to the United States. The introduction of modern medical and sanitary reforms in these areas curbed the Malthusian forces of communicable and childhood diseases. As a consequence, the populations of Mexico and the 25 countries and 10 dependencies in the Caribbean grew at a high 3 percent annual rate and doubled from World War II to the 1970s. The Moslem Middle East and south Asia, especially the Indian subcontinent and the Philippines, also experienced skyrocketing population growth. These areas became increasingly important in sending immigrants because their economies had made only preliminary advances toward establishing an industrial-technological base that could absorb the surplus population.[11]

Educated elites, growing in size in modernizing countries, encountered limits to the full application of their talents. Moreover, repressive political conditions alienated and frustrated them. The restrictions of homeland life induced talented personnel to seek new outlets in the United States. The so-called brain drain of highly trained human capital flowed from Asia, Latin America, and the Middle East.[12]

War and political persecution in the developing and newly independent nations of the Third World produced a flow of refugees to the United States. Congress established special provisions for the admission of these displaced peoples.

Economic expansion in the United States after World War II made conditions highly attractive to newcomers. From the 1940s to the 1970s, real wages rose 3 percent per year and average family income doubled. These three decades were the greatest period of economic growth in the nation's history. White-collar jobs grew in number and variety, while the lowest skilled manual jobs shrank in numbers. The rising curve of economic growth flattened out in the late 1970s and 1980s. To the poor and the disadvantaged in the Third World, however, American opportunity, though diminished, shone brighter than the chances available at home. Confidence in the room available in the economy also made U.S. natives favorably disposed toward accepting more newcomers.

After World War II, the globe shrank through a communications revolution that spread knowledge about the United States to remote regions of the Third World. Television, movies, radio, and magazines inspired emigrants with the image of the American standard of living. Far-flung regions of Asia, Latin America, and Africa were also brought closer by the airplane revolution. By the 1960s jumbo jets had supplanted the old immigrant steamships as the principal conveyance of immigrants. Airports in Miami and Los Angeles became the new versions of Ellis Island.

## GAUGING THE FLOW OF ANNUAL IMMIGRATION

Annual immigration can be broken down into periods and measured in different ways. A key measure is **net immigration,** the yearly excess of immigrant arrivals over departures. Keeping track of net immigration in different historical intervals is the first step toward gauging the impact of immigration on the host society. The net immigration figure provides the quantity that actually added to the growth of population, by separating those newcomers who returned home.

These return migrants became a major factor by the end of the nineteenth century. A large share of immigrants from southern and eastern Europe, Latin America, and Asia returned home (Table 18-2). Each year there was an average of more than 50 return migrants for every 100 immigrant arrivals among the Chinese, Bulgarian-Serbian-Montenegrins, Greeks, Romanians, Russians, and Spanish; and more than 40 return

**TABLE 18-2. Rates of Return Migration by Average Number of Annual Emigrant Departures (1908–1924) per 100 Average Annual Immigrant Arrivals (1899–1924), by Ethnic Group**

| | |
|---|---:|
| **Asiatic:** | |
| Chinese | 132.9 |
| East Indian | 41.9 |
| Japanese | 26.1 |
| Korean | 16.9 |
| Armenian | 18.1 |
| Syrian | 23.1 |
| Turkish | 80.5 |
| **Eastern European:** | |
| Hebrew | 4.3 |
| Bohemian, Moravian | 15.5 |
| Bulgarian, Serbian, Montenegrin | 87.4 |
| Croatian, Slovenian | 36.3 |
| Dalmatian, Bosnian, Herzegovenian | 26.3 |
| Lithuanian | 20.3 |
| Hungarian | 46.5 |
| Polish | 33.0 |
| Romanian | 66.0 |
| Russian | 65.0 |
| Ruthenian | 16.7 |
| Slovak | 36.5 |
| **Southern European:** | |
| Greek | 53.7 |
| Italian | 45.6 |
| Portuguese | 35.3 |
| Spanish | 51.9 |
| **Northern European:** | |
| Dutch, Flemish | 19.1 |
| Finnish | 22.0 |
| French | 48.2 |
| German | 13.7 |
| Scandinavian | 15.4 |
| British | 20.2 |
| Irish | 8.9 |
| **American:** | |
| Cuban | 49.6 |
| Mexican | 24.1 |
| West Indian | 47.3 |
| **African:** | |
| Negro | 27.0 |

*Source:* Thomas Archdeacon, *Becoming American: An Ethnic History*, Table V-3, pp. 118–119. Copyright © 1983 by The Free Press. Adapted with permission of The Free Press, a Division of Macmillan, Inc.

migrants for every 100 immigrant arrivals among the East Indians, Hungarians, Italians, French, Cubans, and West Indians. These transient laborers journeyed to the United States to earn income sent home in remittances or to be brought home through a future return. Those from Europe were often called "birds of passage" and those from Asia "sojourners." Important exceptions to this general tendency toward increased return migration existed, however. Armenians, Syrians, and Jews exhibited some of the lowest rates of return. They had little interest in going back to homelands under the oppressive control of Turkish and Russian potentates.

Despite the growth in return migration, net immigration increased because the gross volume of annual immigration grew even faster. Thus, in the nineteenth century, net immigration per decade climbed, with some fluctuations, from 123,000 in the 1820s, to 2.6 million in the 1850s, to 5 million in the 1880s (Table 18-1). In the first decade of the twentieth century, net immigration reached a peak level of 6.3 million arrivals. The world war and immigration restriction slashed net totals to 3 million in the 1920s. In the 1930s, the Depression and international tensions combined with quota restrictions to produce a net loss from immigration. Immigrants going back home outnumbered those who were arriving. After World War II and the lifting of national origins quotas, net immigration sprang back to 3.1 million in the 1950s and 4 million in the 1960s. Net immigration in recent decades approached totals in the high tide of American immigration from 1880 to 1930.

The net influx in each decade seems quite large but does not in itself provide a measure of its effect on the host society. In assessing the impact of immigration, it is important to relate the size of the influx to the size of the host population. The **rate of immigration**—the ratio of influx to host population—provides a crude but helpful index of the amount of pressure immigration exerted on both the resources and the institutions of the receiving society. The arrival of 3 million immigrants in a decade can have different effects, depending on whether the newcomers enter a country with a large or a small population.

The rate of immigration—statistically represented as the gross or net annual number of immigrants per 1,000 of the receiving population—began to soar in the 1830s and 1840s (Table 18.1). But in this period rapid growth of the native population and the economy provided a cushion for absorbing the new arrivals. Because the native population grew at a rate sufficient to maintain a demographic advantage over the immigrant population, it was large enough to stay in control of institutions and cultural processes. Economic growth also kept pace with the rate of immigration. In the 15- to 20-year periods of economic growth, long, gradual rises in the rate of immigration occurred. The peak rates of immigration in these long-trend upswings existed in 1851–1854, 1866–1873, 1881–1883, 1905–1907, and 1921–1924. The rate of immigration during these long-term upswings never exceeded 16 immigrants per 1,000 of population in each year. The rate of immigration plummeted into deep valleys during the depressions of 1877 and 1893, and the recession after World War I. In these low troughs, only 3 immigrants per 1,000 of population trickled in.

Immigration tended to respond to a prior rise in economic activity in the United States. That immigration grew in reaction to American opportunity was indicated by the consistent lag of immigration behind rises in wages and declines in unemployment.[13]

Since the 1950s, when net immigration climbed back to 3 to 4 million arrivals each decade, the host society has had a much greater capacity to absorb new arrivals. Three to 4 million new arrivals a decade

was an order of magnitude comparable to the immigration of the 1890s. But in the 1950s and 1960s this influx did not produce as much economic strain because the nation's GNP was 20 times larger than in the 1890s. Moreover, because the nation's population was three times greater, the numerical advantage of natives over immigrants maintained powerful assimilative forces in the social environment.

Throughout history, immigration did not increase faster than the capacity of the population and the economy to absorb it. That capacity has been greater than ever in the late twentieth century.

## THE CHANGING CHARACTERISTICS OF IMMIGRANTS

Throughout the period of free immigration, the majority of newcomers were purposeful, able-bodied young persons whose services were greatly demanded. They migrated as young adults for they planned to spend their most productive years working to get ahead. They were eager to seize available opportunities in the nation's multiplying industries. They were in the prime of their physical vigor, and most were males who could perform heavy physical labor. More than two out of three of immigrants in the nineteenth century were between 15 and 40 years of age, and male immigrants constituted 60 percent of all total arrivals (Tables 18-3 and 18-4). In the period of the new immigration from 1890 to 1920, the proportion of prime-aged newcomers, 14 to 44 years old, hovered around 80 percent, and the preponderance of male immigrants rose slightly, to nearly 70 percent.

Although no systematic data provide information on the marital status of newcomers arriving in the early nineteenth century, scattered evidence suggests that at least half came as single persons. Most of these

**TABLE 18-3.   Distribution of Alien Immigrants by Sex, 1831–1989**

| Year | Males | Females |
|------|-------|---------|
| 1831–1835 | 65.6 | 34.4 |
| 1836–1840 | 63.3 | 36.7 |
| 1841–1845 | 58.3 | 41.7 |
| 1846–1850 | 59.8 | 40.2 |
| 1851–1855 | 57.8 | 42.2 |
| 1857–1860 | 58.1 | 41.9 |
| 1861–1865 | 59.5 | 40.5 |
| 1866–1870 | 61.0 | 39.0 |
| 1871–1875 | 60.4 | 39.6 |
| 1876–1880 | 62.8 | 37.2 |
| 1881–1885 | 60.5 | 39.5 |
| 1886–1890 | 61.6 | 38.4 |
| 1891–1895 | 61.2 | 38.8 |
| 1896–1900 | 61.6 | 38.4 |
| 1901–1905 | 69.8 | 30.2 |
| 1906–1910 | 69.7 | 30.3 |
| 1911–1915 | 65.0 | 35.0 |
| 1916–1920 | 58.3 | 41.7 |
| 1921–1924 | 56.5 | 43.5 |
| 1925–1929 | 60.0 | 40.0 |
| 1930–1934 | 45.2 | 54.8 |
| 1935–1939 | 44.0 | 56.0 |
| 1936–1940 | 45.2 | 54.8 |
| 1941–1945 | 41.0 | 59.0 |
| 1946–1950 | 40.3 | 59.7 |
| 1951–1960 | 45.9 | 54.1 |
| 1961–1970 | 44.8 | 55.2 |
| 1971–1979 | 46.9 | 53.1 |
| 1982–1985 | 50.4 | 49.6 |
| 1986–1989 | 50.2 | 48.8 |

*Sources:* Imre Ferenzci and Walter F. Willcox, *International Migrations* (New York: National Bureau of Economic Research, 1929–1931), Vol. 1, p. 211; U. S. Bureau of the Census, *Statistical Abstract of the United States, 1942*, p. 123; *Statistical Abstract of the United States, 1954*, p. 106; *Statistical Abstract of the United States, 1984*, p. 93. Compiled from *Statistical Yearbook of the Immigration and Naturalization Service, 1985*, p. 46; *Statistical Yearbook, 1989*, p. 24.

single individuals were also young adult males.

Immigrants by and large were not peasants with few skills for an urban economy. From 1820 to 1920 the average each decade of farm laborers (so often pictured as forming the bulk of the manpower flow) only ranged from 11 percent to 32 percent (Table 18-5). Industrial and mining workers constituted nearly as large a proportion of all newcomers as did farm laborers. The largest share of gainfully employed immigrants, around half entering from 1851 and World War I, were employed in domestic service and urban general labor. It must be realized, however, that many of these nonagricultural employees probably had engaged in farm labor at an earlier point in their working lives. As the historian Oscar Handlin has pointed out, immigration was only a later stage in the lives of people "originally set in motion decades earlier." "Here and there," Handlin noted, "were peasants deprived of their land years ago, but unwilling to leave the country of their birth. Perhaps they worked in the factories of nearby cities or toiled as laborers for the gentry, until some more fortunate cousin or uncle from across the Atlantic sent on the redeeming ticket."[14] The most highly skilled immigrants reporting occupations in "liberal professions and public service" constituted a minute fraction of total arrivals, less than 2 percent from 1890 to 1920.

The characteristics of immigrants changed significantly in the late twentieth century. In the 1960s a relative decline began in the traditional dominance of immigration from Europe (Table 18-6). By the 1980s only 11 percent of the total immigration came from Europe, as compared to 90 percent in 1900. The flow from Asia grew faster than from other continents. By the early 1980s, nearly half of all immigrants came from Asian points of origin.

The newest immigration was marked by an increase in human capital flows. It reflected the development of admissions policies that favored occupational preference. In the 1970s, 25 percent of immigrants were professionals, and over 40 percent were white-collar employees (Table 18-5).

The human-capital migration was counterbalanced by an unprecedented wave of undocumented alien laborers. Poor and highly transient, the numbers of **undocu-**

**TABLE 18-4.  Alien Immigrants to the United States by Age, 1868–1989**

| Year | Total Number | Percentage Distribution by Age | | |
|------|------|------|------|------|
| | | Under 15 | 15–40 | Over 40 |
| 1868–1870 | 1,022,160 | 22.2 | 65.7 | 12.1 |
| 1871–1875 | 1,726,796 | 21.7 | 64.6 | 13.7 |
| 1876–1880 | 1,085,395 | 18.2 | 70.8 | 11.0 |
| 1881–1885 | 2,975,683 | 23.0 | 66.5 | 10.5 |
| 1886–1890 | 2,270,930 | 19.2 | 70.2 | 10.6 |
| 1891–1895 | 2,280,735 | 13.9 | 79.3 | 6.8 |
| 1896–1900[a] | 1,563,685 | 14.6 | 76.9 | 8.5 |
| | | Under 14 | 14–44 | Over 44 |
| 1901–1905 | 3,833,076 | 12.1 | 82.5 | 5.4 |
| 1906–1910 | 4,962,310 | 12.0 | 83.4 | 4.6 |
| 1911–1915 | 4,459,831 | 13.2 | 80.9 | 5.9 |
| 1916–1920[b] | 1,275,980 | 17.6 | 71.8 | 1u.3 |
| | | Under 16 | 16–44 | Over 44 |
| 1921–1924 | 2,344,599 | 18.5 | 72.3 | 9.2 |
| 1925–1929 | 1,520,910 | 16.3 | 74.7 | 9.0 |
| 1930–1934 | 426,954 | 17.4 | 70.5 | 12.1 |
| 1935–1939 | 272,422 | 16.3 | 66.5 | 17.2 |
| 1936–1940 | 308,222 | 15.3 | 66.1 | 18.6 |
| 1941–1945 | 170,952 | 14.4 | 62.9 | 22.7 |
| 1946–1950 | 864,087 | 15.9 | 66.6 | 17.5 |
| 1951–1960 | 2,515,479 | 22.9 | 63.5 | 13.6 |
| 1961–1970 | 3,321,677 | 25.5 | 60.7 | 13.8 |
| 1971–1979 | 3,962,000 | 26.1 | 59.3 | 14.6 |
| 1980–1989 | 6,332,218 | 19.8 | 64.4 | 15.8 |

[a] For 1899 and 1900, age groups were under 14, 14–44, and over 44.

[b] For 1918 to 1920, age groups were under 16, 16–44, and over 44.

*Sources:* Imre Ferenzci and Walter F. Willcox, *International Migrations* (New York: National Bureau of Economic Research, 1929), Vol. 1, p. 214; U. S. Bureau of the Census, *Statistical Abstract of the United States, 1942*, p. 123; *Statistical Abstract of the United States, 1954*, p. 106; *Statistical Abstract of the United States, 1962*, p. 99; *Statistical Abstract of the United States, 1984*, p. 93; *Statistical Yearbook of the Immigration and Naturalization Service, 1989*, p. 24.

**mented immigrants** were estimated to reach several million in the early 1980s.

The newest immigration also reflected the transformation of the labor force, in which employment opportunities for females became an important new pull factor, while heavy manual labor jobs historically attracting male immigrants declined. For the first time in history females outnumbered males in the influx. Admissions policies that favored family reunification also increased the immigration of women. Preference for family reunion made the proportion of children and older adults grow to double their levels in the early twentieth century. Thus, immigration in the late twentieth century was more heterogeneous and balanced in its demographic aspects than the proletarian, young male stream of the early twentieth century.

**TABLE 18-5.   Employed Immigrants by Occupation, 1901–1985 (Percentage Distribution)**

|  | 1901–1910 | 1911–1920 | 1921–1930 | 1931–1940 | 1941–1945 | 1946–1950 |
|---|---|---|---|---|---|---|
| Professional | 1.4 | 2.7 | 4.5 | 17.3 | 24.2 | 16.2 |
| Proprietors, managers | 2.7 | 2.7 | 3.5 | 15.3 | 15.2 | 7.1 |
| Clerical, sales | 1.5 | *a* | 7.0 | 10.6 | 16.7 | 17.5 |
| Craftsmen, foremen | 17.8 | 22.4 | 23.7 | 19.3 | 21.9 | 30.7 |
| Farmers, farm managers | 1.6 | 2.2 | 4.2 | 4.2 | 2.3 | 9.1 |
| Farm laborers | 24.5 | 27.2 | 8.5 | 2.9 | 1.1 | 1.6 |
| Laborers | 35.1 | 25.7 | 24.7 | 8.6 | 5.2 | 5.3 |
| Domestics | 14.1 | 16.8 | 17.2 | 15.0 | 7.8 | 7.5 |
| Service | 1.3 | 0.4 | 6.0 | 6.7 | 5.6 | 4.9 |

|  | 1951–1960 | 1961–1970 | 1971–1979*f* | 1982–1985 | 1986–1989 |
|---|---|---|---|---|---|
| Professional | 15.6 | 23.0 | 25.0 | 19.4 | 13.9 |
| Managers | 4.5 | 4.5 | 7.3 | 9.5 | 7.4 |
| Sales | *b* | *b* | 2.1 | 4.3 | 4.4 |
| Clerical | 16.7 | 16.7 | 9.7 | 9.2 | 8.4 |
| Craftsmen | 16.6 | 14.1 | 12.2 | 11.5 | 11.5 |
| Operatives (nontransport) | 14.3 | 11.1 | 13.8 | 22.7 | 26.0 |
| Transport operatives | *c* | *c* | 0.2 | *c* | *c* |
| Laborers | 11.3 | 8.8 | 9.0 | *c* | *c* |
| Farmers, farm managers | 4.2 | 1.8 | 1.0 | 5.0 | 5.3 |
| Farm laborers | 3.7 | 3.9 | 4.4 | *d* | *d* |
| Service workers | 5.9 | 7.4 | 9.4 | 18.3 | 23.0 |
| Household workers | 8.0 | 8.7 | 5.2 | *e* | *e* |

*a* Combined with proprietors and managers.

*b* Sales workers included with clerical.

*c* Transport operatives or laborers included with operatives.

*d* Farm laborers included with farmers and farm managers.

*e* Household workers included with service workers.

*f* No data available for 1980–1981.

*Sources:* Conrad Taueber and Irene Taeuber, *Changing Population of the United States* (New York: John Wiley, 1958), p. 70; *Statistical Abstract of the United States, 1984,* p. 93; Commissioner General of Immigration, *Annual Reports,* 1927, Tables 96, 97. Compiled from *Statistical Yearbook of the Immigration and Naturalization Service, 1985– 1989.*

## THE IMPACT OF IMMIGRATION

### Immigration and Population Growth

Some observers of the late nineteenth century feared that immigration retarded native population growth. They complained that immigrants preempted the population growth that would have occurred naturally.

The competition with immigrants for survival, it was said, depressed native fertility. Francis Amasa Walker, an influential economist and president of MIT from 1881 to 1897, argued forcefully that immigration retarded the increase of the native stock in an article bearing the interesting title "Immigration and Degradation."

Historical evidence casts doubt upon

**TABLE 18-6.  Percentage of Immigrants by Area of Origin, 1961–1970, 1971–1980, 1981–1988**

|  | 1961–1970 | 1971–1980 | 1981–1988 |
|---|---|---|---|
| Europe | 37.3 | 17.8 | 10.8 |
| Asia | 13.4 | 36.4 | 46.0 |
| North America | 40.7 | 36.6 | 33.1 |
| South America | 6.9 | 6.3 | 6.6 |
| Africa | 1.2 | 2.0 | 2.8 |
| Australia | 0.3 | 0.3 | 0.2 |
| New Zealand | 0.1 | 0.1 | 0.1 |
| Other | 0.2 | 0.4 | 0.4 |

*Sources:* Compiled from *Statistical Abstract of the United States, 1984, 1990.*

this "race suicide" theory of immigration. The native population continued to grow at an ample rate even in the heaviest periods of immigration. When net immigration is compared to the natural increase of population, it becomes evident that natural increase, not immigration, produced the bulk of population growth. In nearly all decades of our national history, immigration contributed less than one-third of the increase in population.[15]

Although immigration probably failed to depress the natural increase of the native population, many immigrant subpopulations grew unusually rapidly through a higher rate of fertility (Table 18-7). This has been a continuous factor in the expansion of the U.S. population since the late nineteenth century. Polish, German, and Irish groups had fertility rates twice as high as those of native white Americans in 1880. A century later, Mexican and Puerto Rican immigrants exhibited fertility rates twice as high as those of native white Americans (who by then included the descendants of immigrant Poles, Germans, and Irish). The continuation of large-scale migration of Mexicans and Puerto Ricans and the high fertility of the newcomers thus seem the most likely sources for the greatest input to total population growth coming from current immigration. As a result of its influence, Mexican and Puerto Rican immigra-

**TABLE 18-7.  Fertility of Ethnic Groups for Selected Periods**

| 1880 Ethnic Group (Detroit Sample) | Number of Children Under Age 5 per 1,000 Women Aged 20–49 |
|---|---|
| Native white American | 470.12 |
| British | 536.28 |
| Canadian | 764.94 |
| Irish | 934.19 |
| German | 944.68 |
| Polish | 1,058.00 |

| 1980 Ethnic Group (U.S. Total) | Number of Live Births Ever per 1,000 Women Aged 15–24 | Number of Live Births Ever per 1,000 Women Aged 25–34 | Number of Live Births Ever per 1,000 Women Aged 35–44 |
|---|---|---|---|
| White | 262 | 1,383 | 2,523 |
| Spanish origin | 317 | 1,476 | 2,639 |
| Mexican | 528 | 2,105 | 3,646 |
| Puerto Rican | 548 | 1,936 | 3,202 |
| Asian/Pacific Islander | 211 | 1,219 | 2,256 |

*Sources:* Olivier Zunz, *The Changing Face of Inequality: Urbanization, Industrial Development, and Immigrants in Detroit, 1880–1920* (Chicago: University of Chicago Press, 1982), p. 74; U.S. Census Bureau, *Population Report, 1980,* Vol. I, Chap. C, Pt. 1, p. 163.

tion can counterbalance the aging of the general population.

It is important to note, however, that very large differences in fertility and natural increase existed among immigrant groups. In 1880 the British ethnic group in Detroit had a fertility rate only slightly higher than that of native whites. And in the late twentieth century, Asian and Pacific Islander groups had fertility rates even lower than that of native whites. Thus, the dynamic effects of high fertility among certain groups have been offset by lower rates among others. If immigration of Asians and Pacific Islanders is sustained at a high level, it will probably offset the fertility of immigrant groups from Latin America and the Caribbean sphere to level out the growth rate of the population caused by immigration. Another mitigating factor is that trends in history show that fertility rates always decline among immigrant groups with the succession of the second and third generations.

## Immigration and Economic Development

The vast influx of 50 million immigrants who arrived since 1820 had all the qualities desired by promoters who needed a dependable form of manpower to propel economic expansion. Developers of the western states and industrial capitalists welcomed the foreigners who would till the virgin prairie or operate the machines in the factories. They felt that constant immigration supplied the catalytic effect of a fluid labor supply that made growth possible. Another group of natives, however, was critical of the role of immigration in the development of the national economy. They asserted that immigration produced a regressive, hasty form of industrialization that lowered wages with harmful effects for the whole economy. Their arguments gained force with the arrival of southern and eastern European immigrants, whom they viewed as an inefficient, dependent form of labor. These **new immigrants,** the critics alleged, as contrasted with the **old immigrants** from northern and western Europe, caused costly accidents, unemployment, the frightening concentration of monopoly capital, and even depressions.

Those who decried the pernicious economic impact of the new immigrants urged restriction. Francis A. Walker, who argued that immigration inhibited the reproduction of natives, also objected that immigration created an unhealthy labor system. In 1911 the U.S. Commission on Immigration issued a multivolume report that attempted to document Walker's earlier warnings.

The pessimists worried about the collapse of the labor market. They believed millions of low-skilled immigrants drove natives out of jobs and lowered wages and the conditions of work. The specter they saw was the future decline of the native worker, the loss of his independence, and his submergence into a permanent proletariat. Immigration as a supply of "cheap labor" spelled the doom of U.S. democracy.

Of course, this dire scenario never transpired. The enormous growth in the scale of manufacturing, achieved through mechanization, reduced the pressure of immigration on the labor market. The increase in scale produced an expansion of the low-skilled labor force, which in turn generated a greater demand for trained supervisory personnel. Immigrants released native artisans to rise to shopkeepers or foremen. In this way it can be said that the flow of new immigrants was an undercurrent that pushed native labor to higher occupational levels. Although the percentage of skilled workers declined after the turn of the century, their absolute numbers increased. Their skills were still in demand because of the overall enlargement of the economy.

Economists and historians feel, however, that immigration has adversely affected economic opportunity for natives in some ways. Immigration seems to have produced short-term lowering of wages for the least skilled native workers. Recently, scholars have discussed the possibility that new immigration from Latin America and Asia has reduced the prospects for blacks to advance.[16]

Nevertheless, the general impact of immigration on the economy appears quite positive. Without a high volume of immigration, the recruitment of an industrial labor force would have proceeded at a much slower rate. Studies have shown that immigrants helped the economy expand by redistributing labor to meet shifting demand. In localities where net immigration was historically high, the rate of economic growth was above average. Without mass immigration, the exploitation of frontier resources would have occurred at a slower pace. A shortage of labor in manufacturing would have impeded the rise of economies of scale, and fewer wage-earners who saved would have appreciably slackened the pace of capital formation. Without high levels of immigration, the GNP would have expanded less rapidly.[17]

The effects of immigration on per capita product are more difficult to grasp. Imaginative guesswork and judicious use of limited data produce a mixed picture. There are indications that immigration helped to raise productivity in the industrial economy. Immigration tended to precede the long upswings in investment and growth until 1870. Furthermore, simply by increasing the size of the total economy and the scale of its constituent productive units through the massive infusion of low-skilled labor, it would appear that immigration enhanced per capita output levels.[18]

The effect of immigration on the age and sex of the labor force was an important influence on productivity trends. First, immigration pushed up the percentage of those in prime working age. Second, it increased the share of males. In an era when women rarely held industrial jobs, immigration insured a large pool of laborers. The positive impact of immigration on per capita production thus lay in the relative enlargement of the producing classes. The age and sex shifts raised the ratio of workers to nonproductive dependents and enlarged the share of workers in their most productive years.

On the other hand, certain effects of immigration counteracted the growth of per capita output caused by these changes. Foreign-born laborers had higher illiteracy and shorter life expectancy than native-born workers. It is possible that without massive immigration, the median schooling and health of the urban labor force would have improved faster. A longer-lived, healthier, and better educated work force might have spurred a faster rise in output per worker.

Also, immigration probably contributed little to the initial elevation of per capita production in the nation's economic history. From 1790 to 1840, per capita output rose to the threshold levels of the late nineteenth and early twentieth centuries. In this period, it should be recalled, the United States experienced a very low rate of immigration. Immigration thus could not have been a primary cause of the "take-off" stage that launched the Industrial Revolution. Instead, its main agencies were technology, capital formation, and organizational innovation that widened markets and produced the factory system.

Because they helped to build a dynamic economy that provided opportunity, immigrants never became a permanent impoverished class. The stable immigrant residents of cities, even the unskilled members of the working class, achieved economic improvement. A substantial fraction of the sons of immigrants were able to move into better jobs than their fathers. They also frequently achieved more education and were more likely to acquire property. Some European groups, such as the Germans and Jews, and non-European groups, such as the Japanese and West Indians, made unusually quick moves up the socioeconomic pyramid. Others, such as the Irish, Italians, and Mexicans, did not attain white-collar occupations and advanced education as rapidly. Nevertheless, over the long term nearly all groups displayed signs of improvement in material welfare. Studies in the 1970s and 1980s showed that when compared to groups derived from northern and western Europe, many groups of southern and eastern European ancestry had equivalent or higher education, income, and less poverty than average. The income levels of Jews, Italians, and Poles were even higher than those of Americans of British descent.[19] The recent arrival of newcomers from Asia, Latin America, Africa, and the Middle East makes it harder to discern their advances, but many of them already are moving into better jobs, starting businesses, and sponsoring the further progress of their children. The social position of immigrant groups improved through a process of cumulative mobility and acculturation from one generation to the next.

## SUMMARY

1. Immigration has been a central feature of American national development from the colonial era to the late twentieth century. Immigration produced significant changes in the direction and speed of American economic and population growth.

2. Immigration was propelled by the net effects of displacing forces in the homeland and attractive forces in the United States. Push and pull forces in the industrial era caused a geometric increase of immigration. Immigration was not a chaotic flight but an organized and structured movement.

3. The history of immigration can be divided into eras defined by the predominance of particular ethnic groups. Moreover, immigration has evolved through stages of progressive ethnic complexity. From the seventeenth century to the late nineteenth century, most immigrants came from northern and western Europe. From the end of the nineteenth century to the early twentieth century, southern and eastern European immigrants predominated, and immigration from Asia and Latin America began. Immigration was severely limited by discriminatory laws from 1924 to 1965. Since 1965, arrivals from Latin America, Asia, the Caribbean, and the Middle East have eclipsed European immigration for the first time.

4. U.S. society has consistently displayed the capacity to absorb mass immigration. Annual gross immigration and net immigration rose in long upswings coincident with phases of economic expansion and declined in long downswings during recession. The ratio of immigration to the size of the host population grew and shrank according to the economic cycle.

5. Immigration has been a key factor promoting economic expansion. Immigration stimulated the growth of the gross national product by increasing the labor force, savers, and consumers that made national commercial markets and industrial economies of scale possible. Immigrants provided the cheap labor power that made mass manufacturing industries practicable. In some ways immigration probably helped to raise per capita output, but in other ways it may have reduced it. Without immigration, the economy would have grown much less in aggregate size or in its constituent units. The standard of living itself might have become lower. The injurious effects of immigration on the status of native workers, by comparison to its positive effects, have been weak. No evidence exists that immigration ever increased unemployment, and adverse effects have been limited to short-term declines in wages for low-skilled workers.

6. On the whole, immigrants to the United States achieved an improved economic life for themselves because they helped to build a dynamic economy that increased overall material welfare. Immigrant groups displayed consistent rates of upward social movement that increased with length of residence and intergenerational succession.

## KEY CONCEPTS FOR REVIEW

Restrictive immigration quotas

Push and pull factors

Demographic transition

Surplus population

Demand pull for labor

Transient labor migration

Chain migration

Net immigration

Rate of immigration

Undocumented immigrants

New immigrants

Old immigrants

## QUESTIONS FOR DISCUSSION

1. Compare and contrast the push forces causing emigration to the United States in the colonial era, the industrial era, and the postindustrial era. What was a "surplus population"?

2. What American pull forces drew immigrants despite large differences in geographic and cultural backgrounds? Compare the relative numbers of immigrants from different countries and regions of the world from the seventeenth century to the twentieth century. Describe the rise of transient migrants, undocumented migrants, and refugees.

3. Discuss the changing levels of annual immigration. What factors caused fluctuations in the size of immigration? Describe the significance of net immigration and the rate of immigration.

4. What were the characteristics of immigrants? Describe the changes in sex distribution, occupational distribution, and age distribution. Summarize the key differences between these distributions in the nineteenth century and the twentieth century.

5. How did immigration contribute to the expansion of the U.S. population? What was its impact on fertility levels?

6. What was the influence of immigration on the evolution of the industrial economy? Assess the effects of immigration on gross national product and per capita gross national product. How did immigration change the scale of economic organization, the status of native workers, and the material status of immigrants themselves?

## NOTES

1. William Bernard, "Immigration: History of U.S. Policy," in Stephan Thernstrom, ed., *Harvard Encyclopedia of American Ethnic Groups* (Cambridge, Mass.: Harvard University Press, 1980); James H. Kettner, *The Development of American Citizenship, 1608–1870* (Chapel Hill, N.C.: University of North Carolina Press, 1978), Chap. 4.

2. Bernard Bailyn, *Voyagers to the West: A Passage in the Peopling of America on the Eve of the Revolution* (New York: Alfred A. Knopf, 1986).

3. Oscar Handlin, *Boston's Immigrants: A Study in Acculturation*, rev. ed. (Cambridge, Mass.: Harvard University Press, 1956), Chap. 3.

4. Thomas J. Archdeacon, *Becoming American: An Ethnic History* (New York: The Free Press, 1983), pp. 121–127.

5. Philip Taylor, *The Distant Magnet: European Emigration to the U.S.A.* (New York: Harper and Row, 1971), Chap. 1 and 3.

6. John Bodnar, *The Transplanted: A History of Immigrants in Urban America* (Bloomington, Ind.: Indiana University Press, 1985), pp. 34–37.

7. Walter Kamphoefner, *The Westfalians: From Germany to Missouri* (Princeton, N.J.: Princeton University Press, 1987), Chap. 1.

8. Eric Wolf, *Europe and the People without History* (Berkeley: University of California Press, 1982).

9. Brinley Thomas, *Migration and the Rhythm of Economic Growth* (Cambridge: Cambridge University Press, 1954).

10. John S. MacDonald and Leatrice D. MacDonald, "Chain Migration, Ethnic Neighborhood Formation, and Social Networks," in Charles Tilly, *An Urban World* (Boston: Little, Brown, 1974), p. 227.

11. Thomas Kessner and Betty Boyd Caroli, *Today's Immigrants: Their Stories* (New York: Oxford University Press, 1982), Introduction, and David M. Reimers, *Still the Golden Door: The Third World Comes to America* (New York: Columbia University Press, 1985), Chaps. 4–5.

12. Maxine Greer Seller, *To Seek America: A History of Ethnic Life in the United States*, rev. ed. (Englewood, N.J.: Jerome S. Ozer, 1989), pp. 294–296.

13. Simon Kuznets and Ernest Rubin, *Immigration and the Foreign Born*, Occasional Paper 46 (New York: National Bureau of Economic Research, 1954), pp. 4–5, 32–37; Richard Easterlin, *Population, Labor Force, and Long Swings in Economic Growth: The American Experience* (New York: National Bureau of Economic Research, 1968), p. 31.

14. Oscar Handlin, *The American People in the Twentieth Century* (Cambridge, Mass.: Harvard University Press, 1954), p. 8.

15. Conrad Taeuber and Irene Taeuber, *The Changing Population of the United States* (New York: John Wiley, 1958), pp. 293–294.

16. Thomas Muller, "Economic Effects of Immigration," in Nathan Glazer, ed., *Clamor at the Gates: The New American Immigration* (San Francisco: Institute for Contemporary Studies, 1985) pp. 109–133.

17. Richard A. Easterlin, "Immigration: Economic and Social Characteristics," in Stephan Thernstrom, Ed., *Harvard Encyclopedia of American Ethnic Groups* (Cambridge, Mass.: Harvard University Press, 1980).

18. W. Elliot Brownlee, *Dynamics of Ascent: A History of the American Economy*, 2nd ed. (New York: Alfred A. Knopf, 1979), pp. 325–326.

19. David L. Featherman and Robert M. Hauser, *Opportunity and Change* (New York: Academic Press, 1978); Andrew M. Greeley, "Ethnic Minorities in the United States: Demographic Perspectives," *International Journal of Group Tensions*, 7, 1977: 64–97; Stanley Lieberson, *A Piece of the Pie: Blacks and White Immigrants Since 1880* (Berkeley: University of California Press, 1981); Thomas Sowell, *Ethnic America: A History* (New York: Basic Books, 1981).

# 19

# *Through the Golden Door*

*T*he adaptability of Asian ethnic groups to conditions in the United States can be seen as a cardinal social achievement, but it has not been a simple and inevitable result. Major barriers to social and economic opportunity impeded the upward mobility of Asian-Americans until after World War II. Factors internal to group life interacted subtly with societal conditions to produce changes. What follows is an examination of the historical conditions and forces enabling Asian Americans to become an unusually productive and functional part of the population.

## HISTORICAL ORIGINS OF ASIAN IMMIGRATION

Labor migration from Asia became a key to the development of the far western states. It was a response to the shortage in the hinterland of a native population, of labor migrants from Europe and Latin America, and of black labor migrants from the American south.

Asian migration to the United States was part of a worldwide exodus from Asia generated by internal upheavals and the arrival of European imperialist power. It was an immense movement that occurred in waves of ethnic succession. Chinese migration arrived from the 1850s until it was restricted by U.S. law in 1882. Japanese immigration began in the 1880s and was curtailed in 1908. Koreans started to immigrate from the early 1900s but were also curbed by 1908. Asian Indians arrived after 1908 but were excluded by 1917. All Asian aliens were completely barred in 1924. But Filipinos, who were U.S. nationals because of the United States' acquisition of the Philippines in 1899, migrated from 1910 until they were restricted in 1934.

In examining the periodic flows of Asian immigration, it is important to realize that the restrictions were not totally exclusive but only excluded selected categories of immigrants. For example, the **Chinese Exclusion Act of 1882** excluded laborers but still permitted other occupational classes of immigrants. Selective exclusion also applied to Japanese and Korean laborers as a result of the so-called **Gentleman's Agreement** the United States negotiated with Japan in 1907–1908, but women, children, and other occupational classes continued to be admitted. Furthermore, immigration laws established categories exempted from exclusion, such as alien spouses or the foreign-born children of U.S. citizens. Because various classes were not excluded, the flow of immigrants from China, Japan, and Korea, though impeded, continued to arrive.

Nevertheless, as a result of the series of restrictions, the largest flows of Asian immigration occurred in a series of bursts. Between 1850 and 1882, 322,000 Chinese immigrants entered the United States. From 1890 to 1924, 290,000 immigrants came from Japan. From 1899 to 1924, 9,200 Koreans and 8,200 Asian Indians immigrated. Between 1910 and 1934, over 50,000 Filipinos arrived. The U.S. territory of Hawaii was another major receiving area. Hawaii was an independent monarchy until 1898, when it was annexed by the United States. Exclusionary immigration laws thereafter applied in the islands to produce a mirror image of the serial immigration to the mainland. In the nineteenth century, 56,000 Chinese journeyed to Hawaii until annexation brought Chinese exclusion. From 1885 to 1924, 230,000 Japanese arrived, and from 1903 to 1924, 9,000 Koreans immigrated. Between 1910 and 1934, 113,000 Filipinos came to the islands.[1]

The policy of selective restriction developed out of a unique conception of Asian civil status. Because Asian immigrants were believed too difficult to assimilate, policymakers categorized them as **aliens ineligible for citizenship.** Asians were regarded as perpetual foreigners within the American nation. As such, their numbers had to be sharply limited. The restrictive immigration law of 1924 thus excluded all Asians on the grounds that they were aliens ineligible for citizenship.

Because the Chinese and Japanese were the earliest immigrant groups from Asia, they long constituted the two largest communities (Table 19-1). In contrast to the hundreds of thousands of Chinese and Japanese who arrived, Korean and Asian Indian immigrants constituted a miniature immigration. The flow from other regions of Asia was even smaller. Few Asian Indians came to the United States compared to the several millions who migrated as laborers to Africa and Southeast Asia.

The majority of Asian newcomers were farm laborers whose overpopulated home communities suffered from weak economic development, political instability, and external commercial disturbances. Geographically localized areas experienced these forms of distress most acutely. As a result, Asian emigration occurred in chain migrations of regionally defined groups. It was similar to the planned and orchestrated movement of German, Italian, and Jewish immigrants who similarly came from very localized homelands.

The early Chinese and Japanese immigrants represented the first case of transient labor migration to the United States. The vast majority were young men sent overseas by their families to obtain new sources of income.[2] In a sense they functioned in two economic systems: the household economy of rural East Asia and the industrializing economy of the United States. Chinese laborers in nineteenth-century America could earn $200 to $300 a year, ten times their annual income in China. Japanese plantation workers in Hawaii earned wages four to six times higher than in Meiji Era Japan.[3] They sent back a steady stream of remittances to provide the margin of survival to their families. From Hawaii, Japanese immigrants sent home $2.6 million before 1900.[4] Many Chinese and Japanese returned home with as much as they could save.

Asian immigrants characterized themselves as "**sojourners.**" Asian transient laborers were not a unique phenomenon. As mentioned in an earlier chapter, the majority of immigrants from southern and eastern Europe also came for temporary work in the United States and for that reason were termed "birds of passage."

Although Asian immigration had a large transient component and was limited by exclusionary immigration laws, Asians were still able to build permanent communities. The Chinese, Japanese, Koreans, Asian Indians, and Filipinos all suffered at first from a highly imbalanced sex ratio; men vastly outnumbered women (Table 19-2). Restrictive policies reduced the time for recruiting marriageable women. Nevertheless, the Chinese were able to start families gradually in the United States and with greater speed in Hawaii. The Japanese and Koreans moved faster than the Chinese from the pattern of transiency by installing an effective system of chain migration of women— marriages arranged through a preliminary exchange of photographs called the "**picture bride system.**" Families thus formed early in the process of community building. Because most Japanese migrated from 1900 to 1920, were closely ranged in age, became

**TABLE 19-1.   Immigration from Asia to the United States, by Country of Former Residence, 1851–1924**

| Decade | China | Japan | Korea[a] | India |
|---|---|---|---|---|
| 1851–1860 | 41,397 | 0 | NA | 43 |
| 1861–1870 | 64,301 | 186 | NA | 69 |
| 1871–1880 | 123,201 | 149 | NA | 163 |
| 1881–1890 | 61,711 | 2,270 | NA | 269 |
| 1891–1900 | 14,799 | 25,942 | 22 | 68 |
| 1901–1910 | 20,605 | 129,797 | 7,697 | 4,713 |
| 1911–1920 | 21,278 | 83,837 | 1,049 | 2,082 |
| 1921–1924 | 20,393 | 29,204 | 375 | 1,311 |

[a] Figures are compiled by "race or people" rather than country of former residence.

*Source:* Compiled from U.S. Commissioner General of Immigration, *Annual Reports*, and U.S. Commission on Immigration, *Reports* (Washington, D.C.: 1912), Vol. III.

**TABLE 19-2.　Sex Ratio among the Chinese and Japanese in the United States and Hawaii (Males per 100 Females), 1860–1940**

| | United States | | Hawaii | |
|---|---|---|---|---|
| Year | Chinese | Japanese | Chinese | Japanese |
| 1860 | 1,860 | NA | NA | NA |
| 1870 | 1,280 | NA | NA | NA |
| 1880 | 2,100 | NA | NA | NA |
| 1890 | 2,680 | 690 | 640 | NA |
| 1900 | 1,890 | 2,370 | 380 | 350 |
| 1910 | 1,430 | 690 | 220 | 220 |
| 1920 | 700 | 190 | 106 | 130 |
| 1930 | 390 | 140 | 130 | 120 |
| 1940 | 280 | 103 | 110 | 110 |

Sources: Computed from U.S. Census Bureau, *Population Reports*, 1860–1950.

permanent residents, and formed families at the same time, the Japanese community was organized along generational lines. The roughly uniform characteristics of the first generation combined with exclusion of a large later immigrant wave to create a coherent first generation known as the **Issei.** The members of this generation produced children at the same time, guaranteeing similar historical and developmental experiences for the second generation, called the **Nisei.**

The Japanese community resembled many European immigrant communities in the salience of family formation. From 1910 to 1940, the children of immigrants multi-

**TABLE 19-3.　Rates of Natural Increase, 1930–1980**

| Year | Chinese | Japanese | Filipino | White |
|---|---|---|---|---|
| 1930 | −0.5 | 14.0 | NA | 7.9 |
| 1940 | −0.8 | 8.3 | NA | 8.2 |
| 1950 | 34.9 | 18.4 | NA | 13.5 |
| 1960 | 17.8 | 22.9 | NA | 13.2 |
| 1970 | 13.3 | 9.7 | NA | 7.9 |
| 1980 | 12.0 | 11.5 | 17.0 | 6.0 |

Source: Compiled from U.S. National Office of Vital Statistics, *Vital Statistics of the U.S.*, *1937–1977*, and National Center for Health Statistics, *Vital Statistics of the United States, 1980* (Washington, D.C.: 1984–1985).

plied by 17 times in the United States and 24 times in Hawaii. The rate of natural increase of the Japanese (the yearly difference between the number of live births and deaths per 1,000 people) was almost twice that of the white population in 1930 (Table 19-3). Fertility rates among the Japanese reached their historic high points about this time (Table 19-4).

**TABLE 19-4.　Fertility of Selected Asian American Groups and Whites, 1920–1980**

| Year | Ethnic Group | Number of Children under 5 Years old per 1,000 Females 15–44 Years old |
|---|---|---|
| 1920 | Japanese | 843 |
| | Chinese | 803 |
| | White | 471 |
| 1930 | Japanese | 709 |
| | Chinese | 858 |
| | Filipino | 933 |
| | White | 463 |
| 1940 | Japanese | 263 |
| | Chinese | 443 |
| | Filipino | 1,356 |
| | Asian Indian | 1,071 |
| | White | 324 |
| 1950 | Japanese | 391 |
| | Chinese | 604 |
| | Filipino | 992 |
| | White | 467 |
| 1960 | Japanese | 447 |
| | Chinese | 604 |
| | Filipino | 779 |
| | White | 546 |
| 1970 | Japanese | 241 |
| | Chinese | 344 |
| | Filipino | 462 |
| | White | 392 |
| 1980 | Japanese | 204 |
| | Chinese | 344 |
| | Filipino | 462 |
| | White | 392 |

Source: Computed from U.S. Census Bureau, *Population Reports* of the Decennial Census, *Special Reports*, and *Subject Reports*.

## THE EVOLUTION OF ASIAN AMERICAN SOCIETY, 1850–1965

### The Rural Frontier: Sojourner Society

In the United States, the sojourner generation acted as a cheap labor force enabling the development of the western infrastructure. In the 1860s, an estimated 12,000 to 14,000 Chinese laborers built the Central Pacific Railroad linking the Pacific coast with eastern Utah to complete the transcontinental railroad. Two out of every three miners in principal mining districts were Chinese. Factory owners in San Francisco developed a preference for the hands of East Asia: in 1870, 64 percent of woolen-mill workers were Chinese and so were 91 percent of the cigar makers.[5] The Chinese comprised the majority of the state's boot and shoemakers. They also worked in laundries and restaurants in a female-short society. They organized these service occupations into mainstays of the West's small business economy.[6] The Chinese were a small minority, only one-tenth of the California population in 1880; but because they were nearly all males of productive age and eagerly sought employment, they actually made up 25 percent of the state's labor force.[7]

Chinese farmers were enterprising pioneers who laid the foundation for commercial agriculture, the "green gold" of California.[8] Through all-male partnership households, composed of several to a dozen members, they created a new form of agriculture. They established farms involving collective manpower and labor intensity. The Chinese reclaimed marginal farmlands and turned them into productive parts of California's food supply apparatus.

The Japanese entered the economy as substitutes for Chinese laborers barred by restrictive legislation. They established retail businesses but faced less favorable economic and social conditions than did their countrymen in Hawaii. The sparseness and dispersion of the Japanese population made for a small, fragmented ethnic market.

Many shopkeepers opened up the same types of businesses the Chinese had found profitable: groceries, laundries, and restaurants.

For most Japanese, however, commercial agriculture became the route of upward mobility. They built upon the work of Chinese farmers who had been instrumental for the development of arable land in the nineteenth century. The steps toward farm ownership began with migratory farm work. Gradually, the laborer was able to save enough to rent farmland. Progress along this entrepreneurial path was rapid. In 1900, only 39 Japanese farmers were recorded in the United States census and they owned less than 5,000 acres. By 1909, 6,000 Japanese farmed under various forms of tenancy, and their total holdings were more than 210,000 acres.

Filipino immigrants, upon their arrival, often went into service occupations in seaport towns. A large contingent later joined the army of migrant farm workers. Along with the "Okies" and the Mexicans, Filipinos constituted the backbone of California's agricultural work force from which the Chinese and Japanese had departed. Korean and Asian Indians augmented these core groups as a supplemental farm labor force.

As versatile low-skilled labor, the Japanese, Koreans, Asian Indians, and Filipinos helped complete the transformation of the rural economy begun by the Chinese. They were indispensable in consolidating the commercial food supply system and the infrastructure for supporting urban population growth. Their labor enabled agricultural and industrial development to reach mature levels of organization.

Despite their positive effects on regional development, Asian immigrants encountered both legal and customary discrimination. Local laws were passed that made it difficult for Asians to carry on small businesses. Labor unions excluded Asians from membership. In 1913 and 1920 California enacted **Anti-Alien land laws** barring "aliens ineligible for citizenship"—all Asian immigrants—from purchasing and leasing agricultural land. These laws were aimed chiefly at Japanese farmers. Asians, however, found ways to circumvent and to compensate for these obstacles.

### Sojourner Society to Middleman Minority

In the United States, the Chinese and Japanese moved in the early twentieth century toward increasing ethnic solidarity and compartmentalization in the surrounding society. They evolved into an American version of a global ethnic phenomenon known as **middleman minorities.** Marx, Simmel, Weber, and Toennies identified this phenomenon. Social scientists have found many examples of such groups, including the Jews in Europe, the Chinese in Southeast Asia, Asian Indians in East Africa, Arabs in West Africa, and Armenians in Turkey. Although they varied in group history and circumstances, they shared a number of compelling similarities.[9]

Middleman minorities were social buffers positioned between indigenous elite strata and the populace, facing considerable hostility from both. Their exclusion was marked by a visible difference such as race. They lacked political power and were dependent upon the controllers of political power. In the United States, the Chinese and Japanese possessed these features.

To a large extent, middleman groups were economic intermediaries, agents distributing the flow of various products and services to consumers. The Chinese and Japanese roles in agricultural commerce, shopkeeping, and personal service had this quality. They were positioned functionally between the producer-owner capitalist class and the working class. This positioning corresponded with intensifying settlement in urban centers. Their isolated social position made the Chinese and Japanese seek economic resources that outsiders could not take away from them. They concentrated on self-employment, the building of human capital, and savings through thrift and underconsumption. They had to look for underoccupied or underdeveloped economic opportunities. This gave them an enterprising and resourceful appearance.

Asians also deviated from the general form of a middleman group in that they assumed important roles as primary rural producers. The Chinese and Japanese engaged in farming, mining, and fishing as independent operators.

Like many middleman groups, the Chinese and Japanese communities sprang from immigration. They maintained connections with their homelands through commerce, return migration, and the sending of remittances. They constituted themselves as a separate community by maintaining a different institutional life and culture. Chinese and Japanese set up separate language schools, practiced ancestor worship, sent children back to Asia for education, and stressed marriage within the group. They transplanted mutual-benefit organizations based on suprafamilial local ties such as the Chinese *hui*, the Korean *kye,* and the Japanese *kenjinkai* and *tanomoshi*. These bodies performed mutual assistance and protection, giving the impression that Chinese and Japanese made progress without reliance on outside aid. These tactics reinforced concepts of group honor and pride.

### Sojourner Society to Insular Ethnic Groups: The Case of Hawaii

In Hawaii, the social structure precluded the evolution of Asians into middleman minorities. As the demographic majority, they constituted the middle class and working class of the community and dominated its social life. They achieved political power through labor organizing and mass party politics.[10] As groups they were not small, politically powerless, and isolated in the middle. They were a principal part of the core of society.

In Hawaii, integration along class lines defined the Chinese and Japanese communities, rather than castelike isolation.[11] The assimilating Koreans reinforced this pattern. The Hawaiian pattern of Asian demographic takeover and class integration resembled those of European immigrant communities after two generations in eastern industrial cities.

### Sojourner Society: Filipino Americans

Filipino communities in the early twentieth century resembled Chinese sojourner communities of the nineteenth century. They were marked by an almost complete absence of women and family life. In Hawaii, the Filipino population persisted on plantations. For Filipinos, who had come latest, the movement to urban jobs and livings was rendered more difficult by the need to compete with preestablished Chinese and Japanese. On the mainland, the annual cycle of transient farm labor migration periodically dissolved communities. Hardly any Filipinos entered the industrial labor force because of the historic tradition of Asian exclusion by unions.

The Filipinos did not establish a mechanism for chain migration like the picture bride system used by the Japanese and Koreans. Like early Chinese rural communities, Filipino communities were evanescent because of the lack of generational succession through family life. The male-to-female ratio was the highest of any ethnic population. In Hawaii, it was 80 to 1 among single Filipinos in 1935; in the United States it was 14 to 1 for the entire Filipino population in 1930. Antimiscegenation laws in the states prevented intermarriage as a way of building families.

### The Beginnings of Metropolitan Society

World War II marked a crucial turning point. The reorganization of community accelerated and took different forms for different groups. In one of the greatest miscarriages of constitutional justice ever, over 110,000 Japanese Americans, two-thirds of whom were U.S. citizens, were evicted and incarcerated, and interned in concentration camps on the false charge that they were disloyal to the United States. The internment destroyed the ghetto communities and the domination of immigrant leaders.

The sojourner society of Filipino Americans also began to show signs of change. In both Hawaii and the United States, the **Tydings-McDuffie Act** of 1934 discouraged return migration to the Philippines because Filipinos knew that the small annual immigrant quota of 50 practically ruled out return to U.S. territory. The law had been designed to keep Filipinos out, but it also kept in a core group that created a permanent community. It stabilized the Filipino community, beginning its changeover from a throwback to nineteenth-century Chinese communities into a permanent and continuously evolving ethnic community. Gradually, family life and permanent settlement were achieved.

After the end of the war, the momentum of change continued. The Japanese found that the climate of persecution had relaxed when they returned to California. As arriving settlers, they were like the newcomers from all over the nation being reshuffled into new communities in California. Policymakers and the public they represented no longer urged persecution of the Japanese. There was even a limited effort at compensating Japanese Americans for the property losses they suffered when they were hastily evicted. In the 1950s, they entered employment fields from which they had been completely excluded before the war. The new American-born leaders stressed assimilation. Rapid mobility in savings, occupation, and education pushed the Nisei into the mainstream of society.

While the Japanese were imprisoned and dispossessed, the Chinese experienced favorable publicity as allies and encountered new opportunties. The war-stimulated demand for industrial manpower opened up jobs outside the Chinatown service economy. Surveying this shift in economic opportunities, a historian noted, "The war indeed gave a new economic beginning to Chinese-American society."[12] Chinese Americans gained employment in shipyards and factories, offices and laboratories. Of special importance was the formation of a nucleus of professionals in the sciences and professions, particularly in engineering, who would lead the new suburban middle class after the war. Moreover, the draft itself helped expose Chinese men to new opportunities. In New York City, 40 percent of the Chinese population, the highest proportion of any nationality group, served in the military.[13] They acquired new training and skills in the armed forces. They used this education as a stepping stone to better jobs. Finally, Chinese immigration within the regular admissions system was started again during wartime. In 1943, a token annual quota of 105 was allotted to China as a good will gesture to an ally. After the war, various displaced persons and war brides acts permitted the migration of Chinese women. The second generation expanded in the Chinese community as the sex ratio achieved more balance. They received the resources of parents who had experienced a boost in opportunity during World War II.

In Hawaii, the Chinese, Japanese, and Koreans moved further into the middle class, and Filipinos began to get a foothold there too. Ethnic social mobility gained expression in the drive for statehood, which culminated successfully in 1959. Chinese and Japanese Americans were elected among Hawaii's first federal representatives. Hiram Fong became the first Chinese American U.S. senator, and Daniel Inouye became the first Japanese American U.S. congressman.

Postwar America was a time of new opportunities for all Asian Americans. The rise out of the "middleman minority" after World War II resembled the movement of Jews out of ghettos in nineteenth-century Europe. For decades, Asians had been ostracized and circumscribed legally. They had built up an enormous reserve of pent-up ambition. They had accumulated the human capital of education, resourcefulness, and organizational discipline.

In 1952 Congress finally lifted the ban against the naturalization of Asian-born immigrants. The elderly flocked to the courts to gain certificates of citizenship. For the first time, the immigrant generation was enfranchised. It was an important symbol of the changes under way.

## THE SECOND WAVE
## OF ASIAN IMMIGRATION

After World War II, token allotments to Asian nations, special refugee admissions, and family reunification for war brides opened the door once more to large numbers of Asian immigrants. With the passage of the Hart-Celler Act of 1965, which reopened regular admissions from Asia, Asian communities received the first mass infusion of newcomers since the early twentieth century.

Asians grew noticeably as a share in the official migrations of the 1970s. In that decade, 1.5 million Asian immigrants entered this country, while European immigrants totaled only 840,000 and documented Mexican immigrants 624,000. In the 1970s, most Asians came from the Philippines and Korea. The dominant position of the Japanese and Chinese population eroded as the Filipino and Korean communities grew faster from accelerating immigration.

Before 1965 Asian immigration came almost wholly from five areas: China, Japan, Korea, the Philippines, and the Indian subcontinent. Korea and India had contributed only a very small flow. After 1965, mass immigration came from all these countries. Koreans and immigrants from the new nations of the Indian subcontinent—India, Bangladesh, and Pakistan—became among the fastest growing groups. The nations of Indochina—Thailand, Laos, Cambodia, and Vietnam—also became the source of a huge new influx (Table 19-5). Smaller streams were added as well from Indonesia, Burma, Pakistan, Sri Lanka, Singapore, and Malaysia. Many Asian immigrants came from locations outside of their original homelands. Chinese and Hindus from the West Indies, for example, migrated to the United States.

Despite its multiple sources, the new influx was composed of three basic elements. First, a substantial flow of poor, low-skilled immigrants entered the country. Chinatowns, especially New York City's, were flooded by newcomers seeking jobs in the service and sweatshop economy. Second, a human-capital migration of highly educated newcomers, members of homeland elites, grew large. Physicians and nurses were heavily represented in the arrivals from the Philippines, Korea, Pakistan, and India. According to one study, the majority of Pakistani male immigrants had a university or professional education, and 90 percent of recent Indian arrivals were classified as

"professional/technical workers" and their dependents. In addition, many foreign students adjusted their status to permanent residency. Third, refugees fleeing revolution, war, and political persecution entered in unprecedented numbers.

The swelling tide of refugees included Chinese, Vietnamese, Cambodians, and Laotians, as well as ethnic Chinese from Vietnam and the Hmong people of Laos. Over 200,000 Asian refugees arrived in the 1970s; from 1981 to 1986, half a million more established new homes in the United States. The refugees experienced a difficult transition to American life. They were thrust suddenly into American conditions after enormous hardships and with little preparation.

Within each of these three broad categories, chain migration of family members enlarged the Asian influx. Immigration policy afforded naturalized citizens the right to bring family members over annual visa limitations. Asians took full advantage of this feature of immigration law and enhanced their numbers.

As a result, a related aspect of the newest immigration from Asia became the growing representation of women. Whereas women made up only a minuscule share of immigrants from Asia before World War II, they have equaled the numbers of men since 1965. Family formation and reunification through the growth of female immigration showed that second-wave Asian newcomers intended to settle permanently. Return migration, so prominent in the first wave, was comparatively small.

**TABLE 19-5. Asian Immigration to the United States by Country of Birth, 1961–1988 (in thousands)**

| Country | 1961–1970 | 1971–1980 | 1981–1988 |
|---|---|---|---|
| Cambodia | 1.2 | 8.4 | 105.3 |
| China (Mainland and Taiwan) | 96.7 | 202.5 | 295.5 |
| Hong Kong | 25.6 | 47.5 | 43.8 |
| India | 31.2 | 176.8 | 200.0 |
| Japan | 38.5 | 47.9 | 32.7 |
| Korea | 35.8 | 272.0 | 272.3 |
| Laos | 0.1 | 22.6 | 122.7 |
| Philippines | 101.5 | 360.2 | 374.5 |
| Thailand | 5.0 | 44.1 | 46.2 |
| Vietnam | 4.6 | 179.7 | 314.9 |

*Source:* Compiled from *Statistical Abstract of the United States, 1990*, Table 7, p. 10.

## METROPOLITAN SOCIETY IN THE AGE OF NEW IMMIGRATION, 1965 TO THE PRESENT

The second-wave immigrants made up the first large and regular influx of Asians since the early twentieth century. They changed the character of Asian ethnic communities. Families multiplied, and a new generation of the children of immigrants were coming of age in the 1980s. In a reversal of prewar demographic patterns, expanding new families submerged the fossilized, elderly male populations. Korean, Filipino, and southeast Asian communities reflected a similar infusion. The decadal growth rate of the Chinese population climbed from 58 percent in 1950–1960 to 85 percent in 1970–1980 (Table 19-6A). In the same interval, the decadal growth rate of the Filipino population rose from 44 percent to 126 percent. The one exception was the Japanese population, which displayed a declining rate of growth. The Filipino and Korean population increased chiefly from immigration. From 1970 to 1980, the Filipino foreign-born population grew 171 percent and the Korean 649 percent (Table 19-6B). The urban population of each group grew faster than the total population (Table 19-6C). Asian Americans settled out of the historic zone of settlement in Hawaii and the West Coast (Table 19-6D). States like New York, New Jersey, Maryland, Illinois, and Texas began to exhibit some of the most sizable concentrations of Asians (Table 19-6E). From 1950 to 1980, the share of total population in the Far West shrank among Chinese from 64 to 50 percent, among Japanese from 87 to 77 percent, and among Filipinos from 86 to 67 percent. By 1980, only 39 percent of all Koreans lived in the Far West. Asian Americans were growing from a regional ethnic population to an increasingly national one.

The new immigration formed pockets of poverty, especially among displaced peoples from southeast Asia. For the 150,000 Vietnamese who came from 1975 to 1980, their ordeal as refugees had been an immense setback. The majority were from educated, urban backgrounds and had strong historic ties to French and American culture, but arriving in destitution they faced a new, hard struggle against poverty and powerlessness. Ethnic Chinese formed a substantial part of the wave from Vietnam.

The Cambodians and Laotians represented a broader social cross-section than the Vietnamese. Many came from poor, rural backgrounds and had little education. Cambodians and Laotians congregated not only in the major metropolitan centers, but also in rural regions and smaller towns. Because their relocation was aided by the government, they were resented for adding to the burdens of welfare.

Some Asian communities were divided by heightened social class divisions. The Chinese community became more sharply split between the middle class and the working class. In New York State, the destination of the poorest Chinese newcomers, Chinese males earned only 58 percent of the median annual income of their white counterparts. The less educated newcomers struggled to forge ahead in Chinatowns. Poor children were pressured to sacrifice schooling for early labor market entry. They exhibited high dropout rates and poor academic performance.[14]

Social mobility, nevertheless, occurred on two fronts. On one front, descendants of first-wave Asian immigrants consolidated their middle-class position and were moving into its upper strata. Their mobility was the product of progress over the span of three or four generations.[15] Education became the chief means of raising income and occupational position (Table 19-7). In 1970, before the arrival of highly educated new immigrants, the Japanese, Chinese, Filipino, and Korean median level of education included some amount of college education. Their mean years of schooling and rate of high school graduation exceeded the averages for whites. On the second front, college-educated, newly arrived immigrants made rapid and impressive economic gains. Many, however, had to take a detour toward small-shopkeeping or lower skilled employment because the language barrier and lack of certification did not allow them to pursue their professions.

Annual family incomes and median male incomes for Asians in both California

**TABLE 19-6.  Demographic Aspects of Asian American Ethnic Groups, 1950–1980**

### A. Total Population in United States (Including Hawaii), 1950–1980

|  | 1950 | 1960 | 1970 | 1980 |
|---|---|---|---|---|
| Chinese, total | 150,005 | 237,292 | 435,062 | 806,040 |
| Percentage increase |  | 58 | 83 | 85 |
| Japanese, total | 326,379 | 464,332 | 591,290 | 700,974 |
| Percentage increase |  | 42 | 27 | 19 |
| Filipino, total | 122,707 | 176,310 | 343,060 | 774,652 |
| Percentage increase |  | 44 | 95 | 126 |
| Korean, total | NA | NA | 69,510 | 354,593 |
| Percentage increase | NA | NA | NA | 410 |

### B. Percentage Increase In Native-Born and Foreign-Born Populations, 1970–1980

|  | Chinese | Japanese | Filipino | Korean |
|---|---|---|---|---|
| Native-born | 103 | 6 | 85 | 110 |
| Foreign-born | 66 | 84 | 171 | 649 |

### C. Percentage Increase in Urban Populations (Standard Metropolitan Statistical Areas), 1970–1980

|  | Chinese | Japanese | Filipino | Korean |
|---|---|---|---|---|
| New York City | 105 | 40 | 302 | 673 |
| San Francisco | 91 | 98 | 214 | NA |
| Honolulu | 9 | 12 | 49 | 89 |
| Los Angeles | 179 | 29 | 268 | 758 |
| Chicago | 90 | 3 | 241 | NA |

### D. Percentage of Population in Far West (California, Oregon, Washington, Hawaii)

|  | Chinese | Japanese | Filipino | Korean |
|---|---|---|---|---|
| 1950 | 64 | 87 | 86 | NA |
| 1960 | 60 | 82 | 81 | NA |
| 1970 | 54 | 77 | 72 | NA |
| 1980 | 50 | 77 | 67 | 39 |

### E. States With Largest Asian American Populations

|  | 1950 |  | 1980 |  |
|---|---|---|---|---|
| Chinese | 1. California | 58,000 | 1. California | 322,300 |
|  | 2. Hawaii | 32,000 | 2. New York | 148,000 |
|  | 3. New York | 20,000 | 3. Hawaii | 56,000 |
|  | 4. Illinois | 4,200 | 4. Illinois | 29,000 |
|  | 5. Massachusetts | 3,600 | 5. Texas | 25,000 |
| Japanese | 1. Hawaii | 184,600 | 1. California | 262,000 |
|  | 2. California | 85,000 | 2. Hawaii | 240,000 |
|  | 3. Illinois | 11,600 | 3. Washington | 26,000 |
|  | 4. Washington | 9,700 | 4. New York | 25,000 |
|  | 5. Colorado | 5,400 | 5. Illinois | 19,000 |

**TABLE 19-6.    Continued**

### E. States With Largest Asian American Populations

| | | 1950 | | | 1980 |
|---|---|---|---|---|---|
| Filipinos | 1. Hawaii | 61,000 | 1. California | 358,000 |
| | 2. California | 40,400 | 2. Hawaii | 134,000 |
| | 3. Washington | 4,300 | 3. Illinois | 44,000 |
| | 4. New York | 3,700 | 4. New York | 34,000 |
| | 5. NA | | 5. New Jersey | 24,000 |
| Koreans | 1. Hawaii | | 1. California | 104,000 |
| | 2. NA | | 2. New York | 34,000 |
| | 3. NA | | 3. Illinois | 24,000 |
| | 4. NA | | 4. Maryland | 15,000 |
| | 5. NA | | 5. Texas | 14,000 |

### F. Percentage of Outmarriages Among Japanese Americans, Los Angeles County, 1924–1972

| Year | Percentage Marrying a non-Japanese |
|---|---|
| 1924–1933 | 2 |
| 1948 | 12 |
| 1959 | 23 |
| 1972 | 49 |

**TABLE 19-7.    Levels of Schooling among Persons 25 Years and Older in Asian Ethnic Groups and the White Population, 1970 and 1980**

| Group | Percentage Graduated from High School | Median Years of School |
|---|---|---|
| **1970** | | |
| Japanese | 68.8 | 12.5 |
| Chinese | 57.8 | 12.4 |
| Filipino | 54.7 | 12.2 |
| Korean | 71.1 | 12.9 |
| White | 54.5 | 12.1 |
| **1980** | | |
| Japanese | 81.6 | 12.9 |
| Chinese | 71.3 | 13.4 |
| Filipino | 74.2 | 14.1 |
| Korean | 78.1 | 13.0 |
| Asian Indian | 80.1 | 16.1 |
| Vietnamese | 62.2 | 12.4 |
| White | 68.8 | 12.5 |

*Source:* Compiled from U.S. Census Bureau, *Population Reports: Summary, 1980,* and *Subject Report 1G,,* 1970.

and New York, the two states with the largest Asian American populations, showed a tendency to rise in comparison with white income levels from 1970 to 1980, except in the case of the Chinese in New York State (Table 19-8). By 1980 Japanese Americans in California had a median family income of $27,000, and Chinese American families earned $24,000, as contrasted with $23,000 for whites. The higher family incomes of some groups was due to the fact that their median annual income for males was higher than for white males. Japanese and Asian Indian men in both California and New York ranked above their white counterparts in income in 1980, thus raising their family incomes above that of whites. The leading rate of male income among the Japanese was attributable to three or four generations of cumulative investment in career education; the unusual annual income for Indian males derived from the heavy representa-

**TABLE 19-8. Median Annual Income as Percentage of White Annual Income, Asian American Males and Families in California and New York, 1970 and 1980**

| | 1970 | | 1980 | |
|---|---|---|---|---|
| Ethnic Group | Male | Family | Male | Family |
| *California:* | | | | |
| Japanese | 112 | 110 | 120 | 120 |
| Chinese | 74 | 99 | 92 | 107 |
| Korean | 85 | NA | 91 | 91 |
| Filipino | 85 | 83 | 81 | 104 |
| Asian Indian | NA | NA | 112 | 114 |
| *New York:* | | | | |
| Japanese | 106 | 110 | 158 | 139 |
| Chinese | 58 | 75 | 58 | 74 |
| Korean | NA | NA | 92 | 92 |
| Filipino | 83 | 107 | 98 | 129 |
| Asian Indian | NA | NA | 104 | 105 |

*Source:* Computed from U.S. Bureau of the Census, *Population Reports* for California and New York, 1970, 1980, and *Subject Reports* on Asian Americans, 1970, 1980.

tion of professionals in health care and technology among recent immigrants. The annual incomes of Chinese males in New York and Filipino males in California, however, lagged behind those of white males. But among these Chinese and Filipino subpopulations family income was closer to the level of white income. The low rate of annual male earnings was probably compensated for by increasing the number of workers in the family, usually through the employment of a spouse.

The social mobility of Asian Americans provoked a backlash among native-born whites and minorities who were struggling economically. Boycotts, intimidation, and violence were directed toward Korean shopkeepers operating in inner-city areas. Some natives felt anxious about the resurgence of Asian immigration and vaguely connected it with dangerous economic competition from Japan, South Korea, and Taiwan. Often seen unsympathetically as benefici-aries of welfare, refugees encountered hostility and ostracism.

Recently, the longer settled parts of the Asian American population have exhibited the declining rate of fertility and natural increase characteristic of the white population. The Chinese and Japanese rates of natural increase fell like that of whites in the late twentieth century (Table 19-3) Their fertility has declined to drop below the rate of native whites (Table 19-4) (see Chapter 18). Low death rates rather than high birth rates accounted for natural increase among Asians. In the first half of the twentieth century, Asian American groups underwent a kind of "catch-up" convergence with the metropolitan norm of the nuclear family and have settled securely into this pattern.

Social scientists pointed to Asian American social mobility and demographic convergence as evidence for the decline of overt discrimination. The Japanese American community in the late twentieth century especially approximated the assimilated stage achieved by European immigrant groups such as the Jews, Armenians, and Germans. Its features were shaped by four to five generations of cumulative social mobility and acculturation. By 1980 Japanese Americans had achieved an annual family income 20 percent higher than the average for whites in California. Over 81 percent had graduated from high school, and the median level of education included a year of college. Japanese Americans were dispersed residentially in middle-class suburbs. They had a longer life expectancy than the average for the country at large. Their rate of political participation in voting and office holding was increasing.

Japanese Americans, like the white population, experienced a slowing rate of population growth. Their rate of natural increase shrank to its lowest historical levels since large numbers of marriageable females arrived after World War I (Table 19-3). Frequent intermarriage (prevented earlier in the century by preference for within-group marriage and antimiscegenation laws) depleted the ranks of the next generation who would have total Japanese American ancestry. In Los Angeles by 1959, the share of Japanese marrying outside the group climbed to 23 percent, and in 1972 it reached 49 percent. In San Francisco and Hawaii the intermarriage rate was over 50 percent. Most of the marriages involved white spouses; next in frequency were marriages to Chinese spouses.[16] The population did not receive a large wave of new immigrants. Since there was little reforeignization of culture, widespread absorption of normal popular culture proceeded. As in the case of American Jews, Japanese Americans began to express concern that they were a disappearing ethnic group as a result of effective assimilation.

## ETHNIC SOLIDARITY AND HISTORIC MOBILITY STRATEGIES

### Mutualism and Group Discipline

**Mutualism**—the ascribed forms of interdependent relations between individuals—was a premigration cultural form that was transplanted to American conditions, where it performed as a system of both economic and social discipline. Asians organized to help out kinfolk and countrymen through sharing and mutual aid. The organizational principles of Asian mutualism made economic progress less an individual enterprise than a collective and cooperative enterprise. Japanese immigrants believed progress was the result of group solidarity, whereas poverty was the result of individualism.[17] This approach to mobility was not unique. Historians have shown that European immigrants orchestrated kin and ethnic ties to organize in a cooperative, collective way for economic gain.

Perhaps the signal embodiment of economic mutualism was the rotating credit associations that Asian immigrants used to raise capital to start a small business or to sponsor a child's education. These arrangements, consisting of several partners who combined their savings to create a pool for borrowing, often based on geographic and linguistic ties, were called the *hui* by the Chinese, the *tanomoshi* by the Japanese, and the *kye* by the Koreans.

Asian economic mutualism before World War II was affected by the absence of viable alternatives. Central arenas for individual economic mobility open to white Americans were closed to Asians. Thus they had to remain within the discipline of the group and its mutualist economy. And dependence or lack of options made the power of the group to extract cooperation and self-sacrifice enormous. External discrimination did not subside to permit wider contacts until after World War II. Thereafter, extreme dependence on mutualism relaxed.

The Confucian system of familism disciplined, socialized, assigned roles, and distributed resources. It resembled European immigrant familism in its emphasis on collective welfare and interdependence between family members. This focus promoted capital accumulation to provide for the continuation of the lineage.

### Economic Strategies: Work, Savings, and Education

Early exclusion from industrial occupations and unions encouraged Asians to develop an expertise in small business. They developed both urban and rural enterprises. Chinese, Japanese, and Korean immigrants owned and managed commercial farms and retail stores. Premigration experience most likely prepared these immigrants for entrepreneurial roles. Commercial practices and attitudes were highly evolved in homeland areas of southern China and Japan.

An Asian American equivalent of the Protestant work ethic existed. It had roots in the imperatives of familial duty, religious asceticism, and the labor-intensive traditions of Asian agriculture. Chinese and Japanese families operated on the principle of labor intensity. All family members were expected to work. In 1979 Asian American families more often than white families had two or even three income earners. Chinese and Japanese immigrants were willing to work long hours or even hold onto two full-time jobs. Employees in small businesses put in very long hours. Recent Korean newcomers have gained reputations for labor intensity in small shopkeeping, with family members working 12 to 16 hours at a stretch in their stores. Among all groups, the general tactic to increase income was to multiply the number of earners and extend work periods.[18]

The work ethic intermeshed with an Asian **savings ethic.** From the earliest Chinese and Japanese sojourners, Asians exercised enormous restraint on expenditure. Recent immigrants from south Asia such as the Indochinese and Asian Indians also practiced the careful husbandry taught by the economic conditions of stringency and scarcity in Asia.

A key aspect of Asian economic adaptation has been an overriding commitment to intergenerational mobility. **Intergenerational mobility strategies** relied on building a secure economic base and using marginal savings to invest in education. A sufficient level of economic mobility was thus required to pay for advanced schooling.[19] Asians subscribed to the belief, also held by groups such as the Jews and Armenians, that education was the route to the best occupations.

A high proportion of late-twentieth-century immigrants from Asia entered the country with professional training or capital that provided rapid availability of resources to invest in their children's schooling. Thus the children of Chinese, Korean, Asian Indian, Pakistani, Bangladeshi, and Filipino professionals and businessmen entered the market for higher education quickly, augmenting the exceptional numbers of Asian American students in leading colleges and universities. Even the children of Vietnamese refugees with few material resources have begun to exhibit unusual achievement in education, garnering the top positions in their graduating secondary classes and progressing toward elite colleges. The prize of education impelled parents to make sacrifices and gave their children enormous motivation to do well in school. These attitudes were extensions of premigration culture, particularly of Asian groups from Confucian-based societies. Highly educated elite newcomers placed a premium on schooling out of their social-class culture as well as deeply rooted traditions.

Through mutual aid, labor intensity, disciplined saving, sponsorship of education, and an emphasis on intergenerational mobility deeply rooted in group experiences, Asians made advances with the gradual growth of opportunities in the United States. Today, the newest arrivals show signs that they are beginning to travel these well-worn steps.

## SUMMARY

1. Asian immigration was the first mass migration to the United States from outside Europe. The first wave occurred in a series of bursts from the end of the nineteenth century to the early twentieth century, because of the sequential recruitment of immigrant labor from China, Japan, Korea, the Philippines, and India. Discriminatory restrictive laws limited the period of free migration from these Asian countries.

2. Asian immigration in the last half of the twentieth century—the second wave—represented a far larger share of total immigration than in the industrial era. Asian immigration has become increasingly diversified in both occupational and ethnic background. A human-capital migration of educated elites has flowed into the United States at the same time that refugees and laborers have arrived.

3. Asian immigrants helped to make the primary development of western rural society an enabling condition for secondary urban-industrial development. The Chinese were the first supply of

migratory labor to help start up economic change. The Japanese, Koreans, Filipinos, and Asian Indians helped complete—as a supplementary labor force—the transition to a mature regional infrastructure. In Hawaii, Asian immigrants supplied the labor for large-scale agricultural production. Recent Asian immigration has supplied an entrepreneurial and highly trained middle class vital for postindustrial economic development. But it also brought a new wave of workers who replenished the low-skilled and service labor sector.

4.   Asian immigrants who arrived in the industrial era—the Chinese, Japanese, Koreans, and Filipinos—demonstrated the capacity to achieve significant mobility over time. Industrial and agricultural workers achieved economic movement through reskilling and small-scale entrepreneurialism. A substantial fraction of the sons and daughters of first-wave immigrants gained more education, acquired more property, and were able to move into better jobs than their parents. Each successive generation has obtained further socioeconomic improvements, by and large.

5.   As an immigrant group, Asians were able to transplant communal and self-help institutions, giving them an organizational advantage in maximizing productivity and social cohesion. Institutions like the *hui*, the *tanomoshi*, the *kye*, and the Confucian code of behavior were typically traditional and rural cultural forms, but they proved effective in an industrializing America.

6.   The tactics for achieving social development included mutual assistance, labor intensity, financial husbandry, education, and the commitment to intergenerational social mobility.

7.   The social and economic development of Asian groups was multifaceted and went forward in stages because of the variety of groups, their subpopulations, and their times of arrival. Social inequality existed among Asians and between Asians and whites. Educational and economic advances though generally above average in magnitude and pace have not been uniform. A clear historic trend emerged among first-wave Asian groups: a rapid transition from a frontier rural mode of social life featuring the absence of families, labor intensity, proletarianization, transiency, and illiteracy to a metropolitan mode based on nuclear families, higher education, white-collar employment, and high per capita family resources. In this general changeover, first-wave Asian groups paralleled European immigrant groups, but it took longer to achieve and the most notable advances came in recent changes.

8.   Before World War II, the social mobility of Asians was distorted and limited by ostracism and discrimination exceeding that confronting the European immigrant. Since then, the universalizing of equal opportunity in the United States has permitted Asian newcomers to advance with more consistency and alacrity. However, competition with achieving Asian groups produced new anxieties and prejudices toward Asians among native whites and minorities. Asian immigration has revealed the changing possibilities for creating a more inclusive society out of elements widely separated by race and culture.

## KEY CONCEPTS FOR REVIEW

Aliens ineligible for citizenship
"Sojourner"
"Picture bride system"
Issei
Nisei
Chinese Exclusion Act
Tydings-McDuffie Act
Middleman minorities
*Hui*

*Kenjinkai*
*Tanomoshi*
*Kye*
Mutualism
Savings ethic
Gentlemen's Agreement
Anti-Alien land laws
Intergenerational mobility strategies

## QUESTIONS FOR DISCUSSION

1. Asian immigration occurred in two separate waves. Compare and contrast the characteristics of the first and second wave. Describe the migration of sojourners, women, post-World War II human-capital migrants, and refugees.

2. Why were Asian immigrants so useful in the development of the Far Western economy? Compare the roles of the Chinese, Japanese, Koreans, Filipinos, and Asian Indians in industrial and agricultural labor.

3. What endeavors served as major avenues of social mobility for Asians? Discuss the role of small business enterprise and the sponsorship of advanced schooling. How did Asians employ traditional ethics and institutions such as the family and mutual benefit associations?

4. As they developed over time, Asian communities went through different forms of social organization. Compare the distinctive features of sojourner society, Asian society in Hawaii, middleman minority society on the mainland, and metropolitan society.

5. Immigration and social mobility were hampered by anti-Asian discriminatory laws and customs. Describe the restrictionist policies toward Asian immigration, the ban on the naturalization of Asian immigrants, and the obstacles to full economic and social opportunities. Why was it difficult to form families? How did the internment of Japanese Americans during World War II affect the development of this ethnic group?

6. How has the social structure and composition of the Asian population changed since World War II? Describe the social and ethnic changes brought about by the second wave of immigration. Describe the social mobility and patterns of integration among the descendants of first-wave immigrants such as the Japanese Americans. To what extent has opportunity expanded and overt discrimination declined?

## NOTES

1. Figures for Asian immigration to the United States were compiled from the statistical tables of U.S. Bureau of Immigration, *Annual Reports*, various years. Immigration totals to Hawaii were obtained from Eleanor Nordyke, *The Peopling of Hawaii*, 2nd ed. (Honolulu: University of Hawaii Press, 1989).

2. Lucy Cheng and Edna Bonacich, *Labor Immigration under Capitalism: Asian Workers in the United States before World War II* (Berkeley: University of California Press, 1984), pp. 27–28.

3. Gunther Barth, *Bitter Strength: A History of the Chinese in the United States, 1850–1870* (Cambridge, Mass.: Harvard University Press, 1964); Yuji Ichioka, *The Issei: The World of the First Generation Japanese Immigrants, 1885–1924* (New York: The Free Press, 1988), p. 46.

4. Alan Moriyama, "The Causes of Emigration: The Background of Japanese Emigration to Hawaii, 1885–1894," in Cheng and Bonacich, *Labor Immigration under Capitalism*, pp. 268–270.

5. Mary Roberts Coolidge, *Chinese Immigration* (New York: Henry Holt and Company, 1909), p. 359.

6. Roger Daniels, *Asian America: Chinese and Japanese in the United States since 1850* (Seattle: University of Washington Press, 1988), pp. 75–81.

7. Him Mark Lai, "Chinese," in Stephan Thernstrom, ed., *Harvard Encyclopedia of American Ethnic Groups* (Cambridge, Mass.: Harvard University Press, 1980).

8. Sucheng Chan, *This Bittersweet Soil: The Chinese in California Agriculture, 1860–1910* (Berkeley: University of California Press, 1986).

9. Edna Bonacich and John Modell, *The Economic Basis of Ethnic Solidarity: Small Business in the Japanese American Community* (Berkeley: University of California Press, 1980), Chap. 2.

10. Lawrence H. Fuchs, *Hawaii Pono: A Social History* (New York: Harcourt, Brace, Jovanovich, 1981).

11. Ronald T. Takaki, *Pau Hana: Plantation Life and Labor in Hawaii, 1835–1920* (Honolulu: University of Hawaii Press, 1983).

12. Shih-shan Henry Tsai, *The Chinese Experience in America* (Bloomington, Ind.: University of Indiana Press, 1986), p. 117.

13. Peter Kwong, *Chinatown, New York: Labor and Politics, 1930–1950* (New York: Monthly Review Press, 1979), pp. 114–115.

14. Peter Kwong, *The New Chinatown* (New York: Hill and Wang, 1987), Chaps. 2, 4.

15. Bonacich and Modell, *The Economic Basis of Ethnic Solidarity*, Chap. 15.

16. Akemi Kikumura and Harry H. L. Kitano, "Interracial Marriage: A Picture of the Japanese

Americans," *Journal of Social Issues, 29*, 1973, pp. 67–81; John N. Tinker, "Intermarriage and Ethnic Boundaries: The Japanese American Case," *Journal of Social Issues, 29*, 1973, pp. 49–66.

17. S. Frank Miyamoto, *Social Solidarity among the Japanese in Seattle* (Seattle: University of Washington Press, 1939); Ivan Light, *Ethnic Enterprise in America: Business and Welfare Among Chinese, Japanese, and Blacks* (Berkeley: University of California Press, 1972), Chaps. 4, 5, 9.

18. Thomas Sowell, *Ethnic America: A History* (New York: Basic Books, 1981), p. 177.

19. John Modell, *The Economics and Politics of Racial Accommodation: The Japanese of Los Angeles, 1900–1942* (Urbana: University of Illinois Press, 1977), Chaps. 6, 7.

# 20

# *Have We Decided to Control Our Borders?*

*I*n 1986, after years of debate, revision, delay, inaction, and political infighting, Congress passed the Immigration Reform and Control Act of 1986 (IRCA), the first major piece of immigration legislation since 1965. It was passed with the explicit purpose of reversing a trend through which the United States had "lost control of our borders." Illegal entry into the United States, along with other abuses like overstaying visas and preparing fraudulent documents, had led to a substantial increase in the number of illegal alien residents.

How substantial? No one knew exactly, but whatever the numbers, they were clearly on the rise. In 1986 alone, there were 1.7 million apprehensions of illegal entrants along the U.S.–Mexican border. How many crossed this border without being apprehended or entered the United States by other routes could only be guessed at. At the same time, legal immigration was also on the rise. From under 300,000 immigrants in 1965 when our policies were liberalized, the number had doubled to over 600,000 in 1986.

In the mid-1980s, then, we were facing a situation in which total immigration was growing, where an increasing number of those arriving were doing so illegally, and where a large proportion of the so-called undocumented aliens were from Latin America and from Mexico in particular. They thus formed part of what was already one of the fastest growing minority groups in the nation. Some observers feared that this was just the beginning of a flood that could, under certain future circumstances, become a tidal wave.

The result was IRCA and the attempt to regain control of our borders. In this chapter, we take up the background of this new phase of our immigration policy, asking why we passed this legislation, what the legislation attempts to do, and how successful or unsuccessful it has been during its first years of operation. We shall also consider another major piece of immigration legislation enacted in November 1990. In contrast to the 1986 legislation, this new law was designed to *increase* immigration to the United States, including the entry of more skilled workers.

## HISPANIC DOORS TO THE UNITED STATES

The problem of illegal aliens in the United States is by no means wholly a Hispanic problem, but it is fairly heavily centered in the northward migration of Mexicans and Central Americans. It was estimated in 1987 that 60 percent of undocumented residents of the United States were from Mexico; a fairly large number come from Central American countries like El Salvador and Guatemala; South American countries, like Colombia, add a smaller but still appreciable number. Clearly, the Mexican border has been a central focus of concern.

### "We were here first, gringo!"

A recent book on U.S. immigration policy since 1820 describes it in terms of a number of "doors"—an "open-door" era; a "door-ajar" era; even a "Dutch door" era.[1] In the case of Hispanic and especially that of Mexican immigration, the metaphor is difficult to apply in the early phases of our continental experience because it was really *their* door that *we* were entering. As is well known, the Southwest, California, and Florida were originally discovered and explored by Spaniards. In 1830 it was Mexico that was trying to close the door on immigration—of U.S. citizens into Texas, which was then part of the Mexican state of Coahuila.

In due course, Texas was annexed to the United States (1845). The **Treaty of Guadalupe Hidalgo** at the end of the **Mexican War** (1848) secured California, New Mexico, Nevada, Arizona, Utah, and Colorado for the United States, with the **Gadsden Purchase** (1853) rounding out our southwestern border. In point of obvious historical fact, much of the territory where today's Mexican immigrants, legal or illegal, are now residing was once officially part of Mexico.

Does this historical background have any relevance to today's Hispanic migrations northward? In some ways, it would seem not. The entire Mexican-origin population in the American Southwest in 1848 was probably around 80,000 persons,[2] about one-fifth of the total population of that area. The Mexicans who have come there since have done so voluntarily, and recently, of course, in great numbers. There is no realistic sense then in which one can speak of Mexicans in the United States today as a "conquered" or "colonized" people. The psychological impact of this history on Mexicans may, however, be a bit more complex. It is noteworthy that Mexicans are the least likely among all immigrant groups to become naturalized U.S. citizens after fulfilling legal residency requirements.

### The Swinging Door, 1900–1965

The last half of the nineteenth century saw very little legal Mexican immigration to the United States, although the border at this time was generally unchecked and entry and exit were easily accomplished. In the second decade of the twentieth century, however, legal immigration began to pick up sharply, and in the 1921–1930 period it reached nearly 500,000 Mexicans, over 11 percent of our total legal immigration. As before, there was a great deal of informal coming and going across the border, with few Mexican laborers actually bothering to pay the officially required head tax.[3]

In terms of the "door" analogy, during the first two-thirds of this century, we might think of the U.S. policy toward Mexican immigrants in terms of a **"swinging door."** During World War I and through the 1920s, while the nation was generally restricting immigration (particularly from southern and eastern Europe and from Asia), Mexican workers were actually welcomed in the United States and encouraged to migrate

by Mexico. In the 16 years between 1910 and 1926, the estimated Mexican population in the United States quintupled.

Then, in 1929, the Great Crash ushered in the decade of the Depression, and thousands of Mexicans, including many legally entitled to remain here, were forcibly returned to their homeland. The immigration door, so wide open a few years before, was now suddenly sent swinging in the opposite direction.

Only to be swung open again after December 7, 1941, when the United States, now engaged in World War II, found itself more than eager to find extra laborers for a manpower-poor, production-booming wartime economy. The fall of 1942 saw the first admissions of Mexican farm workers under the so-called **bracero program.** Mexicans were now being formally and legally embraced as useful additions to the U.S. labor force, a program that continued with various modifications through 1964.

But although the door was swinging open at this time, in another sense efforts were soon being made to close it, at least partially. Legal admissions under the bracero program did not meet the desires either of Mexican workers to work in the United States or of U.S. growers and other employers to hire them. Thus, along with expanded legal migration to the United States, we also had greatly expanded illegal entry across the Mexican border. In reaction, the Immigration and Naturalization Service (INS) launched "Operation Wetback" in California and then in Texas in 1954. Almost immediately, the INS proclaimed this operation a success. "The so-called 'wetback' problem no longer exists," it stated in 1955. "The border has been secured."[4]

But this particular door did not remain closed for long. Although the number of apprehended illegals fell for a few years, it began to rise again in the early 1960s. In fact, the nation was just about to enter a period when the number of undocumented aliens would increase dramatically.

### 1965 to 1986

As Figure 20-1 shows, the number of illegal immigrants apprehended between 1965 and 1986 rose sharply—from about 110,000 to 1,670,000. This period saw many other changes on the immigration front as well. There was a rise in legal immigration to the United States, averaging nearly twice as many persons per year in the 1970s and early 1980s as in the 1950s and early 1960s. An increasing percentage of legal immigration was from Latin America, rising from 22.5 percent in the decade of the 1950s to 40.3 percent in the decade of the 1970s. Meanwhile, the bracero program for migrant farm workers had been ended. Refugees had become an important element in our immigration picture, including the 125,000 Cubans exported to the United States by Castro via the Mariel Boatlift in 1980. Family preferences (as opposed to the earlier nations of origin principle) had become a central criterion of our general immigration policy, meaning that once here,

immigrants could soon be followed by large numbers of relatives.

Many of these changes tended to intensify concern about the problem of **illegal immigration.** Our Hispanic population was now growing rapidly. Furthermore, the Mexican economy, once developing quite well, then later propped up by high oil prices, was entering a period of economic disaster. Unemployment was rampant, international debt was growing, the peso was perpetually in decline. In Central America, moreover, war, revolution, and other political and economic disasters seemed endemic. The ending of the bracero program had turned many previously legal entrants into the United States into illegals. The Mariel boatlift, under cover of which Fidel Castro had sent a number of criminals to south Florida, had soured many Americans on our increasing levels of immigration, particularly Hispanic immigration.

Beginning with a spirit of **liberalization,** the period from 1965 to 1986 saw the U.S. public shift increasingly toward concern over our immigration policies. This concern was focused on many different groups— Haitians, Dominicans, Vietnamese, Mariel Cubans, and others—but especially on those millions who, under cover of darkness, were crossing the increasingly porous 2,000 miles of border we shared with Mexico.

## WHY SHOULD THE UNITED STATES HAVE BEEN CONCERNED?

As a nation, we have always proudly declared ourselves a "nation of immigrants." Why then did we not simply welcome this new flow of immigrants, legal or illegal? Some Americans did, and in fact there were advocates of completely open borders for both people and goods as our appropriate policy. Other Americans, however, found a number of problems with such a solution:

*Concern over Controlling Our Borders.* Much of the discussion of the flood of

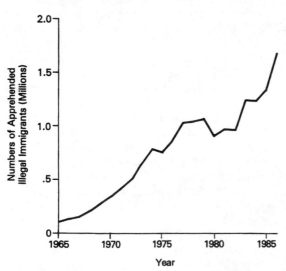

**FIGURE 20-1:   Number of Apprehended Illegal Immigrants, 1965–1986**

*Source:* U.S. Department of Justice, Annual Reports of the Immigration and Naturalization Service.

undocumented aliens was framed in terms of the fact that, as stated by Attorney William French Smith in 1981, "we have lost control of our borders."[5] In a certain sense, there is less to this argument than might appear at first sight. We have already mentioned that one of the reasons for the increase in illegal migrants from Mexico was the fact that we had abolished the bracero program under which many farm workers had entered legally. If, on other grounds, we decided that we wanted more workers from Mexico and other Hispanic nations, we could simply admit them legally, thus rendering the question of border control irrelevant. (This is a bit like solving the illegal drug problem by legalizing drugs.) The counterargument, however, is that under these circumstances the number of legal immigrants would soon soar to impossible levels (in the drug analogy, the number of users would soar), meaning that we would still have to limit border access, raising the national sovereignty issue again. In any event, numerous polls of Americans during the late 1970s and 1980s suggested that a great majority, including a majority of Hispanic Americans, felt that we should gain better control of our borders.

*Population Size and Environmentalism.* However high any legal limit on immigration was set, it was argued (as just noted) that the pressures to enter the United States would exceed that limit and immediately confront us with the illegal alien problem all over again. All legalization would have accomplished would be to raise the general level of migration (legal plus illegal) to this country. The argument was made: (a) that pressures for such large-scale migration already existed and were bound to intensify; and (b) that the United States already had or would soon have a population of sufficient or even excessive overall size. Without control, immigrants would flood in, and such a flood would be harmful to the nation, at least in the long run.

As far as point (a) is concerned, the obvious source of worry was the extremely high rate of population growth exhibited in Mexico, Central America, and, indeed, in the Third World generally. Mexican population had nearly quadrupled between the end of World War II and 1986 (from 22 million to 86 million); Mexico City, with a population of 3 million in 1950, had reached 18 million by 1986, far larger than any North American metropolis. With an economy that seemed to be addicted to corrupt, inefficiently run, state-owned, capital-intensive enterprises, population growth, even though somewhat reduced in the 1980s, still far exceeded job growth. With heavy unemployment, with wages only a fraction of the North American level even for those lucky enough to be employed, Mexico alone seemed capable of supplying millions of job-seeking migrants each year. Adding in the Caribbean, Central America, and the rest of South America (not to mention the refugees and job seekers from other Third World countries), the *potential* inflow dwarfed anything in our historical experience.

And this was happening, or so many commentators argued, when the historic advantages of immigration had disappeared (point (b) above). There were no longer any economies of scale to be gained from further increasing our population size. Furthermore, there were clear environmental *dis*advantages to further population growth—smog, noise, crowding, traffic, toxic wastes. Mexico City itself could stand as an example of what overcrowding does. It has the "most acute traffic and smog problems in the Western Hemisphere. One 1985 study found that the poisonous atmosphere caused 100,000 deaths annually."[6] Since Los Angeles, an important receiving area for Hispanic immigrants, was already failing to meet U.S. clean air standards, how could we even think of allowing further mass immigration to occur?

*Labor Supply Considerations.* Of course, as we noted in the very first chapter of this book, by the mid-1980s some Americans were worried about our below-replacement-level fertility rate and the prospect of future population decline. From their point of view, adding additional Americans either through higher birth rates or through immigration could be counted a blessing rather than a curse. Moreover, the argument could be made that we had a very specific problem facing us where immigration would distinctly help: the predictably low level of young job entrants because of our continuing Baby Bust. The United States would be facing a labor shortage; Mexico and Central America were producing huge labor surpluses; what better solution than to solve both problems through the free flow of labor resources across the border?

There were, however, two important counterarguments to this position. The *first* point was that, in view of the vast differences in wage rates between the United States and Mexico and other Third World countries—differing by a factor of 6, 7, or even 10 to 1—and in view of the vast populations of potential laborers available, the effect of free labor flows into the United States would be to lower our general wage rate substantially, the benefits accruing to the owners of capital and land, already the more well-to-do members of our population.

The *second* point was that since the entering laborers would be generally poorly educated and unskilled, the groups that would be most severely harmed would be similar groups already in the United States, notably other Hispanics, refugees, recent immigrants already here, and American blacks. *Within* the labor force, highly skilled workers might very well be positively affected by this influx of the unskilled, because of the general expansion of demand they bring with them, and/or other factors. Those who stand to be hurt are the poor and unskilled. Walter Fogel wrote in the early 1980s:

> Skilled workers, and those with the ability to advance occupationally, may . . . benefit

from the economic expansion immigration brings. Unskilled workers will suffer harm from their immigrant competitors unless the former possess the abilities and means for job upgrading. . . . It is unconscionable for the U.S. to permit immigration practices that harm the poorest people in the resident population while providing benefits for most others, including particularly large benefits for the owners of capital and land. . . . It is ironic that "free entry" from abroad prevails in the lowest-paid U.S. labor markets, while nearly all the better-paid occupations are protected from entry by qualified foreigners.[7]

In fact, Fogel attributed the high unemployment and low labor force participation of young black males in the 1970s at least in part to the "unsanctioned immigration" of that period.

Of course, these arguments, too, have their counters. Were the illegal aliens of the 1970s and early 1980s really competing with domestic workers, or were they, in fact, simply taking jobs that most Americans, including many black Americans, considered beneath them? Thus, in another study published not long before IRCA was adopted, Mexican scholar Jorge Bustamante wrote:

> The U.S. economy requires unskilled labor; nevertheless, its society is not prepared to produce unskilled labor. The educational system in the United States is based on values and aspirations that make certain jobs undesirable. Thus even with the high levels of unemployment in the United States and even though some U.S. citizens have no or very slight labor skills, they do not attempt to satisfy the market demands to which the Mexican worker is ready to respond. In this way, the United States acquires a factor of production that is in insufficient supply, and therefore must be imported from abroad.[8]

Which point of view is correct? A general survey of studies in the *Journal of Economic Literature* in December 1986 found that although many scholars believed that unskilled domestic workers are harmed by the immigration of unskilled workers, these effects are probably "not sizable." Even this conclusion is qualified, however, by the fact that most studies of this issue have been imperfect and that, in many cases, adequate time-series data are not yet available.[9]

In any event, polls in the early 1980s showing that a majority of Hispanic and black Americans favored sanctions against employers who hired illegal aliens demonstrated that most poor people in the United States *believed* that their economic position was being worsened by the large number of border crossings that were occurring. Furthermore, as far as labor market considerations are concerned, there was the genuine sympathy that many Americans felt for the undocumented workers themselves. Illegally in the country, they offered a natural target for exploitation by unscrupulous employers. Reports of the subhuman conditions in which many illegals were living also fed the growing belief that this was no way for a civilized country to handle its labor shortages.

### Utilization of Public Services.

Another consideration that fueled the growing demand for immigration reform in the early 1980s was the feeling that the illegals were beginning to place serious demands on the public purse. This seemed clearly true with respect to welfare payments and other public expenses for specific groups like the Vietnamese boat people and the Mariel Cubans. Moreover, in 1981, in the case of *Doe* v. *Plyler,* the Supreme Court determined that illegal alien children were eligible for free public education. Although Congress had, in many instances, denied illegals eligibility for welfare, subsidized housing, and other services, a number of court decisions went in the other direction. In April 1986, for example, public housing officials in Los Angeles estimated that illegal aliens were living in at least 30 percent of California's 500,000 public housing units, and possibly a much higher percentage.[10]

Even in the case of legal immigrants, it is difficult to estimate accurately their net impact on public transfers and taxes. Some studies suggest that, on the whole, families headed by legal immigrants receive about the same level of transfer payments as do families of native Americans of comparable age and other demographic characteristics. The evidence is incomplete, however, and to be comprehensive would have to take into account the possible secondary effect of immigration on transfer payments and taxes paid by domestic workers. Needless to say, estimates of transfer and tax payments in the case of illegal aliens—whose total numbers have themselves been subject to widely varying estimates—are even more complex. Employed illegal aliens do often pay income and Social Security taxes, perhaps in as high as 75 percent of cases. Also, since they are characteristically young, male workers, separated from their families, they frequently make little use of welfare and other public services. Thus, in net terms, they may well represent a plus rather than a minus as far as being a drain on the public exchequer is concerned.[11]

One effort to determine the impact of immigrants in Los Angeles County on local and state revenues concluded that, in 1980, each immigrant family cost slightly more in services than they paid in state and local taxes. The impact of Mexican immigrants on state and local finances was greater: "benefits received outweighed taxes paid by a factor of 2 to 1." The main reasons were low Mexican earnings and large Mexican families: "Each Mexican immigrant household enrolled an average of 2.25 times the number of children in elementary and secondary schools as the average Los Angeles County household." This analysis, however, was limited to immigrants enumerated in the 1980 census, primarily legal immigrants. When one takes into account the impact of illegal immigrants, largely uncounted, the balance changes since, as already mentioned, so many of these were young and unaccompanied by families.[12]

At the federal level, the balance between benefits and expenditures changes once again. One economist, Julian Simon, argues that working-age immigrants pay more in income and Social Security taxes than they receive in benefits, and adds that, in the long run, immigrants as producers, and as contributors to a larger consuming market, stimulate greater and more efficient production. He considers them a net economic benefit.[13] By contrast, another economist, George J. Borjas, has calculated that over the life cycle of recent immigrants, the lifetime welfare costs of a typical household that immigrated in the 1970s will be $12,746 (in 1989 dollars), as compared to the lifetime welfare costs of a typical native household of the 1970s of $7,909.[14]

Under any circumstances, the low earnings of many new immigrants could pose a problem. At a minimum, the high poverty rate of Hispanic Americans suggested to many observers the possibility of substantial future welfare burdens if unrestrained immigration should be allowed.

## THE IMMIGRATION REFORM AND CONTROL ACT OF 1986

The concerns just discussed became greater and greater as the number of apprehended illegals increased in the 1970s and early 1980s (Figure 20-1). Despite this fact, efforts to pass legislation addressed to this problem followed a very circuitous route, and, indeed, in the early months of 1986, immigration reform was widely regarded as a dead issue. The problem was that although there was considerable agreement that *some* bill was needed, there was hardly a provision of any of the proposed pieces of legislation that could not find serious opponents somewhere.

A central issue from the beginning was whether illegal immigration should be controlled by means of sanctions—fines, penalties, even imprisonment—applied to employers who knowingly hired illegals. One

of the oddities of U.S. immigration law had been that, while it might be illegal for a person to be in the country, and while that person, if found, could be deported, it was nevertheless *not* illegal to hire and employ that person. Clearly, if one wanted to get serious about illegal aliens, one would have to make it illegal to hire them, and, to give more than lip service to this notion, to develop serious penalties for those who did so.

Such an approach, however, ran into opposition from growers and other employers, who felt that the basic laws of supply and demand, including the provision of cheap labor for their particular enterprises, were being interfered with. Civil rights activists foresaw the possibility that the law would become a vehicle for discrimination against all Hispanics, further damaging their already vulnerable position in the U.S. economy. Moreover, some critics felt quite simply that such a law was unworkable. Many countries had adopted employer sanctions; indeed, by 1986, 11 states, including California as early as 1971, had adopted legislation prohibiting the knowing employment of illegal aliens. The state laws had not been enforced, and it was arguable (although opinions differed) that the experience of other countries had shown such legislation to be ineffective.

As a result, the legislation that was finally signed into law on November 6, 1986, contained a variety of complex compromises, none of which was perfectly satisfactory to any single member of Congress. The main provisions of the **Immigration Reform and Control Act (IRCA)**, often called the Simpson-Rodino law after its Senate and House sponsors, were as follows:

1. *Employer Sanctions.* It became unlawful to "knowingly" hire, recruit, or refer for a fee any "unauthorized alien." How can the employer know? A variety of documents can be taken in evidence (passport, Social Security card, driver's license, etc.) with the employer essentially being required to com-

ply "in good faith" with the verification procedures. An employer's failure to do so after an initial transition period makes the employer subject to graduated civil penalties, ranging from $250 to $10,000 per unauthorized alien, and to criminal penalties, with up to six months in prison, where there is a "pattern or practice" of violations.

2. *Legalization of Undocumented Alien Residents.* The "**amnesty**" **provisions** of the law permitted aliens who had continuously resided in the United States in an unlawful status since before January 1, 1982, to be eligible for temporary resident status. The law further provided that these legalized aliens can adjust to permanent resident status after 18 months if the alien has resided continuously in the United States during that time, is generally admissible on other grounds, and demonstrates a minimal knowledge of English and of U.S. history and government.

3. *Agricultural Workers.* There are a number of rather complicated provisions designed to meet U.S. needs for **agricultural workers.** These include arrangements for expediting grower requests for temporary agricultural laborers from abroad; the establishment of conditions under which agricultural workers can apply for permanent resident status; and provisions for "replenishment workers" from abroad for the years 1990–1993 if the secretaries of labor and agriculture certify that a shortage of agricultural workers exists.

There are a number of other provisions relative to the main changes noted above. For example, there is an antidiscrimination provision, obviously designed to meet the objection that employers, to avoid possible complications, will hesitate to hire any Hispanic-looking individuals. There is a provision that allows agricultural workers who receive temporary resident status to leave agriculture and work in other fields. Also, there are various fiscal provisions designed to beef up the enforcement activities of the INS, and to reimburse state and local governments for certain public assistance and medical costs involved in the amnesty effort.

In short, the law legalized the *previously* illegal; took steps to reduce the number of *new* illegals entering the country; and, in the agricultural programs, created a complex arrangement whereby agricultural workers can be fed into the *general* U.S. economy and then, for a time at least, "replenished" by new temporary workers should farm labor shortages develop.

## WHAT HAS BEEN THE EFFECT OF IRCA?

At the time of its passage, it was so widely (though, of course, not universally) stated that IRCA could not possibly work that our first question has to be: Is there any evidence at all that IRCA has produced the results that were intended? In particular, has the flow of illegals been reduced? And how did the undocumented respond to the amnesty offer?

### Reduction of Illegal Immigration

There is substantial evidence to suggest that the new immigration law did reduce illegal immigration during the first two or three years after its passage. A 1990 study by the INS provided an indirect measurement of changes in the flows of illegal aliens into the United States after IRCA as compared to before IRCA.[15] These measurements, presented in Figure 20-2, do not refer to the number of illegal aliens resident in the United States at any given moment in time, but to flows across the border. Clearly, some individuals cross the border many times in any given period. Furthermore, these measurements refer only to apprehensions by the Border Patrol on the U.S.–Mexican border on a per officer hour basis. Many illegals are not apprehended, the number of officer hours varies, illegals enter by other routes, and so on.

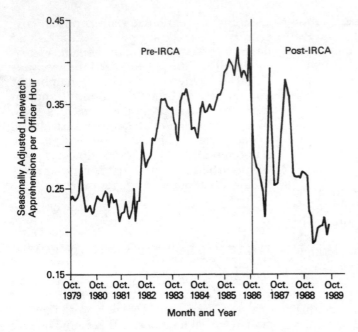

**FIGURE 20-2: Seasonally Adjusted Linewatch Apprehensions per Hour, October 1979–September 1989**

*Source:* Michael D. Hoefer, "Background of U.S. Immigration Policy Reform" (mimeographed), Statistics Division, U.S. Immigration and Naturalization Service, 1990, Chart 2.

Given these qualifications, it would nevertheless seem that the flow of illegals definitely fell after IRCA as compared to before IRCA. The total number of border apprehensions fell from about 1.7 million in 1986 to around 900,000 in 1989—still a large figure but a substantial decrease.

How much of this decrease was *due* to IRCA and to employer sanctions in particular is much harder to say. Employer sanctions were not actually applied until August 1987, and the first fines were not levied until June 1988. As of October 1989, the INS had conducted 26,356 investigations and levied $15.5 million in fines, of which $4.0 million had been collected. Thus, the sharp decline in apprehensions in late 1986 and early 1987 obviously occurred not in *response* to employer sanctions but in *anticipation* of the effects of the law. Mexican newspapers had suggested that there might be mass deportations under IRCA, as there had been under the bracero program. Also, illegals who previously commuted may have decided to stay put in the United States in order to be eligible for legalization. Fur-

thermore, in judging the figures, it must be remembered that the legalization program *in itself* was bound to reduce the numbers of *il*legals crossing the border. This was particularly true of the legalization program for temporary agricultural workers.[16]

An attempt to take these and other factors into account was made in a model developed by Michael White and Frank Bean of the Urban Institute and Thomas Espenshade of Princeton University. Their other factors include such variables as the rate of population growth in Mexico and relative U.S./Mexican wage and unemployment rates. Their general conclusion was:

We estimate an overall decline in apprehensions between November 1986 and September 1988 of nearly 700,000 or about 35 percent below the level that would be anticipated in the absence of IRCA. About 12 percent of this decline is due to changes in INS effort, about 17 percent is due to the agricultural legalization program, and the remaining 71 percent is due to the component we call the deterrent effect of IRCA.

In short, they suggested "that the new legislation has slowed the rate of undocumented migration across the southern border of the United States, but this reduction is not as large as many have claimed."[17]

Experience subsequent to this report suggests that illegal immigration has begun to rise again, with border apprehensions in 1990 going over one million, a nearly 200,000 increase over 1989. This reinforces the view of those who believe that sanctions have failed to resolve the illegal immigration problem, although it can be argued that the law certainly stemmed what had been a sharp *rate of increase* of illegal immigration. Also, it can be argued that the promised increase in funding for the INS never really came through—with more resources, it is claimed, far more could have been accomplished.

### Effects of the Legalization Program

The second question—the effects of the amnesty program—is more easily answered in the sense that the period of application has ended: for illegal aliens resident in the United States since 1982, on May 4, 1988; and for special agricultural workers, on November 30, 1988. (In both groups, there were effective extensions in some cases.) The monthly application figures are shown in Figure 20-3. The totals were 1.8 million under the legalization program and 1.3 million under the agricultural worker program, for a total of 3.1 million applications. Under the legalization program, about 70 percent were from Mexico, and in the agricultural program around 82 percent.

Was this a successful effort or not? At the beginning, many observers felt that it

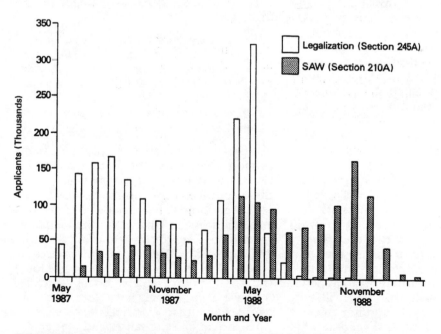

**FIGURE 20-3:   Legalization Applicants by Month of Application, May 1987–March 1989**

*Source:*   Michael D. Hoefer, "Background of U.S. Immigration Policy Reform" (mimeographed), Statistics Division, U.S. Immigration and Naturalization Service, 1990, Chart 1.

was not working successfully at all, but then they did not take into account the huge last-minute surges in applications; witness the April and May 1988 flood of legalization applicants. In general, the success of the program must be measured in terms of the numbers of illegal aliens presumed to be in the country at the time the law was passed. Did we legalize a large or small fraction of that number? This number has been subject to widely varying estimates, although an in-between estimate is that there were probably 3 to 5 million illegals resident in the United States in 1986.

In this context, the 3.1 million total should probably be regarded as quite successful, and this despite the fact that many of the later agricultural worker applications appear to have been fraudulent. Insofar as it was our object to legalize our illegal population—particularly that portion of it that had been resident for a number of years—we appear to have achieved our purposes fairly well. This, of course, says nothing about the illegal population that has been formed since the legislation was passed. Though smaller than it might have been without IRCA, such an illegal population clearly does still exist and is growing.

## AN UNDERLYING QUESTION

The experience under IRCA strongly suggests that the United States has not seen the last of the issue of illegal immigrants. Not only does the number appear to be growing again, but it can be argued that the amnesty experience virtually guarantees that this growth will continue. Present and future illegals may easily decide that the experience could be repeated—that if they will only hang in there long enough, another amnesty program will come along and validate what previously had been considered invalid.

The employer sanctions approach also has certain fairly obvious drawbacks. In some respects, it can be criticized because it is so easy to get around. The counterfeiting

of fake documents has become a major industry around the Mexican border.[18] Because employers are not required to verify the Social Security or "green cards" (permanent residency documents) presented to them by job applicants, the possibility of knowingly or unknowingly hiring illegals is all too apparent. On the other hand, employers fearful of the law may go in quite the opposite direction. A well-publicized 1990 General Accounting Office (GAO) report found that **employer discrimination** was increasing against perfectly legal but "foreign-appearing, foreign-sounding" Hispanics. This prompted Senator Edward Kennedy to argue that unless such discrimination was reduced, sanctions would have to be repealed.

These various considerations have convinced some observers that a quite different approach to illegal immigration should be tried. The underlying issue might be put this way:

*Should we concentrate on trying to restrict immigration from Mexico and other Latin American countries, or should we focus much more on helping these countries achieve vigorous economic growth and political stability at home so that the pressures for emigration to the United States are reduced?*

Given the negative character of immigration restrictions and border apprehensions, the positive suggestion that we help these countries close the gap between themselves and the United States sounds very appealing. As an editorial in the *Wall Street Journal* put it succinctly, "fostering economic growth in Latin America and other areas of potential conflict is the only way to reduce the numbers of people who feel compelled to leave their homes. That means encouraging countries to lower incentive-killing tax rates, break up state-sanctioned monopolies and free flourishing underground economies."[19]

Unfortunately, this last sentence indicates one of the major difficulties of this particular approach. Any serious attempt by the United States to foster this (or any other) particular set of politicoeconomic policies in a Latin neighbor would be regarded as a gross interference with that country's sovereignty. Even simple foreign aid, with no strings attached, is a very complex matter and by no means certain to produce positive economic results (see Chapter 25, pp. 452–453).

What this means is that the range of actually effective U.S. policies for implementing this positive-sounding approach is very limited. Of course, economic and political progress may occur in these countries quite independently of our policies. By 1990 the new president of Mexico, Carlos Salinas de Gortari, a U.S.-trained economist, had already taken a number of badly required steps to restore the vigor of Mexico's economy and the political integrity of its government. There is no intrinsic resource constraint or other limitation that prevents Mexico or the countries of Central America or the Caribbean from achieving economic development.

Such development could conceivably help reduce pressures to emigrate to the United States, though even this point is somewhat in doubt. Historically, immigrants have come not from the lowest layers of very poor societies but, rather, from the lower end of the *middle* of the economic spectrum. "This is a significant point," notes economist Sidney Weintraub, ". . . because it means that increased economic opportunity in the sending country may not translate immediately into reduced emigration. It may lead to the reverse."[20] In the case of Mexico, immigration today often does come from groups of very poor, landless peasants from rural areas, and this might be reduced by better employment opportunities within the Mexican economy. Still, it is doubtful that any realistic economic developments in Mexico or the other relevant countries will substantially reduce migratory pressures in the next decade or two. Thus, the effective choice as far as illegal immigration is concerned would appear to be either to continue the sanctions, imperfect as they are, or to agree to accept a truly enormous inflow of undocumented migrants.

## IMMIGRATION ISSUES FOR THE 1990S

We return at this point to the possibility raised earlier in the chapter that we should simply accept this potentially large inflow of immigrants and give up any serious attempt to restrict their numbers. One reason for doing this in the case of Mexican and other Hispanic immigration lies in the field of international relations. A fear sometimes expressed by those who worry about our periodic crackdowns on Hispanic illegals is that we may be denying Mexico and Central America a badly needed "safety valve" for their own populations. The worst scenario, it can be argued, is for the United States to tighten the screws too firmly, turning the vast unemployed or underemployed populations to the south into potentially explosive mobs who not only would create enormous political and economic instability in those countries, but would inflame them with hostility toward the United States. The installation of regimes actively antagonistic to this country cannot be ruled out. Thus, there is definitely *an* argument for allowing as much Hispanic immigration as possible on the grounds that we would prefer, other things equal, to have friendly relations with our neighboring countries.

This argument can be further buttressed by some of the U.S. labor market considerations that we mentioned earlier. Our own native population is growing very slowly; the Baby Bust has meant a particularly slow growth of young entrants into the labor force; also, we need workers who will do the kinds of jobs, whether in the fields, in construction, or in services, that many native citizens consider beneath them.

There arguments all have comebacks, some of which we have discussed earlier. We can now add two further considerations that must give us pause before this approach is fully endorsed. The first has to do with a *qualitative* issue, namely, the skills of the entering immigrants. Most studies of the projected labor force of the U.S. economy suggest that the *major* problem facing our economy in the future is likely to be an imbalance of supply and demand, with too few skilled workers for the jobs available for them and too many unskilled workers for the jobs available for them.[21]

One problem with allowing massive immigration from Latin America is that the workers who migrate are predominantly unskilled and poorly educated. These characteristics run counter to the basic economic needs of the United States in the years ahead and, indeed, to recent changes in our immigration philosophy. On November 29, 1990, President Bush signed into law a major overhaul of our immigration regulations. This new legislation increased overall legal immigration levels from 540,000 in 1989 to 700,000 for each of the subsequent three years (then stabilizing at 675,000 a year). What is most notable for the purposes of our present discussion, however, is that half that increase is reserved for immigrants with desirable employment skills. Their number is to be raised from 54,000 to 140,000. A further 10,000 visas are to be set aside for investors who have $500,000 or more to invest in businesses that create new jobs. Although the legislation continues the previous policy of favoring applicants with relatives in the United States, the *new* element is the emphasis on skills, and also on strengthening immigration from certain European countries (Ireland, Poland, and Italy, in particular) to balance out recent increases from Asia and Latin America. One problem with simply opening our doors to the south, then, is that the immigrants who may flood in may not possess the skills the nation needs and is now explicitly seeking.[22]

A second problem is more *quantitative* in character. If we relax our efforts to control the borders, then it seems probable that there will, in fact, be very substantial increases in Mexican and other Hispanic migration to the United States. This will lead to a major expansion in our Hispanic American population beyond what is already guaranteed to occur in a very rapidly increasing part of our domestic population. Furthermore, since even our revised legal immigration policies are based heavily on favoring family members and relatives, the more legal immigrants we admit in one phase, the greater will be the admission of, or at least pressure to admit, further immigrants from those very same regions. With Mexican Americans already having a much higher fertility rate than white non-Hispanic Americans and also a higher rate than blacks, one can envisage the possibility of a historically unprecedented growth in a single minority group in the United States, and one with very strong cultural, linguistic, and political ties to a country or countries outside the United States.

Given then the virtual certainty that a more relaxed immigration policy would lead to vast numbers of Mexicans and other Hispanics entering this country, a big issue is whether such a large group, and especially one with its particular history, can be appropriately absorbed into the American mainstream. Are we dealing with a fundamentally new phenomenon here? Or will Mexicans and other Hispanics, while keeping their own ethnic and cultural identities, be able to become "Americans" more or less to the same degree as other immigrant groups in the past?

To this important question, we turn our attention in the next chapter.

## SUMMARY

1. Immigration to the United States from Mexico and other Latin American countries has followed a shifting pattern over the years as economic conditions and government policies have fluctuated.

2. In the period after 1965, when U.S. immigration policies had been somewhat liberalized, concern gradually mounted over the increasing number of illegal aliens who were entering the United States, particularly across the U.S.–Mexican border. It was widely stated that we had "lost control of our borders."

3. This concern, along with other worries about population size, the environment, the effect of low-wage immigrants on low-wage American workers, and the potential drain of immigrants on education and other public services, led in 1986 to the passage of the Immigration Reform and Control Act. Even at the time of passage there were great disagreements about the need to control immigration (Didn't we need immigrants for our labor force? Didn't many immigrants contribute more in taxes than they received in public benefits?) and about the wisdom of employer sanctions as a method (this tool has never worked very well in the past; also, it could easily lead to discrimination against Hispanics and other minorities). Still, IRCA did pass with employer sanction provisions, along with provisions for amnesty for current illegal aliens and for supplying future agricultural workers.

4. Experience through 1990 suggested that the flow of illegal aliens had been reduced (border apprehensions were halved between 1986 and the end of 1989) and that a substantial number of aliens (3.1 million) had taken advantage of the opportunity to apply for legal status. However, there were already ominous signs that the flow of illegals was beginning to increase again, and there was also some evidence of increased discrimination against legal Hispanic residents when they applied for jobs.

5. Underlying the debate about our future policy with respect to illegal immigrants is the issue of whether it would be better to try to promote economic development in Mexico and other Latin countries so that potential immigrants would remain at home, rather than to adopt a restrictive approach. Opportunities for promoting such development are, however, somewhat limited, and it is doubtful that such measures as the United States could take would do much to stem the inflow of illegals.

6. Welcoming a large number of legal immigrants has the advantage that it would help maintain friendly relations with our Latin neighbors, although, if taken too far, it would raise the issue of (a) the future balance of skilled versus unskilled workers in the U.S. economy, and (b) the ability of the United States to assimilate what would be a very rapidly growing minority group with strong ties to Mexico and other Latin countries. Emphasis on increasing the immigration of skilled workers was a significant element of a major overhaul of U.S. immigration laws in 1990.

## KEY CONCEPTS FOR REVIEW

Mexican-U.S. history
   early Spanish exploration
   Mexican War
   Treaty of Guadalupe Hidalgo
   Gadsden Purchase

"Swinging door" policies

Liberalization of U.S. policy in 1965

Rise in illegal immigration

"We have lost control of our borders"

Environmental, labor force, public expenditure issues

Bracero program

Immigration Reform and Control Act (IRCA) (1986)
   employer sanctions
   amnesty provisions
   agricultural workers

Border apprehensions

Employer discrimination against Hispanic workers

Problems of economic conditions and political stability in Latin America

Problems of assimilation of Hispanic immigrants

Skilled versus unskilled immigrants

1990 immigration reform

## QUESTIONS FOR DISCUSSION

1. Does the fact that the American Southwest was once largely Mexican seem to you to be relevant or irrelevant to the setting of U.S. immigration policies with regard to present-day Mexico? Explain your answer.

2. "The simple solution to the problem of controlling our borders is to make all immigration, excepting felons and known criminals, legal and open. Then our borders cannot be violated by illegal entry since, practically speaking, all entry will be legal." Discuss.

3. Since both "conservatives" and "liberals" saw much to object to in the Immigration Reform and Control Act of 1986, it was surprising even to the bill's sponsors that it eventually passed. Explain why you think groups on opposite sides of the political spectrum might object to this law. Can you find reasons that groups on opposite sides of the political spectrum might also support the law?

4. What economic pressures on both sides of the U.S.–Mexican border might tend to weaken the effectiveness of employer sanctions? What has experience shown to date about the effectiveness of such sanctions?

5. Do you consider economic aid to Mexico, Central America, and Caribbean nations a fruitful way of keeping emigration from those countries within reasonable limits in the future? Explain why or why not.

6. What is new about the immigration policy embedded in the 1990 overhaul of our immigration laws? Does this new emphasis have any bearing on the issue of large-scale immigration from Mexico and other Latin countries?

## NOTES

1. See Michael C. LeMay, *From Open Door to Dutch Door* (New York: Praeger, 1987).
2. Frank D. Bean and Marta Tienda, *The Hispanic Population of the United States* (New York: Russell Sage Foundation, 1987), p. 107.
3. Thomas Weyr, *Hispanic U.S.A.: Breaking the Melting Pot* (New York: Harper & Row, 1988), p. 17. Much of this section relies on Weyr's account.
4. Ibid., p. 19.
5. Smith is quoted in David E. Simcox, ed., *U.S. Immigration in the 1980s: Reappraisal and Reform* (Boulder, Colo.: Westview Press, 1988), p. 4.
6. Michael C. Mayer and William L. Sherman, *The Course of Mexican History*, 3rd ed. (New York: Oxford University Press, 1987), p. 695. Some of the issues taken up briefly in this chapter will be considered more comprehensively in Chapter 25, "The United States and the World Population Explosion."
7. Walter Fogel, "Immigrants and the Labor Market," in Demetrios G. Papademetriou and Mark J. Miller, eds., *The Unavoidable Issue: U.S. Immigration Policy in the 1980s* (Philadelphia: Institute for the Study of Human Issues, 1983), p. 88.
8. Jorge A. Bustamante, "Mexican Migration to the United States: De Facto Rules," in Peggy B. Musgrave, ed., *Mexico and the United States: Studies in Economic Interaction* (Boulder Colo.: Westview Press, 1985), p. 189.
9. Michael J. Greenwood and John M. McDowell,

"The Factor Consequences of U.S. Immigration." *Journal of Economic Literature,* 24, December 1986, p. 1767. The authors note that "empirical conclusions regarding the effects of immigration on U.S. workers have frequently been based on circumstantial rather than direct evidence." They find that, even today, in many cases, "appropriate time-series data have not yet been generated or identified" (p. 1769). Their recommendation: More research is needed on these important matters.
10. Simcox, *U.S. Immigration,* p. 39.
11. See discussion in Greenwood and McDowell, "The Factor Consequences of U.S. Immigration," pp. 1757–1760. They give references there to the work of a number of scholars who have studied taxes and transfer payments as they relate to legal and illegal immigrants.
12. Thomas Muller and Thomas J. Espenshade, *The Fourth Wave: Mexico's Newest Immigrants* (Washington, D.C.: Urban Institute Press, 1985), pp. 142–144.
13. Julian L. Simon, *The Economic Consequences of Immigration* (Cambridge, Mass.: Basil Blackwell, 1989), Chaps. 6, 8.
14. George J. Borjas, "Immigrants—Not What They Used to Be," *Wall Street Journal,* November 8, 1990. Also see Borjas, *Friends or Strangers: The Impact of Immigrants on the U.S. Economy* (New York: Basic Books, 1990).
15. Michael D. Hoefer, "Background of U.S. Immi-

gration Policy Reform," mimeographed, Statistics Division, U.S. Immigration and Naturalization Service, 1990.

16. Ibid., p. 18.

17. Michael J. White, Frank D. Bean, and Thomas J. Espenshade, "The U.S. Immigration Reform and Control Act and Undocumented Migration to the United States," *PRIP-UI-5* (Washington, D.C.: Program for Research on Immigration Policy, 1989), pp. 20, 23.

18. A 1989 survey by the immigration service found that of 900 aliens, 233 admitted having fake Social Security cards and 142 fake "green cards." It was believed that the actual number of fraudulent documents was higher than this. Richard W. Stevenson, "Growing Problem: Aliens with Fake Documents," *New York Times*, August 4, 1990.

19. "Bus People," *Wall Street Journal*, February 26, 1987.

20. Sidney Weintraub, "Illegal Immigration and U.S. Foreign Economic Policy," in Papademetriou and Miller, eds., *The Unavoidable Issue*, p. 187.

21. This is a main conclusion of Gary Burtless and others who have been studying the future U.S. job market. Thus Burtless writes that "the demand for skilled workers has been growing faster than the supply and the demand for unskilled workers has fallen faster than the supply." Gary Burtless, ed., *A Future of Lousy Jobs?* (Washington, D.C.: Brookings Institution, 1990), p. 30.

22. It should be said that Third World countries may not particularly applaud our new approach to immigration. From the point of view of the *sending* countries, a U.S. policy of emphasizing skills and professional qualifications could easily subject us to the charge of promoting a "brain drain" from these countries. Already, some Latin American officials are aware that they may be losing some of their best people to the United States. Thus, President Carlos Salinas of Mexico has said: "The people who emigrate to the U.S. are so enterprising, so daring, that they are obviously the kind of people we would like to keep in Mexico." Quoted by James Reston, in "Mexico's next president talks of new generation taking over, getting our ear," *Fort Lauderdale Sun-Sentinel*, February 17, 1988.

# 21

# The Hispanics: Is the Pot Still Melting?

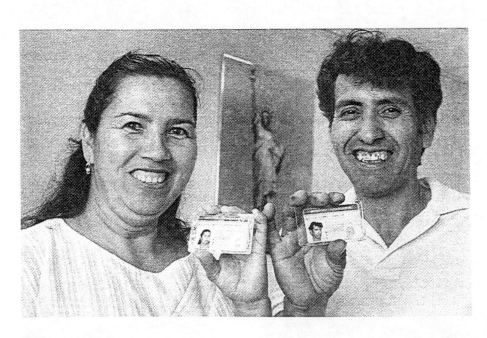

*W*hat the growing Hispanic presence means for the ethnic landscape of the United States is a source of continuing debate.

## ASSIMILATION AND PLURALISM

At one extreme is the demand for a "complete renunciation of the immigrant's ancestral culture in favor of the behavior and values of the Anglo-Saxon core group."[1] Cultural pluralism—its opposite—demands equal treatment for all groups, whether or not they choose to retain distinctive ethnic traits. It expects that the maintenance of distinctiveness, including the speaking of a non-English language, will not impair civic functioning or undermine national policy. Between these extremes of **Anglo-conformity** and **cultural pluralism** are various other possibilities. Close to the assimilationist pole is the "**melting pot**"[2] which assumes that culturally distinct groups will make some contribution to the emerging American culture without altering its basic composition, even as they themselves are transformed. Recent references to the "salad bowl" are closer to the pluralist pole in that each cultural group is expected to retain most of its original culture while contributing to the overall composition.[3]

Whatever model of assimilation one subscribes to, the rapid growth of the Hispanic population,[4] contrasted with slower growth among blacks and still slower growth among non-Hispanic whites,[5] raises questions about the social and cultural significance of the increasing Hispanic presence in the United States. Is the rapid rise of Hispanics (a group itself composed of many distinct groups) simply yet another stage in the history of expanding American cultural diversity, or will it undermine a necessary minimal degree of political unity? Does the size of Hispanic groups, and their dominance in key immigrant-attracting areas such as southern California and southern Florida, introduce a new and unfamiliar theme in the history of American immigration? Does the connection of the largest among the Hispanic groups, the Mexican Americans, to a home country just over the border require a special political relationship with the United States? Is the persistence of Spanish language use among Hispanic groups a matter of concern?

These questions do not admit easy answers, but they are at the core of present debates on how the increasing Hispanic presence will influence the United States in the near and distant future. To a large extent, the social and cultural impact of Hispanics on the United States depends on demographics: How many are there? Where do they live? What do they do? Equally important in shaping the experiences of Hispanics, as well as the prospects for and character of their integration, are conditions in the United States that influence tolerance for ethnic diversity: the state of the economy, public sentiment toward immigration, and perceptions of how acculturation and assimilation processes are working among Hispanics.

Hispanics include no less than 23 different national identities, all using the same language, which considerably complicates any consideration of prospects for their integration. The rapid growth of Hispanics since 1960, coupled with persisting regional concentration, raises concerns about whether Spanish-speaking groups can become socially and culturally integrated. And among the most nativist segments of society, the growing Hispanic presence also conjures fears about the potential "Latinization" or "Hispanicization" of the United States. These nativist sentiments are particularly evident in areas where Hispanics are highly concentrated. In those areas, the demographic impact of Hispanics is awesome.

For example, a recent report on the changing population of Texas projected that in the 1990s non-Hispanic whites (called "Anglos" in the Southwest) would no longer make up the majority of children enrolled in the public schools.[6] This was already true in 1986 for the lower grades. Hispanics are the dominant ethnic group in El Paso, San Antonio, and Miami. The Population Reference Bureau recently estimated that if current demographic trends continue, by the year 2010 non-Hispanic whites will no longer hold a statewide majority in California and Texas.[7] Of course, it does not automatically follow that a Hispanic majority will reverse the course of acculturation and assimilation of Spanish-speaking ethnic populations. Size does not automatically ensure power, nor is the Hispanic population a monolithic entity.

History, opportunity, race, and class will be decisive in shaping the assimilation and acculturation of Hispanics. Just as the waves of immigrants from western and eastern Europe confronted unique opportunities and experienced diverse integration experiences, so too the immigrants from Latin America have encountered circumstances that differentiate their paths of acculturation according to the time of their arrival, the country of their origin, the social class that characterizes them, and the degree to which they are seen as racially different.

Two general scenarios suggest themselves. One—the classic assimilation scenario—is that the observed differences in the social and economic standing of Hispanics will disappear with time, irrespective of country of origin or period of arrival. Evidence that earlier arrivals fare better than later arrivals would lend support to this interpretation. An alternative scenario would emphasize the role of unique historical circumstances and cultural differences for Hispanics, or major groups among them, such as Mexicans, Cubans, and Puerto Ricans.

To unravel these themes, we begin with a discussion of the growth of the Hispanic population since 1960, focusing on the post-1980 period, and considering what recent trends portend for the twenty-first century. Subsequently we describe the socioeconomic diversity of Hispanic minorities along national origin lines because rather different integration experiences characterize the major Hispanic national origin groups.[8] As their numbers increase, politics also become increasingly important in shaping the integration prospects, and the social, economic, and cultural development of Hispanic-origin groups. Accordingly, a later section will amplify on the powerful social implications of Hispanic demographics by discussing the political significance of their growing numbers, residential concentration, and linguistic diversity.

## HISPANIC DEMOGRAPHICS

Although the Hispanic presence in the United States predates the formation of the nation as we know it today, until 1960 Hispanics were not known to most observers outside the Southwest or the Northeast. Until World War II, virtually all people currently classified as *Hispanics* were of Mexican origin.[9] Other long-standing Hispanic communities include the Cubans in Florida, whose presence dates from the 1860s, and the Puerto Ricans in New York, who established small settlements on the U.S. mainland after their homeland became a possession of the United States in 1898. Compared to Mexicans residing in the Southwest, however, these communities were invisible at a national level because they were tiny and geographically contained.

This picture changed radically after World War II. The heavy migration from Puerto Rico to the mainland during the 1950s and continuing through the 1960s increased the Hispanic presence in the Northeast, while the admission of Cuban refugees following the Cuban Revolution in 1959 did the same in southern Florida and some northeastern labor markets. Immigration has figured prominently in the growth of the Hispanic population since 1941, but even more since 1965. Thus, since the mid-1960s, the Hispanic population, once perceived as consisting of separate and small regional populations, was increasingly seen as a national minority that was regionally distributed. This latter perception, moreover, had implications for the label used to describe the population, a point we discuss later.

Table 21-1 summarizes the growth of the U.S. Hispanic population since 1960, when the estimated population hovered around 7 million. By 1980 the Hispanic population had essentially doubled, and if current growth trajectories continue, the 1990 census should enumerate around 21 million Hispanics, representing a threefold increase during a 30-year period! This growth is phenomenal by any standard, but it is all the more so in light of evidence that the growth of the non-Hispanic white population has slowed. Consequently, the share of the total population made up of Hispanics has risen steadily, from approximately 4 percent in 1960 to 8 percent in 1989.

The 34 percent increase of Hispanics during the 1960s is well below the 61 percent growth recorded during the 1970s—from 9.1 to 14.6 million. However, the 61 percent increase is in part an artifact of the vast improvement in population coverage in 1980 combined with the serious Hispanic undercount in 1970. That is, changes in the design of the 1980 census questionnaire, and particularly the decision to include an item that solicited responses on Spanish/Hispanic origin or descent on the 100 percent questionnaire, resulted in a higher response rate of Hispanics in 1980.[10] Changes in the census forms, while improving coverage, also served to increase the enumeration of undocumented aliens. These problems—the undercount of Hispanics in 1970 and the uncertainty about the number of undocumented aliens included in the 1980, but especially the 1970 census—render estimates of the Hispanic population growth during the 1970s approximate at best.

In recognition of the 1970 census undercount, the Population Reference Bureau produced an adjusted estimate of 10.5 million Hispanics—1.4 million, or 15.4 percent higher than the official Census Bureau enumeration. This adjustment for undercount suggests that the Hispanic population increased 39 percent during the 1970s, a growth pattern more consistent with the growth recorded for the 1960s and, subsequently, for the 1980s. Recent estimates based on the *Current Population Survey* show that the vigorous growth of the Hispanic population continued unabated during the 1980s. Approximately 5.5 million Hispanics were added to the U.S. population between 1980 and 1989—an increase of 38 percent.

Figure 21-1 indicates that the major nationality groups did not contribute uniformly to the phenomenal growth of the Hispanic population, and that these differ-

**TABLE 21-1.   Growth of the U.S. Hispanic Population, 1960–1989 (in millions)**

| Year | Total U.S. Population | Hispanic Population | Hispanic Interperiod Increase | Hispanic as Percentage of U.S. Population |
|------|-----------------------|---------------------|-------------------------------|-------------------------------------------|
| 1960 | 179.3 | 6.9 | – | 3.9% |
| 1970[a] | 203.2 | 9.1 | 2.2 | 4.5 |
| 1970[b] | 203.2 | 10.5 | 3.6 | 5.2 |
| 1980 | 226.5 | 14.6 | 4.1 | 6.4 |
| 1985 | 234.0 | 16.9 | 2.3 | 7.2 |
| 1989 | 243.7 | 20.1 | 3.2 | 8.3 |

[a] Official Census Bureau enumeration.

[b] Adjusted estimate prepared by the Population Reference Bureau.

*Sources:*   Frank D. Bean and Marta Tienda, *The Hispanic Population of the United States* (New York: Russell Sage Fundation, 1987); *Current Population Survey Reports,* March 1987 and 1988.

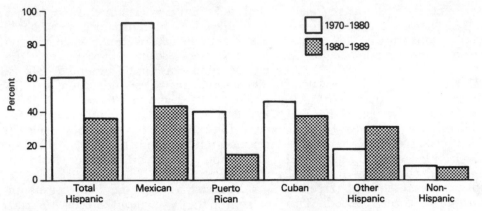

**FIGURE 21-1:   Growth of Hispanic Population, 1970–1980 and 1980–1989 (Percentage Change)**

*Source:*   U.S. Bureau of the Census. *The Condition of Hispanics in America Today* (1984) and 1989 Supplementary Report CB89-158.

ences appear to be widening rather than narrowing over time. Obviously, the disproportionate increase of Mexicans between 1970 and 1980 was driven by the Mexican undercount in 1970. One might also want to attribute part of the Puerto Rican and Cuban increase during the 1970s to improved enumeration procedures in 1980. But neither of these caveats weakens the point that the Hispanic population grew at a pace considerably greater than the non-Hispanic white population, which increased 9 percent during the 1970s. This contrasts with 41 percent for Puerto Ricans, 47 percent for Cubans, and 19 percent for Other Hispanics.

Following the pattern of the previous decade, the largest growth was experienced by the Mexican-origin population, which expanded a whopping 44 percent between 1980 and 1989. The Cuban and Other Hispanic populations grew by 38 and 32 percent, respectively, while Puerto Ricans increased by a modest 15 percent. Immigration figured prominently in the growth of the Mexican, Cuban, and Other Hispanic groups, but not in that of the Puerto Ricans, whose net migration to the mainland has not been a major growth factor during the 1980s. By contrast to the Hispanic popula-

tion, the non-Hispanic white population increased a meager 8 percent between 1980 and 1989.

These differential increases among the major national-origin groups have begun to alter the composition of the Hispanic population. Figure 21-2 shows that three out of every four Hispanics is of either Mexican or Puerto Rican origin, as was true in 1980. Owing to the rapid increase of Mexicans during the last decade, however, the Mexican share of the total Hispanic population has increased from 60 to 63 percent, while the Puerto Rican share has declined, from 14 to 12 percent. Furthermore, the Central and South American population has risen from 7 to 12 percent of the total, while the Other Hispanics declined from 14 to 8 percent.

A further demographic change of importance is illustrated in Table 21-2, which disaggregates the category "Central and South Americans" into 16 countries and two residual categories. The national origins of this diverse and rapidly growing category of Hispanics have been shifting from decade to decade, depending on economic and political circumstances. By 1980 over one-third of Hispanics from Central America and the Caribbean traced their origins to a single country—the Dominican Republic—whereas less than 20 percent did so two decades earlier. Further, the escalating military and political turbulence in El Salvador and Colombia has left its imprint on the Hispanic immigrant streams from Central and South America.

Immigration is the primary determinant of growth of the Hispanic population from Central and South America. Approximately 80 percent of those enumerated in the 1980 census from Central and South America were foreign-born, compared to roughly one-quarter of Mexicans and 17 percent of Other Hispanics.[11] Just under half (49 percent of Central Americans and Dominicans versus 47 percent of South Americans) of the Hispanic population of Central and South American enumerated in 1980 arrived after 1970. Because of their relatively recent arrival in the United States, Central and South Americans represent embryonic Hispanic communities whose ethnic impact lies ahead.

Just how immigration will continue to fuel the growth of the Central and South American communities in the United States is uncertain. These outcomes hinge on U.S. foreign policy toward Central America as well as on revisions in immigration legislation. Future reforms may result in a more restrictive and selective policy.[12] The greatest unknown about immigration concerns the flow of illegal migrants—its volume and source countries—and whether the recent reforms will be successful in stemming this stream. On this subject, the research community is divided.

The visibility of distinct Hispanic communities is heightened by persisting regional concentration along national origin lines. In 1989, two states—California and Texas—housed half of all Hispanics residing in the United States. The majority of these Hispanics are of Mexican origin. Central and South Americans—Salvadorans, Guatemalans, and Nicaraguans—are also concentrated in California and Texas. Arizona, New Mexico, and Colorado account for an additional 8 to 9 percent of all Hispanics, these predominantly of Mexican origin. The majority of Puerto Ricans reside

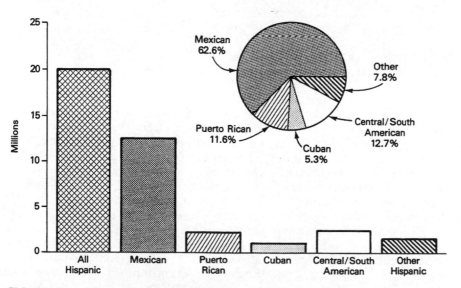

**FIGURE 21-2: Persons of Hispanic Origin in the United States, 1989**

*Source:* U.S. Bureau of the Census, Supplementary Report CB89-158, 1989.

**TABLE 21-2.    Country-of-Origin Distribution of the Central and South American Origin Population, 1960–1980**

| Country of Origin | 1960 | 1970 | 1980 |
|---|---|---|---|
| **Central America and the Caribbean**[a]**:** | | | |
| Dominican Republic | 16.5 | 30.1 | 35.4 |
| El Salvador | 9.2 | 10.7 | 18.4 |
| Guatemala | 9.7 | 10.1 | 12.5 |
| Nicaragua | 15.7 | 12.9 | 9.1 |
| Panama | 25.1 | 13.2 | 8.5 |
| Honduras | 14.9 | 13.8 | 7.7 |
| Costa Rica | 8.8 | 9.2 | 5.5 |
| Other Central American | — | — | 2.9 |
| Total | 99.9 | 100.0 | 100.0 |
| **South America:** | | | |
| Colombia | 14.8 | 23.3 | 33.1 |
| Ecuador | 8.2 | 13.8 | 20.1 |
| Peru | 8.1 | 10.0 | 12.9 |
| Argentina | 22.6 | 21.2 | 11.3 |
| Chile | 9.9 | 5.8 | 7.6 |
| Venezuela | 11.6 | 6.1 | 6.3 |
| Bolivia | 1.9 | 3.5 | 3.1 |
| Uruguay | 2.2 | 2.2 | 2.6 |
| Paraguay | 0.4 | 0.9 | 0.5 |
| Other South American | 20.2[b] | 13.2[b] | 2.5 |
| Total | 99.9 | 100.0 | 100.0 |
| Central American as percentage of pooled | 44.2 | 42.5 | 52.2 |
| South American as percentage of pooled | 55.7 | 57.6 | 47.7 |

[a] This refers to the Spanish-speaking Caribbean, excluding Cuba and Puerto Rico, countries considered separately.

[b] Includes other Central Americans.

*Source:*    Computed from 1960, 1970, and 1980 Public Use Microdata Samples files.

in New Jersey and New York, while Cubans are bimodally distributed between Florida and New York. A rising share of Hispanics reside outside the nine states where they have concentrated. Within regions or states, Hispanics remain disproportionately concentrated in the large metropolitan centers. Within these centers, residential segregation continues to keep Hispanics—but particularly those of recent immigrant origin and those of low socioeconomic status—apart from non-Hispanic whites (see Figure 21-3).

What the 1990s portend in terms of geographic assimilation is a large and looming question. There is ample evidence that Hispanics have already left a strong imprint on the ethnic landscape of the United States. This influence is evident in the Mexican flavor of the American Southwest, the strong Cuban presence in Miami and the Puerto Rican, and the Colombian and Dominican presence in New York City. Hispanic settlements are also visible in other large cities such as Chicago, with its sizable Mexican and Puerto Rican communities. Embryonic communities that trace their origins to many places other than Mexico, Puerto Rico, and Cuba are proliferating. Future immigration trends, which are difficult to predict, will determine which nationality groups remain separately identifiable, and which fade into a residual ethnic category distinguished by the Spanish language and a region of origin.

## A MULTIPLICITY OF HISPANICS

The generic terms **Latino** or **Hispanic** call to mind an ethnic image far less precise than the terms Mexican, Colombian, Dominican, or Cuban. Despite their popular use, these generic terms obscure pronounced economic, social, and cultural differences among peoples of Latin American origin. Products of the 1970s in response to the growing national visibility of Spanish-origin peoples combined with political pressure for self-identification, the labels *Spanish Origin* and *Hispanic* were coined as terms of convenience for official reporting purposes. Both labels have limited ethnic content, but they serve as a general umbrella to identify persons of Latin American origin in the United States.

Common ancestral ties to Spain and Latin America—the most visible being retention of the Spanish language—should not give rise to a mistaken impression of cultural and, by extension, socioeconomic similarity among the Hispanic nationalities. The diverse immigration histories and settlement patterns of Mexicans, Puerto Ricans, Cubans, and persons from Central and South America have created distinct subpopulations, with discernible demographic characteristics and with apparently unequal prospects of socioeconomic success in the United States. Evidence of persisting—and in some instances widening—social and economic differences along national origin lines necessitates a careful scrutiny of the historical experiences of these groups to better understand their contemporary and future prospects in the United States.

### The Seeds of Diversity

To understand the heterogeneity of the Hispanic populations, we must describe briefly the circumstances that led to. the establishment of the distinct communities that currently are subsumed under the rubric *Hispanic*. Nelson and Tienda's analytical framework for describing the emergence of Hispanic ethnicities focuses on three broad sociohistorical processes.[13] These are: (1) **mode of entry**—that is, whether the groups trace their emergence to conquest or migrated voluntarily; (2) **mode of integration**—that is, whether the groups were positively or negatively received by the host society; and (3) **mode of reaffirmation**—that is, whether national origin acquires a largely symbolic meaning or whether it is tightly intertwined with economic and social standing, and hence virtually synonymous

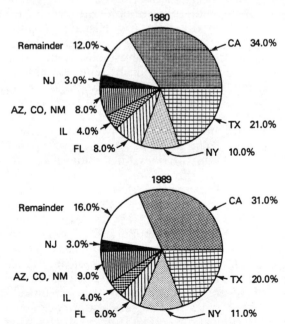

**FIGURE 21-3: Distribution of the Hispanic Population in the United States**

*Sources:* U.S. Bureau of the Census, 1980, and 1989 Supplementary Reports, *The Condition of Hispanics in America Today;* 1984, 1980 Public Use Microdata Sample files.

with minority status. Because it stimulates critical thinking about the ethnic versus the economic content of Hispanic nationalities, we will use the Nelson-Tienda framework to assess the long-term integration prospects of Hispanics.

On these three processes that structure Hispanic ethnicity, there is considerable heterogeneity among the national-origin groups. For example, Mexican and Puerto Rican communities originated through annexation, although massive and voluntary **wage-labor migration** flows ensued and have served as the predominant mode of entry for both these groups. The Cuban presence, on the other hand, was precipitated by events that resulted in their definition as **political** refugees. This status gave them access to refugee assistance, whose symbolic value exceeded its economic value because it purchased immediate legitimacy and acceptance from the host society. How well immigrants ultimately fare in their host societies depends on several factors, including the timing and volume of the flows; the social and demographic composition of the flows; the settlement, consumption, and expenditure patterns of migrants; and the **auspices of migration**—that is, the complex set of social and economic arrangements that organize the migration streams.

The newest wage-labor migrants to the United States are Dominicans, Colombians, Salvadorans, and Guatemalans. These immigrant groups differ from one another in the extent to which political factors precipitated the flows. Unlike Cuban refugees, Salvadorans and Guatemalans have yet to be officially recognized as refugees. Theirs is not even a story of tacit acceptance, but rather one of clandestine entry and continual legal and political struggles for recognition. Adding to the complexity of the picture, these new labor streams from Central and South America share with Mexican migrants the presence of a growing illegal population. This circumstance undermines the political leverage these groups can exert even as their size swells.

Although the distinction between economic migrants and political refugees is neither clearly demarcated nor permanent, the initial mode of reception appears to affect the longer term integration experiences of immigrant groups. Nelson and Tienda argue that the period of entry combined with the circumstances that initiated each flow decisively shapes both the geographical distribution and the socioeconomic position of each group. The changing climate of prejudice and xenophobic sentiment, shifting economic conditions, and legal prescriptions governing immigration flows and labor practices all play decisive roles in shaping patterns of contact between immigrant groups and the host society. These differences are summarized in Table 21-3.

A brief comparison of wage-labor migrants is instructive for illustrating how diverse modes of entry and integration have served to diversify the Hispanic populations. Despite the very different circumstances leading to the establishment of the Puerto Rican, Mexican, and Dominican communities in the United States, there are several parallels among them that are pertinent to an understanding of the contemporary socioeconomic position of these groups. First, all three represent wage-labor flows destined for unskilled blue-collar jobs. Second, all three groups were destined for regional labor markets—the industrial Northeast in the case of Puerto Ricans, the agricultural Southwest in the case of Mexicans, and the New York City apparel industry in the case of Dominicans. Third, like Mexicans in the Southwest, Puerto Ricans in the Northeast have been the victims of severe discrimination and prejudice.[14] There exists less empirical evidence about discrimination against Dominicans, but their economic fate seems to be more promising than that of Puerto Ricans despite the advantage of citizenship and legal status the latter have.

Similarities among the Mexican, Puerto Rican, and Dominican wage-labor migration

**TABLE 21-3. Modalities of Hispanic Integration**

| Group | Mode of Entry | Mode of Integration | Mode of Reaffirmation |
|---|---|---|---|
| Mexicans | Territorial annexation; subsequently, massive wage labor flows, including growing undocumented components | Concentrated in Southwest; extreme discrimination; relegation to unskilled "Mexican" jobs for decades | Immigrant minority |
| Puerto Ricans | Territorial incorporation; subsequent wage labor flows which reversed themselves during cyclical downturns | Concentration in Northeast; relegation to second-class citizenship; benign neglect that eventuated in displacement as economy contracted | Citizen minority |
| Cubans | Political refugees; multiple waves differentiated by class background | Refugee assistance purchased political legitimacy and permitted establishment of Cuban economic enclave | Ethnic entrepreneurs |
| Central Americans | Brain drain migrants initially; unofficial political refugees subsequently | In progress, shaped by presence of growing anti-immigrant sentiment and U.S. foreign policy | Immigrant minorities |
| South Americans | Brain drain migrants initially; wage labor flows subsequently with large undocumented component | In progress, shaped by presence of growing illegal segment, growing anti-immigrant sentiment and unskilled labor requirements in Northeast and California | Immigrant minorities and ethnic groups |

experiences should not be overstated, however. Unlike Mexicans, who entered U.S. labor markets largely as agricultural workers, Puerto Rican migrants have been almost exclusively urban-based and concentrated in the manufacturing and service sectors of New York City. This circumstance, coupled with the industrial restructuring of the New York City labor market away from the types of union jobs formerly held by Puerto Ricans, may seem to explain why the economic welfare of Puerto Ricans has declined since 1970. However, the relative economic success of Dominicans in New York City challenges this interpretation. Finally, the fact that Puerto Ricans are citizens by birth differentiates their entry to the mainland society from that of Mexicans and Dominicans, particularly those who enter in an undocumented status. Theoretically, their citizenship could give them greater political leverage in lobbying for their interests, but in practice this has not occurred.

Ethnic reaffirmation can occur only after immigrant communities have a solid foundation (i.e., numerical base and social organization) in the host society. Ethnic labels are partly imposed by the host society and partly taken by the immigrant groups who wish to maintain their ethnic identity. Groups with a relatively successful economic adaptation often use their national heritage as a basis for economic relationships. Cuban entrepreneurs are a prime example, but a similar phenomenon occurs among Jews and Asian groups as well. Groups less successful in penetrating the social hierarchies of the host society become immigrant minorities—that is, ethnic groups who also are economically disadvantaged. These are groups for whom class position and national origin are inextricably linked because opportunities have been shut off, as seems to have occurred for Puerto Ricans, or because illegal status forces many into the underground economy, as has occurred among large segments of Dominican, Colombian, and Mexican labor pools.

For each group of Hispanics we find a somewhat different social and economic profile. There is a clear ranking of the major groups, with Cubans enjoying the highest status and Puerto Ricans the lowest. Because each group brought a variety of backgrounds and confronted distinct reception factors, integration experiences should be equally varied. Thus, contemporary expressions of Hispanic ethnicity cannot embrace a common Latin American or Spanish culture.

### A Profile of Socioeconomic Diversity

This section documents the educational standing, labor force participation, occupational position, and income status of the major Hispanic groups. Changes in education and employment standing are crucial for assessing whether socioeconomic parity with the host population is being achieved, and whether group differences in socioeconomic standing are narrowing over time.

*Educational Standing.* Table 21-4, which summarizes the changes in median education of Hispanics between 1960 and

**TABLE 21-4. Median Education of Persons Aged 25 and Over by Race and Hispanic National Origin, 1960–1988**

|  | 1960 | 1970 | 1980 | 1988 |
|---|---|---|---|---|
| Mexican | 6.4 | 8.2 | 9.1 | 10.8 |
| Puerto Rican | 7.5 | 8.2 | 10.0 | 12.0 |
| Cuban | 8.4 | 10.0 | 11.7 | 12.4 |
| Central/South American | 11.6 | 11.7 | 11.7 | 12.4 |
| Blacks | 8.0 | 10.0 | 12.0 | 12.4[a] |
| Non-Hispanic whites | 11.0 | 12.0 | 12.0 | 12.7[a] |

[a] March 1987 data.

*Source:* 1960, 1970, and 1980 Public Use Microdata Samples files; March 1987–1989 *Current Population Survey Reports.*

1988, shows that the median education level of all Hispanics has risen and converged with that of the non-Hispanic white population. Whereas in 1960 the median education of all Hispanic groups except those of Central and South American origin lagged behind that of non-Hispanic whites, by 1988 only the schooling level of Mexicans was significantly lower than that of other Hispanics, non-Hispanic whites, or blacks. The higher schooling level of Central and South Americans reflects the high selectivity of the early immigrant cohorts.

Optimism about the educational progress of Hispanics since 1960 must be tempered because measures of central tendency conceal considerable variation within groups. High school noncompletion rates remain disturbingly high for Mexicans and Puerto Ricans. If the problem were simply a matter of linguistic differences and immigrant status, then similar unsatisfactory outcomes would be expected for southeast Asian minorities, who also arrived with linguistic and economic handicaps. Furthermore, the Cuban experience undermines allegations that poor educational achievement among Chicanos and Puerto Ricans results from the immigrant composition of these groups. Despite the linguistic and cultural difficulties Cuban children confronted initially, most, like Asians, were able to overcome these handicaps and did not experience dropout rates comparable to those of Mexicans and Puerto Ricans. Even black youths complete high school at higher rates than Mexicans and Puerto Ricans, despite the more severe prejudice and economic disadvantages they encounter. Their status as immigrants or the children of immigrants, lacking command of English, cannot account for Hispanic educational underachievement.

The poor educational performance of Hispanics has profound consequences because it will limit the employment and income opportunities of future generations. Not only will continued immigration diversify the educational composition of Hispanics in the future, but so also will the unequal performance of native-born youth. The labor market consequences of these processes are already evident, as the following section shows.

*Labor Force Participation.* Table 21-5 summarizes national trends in labor force participation between 1960 and 1985 for the major Hispanic nationality groups. Non-Hispanic whites provide the metric for determining whether Hispanics are achieving labor market parity with the host population, while blacks provide the standard for identifying minority status.

For the pooled Hispanic population, Bean and Tienda showed that men's labor force participation rates fell during the 1960s (from 86 to 82 percent), but remained constant throughout the 1970s.[15] Activity rates of Hispanic men converged over time with those of non-Hispanic white men, providing some evidence of approach to socioeconomic parity. Participation rates of black men, lower than Hispanic or white rates in 1960, reached a low in 1980 and recovered slightly by 1985. Women's participation rates, by contrast, increased steadily between 1960 and 1985.

But there are also striking differences among the national origin groups. The pattern of growing labor force participation by Cuban women, women of Central and South American origin, and both black and white women, coupled with low participation by Puerto Rican women, persisted over the 25 year period. The deviant participation profile of Puerto Rican women has yet to be explained and is all the more puzzling because Dominican women, who have been subjected to similar economic forces as Puerto Ricans, have maintained a tight labor market attachment. The labor force expe-

**TABLE 21-5. Labor Force Participation Rates of Persons Aged 16–64 by Race, Hispanic National Origin, and Gender, 1960–1985**

| Year | Gender | Mexican | Puerto Rican | Cuban | Central and South American | Other Hispanic | Black | Non-Hispanic White |
|------|--------|---------|--------------|-------|----------------------------|----------------|-------|--------------------|
| 1960 | Men    | 85.7    | 84.7         | 87.1  | 83.6                       | 88.9           | 80.6  | 88.5               |
|      | Women  | 31.5    | 40.3         | 51.5  | 49.0                       | 33.5           | 47.2  | 39.5               |
| 1970 | Men    | 81.9    | 77.8         | 86.0  | 83.2                       | 83.9           | 75.2  | 85.4               |
|      | Women  | 39.6    | 32.9         | 52.8  | 52.1                       | 45.4           | 51.1  | 46.6               |
| 1980 | Men    | 83.5    | 73.8         | 85.0  | 82.5                       | 81.3           | 73.3  | 84.6               |
|      | Women  | 52.0    | 41.7         | 64.2  | 57.6                       | 57.4           | 61.1  | 57.9               |
| 1985 | Men    | 86.0    | 70.2         | 85.3  | 84.9                       | 80.6           | 74.0  | 85.7               |
|      | Women  | 54.9    | 40.2         | 68.3  | 58.5                       | 59.9           | 62.7  | 65.2               |

*Source:* 1960, 1970, and 1980 Public Use Microdata Samples files; March 1985 *Current Population Survey.*

rience of Mexican men contrasts sharply with that of Puerto Rican men in that the former actually *increased* their market activity during the 1970s—a time when the labor force activity rates of men generally declined. In fact, while the labor force activity rates of Mexican, Cuban, and Central and South American men converged with those of Anglo men, those of Puerto Rican men have converged with those of black men.

In summary, Puerto Ricans have become the most disadvantaged of all Hispanic groups. At the other extreme, Cubans have become virtually indistinguishable from non-Hispanic whites. Theirs is a swift socioeconomic assimilation process—at least for those who arrived before 1980.

*Occupational Placement.* Changes in the occupations of Hispanics provide further evidence of diversity along national origin lines. Occupation is crucial for defining relative social standing. The most important source of change in the employment structure over the past half century has been the industrial transformation of production involving the growth of service industries and the decline of the extraction industries

**TABLE 21-6A.    Occupational Distribution of Black, White, and Hispanic Male Workers, by Nationality, 1970–1985**

| Year and Broad Occupational Groups | Mexican | Puerto Rican | Cuban | Central and South American | Other Hispanic | Black | Non-Hispanic White |
|---|---|---|---|---|---|---|---|
| **1970:** | | | | | | | |
| Upper white-collar | 10.5 | 8.6 | 20.0 | 22.6 | 21.3 | 11.6 | 14.2 |
| Lower white-collar | 9.6 | 15.3 | 16.7 | 17.3 | 12.3 | 27.4 | 43.1 |
| Upper blue-collar | 19.9 | 15.4 | 18.9 | 19.5 | 17.2 | 1.5 | 1.9 |
| Lower blue-collar | 40.5 | 40.4 | 29.8 | 27.5 | 32.3 | 35.3 | 18.3 |
| Service workers | 10.8 | 18.8 | 13.8 | 12.9 | 12.3 | 18.7 | 9.8 |
| Farm workers | 8.6 | 1.4 | 0.9 | 0.2 | 4.7 | 2.9 | 1.1 |
| Total[a] | 100.1 | 99.9 | 100.1 | 100.0 | 100.1 | 100.1 | 100.1 |
| **1980** | | | | | | | |
| Upper white-collar | 11.8 | 14.2 | 27.2 | 20.3 | 22.1 | 16.6 | 32.6 |
| Lower white-collar | 9.2 | 14.7 | 17.7 | 14.5 | 13.3 | 14.2 | 12.3 |
| Upper blue-collar | 19.6 | 16.0 | 17.0 | 18.0 | 18.7 | 15.8 | 21.4 |
| Lower blue-collar | 39.9 | 35.7 | 25.3 | 30.6 | 29.8 | 35.4 | 23.6 |
| Service workers | 12.3 | 18.0 | 12.2 | 16.2 | 14.1 | 16.9 | 9.2 |
| Farm workers | 7.1 | 1.4 | 0.5 | 0.4 | 2.2 | 1.2 | 0.9 |
| Total[a] | 99.9 | 100.0 | 99.9 | 100.0 | 100.2 | 100.1 | 100.0 |
| **1985:** | | | | | | | |
| Upper white-collar | 10.7 | 16.3 | 25.4 | 19.6 | 25.8 | 14.8 | 33.9 |
| Lower white-collar | 8.9 | 16.3 | 12.4 | 11.3 | 11.9 | 10.9 | 13.3 |
| Upper blue-collar | 21.4 | 15.7 | 21.0 | 20.8 | 18.9 | 14.1 | 20.4 |
| Lower blue-collar | 38.3 | 29.5 | 32.2 | 28.5 | 28.3 | 37.5 | 23.3 |
| Service workers | 13.4 | 21.7 | 9.1 | 18.4 | 14.0 | 21.0 | 8.1 |
| Farm workers | 7.3 | 0.5 | 0.0 | 1.3 | 1.1 | 1.7 | 1.1 |
| Total[a] | 100.0 | 100.0 | 100.1 | 99.9 | 100.0 | 100.0 | 100.0 |

[a] Numbers may not sum to 100 percent because of rounding.

*Source:*   1960, 1970, and 1980 Public Use Microdata Samples files; March 1985 *Current Population Survey.*

(e.g., agriculture and mining). These changes have fostered the relative decline of blue-collar occupations while increasing the relative share of white-collar jobs. As a result of these macrostructural changes in the organization of work, Hispanics experienced variable amounts of occupational upgrading. This is evident in an increased representation in white-collar occupations of all gender and national origin groups, except Central and South American men (see Table 21-6).

The amount and pace of occupational upgrading differed markedly by gender and national origin. The share of Puerto Ricans holding upper white-collar jobs in 1980 and 1985 exceeded the shares of Mexicans so employed, which seems partly to contradict the story based on labor force participation, which showed Puerto Ricans to be the most disadvantaged Hispanics. Two factors account for this apparent anomaly. First, the higher representation of Puerto Ricans in white-collar occupations reflects the highly urban residence pattern of this population, especially when compared to Mexicans. Second, and more important, this result reflects the positive selection of Puerto Rican work-

**TABLE 21-6B. Occupational Distribution of Black, White, and Hispanic Female Workers, by Nationality, 1970–1985**

| Year and Broad Occupational Groups | Mexican | Puerto Rican | Cuban | Central and South American | Other Hispanic | Black | Non-Hispanic White |
|---|---|---|---|---|---|---|---|
| **1970:** | | | | | | | |
| Upper white-collar | 8.1 | 8.6 | 10.6 | 18.5 | 15.4 | 11.6 | 17.5 |
| Lower white-collar | 33.3 | 32.3 | 31.3 | 35.7 | 37.3 | 27.4 | 43.1 |
| Upper blue-collar | 2.1 | 2.4 | 2.3 | 1.6 | 1.9 | 1.5 | 1.9 |
| Lower blue-collar | 25.4 | 44.0 | 42.1 | 29.8 | 21.6 | 17.3 | 18.3 |
| Service workers | 25.7 | 12.4 | 13.0 | 19.2 | 22.3 | 41.2 | 18.9 |
| Farm workers | 5.4 | 0.3 | 0.6 | 0.2 | 1.6 | 1.1 | 0.5 |
| Total[a] | 100.0 | 100.0 | 99.9 | 100.0 | 100.1 | 100.1 | 100.2 |
| **1980:** | | | | | | | |
| Upper white-collar | 11.6 | 14.3 | 17.4 | 13.4 | 18.8 | 18.8 | 24.3 |
| Lower white-collar | 33.4 | 38.8 | 40.1 | 29.2 | 39.8 | 31.8 | 41.1 |
| Upper blue-collar | 2.5 | 3.0 | 2.9 | 3.2 | 2.4 | 1.7 | 2.3 |
| Lower blue-collar | 25.2 | 28.1 | 27.4 | 32.3 | 16.0 | 15.2 | 14.4 |
| Service workers | 22.7 | 15.3 | 12.0 | 21.7 | 22.1 | 32.2 | 17.6 |
| Farm workers | 4.6 | 0.4 | 0.2 | 0.3 | 0.9 | 0.4 | 0.4 |
| Total[a] | 100.0 | 99.9 | 100.0 | 100.1 | 100.0 | 100.1 | 100.1 |
| **1985:** | | | | | | | |
| Upper white-collar | 14.3 | 17.0 | 19.1 | 15.9 | 18.2 | 19.4 | 29.0 |
| Lower white-collar | 36.6 | 38.1 | 38.6 | 30.9 | 43.3 | 34.4 | 41.8 |
| Upper blue-collar | 2.5 | 1.0 | 0.8 | 0.6 | 2.4 | 1.5 | 1.7 |
| Lower blue-collar | 20.3 | 20.9 | 28.2 | 27.1 | 13.0 | 14.6 | 9.9 |
| Service workers | 23.3 | 22.8 | 13.4 | 25.0 | 23.1 | 29.7 | 17.1 |
| Farm workers | 2.9 | 0.3 | 0.0 | 0.5 | 0.0 | 0.4 | 0.5 |
| Total[a] | 99.9 | 100.1 | 100.0 | 100.0 | 100.0 | 100.0 | 100.0 |

[a] Numbers may not sum to 100 percent because of rounding.

*Source:* 1960, 1970, and 1980 Public Use Microdata Samples files; March 1985 *Current Population Survey.*

ers with jobs. In other words, the occupational profile presented in Tables 21-6A and 21-6B is based on the subset of workers who manage to secure jobs, which for Puerto Ricans represents a declining share of those eligible to work. Puerto Ricans who work do quite well, but an increasing share have no job at all. This suggests a pattern of social and economic bifurcation among Puerto Ricans, which finds additional support in indicators of income and poverty.[16]

A second message relayed by the occupational profiles is that the pattern of occupational change depends on the initial configuration. For example, Mexicans, whose mode of entry into the U.S. labor market was through agriculture, experienced the greatest declines in farm occupations. Yet vestiges of the past persist. As recently as 1985 the Mexican presence in farm occupations, mainly in laborer rather than operator jobs, far exceeded that observed for other Hispanics. The decreased participation of Mexicans in farming pursuits was offset by a greater presence in white-collar and upper blue-collar jobs. Mexican-origin women increased their representation in upper white-collar jobs, a shift made possible by declining jobs in farming and domestic service.

Declining farm employment had little bearing on changes in the occupational structure of non-Mexican groups because of their highly urban settlement patterns. For Puerto Ricans, the most striking occupational changes revolved around the sharply declining shares of lower blue-collar workers, a decline of 23 percentage points for women and 11 percentage points for men between 1970 and 1985. This precipitous drop in Puerto Rican blue-collar employment—a direct consequence of the industrial restructuring of the New York City labor market—translated into an increased representation of men in upper blue- and white-collar occupations, and an increase of women in white-collar occupations. But recall that the seemingly impressive occupational upgrading experienced by Puerto Ri-

cans must be interpreted as a highly selective process whereby those most likely to succeed have remained in the labor force, while those with limited prospects for occupational mobility have dropped out altogether.

The Cuban socioeconomic success story emerges clearly in the pattern of occupational change between 1970 and 1985. By 1985, 38 percent of employed Cuban men and 58 percent of employed Cuban women worked in white-collar jobs, compared to 25 and 34 percent, respectively, in 1960. This impressive occupational mobility was facilitated by the recovery of positions similar to those the refugees had held in Cuba, after experiencing initial downward mobility as a result of their limited English skills and the need for professionals to recertify their credentials. However, the imprint of the "Mariel" exodus during April 1980 is evident in the lowered representation of Cuban men in upper white-collar jobs by 1985. The working-class origins of this recent refugee cohort resulted in a swelling of male employment in lower blue-collar jobs.

Although Central and South Americans are often grouped with Cubans as holding a relatively high status in the U.S. labor force, this was truer for the 1960s and 1970s than the 1980s. Moreover, this group differs from the Cubans in two important respects: (1) This group *decreased* its representation in white-collar jobs during the 1970s, and consequently (2) the relative share of Central and South American workers holding white-collar jobs in 1985 was lower than it had been previously. The changing country-of-origin composition of the Central and South American population during the 1970s (discussed earlier), which ended the "brain drain"—that is, the flight of highly educated and skilled persons—largely explains the shifting occupational configuration of Central and South Americans.

In general, Hispanics enjoy a higher occupational standing than blacks but are far from occupational parity with non-Hispanic whites. Persons of Mexican and Puerto Rican origin lag furthest behind, and increasingly so do migrants from Central and South America. Moreover, the economic standing of Hispanics depends on their ability to secure jobs in the first place, and secondarily on *what types* of jobs they secure.

*Family Economic Well-Being.* Differences in the median family incomes of Hispanics are especially instructive about the extent of economic assimilation experienced by Hispanics. Figure 21-4 traces changes in median family incomes since 1969 in constant dollars. During the 1970s median family incomes of blacks and whites increased 8 and 6 percent, respectively, in real terms. While Mexicans and Cubans enjoyed an 18 to 20 percent real increase in median family income, families of Puerto Rican and Central or South American origin weathered real *declines* ranging from 4 to 6 percent. For Central and South Americans, this fall largely was precipitated by changes in the class composition of recent immigrants, coupled with the deleterious effects of the recession during the mid-1970s. This economic downturn had an adverse impact on

Puerto Ricans, whose labor market position was undermined by the confluence of several factors, including the weakened union bargaining power in the textile industry, the decline in unskilled operative jobs in northeastern labor markets, and the influx of new immigrants from Colombia and the Dominican Republic who were readily available to work in menial service jobs at minimum wages. Although the steep economic downswing during the early 1980s affected incomes of all groups, its deleterious impact apparently was most pronounced among minorities and ethnic groups. As a result, much of the convergence in family incomes between Hispanics and non-Hispanic whites achieved during the 1970s was undermined.

The evolving differentials in median family incomes underscore the profound significance of distinct **modes of incorporation** among Hispanic groups. It is apparent that the term *Hispanic*, suggesting common group experience, is not useful in portraying the diverse socioeconomic integration experiences of the Hispanic national-origin groups. Do these differences in socioeconomic integration affect residen-

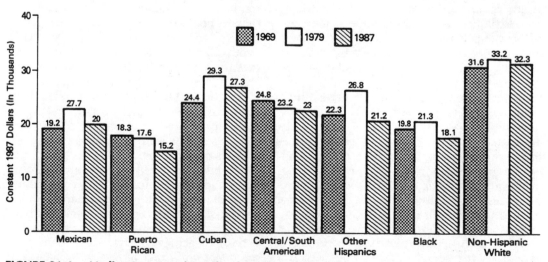

**FIGURE 21-4: Median Income of Families by Race, 1970–1988**

*Source:* U.S. Bureau of the Census, 1989; Supplementary Report CB89-158, March 1988; *Current Population Report, 1988*, Series P-20, Nos. 437, 438.

tial segregation and political and linguistic integration? We consider these implications in the final section.

## PROSPECTS FOR INTEGRATION: SPATIAL, CULTURAL, AND POLITICAL ISSUES

**Residential patterns** are an important indicator of social integration because social resources are unevenly distributed in space and because spatial arrangements shape the expression of cultural diversity. The concentration of ethnic groups in physical space allows native languages to flourish and makes ethnic enterprises and institutions viable. Some investigators unfortunately interpret these phenomena as constituting evidence that selected ethnic groups have limited integration prospects because they either refuse to be or cannot be accommodated into the mainstream.

Recent evidence showing that Hispanic residential concentration increased during the 1970s could be used to support such beliefs. However, this is primarily an effect of increasing immigration, and the subsequent replacement of non-Hispanic whites by Hispanics as their numbers increase. Aiding this process is the socioeconomic distance between recent immigrants and the settled non-Hispanic white population, and the immigrant adjustment process. The latter is facilitated by residence in areas where social supports needed to find jobs and housing are readily available.[17] Friendship and kinship networks promote the settlement of recent arrivals in areas of high ethnic concentration. During periods of economic austerity, the need for social supports increases, thereby encouraging ethnic groups to turn inward.

Concentration in ethnic neighborhoods, coupled with an increased use of ethnicity as a basis for social organization, also is a reaction to perceived rejection by the dominant society.[18] Thus, when ethnically distinct groups are denied access to the opportunities enjoyed by the dominant population, group members elaborate social ties among themselves. In the face of interethnic tension and economic adversity, compatriots furnish the social supports needed for adequate, if not equal, functioning in the host society. Expressions of Hispanic culture, most prominently the Spanish language, become an enduring rather than a transitional feature of Hispanic neighborhoods because they are preserved by ethnic encapsulation. Thus, we may see ethnic resilience as the *consequence* of unequal integration experiences, rather than their cause. Alternatively, for successful ethnic entrepreneurs, like the Cubans in Miami, ethnic encapsulation provides a basis for strengthening economic ties. This partly explains the success of the Cuban economic enclave in Miami.

### Linguistic Pluralism

At the outset of this chapter we noted that the issue of integration lies at the core of a philosophical debate about whether assimilation should pursue an Anglo-conformity or some variant of a pluralism model. The language issue is crucial in this debate because it is the target of political efforts to assimilate ethnically distinct groups, and because high levels of Spanish retention have been blamed for the disadvantaged economic status of the Hispanic population. The pluralism versus Anglo-conformity debate with respect to language maintenance is emotionally charged and invites diametrically opposed views, each with its own compelling logic.

While there exists considerable controversy about the socioeconomic consequences of bilingualism, the preponderance of research shows that Spanish retention per se (bilingualism) does *not* hinder the social and economic achievements of Hispanics, *provided that proficiency in English* is acquired.[19] This conclusion is based on evidence showing that Spanish retention is inconsequential for occupational status or earnings among those who are proficient in English. Furthermore, there is some evidence that bilingualism may actually be an asset, but only among the middle class, who are able to convert this skill to social and financial resources. Unfortunately, though, most bilingual Hispanics are neither middle class nor highly proficient in English. For them, bilingual education may be a barrier to English proficiency, as critics charge.[20]

Spanish retention or, more generally, linguistic diversity is *not* incompatible with social and economic integration of Hispanics because Spanish retention and English proficiency are not mutually exclusive. If language retention as an expression of cultural diversity is not a major obstacle to the social and economic integration of Hispanics— and the preponderance of empirical research suggests that cultural factors give way to class and social background factors as key determinants of social standing—the critical question becomes: Why does there persist a close association between Hispanic national origin and low social standing? Two scenarios suggest themselves.

One is a replenishment and composition argument. That is, as earlier arrivals and their native offspring move up the social escalator, new immigrant cohorts of low social origins and who are destined for low-status jobs enter on the bottom step. This replenishment argument is congruent with the experience of European ethnic groups who, upon entering the U.S. labor market, occupied the lowest status jobs, but with the passage of time and generations improved their position in the host society. This replenishment argument is essentially a variant of the assimilation model proposed by Milton Gordon in his classic statement on assimilation.[21] What is crucial for interpreting the experience of early European groups is that immigration virtually ceased, thereby eliminating the compositional changes produced by replenishment of new cohorts at the bottom of the social escalator.[22] For Hispanics, the replenishment process continues unabated and is only partly shaped by formal admission criteria, as the large volume of undocumented immigrants testifies. This could change, however, if the 1986 Immigration Reform and Control Act is successful in reducing illegal immigration.

Thus, given the relative recency of the immigrant streams from Central and South America and the Dominican Republic, the low aggregate social standing of these groups largely reflects their limited experience with U.S. institutions and labor market, and one may expect that with the passage of time (and assuming an end to immigration from these sources) these immigrant groups will, like their European predecessors, move up the social ladder. But this interpretation does not explain why native-born persons of Mexican ancestry are relatively less successful in educational, labor market, or political spheres than recent immigrants from Cuba, or why recent immigrants from Colombia and the Dominican Republic participate in the labor force at rates exceeding those of Puerto Ricans who are U.S. citizens by birth.

Thus, an alternative scenario projects over the long term relatively limited social mobility, particularly for those groups whose ethnic distinctiveness is most pronounced and whose class backgrounds place them on the bottom step. This interpretation accords greater weight to the complex set of circumstances that define distinct *modes of incorporation* for the various Hispanic groups. Unfortunately, it is too early to evaluate the relative merits of both predictions, primarily because the replenishment process is very much alive, and because the future of immigration is indeterminate. The socioeconomic fate of Hispanics also will be shaped decisively by the extent to which the national-origin groups participate in the political process and, in particular, the extent to which Hispanic elected and appointed officials use ethnicity as a criterion for defining their political agendas. This future also is uncertain, as the next section shows.

## Political Participation and Hispanic Interests

The rapid growth of the Hispanic population since 1960, coupled with its residential concentration, provides conditions for increasing participation in the political process. The Southwest Voter Research Institute notes that the reapportionment and redistricting process following the 1990 census could increase opportunities for Hispanic representation in Congress.[23] Population projections indicate that Texas, Arizona, and California—three states with large Hispanic populations—stand to gain as many as 10 new congressional seats. As we argued at the outset, however, size does not ensure power. This is evident in the relative underrepresentation of Hispanics in elective offices at all levels. Although Hispanics represent 8 percent of the U.S. population, they hold less than 2 percent of elected offices. In 1989 Hispanics held 9 seats in Congress, less than 2 percent.

Hispanics do not represent a unified political force nationally. But in communities with large Spanish-speaking populations, Hispanic politicians have emerged and political platforms have been mobilized around common ethnic issues. Cuban and Mexican mayors have been elected in Miami and San Antonio, respectively. Hispanic governors have been elected in Florida, Colorado, and Arizona. At the national level, Hispanic politicians have created the Hispanic Caucus, a fragile alliance attuned to Hispanic issues, but its cohesion as a national political force has yet to be tested. Nevertheless, its existence testifies to the political presence of Hispanics.

Greater numbers, though a necessary condition to increase Hispanic representation, are insufficient to guarantee it. An age structure with a large share of the population under 18 years, coupled with low rates of naturalization among the foreign-born, reduces the size of the Hispanic electorate. A further major challenge ahead is ensuring that Hispanics vote, and past experience has demonstrated that this is a serious problem. Despite their increasing share of the total population, Hispanics represent approximately 7 percent of the adult population and between 2 and 4 percent of the voters. Voter turnout also varies by national origin: Cuban voter turnout exceeds that of Mexicans and Puerto Ricans. Moreover, class interests and political history leads to a split by party affiliation. Cubans vote Republican, in the main, while Mexicans and Puerto Ricans lean towards the Democrats. Hence, differentiation along national origin lines potentially undermines efforts to build a united front on behalf of Hispanic interests, despite the presence of common ethnic concerns, such as the future of immigration policy and the financing of bicultural education programs. Thus, Hispanic political cohesiveness will remain frail and unpredictable for some time to·come.

## SUMMARY

1.  The rapid increase of the Hispanic population has raised concerns about whether large numbers of an ethnically distinct but highly differentiated population can be integrated into Anglo-American society. Prominent among the reasons for these concerns are: (1) the rapid demographic growth of Hispanics combined with pronounced regional concentration; (2) increasing population heterogeneity along national-origin lines; (3) the growing political force represented by greater numbers of spatially concentrated Hispanics; and (4) the reappearance of immigration policy on the political agenda. Recent controversy about illegal immigration has further increased public awareness of the Hispanic presence in the United States and has been the source of considerable misunderstanding and tension.

2.  However, the extensive heterogeneity of Hispanics suggests, against many current fears, a diversified social and political imprint on the United States, and dissimilar trajectories of "Americani-

zation.'' Integration experiences will depend on the diverse historical contexts that gave rise to the migrant streams from each country, the timing of arrival, reception factors in the host communities, and differences in the class composition and social backgrounds of the migrants.

3. For the general public and lay politicians, the fears of cultural pluralism have been aroused by the regional and metropolitan concentration of Hispanics, the slowdown in the process of residential succession, heightened awareness of Spanish retention, and the resurgence of ethnicity or common national ties as a basis for social functioning. These and other indicators of cultural pluralism have been misunderstood, and consequently the persistence of ethnic markers has been interpreted as evidence of an inability or an unwillingness on the part of Hispanics to become integrated into the mainstream of U.S. society and the U.S. economy. But such interpretations confuse the causes and consequences of the persisting association between national origin and low social standing. Further, they underestimate the significance of intragroup divisions along ethnic lines. A static picture emphasizing socioeconomic problems and cultural differentiation fails to capture the dynamism inherent in both the settlement and the integration process, as well as the increasing heterogeneity among Hispanics.

4. The main theme of this chapter is that Hispanics do not represent a unified ethnic group that can easily mobilize behind common social goals.[8] Evidence of increasing rather than decreasing social and economic differences along national-origin lines undermines the apparent unity subsumed under a common label and frail political coalitions. Although it is conceivable that Hispanic elected and appointed officials may unite to gain concessions that benefit all Hispanic ethnic constituencies, few issues unite Hispanics across class lines and can sustain ethnic coalition politics on a sustained basis. The political alliances that may have emerged to promote specific ethnic issues, such as bilingual education or a liberal immigration policy, are precarious.

5. It is difficult to project the nature of U.S. ethnic relations into the future, but continued high levels of immigration from Latin America virtually insure that the Hispanic imprints on the United States will become more pronounced over the next decade or two. Tendencies for spatial concentration coupled with large immigrant cohorts will enhance the visibility of Hispanics in the United States and will also lead to downward pressure on the class position of all nationality groups except the Cubans. But it would be a mistake to leave the impression that Hispanics have not been assimilating. The trend toward a language shift away from Spanish— one that has proceeded most rapidly among Cubans—is stark testimony to this fact. Again, what remains to be explained is the higher rate of Spanish retention among native-born Mexicans and Puerto Ricans.

## KEY CONCEPTS FOR REVIEW

Assimilation: Anglo-conformity, cultural pluralism, and the melting pot

Ethnic labels: Latino versus Hispanic

Modes of incorporation: entry, integration, and reaffirmation

Auspices of migration

Political versus wage-labor (economic) migrants

Residential patterns

## QUESTIONS FOR DISCUSSION

1. How has the national origin composition of the Hispanic population changed since 1960, and what factors explain this shift?

2. What is the social significance of regional concentration for the Hispanic population?

3. What is meant by a *mode of incorporation,* and what implications does it have for the integration of Hispanic groups?

4. Compare and contrast the labor market position of Hispanics in terms of labor force participation and occupational standing.

5.  How does linguistic diversity bear on the social integration prospects of Hispanics?

6.  Under what conditions can Hispanics become

a viable political force in the future, and how will this influence their positioning in U.S. society?

## NOTES

1.  Milton Gordon, *Assimilation in American Life* (New York: Oxford University Press, 1964).
2.  Originally the "smelting pot," a rather fiercer image, which evokes a crucible in which metals are transformed into something quite different; the "melting pot" implies the possibility of a cooking utensil in which some aspects of the original ingredients survive.
3.  F. Ray Marshall and Leon F. Bouvier, *Population Change and the Future of Texas* (Washington, D.C.: Population Reference Bureau, 1986).
4.  We use the term *Hispanic* because that is the term used by the Census Bureau for Spanish-speaking groups from the various countries of Latin America. *Latino* is becoming more popular to refer to Spanish-speaking groups. Names can change rapidly: *black* replaced *Negro,* and *Hispanic* may not long prevail as the most common term for immigrants from the Spanish-speaking countries of the New World and their descendants. *Hispanic* itself replaced the term *Spanish-surname,* used during the 1950s and 1960s, and *Spanish origin,* used in 1970.
5.  Clumsy as the term *non-Hispanic whites* is, there seems to be no decent alternative. *Anglo,* widely used in the Southwest and Miami in Dade County to refer to non-Hispanic groups, includes groups (such as Jews, and descendants of other southern European, eastern European, and Near Eastern groups) who would find the appellation *Anglo* odd. It is also not in common use in other major centers of Hispanic populations, such as New York City and Chicago. *Non-Hispanic white* also has the virtue of being the term the Census Bureau uses.
6.  Marshall and Bouvier, *Population Change,* pp. 52–53.
7.  Population Reference Bureau, *America in the 21st Century: A Demographic Overview* (Washington, D.C.: Population Reference Bureau, 1989).
8.  Classifying all Hispanics as a "minority" population is problematic in the sense that the label *minority* customarily is used to refer to groups that are both numerically small and economically disadvantaged. Many of the Hispanic subpopulations are not economically disadvantaged, particularly those of Cuban origin and those of South American origin who arrived during the 1960s—the so-called brain drain migrants. Politically and administratively (for example, in regulations requiring government contractors or local school districts to

report on numbers of specific minority groups), Hispanics are considered a minority, and using only numerical considerations, the labeling of Hispanics as a minority is appropriate.
9.  These included descendants of the original Spanish settlers in what is presently New Mexico and Colorado (known as *Hispanos*), offspring of Mexicans who became U.S. citizens under the 1848 Treaty of Guadalupe Hidalgo, and immigrants from Mexico who had been recruited since the turn of the century to work in agriculture, mining, and the expanding railroad industry.
10.  Prior to 1980 the Hispanic population was identified through a battery of items that were asked of a sample of the total population ranging from 5 percent to 20 percent. Despite the fact that several identifiers were used in 1970, none yielded an accurate population estimate. Consequently, for the 1980 questionnaire, an item to identify Hispanics was included in the schedule administered to all households. These changes were implemented largely in response to political pressure to improve the undercount of Hispanics in the 1970 census. The improved enumeration in 1980 also was facilitated by an expanded public relations campaign aimed at encouraging Hispanics to complete the census questionnaire, irrespective of legal status.
11.  See Frank D. Bean and Manta Tienda, *The Hispanic Population of the United States* (New York: Russell Sage Foundation, 1987), Table 4.4.
12.  Whereas the 1986 Immigration Reform and Control Act focused on undocumented immigration and left the preference system essentially untouched, legislation passed in 1990 placed a greater premium on occupational skills as a criterion for admission (see Chapter 20, this volume).
13.  Candace Nelson and Marta Tienda, "The Structuring of Hispanic Ethnicity: Historical and Contemporary Perspectives," *Ethnic and Racial Studies,* 8(1), 1985, 49–74.
14.  U.S. Commission on Civil Rights, *Puerto Ricans in the United States: An Uncertain Future* (Washington, D.C.: U.S. Government Printing Office, 1976).
15.  Bean and Tienda, *The Hispanic Population.*
16.  See Marta Tienda and Lief Jensen, "Poverty and Minorities: A Quarter Century Profile of Color and Socioeconomic Disadvantage," in Gary D. Sandefur and Marta Tienda, eds., *Divided Opportunities,* pp. 265–270 (New York: Plenum, 1988).

17. Douglas S. Massey and Nancy A. Denton, "Spatial Assimilation as a Socioeconomic Outcome," *American Sociological Review, 50,* 1985, 94–105.

18. Portes Alejandro and Robert L. Bach, *Latin Journey* (Berkeley: University of California Press, 1985).

19. Marta Tienda and Lisa J. Neidert, "Language, Education, and the Socioeconomic Achievement of Hispanic Origin Men," *Social Science Quarterly, 65*(2), 1984, 533.

20. For evidence on bilingualism as a resource, see David E. Lopez, "The Social Consequences of Chicano Home/School Bilingualism," *Social Problems, 24,* December 1976, 234–246, and Marta Tienda, "Sex, Ethnicity and Chicano Status Attainment," *International Migration Review, 16*(2), 1982, 435–472. For criticisms of bilingual education policies, see Abigail M. Thernstrom "Bilingual Miseducation," *Commentary,* Feb. 1990, pp. 44–48, and Rosalie Porter, *Forked Tongue: The Politics of Bilingual Education* (New York: Basic Books, 1990).

21. Gordon, *Assimilation in American Life.*

22. This is essentially what Stanley Lieberson argues in *A Piece of the Pie* (Berkeley: University of California Press, 1980) when comparing blacks to the second major wave of European immigrants.

23. *Southwest Voter Research Notes,* 3(2), October 1989.

# Part VI
# *OUR POSTERITY*

# 22

# Can We Live Long and Live Well?

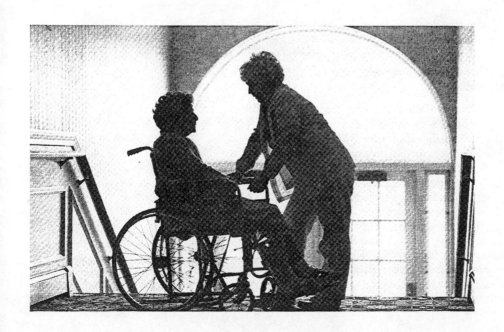

*I*n Part VI, we shall be exploring the population future that may await ourselves and our posterity. The issues we consider necessarily involve speculation about matters that cannot be determined unequivocally at this time. Still, we know that our present situation is unlikely to persist, that major changes of one kind or another will be occurring, and that we would be well advised to sketch out some of the scenarios that may develop in the decades ahead.

In no part of our work is this effort more necessary than in the matter of the length of human life. For we are not only virtually certain that our life expectancy will continue to increase, but many observers believe that we are on the verge of revolutionary changes in human life span. How long can we live? What would be the consequences of very long lives on our state of health, our economy, our relations with other generations, our life-styles?

## SQUARING THE CURVE

There are really two different ways in which our life expectancies may be extended in the future: increasing our chances of surviving to a given maximum life span, and extending the maximum life span.

### Continuing Our Historic Progress against Mortality

We begin with what has been our traditional pattern of advance. When we introduced the Aging Society (Chapter 5), we spoke of "squaring" the population pyramid as the society's fertility rate fell and the proportion of older people increased. We now use the term *squaring* in a different sense to refer to survival curves. These curves have nothing to do with fertility rates and simply express the probabilities of survival (expressed as a percentage) of individuals to different ages in a population at a given time. Thus, the probability of an individual surviving to age 2 is higher than

the probability of surviving to age 5, or 30, or 80, and so on.

In Figure 22-1, we show three curves: the **survival curves** for the United States in 1900 and 1987, and a theoretical upper limit to our survival curve on the assumption that our maximum life span remains fixed at around 110 years. If literally every newborn lived to be 110 and then died, this upper limit would be represented by a 90-degree angle curve that went across at 100 percent to age 110 and then went down vertically to zero percent. The curve would be perfectly "squared." In fact, however, it is beyond the realm of possibility that no one would ever die along the way; if nothing else, accidents would guarantee some earlier fatalities. Also, there are wars, homicides, suicides, inherited birth defects that lead to death, and the like. The best one could hope for is that we continue moving in the future as we did between 1900 and 1987—in the general direction of "squaring" our survival curve. And, indeed, everyone agrees that our future advance will continue in this direction and that our survival curve

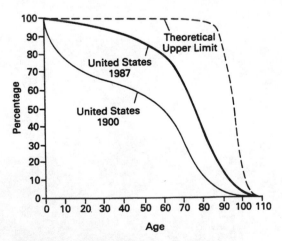

**FIGURE 22-1: Survival Curves**
These curves show the percentages of the U.S. population surviving to different ages. Assuming a fixed maximum life span of 110, further "curve-squaring" could take us out to the theoretical upper limit shown above.

in, say, the year 2080 will be to the right of that for 1987.

### The Debate over the Rate of Advance

But how far to the right? At this point, we must accept the fact that experts disagree on the probable rate of advance; we must content ourselves with indicating the range of possibilities projected by qualified observers. We know from our earlier discussions that the Census Bureau projects different future life expectancies in its High, Middle, and Low (and other) Series. In 1989, these ranged from a Low Series estimate for life expectancy at birth in the year 2080 of 77.9 years to a High Series estimate of 88.0 years. Interestingly enough, this high estimate is 2.1 years higher than the estimate made just five years before (in 1984).

But is it high enough yet? In 1988, while the Census Bureau was developing these projections, a study published in the *Milbank Quarterly* suggested that the bureau might be considerably underestimating future increases in life expectancies. The authors offered this description of their alternative projection:

> The projections of the Census Bureau and the Social Security Administration have used the assumption that the mortality decline seen in the past two decades cannot continue. In this article, an alternative projection is presented that uses the assumption that the recent level of mortality decline could be sustained for the next half century as a result of continued advances in prevention and therapy of the common causes of death, as well as by potential biomedical breakthroughs.[1]

Using the assumption of a 2 percent annual mortality decline (the rate observed in the United States between 1968 and 1980), they project average life expectancies at birth in the year 2040 at 85.9 years for American males and 91.5 years for American females. The contrasting Middle Series Census Bureau projections for 2040 are 75.9 and 82.8 years, respectively. The consequences of these differences are shown in Table 22-1. Not only would we have many more 65-and-older persons on the 2 percent mortality decline assumption (86.8 million versus 68.1 million in the year 2040), but the distribution of these elderly would be heavily tilted toward the older old. In particular, there would be *nearly a doubling* of the number of 85-and-over persons (from 12.3 to 23.5 million in 2040). Authors Guralnik, Yanagishita, and Schneider do not claim any great confidence in their own projections, but they do in fact describe a number of reasons for believing that they are at least as likely as those from the Census Bureau. Clearly, our future will be greatly affected by which experts' projections—and there are many others beside these two—turn out to be the more accurate.[2]

## HOW LONG *COULD* WE LIVE?

If there is a debate about the future rate of advance of our "curve-squaring" technologies, there is even greater uncertainty about the second main way in which our life expectancies might be increased—that is, by extending the maximum human life span.

### Extension of the Maximum Life Span

As we have often said before, **maximum human life span** appears to have been relatively fixed during the course of human history. In the absence of intervention, it also appears to be relatively fixed for other species—the tortoise at 150 years, the whale at 50, the dog at 20, the mouse at 3.5, and so on.

Of course, if we go far back beyond historical records into our evolutionary past, there is evidence of a lengthening of the life spans of mammals, and of human beings in particular. Life span has tended to increase with brain size, and, over millions of

**TABLE 22-1. Alternative Projections of Life Expectancy and of Older Population, 2040**

| | Census Bureau, 1989 Middle Series | | Assumption of 2% Annual Mortality Decline | |
|---|---|---|---|---|
| | *Male* | *Female* | *Male* | *Female* |
| Life expectancy from birth (years) | 75.9 | 82.8 | 85.9 | 91.5 |
| Population (in thousands) | | | | |
| Ages: | | | | |
| 65–74 | | 30,808 | | 32,075 |
| 75–84 | | 25,050 | | 31,212 |
| 85+ | | 12,251 | | 23,519 |
| Total 65+ | | 68,109 | | 86,805 |
| Percentage distribution of 65+ population by age group (percentages)[a] | | | | |
| 65–74 | | 45.2 | | 37.0 |
| 75–84 | | 36.8 | | 36.0 |
| 85+ | | 18.0 | | 27.1 |

*Note:* Both projections assume Middle Series fertility and migration assumptions.

[a] Totals may not equal 100 percent because of rounding.

*Sources:* Based on Gregory Spencer, "Projections of the Population of the United States by Age, Sex, and Race: 1988 to 2080," U.S. Bureau of the Census, *Current Population Reports*, Series P-25, No. 1018, 1989, and Jack M. Guralnik, Machiko Yanagishita, and Edward L. Schneider, "Projecting the Older Population of the United States: Lessons from the Past and Prospects for the Future," *Milbank Quarterly,* 66(2), 1988, Table 5, p. 302.

years, the brain weight of humans is estimated to have increased from around 1.7 to 3.1 pounds. In terms of the time perspective of our own study, however, our maximum life span has been constant, and any extension of that span would represent an unprecedented accomplishment.

Graphically, as we see in Figure 22-2a, such an accomplishment would involve a shifting out of our survival curve to the right of the diagram. Such a shift would be qualitatively different from the "**curve-squaring**" **advances** just discussed, although, of course, we might have technological advances that both extended the survival curve and squared it at the same time. In terms of our population pyramid (or rectangle), the effect of span extension would be to raise the height of the pyramid (Figure 22-2b).

### Theories of Aging

Whether such advances will be possible will depend on the nature of the aging process in human beings, our understanding of that process, and, finally, our ability (and willingness) to intervene and alter that process. At the present time, there is no agreement either on the nature of the process or on our ultimate ability to understand and control it. Nevertheless, there has been an outpouring of theories of aging during recent decades, and it is clear that, with the extraordinarily rapid advances now occurring in molecular biology, neurobiology, and immunology, the possibilities for understanding and control are increasing geometrically. Even a list of the main theories of aging, apart from their numerous variations, would be quite extensive. Investigators have suggested that the aging process may be significantly affected by the following factors, among many others:

- Diet restriction
- Body temperature
- The excessive or deficient release of certain hormones

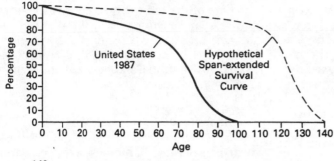

**FIGURE 22-2a:   Survival Curves with Span Extension**

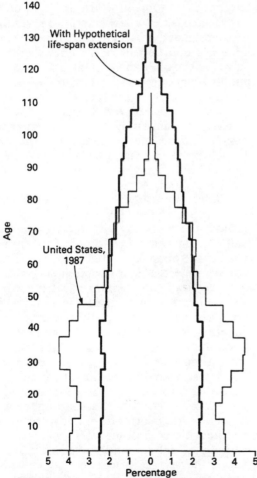

**FIGURE 22-2b:   Population Pyramids, United States, 1987 and with Hypothetical Life Span Extension**

Note that the areas of these two pyramids are equal, each representing 100 percent of the relevant population.

- The accumulation of certain insoluble lipofuscins within cells
- Errors in DNA transcriptions
- The accumulation of certain destructive "free radicals"
- Fundamental limits on the reproductive capacities of human cells
- The action of certain limited clusters of genes such as the "major histocompatibility complex"
- The effect of "longevity-assurance" genes
- The presence in senescent cells of substances that inhibit DNA synthesis
- Cross-linkage effects either within or between protein molecules
- Genes such as "Age-1" that promote fecundity at the expense of shortening life span

Within this wide range of theories there is also a variation in the most fruitful general approach: whether at the level of the molecule, cell, or organ system; whether from the point of view of a wear-and-tear approach or a genetic programming approach; whether, in terms of genetic programming, to look for mechanisms that promote aging and death, or to look for mechanisms that promote longevity as a counterweight to normal survival activities, like breathing, that have undesirable side effects. With respect to this last point, it can be argued that since animals in the wild never live long enough to grow old, there is no *evolutionary reason* for aging and death to be programmed into our genes. What *is* necessary, according to this argument, is to have genes that protect us against the hazards of living—that is, **longevity-assurance genes** that keep us alive long enough to reproduce and raise our young.

Despite this range of theories and often conflicting angles of approach, there have been some important lines of research that suggest to many investigators that the subject is far from hopeless:

*1. Diet Restriction.* One of the more persistent themes in the field is that a suitably planned diet reduction may lead to major life span extension. Evidence here goes back to the late 1920s with the experiments of Clive M. McCay of Cornell on the effects of **diet restriction** on the life spans of male rats. In a series of papers beginning in 1935, McCay claimed that, by severely restricting the diet of one group of rats (while maintaining crucial nutrients), he was able to achieve major increases in life spans as compared to a control group of rats who were fed, at will, as much as they wanted. Calorie restrictions of 50 percent led roughly to a doubling of life spans, while restrictions of 25 percent led to about a one-third increase.

These results were substantially confirmed in the 1960s and 1970s by Morris Ross of the Institute of Cancer Research in Philadelphia. Ross found maximum life span among the well-fed rats to be 1,000 to 1,099 days, while that of the calorie-restricted rats was 1,600 to 1,699 days. In the 1980s, physiologist Edward J. Masoro of the University of Texas (San Antonio), reduced calorie intake by 60 percent and produced healthy, active rats with a 50 percent increase in life span. Similar results have been found with other species, for example, the microorganism *Tokophyra*. Freely feeding *Tokophyra* lasted only 10 days; by reduced feedings, life span was extended to 80 days, a dramatic 800 percent increase.

One of the most respected investigators of life span extension, Roy L. Walford of the University of California at Los Angeles, has in fact been practicing diet restriction as his own personal experiment in human longevity.[3]

*2. Cell Division and the "Hayflick Limit."* Some gerontologists date the effective beginnings of modern aging research to the publication in 1961 of a paper by microbiologist Leonard Hayflick presenting evidence that there was a limit to the number of times that human cells would divide in vitro before they died.[4] Hayflick's experiments suggested that a range of 50 (plus or minus 10) doublings was characteristic of a particular strain of fibroblasts (the WI-38 strain). This limit (now widely known as the **Hayflick limit**) was in contrast to the previously prevailing view that cells, if properly fed and maintained in culture, were essentially immortal.

There are many conflicting views of the significance of the Hayflick limit. There is always the difficulty of inferring results achieved in vitro to conditions applying to the human organism—that is, in vivo. Thus, for example, the 50 or so doublings Hayflick achieved took only months in vitro; clearly, this is much shorter than the human life span which is a matter of many years. Transplanting older cells to younger animals has been shown to extend the life of the former, suggesting that it is not just the cell itself, but its surrounding environment as well, that affects its life span. Some experiments have shown further that adding certain substances (like cortisone or hydrocortisone) to the culture medium can increase the number of cell doublings even in vitro. In short, the subject is unavoidably complex. Still, the concept that human beings are genetically programmed to age, and ultimately to die, and that this biological "clock" (or one of our biological "clocks") may be located in the cell itself is one that has produced important and continuing research in the field of span extension. It has even been suggested that this cellular clock could be a kind of backup mechanism, guaranteeing the ultimate death of an individual in case other clocks (say, in the brain) or simple wear-and-tear fail to get us first.[5]

*3. Free Radical Theories.* One of the more fundamental notions that appears in many theories of aging is that we grow old as a result of the side effects of normal processes necessary for survival. One such process is breathing. And the side effect emphasized by doctor/chemist Denham Harman as far back as 1956 was the formation of oxygen **"free radicals,"** oxygen molecules with unpaired electrons.[6] These molecules seek additional electrons and, in taking electrons from other molecules, create other free radicals, which can continue the general onslaught on the human body. Free radicals have, in one way or another, been implicated in such degenerative diseases as cancer, heart disease, stroke, Parkinson's disease, cataracts, and emphysema. And, according to Harman and other scientists working in this area, they may cause damage to cells and DNA, reprogram our genes, and in general contribute to the aging and decay of the organism as a whole.

More recent research has shown that the adverse effects of free radicals on bodily tissues are to some degree counteracted by various antioxidants and repair enzymes that either neutralize the free radicals or mop up or repair the damage they have caused. The degree of antioxidant protection in the body may be regulated by our genes, meaning that those species with greater protection against the effects of free radicals will have longer life spans than those that have less protection. This, then, would be an example of a theory that postulated genes that promote longer life, rather than genes that are specifically programmed to produce aging and death.

*4. The Immune System.* Not unrelated to the free radical theories (because free radicals may do damage to our immune system) are numerous hypotheses that implicate the immune system in the aging process. As we age, our immune system deteriorates in two ways: (1) Our protection against outside invaders becomes weakened, and (2) there is an increase in autoimmune disorders (like rheumatoid arthritis) in which the body essentially attacks itself as "foreign." In one view, aging is essentially an increasing process of self-rejection. In his *Immunologic Theory of Aging* (1969), Roy Walford suggested that the end of life involves a serious deterioration in our capacity for self-recognition. Walford (whose interest in diet restriction we mentioned earlier) has also advanced the hypothesis that aging may be controlled by a relatively small number of genes, those involved in the "major histocompatibility complex," which determine, for example, the matching of tissues for successful organ transplants.

Other researchers, like Allan Goldstein, chairman of the Biochemistry Department at George Washington University, have stressed the role of the thymus gland, the master gland of the immune system. The thymus gland shrinks throughout our lives, with a noticeable decrease in the production of a family of hormones called "thymosins." These thymosins activate T-cells, which kill foreign organisms and cancer cells, help develop antibodies, and also suppress autoimmune reactions in which the immune system attacks the body's own tissues. Insofar as aging involves a failure of the immune system to function properly, the role of thymosins may prove to be critical.

*5. Aging as a Product of Multiple Factors.* Thymosins are one class of substances that may affect longevity, but there are numerous hormones, enzymes, proteins, and other chemical compounds that have been implicated in the aging process. Much has been made of the role of DHEA (de-hydroepiandrosterone), a protector of the thymus gland; DECO (decreasing oxygen consumption hormone), the so-called death hormone; SOD (superoxide dismutase), an important antioxidant; fibronectin, a protein that holds cells in position and helps young cells retain their shape; or an undetermined (as of this writing) protein present in senescent cells that inhibits DNA synthesis and effectively shuts these cells down.

It is important to mention this great variety of approaches because, while some years ago many researchers were seeking a single gene that might be responsible for the aging process, scientists currently believe there are many factors involved. At a 1989 conference on aging in Santa Fe, Thomas E. Johnson of the University of Colorado, discoverer of the "Age-1 gene," concluded: "We're not looking for single causes any more. Aging is a mixture of multiple causes."[7] Thus, while future progress is likely to rule out some of the current leads as erroneous, it is also quite possible that many of them may be found to be relevant, probably in complicated and interconnected ways. The general spirit of the conference was decidedly optimistic: The analysis of aging, it was argued, is now itself coming of age.

## But Is Aging Subject to Intervention and Control?

In the absence of any generally accepted theory, or theories, of aging, scientists cannot know whether the process will ever be amenable to human intervention. (Whether such intervention *should* be contemplated is another question.) On the whole, however, most researchers in the field believe that such interventions will be possible. There is already the rather compelling evidence of span extension in certain animal species through diet restriction. Lowered body temperature (hypothermia) has apparently achieved the same result in certain cases. More complicated results in animal experi-

ments have been achieved through parabiosis—joining the younger and older member of the same species so that they share a common blood supply—or the surgical removal of the pituitary gland, combined with supplementary doses of thyroxine.

Successful interventions obviously will depend on what factors prove most crucial in the aging process. Thus, if "free radicals" are serious culprits, then intervention may involve the administration of well-known antioxidants like SOD, Vitamin E, beta carotene, glutathione, and selenium. If DNA repair is crucial, then such repair might be stimulated by inducing low levels of damage that bring forth large rates of repair, or by "tricking" cells into thinking that damage has occurred in order to stimulate the repair process. Insofar as the aging process is basically genetic in nature, the enormous recent progress in biogenetics, including the plan to plot out the entire human genome (see Chapter 26), strongly suggests that both understanding and control will increase dramatically in the next century.

Not that progress along these lines will necessarily be easy or to everyone's taste. For example, Richard Cutler, one of the most creative (and sometimes controversial) figures in gerontology, has suggested that major gains in longevity might ultimately depend on **neoteny**, or the retention into adulthood of early, childlike developmental features. These long-lived neotenous humans would likely have brains twice as large as ours, meaning that their heads would be too large to survive the journey down the birth canal, meaning in turn that babies in this distant future would have to be conceived and sustained outside the womb by artificial means. This method is likely to be used, Cutler believes, whether we achieve major longevity gains or not.[8]

Despite all qualifications, one conclusion should command close to universal assent:

*There is now a serious possibility that life span extension may be achieved within the next cen-*

*tury, half century, or even sooner. Whether the gains may be a few years or qualitatively revolutionary gains of 50 or 100 years or even more, only time will tell. But it is no longer considered quackery or science fiction to imagine that these major extensions will take place. In this, as in many other respects, human evolution may increasingly be coming under human control.*

## HOW WELL WILL WE BE?

If major advances in mortality reduction do occur, will improvements in morbidity be far behind? Will our increases in life expectancy be largely in years of good health or in years of disability?

When we last discussed this subject (Chapter 8), we saw that no firm conclusion could be reached on the mortality/morbidity issue as far as our past experience is concerned. In that earlier discussion, we did, however, note one hopeful possibility: namely, that if the number of unhealthy years is on the increase, there will almost certainly be—and we see evidence of this already—a more vigorous focus on issues of *health* as opposed to simple *longevity*. History strongly suggests that, as problems develop—in this case, increased morbidity—we will devote our efforts specifically to those problems, and with reasonable hope of success.

Do we have any other reasons to believe that our longer lives of the future may be lived in good health?

### Good Health at Older Ages Can Be Promoted by Our Behavior

One major reason for some optimism on this matter is that modern research has shown that many of the negative effects of aging, whether physical or mental, can be offset by our own efforts. In principle, this result should apply whether our longer lives

are achieved through curve-squaring technologies or through life-span extension.

*1. Physical: Exercise and Diet.* Numerous studies have shown that virtually all the characteristic signs of physical decline with age—reduced lung capacity, decreased heart stroke volume, increased tendencies to blood clotting, loss of muscle fiber, reduced calcium and increased bone loss, and the like—can be either slowed down or, for long periods, actually reversed by an appropriate exercise regimen. According to Dr. Roy J. Shephard of the University of Toronto, a simple routine of "little more than rapid walking for 30 minutes at a time three or four times a week ... can provide 10 years of rejuvenation."[9]

Where specific ailments, like arthritis or osteoporosis, are involved, vigorous exercise may not be possible (although weight-bearing exercises may be effective with osteoporosis), but diet may have important effects. Recent evidence, for example, suggests that osteoporosis, which involves increasingly brittle bones and the greater risk of hip fractures among the elderly, may result in part from vitamin D deficiency. Studies at Tufts University have found that some 40 percent of hip fracture victims among the elderly are lacking in adequate vitamin D.

Other studies have shown that older people can gain additional muscle mass and strength through exercise; that Seventh Day Adventists live not only longer but healthier lives than the rest of us because of their good health habits (exercise, vegetarianism, nonsmoking); and that centenarians, when they are not afflicted by Alzheimer's disease or other forms of dementia, live surprisingly healthy lives right up until the end. According to David R. Wekstein, of the Sanders-Brown Center on Aging at the University of Kentucky: "We have no information on any centenarian developing a prolonged illness. They get sick and die in the space of about a week.... It's almost as if they have read the guidelines of good health from the American Heart Association and the American Cancer Society."[10]

From a physical point of view, then, the notion of inevitable decline into disability with old age can no longer be accepted. Not only longevity but good health is significantly affected by our own habits; habits that can and should benefit from improved medical knowledge and research.

*2. Improvement in Mental Functioning.* Perhaps the greatest single worry about debility in old age, however, has to do with impaired mental functioning. Some 35 to 40 percent of those centenarians studied in Kentucky showed evidence of dementia. We have mentioned previously (Chapter 8, pp. 136–137) the enormous importance of Alzheimer's disease and of the research going forward to address that problem.

Apart from specific mental diseases and illnesses, however, another major conclusion of modern research is that "senility" is by no means the inevitable accompaniment of old age. All people who grow old are aware of the slowing down of certain mental functions, and most of them have read about the loss of brain cells (100,000 a day after age 30 is a statistic sometimes cited). The researches of numerous scientists and social scientists suggest, however, that the fears of decline are exaggerated and that, with an enriched, challenging environment in which the elderly are encouraged to use their mental abilities, there can in fact be considerable *improvement* in intellectual functioning.

Some examples: Experiments by Marian Diamond found that when rats were kept in an enriched environment, with toys and other stimuli, they developed increased brain size; more glial cells, which provide nutrients for neurons; and a greater number of dendrites, the cell projections by which nerve cells communicate. Studies by K. Warner Schaie have shown that, to the age of 60, almost none of the members of a Seattle health maintenance organization exhibited any clear declines on cognitive tests over a seven-year period. Even up to age 80, less than half of this group showed a measurable decline in such tests. Other studies by Schaie, Paul Baltes, and Sherry L. Willis have demonstrated the marked improvement on cognitive tests that can be achieved through the training of the elderly. Indeed, evidence is building up that, while old persons may have some mental deficits, they also may have certain advantages. Slower to perform some tasks, they may compensate by performing them more accurately. There is also, of course, the buildup of experience with age, the possibility of a certain old-fashioned "wisdom." It is no accident that, in certain fields of endeavor, older people have higher levels of achievement than younger, and that, for certain individuals, their greatest intellectual and artistic achievements have come near the ends of their lives.[11]

The major conclusion, then, would seem to be that the notion of an early onset of intellectual decline that continues inexorably on to total "senility" is misleading and that, barring genetic defect and given proper preventive steps, such decline as does naturally occur may be reduced and even reversed. In this respect, mental exercise may play the same role for the mind that physical exercise does for the body. Provide older individuals with sufficient mental activity and challenge, and their capacity to function well until quite late in life may be greatly enhanced.

### Extending the Number of Youthful Years

The above comments apply whether our future increases in life expectancy are due to curve squaring or span extension. Many enthusiasts for the latter are, however, convinced that by slowing down the general process of aging, we may achieve not only major gains in longevity but also major gains in the health of our population: We will live many more years and they will be, on the whole, healthy years. This conclusion can be reached by two routes:

1. *A great deal of serious illness occurs near the end of life; if, therefore, we push the end of life further and further ahead, we will enjoy better health through the majority of our additional years.* We mentioned this concept in passing when we were discussing health care costs in Chapter 8 (p. 135, note 12). Health economist Victor R. Fuchs has suggested that instead of focusing our attention on the number of years we can expect to live from birth, we should focus on the number of years we can expect to live until death. If we think of morbidity as increasing with age and if we define age not in terms of years from birth but in terms of years from death, then we could argue that today's elderly are actually growing "younger" all the time and that their susceptibility to serious diseases is growing less at each chronologically measured age. According to this view, extending life span will not result in more old old people (those near death) but in more young old people (those with advanced ages by present standards, but still very far from death.)

2. *The best way* (it is argued) *to "cure" the diseases of old age, like cancer, heart disease, diabetes, stroke, arthritis, senile dementia, and others, is by building up our resistance to these diseases. The best possible resistance, in general, is to be young. By slowing down the aging process, we remain younger longer and therefore are able to postpone these diseases until much later in life.* This argument can also be buttressed by a further argument, namely that as we conduct our research into the aging process, we will also inevitably be studying the causes of the diseases that increase with age. Thus, it is very possible that, each time we gain a longevity victory, we may also be gaining a victory against one or more diseases to which the elderly have been particularly susceptible. If, for example, aging is connected in one way or another with malfunctions of the immune system, then by slowing the

process of aging one may also be preventing, inhibiting, or even curing ailments like rheumatoid arthritis that have a strong autoimmune component. Essentially, this line of argument says that by achieving control of the aging process, we also achieve control of a major factor that makes people vulnerable to illness. Much longer life—youthful life—and much better health could ultimately go together.

These optimistic arguments can be summed up in a diagram adapted from Roy L. Walford's book *Maximum Life Span* (Figure 22-3). Here we see the clustering of the major diseases of old age and the occurrence of senile dementia in the area of the survival curve that shows accelerating decline: in today's world in the seventies and eighties; in tomorrow's hypothetical world, in the hundreds and above. The years of general good health, physical and mental, have been substantially increased.

This is the optimistic view. The opposite view, of course, is that, as at present, we can make no clear judgment about the future course of morbidity in relation to mortality. To which these more conservative and cautious observers might add: *Do not forget that if you are wrong, and adding to maximum life span simply increases the number of frail, infirm, and demented individuals, then your great "achievement" will prove, in fact, to be a massive tragedy.*

## SOCIOECONOMIC CONSEQUENCES OF VERY LONG LIVES

Whether a long-lived society would be desirable, or even viable, in a socioeconomic sense would depend in part on the issue we have just discussed: the health of the population. But there are other issues as well.

### The Economics of Span Extension

If we are worried about Social Security and the general problem of elderly de-

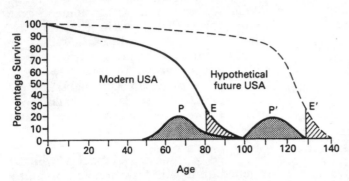

**FIGURE 22-3: The Possible Effect of Extension of Maximum Life Span**
Possible effects of extension of maximum life span in modern United States and in a hypothetical future United States, or the frequency at different ages of the major diseases of aging (*P* and *P¹*) and on the occurrence of feeble or senile oldsters (*E* and *E¹*) in the population.

*Source:* Adapted from Roy L. Walford, *Maximum Life Span*, Figure 2–1, p. 16. Reprinted by permission of W.W. Norton & Co.

pendency in today's United States, with a median age in the early thirties, what will our future economic problems be if we have been seriously underestimating potential gains in our life expectancy? What we might call optimistic news from a general human point of view might be considered very pessimistic news from that of a Social Security actuary. (See Box.)

It seems fairly obvious that the truly long-lived society would have to organize its work and retirement habits differently from those common in the United States today. If we begin living well past 100, it would be extremely difficult to sustain today's average retirement age of around 62, let alone the continuing trend toward earlier retirement. Assuming that the health of our older citizens was reasonably good and that, in effect, there were more young old people at each chronological age, then there would be no physical difficulty about increasing the retirement age roughly in proportion to our increases in longevity. This would be all the more possible since the trend away from heavy physical labor and toward service-sector employment is very likely to continue.

Interestingly, a case can be made that in a span-extended society, the economic costs of Social Security would be rather *less* burdensome than in a shorter lived society. Let us assume that the additional numbers of elderly citizens we are accruing are the young old—that is, that the 70-year-old is

effectively a 35-year-old, that the 100-year-old is a 50-year-old. Let us assume further that work span and life span increase in the same proportion, say, double. Thus, we are contrasting an economy in which people work for 40 years and retire for 10 years with one in which people work for 80 years and retire for 20 years.

Such contrasting economies have been studied by Laurence J. Kotlikoff, chairman of the Department of Economics at Boston University. His "major conclusion" is that "the expansion of work span and total life span should significantly increase economic welfare, which is measured as average consumption over an individual's lifetime; increasing the length of life, including productive life, appears to permit a higher level of consumption in every year that an individual is alive."[13]

The reasoning behind this conclusion is roughly the following:

*People save in order to provide for their old age. If we keep the proportion of retirement years to working years constant, then the fraction of income they save each year should remain unchanged no matter what the absolute length of their working or retirement years is. However, when life span, and thus both working and retirement years, is increased absolutely, then the total amount of savings the average individual will accumulate during his lifetime will increase in the same degree. At any*

EXCHANGE BETWEEN SENATOR JOHN R. CHAFEE OF RHODE ISLAND
AND FRANCISCO R. BAYO, DEPUTY CHIEF ACTUARY, SOCIAL SECURITY ADMINISTRATION

Senator Chafee: "Optimistic" to me would mean people living longer. I take it "optimistic" to you is the contrary. You look at it strictly from a cash point of view, don't you? "Optimistic" to you means that they will be dying earlier? I do not mean to be harsh, but is that about the way it is?

Mr. Bayo: That is correct, Mr. Chairman. The labeling is done according to . . .

Senator Chafee: That is a little ghoulish. "Optimistic" means people will die at a very satisfactory rate, is that right?

Mr. Bayo: Yes.

Senator Chafee: And pessimism comes over your organization when you find people living longer, is that right?

Mr. Bayo: The set of assumptions that results in the highest cost to the Social Security program is labeled "pessimistic" and includes the highest rate of (de)crease in mortality, because people living longer and receiving benefits longer will increase the cost of the program.

Senator Chafee: Well, in my presentation, I reverse your terms. I think we want to say it is optimistic when people live longer, but you are looking at it strictly from a cash point of view.[12]

*given moment of time, the average individual will have accumulated more savings in the span-extended case. Since accumulated savings represent accumulated capital, each worker in the span-extended society will have more capital to work with. More capital to work with means higher output levels.*

On these assumptions, then, productivity increases in the span-extended society even when there is no increase in the proportion of one's longer life devoted to productive work. Making various other technical assumptions, Kotlikoff concludes that the span-extended economy would enjoy an 18 percent per capita output advantage over the shorter lived society. With this output advantage, and with the assumed proportion of retirement to work years unchanged, Social Security benefits should be *easier* to sustain in this very long lived society—an "optimistic" outcome on both human and economic grounds.

### Social and Institutional Changes

It is easy to say that we will extend work span from, say, 40 years to 80 years, but in considering such large changes we are likely to face, in intensified fashion, all those issues

we considered earlier (Chapter 7) in connection with the retirement decision. Before we accept any forecasts of increased productivity in the span-extended society, we would want to know how such a society would deal with three issues:

1. *Obsolescent skills:* When we consider the revolutions in products and technologies of production that occur each decade (and even annually), we realize that workers who spend anything like eight decades on a given line of work will find that the skills they began with may well be wholly irrelevant to the production process they face later in their working lives. Indeed, the product they produce later may be wholly different from the product they produced earlier, perhaps from a completely new sector of the economy. Young at heart or not, how can workers stay on top of new technologies over such a long period of time?

2. *Crowding at the top:* We also have our job pyramid versus population rectangle question again. If the chronologically older citizens insist on remaining in the work force (and, of course, if they all retired, we would be in deep trouble), and if they cluster at

the top of the job pyramid, then the chances of the average young worker reaching the top are thereby diminished. This is a potential problem with any population rectangle, but it is more serious in the span-extended society because everyone's average length of participation in the labor force is greatly increased. Twenty years without advancement may be hard to take, thirty years much harder. Forty or fifty years? Perhaps that would be unacceptably long for many of us.

3. *The overhanging threat of boredom:* Unacceptably long and perhaps unrelievedly boring. Many scientists and scholars (including scholars of the aging process) are in highly exciting fields with new developments lurking around every corner, fresh experiments to be run, new books to be written. As we have indicated earlier in our study, however, polls show that many and perhaps most Americans who retire early are happy to have done so, and one of the main reasons given is a simple one: They do not have to go to work anymore. If we increase the lengths of those already not-very-satisfying careers by 50 or 100 percent, how can we possibly imagine that workers will want to stick with them? Will not everyone be clamoring for a proportionately much earlier retirement than today? And what then happens to our elderly dependency burden in the years ahead?

Of course, one could argue that increasing the number of *retirement* years would also pose the problem of boredom in a significant way. How many trips can one take? How many game shows can be watched? How much gardening can one do? How much napping?

What these three obvious problems mean is that the kinds of institutional and attitudinal changes we discussed earlier in this book would become not merely desiderata but absolute prerequisites for a viable span-extended society. The key is continuing training, retraining, and education at all levels, from basic to professional, and at all stages of life, from childhood to the most advanced ages. Education is the enemy of obsolescence and the foe of boredom. It is also, as we have suggested, a major way in which these increasingly old individuals (chronologically speaking) of our span-extended society can remain increasingly young (in terms of retaining and improving their mental functioning). In truth, there is a "virtuous cycle" here: education provides the kind of challenge to older people that increases their capacity to learn and makes them capable of *being* educated even quite late in life.

Furthermore, the span-extended society does provide the necessary years to increase the time the average individual spends in training and education. In our earlier example, we spoke of doubling work and retirement years (from 40 to 80 and 10 to 20, respectively). By the same general logic, we would only be keeping proportions constant by doubling the average number of years an individual spent in training and education over the course of a lifetime, say, from 20 to 40. Just as we might build up society's tangible capital by saving more over our longer lives, so we also might build up more intellectual capital by spending more years in school, or in training programs, or in self-improvement activities.

Almost certainly, this educational activity would not be concentrated wholly or even mainly in our youth. We might well start out very much as we do today, finishing high school, and perhaps college or even a professional school. What would be new would be major interruptions for further training and education later on in life. If we follow the pattern of the multiple-career lifestyle (see p. 121), then we might want to take sabbaticals of one, two, or even several years in the middle of our lives, preparing, say, to become a lawyer after a 30- or 40-year career as a physician. There could be costs to such career changing (Kotlikoff suggests that this pattern might lower productivity to some degree), but the advantages in terms of avoiding obsolescence, of making room at the top (in one's previous profession) for young people moving up, and above all of averting the mind-numbing repetitive pattern of an excessively prolonged single career—all these suggest that the move to a multiple-career life-style, already in considerable vogue today, will greatly shape the future of the long-lived society.

## GENERATIONAL RELATIONS

Much of what we have said so far seems reasonably hopeful about the possibility of living well in a long-lived society, whether in terms of health, economics, or social institutions. One might expect that much the same could be said about the relations among the several generations in such a society. If, as we have suggested, there is no intrinsic problem in these other areas, then there would seem to be no particular reason to expect any great struggle between generations over the disposal of society's resources. Since both young and old can be reasonably well off in the long-lived society, why should we anticipate the intergenerational warfare that some observers have seen looming on the horizon?

Although the potential battle over resources has probably been overstated, we should not imagine that relations between generations in the span-extended society will be exactly the same as they were in the past. In one respect, they may be much better. For the longer each of us lives, the greater the possibility for *adult* relationships to develop between different generations. This is obviously the case today with our children; it is increasingly the case with our grandchildren, who may be well into their adulthood while their grandparents are still living. With curve-squaring technologies at work, and even more with span extension, *multiple generations* of a given family, all surviving together, all adults, may become

commonplace. Intergenerational adult friendships and companionship could be important assets of the long-lived society.

At the same time, one must recognize that this pattern involves a considerable wrenching of the traditional concept of intergenerational relationships. In a certain sense, in the old days, each generation was seen to be working for and deriving satisfactions from the benefits that were to accrue to subsequent generations. Parents lived, as it were, for their children, they in turn for their own children, and all of us ultimately for generations unseen.

In the span-extended society, however, those future generations are definitely "seen," and "seen" today. It is one thing to pass the torch to the next runner and then drop out of the race. It is another thing to have the torch wrenched out of your hands while you are still around, eager to continue the race yourself. In the multiple-generation society that lies ahead of us, would the older generations really take that much pleasure in handing over the management and control to the new group (actually groups) coming up, or would they, on the contrary, feel that the latter were trying to take over and displace them while they still felt themselves to be in their prime?

Might it not be that, multiple careers notwithstanding, the fundamental relations among generations living side by side, possibly as many as six, seven, eight at a time, would be highly competitive rather than complementary? Could we be creating a world where, instead of observing the harmonious parade of the generations marching off into the future, each generation was suspiciously eyeing those ahead and those behind, making sure that none was gaining special advantages?

Where this issue comes up most strongly, of course, is in the concept of the family, humankind's traditional institution for ensuring the perpetuation and continuity of the generations. To the future of this concept, therefore, we turn our attention in the next chapter.

## SUMMARY

1.  Increases in American life expectancy in the next century may occur either through increasing our chances of surviving to a given maximum life span, or extending maximum life span, or both.

2.  There will undoubtedly be improvements due to the traditional route ("curve squaring"), but there is considerable disagreement as to how great these improvements will be. Estimates of the gains for the next half century range from a few years to as much as 15 years or even more.

3.  Some scientists believe that much longer increases in life expectancy will be achieved by our growing understanding and control of the aging process, resulting in the extension of maximum life span. There are now many different theories of aging being developed. They focus on such varied topics as diet restriction, cell division and the Hayflick limit, the effects of "free radicals," the workings of the immune system, and "longevity-assurance genes," as well as many other genetic, hormonal, metabolic, and other phenomena. A growing consensus is that aging will prove to be a mixture of multiple causes rather than the product of a single factor.

4.  Just as the relationship between morbidity and mortality has been complex in the past, so it is difficult to predict how healthy a long-lived society will be. One factor that should make for better health, both physical and mental, is our ability to improve our health by our own behavior. Through physical and mental exercise and diet, many Americans should be able to maintain a high level of functionality even into quite advanced ages.

5.  Also, some (but not all) observers believe that, if our gains in life expectancy come as a result of life span extension, we may be able to concentrate our years of infirmity, and also of senile dementia, in the last (or near-death) years of our lives. This could mean a large expansion in the number of our healthy years.

6.  In principle, there is no socioeconomic reason that a very long-lived society could not be viable. If individuals save and accumulate more capital for their longer old ages, income per capita in such a society could even be higher than at present.

7.  Such optimism will be warranted, however, only if such a society can handle problems like obsolescent skills, crowding at the top of the job pyramid, possible competitive relations among multiple generations, and general boredom. These and other problems will undoubtedly require many changes in life patterns in the long-lived society, including multiple career paths and, especially, lifelong educational opportunities.

## KEY CONCEPTS FOR REVIEW

Survival curves

"Curve-squaring" advances

The aging process

Maximum human life span

Diet restriction

Hayflick limit

Free radical theories

Longevity-assurance genes

Neoteny

Wear-and-tear versus genetic clock theories of aging

Aging as a product of multiple causes

Behavioral effects on physical and mental functioning

Capital accumulation in the long-lived society

Problems of obsolescence, job structures, generational relations, boredom

Key role of lifelong education

## QUESTIONS FOR DISCUSSION

1. Explain the difference between gains in life expectancy due to "curve-squaring" and those due to extension of maximum life span. Although they are different, is there any reason that these two developments could not occur simultaneously?

2. Why do some scientists claim that there is no *evolutionary* reason for aging and death to be programmed into our genes? What has this argument to do with the search for "longevity-assurance" genes?

3. "One main reason that we can expect a span-extended society to be a healthy one is that the search for the key to aging will most probably lead at the same time to (a) span extension and (b) the understanding and control of many chronic diseases." Discuss.

4. Cite some examples of how by mental challenge and physical exercise people can remain "younger" than their years. Can you add support to this hypothesis from your own observations of senior citizens you know?

5. Given that we worry about the economic burdens of the Aging Society even in the absence of extended human life spans, how could such a society possibly be viable if we live 50 percent or even 100 percent longer than we do today?

6. Describe how you feel our formal educational system should be reformed in this Aging Society of ours, and also in a possible span-extended society of the future.

## NOTES

1. Jack M. Guralnik, Machiko Yanagishita, and Edward L. Schneider, "Projecting the Older Population of the United States: Lessons from the Past and Prospects for the Future," *Milbank Quarterly*, 66(2), 1988, p. 305. Guralnik and Yanagishita are from the National Institute on Aging; Schneider is Dean of Gerontology at the University of Southern California.

2. One recent study arrives at a rather conservative conclusion, at least with respect to the prospects of what we have called "curve-squaring" advances: "The data presented here indicate that life expectancy should not exceed 85 years at birth . . . unless major breakthroughs occur in controlling the fundamental rate of aging." S. J. Olshansky, B. A. Carnes, C. Cassel, "In Search of Methuselah: Estimating the Upper Limits to Human Longevity," *Science*, 250, November 2, 1990, p. 638.

3. The original article on diet restriction was C. M. McCay, M. F. Crowell, and L. A. Maynard, "The Effect of Retarded Growth upon the Length of Life Span and upon the Ultimate Body Size," *Journal of Nutrition, 10*, 1935, pp. 63–79. See also Morris H. Ross, "Nutritional Regulation of Longevity," in J. A. Behnke, C. A. Finch, and G. B. Moment, eds., *The Biology of Aging* (New York: Plenum Press, 1978), and Roy L. Walford, *Maximum Life Span* (New York: Norton, 1983), esp. Chapter 5. It should be noted that although evidence of the effectiveness of diet restriction in promoting longevity is substantial, some critics have pointed out that allowing rats to feed ad libitum in the control group is itself unnatural—that is, is not the way things happen in the wild. Possibly the control group rats are dying early because they are *overfed*.

4. The classic paper was L. Hayflick, "The Serial Cultivation of Human Diploid Cell Strains," *Experimental Cell Research, 25,* 1961.

5. For an attempt to synthesize aging research in terms of both wear-and-tear theories and biological clock theories, see the analysis of science reporter Albert Rosenfeld in *Prolongevity II* (New York: Knopf, 1985), esp. Chapter 16, "Putting It All Together."

6. D. Harman, "Aging: A Theory Based on Free Radical and Radiation Chemistry," *Journal of Gerontology, 11,* 1956.

7. Thomas E. Johnson, quoted in *Scientific American,* May 1989, p. 17.

8. In an interview for *Omni* magazine (October 1986), Cutler is quoted as follows: "Whether we evolve into the species of *Homo futurus* [large-brained, neotenous beings] or not, female pregnancy is likely soon to become a thing of the past. *All* babies would be conceived and raised outside the womb. By eliminating nine months of pregnancy, a woman would gain many advantages, even increasing her life span." Cutler's free-wheeling and imaginative views have sometimes put him at odds

with the establishment in the longevity field. For an account of some of his travails, see Carol Kahn, *Beyond the Helix: DNA and the Quest for Longevity* (New York: Times Books, 1985), esp. Chapters 4 and 10.

9. Quoted in Erik Eckholm, "Aging: Studies Point Toward Ways to Slow It," *New York Times*, June 10, 1986, p. C3.

10. David R. Wekstein, quoted in David Holzman, "To Find a Way to Age in Health," *Insight*, April 10, 1989, pp. 13–14.

11. For a brief survey of the accomplishments of the elderly, see K. Warner Schaie and James Geiwitz, *Adult Development and Aging* (Boston: Little, Brown, 1982), esp. pp. 413–418. Among other substantial accomplishments, they note: "Michelangelo, for example, finished painting *The Last Judgment,* one of the most famous pictures in the world, at sixty-six. At seventy, he completed the dome of St. Peter's in Rome. Goethe was eighty-two when he finished *Faust.* Wagner finished *Gotterdammerung* at sixty-three. Verdi produced *Otello* at seventy-four and *Falstaff* at eighty. Cervantes wrote *Don Quixote* at sixty-eight" (p. 415).

12. Hearing before the Subcommittee on Savings, Pensions, and Investment Policy of the Committee on Finance, U.S. Senate, 98th Congress, 1st Session, July 15, 1983.

13. L. J. Kotlikoff, "Some Economic Implications of Life Span Extension," in J. March, J. L. McGaugh, and S. B. Kiesler, eds., *Aging: Biology and Behavior* (New York: Academic Press, 1982), p. 98.

# 23

# Does the Family
# Have a Future?

The family is an intermediate unit in our society in two respects. First, it is a bridge between the generations. The generation of young adults who form families provides, through its productive efforts and through its emotional support, crucial sustenance both for the elderly and for children. Second, it is a bridge between the individual member of society and the society as a whole. Individuals alone cannot survive. An all-encompassing society, as shown by the experience of totalitarian states, is hopelessly inefficient, coercive, and not viable in the long run. Between the microcosm and the macrocosm exist smaller social units, of which the family has historically been the most significant and enduring.

But can this larger-than-individual but smaller-than-social unit continue to persist in the future with anything like its historic vitality? Some observers argue that it is under assault from both ends of the spectrum: from rampant individualism on the one hand and from the encroachments of the modern welfare state on the other. At the same time, the possibilities of intergenerational conflict discussed in the last chapter raise questions about the willingness of any given generation to subordinate what it believes to be its own interests to other generations, younger or older.

Speculations about the future of the family, then, must rank high in our concerns over the kind of posterity we are bequeathing to twenty-first-century America.

## WHAT "FAMILY" ARE WE TALKING ABOUT?

In 1980, in response to then-President Carter's worries about the state of the American family, a White House conference was held to study the matter. By common consent, the conference produced nothing of any real interest or value, except perhaps its own name. For what started out as an expression of concern about the declining fortunes of *the* American family became officially the White House Conference on Famil*ies.* This change expresses a dilemma that anyone concerned with this subject must face. As we have indicated in earlier chapters, the "traditional" American family—with a permanently married husband and wife, their own natural children, and a husband-provider and wife-homemaker division of labor—is no longer the characteristic U.S. family arrangement and, indeed, is an increasingly exceptional arrangement. Mothers of young children are now typically in the labor force. Never-married mothers, absent fathers, divorced and separated couples, childless couples, unmarried cohabiting couples, couples of the same sex living together—all these variations do exist and will almost certainly continue to exist in the future.

Claims that important trends, like divorce, have now reversed themselves are so far not sustained by serious scholarly research. In 1987, for example, pollster Louis Harris suggested that "marriage might just be making a strong comeback and divorce might be on the wane," adding the incredible statement that "almost 90 percent of all marriages survive."[1] To which scholars Teresa Martin and Larry Bumpass replied that "of first marriages occurring in 1975, one-third had already been disrupted by 1985." They noted further that "even though the long-term increase in marital instability may have plateaued since 1980, the level remains very high." In particular, their research suggests that "about two-thirds of all first marriages are likely to disrupt." Correcting for various other variables (like age at marriage), they conclude also that second marriages tend to disrupt at about the same rate as first marriages.[2]

The point is that, as a matter of empirical fact, *families* (plural), not **the** *family,* are what we are confronted with in present-day America. It must be understood, moreover, that what people refer to as "families" now covers a truly enormous range of variations. A widely reported 1988 poll of 1,200 randomly selected adults, conducted by the

Massachusetts Mutual Life Insurance Company, revealed that less than one-quarter of respondents defined the family in terms of people related by blood, marriage, or adoption (the Census Bureau definition), whereas nearly three-quarters defined it as "a group of people who love and care for each other."

In a Special Edition of *Newsweek* (Winter–Spring 1990) devoted entirely to the "21st Century Family," a variety of legal decisions broadening the concept of the family were noted. Particularly interesting was the New York State Court of Appeals decision holding that the survivor of a homosexual couple had the same rights to a rent-controlled apartment as would a surviving husband or wife. The court then set standards for a "family": (1) the "exclusivity and longevity of a relationship"; (2) the "level of emotional and financial commitment"; (3) how the couple "conducted their everyday lives and held themselves out to society"; and (4) the "reliance placed upon one another for daily services."[3]

Needless to say, if the family is defined in such broad, affectional terms, then the answer to our question, "Does the family have a future?," is obvious. Of course, it does. For as long as there is a future human population of any sort, there are bound to be numerous individuals bound together in various forms of loving, caring relationships. The question is trivialized by such broad definitions.

Our dilemma arises quite simply because, although we can trivialize the question if we wish, we cannot escape the underlying concern that raised the question in the first place. The existence of so many different kinds of "families" does not mean that there may not be different social, economic, and political consequences from each particular type of family. Concern about "the family" may, in fact, arise precisely because one relatively narrowly defined type of family is losing ground to a wide variety of other types.

Our question, then, must be framed with respect to a somewhat more specifically defined concept of the family. Clearly, we cannot go all the way back to the "traditional" family as defined in Chapter 9. The sharp division of labor between husbands and wives (sole provider versus happy homemaker) is clearly a thing of the past under almost any conceivable circumstances. Some of the essence of the "traditional" concept can be retained, however, if we emphasize the relative stability of the relationships of family members over time, and if we specifically include the raising of children as an ordinary and characteristic function of the family unit. In the discussion that follows, then, we shall think of "the family" in these terms:

*The family unit is conceived to consist of a husband and wife, usually though not necessarily formally married, and children, usually though not necessarily genetically related to both parents. In any case, the family unit takes a major responsibility for the care and nurture of the children when they are young. The family unit has sufficient permanence so that emotional ties among family members usually persist through life, including old age. Indeed, the memory of deceased family members will ordinarily remain with the living long after the former have departed.*

Obviously, there are other universally accepted types of family not included in this definition (childless couples, for example). Also, although the definition is necessarily loose, it is not as broad as people who "love and care for each other." Specifically, the raising of children is considered an essential feature; also, the reasonable permanence of relationships is called for.

What the definition attempts to do is catch the essential flavor of that institution about whose possible disappearance many Americans are greatly concerned. When we ask, "Does the family have a future?," we are asking whether this particular form of family unit is likely to be viable in a large number, and possibly a majority, of interpersonal relationships over the next several decades.[4]

## THE "INEVITABLE" DECLINE OF THE FAMILY

We begin with the case for the prosecution. Many commentators argue that the family unit we have described is essentially a vanishing phenomenon, for a variety of inter-related reasons:

### Basic Demographics

An important underlying change that has occurred over the past century or more has been the diminishing importance of the child-rearing function in the lives of most Americans. This diminished role is, from one point of view, a simple function of two basic demographic changes: (1) sharply lowered fertility and (2) substantially increased life expectancies. In 1976 Mary Jo Bane reported on comparisons of the hypothetical **life cycles** of women born in 1846–1855 and those born a century later, in 1946–1955. (Table 23-1)

**TABLE 23-1.   Hypothetical Life Cycles: Mean Ages at Major Events of Women in Nineteenth, Mid-Twentieth, and Late Twentieth Centuries**

|  | Born | |
| --- | --- | --- |
|  | 1846–1855 (6 Children) | 1946–1955 (2 Children) |
| First marriage | 22.0 | 20.8 |
| Birth of first child | 23.5 | 22.3 |
| Birth of last child | 36.0 | 24.8 |
| Last child reaches age 6 | 42.0 | 30.8 |
| First marriage of last child | 58.9 | 47.7 |
| Death of spouse | 56.4 | 67.7 |
| Own death | 60.7 | 77.1 |

*Source:* Mary Jo Bane, *Here to Stay: American Families in the Twentieth Century*, Table 2-1, p. 25. Copyright © 1976 by Mary Jo Bane. Reprinted by permission of Basic Books, a division of HarperCollins Publishers, Inc.

The historic decline in the percentage of a woman's married life devoted to raising children is quite striking. If we focus on the first six years of the children's lives, then our hypothetical mid-nineteenth-century woman could expect to spend 18.5 years out of a marriage of 34.4 years with a child under age 6 in the house—that is, 54 percent of her married life. With women born in the mid-twentieth century, it is estimated that they will have spent 8.5 years out of a marriage of 46.9 years with children under 6 at home—that is, only 18 percent of their married lives. Given that life expectancies are still increasing, this percentage will presumably fall even further for future cohorts of married women.

Similar calculations can be made for the percentage of a woman's entire life devoted to small children; or for the percentage of her married life when the children are below, say, age 18; or for the percentage of her married life before the last child gets married; and so on. In each case, one finds a tremendous drop in the percentage of time that a woman (or her husband) is involved with the rearing of children. If one were to carry these calculations back even further in time—say, to the mid-eighteenth century—the results would be more striking. American women had even more children then, and life expectancies were shorter. For a considerable number of women—those who would die in their last childbirth—virtually the whole of their married lives would have been given over to the rearing of young children.

Insofar as we have defined our family unit as having a central function in the rearing of children, it can be argued that that central function is simply less important now in the objective sense of time expended. We may also face increasing childlessness, according to Alvin Toffler's *Future Shock:*

We may expect many among the people of the future to carry the streamlining process a step further by remaining childless, cutting the family down to its most elemental components, a man and a woman. Two people, perhaps with matched careers, will prove more efficient at navigating through education and social shoals, through job changes and geographic relocations, than the ordinary child-cluttered family.[5]

It can be argued further that the diminished role of children creates a psychological void that must be filled with other activities, many of which—like career building on the part of both husband and wife—will be irrelevant to, or even in many cases in opposition to, the continuation of a stable married life. The Toffler quote conveys the possibility of the conflict that develops when other objectives—for example, "matched careers"—are seen to be complicated by "child-cluttered" homes.

### Economic Considerations

Economic considerations are likely to affect the future of the family in a variety of ways, including their indirect effects on underlying demographics, especially continued low fertility (see Chapter 3, pp. 44–49). Perhaps the most clear-cut direct effect is that mentioned at the end of the previous paragraph—namely, the impact of **career-building activities** on the part of both husband and wife on the stability of the marital union. It can be argued that as personal satisfactions for women move increasingly toward careers and away from child rearing, the glue cementing the marriage together will become increasingly weak. The rearing of children will pose serious career problems for any ambitious woman because these responsibilities are likely to come at a time when her career would normally begin to take off. She will be constantly "out of sync" in terms of the more straightforward and continuous career paths of her male competitors.

Furthermore, her husband is likely to become a competitor as well, at least in the sense that "matched careers" *à la* Toffler are a great rarity in real life. For the woman to do *too* well may, as we have mentioned

earlier in our study, cause psychological problems for her husband; also, when she does very well, the woman will have achieved a degree of economic independence that will enable her to manage financially without a husband. Synchronization problems involving two careers will, at best, call for complicated adjustments (Whose career move takes priority? Do we live apart? Commute? Or what?) which also may place strains on the marriage.

Thus, the shift from homemaking to career-building activities on the part of women can be viewed as (1) weakening the positive forces holding the marriage together (children, complementary activities of husband and wife, economic dependence of the wife), while, at the same time, (2) reinforcing the negative aspects of marriage (restricting time, freedom of maneuver, career flexibility). In general, in the case of the marriages of white women, improved economic options for women are thus seen as a major and continuing factor in promoting increasing divorce and decreasing remarriage.

Economic considerations can, however, also work in a different way, as they appear to do in the black community, in this case leading not so much to divorce and separation as to an increase in the number of never-married mothers.[6] This involves the hypothesis that lack of employment opportunities for young black males may be a major factor in the failure of so many young black mothers to find suitable husbands (see Chapters 13 and, especially, Chapter 15). Even in this case, however, improved economic options for women—including cash and noncash welfare benefits—may play a role in the increase in never-married mothers.

Broadly speaking, it can be argued that economic need, like the bearing and rearing of children, provided an important reason for the formation of families and for their relative permanence over time. The richer the society, and in particular the greater the number of options for women—heretofore the economically dependent sex—the less likely are marital unions to remain intact.

## General Sociopolitical Trends

Numerous general trends also are likely (it is argued) to lead to the further decline of the family in the future. These include:

***Individualism and the Desire for Self-Realization.***   Whether Americans are increasingly narcissistic, as some commentators have claimed, there is little doubt that the goal of self-realization, whether in terms of materialistic achievement, sexual fulfillment, good health, or intellectual and spiritual values, has become very prominent in recent years. The family is, in its essence, an intergenerational unit. It is possible that the modern emphasis on **self-fulfillment**—often including fulfillment with different sexual partners—conflicts with the intrinsically selfless, even self-sacrificing, qualities we expect in family life.

***Choice and Pluralism.***   Whether in terms of race, ethnicity, sexual preference, or virtually any other dimension of modern life, today's America places a high value on pluralism and free choice. Our earlier discussion of famil*ies* (as opposed to *the* family) suggests a strong trend in U.S. society to accept variation and choice in all our social institutions. Thus, anyone who tries to promote a particular kind of institution—such as the family, however defined—runs up against a strong countercurrent arguing that each person's or group's choices are as valid as anyone else's, and that no one has a right to impose his or her solutions on other members of the community. (This tendency is sometimes described—usually by its critics—as *moral relativism.*)

***The Importance of the Principle of Equality.***   Although it is relativistic in many respects, modern U.S. society has reserved a special place for the **principle of equality.** With the great civil rights and women's rights movements of recent decades, there has been a substantial attempt to remove discrimination in many walks of U.S. life, and even to extend the principle of equality of opportunity in the direction of the stronger principle of equality of result. The point here is that the private institution of the family, because it provides very different levels of income, educational resources, emotional nurture, and care to certain individuals compared to other less fortunate individuals, is an essential source of inequality in any society. How can the poor immigrant or ghetto child, with little or no family economic or cultural resources in his or her background, hope to compete equally with the child whose parents are highly educated, can afford the best schools for their offspring, and will leave a comfortable inheritance to help ward off future financial strains? The principle of equality, applied strenuously enough, leads to attempts to reduce the exceptional family advantages of some and to decrease the family disadvantages of others—in short, to achieve a redistribution of wealth, income, education, job opportunities, and the like in favor of the less fortunate members of society. In this case, the family is weakened not by the forces of individualism but by those favoring collective—that is, state—action.

***Growth of the Welfare State.***   Government expenditures, including transfer payments, rose from under 20 percent of U.S. GNP in the 1930s to around 35 percent in the late 1980s. Much of this growth occurred in the category "Payments for Individuals," covering retirement, unemployment, medical care, food, nutrition, and public assistance, and other such programs, most of which have a strong redistributional component. In 1940 such expenditures were less than one-fifth of the federal budget; by 1990 they were over half of that budget. The point is that many of these expenditures took over functions that were once largely the responsibility of families. This is particularly true of the very large expenditures with respect to the elderly—Social Security and Medicare—though also to a lesser degree expenditures for the poor, such as Medicaid, Aid to Families with Dependent Children, food stamps, and the like. Many observers feel that the state must assume further responsibilities in areas at the heart of the family experience—day care for preschoolers in particular. The family, it is believed, can no longer fulfill its responsibilities without substantial state intervention.

In short, the family is seen to be increasingly inadequate to meet either individualistic desires for choice and self-fulfillment or social responsibilities to ensure a more equal distribution of society's resources and protection for its vulnerable members. An institution of only passing, historical interest, the family's further decline is virtually guaranteed.

## THE "INEVITABLE" RESURRECTION OF THE FAMILY

Although the foregoing arguments are convincing to many, other observers believe that the pendulum is due to swing back again, and, indeed, has already swung back to some degree, in the direction of restoring a more stable family life. Many of the negative trends that seemed so overwhelming in the 1960s and 1970s are seen to have slowed down or even reversed themselves, while a positive appreciation of the benefits of family life is expressed daily in newspaper and magazine articles, best-selling books, television shows, and movies. Corresponding to the decline of the family arguments are these predicting its resurrection.

### Demographics Favoring the Family

The very same numbers shown in Table 23-1 can be used to support the view that family life can and will be much more satisfactory in the future than in the past. With respect to the child-rearing function, longer life expectancies and fewer children mean that the average parent will have to devote only a very small fraction of his or her life to bringing up children within the family context. Insofar as parents, and women in particular, feel the stress of conflict between career and family objectives, low fertility and continually increasing life expectancies should *ease*, not intensify, that stress. One obvious solution to the conflict is called "sequencing": taking a few years off early in one's career to raise very young children within the family context, often continuing with some part-time work during this period, and then subsequently returning full time into the career stream. The point is that longer and longer life expectancies—with the possibility also of longer life *spans*—should allow more total room for both career and family objectives. Indeed, very long lives, with career objectives only, could easily become boring: Raising children could provide interest, variety, and depth to most lives.

Furthermore, longer life expectancies, as we have noted before, provide the opportunity for more **intergenerational family contacts** between *adult* family members than in the past. In a large, impersonal, rapidly changing world, such long-lasting relationships may be of particular importance to our sense of security and even sanity.

### The Unfortunate Economics of Single-Parent Families

It is odd—family advocates are likely to say—that anyone should use "economic considerations" as grounds for expecting a further decline in family life. For there is little doubt, they claim, that the breakdown of family life today is a major factor behind our central economic problems. These problems are both immediate and long run.

The ***immediate* problem** is **poverty,** and especially the poverty of women and of children brought up in single-parent homes. We have already indicated that there is some dispute on this matter (see pp. 261–263), but many observers would accept the verdict of sociologists Roger Wojtkiewicz, Sara McLanahan, and Irwin Garfinkel:

> There is much debate over the psychological effects of growing up in a female-headed family, but the economic consequences are clear. Nearly half the female-headed families with children have incomes below the official poverty line, and nearly half depend on welfare for a major proportion of their income. Indeed, the growth of female-headed families is a proximate cause of two widely cited trends: the feminization of poverty and the decline in the economic position of children relative to the elderly.[7]

Family proponents believe that a major reason for the ultimate resurrection of the family will be that single-parent families have proved not to be economically viable.

The **long-run economic problem** with family breakdown may be even more serious, although, of course, it is partly related to the poverty problem. Children brought up in poverty, particularly when it is within a generally impoverished community setting, are likely to face many obstacles as they try to improve their status later in life. However, it is not just poverty per se that is the problem, but lack of crucial family support in the specific area of education and training. With no father available and a mother who may be working to supplement inadequate welfare benefits (or to qualify for them), the child may lack the family interest, encouragement, and pressure to perform well in school. Indeed, in an age where our school system itself is in crisis (see Chapter 17), without family interest, encouragement, and pressure *on the schools,* classrooms around the country may continue to produce half-literate, mathematically incompetent, geographically and culturally ignorant graduates (or dropouts) who will be wholly inadequate to the task of staffing the future labor force of our high-technology society. The family, it is argued, is essential not only to the personal well-being of the coming generations, but also to our collective well-being in a world of fierce international economic competition.

## Societal Trends Have Been Changing Direction

Americans have shown an increasing awareness that many of the trends of the 1960s and 1970s—as, for example, the early celebration of the drug culture—have been leading to personal tragedy and social dead ends. More recent trends (it is argued) are very favorable to the resurrection of family life:

***Winding Down of the Sexual Revolution.*** All polls suggest that a great majority of Americans believe that married people are happier than singles, however "swinging" their existence may seem to be. The free-wheeling sexuality of the 1960s has received very critical press notices in recent years, particularly since the advent of AIDS. Cheryl Russell, editor-in-chief of *American Demographics,* puts it unequivocally: "The fear of AIDS will end the sexual revolution. After a 25-year hiatus, once again there is good reason to say no: Fear of death is a cold shower for casual sex, a more effective deterrent than fear of pregnancy. This fact is likely to make marriage more popular, especially among the young."[8] Whether AIDS will have this effect over the long run is unclear, particularly since over a sufficiently long run scientific research may develop either a prevention or cure for the disease. Under any circumstances, however, it is argued that the rampant search for individual and especially sexual fulfillment in the 1960s and 1970s was an aberration, not a portent of the future, and that U.S. society is now settling back into a more reasonable and balanced view in this area of life.

***A Critique of Divorce.*** A 1989 Gallup/ *Newsweek* poll found that 70 percent of respondents believed that when husbands and wives with young children were not getting along, it was better to separate than to raise the children in a hostile atmosphere.[9] Nevertheless, it is also true that the 1980s saw an increasing awareness throughout the country that **divorce** was a solution that involved a great many problems of its own. We have already mentioned the problem of poverty in the case of female-headed households. This poverty extends to women quite late in life since, in many cases, divorces are now taking place with older couples, where the remarriage rate for women is very low. In 1987, the poverty rate for divorced women aged 65 years and over was 23.9 percent, compared to 5.7 percent for elderly married women with spouse present.[10]

There is also evidence that divorced persons are less healthy than married persons. In Figure 23-1, we contrast the average number of days in bed in 1987 for women and men in various age groups. In each category, married persons do better than divorcees. Although there are problems of interpretation here (Do healthy people tend to stay married longer?), the authors of this study note both that married people tend to have better "health habits" (smoking, drinking, etc.) than the divorced, and that divorce itself causes "stress, resulting in weight change, stomach upset, fatigue, appetite loss, headaches, nervousness, nightmares, difficulty in sleeping, and tension." They conclude: "No wonder divorced men and women are more likely than the married to suffer from chronic conditions and acute illnesses and injuries."[11]

Furthermore, although children may sometimes do better after divorce than in a highly stressful marital situation, there is increasing awareness that children raised by single parents or in stepfamilies may face very difficult psychological and developmental adjustments. We have already noted the increase in emotional and behavioral problems of children in mother-only and mother-stepfather families (Chapter 14). There are other hazards too. Children in stepfamilies are more likely to be subject to sexual abuse than are children in ordinary

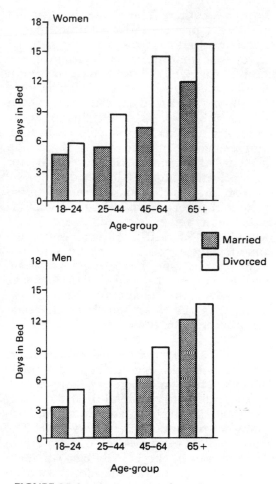

**FIGURE 23-1: Average Number of Days in Bed, 1987, by Marital Status**

*Source:* Barbara Foley Wilson and Charlotte Schoenborn, "A Healthy Marriage," *American Demographics,* November 1989. Data are from National Health Information Survey.

families. A quite general hazard that all such children face is the possibility that the new marriage may break up. Says Andrew Cherlin, professor of sociology at Johns Hopkins University: "Remarriages are very fragile. There's a high rate of divorce for the first several years, almost as though these couples have gone through one bad marriage and they're determined not to go through another. Their antennae are up and they're prepared to leave if necessary." A striking finding from a recent national survey was that nearly a quarter of the children surveyed did not include their step-siblings as members of their family even though they were all living together.[12] Often lacking in both depth of attachment and a sense of permanence, the children in step-families may in many cases fail to develop the sense of personal security necessary for a smooth transition to adulthood.

For all these reasons, divorces—often prompted, according to critics, by unrealistic expectations and exaggerated notions of the possibilities of self-fulfillment—may become less fashionable as their adverse consequences become increasingly apparent. Trying harder to make the marriage "work"—for the benefit of the marriage partners as well as for the children—could easily become the newer trend.

***The Countertrend toward Privatization.*** Finally, those who expect a return to family values will note that there is a national and, indeed, international trend these days away from state intervention and toward the privatization of economic and social life. The most obvious examples, of course, are in the countries of the Eastern bloc where, in 1990 and 1991, one of the most extraordinary revolutions in human history was occurring. If a key word in the early postwar era was *equality*, in the last decade, the key word may well have been *incentives*. In the Soviet Union and its former satellite nations, centrally planned economies have been pronounced a failure by their own leaders, largely because they have failed to provide sufficient incentives for creative, productive enterprise and simple hard work. Although the path that the Soviet Union will take remains uncertain—there are strong vested interests opposed to change—the universal solution among the other former Warsaw Pact nations has been to introduce private incentives in a much more decentralized political-economic system. The emphasis is

on units much smaller than the central planning boards of the state; that is, the attempt is to find a middle ground between carte blanche individualism, on the one hand, and the dominant, overarching state on the other.

Such trends are also apparent, in varying degrees, in the Western democracies. Most European countries have practiced some degree of privatization during the 1980s—in some cases, as in Great Britain under the Conservatives, restoring certain nationalized industries to the private sector. Even Sweden, the most advanced "welfare state" in Europe, has been seeking to reduce taxes and restore private incentives. In the United States, the so-called Reagan revolution, though less powerful in its effects than some proponents, and also some critics, have believed, nevertheless definitely contributed to a slowing down of the growth of government in the economy. While total federal, state, and local expenditures almost doubled as a percentage of GNP from 1947 to 1982, the percentage was essentially constant from 1982 to 1990.

In the course of this counterrevolution against the seemingly inexorable expansion of the welfare state, many Americans have become conscious of things that the government does not do particularly well. As we have seen, the War on Poverty was not as successful as its original proponents had anticipated. In 1990 there was even some discussion of "privatizing" at least part of our Social Security program (as a number of other countries have done), a subject that would have been almost completely taboo as recently as the mid-1980s.

In short, those who believe that the family is on the verge of a comeback argue that both extremes—whether the steady encroachments of the welfare state or rampant, self-centered individualism—have proved inadequate. The family as an essential unit for raising and educating the young; securing the interests of men and women; protecting and helping the poor, the elderly, and the infirm; and providing for stable, long-run emotional commitments between human beings both within and across generations—this unit has proved itself more invaluable than even its advocates had imagined. Its resurrection is inevitable!

## THE FAMILY AND THE CORPORATION

Whether the foregoing pro-family arguments are mainly wishful thinking remains to be seen. One thing is fairly certain, however, and that is that if the family is to be restored to anything like its vigor in the earlier twentieth century, a number of changes in other areas of the society will have to occur. These changes will be required in both the private and public sectors. Absent such changes, the drift toward family breakdown may well be resumed.

Perhaps the most significant changes in the private sector have to do with the accommodations business corporations and other private enterprises make to what almost everyone believes is a desirable (and, in any event, irrevocable) modern development: the large-scale entry of American women into the labor force. The single breadwinner/homebound wife model is clearly anachronistic. Can society adapt to

the new model of the family in such a way that crucial functions—especially parental nurturing and care for children—can still be achieved in a familial context?

It should be noted that a number of changes are already occurring in U.S. corporations in recognition of the fact that working women, and working mothers in particular, are now an indispensable part of their labor force. One widespread change is the increased availability of maternity leave benefits. Table 23-2 shows the striking changes in maternity leave arrangements that occurred between the 1960s and the 1980s for working women at the time of their first births. Those who received some benefits almost tripled (from 16.0 to 46.6 percent), while those who stopped working, either quitting or being let go, fell from around two-thirds to one-third. The category of "unpaid leave"—essentially involving an informal understanding that the woman would return to work after a specified period of time—also increased. Furthermore, the percentage of those receiving benefits who got cash payments for all or part of their leaves of absence increased from 50 to 81 percent over these two decades.

An important result of corporate maternity leave policy is indicated in Figure

**TABLE 23-2.   Percentage Distribution of Leave Arrangements, 1961–1965 to 1981–1985**

| | *Year of First Birth* | | | | |
| *Type of Leave* | *1981–85* | *1976–80* | *1971–75* | *1966–70* | *1961–65* |
|---|---|---|---|---|---|
| Number of Women (thousands) | 5,239 | 4,414 | 3,700 | 3,435 | 2,797 |
| Total (percentages)[a] | 100.0 | 100.0 | 100.0 | 100.0 | 100.0 |
| Quit job | 28.3 | 41.3 | 51.1 | 58.9 | 62.8 |
| Maternity/sick/paid leave | 46.6 | 34.0 | 23.4 | 18.3 | 16.0 |
| Unpaid leave | 20.3 | 20.2 | 20.8 | 17.6 | 14.1 |
| Let go from job | 4.6 | 4.9 | 4.6 | 4.2 | 5.0 |
| Never stopped work | 2.8 | 2.0 | 1.7 | 1.4 | 2.7 |

*Note:*  Leave arrangements refer to those used by women who worked during their first pregnancy.

[a] Individual leave arrangements exceed 100.0 percent because of multiple answers.

*Source:*  Martin O'Connell, U.S. Bureau of the Census, "Maternity Leave Arrangements, 1961–1985," Table 2. Paper presented at the annual meetings of the American Statistical Association, August 7, 1989.

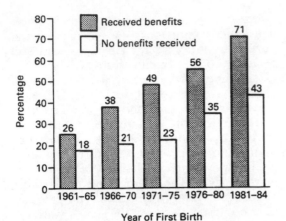

**FIGURE 23-2: Percentage of Women Working within Six Months of Child's Birth, by Maternity Leave Arrangements During Pregnancy, 1961–1965 to 1981–1984**

*Source:* Adapted from Martin O'Connell, U.S. Bureau of the Census, "Maternity Leave Arrangements, 1961–1985," Figure 9. Paper presented at the annual meetings of the American Statistical Association, August 7, 1989.

23-2, where it can be seen that, in 1981–1984, 71 percent of women who received benefits returned to work within six months of their child's birth, as compared to 43 percent who had not received such benefits. These numbers strongly suggest that maternity leaves may be very much in the interest of the corporation in that they help to minimize work time lost due to the birth of children, and thus assure relative stability of the firm's work force.

At the same time, however, it is not so clear that these particular corporate changes are in any way pro-family. For it seems evident both in the gap between benefit receivers and nonreceivers, and in the upward drift of the bars from the 1960s to the 1980s, that there is a strong general tendency to reduce time lost through pregnancy and birth. In the 1960s, over three-quarters of women who worked during pregnancy lost a year or more of work after the birth took place. Twenty years later,

only about one-third gave up work for a year or more. Essentially, then, corporate maternity leave policy, while more responsive to women's employment needs, and very probably highly desirable from the point of view of the corporation's hiring practices, is basically a factor favoring infant and early child care outside, and not within, the family unit.

Returning, then, to our central question, we ask: Can business corporations take steps that, while encouraging women to be active in the labor force, nevertheless also encourage active parental care for infants and young children? One approach to this problem attracted much attention, and controversy, at the end of the 1980s. It was suggested that women should be divided into two groups, **career-primary** and **career-and-family** women. The proposal appeared in the *Harvard Business Review* and immediately earned for its author, corporate consultant Felice N. Schwartz, national publicity as the advocate of a **"mommy track."**[13]

Schwartz begins with the proposition that, because of approaching labor shortages, women are in much demand in business and have, in fact, moved from a buyer's to a seller's market. All women should benefit from this position, including the small but definite group of women who, like many men, put their careers first. Such a group will either have no children (she notes that 90 percent of executive men but only 35 percent of executive women have children by the age of 40) or give over the care of their children to others. In the case of these career-primary women, the corporation, she believes, should try to identify them early, give them serious responsibility, expect them to make deep personal commitments to their work, include them in every kind of communication, and take whatever other steps are needed to eliminate the generally greater obstacles that women, compared to men, face in climbing the corporate ladder.

The main purpose of Schwartz's article, however, is to deal with the "majority of women," those "who want to pursue serious careers while participating actively in the rearing of children"[14]—hence the nickname "mommy track." In addition to discussing maternity leave, better child care facilities, parental leave for fathers, and the like, she stresses the concept of **flexibility:**

> In its simplest form, flexibility is the freedom to take time off—a couple of hours, a day, a week—or to do some work at home and some at the office, an arrangement that communication technology makes increasingly feasible. At the complex end of the spectrum are alternative work schedules that permit the woman to work less than full-time and her employer to reap the benefits of her experience and, with careful planning, the top level of her abilities.
>
> Part-time employment is the single greatest inducement to getting women back on the job expeditiously and the provision women themselves most desire. . . . I believe, however, that shared employment is the most promising and will be the most widespread form of flexible scheduling in the future. It is feasible at every level of the corporation except at the pinnacle, for both the short and the long term. It involves two people taking responsibility for one job.[15]

This approach is clearly compatible with the concept of "sequencing," which we mentioned earlier. Work at home, part-time work at the office, a gradual resumption of full-time work when the children are past infancy and ready for school, or even preschool—all this makes for a hopeful blend of satisfactory, if not stellar, career building and parental participation in the rearing of children.

Still, many women were, and are, unhappy with this approach. One obvious question is: Why should this special burden of adjustment be placed on women? Why not on men as well? What we should really be talking about, it is said, is not a "mommy track," but a *parent* track."[16] But there are other questions, too. Notwithstanding the miracles of modern communications technology, there is much evidence that working

at home—especially in the company of very young children—takes both a very special job and a very special parent. It is certainly not the panacea once hoped for. Also, it should be said that most women feel that, if they go part time, their long-run careers will suffer heavily for it. Thus, for example, IBM in 1989 was offering a three-year flexible-time program under which female employees could work part time. However, IBM policy, although the company is considered one of the most "enlightened" in corporate America, did not count part-time work as progress in one's full-time career.[17]

From the corporation's point of view, moreover, all of these flexible arrangements—as Schwartz fully recognizes—tend to be expensive. Her response is that women's productive talents are worth the extra cost; that firms that do not follow such policies will face huge retraining costs if experienced female employees do not return to them after having children; and that businesses really have no choice in the matter. Women are vital to the work force of today and the foreseeable future, and they will ultimately go wherever their needs are best met.

## PUBLIC POLICY TOWARD THE FAMILY

What of public policy toward the family? Can the government, which has historically tended to take over responsibilities traditionally borne by the family, actually act in such a way as to promote the family unit? Should it do so, if it could?

It should be said immediately that one of the major thrusts of current U.S. government policy is still in the direction of displacing family functions. We have previously discussed the child care legislation passed in 1990 (Chapter 16). Although everyone agrees that improving the quality of day care in the United States is a worthy objective, and although the 1990 legislation was advertised specifically as a pro-family initiative, there is little doubt that in subsidizing extra-family day care, the government is facilitating the transfer of family functions to the state.

It is clear, however, that there are numerous actions the government *could* take to enhance the role of the family if it so chose. In an article in *The Public Interest* (Winter 1989), Allan Carlson proposed various tax changes that might support family objectives. These included increased tax credits for children and a doubling of the 1989 personal exemption for children of $2,000 to $4,000. It should be noted that this exemption rose from $600 in 1948 to $2,000 in 1989, an increase of three and one-third times, while the consumer price index (CPI) rose roughly fivefold. In other words, the *real* value of the personal exemption for children was substantially lower in 1989 than it was in the far less well-to-do U.S. economy of the late 1940s.[18]

To pay for these tax credits and tax reductions, Carlson urges an increase in the progressivity of our federal income tax. Such an increase would involve a rise in *marginal* tax rates (taxes on additional dollars of income), a policy opposed by many supply-siders who argue that high marginal tax rates reduce incentives to work and invest. In a sense, however, it is this disincentive effect—at least as far as parental labor is concerned—that Carlson wishes to achieve. Should an extra hour of a parent's labor be spent in the marketplace or in "home production," and, specifically, in caring for children? Because home production is not taxed, high marginal rates, by discouraging additional labor in the marketplace, are in effect encouraging additional labor at home. This is only fair, Carlson feels, in that the parent who stays at home to care for children faces a tremendous "opportunity cost": "such a parent must sacrifice extra income and possible future career advancement."[19]

The mention of "career advancement" is important here, because one of the great problems with raising young children at home, as we have noted, is that the parent's

career is often interrupted at a critical point such that it becomes very hard to get back on track again in the future. This inherent difficulty of the "sequencing" approach is only aggravated by the tendency of corporations to view part-time interim work as little more than treading water.

There could, however, be public policies directed explicitly to the problem of interrupted careers. We have, indeed, a perfect and extremely successful model addressed to this very problem—the reason for the interrupted careers in this case being World War II. At that time, it was largely men's careers (and/or education) that were being interrupted in midstream, and what the government did, through the GI Bill of Rights, was to provide a substantial subsidy for these individuals to return to, or start up, a program of education and training that would prepare them for returning to civilian life. All this suggests that a **Parental Bill of Rights**—in this case, addressed largely, though not wholly, to the needs of women—could be formulated, under which the parent who stayed at home would accumulate credits toward future educational expenses, both tuition and living allowances, which would smooth the transition not from war to peace, but from family-centered to market-centered production. This subsidy could be used at any level of education, from finishing high school to starting medical school, from liberal arts to specifically vocational training. It would, in effect, be the pro-family counterweight to the kind of subsidy now being initiated for women who wish to place their children in day care so that they can take jobs in the marketplace.

In general, it seems clear, at both the public and the private level, that if Americans wish to promote family life—if not of the "traditional" kind then at least of a recognizable kind (as in our loose definition)—ways can be found to do so. The larger question really has to do with purpose: Do we really wish to do so? In our final Postscript (pp. 471–472), we shall briefly discuss developments in biogenetics that could, if implemented someday, undermine the entire genetic structure of family relationships. But even in the here and now, deep questions arise. To many Americans, Sweden, for example, would appear to have taken enormous strides away from any recognizable concept of family life. Nearly half the new babies in Sweden are born out of wedlock; more than half of Swedish couples are living in "consensual unions"; divorce rates are high; virtually all mothers of young children are in the labor force; government-subsidized day care is universally available; paternal as well as maternal leaves are generously paid for—in short, virtually all the trends away from family to state responsibility that we noted in our own country have, in Sweden, been carried one step, or really several steps, further.

One of the large questions for the future of the family in the United States will be whether the Swedish model—currently under some financial pressure because of Sweden's exceedingly high tax rates—is: (1) relevant to our national situation (Sweden is a very small, ethnically and culturally homogeneous society) and (2) desirable as a future goal to strive for (what *are* the long-run implications of a society virtually bereft of family ties?)

Thus, our longer term question is likely to be not whether there is a way, but what is the will that we wish our future way to express.

## SUMMARY

1. The great variety of current "families" raises a question about what is "the family" whose future we are considering. Still, the two-parent family of a reasonably permanent nature, with those parents taking a serious responsibility for the raising of their children, is what most people have in mind when they express concern about the "future of the family."

2. Many people believe that a family unit such as this is basically on the way out for a variety of reasons:

a. *Demographic:* As parents live longer and have fewer children, the central function of the family is appreciably weakened.

b. *Economic:* The large-scale shift from homemaking to career building by U.S. women weakens the economic ties that hold marriages together and also reinforces the negative aspects of marriage and child rearing as far as the woman's career is concerned.

c. *Sociopolitical trends:* A variety of trends, including increased desires for individual self-fulfillment, a relativistic and pluralistic outlook, the principle of equality, and the growing welfare state all tend to make the family either irrelevant or an obstacle to other higher priority goals.

3. Other commentators argue that the institution of the family is due for a resurrection for other reasons:

a. *Demographic:* Longer life expectancies and fewer children mean that couples can easily have time to discharge their parental responsibilities to their children and still fulfill other goals.

b. *Economic:* It is only through a revitalized family that our country's poverty problems are likely to be solved, both in the short run and the long run.

c. *Societal trends:* a number of more recent trends, including a moderating of the sexual revolution, increasing awareness of the costs of divorce, and a countertrend to privatization as opposed to growing welfare state dependency, have made the family seem more valuable to society than ever.

4. Corporate policies to promote family objectives with various flexible employment arrangements are clearly possible, although many women find that any suggestion of a "mommy track" is likely to run counter to their long-run interests.

5. The state can also adopt various pro-family policies if it wishes, including a Parental Bill of Rights that would help the spouse who takes time

off to raise the children to prepare for a return to the labor force. Given that state policies can also undermine the family, however, it is not clear that expansion of state activity will necessarily tend to be pro-family, or, for that matter, that the future of the family is very secure in general.

## KEY CONCEPTS FOR REVIEW

*The* family versus famil*ies*

Changing life cycles

Career-building activities

Individualism

Self-fulfillment

Pluralism

Principle of equality

Welfare state

Intergenerational adult relationships

Poverty and family breakdown
    short-run
    long-run

Reactions to the sexual revolution

Costs of divorce

Privatization

Corporate employment
policies and the family
    career-primary women
    career-and-family women

"Mommy track"

Flexibility

Government family policies
    taxes
    Parental Bill of Rights

## QUESTIONS FOR DISCUSSION

1. Compare the brief definition of "the family" in this chapter with the longer definition of the "traditional" American family in Chapter 9 (pp. 145–146). What are the major differences you notice? Explain why such changes in definition were required.

2. Since the title and principal subject of this book is "our changing population," discuss the many different ways in which changes in our population—mortality, fertility, and immigration—might affect the future of the American family.

3. Considering economic factors in isolation, do you think that, on the whole, they make it more or less likely that family institutions will survive into the future? Would you agree that there are likely to be important economic costs either

way—that is, with a declining family *or* with a resurrected family? What costs do you foresee?

4. "Corporations should never adopt the concept of a 'mommy track'; what they all need is a 'parent track.' " Discuss.

5. Give examples of public programs that (a) might weaken or (b) might strengthen the American family. Give arguments in favor of programs of both kinds, and then design a general version of your own family policy. Do you think these policies will make a great deal of difference or very little difference in the long run?

6. Is it important to have institutions in the society that are smaller than the state but larger than the individual? Explain your answer.

## NOTES

1. Louis Harris, *Inside America* (New York: Vintage Books, 1987), p. 86.
2. Teresa Castro Martin and Larry L. Bumpass, "Recent Trends in Marital Disruption," *Demography*, 26(1), February 1989, pp. 46–49.

3. Jerrold K. Footlick, "What Happened to the Family?," *Newsweek*, Special Edition, Winter–Spring 1990, p. 18. About such broad definitions of the family, Footlick quotes social critic Midge Dexter: "You can define 'family' any way you want to, but

you can't fool Mother Nature. A family is a mommy and a daddy and their children."

4. Since the question of "*the* family" versus "famil*ies*" confronts everyone who studies this particular field, there is a large literature discussing the matter. For further reference, the reader may wish to consult John Scanzoni, *Shaping Tomorrow's Families: Theory and Policy for the 21st Century* (Beverly Hills, Calif.: Sage Publications, 1983). Scanzoni devotes a whole section to the disputes between different groups in connection with the 1980 White House Conference on Families. He also develops what he believes is a crucial distinction between a "morphostatic" view of the family and a "morphogenetic" view. The former emphasizes a sense of sameness, resistance to change, and the attempt to preserve a given equilibrium. The latter emphasizes the creation of new structures and arrangements in response to changing conditions. The morphostatic view tends to be held by conservatives who like to think of "the family"; the morphogenetic view tends to be held by liberals, who think in terms of "families." Further discussion can also be found in Brigette Berger and Peter L. Berger, *The War Over the Family: Capturing the Middle Ground* (Garden City, N.Y.: Anchor Press/Doubleday, 1983). In particular, they argue that there is a danger in translating the *empirical fact* of diversity in family arrangements into a *norm* of diversity (p. 63) See also Faith Robertson Eliot, *The Family: Change or Continuity?* (Atlantic Highlands, N.J.: Humanities International Press, 1986), where a valiant attempt by a British sociologist to answer the question "What is the family?" seems to end in total confusion (pp. 4–8.)

5. Alvin Toffler, *Future Shock* (New York: Bantam Books, 1970), p. 242.

6. For a discussion of the different pattern of female-headed households in black and white families, see Roger A. Wojtkiewicz, Sara S. McLanahan, and Irwin Garfinkel, "The Growth of Families Headed by Women, 1950–1980," *Demography*, 27(1), February 1990.

7. Ibid., p. 19. Economists James P. Smith and Michael Ward state this conclusion even more firmly: ". . . the feminization of poverty has its origins exclusively in the growth of female-headed families." Smith and Ward, "Women in the Labor Market and in the Family," *Journal of Economic Perspectives*, 3(1), Winter 1989, p. 20.

8. Cheryl Russell is quoted in the *Wall Street Journal*, March 3, 1987. Whether the predicted end of the sexual revolution will in fact occur cannot yet be determined. So far, studies among teenagers suggest that premarital sex and multiple sex partners are *increasing* rather than decreasing. In the years between 1985 and 1988, the percentage of women aged 15–19 who had engaged in premarital sexual intercourse is estimated to have increased from 44.1 percent to 51.5 percent. William Pratt, "Premarital Sexual Experience Among Adolescent Women-United States, 1970–1988," *Morbidity and Mortality Weekly Report*, Centers for Disease Control, Vol. 39, Nos. 51 & 52, January 4, 1991, pp. 929–932.

9. *Newsweek*, Special Edition, Winter–Spring 1990, p. 18. A recent study, giving partial support to this position, is A. J. Cherlin et. al., "Longitudinal Studies of Effects of Divorce on Children in Great Britain and the United States," *Science*, 252, June 7, 1991. This study suggests that family conflict and other conditions before divorce may explain a considerable part of the behavioral and other problems of children after divorce. A possible criticism of this study is that it does not consider the effect of an easily accessible and socially acceptable divorce option on the likelihood of family problems arising before divorce actually occurs.

10. "Studies in Marriage and the Family," U.S. Bureau of the Census, *Current Population Reports*, Series P-23, No. 162, Table J, p. 10. This same table also suggests costs of divorce for elderly *men*. The poverty rate for divorced men 65 and older in 1987 was 19.1 percent, as compared to 5.9 percent for married men with spouse present.

11. Barbara Foley Wilson and Charlotte Schoenborn, "A Healthy Marriage," *American Demographics*, November 1989, p. 43.

12. Barbara Kantrowitz and Pat Wingert, "Step by Step," in *Newsweek*, Special Edition, Winter–Spring 1990, p. 34. The Andrew Cherlin quotation is also taken from this article.

13. Felice N. Schwartz, "Management Women and the New Facts of Life," *Harvard Business Review*, January–February 1989, pp. 65–76.

14. Ibid., p. 70.

15. Ibid., p. 73.

16. Ronnie Sandroff, "Why Pro-Family Policies Are Good for Business and America," *Working Woman*, November 1989, p. 126.

17. Ellen Forman, "On Track," *Fort Lauderdale Sun-Sentinel*, March 19, 1989, p. 21a.

18. Between 1989 and 1991, there was an increase in the exemption for children from $2,000 to $2,150, still insufficient to keep pace with inflation over those two years.

19. Allan Carlson, "A Pro-Family Income Tax," *The Public Interest*, Winter 1989, No. 4, p. 75.

# 24

# Will the Poor
# Always Be with Us?

*H*ow will the **distribution of income** in the United States change in the future? More specifically: Will the percentage of Americans in poverty tend to increase, decrease, or remain about the same? Will the poor always be with us or, as many policymakers believed in the early 1960s, will our "affluent society" easily be able to rid itself of the scourge of poverty once and for all?

These questions are very relevant to the subject matter of this book—our changing population—for demographic factors clearly will affect the income distribution of our future society, at the same time as the income distribution of that society is likely to affect its underlying demographics. We have, in short, a complex interaction here, and we shall not expect simple answers to our deceptively simple-looking questions.

## INCOME DISTRIBUTION OVER TIME

Not that such simple answers haven't been given in the past. The centerpiece of the Ricardian analysis which we considered in our very first chapter (pp. 9–10) was a theory of long-run changes in income distribution. Wages for the great mass of laborers tended over time to be kept near the "subsistence level" by population growth. Meanwhile, the law of diminishing returns guaranteed that the profits of capitalists would also tend to fall over time. The only group that benefited in the course of the natural progress of society was the landowning class, whose land (or other natural resources) was increasingly in demand as population grew.

In the mid-nineteenth century, Karl Marx called the Malthusian population doctrine, on which the Ricardian theory rested, a "libel on the human race." He wished to prove that the problem of general poverty was due not to biological factors (the tendency of the poor to overreproduce) but to historically conditioned socioeconomic structures, of which capitalism was the latest manifestation. Nevertheless, his theory of

income distribution came out looking a bit like Ricardo's. (Marx himself acknowledged a debt to the writings of Ricardo.) In Marx's view, the masses tended to become poorer and poorer ("immiserization"). Also, as in Ricardo, capitalists tended to see their profits get squeezed over time. The argument, however, was quite different. The reason the workers never could earn above subsistence wages was that, whenever wages started to rise, the capitalists would displace laborers with machinery. Since a fundamental tenet of Marx's thought was that labor was the ultimate source of all economic value, however, the capitalist was unknowingly undoing himself by replacing labor with machinery. He did keep wages down— essentially by creating a large army of unemployed workers—but he was also destroying his ultimate profit source. In short, he was killing the "goose that laid the golden egg."

All this general misery, of course, would end with the revolution and the advent of communism. At that time, the ultimate rule governing income distribution would be, "From each according to his ability, to each according to his need." Just how badly mistaken Marx was in his estimate of the economic powers of future communism, we discuss briefly in our next chapter.

From our point of view, a much more interesting approach to the question of income distribution over time can be found in the work of the late Nobel Prize–winning economist Simon Kuznets. Kuznets did not provide a sweeping synthesis like that of Ricardo or Marx, but he did attempt to make a number of empirical generalizations on the basis of a much longer historical record than was available to either of his predecessors.

In writings in the 1950s and 1960s,[1] Kuznets suggested that the general experience of industrial nations like the United States, Great Britain, and Sweden was to move from *increasing inequality* in income distribution in the first phases of industrialization toward *increasing equality* in the later stages. In a relative sense at least, although poverty might get worse when the transition from an agrarian to an industrialized world began, later on it would certainly lessen, with both the number and percentage of poor people tending to decline over time.

A variety of reasons could account for this general pattern. Before industrialization occurs, there may be some extremely well-to-do groups in the society (as we find today, for example, in certain elite groups in very poor less developed countries, or LDCs), but they tend to be a very small proportion of the total population. When development occurs and more people move into high-income occupations, this may increase the degree of inequality overall by reducing the *share* of the total national income going to the poor.[2] Later on, as more and more workers move into high-productivity sectors, and as the productivity of the traditional agricultural sector also improves, there may be an increasing middle class and a move toward greater equality overall. This tendency may be abetted by a variety of factors: the spread of education to all classes of the society, the decline of property incomes (the opposite of the Ricardian prediction), and a more egalitarian philosophy that prompts the state to intervene with various welfare, social security, and other income-redistributing legislation.

In Figure 24-1, we present one empirical attempt (1976) to relate the stage of economic development of 66 different countries (measured by their per capita real GNP) to their income distributions (measured by the percentage of national income going to the top 20 percent of income recipients and the percentage going to the poorest 40 percent.) This study, by M. S. Ahluwalia,[3] tends roughly to confirm the Kuznets hypothesis. In very poor countries, income is fairly evenly distributed (virtually everybody is poor); then, as we consider countries with slightly higher per capita incomes, the share of the rich tends to rise and the share of the poor to fall. With still higher average levels of per capita income, we move back toward a more equal distribution of income.

This, of course, deals with historical development. What of the future? In the case of the United States, Kuznets, writing in 1979 and 1980,[4] feared that we might be facing a tendency toward greater *in*equality again. He attributed this possibility to demographic factors and, in particular, to the tendency of lower income groups in the nation to outreproduce higher income

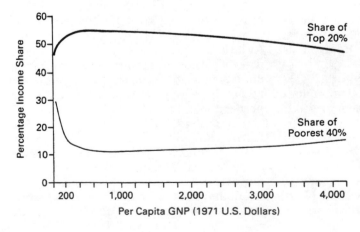

**FIGURE 24-1: Income Shares and Economic Development**

*Source:* M. S. Ahluwalia, "Income Inequality: Some Dimensions of the Problem," in H. Chenery et al., *Redistribution with Growth* © 1974 by The International Bank for Reconstruction and Development and The World Bank. Reprinted by permission of Oxford University Press, Inc.

groups. We will return to this point in a moment.

## A RISING TIDE OR A GREAT U-TURN?

As we mentioned in some of our earlier discussions of poverty in the United States, it makes a great difference whether we are talking about *absolute poverty* or *relative poverty*. Figure 24-1 is concerned with relative shares of rich and poor. As we move to the right in the diagram, we are dealing with countries with higher and higher per capita incomes. Even if the percentage of income going to the poorest 40 percent of the population did not rise in the course of economic development, rising per capita incomes would virtually guarantee us a constant decline in the amount of absolute poverty over time. In this absolute sense, the answer to our question—Will the poor always be with us?—seems to be perfectly clear. It would be: No, the poor will not always be with us. Or, at least, the poor who remain with us will be a constantly diminishing proportion of our total population.

In a very broad sense, thinking historically, this answer is obviously true. There is incomparably more absolute poverty in a poor country like Bangladesh or Ethiopia than there is in a country like the United States, Britain, or Sweden. The same applies to the latter countries at, say, the beginning of the eighteenth or nineteenth centuries as compared with those same countries today.

A major reason that this decline in absolute poverty has taken place in the industrial nations, and why many people expect this decline to continue in the future, can be expressed in a simple phrase, a favorite expression of the late John F. Kennedy: "**A rising tide lifts all boats.**" The "rising tide" refers to the increases in overall wages, living standards, education, job opportunities, and the like that have been characteristic of our past history. This rising tide might, of course, not "lift all boats" equally. It is even conceivable that it might

lift the boats of the rich far more than the boats of the poor. In this case, general economic progress might be accompanied by an increase in *relative* poverty. But as long as the tide lifts all boats to at least some degree, then economic progress should reduce, and in the long run virtually abolish, *absolute* poverty.

But can this be counted on for the future? Political economists Bennett Harrison of MIT and Barry Bluestone of the University of Massachusetts believe not, unless a massive restructuring of our economy occurs. Although their views are by no means universally accepted, they argue that the past 15 years have seen a dramatic shift—a "**great U-turn**" in income distribution in the United States. They exhibit graphs similar to Figures 24-2 through 24-4 to show that average weekly real earnings of workers have declined considerably since the early 1970s, that real median income has been stagnant during that period, and that an index of family income inequality has risen sharply since the end of the 1960s.[5] They also note that poverty has been increasing in recent years, both absolutely and relatively. In 1989, there were over 8 million more Americans below the official poverty level (an absolute standard) than in 1973. The percentage of Americans in poverty also increased during that time, from 11.1 to 12.8 percent.

Apparently, either the "tide" is not rising sufficiently rapidly, or perhaps a number of "boats" have been left stranded on the shore. In either event, it would seem that this metaphor no longer guarantees a poverty-diminished future. We had more poor people in the United States in the late 1980s than we did in the 1970s.

Of course, it should be said that the particular numbers and diagrams used to describe recent trends sometimes make them look more ominous than they are. We have often mentioned the difficulties of finding adequate measures of "poverty" (pp. 254–255). Figure 24-4 is a good example of potentially misleading graphics. It seems to

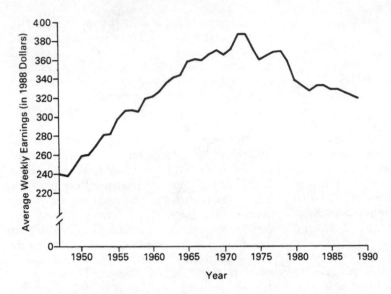

**FIGURE 24-2: Real Average Weekly Earnings, 1947-1989 (in 1988 Dollars)**

*Source:* Council of Economic Advisers, *Economic Report of the President, 1990* (Washington, D.C.: U.S. Government Printing Office, 1990). Adapted by the authors.

show an index of family income inequality that is zooming skyward. Yet if we look at the numbers on which this diagram is based, we might come to a rather different conclusion. In Tables 24-1 and 24-2, we show income distribution in the United States over the period 1947 to 1988 by quintiles, first for families and then for unrelated individuals. Looking at these numbers, one does not get a sense of any massive trend toward inequality in recent years. Considering similar numbers (1947 to 1984), University of Maryland expert Frank Levy says that "the most obvious feature of the postwar family income distribution was its stability" and that "the income distribution of

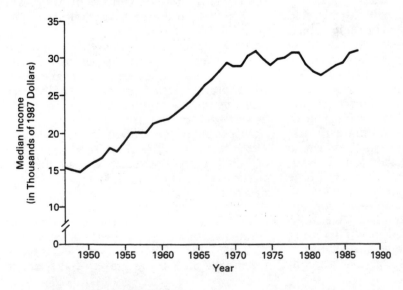

**FIGURE 24-3: Real Median Income, Families and Unrelated Individuals, 1947–1987 (in 1987 dollars)**

*Source:* U.S. Bureau of the Census, *Current Population Reports,* Series P-60, No. 162, Table 11.

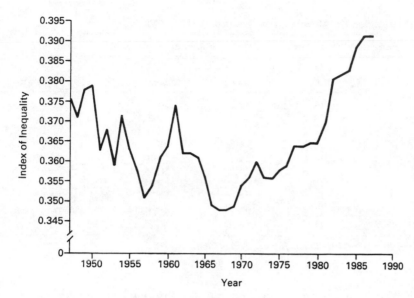

**FIGURE 24-4:  Family Income Inequality, 1947–1987 (GINI Index)**

*Source:* Adapted from Bennett Harrison and Barry Bluestone, *The Great U-Turn: Corporate Restructuring and the Polarizing of America* (New York: Basic Books, 1988), Figure 1-3.

unrelated individuals shows a modest trend toward greater equality throughout the postwar period."[6]

Not that Levy himself is all that sanguine about what has been happening. He notes that in the 1950s and 1960s, 40-year-old men could expect to have their incomes increase anywhere from 25 to 36 percent by the time they were 50. In 1973, however, 40-year-old-men saw their average incomes *fall* (by about 14 percent) in real dollars by the time they reached 50 (1983). Young men leaving home to go out into the world used to be able to match or improve on their fathers' earnings very quickly, but, Levy notes, this ceased to be so in the 1970s and early 1980s. He also mentions the increase in poverty during this period, as discussed earlier. Finally, he suggests that our real problem may not be inequality of

**TABLE 24-1.  U.S. Family Income Distribution, 1947–1989**

| | *Percentage of Family Income Going to Different Quintiles* | | | | | |
|---|---|---|---|---|---|---|
| | *1st (Poorest)* | *2nd* | *3rd* | *4th* | *5th (Richest)* | *Top 5 Percent* |
| 1947 | 5.0 | 11.9 | 17.0 | 23.1 | 43.0 | 17.5 |
| 1949 | 4.5 | 11.9 | 17.3 | 23.5 | 42.7 | 16.9 |
| 1954 | 4.5 | 12.1 | 17.7 | 23.9 | 41.8 | 16.3 |
| 1959 | 4.9 | 12.3 | 17.9 | 23.8 | 41.1 | 15.9 |
| 1964 | 5.1 | 12.0 | 17.7 | 24.0 | 41.2 | 15.9 |
| 1969 | 5.6 | 12.4 | 17.7 | 23.7 | 40.6 | 15.6 |
| 1974 | 5.5 | 12.0 | 17.5 | 24.0 | 41.0 | 15.5 |
| 1979 | 5.2 | 11.6 | 17.5 | 24.1 | 41.7 | 15.8 |
| 1984 | 4.7 | 11.0 | 17.0 | 24.4 | 42.9 | 16.0 |
| 1989 | 4.6 | 10.6 | 16.5 | 23.7 | 44.6 | 17.9 |

*Source:*   U.S. Bureau of the Census, *Current Population Reports*, Series P-60, Nos. 146, 149, 166, 168.

**TABLE 24-2.  U.S. Income Distribution for Unrelated Individuals, 1947–1988**

| | *Percentage of Income of Unrelated Individuals by Quintiles* | | | | | |
|---|---|---|---|---|---|---|
| | *1st* *(Poorest)* | *2nd* | *3rd* | *4th* | *5th* *(Richest)* | *Top 5 Percent* |
| 1947 | 2.0 | 6.2 | 12.7 | 22.5 | 56.6 | 29.3 |
| 1949 | 2.4 | 7.5 | 14.3 | 26.0 | 49.8 | 19.4 |
| 1954 | 2.4 | 7.1 | 13.1 | 24.8 | 52.6 | 22.2 |
| 1959 | 1.4 | 7.2 | 13.2 | 24.8 | 53.4 | 22.1 |
| 1964 | 2.5 | 7.1 | 12.8 | 24.4 | 53.2 | 22.9 |
| 1969 | 3.3 | 7.8 | 13.8 | 24.3 | 50.9 | 20.7 |
| 1974 | 4.2 | 8.9 | 14.6 | 24.1 | 48.3 | 19.5 |
| 1979 | 4.0 | 9.2 | 15.3 | 24.3 | 47.2 | 18.5 |
| 1984 | 3.8 | 8.9 | 15.2 | 24.1 | 48.1 | 19.1 |
| 1988 | 3.7 | 8.7 | 15.0 | 23.8 | 48.8 | 20.3 |

*Source:*  U.S. Bureau of the Census, *Current Population Reports*, Series P-60, No. 166, p. 31.

current income, but a rapidly increasing *inequality of prospects*, "an inequality in the chance that a family will enjoy the "middle-class dream."[7]

## POSSIBLE SOURCES OF FUTURE POVERTY

Many special circumstances can be called upon to explain the economic slowdown of the 1970s and early 1980s suggested by Figures 24-2 and 24-3—for example, the energy crises engineered by OPEC, the ensuing stagflation, the sharp recession of 1982–1983 as the government tried to clamp down on inflation, and so on.[8] Still, the numbers are sufficiently discouraging to make one wonder whether the United States has, indeed, made some kind of permanent U-turn on the poverty front. Is it possible that the number of American poor—poor even in the absolute sense— will keep on increasing in the future as it has over the past two decades?

Let us first list some of the possible **sources of future poverty** in the United States; subsequently, we shall comment on

how changes in our population may interact with these particular factors. Briefly, poverty is likely to increase if any of the following problems occur.

### Economic Slowdown

If the great engine of U.S. economic growth slows down in the coming decades (as it did in the 1973–1983) decade, then the prospects of more and more people escaping poverty will be greatly diminished. Historically, economic growth has provided: (1) abundant jobs for a growing population, and (2) increases in output per capita and per employed worker that have made possible higher incomes for all groups in the society, including the poor. More jobs and **increasing worker productivity**—these have been the main forces responsible for the historic reductions in poverty in all industrial nations. Is there anything to suggest that these forces will cease to operate so successfully in the future? Are we passing through some kind of economic watershed where our ability to provide jobs—decent, high-paying jobs—and/or our ability to improve our technological prowess is failing us?

## Differential Fertility

In general, low-income groups in the United States have higher fertility rates than higher income groups. This has always been true historically, but, in the past, population growth rates for low-income groups—as, for example, black Americans—were diminished by higher mortality rates. As mentioned before, Simon Kuznets was concerned about this problem of **differential fertility.** He noted that, because of higher fertility, more children than adults are in low-income families. In 1960, on a per person basis, "the average family income of the universe of children is about 30 percent lower than the average income of the universe of adults." And the potential problem with this is that "lower income levels of parents mean proportionately lower investment in the quality of the descendants and hence possibly lower growth rates in per capita income of the lower income groups and their descendants." This could result in a "widening of income inequality" and possibly a slower rate of growth of GNP in general.[9]

## Weakened Family Structures

In the last chapter, we discussed in some detail possible futures for the American family and its many variants. Clearly, if the trends toward divorce, separation, never-married mothers (and fathers), and, in general, toward single-parent child rearing continue, then this will make it more difficult to eliminate both absolute and relative poverty in the United States in the twenty-first century. To some degree this is just a simple matter of arithmetic. Since it takes more income for a family to live in two separate households than for the same number of people to live in a single household, then any breakup of family units tends directly to increase the number of people living in poverty.[10]

Of course, the problems of weakened **family structures** are by no means confined to simple arithmetic calculations. The great difficulty facing single parents (almost always mothers) in trying both to raise children *and* to earn money has been discussed at length in previous chapters. In 1988, even after government cash *and* noncash transfers, the poverty rate in female-headed families with children was above 38 percent. This poverty also lasts much longer than that which occurs in two-parent families. Here we have the same potential problem of inadequate investment in children that Kuznets discussed in relation to differential fertility. Since we have considered family structure at length in the previous chapter, we shall make only a few further references to the problem in this chapter.

## Failure of Welfare Programs

One of the reasons, mentioned earlier, to expect a more equal distribution of income over time is that governments in most economically advanced countries, including the United States, have actively sought to redistribute income so as to assist the ill, elderly, handicapped, and needy. The "welfare state," though varying in scope in different countries, has been a major factor throughout the industrialized world.

Why, then, would we list the "**failure of welfare programs**" as a possible factor leading to greater income inequality in the future and possibly to increased poverty?

There are really two diametrically opposed answers to this question. *Answer One* is that, in many industrialized nations, and certainly in the United States, there has been a reaction against the expansion of the welfare state that characterized the 40 years from the mid-1930s to the mid-1970s. The "failure" of our welfare programs, according to this answer, is to provide sufficient assistance to those in need. We have been retrenching on many vital programs, especially Aid to Families with Dependent Children (AFDC). If our present retrenchments are not reversed and if new initiatives (like the recent child care legislation) are not expanded, then our welfare system will continue to be a "failure" and poverty in America will persist indefinitely into the future.

*Answer Two* (which, like *Answer One,* we have encountered in earlier chapters) states that the "failure" of the welfare system lies not in its niggardliness but in its almost inexorable tendency to expand and to weaken both the motives and institutions by which Americans have historically worked their ways out of poverty. In its most simplistic statement, this view argues that the welfare system subsidizes poverty and, as any first-year economics student can tell you, when you subsidize an activity you tend to get more of it. In more complex versions, this second answer notes that the welfare system may weaken those very institutions, notably the family, that must be strengthened if poverty in this country is ever to be eliminated. Thus, to take the child care example, by subsidizing child care outside the home so that single mothers can work, one simply makes it that much easier to *be* a single mother—that is, to avoid the more complex, but ultimately poverty-reducing, effort to have and rear children within a two-parent household.

## THE GREAT PRODUCTIVITY QUESTION

Of all the factors just mentioned, probably none is of greater relevance for the future of poverty in the United States than the ability of our economy to generate higher and higher real incomes in the future as we did over the course of our historic past. If not all boats, a rising tide certainly lifts *many* boats. Will good jobs be available in the future for those willing and eager to take them? Will the productivity of U.S. workers increase in the years ahead, level off, possibly even decline? On this issue, as we have noted in other contexts (for example, the

viability of our Social Security and health care systems), a great deal depends.

Although there are many different opinions on the subject, no general answer to this question can be given. The fact is that the fundamental causes of our recent productivity slowdown are still surrounded by a certain air of mystery. Extending these uncertain explanations into the future only increases their shakiness. We are moving more and more into a service-providing as opposed to goods-producing economy. Is there something intrinsic about service industries that condemns them to slower productivity growth than we found earlier in agriculture and manufacturing? We are experiencing very low levels of personal saving; the government budget deficit means (to most economists) that the government is engaged in negative saving (dissaving). Does this mean that we will not have the resources necessary to invest in our future? For that matter, how about foreign competition? Are all the really good, high-paid, high-productivity jobs disappearing from this country as enterprising foreign nations outcompete us and leave us in the dust?

Such questions are well outside the province of this book and, in any event, have no definitive answers. Indeed, we do not even know at this juncture how large the recent productivity growth slowdown in this country actually has been. Productivity specialist John Kendrick, for example, believes that most estimates of our real GNP (which essentially provides the numerator of productivity estimates) significantly understate our rate of economic growth. This is because in a number of service sectors, where output is hard to measure, government statisticians use labor inputs as a proxy measure for output, a method that guarantees zero **measured labor productivity** growth in these sectors even though **true productivity** may be growing substantially. Furthermore, there are well-known errors in the way statisticians adjust for price changes and for improvements in the quality of goods. Kendrick suspects that such problems may have led us to exaggerate our recent productivity growth slowdown or, if not that, at least to underestimate our entire rate of economic growth between 1948 and 1988.[11] (Incidentally, if Kendrick is right, and our real incomes are actually higher than we had thought them, then the amount of absolute poverty in the United States in the late 1980s would also be considerably less than official measurements suggest.)

Failing a general answer to the great productivity question, we can nevertheless indicate specific effects that our changing population may have on productivity growth in the future. Briefly, there are two such effects, and they very probably will work in opposite directions.

**1. Changing Age and Experience Structure of Our Labor Force.** This first effect should be favorable. In the 1970s, one of the reasons given for our slower productivity growth was that, with the Baby Boomers coming of working age and with the dramatic increase in the number of women entering the job market, the levels of **age and work experience in our labor force** fell considerably. We had suddenly to cope with a young, inexperienced group of labor force entrants, and labor productivity dropped in consequence. By the same token, the decades of the 1990s and the early twenty-first century will see the impact of the Baby Bust. All the talk today is not of a surplus of new entrants into the labor market but of a potential labor shortage. This means that the level of experience in our labor force—few new entrants because of the Baby Bust plus the fact that many women are already working, *and* that the Baby Boomers are entering the most productive years of their lives—will increase sharply. This should mean not only higher productivity but also a very good job market for young labor force entrants. The latter effect may have a direct impact on employment opportunities for young black males. Insofar as the absence of such opportunities is a major factor in black poverty (see above,

pp. 264–266), then it will have a similarly direct and positive impact on our national poverty percentages in the coming decades. Of course, other demographic changes—if, say, we were to sharply increase immigration—might lessen this favorable effect on black employment opportunities.

**2. Possible Mismatch of Jobs and Skills.** To achieve the productivity growth necessary to reduce future poverty, most experts believe that there will be increasing demands on the technological skills of our work force. The Labor Department, for example, has estimated that between 1984 and 1995, high-skill jobs will increase by 23 percent, compared with an increase of only 12 percent in low-skill jobs. A problem arises in meeting this demand, however, because of general deficiencies in our educational system, which we discussed in Chapter 17, and also because of the changing racial and ethnic composition of our work force. Blacks, Hispanics, and other minority groups supplied only 18 percent of the net increase in our labor force between 1970 and 1985, but these groups will provide an estimated 29 percent of the net addition between 1985 and the year 2000. Since educational and achievement levels are currently lower for blacks and the majority of Hispanic groups, the prospect has been raised that there will be a mismatch between the jobs necessary to maintain high productivity growth and the skills available for filling those jobs.

We are not, incidentally, talking about extremely high levels of skills here, but of a minimum competence in language and computational ability. In these terms, the National Assessment of Educational Progress in 1978 determined that whereas 13 percent of all American 17-year-olds could be judged to be "functionally illiterate," the corresponding figures for that age group among blacks was 56 percent and among Hispanics 44 percent.[12]

There may also be a mismatch between jobs and people in terms of location. Many jobs, particularly low-skill, entry-level jobs, may be outside the inner cities, in suburban shopping malls and rural areas difficult to reach for the urban poor. Thus, there is the prospect of a deficit of entry-level jobs in the cities where the workers are, and a deficit of workers in the suburbs where the jobs are.

None of these difficulties will necessarily be decisive, and there is the underlying favorable condition mentioned before—a future of relatively high demand for new workers—but still, it is clear that, as far as productivity growth is concerned, demographic factors are likely to cut both ways, negatively as well as positively.

## THE DIFFERENTIAL FERTILITY QUESTION

Differential **fertility** is an important reason that the proportion of blacks and Hispanics in our future labor force will increase. (Immigration, of course, is another factor in the case of Hispanics.) What do we make of the Kuznets argument that the higher fertility rates of poor people pose a serious obstacle to the elimination of poverty and income inequality in the United States in the coming decades?

### Historical Mobility

Historically, differential fertility among income classes has not proved a major obstacle to the upward mobility of the poor. As noted earlier, it has more or less always been the case that Americans in the lower economic classes have had more children than the well-to-do, yet the overall historic trend in this country has been toward the reduction of absolute poverty and toward at least some reduction in relative income inequality. Indeed, it has been argued that differential fertility, along with heavy immigration in the late nineteenth and early twentieth centuries, created an important "push" factor stimulating upward mobility in the United States. One obvious example

would be the shift of workers from rural and farm areas, where higher fertility created a surplus labor force, to urban and factory employment, often with jobs that paid more and were higher in the "stratification hierarchy."[13] In short, as better jobs became available in the course of industrialization (in our own day, these would be the high-skill, high-tech jobs mentioned earlier), the labor surplus created by higher fertility among the poor provided the labor pool from which these better jobs were filled.

To complete the story: As the children of the poor adjusted to their new work conditions and higher incomes—and, in the case of immigrants, to their adopted nation—they themselves had fewer children, and the problem disappeared. Poor people, whether immigrants or native-born, remained poor and produced large families only for a generation or two. Then they were swallowed up in the mainstream of middle-class, unpoor, declining-fertility Americans.

### Minority Group Status versus Social Characteristics

This above generalized description may not, however, fit all groups in our society to the same degree. One of today's great concerns is precisely that some minority groups may become trapped in a kind of vicious circle of poverty that may last well beyond the second generation. Moreover, when it comes to the fertility behavior of minority groups, the pattern described in the previous section should more properly be thought of as one of two competing hypotheses.[14]

Briefly, the first hypothesis is that fertility patterns in all groups in the society are determined by their social and economic circumstances. This is the so-called **social characteristics hypothesis.** According to this view, as various groups, whether native or immigrant, move up the economic ladder, receive more years of education, and are assimilated into the social and cultural mainstream of U.S. society, their fertility patterns will show the same characteristics as those of the majority of Americans. Thus, in our earlier brief description, we describe poor, high-fertility groups becoming low-fertility groups as they rise in the socioeconomic stream. This is an example of the "social characteristics" approach.

A competing view is that minority groups will often tend to have different patterns from those of the majority population even when their socioeconomic characteristics are the same. At any given socioeconomic level, they may have higher, or lower, fertility rates than the majority population simply by virtue of their being a minority group in the society, with the different history, background, and insecurities that such a status may imply. Thus, this hypothesis is called the **minority group status hypothesis.**

This hypothesis was first advanced by Calvin Goldscheider and Peter R. Uhlenberg in 1969. They argued that well-educated blacks, Jews, and Japanese Americans all tended to have *lower* fertility rates than average Americans at the same high socioeconomic level. They concluded that "the insecurities of minority group membership operate to depress fertility below majority levels." This conclusion was qualified, however, with the major exception that there be "no pro-natalist ideology associated with the minority group and no norm discouraging the use of efficient contraceptives." The qualification was necessary because the authors found that, in the case of the Catholic minority group, fertility rates were generally higher than simple socioeconomic characteristics would predict.[15]

Can we choose between these two hypotheses with respect to two of our large minority groups—blacks and Hispanics—both of which have high fertility and poverty rates?

### Black Fertility Trends

A great deal of research has been devoted to determining whether black fertility

rates conform better to the social characteristics or minority group status hypothesis. One study, by sociologist Nan E. Johnson, suggested the possibility of what she called a "weak" form of the characteristics hypothesis. In Figure 24-5a, we represent a "strong" form of the characteristics hypothesis using "education" as a proxy variable to represent socioeconomic characteristics. Here, black and white fertility rates are identical at each level of education, the difference between them at any given moment of historical time simply reflecting the fact that blacks have lagged behind whites in terms of socioeconomic status. A "strong" form of the minority group status hypothesis is shown in Figure 24-5b, where blacks have higher fertility at low educational levels but lower fertility at high educational levels. What Johnson's research suggested was that a "weak" form of the characteristics hypothesis was the most appropriate. This is shown in Figure 24-5c, where blacks at low socioeconomic levels have higher fertility rates than whites but where, beginning at a certain point (say, once they enter that elusive state called the "middle class"), black fertility behavior becomes the same as that of whites.[16]

More recent research, however, suggests that racial differences in fertility appear at all economic levels to at least some degree, suggesting that the minority group status approach may have a slight explanatory edge. For example, Farley and Allen note that while "social, demographic, and economic factors influence the childbearing of black and white women in much the same manner ... the fertility of black women exceeds that of white women in almost all categories of every variable." They caution against the simple view that "the racial gap is declining."[17]

Are black and white fertility rates likely to converge in the future? The Census Bureau Middle Series projections, we recall, suggested that they would by the middle of the next century (p. 217). As Figure 24-6 shows, in an absolute sense, the differ-

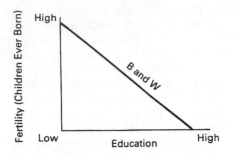

**FIGURE 24-5a:   Characteristics Hypothesis ("Strong" Form)**

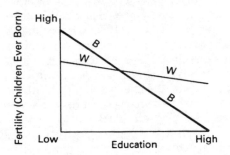

**FIGURE 24-5b:   Minority Group Status Hypothesis ("Strong" Form)**

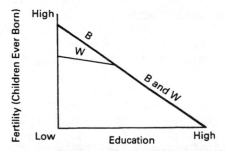

**FIGURE 24-5c:   Characteristics Hypothesis ("Weak" Form)**

**FIGURE 24-5:   Black and White Fertility Hypotheses**

*Source:*   Nan E. Johnson, "Minority-Group Status and the Fertility of Black Americans, 1970: A New Look," *American Journal of Sociology, 84*(6), May 1979, p. 1388. Reprinted by permission of The University of Chicago, publisher.

ence between black and white fertility rates narrowed sharply from the peak of the Baby Boom in the late 1950s. In a *relative* sense, however (black divided by white fertility rates), there has really been no significant change in the last half century. About 30 percent higher than the white rate in 1940, black fertility remained about 30 percent higher in 1988.

What all this means in terms of poverty is that there is no easy escape promised us from the concerns expressed by the late Simon Kuznets. The fertility rates of blacks in low economic groups will very probably continue to be higher than those of blacks in higher economic groups and also higher than those of whites in comparably low economic groups.

### Hispanic Trends

Another minority group that shows high fertility and high poverty rates is the American Hispanic population. Hispanic population growth, fed by immigration as well as high fertility, is expected to be much more rapid than black population growth during the coming decades. Over the next century, for example, Hispanics could roughly triple as a percentage of the U.S. population. Meanwhile, the poverty rates for Hispanic-origin families are high: 23.4 percent in 1989, compared with 7.8 percent for white families. Their dropout rates in school substantially exceed those of other ethnic groups. In 1989, 33.0 percent of Hispanics aged 16 to 24 had not completed high school and were not currently enrolled in school. The comparable figure for whites was 12.4 percent and for blacks, 13.8 percent. The percentage of Hispanics 25 years and over who have completed less than five years of school is more than twice that of blacks.

Given these numbers, it would obviously be very desirable to be able to generalize about the future course of both immigration and fertility among Hispanics. The two may very well be intertwined, in that the size of the Hispanic population and the continuing

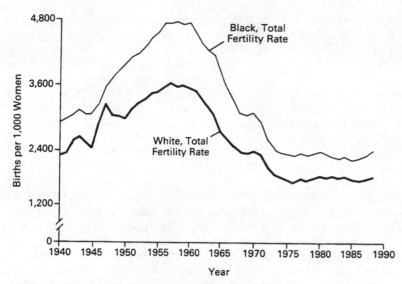

**FIGURE 24-6a:  Trends in the Total Fertility Rate by Race, 1940–1988**

*Source:*  Robert D. Grove and Alice M. Hetzel, *Vital Statistics Rates in the United States: 1940–1960* (Washington, D.C.: U.S. Government Printing Office, 1968), Table 12; National Center for Health Statistics, *Vital Statistics of the United States: 1981*. Vol. 1, Table 1-4; *Monthly Vital Statistics Report*, Vol. 35, No. 4 supplement, July 18, 1986, Table 4, Vol. 35, No. 6 supplement (2), September 26, 1986, Table 2. *Monthly Vital Statistics Report*, Advance Report of Final Natality Statistics, 1988, Vol. 39. No. 4 supplement, August 15, 1990, Table 4.

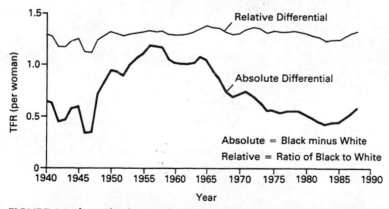

**FIGURE 24-6b:  Absolute and Relative Differentials between Black and White Total Fertility Rates, 1940–1988.**

access to a large immigrant pool may influence cultural norms, which, in turn, may influence fertility rates. This may be especially true in the case of Mexican Americans, where the potential pool is enormous; the possibilities of access, entry, exit, and reentry are likely to remain relatively high; and the concentration of Hispanics in a geographical area (which, in fact, once belonged to Mexico) is great. Is it possible that high,

Third World–style fertility rates might maintain themselves in the American West and Southwest, increasing the number of persons below the poverty level at a rapid rate?

This outcome seems improbable, but it must be said that we have much less good statistical evidence on American Hispanics than we do in the case of blacks. In trying to apply different fertility hypotheses to the case of Hispanic Americans, Frank Bean and Marta Tienda suggest that there are elements of both the social characteristics hypothesis and the minority group status hypothesis that apply. They also mention two other somewhat different hypotheses, including what they call the **subcultural hypothesis.** This hypothesis, relevant to immigrant groups, suggests that fertility rates may be affected by the cultural values of the immigrants' country of origin— in the Mexican case, including the tendency of "women finding their greatest satisfaction in the bearing and raising of children."[18]

Their conclusion is that one cannot fully rule out any of the competing hypotheses. In terms of social characteristics, age composition, education, and women's labor force participation rates are all important elements in explaining why Hispanic fertility is higher than that of non-Hispanic white women. Different educational levels, for example, may explain anywhere between one-third and two-thirds of the fertility gap.

However, differences remain even after socioeconomic factors have been taken into account, and Bean and Tienda offer as a tentative explanation a mixture of the hypotheses. In the early years of childbearing, Hispanic women may respond to the norms and values of a group that places a high value on fertility; as they grow older, economic factors and, indeed, the minority group hypothesis may come into play, reducing their fertility later in their lives.[19]

It is, however, impossible at this point in time to project future Hispanic American fertility with any confidence. The poor educational experience of this group to date, plus the various factors that may make the persistence of norms from their countries of origin more likely, do suggest, however, that the escape from the Kuznets problem may be no easier, and perhaps more difficult, than it may prove to be in the case of black Americans.

## CAN THE STATE HELP FIND THE SOLUTION?

In our discussion so far, we have been left with large question marks about our future productivity growth and about the effects of differential fertility on poverty trends in coming decades. Since we know from the previous chapter that the future of the two-parent family is far from secure, we have to acknowledge at this point that the "poor"—perhaps quite a large number of "poor"—may continue to "be with us" in the future.

Unless, of course, public policies can be devised to eliminate the bulk of whatever poverty remains. But is public intervention part of the solution or part of the problem? We summarize, first, the dilemmas facing public policy in this area and then indicate some approaches that are being widely discussed as we enter the decade of the 1990s.

### Dilemmas of Welfare Policy

In his well-received book (*Poor Support: Poverty in the American Family*), Harvard University's David Ellwood describes three **"conundrums" affecting America's welfare policy:**[19]

1. *The security–work conundrum:* "When you give people money, you reduce the pressure on them to work and care for themselves."

2. *The assistance–family structure conundrum:* "The economic insecurity of single-parent families leads to a natural desire to provide some level of support through wel-

fare, yet such aid creates a potential for the formation and perpetuation of single-parent families."

3.  *The targeting–isolation conundrum:* "A natural goal of policy is to target services to those who are most in need, but the more effectively you target, the more you tend to isolate people who receive the services from the economic and political mainstream."

How important are these conundrums? Do they mean that, in total, welfare policy is bound to be a failure, no matter how it is shaped? Or are they simply inconveniences along the way?

Much depends on how large the specified effects are. For example, most careful studies of the effect of welfare payments suggest that they have relatively little effect on family formation. Yet most poor people, as well as most Americans in general, believe that the effects are quite large. Furthermore, although there are some conjectures, there is no generally accepted theory of why single-parent families have grown so rapidly in recent decades, particularly among blacks in poverty.[20]

Often these conundrums have curious effects. Ellwood notes, for example, that when certain poor people were given work vouchers that promised prospective employers that the government would pay a part of their wages—thereby making it cheaper for employers to hire them—these workers had *lower* levels of employment than a control group that received no vouchers. Effectively, the vouchers stigmatized these workers as bad risks. In an age when we are worried about the possibility of an isolated "underclass" developing, this targeting–isolation conundrum could become quite serious. Yet how do you help the poor at all without setting them apart to at least some degree?

At this abstract level, perhaps the only real conclusion one can reach is that, whether generally helpful or hurtful, the large-scale provision of welfare assistance to the poor is certainly no panacea as far as future poverty in the United States is concerned.

## Money versus Structured Assistance

In a famous literary conversation, F. Scott Fitzgerald told Ernest Hemingway that he thought the rich were different from the rest of us. To which Hemingway replied: "Yes, they have more money than we do." Reversing the income groups, could we accept a Hemingwayesque answer about the way the poor are different from the rest of us? "Yes, they have less money than we do."

Social scientists once thought so, and the natural result of such thinking was to construct one version or another of a guaranteed annual income (usually disguised so that its real nature would be somewhat hidden from view). The poor needed only one thing: money. Give them money and poverty would disappear. Of course, you had to be careful how you did this. If, for example, you gave money only to single-parent families, denying it when the husband was present, you clearly ran the risk of creating incentives for marital breakup. Also, there were work incentives to be worried about: If an equal amount of money was cut off when you began earning money on your own, then clearly you'd be very hesitant about taking anything less than a very good (and probably unavailable) job. So *some* structure was necessary, but the ideal might well be to minimize the structure and concentrate as far as possible on getting to the poor what the poor needed: money.

Unfortunately, none of this worked quite as well as expected. One of the problems occurred in connection with the famous SIME-DIME experiment (Seattle Income Maintenance Experiment–Denver Income Maintenance Experiment) of the early 1970s. Although the program was specifically designed not to penalize two-parent families, the income guarantees seemed on first investigation to have led to a major increase (compared to control groups) in marital dissolutions in a three-year period: 37 percent for Hispanics, 43 percent for blacks, and 63 percent for whites. More money, in itself, could apparently produce destructive changes in family patterns.

Actually, subsequent research has cast some doubts on this influential finding. A more recent study by Glen Cain and Douglas A. Wissoker finds only a 14 percent higher rate of marital breakup, a result that is statistically insignificant and that is further reduced when certain biases are taken into account. Even Cain and Wissoker acknowledge, however, that income maintenance programs may increase the number of single-parent households in other ways than through marital breakup.[21]

But if at least some structure seems necessary, *what* structure?

Without asserting that our governmental welfare policy is in any way the key to eliminating future poverty in the United States, one suspects that it will ultimately be most helpful (or least harmful) if it follows three broad guidelines:

1. *Focus more on the causes of poverty than its symptoms.* This is the major positive theme of David Ellwood's research. He tries to classify the poor into different categories (for example, the working poor in two-parent families, poor single-parent families, and ghetto families), and then to design a welfare program that addresses the quite different needs of each of these groups.

2. *Include education, training, and actual work in welfare programs to a much higher degree than in the past.* Not everyone agrees with this prescription (see above, p. 267). Some believe that education and training produce little or no measurable benefits, particularly for the persistently poor. Others note that "workfare" makes little sense for the single mother with small children at home; furthermore, the notion of workfare still carries a stigma in the eyes of some observers. On the whole, however, both liberals and conservatives are coming to agree that provision of training and work in welfare programs is a highly desirable feature, partly in the hope of saving money, but more significantly as providing an enabling path by which the poor may join the national mainstream. As far as "stigma" is concerned, it seems difficult to believe that more disapprobation would be attached to those who work for their welfare checks in one way or another than to those who receive them specifically for not working.

3. *Finally, welfare programs should be designed as much as possible so as not to further destabilize the two-parent family.* Indeed, this prescription should probably be applied to all government policies, making certain that married couples with children are in no way put at a disadvantage as compared to single individuals or childless couples. Also, these policies should be carefully weighed so that they do not subtly undermine the family by having the state take over functions for which families were responsible in the past.

We have often discussed the issue of publicly provided child care in this connection. Giving families free or publicly subsidized day care for young toddlers can obviously help many poor families, including single-parent families, where such assistance may permit the mother to work and thus acquire the skills necessary for eventual departure from the welfare rolls.

Such a policy, however, also potentially weakens the family by removing, or reducing, its role as provider of nurture, care, and instruction for the very young. Thus, it can be argued that, *if* the state gets involved in subsidizing out-of-home care for poor children, then, at a minimum, it should provide equal subsidies for those who care for their children at home. This could be in the form of a Parental Bill of Rights plan, as we discussed at the end of the last chapter.

Clearly, there are many variations on this and other schemes, the main characteristic of which is to make sure (or as sure as is humanly possible) that, in supporting the poor, we are not indirectly contributing to the structural changes in our society that tend to perpetuate poverty.

This will not be an easy task. And it is quite possible that at least some "poor" will "always be with us," despite our best efforts.

Still, the three guidelines suggested here do offer a starting place, based on what is now at least a quarter of a century of experience in formulating explicit poverty programs.

## SUMMARY

1. Broad theories of income distribution over time, like those of Ricardo or Marx, often predicted the perpetuation of poverty at least for some time in the future. The empirical researches of Simon Kuznets suggested that, with economic development, income tends to be distributed first more unequally and then more equally. Kuznets, however, worried about the higher reproduction rates of poor people in terms of perpetuating future inequality.

2. In the United States, a "rising tide" of general economic progress has tended to reduce absolute poverty over time, but some observers have wondered if we have not made a "great U-turn" on the poverty front in recent years, with more poor people and a greater inequality of income distribution showing up in some economic statistics.

3. Poverty in the United States is likely to persist in the future if there is an economic slowdown, if family structures are weak, if differential fertility greatly increases the number of poor people, and if public welfare programs fail. Ironically, there is disagreement as to whether these programs are currently failing because they are inadequate in scope or because, by weakening incentives and family structures, they create conditions that actually contribute to poverty.

4. Future economic growth is difficult to predict, but our changing population is likely to have two opposite effects on future growth. Because of the Baby Bust, the ratio of new, inexperienced workers to older, experienced workers will fall compared to recent years. This should improve productivity and should also create a good job market for young blacks and other minority workers. At the same time, the relatively low educational level of these young workers suggests a possible mismatch of skills and jobs in our increasingly high-tech world.

5. The higher fertility of poor people, including large minority groups like blacks and Hispanics, could pose obstacles to the reduction of poverty in the future, although historically this has not been a severe problem. It remains to be seen whether black and Hispanic fertility remains high or adjusts to prevailing majority rates as socioeconomic levels rise over time.

6. Although not the panacea they were once believed to be, public welfare programs may be able to help reduce poverty if they focus more on its causes than its symptoms; if they include training, education, and actual work experience rather than simple welfare payments; and if they are shaped, insofar as possible, in such a way that they do not further destabilize the two-parent family.

7. Given the weaknesses of the two-parent family noted in Chapter 23, and the other obstacles developed in this chapter, it is obvious that *some* poor people are likely "always to be with us," although their number will certainly be reduced if economic growth is sufficiently vigorous.

## KEY CONCEPTS FOR REVIEW

Theories of income distribution
    Ricardo
    Marx
    Kuznets
"A rising tide lifts all boats"
"The great U-turn"
U.S. income distribution, 1947–1988
Measures of inequality

Factors affecting future poverty
    productivity growth
    differential fertility
    family structures
    welfare programs
Measured versus true labor productivity
Changing age and experience of our labor force
Mismatch of jobs and skills

Fertility hypotheses
   social characteristics
   minority group status
   subcultural
Welfare policy conundrums

security–work
assistance–family structure
targeting–isolation
Criteria for future welfare programs

## QUESTIONS FOR DISCUSSION

1. The actual experience of a number of countries suggests a certain pattern in the trends of income distribution over time. What are these patterns? How would you explain them? Do they give much support to older theories of income distribution like those of Ricardo or Marx?

2. Thinking of U.S. history since colonial times, would you find the metaphor of a "rising tide" a useful way to describe our experience with absolute poverty? With relative poverty? How about the last 15 years? Which metaphor appeals most, a "rising tide" or a "great U-turn"? Or does neither seem accurate?

3. List and briefly discuss the major factors that may affect the degree of poverty the U.S. population will experience in the future.

4. Explain how our changing population may affect our future productivity growth (a) positively and (b) negatively? On balance, do you feel these factors will tend to help reduce poverty in this country?

5. What are the different major hypotheses used to explain the fertility experience of minority and immigrant groups as compared to that of the native white majority? Show the difficulties of applying these hypotheses to future black and Hispanic population growth.

6. Design and defend your own basic welfare policy for the United States as we head toward the twenty-first century.

## NOTES

1. Simon Kuznets, "Economic Growth and Income Inequality," American Economic Review, *45*(1), March 1955, pp. 1–28; and *Modern Economic Growth* (New Haven: Yale University Press, 1966).
2. See Lars Osberg, *Economic Inequality in the United States* (Armonk, N.Y.: M. E. Sharpe, 1984), esp. Chapter 12.
3. M. S. Ahluwalia, "Income Inequality: Some Dimensions of the Problem," in H. Chenery et al., *Redistribution with Growth* (London: World Bank, Oxford University Press, 1976).
4. Simon Kuznets, *Growth, Population and Income Distribution* (New York: Norton, 1979), and "Notes on Demographic Change," in Martin Feldstein, ed., *The American Economy in Transition* (Chicago: University of Chicago Press, 1980).
5. Figures 24-2 through 24-4 are updated and revised versions of Figures 1.1 through 1.3 from Bennett Harrison and Barry Bluestone, *The Great U-Turn: Corporate Restructuring and the Polarizing of America* (New York: Basic Books, 1988), pp. 6, 7. The GINI index, referred to in Figure 24-4, is a frequently used measure of income inequality. Essentially, it measures the degree to which the income distribution departs from perfect equality. If everyone had the same income, the GINI index

(or coefficient) would be zero. If all income were received by one person (with nothing for anyone else), we would have a GINI index of 1.0. For a simple presentation of this measure, see Frank Levy, *Dollars and Dreams: The Changing American Income Distribution* (New York: Russell Sage Foundation, 1987), Appendix E.
6. Frank Levy, *Dollars and Dreams*, pp. 14, 16. It should be noted, however, that Levy's comments were made on data only up to 1984. Most indices suggest further moves toward income inequality in the period 1984–1989. See, for example, U.S. Bureau of the Census, *Current Population Reports*, Series P-60, No. 168, pp. 5–7.
7. Ibid., pp. 6, 79–82.
8. Edward F. Denison, perhaps the United States' leading authority on productivity growth, analyzes 18 separate factors to account for the slowdown of U.S. productivity growth between 1964–1973 and 1973–1979, but even after these factors are taken into account, a large "residual productivity" factor remains to be explained. The subject, to say the least, is complex. See Edward F. Denison, *Trends in American Economic Growth, 1929–1982* (Washington, D.C.: Brookings Institution, 1985).

9. Simon Kuznets, *Growth, Population and Income Distribution* (New York: Norton, 1979), pp. 294, 307.

10. Consider, for example, a family of four (a) living as a single unit or (b) living as two units with, say, the husband in a single unit and the wife and two children in a single unit. In 1989 the poverty threshhold for a family of four was $12,100; for a single individual, it was $5,980; and for a family of three, it was $10,060. Suppose now that the husband is the only employed member of the family, that his income is $12,500, and that after the divorce or separation it is divided equally on a per capita basis between the two households— that is, three-quarters, or $9,375, to the ex-wife and children, and one-quarter, or $3,125, for the husband. Simple inspection reveals that, before the family breakup, we had a family of four persons above the poverty level, whereas after the breakup, we have a husband below the poverty level and a mother and two children below the poverty level. Total income has remained the same; what has changed is the cost of maintaining separate households.

11. John W. Kendrick, "The Economy's Even Better Than It Looks," *Wall Street Journal*, October 24, 1989. For a long-term view of U.S. productivity performance, see William J. Baumol, Sue Anne Batey Blackman, and Edward N. Wolff, *Productivity and American Leadership: The Long View* (Cambridge and London: The MIT Press, 1989). Also see the review of this book, Jeffrey G. Williamson, "Productivity and American leadership: A Review Article," *Journal of Economic Literature* XXIX(1), March 1991, pp. 51–68.

12. John Palmer and Gregory B. Mills, "Budget Policy," in John Palmer and Isabel V. Sawhill, eds., *The Reagan Experiment* (Washington, D.C.: Urban Institute Press, 1982), p. 78.

13. Leonard Beeghley, *The Structure of Social Stratification in the United States* (Boston: Allyn and Bacon, 1989), p. 76.

14. Actually, there are more than two competing hypotheses, as noted on p. 438. Some writers have distinguished four categories of hypotheses depending on the weight given subcultural, sociodemographic, social psychological, or economic factors. See Frank D. Bean and Marta Tienda, *The Hispanic Population of the United States* (New York: Russell Sage Foundation, 1987), pp. 209–214.

15. Calvin Goldscheider and Peter R. Uhlenberg, "Minority Group Status and Fertility," *American Journal of Sociology*, 74, January 1969.

16. Nan E. Johnson, "Minority-Group Status and the Fertility of Black Americans, 1970: A New Look," *American Journal of Sociology*, 84(6), May 1979. For symmetry, we should note that there is a fourth possibility that could be added to Figure 24-5—

namely, a "weak" form of the minority group status hypothesis. It would look like this:

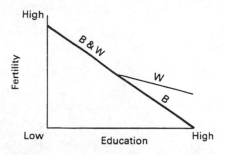

Since black fertility at low income/education levels is definitely higher than that of whites, however, this fourth possibility has no relevance for our discussion.

17. Farley and Allen, *The Color Line and the Quality of Life in America* (New York: Russell Sage Foundation, 1987), pp. 94–95.

18. Bean and Tienda, *The Hispanic Population*, p. 210. It hardly needs saying that the relevant "cultural values" vary strikingly among different Hispanic groups. As we have noted earlier in this book, for example, Cuban fertility rates in the United States tend to be lower not only than Mexican and Puerto Rican rates, but also than non-Hispanic white rates.

19. David T. Ellwood, *Poor Support: Poverty in the American Family* (New York: Basic Books, 1988), pp. 18–25. Ellwood uses a dictionary definition of *conundrum* as "a problem admitting of no satisfactory solution." His own personal definition is: "A conundrum is a damned-if-you-do and damned-if-you-don't situation" (p. 18).

20. See our discussion of this issue in Chapter 15, especially pp. 263–266. Although considering the labor force problems of young black men is a promising approach to the single-parent problem, those labor force problems have themselves not yet been fully or satisfactorily explained.

21. They write: "Marital breakups by already married couples are not as likely to be affected by income maintenance plans as are other behaviors that increase the number of single parents, namely births to unwed mothers who remain unmarried; previously married women who choose to remain unmarried; and single parents who live separately from an extended family." Glen G. Cain and Douglas A. Wissoker, "Do Income Maintenance Programs Break Up Marriages? A Reevaluation of SIME-DIME," *Focus*, University of Wisconsin–Madison Institute for Research on Poverty, *10*(4), Winter 1987–1988, p. 14.

# 25

# *The United States and the World Population Explosion*

Although this is a book about population change in the United States, we have had several occasions to mention global population concerns. In this chapter, we shall briefly discuss those global concerns, focusing especially on the relationship between U.S. population growth and population growth outside our borders. In what is increasingly a one-world context, linked by rapid transportation and telecommunications ties, it is more than ever true that no nation can be an island unto itself.

Is the world population explosion, of which we have read so much, on the verge of bringing starvation and tragedy to the **less developed countries (LDCs)**? What is the significance of that **population explosion** for the United States and the industrial democracies of the world in general? Just to state those questions is enough to indicate that the following pages deal with a subject matter on which expert opinion is often sharply divided.

## BIRTH DEARTH
## VERSUS POPULATION EXPLOSION

One thing on which there is no difference of opinion at all is that the population of the United States (and of other presently developed nations) will decline sharply *relative* to the populations of the LDCs over the next century. How large that relative decline will be will depend on many factors. We know from our earlier discussions that the Census Bureau projections for the U.S. population over the next century cover an extraordinarily wide range of possibilities (see p. 15). Projecting for the LDCs is more perilous still. Even estimating the *present* populations of many of these nations involves more guesswork than one would ideally like.

Since we have already referred to Ben Wattenberg's book, *The Birth Dearth* (p. 14) and since we will be considering some of his arguments in a moment, we reproduce here Wattenberg's estimates of global population

growth (Figures 25-1 through 25-3). The categories covered in the graphs are:

• *Industrial democracies:* Includes Canada, the United States, Australia, New Zealand, Japan, Austria, Belgium, Denmark, Finland, France, West Germany, Iceland, the United Kingdom, Italy, Luxembourg, the Netherlands, Norway, Spain, Sweden, and Switzerland (Figure 25-1).

• *Less developed countries:* Includes all nations of Africa, Asia, and Central and South America, except Japan (Figure 25-2).

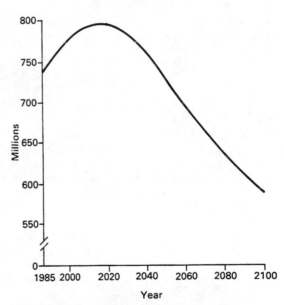

**FIGURE 25-1: Projected Population of the Industrial Democracies, 1985–2100**

*Note:* Industrial democracies include Canada, the United States, Australia, New Zealand, Japan, Austria, Belgium, Denmark, Finland, France, West Germany, Iceland, Italy, Luxembourg, the Netherlands, Norway, Spain, Sweden, Switzerland, the United Kingdom.
*Source:* Special World Bank projections. Figures 25-1, 25-2, and 25-3 are adapted from Ben J. Wattenberg, *The Birth Dearth* (New York: Pharos Books, 1987), Charts 4-B, 4-I, and 4-J, respectively.

445

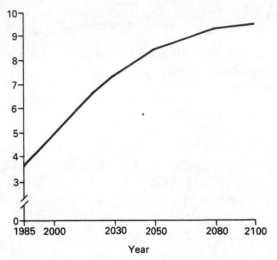

**FIGURE 25-2: Projected Population of the Less Developed Countries, 1985–2100**

*Note:* Less developed countries include all nations of Africa, Asia, and Central and South America, except Japan.
*Source: World Population Projections 1984,* World Bank.

• *Rest of the world:* This category (Figure 25-3) lumps together the LDCs plus what Wattenberg in 1987 called the "industrial Communist world": the USSR, Albania, Bulgaria, Czechoslovakia, East Germany, Hungary, Poland, and Romania.

As we shall point out later in the chapter, the choice of countries to be included under each of these headings is a matter of great interest to us, especially in relationship to evaluating Wattenberg's concerns.

The basis of these concerns is most clearly shown in Figure 25-3. This diagram indicates that even during a recent 35-year period (1950–1985), while the populations of the industrial democracies were still growing fairly briskly, they were losing ground to the much more rapid rates of population growth elsewhere. During these years, the *actual* population of the industrial democracies as a percentage of world pop-

ulation declined from 22 percent to 15 percent.

The *projected* figures suggest "free fall" rather than decline. By 2030, the industrial democracies are projected to have only 9 percent of the world's population; by the year 2100, only 5 percent. These projections are generally in line with those made by other professionals in the field. Table 25-1 presents the U.S. Census Bureau's rankings

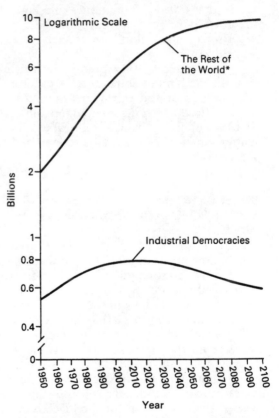

**FIGURE 25-3: World Population By Group, 1950–2100**

*Note:* The rest of the world includes the LDCs plus the USSR, Albania, Bulgaria, Czechoslovakia, East Germany, Hungary, Poland, and Romania.
*Source:* Actual population levels, *World Population Prospects,* United Nations, 1985. Projections for industrial democracies, Special World Bank projection. For rest of world, *World Population Projections 1984,* World Bank.

**TABLE 25-1.  World's 20 Largest Countries, 1988 and 2050
(Population in Millions)**

| 1988 | | 2050 | |
|---|---|---|---|
| *Country* | *Population* | *Country* | *Population* |
| China | 1,088 | India | 1,591 |
| India | 817 | China | 1,555 |
| USSR | 286 | Nigeria | 471 |
| United States | 246 | Pakistan | 424 |
| Indonesia | 184 | USSR | 386 |
| Brazil | 151 | Brazil | 368 |
| Japan | 123 | Indonesia | 360 |
| Nigeria | 112 | United States | 299 |
| Bangladesh | 110 | Bangladesh | 266 |
| Pakistan | 107 | Iran | 252 |
| Mexico | 84 | Ethiopia | 243 |
| Vietnam | 65 | Philippines | 204 |
| Philippines | 63 | Mexico | 169 |
| West Germany | 61 | Vietnam | 166 |
| Italy | 57 | Kenya | 166 |
| Britain | 57 | Zaire | 158 |
| France | 56 | Egypt | 142 |
| Thailand | 55 | Tanzania | 133 |
| Turkey | 54 | Turkey | 120 |
| Egypt | 53 | Japan | 115 |

*Source:* U.S. Bureau of the Census, *World Population Profile, 1987*, Table 3, pp. 39–43.

of the world's 20 largest countries in 1988 and as projected to the year 2050.

The relative demographic decline of the United States and the other industrial democracies is quite apparent from this table. The United States falls from fourth to eighth on the list; West Germany, Italy, Britain, and France drop out of the top 20 altogether; Japan barely hangs on in last place. Nigeria, Pakistan, Brazil, and Indonesia will all march past the United States. Japan will have only two-thirds the population of Mexico and less than half that of Iran or Ethiopia. Bangladesh could easily have a greater population than Germany, Britain, Italy, and France *combined.* In the course of these changes, world population

is projected to increase from around 5 billion in 1988 to around 11 billion by the year 2050.

## PROGRESS OR POVERTY?

In discussing the potential impact of these large population changes on the United States and the rest of the industrialized world, one cannot avoid making certain judgments about the likely success or failure of the various developmental efforts underway in the LDCs. In Chapter 1, we mentioned that the rather pessimistic outlook of the 1960s and early 1970s had given way to a somewhat more optimistic frame of mind in the 1980s. This optimism (as we shall note presently) is by no means fully shared, but it does have at least some empirical basis.

### Postwar Development in the LDCs

Contrary to some fears, and despite their very rapid rates of population growth, substantial economic development has occurred in many of the LDCs since the end of World War II. For the period 1955–1980, Professor Gerald M. Meier, a long-time student of the development process, writes:

> After the preceding centuries of near stagnation, there has been unprecedented growth in national output and the value of output available per person in poor countries. . . . Indeed, the average rate of growth in GNP per head was 3.1 percent (including China)—a remarkable rate.

Meier then goes on to compare the performance of the LDCs today with the historic performance of the developed nations, including the United States. He concludes:

> Compared with their own past records and the records of the presently developed countries in their initial phases of development, many LDCs have exceeded expectations in the growth of GNP and GNP per head. . . . The period since 1950 can certainly be viewed as the best period in history for people in the poor countries of the world.[1]

This assessment was not atypical in the 1980s. In a 1982 report on a Nobel Symposium on Population Growth and World Development, the same theme reappeared frequently: "An optimistic frame of mind was engendered because there seemed reason to hope that in the next 20 or 50 years output of food could rise more quickly than the growth of population, even if presently available technological opportunities were exploited only partially."[2] In this symposium, Nobel laureate economist Wassily Leontief used his input–output techniques to attempt a forecast of output per capita for the LDCs over the next few decades (to 2030). He and his colleague, Ira Sohn, developed both a "pessimistic" and an "optimistic" forecast. It is notable that the "pessimistic" projection, even for the "resource-poor" LDCs, forecasts annual rates of growth of output per capita of between 1.38 and 1.52 percent. These rates are comparable to those achieved by the Western nations in the half century before World War I. Furthermore, if the "optimistic" projection proves valid, the rate of improvement in living standards would exceed 2 percent per year and would be higher than the historic performance of the West.[3]

Another major effort to assess the growth performance of the LDCs was the 1985 study by Lloyd Reynolds, former chairman of the economics department at Yale and founder of Yale's Economic Growth Center. In *Economic Growth in the Third World, 1850–1980*, Reynolds distinguishes between **extensive growth,** where a country's total production is just keeping pace with its population growth, and **intensive growth,** where total production grows faster than population—that is, where there is an increase in per capita output. He calls the period when extensive growth gives way to intensive growth the "turning point." What is interesting is that when Reynolds looks at a number of the most populous of the LDCs—China, India, Pakistan, Indonesia, Egypt—he finds that the transition to positive per capita income growth occurred after World War II. This is to say that the "turning points" in these countries (whose populations include well over half the population of all LDCs together) occurred *when the postwar population explosions within their borders were at or near their peaks.*[4]

Indeed, some scholars believe that population growth may be an important factor in stimulating technological improvements in a country's economy, particularly in the pivotal agricultural sector. Economist Mitchell Kellman has developed a number of theoretical models to describe the relations of population growth to food production in both the developed world and the LDCs. One of these is the **induced innovation** model: "An induced innovation process, triggered by demographic or density pressures, may affect the choice of a new technology so as to economize on the scarce factor [land]." He finds this model widely applicable to historical development in the West and suggests that "a framework incorporating demographically induced technological shifts should prove superior to a Malthusian, diminishing-returns framework in understanding the essentials of the food/population problem facing today's less developed world."[5] In short, population pressures, while a problem in some respects, may in another respect be part of the solution to that very same problem.

### Evidence of Falling Fertility Rates

Although population growth may spur agricultural progress in certain instances, it seems clear that continued growth in numbers at modern rates must eventually come to a halt if human life on this planet is to survive under anything like acceptable conditions. What is the ultimate "carrying capacity" of the earth? No one knows, and recent estimates are absurdly at variance, ranging from 7 billion people (a fractional increase above present numbers) to 100 or even 150 billion people.[6]

Even the latter figures, if accepted, imply a cessation of world population growth in what, historically speaking, would be a rather brief period of time. In other words, we can assume that the reduction of population growth in the LDCs, fairly rapidly and in the fairly near future, is a desirable and very probably necessary condition for the elimination of poverty in those nations. Fortunately, there is considerable evidence that the groundwork for such a reduction is being laid in many of the LDCs, including most of the more populous LDCs.

In Reynolds's comprehensive study, it was found that of 37 countries covered,

birth rates declined in 35 over the period 1960 to 1980 (the two exceptions were Uganda and the Sudan). In this group of 37 (China not included), he found that the most rapid declines in birth rates were, on average, in those countries that made the most rapid economic progress. These declines were in many cases enormously rapid. In the brief space of 20 years, the birth rate fell in South Korea by 44 percent, in Taiwan by 48 percent, in Thailand by 32 percent, in Malaysia by 31 percent, in Brazil by 30 percent, in Turkey by 26 percent, and in Indonesia by 24 percent. Reynolds's general conclusion: "The decline of birth rates in the industrialized countries, accompanying their increasing affluence, is a familiar story. This process now seems to be setting in throughout most of the third world."[7]

Richard Easterlin and Eileen Crimmins have developed a supply-and-demand analysis of fertility change, applying it to both household data and aggregate population data in a selected group of LDCs (Sri Lanka, Colombia, India, and Taiwan). Their overall conclusion is similar to that of Reynolds:

> The lesson of the present analysis is that the process of socioeconomic modernization that lies behind the increased growth rates both of population and per capita income is also operating to bring about fertility reduction. . . . Thus, this analysis of the causes of the fertility revolution leads to a view of the population explosion as a transient phenomenon.[8]

Indeed, in the Easterlin-Crimmins model, the fall in the death rates of the LDCs (the prime cause of their population explosions), brought about largely by the public health revolution imported from the West, tends strongly to lead to fertility reduction. As the supply of children increases, families in the LDCs have an increased motivation to practice birth control. Governments get into the act, propagandizing for fewer children, establishing family-planning clinics, raising the legal age for marriage, instituting systems of rewards (for small families) and penalties (for large families). Thus, we have not only the generalized forces of socioeconomic development tending to bring down the fertility rate (as in the West), but also conscious social policies operating through the political process to promote fertility decline (unlike the West).

The most striking example of this newer element is to be found in the case of **China.** Since China's population includes more than one-quarter of the entire underdeveloped world, its performance actually has a major weight in the overall totals for both development and population control. Briefly, China's policy in urban areas is based on a "one-couple-one-child" principle, this principle being enforced through penalties, rewards, publicity, persuasion, and coercion. Elaborately organized "visits" are paid to youths, newlyweds, and recent parents to convince them of the importance of birth control; women are subjected to frequent X-ray and gynecological exams to make sure that they are not violating the one-child rule; sterilization and abortion are frequently and strongly "recommended." Western observers have written of forced abortions occurring even in the ninth month; also, since there is a strong traditional and economically based preference for sons, the one-child rule has led to many alleged incidents of female infanticide. Other Western observers, however, feel that these charges of force and coercion are highly exaggerated:[9]

Under any interpretation, there is little doubt that China has practiced a vigorous family-planning policy in recent years and with demonstrable results. During the period 1962–1973, China's average annual population growth is estimated at 2.6 percent. By 1985 the rate of growth had fallen to 1.1 percent. Between 1970 and 1980, its birth rate fell from an estimated 36 per thousand to 19 per thousand. Its total fertility rate (TFR) has also fallen sharply and is now fairly close to the replacement rate. Ultimately, of course, a one-couple-one-

child policy implies a TFR in the vicinity of 1, and a declining population.

Since China has also achieved major economic development during the postwar period (estimated at 4 percent per year per capita GNP growth from 1952 to 1979), it stands as both evidence and example of the possibility of achieving economic growth and population control simultaneously.

### Too Rosy a Picture?

China also, however, serves to remind us of certain cautions that should be observed when it comes to generalizing about the population explosion in the LDCs. For one thing, the fact that a policy is successful at one time does not mean that it will continue to be so as conditions change. Whether because of the higher incomes of Chinese workers or the economic liberalization policies of the government in the mid-1980s, Chinese population growth began to rise again, going from the rather remarkable 1.1 percent of 1985 to an estimated 1.44 percent in 1987. (One theory was that families, being richer, could now pay the government fines and have the additional children.)

Also, policies can change. This has been a major problem under the modern Chinese communist regime. At one point, Chairman Mao was actually urging the Chinese to have *more* children, a big population being, he argued, China's major asset. Since the 1989 crackdown on student protesters and the subsequent pullback from liberalization policies, it has been unclear what China's future population policy or general economic policy might be.

But if the Chinese example raises certain caution flags, experiences elsewhere in the less developed world are even more unsettling. In this connection, **sub-Saharan Africa** is a major and telling case in point. Twenty-two of the world's 36 poorest nations are in this region. Over the past 40 years there has been a major increase in life expectancies in Africa; the crude death rate fell by one-third in sub-Saharan Africa in just two decades. But the birth rate has remained basically constant—and high. This region is thus the only major region of the world that has shown an *increasing* rate of population growth in recent decades, rising from about 2.5 percent a year in the 1960s to around 3 percent in the mid-1980s. At this rate of increase, population doubles in 23 years.

Nor has food production been able to keep pace with this enormous population pressure. Per capita grain production has been falling ever since the late 1960s, when it had barely reached a "subsistence level" of production. In many African countries, despite the introduction of some new technologies, grain yields per hectare are also falling. Indeed, in the effort to expand production, Africa is encountering what many observers feel is a serious deterioration of its agricultural resource base through erosion, soil degradation, deforestation, and desertification. Now requiring food as well as other crucial imports, many of these nations also face declining prices for some of their commodity exports and a potentially crushing external debt problem. The result, in many cases, has been *declining* annual per capita incomes. Examples for the period 1965–1986: Zaire, −2.2 percent annual per capita GNP growth; Uganda, −2.6 percent; Tanzania, −0.3 percent; Niger, −2.2 percent; Zambia, −1.7 percent; Ghana, −1.7 percent; Senegal, −0.6 percent.

Nor, finally, has government policy to control population growth been very effective in sub-Saharan Africa. It is only recently that most African governments have awakened to the need for population control policies, and the impact of such policies as there are is very much in doubt. Kenya, for example, was one of the earliest African nations to attempt officially to reduce its rate of population growth, yet in 1988 the World Bank estimated Kenya's annual population growth at 4.1 percent, one of the highest in the world. The extent of the problem is indicated by the fact that, in 1989, Kenya's Demographic and Health Survey announced with pride that, from 1983 to 1988, the fertility rate had dropped from 7.7 to 6.7. (Recall that the U.S. rate in 1989 was 1.9.) Moreover, government policies in many of these countries may well have contributed to the problems of supporting these growing populations. "African agriculture's decline throughout the 1970s and 1980s," writes one commentator, "is now widely understood to be due primarily to African governments' penchant for state marketing boards."[10] Overactive governments, although they may help in certain connections, can also be major obstacles to development in other respects.

All these facts about sub-Saharan Africa must be put into a context that makes them even more disturbing: In a number of African countries, nearly half the population is under 15. With the youngest age structure of any major region of the world, Africa is guaranteed to have very substantial population growth even with sharply declining fertility. Since fertility remains stubbornly high, and since death rates remain comparatively low, the possibility of a truly unsustainable population explosion in sub-Saharan Africa cannot be ruled out.

Thus, a tragic Malthusian solution, with mortality rates ("positive checks") rising to choke off the excess numbers produced originally by the public health revolution, cannot be ruled out either. Drought, famine, malnutrition, plague (for example, the spread of AIDS)—all these ancient scourges could reappear in modern dress.

## IMPACTS ON THE UNITED STATES AND THE WEST

The foregoing brief summary does little justice to a large subject, which could easily command many books in itself. It is enough, however, to serve as a basis for our more specific question: What are the likely impacts of the world population explosion on the United States and other developed nations in the future? Even given the most hopeful possible scenario for economic development and fertility control in the poor countries of the world, their populations are bound to grow substantially in the decades ahead because of their young age structures. Africa is the most notable example of this problem, but it is by no means alone. In the LDCs in general, more than one-third of the populations are under 15.

Also, we must face the paradoxical possibility that "successful" development beyond our borders might pose as many, or more, problems for us than "failed" development. We group the impact of the world's population explosion on the United States and the West under three headings: **humanitarian considerations, ecological and environmental concerns,** and **geopolitical concerns.** We now comment briefly on each.

### Humanitarian Considerations

If the development process were to fail in a number of the LDCs, in part at least because of out-of-control population growth, then the United States and other industrialized nations would confront a world that was ever more sharply divided between highly affluent societies and societies in which poverty, malnutrition, and early mortality were rampant. It can be argued that, from the point of view of economic self-interest, the economically developed countries would fare less well in such a world than in a world where the LDCs became vigorous trading partners and contributors to global GNP.

Putting self-interest aside, however, we must give at least some weight to the humanitarian aspects of such a cruel division of mankind. Because of the media, it is quite impossible for American and European citizens to be unaware of gross poverty and the premature deaths of infants and children, wherever in the world they may occur. In this respect, we have a long history of both public and private concern. Exactly how this concern will, or should, be ex-

pressed is a different matter. Here are some of the various possibilities.

*1. Allow increased emigration from the LDCs to the United States (and other economically advanced countries).* We have already mentioned this approach in Chapter 20. All that needs to be added here is that there is no way that any imaginable increase in **immigration** to the United States could have more than a trivial effect on the population conditions of the LDCs as a whole. Look back again at Table 25-1. The projected *increases* in the populations of the LDCs in this table by the year 2050 are simply too huge to be dealt with by any conceivable immigration policy of the Western world. By that year, for example, China and India alone are projected to have a 1.2 billion *gain* in their populations—four times the total U.S. population projected for that year. Brazil and Mexico together *add on* the equivalent of the projected U.S. population. In this larger picture, our immigration policy would be a virtual irrelevance.

*2. Substantially increase our foreign aid program.* Since there is essentially no way we can bring in vast numbers of people to share our wealth, we have the option of exporting our wealth to where the people are. The basic humanitarian justification for **foreign aid** is twofold: (1) It relieves immediate suffering, as in the case of the typical famine relief programs; (2) it provides the capital and technological know-how required for the poor country to get started on the path of modern development. In the case of countries where the population explosion is deemed to be a major part of the problem, such aid could involve assistance in the specific area of family planning.

This last point indicates one of the more obvious ways in which foreign assistance might contribute to the long-run development prospects of an overpopulated country. However, it also indicates one of the problems involved in securing such assistance from donor countries, particularly, we might say, from the United States. For there has been a considerable debate in this country about family planning in general, and about abortion in particular, especially abortion when used as a method of birth control. In 1985 and 1986, the United States withdrew its budgeted contribution to the United Nations Fund for Population Activities because that organization was participating "in the management of a programme of coercive abortion and sterilization in China."[11] One of the difficulties in implementing any major foreign aid program comes from the frequent differences of policy (including basically different political systems) between donor nations and recipients.

More generally, there is now a serious question as to whether, in total, foreign aid tends to promote development in the LDCs, or whether, for a variety of reasons, it may actually inhibit development. It has been argued that China, which essentially received no foreign aid during most of its postwar development, has performed better than countries, like India, that were aid recipients. It has even been argued that South Korea and Taiwan, two of the LDCs whose economic "miracles" have now promoted them to NICs ("newly industrialized countries"), *really* took off economically only after U.S. aid was sharply reduced.[12] A major problem is that aid may negatively affect domestic production incentives. The importation of food, for example, can reduce prices and incomes for domestic farmers, thus discouraging development in the crucial agricultural sector. When this problem is compounded by government policies designed to provide cheap, subsidized food to the urban middle classes (on whose support the fate of those in power may depend), the disincentives to farmers may create serious rural stagnation.

The issue is by no means settled. Many of the populous LDCs face enormous international debt problems, and in some instances it is difficult to see how any development can be achieved without aid, if only

in the form of a partial forgiveness of debt. Still, it must be said that the enthusiasm for foreign aid of the 1950s and 1960s (much of it based on the quite different experience of the Marshall Plan and the European and Japanese recoveries after World War II) had given way to a more cautious and skeptical approach by the late 1980s. Aid from the developed nations has been declining as a percentage of their GNPs for many years; in the United States in 1990, it had fallen to well under a quarter of 1 percent of GNP.

*3. By promoting vigorous growth in our own economies, and keeping our markets open to the exports of the LDCs, create favorable conditions for the latter to develop.* If neither foreign aid nor increased emigration offers the LDCs a sure route to development, a third route—though no panacea in itself—promises at least highly favorable conditions for such development to occur. Under this third approach, the LDCs essentially manage their development efforts themselves; what the economically advanced nations give them is the clear opportunity to do so. As long as our economies are prosperous and expanding, they will provide markets for the goods of the LDCs, and these markets in turn will provide sharp incentives for LDC producers to expand output in response.

Even this path has its difficulties, including the obvious one that producers in the developed countries may not eagerly welcome the competition from producers in the LDCs. We have clear examples of this already in the frequent demands in the United States that Japan, and now Korea and Taiwan, take steps to reduce their trade surpluses with this country. Protectionist sentiment has risen sharply in recent years. Japan itself is said now to be quite concerned about the inroads of the four "tigers" of the Far East: South Korea, Taiwan, Singapore, and Hong Kong. One can only imagine what the reaction may be if and when the great giants of Asia, China, and India become truly competitive in world markets.

Thus, even this third route is not without its hazards. Still, its promise is substantial and requires from the West no special favors, only that it keep its own economies from languishing (presumably an objective of the United States and the other industrial nations anyway) and keep its doors open to free and fair **trade** with its rising competitors.

## Ecological and Environmental Concerns

The humanitarian concerns that we have just discussed arise when we contemplate the enormous problems that the population explosion may create for the LDCs. The solution to those concerns would involve the rapid development of those countries and, in due course, a reduction in their rates of population growth.

This solution, however, is really where the next *problem* begins. Can the world sustain the massive resource and environmental demands that the "successful" development of the billions of people in the LDCs may place on the planet? Roger L. Conner, a scholar at the Brookings Institution, writes that there is a new "myth" going around: that "population growth has no significant impact on pollution, natural resources, or the quality of life." As an antidote, he suggests looking at Los Angeles:

> Despite the best pollution controls technology provides, the air in the Los Angeles region violates the clean air act's health standards more than 100 days a year. That is because reductions in the pollutants each car emits have been overwhelmed by the increased number of people driving. . . . Overcrowding and traffic congestion are only the tip of the iceberg. Irreversible ecological changes brought on by the needs of an expanding population are far more serious. The exhaustion of groundwater supplies, destruction of agricultural land, erosion of topsoil, loss of wilderness and natural

areas, filled-in wetlands, and diminished wildlife habitat are only part of the list.[13]

This was written with respect to the United States, where our average population density is under 70 people per square mile. Contrast this with China (300 per square mile), India (600), and Bangladesh (1,800). Consider further that, given the age structures of all the LDCs, further population growth is certain to occur even with successful development and population programs. Bangladesh, one of the world's most crowded nations, is projected to more than double its size by 2050 (Table 25-1), reaching well over 4,000 people per square mile. As far as cities are concerned, Mexico City, expected to reach 28 million by the year 2000, will soon make present-day Los Angeles look like a rather small town.

If the population explosion is an ecological threat even without massive increases in GNP, will not modern development—with its enormous utilization of resources and its vast production of pollutants—transform that explosion into an ecological disaster? A disaster, moreover, that will have clear effects on the world's environment, including that of the United States and the other previously developed nations?

No one can possibly give, or expect, a simple answer to this question. Even to begin a discussion of the topic requires that one cope with three very difficult issues:

*1. Do we already have a global environmental crisis in the making?* With all the talk of acid rain, ozone depletion, and the greenhouse effect, it might seem that the answer to this question is obvious. In ancient times, it is said, we were quite capable of polluting our environment, but only in a rather modest, "local" way. Now we are capable of affecting the basic ecology of the entire planet and, in fact, are doing so in a number of quite specific ways. Sulfur emissions from coal-fired furnaces are producing the **acid rain** that is destroying our lakes and forests; **CFCs** (chlorofluorocarbons) from air-conditioners, refrigerators, aerosols, and plastics are destroying the world's ozone layer and exposing us to hazardous ultraviolet rays; fossil fuel combustion is producing excessive carbon dioxide in the atmosphere, leading to the "**greenhouse effect**," a warming of the earth's temperature, ultimate coastal flooding, and other possible disasters. The catalogue goes on, with the LDCs, as they destroy **rain forests** and soil fertility, now beginning to add seriously to the crisis already created by the industrial nations of the world.

The truth is, however, that very few of these effects have been demonstrated in a fully scientific fashion. Probably the best known representative of this group of forthcoming global crises is the "greenhouse effect." Recent climate models run on supercomputers have lowered the estimates of global warming from 5.5 degrees Celsius during the next century to 1.9 or even 1.6 degrees Celsius. By including more detailed representations of clouds and oceans in the models, and by taking into account the possibility that human activity may lead to pollutants that increase the amount of light and heat that the earth reflects back into space (thus cooling the earth's surface), these later models raise the possibility that earlier greenhouse warnings were seriously overstated. A minority view even has it that the effect might on balance be favorable, because of its complicated impact on extending growing seasons and lessening the likelihood of droughts.[14]

This is not to deny the possibility of future global ecological disasters (or of the wisdom of preparing for them in advance); it is simply to state that, in important ways, the extent of these potential threats is not known accurately.

*2. To what degree can technological or other solutions be found to the global environmental crises that may emerge?* Given that the nature of the problems is still unclear in many cases, the nature of possible solutions to the problems is necessarily un-

clear as well. Essentially, the modernization process in the West has been based on a belief that humanity is capable of mastering its own destiny, including finding reasonable solutions to problems of its own creation. There are some technical reasons for believing that pollution poses a particular challenge to this faith—mainly because pollution characteristically involves certain "externalities." By this, we mean that the "polluter" is often able to gain by his pollution while the true costs of the pollution are borne "externally" by the society as a whole. On the other hand, there are also potential ways around this problem. Increasingly, the "polluter pays" principle is recognized as a way of "internalizing" the social costs of pollution.

*3. Which is more to blame for the world's environmental dangers—the population explosion or industrialization?* Are the world's numbers our real problem, or is the more serious threat from the world's growing production (global GNP)? Recall from our brief discussion in Chapter 1 that Dr. Paul Ehrlich considered the birth of an American baby to be 57 times the ecological disaster of the birth of an Indian baby because of the resources consumed and the wastes produced per capita in the United States as compared to India. Many studies strongly suggest that it is production rather than population that is primarily responsible for pollution and other environmental problems the world over.[15]

Insofar as this is the case, then, the shifting balance of the world's population suggested in Figure 25-3 should at least partially offset the environmental threat posed by the general increase in the world's total population. The number of low-GNP-per-capita producers in the world (LDC populations) is increasing relatively to the number of high-GNP-per-capita producers (the United States and other industrial democracy populations). By the time the LDCs catch up with the industrial democracies in terms of GNP per capita, possibly their population explosions will have been totally defused. Possibly, indeed, their populations, as many observers predict for the Western countries, will then enter a general period of decline.

## Geopolitical Concerns

None of the concerns we have just discussed was central to the arguments of Ben Wattenberg, whose book, *The Birth Dearth,* was subtitled, "What Happens When People in Free Countries Don't Have Enough Babies?" Indeed, Wattenberg's general solution called for an increase in the number of babies in the United States and the other **industrial democracies.** As to the possible impact of an increase in these high-GNP-producing populations on the world's environment, his response was given in one sentence: "Some of the most densely populated countries are environmentally advanced—like Switzerland."[16]

Wattenberg was concerned precisely because the industrial democracies are not growing fast enough to keep up with the rest of the world. Population growth and successful development in these other nations would be a problem for us, not on ecological grounds, but because it would threaten our power and influence in the world, and hence freedom and other important values of Western civilization.

On inspection, there is much less to this idea than might at first sight appear. We mentioned earlier that it was important to take note of the lists of countries under each of Wattenberg's three headings. As soon as we do so, we realize that we cannot really be talking about "Western" civilization, since our "industrial democracies" include Japan. However much Japan may have been influenced by the "West," it can hardly be said to be more a product of "Western civilization" than Czechoslovakia or Poland or, for that matter, European Russia, all of which are excluded from the "industrial democracy" group.

Clearly, what we are talking about here is not an ethnic or geographical division but a division on politicoeconomic grounds. Wattenberg's "industrial democracies" are countries that (1) subscribe, on the political side, to such democratic values and procedures as free elections with competing political parties, the rule of law, and respect for certain basic individual rights and freedoms; (2) subscribe, with enormous variations, to an economic system that, despite large public intervention, relies substantially on market mechanisms, supply-and-demand pricing of the factors of production, and the private ownership of real property and capital goods; and, finally, (3) have achieved significant industrialization and economic growth.

Thus, we can define Wattenberg's problem more specifically by asking whether the populations of nations subscribing to these values and achieving substantial economic growth are declining relative to the rest of the world. Is the geopolitical influence of such nations on the decline?

Actually, it is closer to the truth to say that the populations and geopolitical influence of such nations are almost certain to increase massively in the years ahead. Indeed, one can go further and say that their influence *and their total populations* have been increasing substantially even in our own era. If we started not where Wattenberg begins (1950) but in the years before or during World War II, we would find our little band of "industrial democracies" to be far smaller than it is today. In the late 1930s, we would certainly have had to exclude Japan, Germany, Italy, and Spain. During the World War II years, we could include very few countries from continental Europe. Indeed, in 1943, the entire list of "industrial democracies" would have been limited to Canada, the United States, Australia, New Zealand, Iceland, the United Kingdom, Sweden, and Switzerland. What a massive expansion there has been since that time purely and simply in population terms!

This is not statistical sleight-of-hand, but an important example to prove an important point. The list of "industrial democracies" is not fixed in concrete at any moment of time. It is highly fluid. It can change almost overnight. It has done so in the past, and will do so in the future.

This argument does not, in itself, necessarily refute Wattenberg's concern. After all, it is possible that the list of "industrial democracies" might contract over time. We might have not only smaller populations in each nation on the list in the future, but also fewer nations.

This, however, is only a theoretical possibility. The overwhelming evidence of our era—surprising even to the most ardent advocates of political and economic democracy—is the enormous vitality of this kind of system and its intimate connection with successful economic growth. At the time of this writing, the formerly communist world is in a state of total disrepair. East Germany has united with West Germany; Hungary, Poland, Czechoslovakia, Bulgaria, and Romania have fled or are fleeing the system as rapidly as they can; the Soviet Union is experiencing the most serious internal upheavals of its 70-plus years of existence. China put down a student uprising in 1989, but most observers feel that the old guard can only hang on for so long. The wave of the future is political and economic democracy. Communism is now the *ancien regime* everywhere, propped up artificially in a few countries, like Cuba, but decaying at an astonishing rate elsewhere.

As far as the LDCs are concerned, it takes an extraordinarily pessimistic frame of mind to believe that, in their efforts to achieve development, they will pin their hopes on this archaic model. How much more likely is it that over the long pull (and Wattenberg is projecting all the way to the year 2100), the list of "industrial democracies"—countries that are both developed and subscribe to politicoeconomic values similar to ours—will expand enormously.

Instead of representing 5 percent of the world's population in the year 2100, they could easily be 15 percent (as today), or 30 percent, or 90 percent.

Western *nations*, like the United States, will be very small in the world's demography in the year 2100; Western *values*—those embodied in relatively free political and economic systems—may very well be more dominant than they are, or ever have been.[17]

## TWO SCENARIOS

Much of what we have said in this chapter can be summarized in **two broad scenarios** of the future concerning the United States and the world population explosion, a pessimistic view and an optimistic view.

### Pessimistic View

Essentially, the pessimistic scenario involves the failure of the LDCs and the semi-industrialized nations of the world to achieve successful modern development. The combination of heavy population growth, increasing pressure on energy and other resources, destruction of land and the agricultural environment, and widespread industrial pollution proves to be more than these countries can handle. Furthermore, since development is not successfully achieved, a major factor promoting lower fertility rates is absent. Such slowing down of population growth as occurs takes place in large part through increases in the death rate due to starvation, malnutrition, increasing famine, and drought. As infant mortality rises, an important reason for lowered fertility vanishes. In bare subsistence societies, many children are needed for economic support and to replace those who die prematurely.

The impact of this failure of worldwide development on the United States and other developed nations could be very unfavorable. In this pessimistic scenario, substantial population growth has occurred in the world at large, and the effect on the world's available resources and environmental quality has been strongly negative. The spillover effects on the industrialized nations are also negative, leading to environmental deterioration (through the greenhouse and various other global effects), resource constraints (energy shortages and the like), and reductions in economic growth rates. Moreover, the geopolitical situation of the industrial democracies may be seriously threatened by the economic failure of the LDCs and also of the former communist bloc regimes. For this failure may prompt recourse to military measures, Third World subversion, and other direct or indirect attacks on an increasingly isolated group of industrial democracies.

Under this scenario, the best the United States and the other industrial democracies could hope for would be to seal themselves off, fortress-like, from the vast majority of the world's still growing populations. Around those fortresses would be billions of poor, envious, antagonistic people, watching and waiting for their chance to topple their rich adversaries, the latter themselves feeling increasingly dissatisfied with their morally impoverished and increasingly polluted physical environment.

### Optimistic View

In sharp contrast, we have a world of the future in which successful development on the part of the LDCs has taken place, increasingly under the auspices of relatively democratic, individualistic, and at least partially market-oriented regimes. A major result of this successful development is that population growth in all these countries has slowed sharply—indeed, even more rapidly than such reductions occurred in the United States, Europe, and Japan. There is no talk any more of population explosions. As country after country heads in the direction of negative population growth, the ques-

tions that arise have much more to do with the effects of declining numbers: Do we have enough young people to support all our aging citizens? Is there any way we can import some more workers from abroad? What happens to the family when people have so few children? (In short, the same questions we have been discussing frequently in this book, as we considered the future of the United States' slowing population growth.)

Because GNP growth is, by hypothesis, still very vigorous in this world of stable (or declining) population, pollution and resource exhaustion could conceivably be even worse than under the pessimistic scenario. What the optimists see here, however, is a continuation of what has essentially been humanity's actual experience with technological change—namely, as problems have developed, scientific and engineering solutions have been found to get around them. As the world's oil supplies run out, energy prices rise sharply, and private and public research is motivated to find new solutions—anything from clean coal to solar power to nuclear fusion. As pollution increases, wisely imposed charges assessed to all polluters motivate a similar search for environmentally sound technologies. In a few cases (if, say, it is found that CFCs clearly do destroy our protective ozone layer), certain products are banned altogether.

Meanwhile, this is a world that has finally adjusted to a condition of permanent peace. This is partly due to the absurdity of war, given the massive destructive powers of the then modern weapons systems. But it is also due to the fact that there are no great population pressures that entice nations into seizing neighboring territories, and, above all, to the fact that successful development worldwide has been accomplished under basically similar politicoeconomic regimes. Ideology is simply no longer a big issue.

Instead of fortresses with moats, this would be far closer to the "One World" dream of Utopians than anyone had previously thought possible.

Perhaps neither of these scenarios has been held in exactly this form by any particular students of the world's population explosion. Still, they do convey the central drift of two different groups of thinkers. In the late 1960s and the early 1970s, the pessimistic scenario attracted most public attention. In the late 1970s and the early to mid-1980s, the optimistic scenario began to rise to prominence. One reason for this, clearly, was that the dire prognostications of the pessimists had in many cases badly missed the mark. Dr. Paul Ehrlich's prediction, which we quoted in Chapter 1 ("The battle to feed humanity is over. In the 1970s and 1980s hundreds of millions of people will starve to death . . ."), seemed by the mid-1980s to be rather alarmist. Similar predictions about the world running out of oil in the matter of a decade or two also

proved inaccurate. We have already noted some doubts about the stronger form of the greenhouse effect hypothesis. We might also add, that by the late 1980s, the shape of the world's great politicoeconomic rivalry had changed drastically. Earlier fears that the communist nations might actually overtake the West economically have proved to be the most overly pessimistic predictions of all.

As we enter the 1990s, awareness of environmental vulnerability seems definitely on the increase again. Not all environmental effects of population growth and economic development have necessarily been overstated. Some may have been seriously understated. Many of the issues here are simply undecided. In short, neither scenario can be altogether ruled out at this point. As with most things in life, the correct answer will undoubtedly lie somewhere between the two extremes.

## SUMMARY

1.  During the next century or more, the proportion of the world's population represented by today's "industrial democracies" (the United States, Britain, France, and so forth) will decline sharply because of more rapid population growth expected in the rest of the world, and especially because of the very rapid population growth expected in today's LDCs.

2.  Experience during the last quarter century in the LDCs has suggested the following:

a.  Rapid economic development can take place even in the face of rapid population growth (the LDCs have, on average, raised their living standards more in recent decades than ever before in their histories).

b.  Development tends to bring about declining fertility as rapidly as it did in the West, or more so (sharply falling fertility rates have been noted in many LDCs, including China).

c.  Successful development and/or population control is not guaranteed in the LDCs in the future (witness China's fluctuating policies

and the possible tragedy-in-the-making in sub-Saharan Africa.)

3.  The relationship of the world population explosion to the United States and other developed nations involves humanitarian, ecological, and geopolitical implications.

4.  The United States and other developed countries could have little humanitarian impact on the fate of the LDCs by allowing increased immigration, and may have scarcely more impact through increased foreign aid. Robust growth in the West, combined with easy access to our markets for LDC exports, could, however, have a major favorable impact.

5.  The ecological effects of the population explosion, particularly when combined with large-scale economic growth in the LDCs, cannot be accurately assessed at this point. Differences of opinion exist with regard to: (a) the seriousness of the threat, (b) the degree to which adequate responses to the threat will be forthcoming, and (c) whether

the threat comes mainly from population growth or from industrialization.

6. The geopolitical threat that the population explosion poses for the "industrial democracies" (as emphasized by Ben Wattenberg) seems unlikely to be serious, in that the spread of both economic development and democracy worldwide seems a much more probable outcome.

7. Still, nothing is certain, and both a pessimistic and an optimistic scenario for the future remain possibilities.

## KEY CONCEPTS FOR REVIEW

Less developed countries (LDCs)

Population explosion

Extensive versus intensive growth

Population-induced innovation

Falling fertility in the LDCs

Chinese population controls

Sub-Saharan Africa
    high fertility
    young age structure
    agricultural decline
    Malthusian prospects?

Impacts of the world population explosion on the West
    humanitarian
    ecological
    geopolitical

Humanitarian considerations: effects of immigration, foreign aid, trade

Ecological dangers
    greenhouse effect, CFCs, acid rain, rain forest loss, desertification

Geopolitical concerns: viability of "industrial democracies"

Two future scenarios

## QUESTIONS FOR DISCUSSION

1. Explain for the benefit of someone unfamiliar with the subject of the population explosion:

    (a) How dramatic it is from a historical point of view. For example, you might point out that India is projected to have a population in the year 2050 equal to three times the *world's* population in the year 1600. Give other examples.

    (b) Why it is so heavily centered in the LDCs.

    (c) How big will be the likely future decline in the U.S., western European, and Japanese shares of the world's total population.

2. "Population growth is hardly the enemy of development in the LDCs. Recent decades have seen the most rapid rates both of population growth and of increasing per capita GNPs these countries have ever known." Does this argument seem valid to you? If valid today, would it necessarily be valid tomorrow?

3. Why is it sometimes claimed that fertility rates in the LDCs may now fall even more rapidly than they did in the earlier experience of the West? Under what circumstances might this fall be slowed down, or even reversed?

4. Given the extent of its problem, do you approve/disapprove/accept as probably necessary China's method of restricting its population growth? Explain your answer.

5. Explain why foreign aid, so helpful in the rebuilding of Europe and Japan after World War II, might be less effective in the case of today's LDCs.

6. Criticize Wattenberg's thesis that the "Free World" is seriously endangered by future world population trends. Why is it much more difficult to dismiss concerns about the ecological impact of future population and development trends?

## NOTES

1. Gerald M. Meier, *Emerging from Poverty* (New York: Oxford University Press, 1984), pp. 55–56.

2. Just Faaland, ed., *Population and the World Economy in the 21st Century*, Norwegian Nobel Institute (New York: St. Martin's Press, 1982), p. 1.

3. Wassily Leontief and Ira Sohn, "Economic Growth," in Faaland, *Population and the World Economy*, pp. 96–127.

4. Lloyd G. Reynolds, *Economic Growth in the Third World, 1850–1980* (New Haven: Yale University Press, 1985).

5. Mitchell Kellman, *World Hunger: A Neo-Malthusian Perspective* (New York: Praeger, 1987), pp. 189, 194.

6. Estimates of the maximum number of people the world could support range from those of C. Clark's "high" estimate (1967) of 150 billion people to B. Gilland's estimate (1983) of 7.5 billion. Still lower estimates have been made in the past. The differences between the various estimates largely reflect the different assumptions on which they are based. For a discussion of these estimates and assumptions, see Sir Kenneth Blaxter, F.R.S., *People, Food and Resources* (Cambridge: Cambridge University Press, 1986), pp. 89–92.

7. Reynolds, *Economic Growth in the Third World*, p. 405.

8. Richard Easterlin and Eileen Crimmins, *The Fertility Revolution: A Supply and Demand Analysis* (Chicago: University of Chicago Press, 1985), p. 191.

9. One Western observer, Stanley P. Johnson, writes: "Throughout my time in China, I in no way gained the impression that the policy of one couple, one child had been imposed coercively on the Chinese people. . . . To describe China's family planning programme as 'organized coercion' is about as far-fetched an accusation as I have ever heard." Stanley P. Johnson, *World Population and the United Nations* (Cambridge: Cambridge University Press, 1987), pp. 298–299. Other commentators make it clear, however, that the line between "persuasion" and "coercion" is often a rather fine one.

10. Melanie S. Tammen, "World Bank Sows Bad Advice in Africa," *Wall Street Journal*, April 13, 1988. A major problem in this connection is the attempt of many African governments to keep food prices low for urban populations at the expense of farmers: "Of all the steps that governments can take to raise agricultural productivity in Africa, a reorientation of food price policies is the most important. Too many governments have followed policies designed to placate urban consumers. Ceiling prices for foodstuffs discourage agricultural investment and modernization." Lester R. Brown and Edward C. Wolf, "Reversing Africa's Decline," in L. R. Brown et al., eds., *State of the World, 1986* (New York: Norton, 1986), p. 190.

11. Johnson, *World Population and the United Nations*, p. 290.

12. One observer who takes this point of view is Melvyn B. Krauss. See his *Development without Aid: Growth, Poverty and Government* (New York: McGraw-Hill, 1983), p. 160. Others, however, would emphasize the enormous amounts of aid Taiwan and South Korea received earlier on.

13. Roger L. Conner, "Answering the Demo-Doomsayers: Five Myths about America's Demographic Future," *Brookings Review*, 7 (4), Fall 1989, pp. 38–39.

14. For a brief review of recent thinking about the "greenhouse effect," see *Scientific American*, 261 (5), November 1989, pp. 17–18.

15. There are actually three factors that can cause pollution: pollution per unit of product, product per unit of population (per capita), and population size. The first two are probably more significant than the third in most cases. See Working Group on Population Growth and Economic Development, *Population Growth and Economic Development: Policy Questions* (Washington, D.C.: National Academy Press, 1986), p. 37. However, the same study admits that the clearing and burning of forests in the LDCs, largely because of population growth, may be responsible for some 23 to 43 percent of the buildup of atmospheric carbon dioxide (p. 35).

16. Ben Wattenberg, *The Birth Dearth: What Happens When People in Free Countries Don't Have Enough Babies* (New York: Pharos Books, 1987), p. 129.

17. What *is* certain to decline is the proportion of the world's population that is of white, European stock. Even *within* countries like the United States and the Soviet Union (where Moslem ethnic groups are growing much more rapidly than the European Russian population), the traditional white majorities are in relative decline. Wattenberg specifically disclaims any concern about such racial and ethnic balances, however. In the terms in which he has posed the debate—essentially in terms of politicoeconomic systems—the decline of the "Free World" seems extremely unlikely.

# Postscript:
# Choosing Our Posterity?

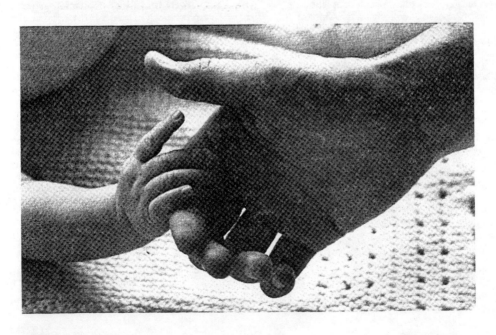

*E*ach chapter in Part VI has been concerned with the future and is therefore speculative. In this Postscript to Part VI, we venture briefly into an even more distant future and necessarily become more speculative still. The reason for doing so is simply stated: The matters we shall touch on here may well have as profound an effect on our future population as any we have discussed in the entire course of this book.

We refer to the biological revolution that has roots going back into the nineteenth century but that was launched in earnest in the decades following World War II. Douglas Costle, former administrator of the Environmental Protection Agency, has said: "While it is probably true that physics was the science of the first half of the century, it is almost certain to be molecular biology in what remains of this century and well into the next."[1] Central to this revolution has been an increased understanding of, and an unprecedented ability to manipulate and alter, the basic genetic constitution of living things. Having long since acquired the power to affect our environment, we are now on the way to acquiring a similar power over human nature at its most fundamental level.

Even the possibility of such a development raises deep questions about the range of choices that may confront us in the future. It also raises complex moral issues. If we acquire practically effective means for shaping our genetic posterity, will we choose to do so? Or will we choose to ignore, restrict, or prohibit any such tampering with the future of the human race? Which choice *should* we make?

## THE DEVELOPING RANGE OF HUMAN CHOICE

In one sense, the scientific developments that have exploded on the world since the discovery of the double-helical structure of DNA (*deoxyribonucleic acid*) by James Watson and Francis Crick in 1953 seem unprecedented in the vistas they have opened up. In another sense, they are the continuation of a long evolutionary development during which the human species has seen an enormous expansion in the range of choices available to it.[2]

In this evolutionary sense, we begin with the gradual emergence of *Homo sapiens* from its biological predecessors through the slow processes of natural selection. In this "hunting-and-gathering" phase, the hominid species, like other animal populations, took the environment basically as a given, and the evolution of human nature was the result of environmental pressures acting selectively to preserve favorable genetic mutations.

In due course, humans took a more active role in shaping their environment, forming agricultural and ultimately industrial societies. Evolution through natural selection became increasingly irrelevant (or was even reversed, some have argued, as modern science and social policy permitted the survival of the weakest as well as the fittest members of the community), while cultural evolution, through the arts, sciences, and socioeconomic factors, became the dominant forces shaping human nature. One part of this more active role in shaping the environment took the form of reshaping the genetic inheritance of various domesticated plants and animals through the process of artificial selection. This was quite different from the regime of natural selection, however, in that "instead of new characteristics being selected according to the advantages they conferred upon the species, they were selected according to whether or not they made the species more useful to man."[3]

As far as humanity is concerned, with the exception of certain horrific attempts at racial genocide (for example, the Nazi-directed holocaust of the 1930s and early 1940s), we have made no attempts at systematic selective breeding and until quite recently lacked fundamental knowledge of how the genetic mechanism functioned. We have, however, been able to exercise an increasing range of choices about our destiny as modern progress has lifted us further and further above the level of bare economic necessity. Indeed, one of those choices—as important as any we have discussed in this book—has been the choice to have fewer and fewer children. In the United States, as we know, this choice has been exercised, with occasional variations, since the beginning of the nineteenth century. In recent years, moreover, we have not only developed much more effective technologies of birth control, but have increasingly used abortion to prevent the birth of unwanted children.

Meanwhile, in the background, knowledge of genetic mechanisms was growing at a fairly undramatic pace from the 1860s on. The Austrian monk Gregor Mendel laid the foundations for the laws of inheritance with his since-famous experiments with peas. Around the beginning of the twentieth century, it was determined that *chromosomes* were the units of inheritance, with each species having its own characteristic number. DNA itself was discovered in 1869, and, before long, its chemical ingredients had been determined. By the 1920s, *RNA (ribonucleic acid)* had also been discovered. But the importance of the two nucleic acids to heredity had not yet been determined.

## THE GENETIC REVOLUTION

From the late 1920s on, a number of experiments, associated with the names of Frederick Griffith, Oswald T. Avery, Alfred Hershey, Martha Chase, and others, gradually established the critical role of DNA as the molecule of heredity. Thus, the stage was set for Watson and Crick in 1953 when they uncovered the double-helical structure of DNA and, in the process, revealed how this structure could enable DNA to reproduce itself, for the two strands, if separated, would each contain all the information necessary to create a duplicate of the entire

molecule. "It has not escaped our notice," Watson and Crick reported, "that the specific pairing we have postulated immediately suggests a possible copying mechanism for the genetic material."[4] In a less academic mode, Crick is quoted as saying: "We have discovered the secret of life!"

We cannot even hope to suggest the vast literature that has developed since this dramatic discovery, nor are we qualified to do so. For our purposes here, we mention only two major developments that have an obvious bearing on the possible future of our changing population. The first is the development of *recombinant DNA* technology, often described as "gene splicing." This technology involves the isolation of a stretch of DNA, including one or more genes, and its insertion into the DNA of another, possibly completely unrelated, organism. First established in the early 1970s, this technology is one of the important tools of "genetic engineering."

A second major development, just in its infancy as we write these pages, is the *human genome project.* The human genome is the entire genetic complement of the human organism. Humans normally have 46 chromosomes (23 pairs), each composed of *genes*, numbering in total perhaps 100,000. The genes in turn are composed of strands of DNA which involve various sequences of four bases—adenine (A), cytosine (C), thymine (T), and guanine (G), which are always paired in a certain way—A with T, C with G. There are perhaps 3 billion of these base pairs in the 46 chromosomes that are found in every cell in the human body (except for the sex cells, which have 23). The genome project involves an attempt to sequence all these base pairs, and thus to determine the chemical makeup of our entire complement of genes and chromosomes. It has been called the greatest single project in the history of biology.

Before considering some of the implications of these revolutionary developments, we should note that there are also numerous other advances taking place in the biological sciences that are relevant to our concerns, including in particular those having to do with the birthing process. One relevant technology is that of *in vitro fertilization* (IVF), or the fertilization of the human egg outside the womb (literally "in glass"). After fertilization, the egg is implanted in the womb of a woman—possibly, though not necessarily, the baby's mother. Thus, among other things, IVF facilitates the use of surrogate mothers (*surrogacy*), a development that has attracted much public attention. Nor must this implantation take place immediately. Gradually, the length of time that the embryo can survive before implantation is being increased. Also, the embryo may be frozen and implanted at a later date. In Australia, where 12 of the world's first 16 "test-tube babies" were born, the first frozen-embryo baby was born in 1984. As of 1989, there were perhaps as many as 10,000 frozen embryos being stored in Australia, raising very tricky legal issues in many instances.[5]

At the other end of the birthing process, modern technology is permitting the survival of younger and younger premature babies—in some cases, babies who are born after only 22 weeks' gestation, often weighing little more than a pound. The obvious ultimate possibility is that the two ends may meet with the combination of IVF and incubator ("artificial womb") dispensing with the human childbearer altogether.

We should also note that our ability to inspect the genetic characteristics of the fetus is improving very rapidly. In the not-so-distant past, parents had to await the birth of their child (and sometimes long after) before determining whether the child had a genetic defect. Various technologies, like amniocentesis and, more recently, chorionic villus sampling have made genetic testing possible well before the child is born. More recently still, a variety of tests have been developed to reduce the necessity for invasive procedures and/or to make very early testing possible. In 1989 no less than three new techniques were reported: work-ing with fetal cells found in the mother's blood; testing an IVF embryo before implantation, as early as a few hours after fertilization; and, in cases where the mother may possibly be carrying a defective gene, testing the egg in vitro even *before* fertilization.[6]

The combination of these new techniques for determining the genetic structure of the unborn child (or even unfertilized egg) with (a) the expansion of our knowledge of the human genome, in its infancy now, but expected to explode in the years ahead, and (b) our ability to alter the genetic structure of organisms through recombinant DNA technology—this confluence of scientific currents, abetted also by computer technology, which makes the work of discovery so much faster in many instances, raises the deepest possible questions about our future. Having made conscious decisions about the *numbers* of children we wish to have, are we now about to embark on a path of choice about the *genetic nature* of those children? Is this the ultimate path along which our population can be expected to change in the next century or two, or perhaps even sooner?

## ACHIEVEMENTS IN PROCESS

It was the expression of dramatic questions, like those just stated, that brought equally dramatic negative responses in the early days of recombinant DNA experiments. Scientists differed among themselves as to the dangers involved in the new technology. Would some new pathogen be created and let loose on an unsuspecting world? Anyway, what right did humankind have to interfere with nature's most basic processes?

In the case of the scientists, the debate led to a three-day meeting in February 1975 at Asilomar, California, where the issues were thrashed out. About a year later, as a result of these discussions, a series of guidelines was drafted by the National Institutes of Health indicating what precautions should be taken to prevent possible dangers to the public. However, the concept of creating new forms of life (including monsters à la Frankenstein) was too alarming to be left there, particularly for some local politicians. In 1976, when Harvard University announced that it planned to go ahead with a proposed recombinant DNA laboratory, the mayor of Cambridge, Alfred Vellucci, decided to intervene. Crowded City Council meetings were held, dotted with such signs as "No Recombination without Representation." There were some who took the affair lightly. A reader wrote to the *Cambridge Chronicle*: "We are amazed that anyone should express concern about the creation of a laboratory at Harvard to experiment with new life forms. A look around Harvard Square at nearly any time of day or night reveals life forms sufficiently grotesque to convince us it is already too late for such protest."[7]

For most scientists, however, it appeared that the danger of this research, in terms of viable, escaped pathogens, was minimal. As far as the creation of a seriously revised human genome—offspring who write music like Mozart and play football like Jim Brown—was concerned, most scientists were all too aware of the complexity of such a task and of how much had to be accomplished before it could be entertained outside the realm of science fiction.

Which is not to say that there haven't already been some accomplishments in the genetic engineering field. Here are a few examples:

• *Applications to agriculture:* There is nothing intrinsically new about playing around with the genes of plants and animals. Farmers were practicing artificial selection long before the structure of DNA was even guessed at. Still, genetic engineering has a wide range of potential applications in this field in increasing the nutritional value of crops, shortening the time it takes to produce new varieties of food plants, creating pest-resistant plants, improving food proc-

essing, and creating superior food-producing animals. With old-fashioned selective breeding, one can produce cows that yield more milk, but with genetic engineering one can precisely duplicate (clone) superior cows, turning animal breeding into a kind of manufacturing process in which uniform quality is assured.[8] Many agricultural specialists believe that the future of genetic engineering in farming is almost limitless.

• *Production of hormones and other pharmaceutical products:* Genetic engineering can lead to the production of hormones, vaccines, blood products, antibiotics, and many other pharmaceuticals. Two of the important early achievements in this field involved the use of genetically engineered microorganisms to make human insulin and human growth hormone. The key here is the universality of the genetic code among living organisms. This makes it possible to take a gene from a human cell, insert it into a bacterium, and have the bacteria manufacture the particular proteins encoded by that gene. The U.S. industry that has been most affected by modern biotechnology to date is, in fact, the pharmaceuticals industry.[9]

• *Prenatal diagnosis of genetic conditions:* We have mentioned the increased ability scientists have to inspect the genetic structure of the human embryo (or the unfertilized egg), as well as our expanding knowledge of the human genome. Together, these make possible the early detection of possible defects in the genetic structure of the embryo, which could lead to serious diseases after the child's birth. Examples of diseases where such detection is now possible include Huntington's disease, cystic fibrosis, sickle cell anemia, Tay-Sachs disease, thalassemia, Down's syndrome, phenylketonuria, and Duchenne's muscular dystrophy. The expansion of the number of detectable genetic defects, including those that may create only a predisposition to certain diseases (cancer, diabetes, heart disease, and the like), is certain to occur in the future, probably quite rapidly.

As we shall see in a moment, much of the promise (or threat) of genetic engineering still lies in the distant future. These examples indicate, however, that the field already has substantial achievements to its credit, with definite gains in a variety of areas predictable for the next few years.

## IMPORTANT CONCERNS ALREADY EXIST

But if these present and predictable achievements already exist, so also do present and predictable concerns. Agricultural applications of genetic engineering have raised alarmed protests because of continuing fears of allowing the release of genetically altered microbes into the environment. In 1987, protesters in California ripped up 2,200 of 2,400 strawberry plants that had been treated with genetically altered bacteria designed to protect the plants from frost. Experiments with animals, such as the injection of human growth hormone genes into pigs in the hope of making them leaner and bigger, have raised philosophical questions about the crossing of species boundaries, particularly where humans and non-human species are involved.

Animal experiments designed for medical research purposes have also run into problems. In 1988 researchers at Harvard University developed a genetically altered laboratory mouse that is particularly susceptible to carcinogens, and therefore will be very useful for further cancer research. Animal rights activists were immediately concerned about the suffering these and other hybrid animals might be put through—a concern intensified by the fact that the inserted gene sequence also affected the sex cells of the mice, meaning that the susceptibility to cancer would be passed on to their descendants. Further concerns were reported when it was announced that Harvard had received a patent for this engineered animal—the first ever issued for a higher animal.

From the point of view of potential changes in our future population, the advances in the prenatal diagnosis of genetic defects are probably the most significant achievements in biotechnology to date. For some people, they will also be the most worrisome.

Some of the issues here are quite complex, but not necessarily unresolvable. In 1989, for example, a pregnant woman, whose first child suffered from cystic fibrosis, had her fetus tested for cystic fibrosis and found that her second child would also have the disease. The insurance company that had paid for the test then announced that, because the child had a preexisting condition, it would not provide medical coverage for the child. In this particular case, under a good deal of outside pressure, the insurance company backed down. But many complications of this sort can be imagined. If a child is to be born with a major life-shortening defect, how much medical care should society devote to the care of that child? A hundred thousand dollars? A million dollars? Ten million? Similar questions occur with regard to educational expenses, college admissions, and the like.

These questions are not intrinsically new ones, as we have basically faced similar issues in the past. In this case, for example, if we discovered that the child had cystic fibrosis after (rather than before) birth, we would still face large questions as to how much society should invest in that particular child. Similar issues arise all the time with regard to low-birth-weight, premature infants whose life expectancies are often extremely short and whose maintenance and health care expenses can be very high.

What is new with early detection is the obvious invitation it extends to abortion. Because for the overwhelming majority of genetic defects discovered today there is no known cure for the disease in question, the parents are not being told, "You and your baby have a problem which we must now treat therapeutically," but, rather, "You and your baby have a problem and, if the baby is in fact born, you and the child will have to live with that problem throughout your life and the child's life as well." Under the circumstances, abortion will seem the appropriate solution to many parents.

Given that abortion in the United States is already widespread, it may seem that nothing particularly new has been added by our expanded genetic knowledge. This does not, however, seem a tenable point of view. There are probably anywhere from 3,000 to 4,000 inherited genetic diseases, and many other diseases—including major killers like heart disease and cancer—undoubtedly have a genetic component. As the human genome project proceeds and our knowledge of genetic effects expands still further, it may be possible to screen embryos for a vast range of disease susceptibility. If the tests are very early and noninvasive, who would not undergo them? And, discovering this or that genetic defect—as would be quite common given the range of possibilities likely to be uncovered—how many will choose to go ahead with what is virtually guaranteed to be an imperfect outcome—an outcome, indeed, that could mean much future suffering for the child and the parents themselves?

This open invitation to abortion may be further underlined by another biomedical advance that is developing concurrently with those on the genetic engineering front, namely the use of fetal cells as a therapeutic tool. Recent experiments have suggested that transplants of human fetal nerve cells into the brains of animals may be effective in treating Parkinson's disease, Alzheimer's disease, and other neurodegenerative conditions. In November 1988, the first U.S. patient received such a transplant and, despite a 20-year history of Parkinson's disease, was reported to have achieved significant improvements in mobility. Reporting in *Science* in November 1989, neurobiologists John T. Hansen and John R. Sladek wrote: "The benefits of studying fetal cells are many, and the clinical potential for their use as therapeutic tools is just now being realized." Also in 1989, however, the federal government renewed its ban on federal support for fetal tissue transplant research. Said Louis W. Sullivan, Secretary of Health and Human Services: "Permitting the human fetal research at issue will increase the incidence of abortion across the country."[10]

On several fronts, then, advances in biomedical technologies are, or seem to be, developing in such a way as to encourage more, perhaps significantly more, abortions in the United States. Some Americans, though not necessarily a majority, disapprove of such a trend. What is of greater interest for our study, however, is that in the case of the genetic advances, the *basis* for abortion is quite different from the characteristic grounds for abortion in the past. In particular, the question ceases to be simply, "Do we or do we not (for whatever reasons) wish to have another baby?"—essentially a quantitative, or numerical, question—and becomes, "Do we or do we not want to have this particular *kind* of baby?"—a qualitative question. Thus choice moves from the already well-established area of numbers (e.g., TFRs of 1.8 or 2.0, as opposed to 3.5 or 7.2) to an essentially new area of qualities (in this case, potential medical problems).

But if genetic defects are on the agenda today, what will be on the agenda tomorrow? Are we starting down a "slippery slope" on which we will not be able to stop until we have totally reshaped the generations ahead who will one day inherit the earth?

## GENE THERAPY

Of course, one response to the concerns just expressed is that the abortion option represents only a temporary stopgap as far as the new technology is concerned. The ultimate object of that technology is not detection, but treatment and cure. We just happen to be, it is argued, at an intermediate stage, where our ability to perform early diagnoses far outdistances our ability to treat the defects in question. When we have a *cure* for, say, cystic fibrosis (or diabetes or any other genetically determined disease), then early detection may simply help us to apply treatment more effectively. The alternative to an unhealthy child will not be abortion, but a healthy child.

Actually, there are many different strands to be considered when we turn to the therapeutic implications of the new biogenetic advances. At least four different types of therapy can be distinguished.[11]

*1. Traditional Disease Therapy Using Genetically Engineered Weapons.* If we conquer a particular infection or form of cancer, leaving the genetic structure of the patient unaffected but using genetically engineered tools, then we raise very few new issues, certainly as far as our future population is concerned. Insofar as the new techniques make possible longer, healthier lives, then they simply join the long line of treatments (antibiotics and the like) by which modern science has been combating disease. In December 1989, newspapers carried reports of a new method of creating "monoclonal antibodies" for potential attacks on diseases like cancer and AIDS. The new method involves inserting genes that carry the blueprint for the antibodies into viruses, which are then used to infect bacteria. The bacteria then begin producing the antibodies, which can later be reproduced in large quantities.[12] Such tools are new, but their use involves no great philosophic problems.

*2. Somatic Cell Gene Therapy.* A different way of combating diseases with a genetic component is to repair or replace the defective gene. Take the case of diabetes. We have already noted that, through genetic engineering, scientists have been able to produce human insulin. When such insulin is taken by a patient, then this would be an example of the kind of traditional disease therapy noted under (1) above. If,

however, the cause of the diabetes is a defective gene, and that gene can be replaced so that the body itself generates the needed insulin, then we have therapy of a very different kind. The beginning steps of such gene therapy have already been taken, and it seems highly probable that it may become widespread in the future.[13] There are, however, many difficulties to be confronted. They involve problems of *delivery* (the gene or genes must enter the right cells and must be able to survive there), *expression* (they must express their products satisfactorily—for example, in the case of diabetes, produce enough insulin to have the desired effect), and *safety* (the entering genes must not harm the cells, or the person, receiving them). If such difficulties are overcome and somatic cell gene therapy becomes widely used, it will be a decidedly novel medical advance, though again not significantly new as far as our future population is concerned. It will simply be another important technology for reducing mortality in our population. It could also have the effect of reducing the incentives for abortion we discussed earlier.

*3. Germline Gene Therapy.* The fundamental reason that somatic cell gene therapy does not affect our future population in any revolutionary way is that, by definition, somatic cells do not include the sperm cells, the egg cells, and the cells that give rise to them. These excluded cells are collectively known as *germline cells*. These are the cells that determine the genetic inheritance of our offspring. In the case of diabetes, germline gene therapy would go beyond (1) insulin injections and (2) replacement of defective insulin-producing genes in, say, the pancreas, and replace the defective genes in the germline cells, thus ensuring that the children of the diabetic individual would not inherit the genetic predisposition to diabetes. The implications of such therapy, if it can ever be provided, are, of course, enormous. For it could mean the possible eradication of those definitely inherited diseases (like, say, sickle cell anemia or hemophilia) to which it was successfully applied. It could also mean the reduction of the future incidence of those many diseases for which there is a genetic predisposition.

Although there is little doubt that germline gene therapy in humans may one day eventuate (genetic transformations in mice have already been shown to be passed on to their offspring), the hurdles to be overcome are widely regarded to be sufficiently serious that experiments in this area are unlikely to be approved until the mechanisms of gene regulation and control are better understood. If and when such understanding develops and the therapy is applied, however, it will definitely mark a new stage in the way in which human populations are propagated, for we will be determining by our actions today not only the *numbers* but also certain *qualities* of our successor generations. In particular, we will be ridding those generations of specific genetic defects that are known to lead to various forms of illness and infirmity. In this sense, we will be "choosing" our posterity in a way heretofore impossible.

*4. Genetic Engineering to "Improve" on Human Nature.* The final potential development in the area of genetic engineering is not really "therapy" in the usual sense at all. Here we would be dealing with "normal" rather than "defective" genes, which we might choose to alter to produce what we consider a "superior" result. We have put quotes around these descriptive words to indicate that defining them involves very complex philosophical concepts. To give a practical example that is already observable today: We have mentioned that one of the successes of genetic engineering has been the production of human growth hormone. This growth hormone can be used to combat a genetic condition known as *dwarfism*. Most people would agree that dwarfism is the result of a genetic "defect." But what of people who are somewhat shorter than the

average, and who feel that their lives are hindered in a variety of ways by this characteristic? Or what of people who are of average height but would prefer to be taller? We know that the parents of many children in the "normal" range of human height seek growth hormone treatment for their offspring today. Should this be regarded as "therapy" for a "defect" or as an attempt simply to "improve upon" Mother Nature?

Whatever vocabulary we use, we can readily see that the move from correcting defects to improving ordinary conditions is a move along a continuum rather than a sharp jump into a new category. The case of human intelligence is perhaps the most obvious of all. Certain individuals are regarded as certifiably "retarded"; a few others are regarded as certifiable "geniuses." In between, we have every imaginable gradation of ability, as well as a huge range of different abilities such that any given individual may be "normal" in some respects, "defective" in others, and "superior" in still others.

Needless to say, the intellectual and technological difficulties of engineering improvements (however defined) in our higher abilities are enormous and could conceivably prove insuperable. Whereas there is fairly general agreement that therapies (1), (2), and (3) may be achievable some day (though not necessarily desirable at any time), genetic engineering to improve the human race in significant ways is still in doubt. Not all questions that we are capable of posing necessarily have practicable answers.

Still, the extreme rapidity of progress in molecular biology these days makes one extremely suspicious of any individual, scientist or not, who suggests that such advances will never be technologically feasible. It is a much safer bet (though it does remain a bet) that, in due course, such advances will occur and that, at some date in the future, humanity will have to decide how to, or how not to, exercise this new power over its own genetic endowment.

*Matrix Breeding grounds*

## POSTERITY CHOICE AND THE PARENTAL CONNECTION

Presuming that that day does come, one of the basic issues that may be raised is the degree to which, in "improving" the human species, we are effectively destroying what remains of the ties that bind parents to their children. If, at the same time that we are engineering "superior" germline cells, we are also moving away from the bearing of children by their natural mothers, we might succeed in severing those ties almost completely.

This question of the "parental connection," as we might call it, is not, of course, the only issue that conscious manipulation of the human gene pool would raise. Many people feel that it is assuming far too Godlike a stance for scientists, or anyone else, to start making drastic revisions in the basic materials of human inheritance. Others feel that, however comforting the assurances that might be given, there is always the possibility of human error in these manipulations. Is it possible that such errors, affecting the gene pool, might prove irreversible? Are we dealing here, as some people feel is the case with nuclear power, with forces of such potency that human beings simply cannot be trusted with them?

And, of course, apart from human error, there is the possibility of human malice and evil intention. Many people fear that the great danger of genetic manipulations is that they may be used, as was believed about the eugenics movement earlier in this century, to rid the world of genes that some people consider "inferior" or "undesirable," including the genes of certain ethnic or racial groups.

All these issues are real and would have to be faced were the cleansing of the human gene pool of "defective" or simply "belownormal" genes to become practically achievable.

Even assuming the best, however—that the technology is available and virtually error-proof; that a wide consensus develops among scientists, governments, and citizens about the proper limits and constraints within which the technology should be applied; and that we really can raise, say, the general level of intelligence, health, and longevity of the human species—even assuming all this, the issue of parental connection would still remain. It might be put this way:

*To the degree that we change the genetic endowment of our children so that it is different from what they would have inherited from us, to that degree we weaken the genetic tie between the generations. Insofar as we produce "better" children, we are producing children who are not quite so much "our" children as they otherwise would have been.*

For the parent who is tone-deaf and slow of foot, it may be satisfying to be able to create a child who, as we said earlier, writes music like Mozart and plays football like Jim Brown, but it is very difficult to see how that parent will see very much of him- or herself in that child. A tall son or daughter may be preferred by short fathers and mothers, but having such a progeny, it will certainly no longer be possible to say how much the child "resembles her mother" or "takes after his father."

Which may not be important.

Or may be. For we are already dealing with a future in which, as we have noted many times, the fate of the family is very much in doubt. If, even now, the care and nurture of the next generation is being given over to nonfamily institutions in a variety of ways, if marriages continue to break up, if the bearing of children begins to be handed over to surrogates or, conceivably, to the nearest laboratory, if—in addition to all this—we begin to endow our children with what have been called "designer genes," as opposed to our own humble, grubby, imperfect, best-we-have-to-offer genes, then what conceivable sense of personal, individualized, parental connection with these children will remain?

Superior as they may be, will we even like them?

Fortunately, perhaps, this total scenario lies far, far in the future. Perhaps less fortunately, some elements of the scenario are already operable, or at least clearly on the horizon.

Now is our chance to ponder both: the immediate and the distant future of our changing population.

## NOTES

1. Steve Olson, *Biotechnology: An Industry Comes of Age* (Washington, D.C.: National Academy Press, 1986), p. 2.

2. For the general reader, there are now numerous accounts of the developments we shall be discussing in this brief postscript. For the discovery of the structure of DNA, a highly interesting, personalized account is given in James D. Watson, *The Double Helix* (New York: Atheneum, 1968). General books describing the succession of crucial discoveries include Burke K. Zimmerman, *Biofuture: Confronting the Genetic Era*, with Foreword by Francis Crick (New York: Plenum Press, 1984); Jeremy Cherfas, *Man-Made Life: An Overview of the Science, Technology and Commerce of Genetic Engineering* (New York: Pantheon, 1982); and Steven S. Hall, *Invisible Frontiers* (New York: Atlantic Monthly Press, 1987). Because change is so rapid in this field, the reader may also wish to consult the numerous periodicals that cover current developments. For those with a strong scientific background, the British journal *Nature*, and the American journals *Science* and the *New England Journal of Medicine*, are very important. A useful summary of the latest from these and other professional journals is provided by *Science News*. For less professional coverage, one can go to the newspapers (for example, the *New York Times* ran a three-part series entitled "New Life: The Promise and Risk of Genetic Engineering," June 9–11, 1987) or to various popular magazines (for example, *Omni* frequently does interviews in this area, and *Modern Maturity* did a Minicourse on genetic engineering, "The Design of Life," in June–July 1989) or, very usefully, to regular issues of *Scientific American*.

3. Brian Stableford, *Future Man: Brave New World or Genetic Nightmare* (New York: Crown, 1984), p. 12.

4. J. D. Watson and F. H. C. Crick, "Molecular Structure of Nucleic Acids: A Structure for Deoxyribose Nucleic Acid," *Nature*, *171*, 1953, p. 738.

5. Such a tricky legal issue arose in Australia when the wealthy parents of some frozen embryos both died in an airplane crash without leaving wills. Did the embryos have a legal right to inherit the $8 million estate left by the couple? In the United States, we have had divorced parents arguing over their frozen embryos, with a judge in Tennessee awarding custody of seven such embryos to the biological mother against the wishes of her ex-husband. See Michael Pirrie, "Reinventing the Law of Human Life," *Wall Street Journal*, September 26, 1989.

6. For accounts of these new testing methods, see *Science News*, *135*, March 4, 1989, p. 132, and *136*, November 18, 1989, p. 325.

7. Quoted in Hall, *Invisible Frontiers*, p. 49.

8. The process of cloning cattle in Wheelock, Texas, is described by Keith Schneider of the *New York Times*: "The . . . genetic mother was a prize Brangus cow that had been treated with hormones before being inseminated in April 1987 with the thawed semen of a valuable Brangus bull. [When] the embryo was five days old and composed of 32 cells, . . . scientists, using microsurgical tools, removed the nuclei from 16 of the embryonic cells. In a separate procedure, they removed the nuclei and part of the cellular material from an equal number of unfertilized bovine eggs collected from ordinary cows. Then researchers transferred the embryonic nuclei into the cavities of the unfertilized eggs, in effect creating a new embryo. The human-made embryos were implanted in surrogate mothers. Eight of the 16 embryos produced calves over a two-week period in January." Keith Schneider, "Cattle Breeders Try Out New Cloning Techniques," *Fort Lauderdale Sun-Sentinel*, February 19, 1988.

9. Olson, *Biotechnology*, p. 18. The pharmaceuticals industry is sufficiently interested in the commercial applications of genetic engineering that it has already witnessed heated fights over patent rights to some of the tools of biotechnology. An example is the 1989 battle between DuPont and Cetus Corporation over patent rights to one of these new tools, polymerase chain reaction, or PCR. Millions and possibly billions of dollars were considered to be at stake.

10. Quotations are from Rick Weiss, "Bypassing the Ban," *Science News*, *136*, December 9, 1989.

11. The following classification, though somewhat different, relies heavily on that of Olson, *Biotechnology*, Chapter 4. Olson's book, published by the National Academy Press, is based on the proceedings of a 1985 conference on genetic engineering sponsored by the Academy Industry Program of the National Academy of Sciences, the National Academy of Engineering, and the Institute of Medicine.

12. The production of "monoclonal antibodies" is a

major tool of modern biotechnology, as important commercially, if not more important, than recombinant DNA technology. The term *monoclonal antibody* is defined as an antibody derived from a single clone of antibody-producing cells. What modern technology has done is to develop means for the production of large quantities of such antibodies in very pure form.

13. In September 1990, a historic step was taken when the first federally approved infusion of genetically engineered cells to cure a disease occurred in the case of a four-year-old girl suffering from an inherited immune disorder called ADA deficiency. Seven months later, in April 1991, the child's immune system still seemed to be responding to the gene-replacement therapy. Meanwhile, a second child with ADA deficiency was receiving similar treatment, and two cancer patients suffering from malignant melanoma had also been treated by gene therapy.

# Appendix: Introduction to Demographic Analysis

In this appendix, we shall introduce some of the problems demographers face and the techniques they use when they attempt to make population estimates and projections. We shall discuss the many sources of information used to analyze the components of population change. We shall also introduce some of the methodological dilemmas demographers encounter as they attempt to answer basic questions about the dynamics of population growth. The appendix thus provides a technical underpinning for many of the topics discussed in more general terms in the text proper.

## I. Basic Factors in Determining Population Size and Composition

As indicated in the text (p. 20), three basic demographic factors are responsible for the size and composition of a given population: *fertility*, which adds residents; *mortality*, which removes them; and *migration*, which can have either net effect. Complete and accurate data on these elements, including the various components of net migration, would perfectly define the resident population.

Many demographic estimates are derived residually by utilizing the logical relationship among these components of change and a procedure known as cohort analysis. A *cohort* is a specific group of individuals whose behavior is traced over time. This group is identified by one or more unchanging characteristics, such as year of birth, sex, and/or race. For instance, we might wish to trace the experiences of a cohort, $c$, comprising white females born in

1915. Given accurate data on the number of such persons born in that year, and their subsequent deaths and international migration, we could estimate the number currently resident in the United States as follows:

$$
\begin{aligned}
\text{Actual} & \\
\text{Resident} &= \text{Births}_c \\
\text{Population}_c &
\end{aligned}
$$

$$
- \begin{array}{l} \text{Total} \\ \text{Deaths}_c \end{array} + \begin{array}{l} \text{Total} \\ \text{Legal} \\ \text{Immigrants}_c \end{array} \quad (1)
$$

$$
+ \begin{array}{l} \text{Total} \\ \text{Illegal} \\ \text{Entrants}_c \end{array} - \begin{array}{l} \text{Total} \\ \text{Emigrants}_c \end{array}
$$

If the cohort has been accurately enumerated at some intermediate time, $t$ (e.g., in the 1980 census), or the census count for time $t$ has been adjusted for all correctable biases to that date, it is possible to bring forward the estimate to time $t + n$ using the same logic:

$$
\begin{aligned}
\text{Projected} & \quad = \quad \text{Enumerated} \\
\text{Population}_{c,t+n} & \quad\quad\;\; \text{Population}_{c,t}
\end{aligned}
$$

$$
- \sum_{y=t}^{y=t+n} \text{Deaths}_{c,y} + \sum_{y=t}^{y=t+n} \left[ \begin{array}{l} \text{Legal} \\ \text{Immigrants}_{c,y} \end{array} \right. \quad (2)
$$

$$
\left. + \begin{array}{l} \text{Illegal} \\ \text{Entrants}_{c,y} \end{array} - \text{Emigrants}_{c,y} \right]
$$

However, the updated estimate is a residual. Therefore, any errors in the components pass directly into the final estimate. Hence, in developing such population estimates, demographers must carefully evaluate and adjust the component information to eliminate potential biases.

## II. Data Sources for Population Estimates and Projections

In attempting to estimate accurately the various factors that affect population size, the U.S. government uses a wide variety of different data sources. This variety is necessary because of the complexity of the problem, particularly when projections are involved.

### A. THE DECENNIAL CENSUS

The keystone on which population estimates and projections rest is census data. The U.S. Constitution (Article 1, Section 2) mandates that an enumeration be made every ten years, so that U.S. representatives and direct taxes can be apportioned according to state populations.

#### Census Underenumeration

Although the intent of the decennial census is to enumerate completely and accurately all persons residing in the United States, this has never been accomplished. The first systematic analysis of census undercount, for the 1940 census, indicated that 5.6 percent of the population, and as many as 12.6 percent of all black males, had been missed by enumerators. Awareness of the nature of this problem focused outreach efforts, and census coverage improved steadily until 1980. By that time just 1.4 percent of the total population, including 8.8 percent of all black males, were believed to have eluded enumeration (Table A-1). The underenumeration of white-and-other women was virtually eliminated (U.S. Bureau of the Census, 1988).

Preliminary reports from the 1990 census indicate that field enumeration levels may have deteriorated substantially during the last census. Just 65 percent of all housing units voluntarily mailed back their 1990 census forms, as compared with 75 percent in 1980. Follow-up efforts have subsequently located 99 percent of the forms sent out, but it has not yet been established what share of the previously uncounted population was thereby located.

Public apathy appears to be a growing problem. A decline in household discretionary time, together with a growing barrage of junk mail and commercial surveys, may have desensitized the public to the importance of enumeration. Whatever the reason, the 1990 enumeration is likely to require a great deal more scrutiny and adjustment than was necessary a decade earlier.

**TABLE A-1.** Estimates of the Percentage of Net Underenumeration by Race and Sex, 1940–1980

|  | 1940 | 1950 | 1960 | 1970 | 1980[a] |
|---|---|---|---|---|---|
| All classes | 5.6 | 4.4 | 3.3 | 2.9 | 1.4 |
| Male | 6.1 | 4.8 | 3.8 | 3.7 | 2.4 |
| Female | 5.2 | 4.1 | 2.8 | 2.2 | 0.4 |
| Black | 10.3 | 9.6 | 8.3 | 8.0 | 5.9 |
| Male | 12.6 | 11.7 | 10.4 | 10.6 | 8.8 |
| Female | 8.0 | 7.5 | 6.2 | 5.6 | 3.1 |
| White and other | 5.1 | 3.8 | 2.7 | 2.2 | 0.7 |
| Male | 5.3 | 4.0 | 3.0 | 2.8 | 1.5 |
| Female | 4.9 | 3.6 | 2.4 | 1.7 | — |

[a] Assuming 3 million net illegal entrants during decade.

*Source:* R. E. Fay, J. S. Passel, and J. G. Robinson, *The Coverage of Population in the 1980 U.S. Census*, Table 3.2. (Washington, D.C.: U.S. Government Printing Office, 1988).

## The Issue of Adjustment

Since the mail-out/mail-back procedure was introduced in 1960, the vast majority of census forms have been handled completely through the mail. Only hard-to-reach populations (such as rural households, the homeless, and persons living in institutions or other group quarters) are still visited by enumerators. But placing the response burden on private households risks nonresponse or the return of incomplete and/or inaccurate information.

Most data users expect, and indeed assume, that official census data are complete and accurate. There are many weighty decisions besides the apportionment of seats in the U.S. House of Representatives that rest on enumeration findings. As the amount of federal funding distributed on this basis has grown, so too have concerns about the social and economic consequences of underenumeration. Hence, the Bureau of the Census now methodically scrutinizes census findings, wherever possible contacting missed households, correcting response errors, and/or ascribing missing values as part of the editing process.

Every housing unit that does not return a census schedule must be visited in person. About 2.5 percent of the population enumerated in 1980 were located in this manner. Where direct contact cannot be established, (another 1.4 percent of the 1980 count), other close-out techniques must be employed. Building on the knowledge that there is a strong correlation between the characteristics of adjacent housing units, information about nearby units may be used to attribute such features as occupancy status, household size, and demographic composition. Even though official counts reflect these corrections, certain demographic groups remain relatively underenumerated.

For purposes of congressional apportionment, the official census counts must be released by the end of the census year.[1] With both voting districts and federal funds tied to these counts, communities and demographic groups with poor response rates have become increasingly vocal about the need to further inflate their official tallies.

### Estimating the Level and Distribution of Undercount

Unfortunately, it is impossible to thoroughly evaluate the extent of underenumeration by the end of the census year.[2] Hence it is customary to release a range of adjusted estimates later on, as an addendum to the official figures. There are two basic methods by which estimates are adjusted. Both are based on a comparison of the enumerated population with various independently derived estimates.

*Demographic Methods.* One method that has been in use since the 1940s is based on demographic analysis. In 1980, independent estimates of the number of residents in each of 64 age-sex-race cohorts were derived from various data sources. These included birth and death registration, adjusted for underregistration; administrative records of legal immigration, from the Immigration and Naturalization Service (INS); independently derived estimates of the population born between 1915 and 1935, when birth registration data were incomplete; estimates of the population aged 65 and over, based on Medicare records adjusted for underenrollment; and analytic estimates of undocumented entries. Unadjusted counts from previous censuses tend to be biased, and are therefore *not* used.

Conceptually, the independent estimate rests on the birth, death, and international migratory experience of each cohort traced from birth to the census date, as in equation (1) above. In reality, since this procedure is applied to each census, it is possible to use adjusted counts from the previous census as a starting point, as in equation (2). A comparison of the expected population with that actually enumerated yields the "error of closure." In 1980,

$$\text{Error of closure}_{80} = \frac{\text{Demographic estimate}_{80}}{\text{(built from 1970 census)}} - \text{Census count}_{80} \quad (3)$$

This initial calculation revealed that in 1980 the enumerated population was actually 5.2 million persons *larger* than had been anticipated on the basis of intercensal births, deaths, and legal migration alone.

Had there been no illegal entries during the decade, the discrepancy would have been attributed entirely to improvements in census coverage. By 1980, however, it was speculated that as many as 12 million illegal aliens might be resident in the United States (Siegel, Passel, and Robinson, 1980). The presence of such individuals in census counts would have masked the omission of a comparable number of expected legal residents. Only by assessing the number of undocumented aliens counted could analysts infer the rate of underenumeration for the legal or, indeed, the total population. The method by which this was accomplished is discussed in detail in the "Immigration" section below.

The demographic method remains an important tool for the evaluation of the 1990 census. However, it does have certain shortcomings. Possible underregistration of recent births (especially for blacks), uncertainty about the size of the undocumented population (which is extremely difficult to measure), and inadequate information about the number of births in cohorts born before 1936 are the main sources of possible error. Also, and most limiting, is the fact that the demographic method provides no information on the geographic distribution of census undercount. The loudest call for census adjustment comes from communities that believe underenumeration has cost them resources to which they are entitled. Geographic detail must be derived in another manner.

***The Post-Enumeration Program (PEP).***
In 1980, this was accomplished with the so-called *Post-Enumeration Program (PEP)*. This method juxtaposed census findings with information from an adjacent month's Current Population Survey (CPS). Each month the CPS interviews respondents from about 56,000 households to obtain information about members' employment and unemployment status.[3] The PEP utilized names selected from this large sample, and from institutional lists, to check the coverage and quality of 1980 census data.

An attempt was made to locate census records corresponding to a sample of individuals in the CPS. Cases in which such a link could not be made provided a basis for estimates of the number, location, and characteristics of those omitted by the census. Similarly, a sample of those enumerated by the census was matched to CPS files to check the validity of census entries. This case-by-case approach yielded information on the attributes of persons enumerated at more than one location (e.g., college students, self-reported on campus and reported by parents in home communities) or at the wrong address (e.g., persons who had moved from the location prior to census day).

Twelve different PEP scenarios were developed, reflecting a broad range of assumptions. The results varied more widely than those of demographic analysis. Although these two major methods reached similar conclusions about the magnitude of underenumeration, they did so fortuitously (through large offsetting differences for both males and females). Compared to demographic analysis, PEP tended to understate the coverage problems of males (particularly blacks) and to overstate those of females.

Of course, deriving estimates of undercount from a sample of persons appearing on a noncensus listing assumes that the independent list is itself complete. To the extent that the census and CPS have difficulty reaching the same demographic groups, omissions on CPS rosters would tend to corroborate census findings rather than expose omissions. Because of this correlation bias, postenumeration estimates of total undercount are less accurate than those derived demographically.

Nonetheless, PEP data fill a very important informational void regarding variations in geographic coverage. The PEP showed that most of the improvements in coverage between 1970 and 1980 occurred in the South. Even so, the vast majority of those omitted in 1980 (73 percent) were still residents of the South.

*Post-Enumeration Survey (PES).* Under growing pressure to adjust census data for underenumeration, the Census Bureau continues to refine its post-enumeration procedures. In 1990 a Post-Enumeration Survey (PES) was conducted (Hogan, 1990). Entire sample blocks were restudied to determine the level of census coverage, duplication, and address misreporting. To preserve the independence of this survey, maps of sample blocks included none of the address or housing unit information gathered for census purposes—this was all regenerated. Approximately 165,000 households were interviewed. The PES records of each of these households were linked, wherever possible, with corresponding 1990 census schedules. Coverage, duplication, and misreporting errors were analyzed for each of 100 separate age-sex-race strata, leading to the development of adjusted population microdata. Records were created for missing individuals, incorporating the characteristics believed to have been underrepresented in the initial enumeration.

As a result of the PES analysis, Census Bureau Director Barbara Everitt Bryant and a majority of in-house experts recommended that the 1990 census count be adjusted. The adjustment would have increased the unadjusted estimate of the U.S. population of 248.7 million by around 5 million people. A disproportionate number of those missed were believed to be minorities—blacks, Hispanics, and Native Americans. However, on July 15, 1991, Secretary of Commerce Robert A. Mosbacher announced that he feared that such an adjustment would open the door to "political tampering with the census in the future," and ruled that the unadjusted figures would continue to be used.

Needless to say, many groups and politicians, especially in the big cities, were outraged by this announcement, and legal efforts to challenge the decision were undertaken. In this textbook, the unadjusted figures are used, as, for the moment at least, they will be used as the basis for all primary census data products.

## B. FERTILITY DATA

As we have seen, birth data are essential to population estimation. The national birth registration system was not fully in place until 1936. Hence, information about births prior to that year is incomplete. Administrative data from the Medicare program, adjusted for underenrollment, provide a basis for estimating the size of cohorts born 65 or more years ago. Birth data for cohorts born prior to 1936 but not yet eligible for Medicare are drawn from analytical estimates by Whelpton (1950) and Coale and Rives (1973).

The completeness of current birth registration data has not been studied since 1964–1968. Overall coverage was nearly complete at that time. Nonetheless, uncertainty about birth data (especially for blacks) is the largest single cause of uncertainty regarding the demographic estimates of coverage.

Birth registration data are used to produce a variety of fertility indices, several of which are described next.

### Crude Birth Rate

The crude birth rate (CBR) is the number of total births per 1,000 of total population during a given year:

$$CBR_t = \frac{B_t}{P_t} \times 1000 \qquad (4)$$

where

$B_t$ = births during year $t$

$P_t$ = midyear population in year $t$

### Age-Specific Birth Rates

Although the crude birth rate is a useful measure, the timing of births (i.e., maternal age) also affects the pace of population growth. Deferred childbearing spaces out generations, thereby slowing the pace of expansion. Thus, population projections must take into account the age at which women bear their children.

Age-specific birth rates ($f_a$) for women in the childbearing ages 15 through 49 are computed using birth registration data and intercensal population estimates, as follows:

$$f_a = \frac{B_a}{P_a} \times 1000 \qquad (5)$$

where

$B_a$ = total annual births registered to women aged $a$

$P_a$ = estimated midyear population of women aged $a$

Trends in these disaggregated rates underlie the different fertility projections.

### Total Fertility Rate

Various schedules of age-specific rates are often condensed into an index of the implicit overall fertility level. The index used to summarize this information is the total fertility rate (TFR), the unweighted sum of a cross-section of annual age-specific birth rates, illustrating the long-run impact of an unchanging schedule of age-specific rates. The TFR can be thought of as the number of children a synthetic cohort of 1,000 women would bear during their reproductive lives if, at every age, they experienced the corresponding age-specific birth

rate from the unchanging schedule. The TFR is computed as:

$$TFR = \sum_{a=15}^{a=49} f_a \times 1,000 \qquad (6)$$

Any schedule of age-specific fertility rates uniquely defines a corresponding TFR, but many different combinations of age-specific rates may lead to the same TFR. Therefore, although this index conveniently summarizes a full schedule of rates, it does not by itself provide sufficient information with which to produce a fertility projection.

## C. MORTALITY DATA

Mortality data are yet another key component of population estimates and projections. Death registration data are now believed to be relatively complete, and do not contribute a great deal of uncertainty to population estimation. Among the more common death indices used are the following.

### Crude Death Rate

The crude death rate (CDR) is the number of total deaths per 1,000 of total population during a given year:

$$CDR_t = \frac{D_t}{P_t} \times 1000 \qquad (7)$$

where

$D_t$ = deaths during year $t$

$P_t$ = midyear population in year $t$

The difference between the crude birth and crude death rates is known as the rate of natural increase (RNI). The RNI illustrates by what margin total births outpace total deaths in a given population during a given year, per thousand of population:

$$RNI_t = CBR_t - CDR_t \qquad (8)$$

### Age-Specific Death Rates

As with fertility, the age at which mortality occurs has a direct bearing on the pace of population growth. The higher the infant mortality rate, the slower will be the pace of expansion. Hence, the first step in projecting mortality patterns is to assess trends in age-specific death rates ($m_a$). These are computed as follows:

$$m_a = \frac{D_a}{P_a} \times 1000 \qquad (9)$$

where

$D_a$ = annual deaths registered among men (or women) aged $a$

$P_a$ = estimated midyear population of men (or women) aged $a$

Although age-specific data are used to develop projections, the resulting mortality scenarios may be summarized in terms of an implicit overall mortality level.

### Life Tables and Life Expectancy Indices

This is accomplished using a single statistic, the life expectancy at birth (denoted $e_0$). This index illustrates the lifetime effects of a given schedule of age-specific mortality rates on a synthetic birth cohort. The life expectancy index indicates the length of time the typical cohort member would live if, at every age, he or she was exposed to the corresponding age-specific risks of death from the reference mortality schedule.

The life table (an example of which is shown in Table A-2) can be interpreted as both:

• A longitudinal profile of the mortality experiences of a single birth cohort of 100,000 persons (called the radix), whose risks of mortality at every age correspond to the age-specific risks in the reference mortality schedule, and

• A cross-sectional profile of the stationary (i.e., unchanging) population that would result if age-specific death rates remained constant and were exactly offset by 100,000 births each year.

The six key functions in a life table are $_nq_x$, $l_x$, $_nd_x$, $_nL_x$, $T_x$, and $e_x$. In life table notation, age at the beginning of a given interval is denoted $x$, while the number of years in the interval is denoted $n$. (Conventional life tables operate on single-year-of-age data, where $n = 1$ and is implicit. Abridged life tables, of which Table A-2 is an example, normally present five-year age groupings, with $n = 5$ being stated explicitly).

The schedule of age-specific life table death rates uniquely defines a stationary population, and corresponds to a specific life expectancy at birth. The upper panel of Table A-2 illustrates the relationship among the six key life table functions.[4]

Assume there exists a population into which 100,000 males are born each year. Throughout each birth cohort's lifetime, members encounter the same age-specific mortality rates as were observed among American males in 1987 ($_nq_x$, column 2). In life table terminology,

$l_x$ denotes the *number of survivors from the initial cohort to exact age x*. For instance, on their twentieth birthday, $l_{20} = 97{,}758$.

$_nq_x$ denotes the *proportion* of all cohort members alive at exact age $x$ *who will die before reaching age x + n*.[5] During the 5 year age interval 20 to 25, .85 percent of all cohort members in this life table die.

$_nd_x$ denotes, of all cohort members surviving to exact age $x$ ($l_x$), and subjected to the risk $_nq_x$, the *number who die before reaching age x + n*. In our example, 834 cohort members, alive at the beginning of age 20, die before their twenty-fifth birthday.

$_nL_x$ denotes the total *number of person-years lived by cohort members during age x* as they pass through that age. All who survive to the beginning of the next age interval are at-

# TABLE A-2. Abridged Life Tables by Sex, United States, 1987

| Age Interval | Proportion Dying | Of 100,000 Born Alive | | Stationary Population | | Average Remaining Lifetime |
|---|---|---|---|---|---|---|
| Period of Life between Two Exact Ages Stated in Years, and by Sex | Proportion of Persons Alive at Beginning of Age Interval Dying During Interval | Number Living at Beginning of Age Interval | Number Dying during Age Interval | In the Age Interval | In This and All Subsequent Age Intervals | Average Number of Years of Life Remaining at Beginning of Age Interval |
| (1) | (2) | (3) | (4) | (5) | (6) | (7) |
| $x$ to $x + n$ | $_nq_x$ | $l_x$ | $_nd_x$ | $_nL_x$ | $T_x$ | $e_x$ |
| MALE | | | | | | |
| 0–1 | .0112 | 100,000 | 1,120 | 99,038 | 7,147,815 | 71.5 |
| 1–5 | .0023 | 98,880 | 224 | 395,001 | 7,048,777 | 71.3 |
| 5–10 | .0015 | 98,656 | 145 | 492,884 | 6,653,776 | 67.4 |
| 10–15 | .0017 | 98,511 | 169 | 492,247 | 6,160,892 | 62.5 |
| 15–20 | .0059 | 98,342 | 584 | 490,403 | 5,668,645 | 57.6 |
| 20–25 | .0085 | 97,758 | 834 | 486,750 | 5,178,242 | 53.0 |
| 25–30 | .0088 | 96,924 | 851 | 482,469 | 4,691,492 | 48.4 |
| 30–35 | .0104 | 96,073 | 1,002 | 477,890 | 4,209,023 | 43.8 |
| 35–40 | .0130 | 95,071 | 1,234 | 472,426 | 3,731,133 | 39.2 |
| 40–45 | .0165 | 93,837 | 1,548 | 465,582 | 3,258,707 | 34.7 |
| 45–50 | .0247 | 92,289 | 2,278 | 456,173 | 2,793,125 | 30.3 |
| 50–55 | .0396 | 90,011 | 3,565 | 441,710 | 2,336,952 | 26.0 |
| 55–60 | .0615 | 86,446 | 5,320 | 419,678 | 1,895,242 | 21.9 |
| 60–65 | .0957 | 81,126 | 7,760 | 387,232 | 1,475,564 | 18.2 |
| 65–70 | .1366 | 73,366 | 10,020 | 342,720 | 1,088,332 | 14.8 |
| 70–75 | .2060 | 63,346 | 13,051 | 284,848 | 745,612 | 11.8 |
| 75–80 | .2949 | 50,295 | 14,830 | 214,531 | 460,764 | 9.2 |
| 80–85 | .4216 | 35,465 | 14,952 | 139,084 | 246,233 | 6.9 |
| 85 and over | 1.0000 | 20,513 | 20,513 | 107,149 | 107,149 | 5.2 |
| FEMALE | | | | | | |
| 0–1 | .0090 | 100,000 | 896 | 99,236 | 7,836,924 | 78.4 |
| 1–5 | .0018 | 99,104 | 177 | 395,993 | 7,737,688 | 78.1 |
| 5–10 | .0010 | 98,927 | 96 | 494,374 | 7,341,695 | 74.2 |
| 10–15 | .0009 | 98,831 | 91 | 493,958 | 6,847,321 | 69.3 |
| 15–20 | .0024 | 98,740 | 237 | 493,145 | 6,353,363 | 64.3 |
| 20–25 | .0027 | 98,503 | 271 | 491,850 | 5,860,218 | 59.5 |
| 25–30 | .0032 | 98,232 | 317 | 490,384 | 5,368,368 | 54.6 |
| 30–35 | .0042 | 97,915 | 409 | 488,600 | 4,877,984 | 49.8 |
| 35–40 | .0058 | 97,506 | 562 | 486,224 | 4,389,384 | 45.0 |
| 40–45 | .0084 | 96,944 | 810 | 482,845 | 3,903,160 | 40.3 |
| 45–50 | .0137 | 96,134 | 1,319 | 477,612 | 3,420,315 | 35.6 |
| 50–55 | .0224 | 94,815 | 2,122 | 469,099 | 2,942,703 | 31.0 |
| 55–60 | .0342 | 92,693 | 3,174 | 455,998 | 2,473,604 | 26.7 |
| 60–65 | .0540 | 89,519 | 4,831 | 436,220 | 2,017,606 | 22.5 |
| 65–70 | .0796 | 84,688 | 6,737 | 407,479 | 1,581,386 | 18.7 |
| 70–75 | .1213 | 77,951 | 9,458 | 367,324 | 1,173,907 | 15.1 |
| 75–80 | .1840 | 68,493 | 12,604 | 312,442 | 806,583 | 11.8 |
| 80–85 | .2937 | 55,889 | 16,416 | 239,551 | 494,141 | 8.8 |
| 85 and over | 1.0000 | 39,473 | 39,473 | 254,590 | 254,590 | 6.4 |

*Source:* U.S. Department of Health and Human Services, *Vital Statistics of the United States, 1987*, Vol. II, Section 6 (Washington, D.C.: U.S. Public Health Service, 1990).

tributed with $n$ years of life (here 5). Except during the first year of life, deaths are assumed to be uniformly distributed throughout the interval. On average, those who die do so midway through the interval, contributing $n/2$ person-years of life. Computationally, $_nL_x$ is approximately [6]

$$_nL_x = \frac{n(l_x + l_{x+n})}{2} \qquad (10)$$

In our example, the 97,758 persons entering ages 20–25 collectively live 486,750 person-years in that interval.

$T_x$ denotes the total *number of person-years lived by the birth cohort beyond exact age x*. In general, this is calculated by cumulating the $L_x$ column from age $x$ to the end of the table, as follows:

$$T_x = \sum_{y=x}^{y=w} L_y \qquad (11)$$

where

$y$ = any age between $x$ and the final year of life

$w$ = the age at which the last cohort member dies.

At age 20, the synthetic birth cohort depicted in Table A-2 collectively looks forward to 5,178,242 more years of life.

$e_x$ denotes the *average years of life remaining beyond exact age x* for cohort members who survive to that exact age. This function is computed as:

$$e_x = \frac{T_x}{l_x} \qquad (12)$$

In our example,

$$e_{20} = \frac{5,178,242}{97,758} = 53.0$$

That is, at age 20 in 1987, the average life expectancy of U.S. males (i.e., the average number of years of life remaining) is estimated to have been 53.0 years.

Although any schedule of age-specific mortality rates uniquely defines a life ex-

pectancy index, many different schedules could generate the same $e_x$ value. Thus, although mortality projections may be described in terms of this summary statistic, they actually imply specific forecasts of the full schedule of age-specific death rates.

## D.   DATA ON GROSS AND NET INTERNATIONAL MIGRATION

Four types of flows make up net international migration: legal immigration, legal emigration, illegal entries, and illegal exits. Only legal immigration is systematically counted. Therefore, estimates of the other flows must be derived analytically.

The Census Bureau and the INS share responsibility for estimating international migration. Census and Current Population Survey data yield periodic estimates of the stock of foreign-born residents in this country. But neither questions nonnaturalized aliens about their legal status.[7] The INS does not monitor the international movement of military dependents, the emigration and return of other U.S. citizens from abroad, or flows to and from Puerto Rico. Aside from border apprehensions, it has no solid data on the entry and exit of undocumented aliens. With so many pieces of the puzzle missing, the estimation of net international flows is as much an art as it is a science.

### Illegal Entries

Conceptually, the size of the undocumented alien population is simply the difference between the number of foreign-born individuals resident in the United States and the number of such persons legally entitled to be so.

Total undocumented population

$$\begin{aligned} &\text{Total resident} &&\text{Legally resident}\\ = {}&\text{foreign-born} &&- \text{ foreign-born} \qquad (13)\\ &\text{population} &&\text{population} \end{aligned}$$

The census provides a count of the foreign-born population. However, the federal government does not monitor the size of the legally resident component. Once an alien has obtained legal resident status, or naturalized, he or she disappears into the larger population. Neither movement abroad nor deaths of these groups are recorded separately.

Until the Alien Registration System was discontinued in 1981, the federal government did enumerate one component of the legally resident foreign-born population: those who had not naturalized. Each January such individuals were required to submit an Alien Registration Form indicating their address, category, and date of admission, as well as certain key demographic characteristics. This provided essential information on both numbers and geographic dispersion. For the other group, naturalized citizens, such information could be obtained more directly from administrative records. Thus in 1980 the count of the illegal population was calculated as:

$$
\begin{array}{l}
\begin{array}{ll}
\text{Estimated} & \text{Foreign-born} \\
\text{undocumented} & \text{population} \\
\text{aliens} & = \text{counted in} \\
\text{counted in} & \text{the census}_{80} \\
\text{the census}_{80} &
\end{array} \\
\hspace{7cm} (14) \\
\begin{array}{ll}
\text{Estimated} & \text{Estimated} \\
\text{naturalized} & \text{legally} \\
- \text{U.S. citizens} & - \text{resident} \\
\text{in the United States}_{80} & \text{aliens in the} \\
& \text{United States}_{80}
\end{array}
\end{array}
$$

On the right side of this equation, the 1980 census provided the first element of information: the size of the enumerated foreign-born population. INS administrative records indicated the second, numbers who had naturalized. The Alien Registration System, adjusted for underreporting, provided the third data item: nonnaturalized but legally resident aliens. (The latter two terms together represent the full legally resident foreign-born population.) By inference, the INS–census team estimated

that approximately 2,057,000 illegally resident foreign-born persons, or illegal aliens, were among those counted by the 1980 census (Warren and Passel, 1987). It was possible to develop a rather detailed profile of these individuals by repeating this calculation for persons born in each of 40 mutually exclusive and exhaustive geographic areas, 13 age groups, two sexes, and four periods of entry.[8]

The passage of the Immigration Reform and Control Act of 1986 (IRCA) enabled 3 million illegal aliens in the country at that time to apply for legal resident status.[9] Their passage from the illegal to the legal side of the ledger, and the imposition of federal sanctions against employers who continue to hire illegal workers, has sustained interest in the size and growth of the undocumented population.

Throughout the 1980s the growth of this group has been monitored using CPS data. However, this process has been greatly complicated by the discontinuation of the Alien Registration System. The present technique conceptually parallels that used in 1980. As before,

$$
\begin{array}{l}
\text{Estimated} \\
\text{undocumented} \\
\text{population} \\
\text{in the CPS} \\
\\
\begin{array}{ll}
\text{Final estimate of} & \text{Final estimate of} \\
\text{total resident} & \text{legally resident} \\
= \text{foreign-born} & - \text{foreign-born} \quad (15) \\
\text{population in} & \text{population in} \\
\text{the CPS} & \text{the CPS}
\end{array}
\end{array}
$$

Now, however, each of the components must be derived from a different source (Woodrow and Passel, 1990b).

The final estimate of the *total* resident foreign-born population rests on an initial CPS count with the following modifications:

$$
\begin{array}{ll}
\text{Final estimate} & \\
\text{resident} & \text{Initial estimate} \\
\text{foreign-born} = & \text{of foreign-born} \\
\text{population in} & \text{population in} \\
\text{the CPS} & \text{the CPS}
\end{array}
$$

$$
\hspace{7cm} (16)
$$

Adjustment    Adjustment for
for CPS non-    CPS misreporting of
+ response on   +   Mexican-born
country of     as native-born
birth

The estimate of the *legally resident* foreign-born population in the United States at the survey date rests on the 1980 adjusted census count, together with the following information on subsequent flows:

$$
\begin{aligned}
&\text{Final estimate} \\
&\text{of legally} \\
&\text{resident} \\
&\text{foreign-born} \\
&\text{in United States at} \\
&\text{survey date}
\end{aligned}
=
\begin{aligned}
&\text{Estimated} \\
&\text{legally} \\
&\text{resident} \\
&\text{foreign-born} \\
&\text{in United States} \\
&\text{in 1980}
\end{aligned}
$$

$$
+
\begin{aligned}
&\text{Legal} \\
&\text{immigration} \\
&\text{from 1980} \\
&\text{to survey date}
\end{aligned}
+
\begin{aligned}
&\text{Applicants} \\
&\text{for IRCA} \\
&\text{legalization}
\end{aligned}
\qquad (17)
$$

$$
-
\begin{aligned}
&\text{Deaths of} \\
&\text{legally} \\
&\text{resident} \\
&\text{foreign-born,} \\
&\text{1980 to} \\
&\text{survey date}
\end{aligned}
-
\begin{aligned}
&\text{Emigration of} \\
&\text{legally resident} \\
&\text{foreign-born} \\
&\text{persons from} \\
&\text{1980 to survey} \\
&\text{date}
\end{aligned}
$$

The difference between the total and the legally resident foreign-born populations is then the CPS estimate of illegally resident aliens, equation (15). As in 1980, separate estimates are still developed for various regions of birth to obtain the most complete possible profile of illegal entrants.

The legalization of about up to 3 million persons at mid-decade obviously reduced the stock of illegal aliens; for several months thereafter the pace of entries also appeared to have slowed. However, Census Bureau analysts estimate that in 1991 the rate of illegal arrivals had returned to pre-IRCA levels.

### Emigration

In recent years the CPS has also been used to examine the pace of emigration (Woodrow and Passel, 1990a). Because em-

igrants are by definition not available for interview, their migratory behavior must be deduced from information supplied by relatives. This is accomplished using multiplicity or network techniques.

All respondents to the July 1987 CPS were queried about the international mobility of specific immediate relatives. Additional questions were asked about emigrants and Americans living abroad. To derive estimates of the actual number who have left the United States, these reports must be weighted for the multiplicity of linkages within the survey (i.e., for the number of resident relatives likely to have reported them). This technique will not be fully validated until it produces consistent estimates from two or more surveys. However, as the first source of empirical data on emigration in three decades, it is regarded as a methodological breakthrough.

### III. Assumptions Underlying Population Projections

These and many other lesser data sources come into play in calculating population projections. The quality of data on the existing population is of utmost importance, and we have seen the lengths to which analysts go to satisfy this need.

Given the appropriate baseline data, the analyst's next concern is to develop an appropriate range of possible paths for future development. Census Bureau projections serve as guidelines for national policy. They must depict the long-term implications of reasonable high, low, and likely trends in each of the components of population change: fertility, mortality, and international migration. These assumptions are derived through an analysis of past trends and observed errors in previous projections.

#### Combining Various Assumptions to Create Alternative Scenarios

The assumptions embodied in the Census Bureau's most recent set of population projections are detailed in Table A-3. Al-

**TABLE A-3.** Base Year and Projected High, Middle, and Low Values for Components of Population Change, 2080, and Resulting Projected Populations

| | Base Year | Level in 2080 | | |
|---|---|---|---|---|
| | | High | Middle | Low |
| Fertility | | | | |
| TFR | 1839[a] | 2200 | 1800 | 1500 |
| Mortality | | | | |
| $e_0$: Total | 75.0[b] | 77.9[c] | 81.2 | 88.0 |
| Male | 71.5[b] | 74.7 | 77.8 | 84.9 |
| Female | 78.5[b] | 81.3 | 84.7 | 91.3 |
| Net international migration (in thousands) | 662 | 800[d] | 500[d] | 300[d] |
| Implicit population (in millions)[e] | | | | |
| Fertility | 244 | 421 | 292 | 219 |
| Mortality | 244 | 279 | 292 | 318 |
| Migration | 244 | 333 | 292 | 265 |

[a] Base year 1985. On a per woman basis, this would be TFR = 1.839.

[b] Base year 1986.

[c] High mortality results in a shorter life expectancy. See the discussion in Chapter 2, p. 20.

[d] Assumed to be constant at this level throughout the projection period.

[e] Assuming the other two factors follow the middle-range path.

*Source:* Gregory Spencer, "Projections of the Population of the United States by Age, Sex, and Race: 1988 to 2080," *Current Population Reports*, Series P. 25, No. 1018 (Washington, D.C.: U.S. Government Printing Office, 1989).

together, 30 separate projection series were published in 1989. These represent all possible combinations of the three fertility, three mortality, and three main immigration scenarios noted in Table A-3. Also included are high, medium, and low growth scenarios assuming the total absence of net immigration.

Although projections are frequently updated, and these may soon be supplanted by another set, much can be learned about population dynamics by studying the relative outcomes of a few key scenarios. The most interesting for this purpose are:

1. The six in which one particular factor varies between high and low extremes while the other two factors are held at midrange ("best guess") levels. These illustrate the pure effects of variability in that single factor.

2. The three in which each component of change reinforces the effect of the other two. These include:

The middle or most likely scenario, in which all three factors are maintained on a middle growth course

The highest growth scenario (low mortality, high fertility, and high immigration)

The lowest growth scenario (high mortality, low fertility, and low immigration)

To grasp the interplay of these three components of growth it is helpful to follow the outcome of each in isolation.

*Fertility.* Today's concerns about impending labor shortages, the aging of the work force, and a contracting population all echo predictions voiced during the Great Depression. As the Baby Boom and Baby Bust have taught us, fertility trends can be volatile and unpredictable.

The middle-range fertility scenario therefore charts a course over the next century implying no change in the total fertility rate.[10] The range of variability cited as reasonable for this factor is between an ultimate increase of 0.4 and an ultimate drop of 0.3 children per woman by the year 2080.

The effects of such variation would be impressive but would emerge slowly. Five years transpire between the birth of a new cohort and its entry into the school system. Accession into the work force lags their birth by 16 or more years, and childbearing can lag by 25 years or more.

Once the cohort becomes reproductively active, however, the compounding effects of second-generation fertility make this factor by far the most powerful potential component of growth (Figure A-1). Over the 90 years ending in 2080, given the assumptions stated in Table A-3, total pop-

ulation could vary by as much as 202 million persons on this basis alone. To place this in context, the total population of the United States in 1987 was about 244 million.

The effect of such fertility variations on age structure would be equally dramatic. Figure A-2 is a different type of age pyramid than that previously shown. It depicts both the absolute size and the age distribution of the U.S. population in the year 2080, given high and low fertility assumptions in Table A-3.[11] The high-fertility scenario produces not only a larger, but a strikingly younger population.

*Immigration.* The factor having the second-largest singular impact on population growth, under assumptions detailed in Table A-3, would be net immigration. Because the net migration balance in the United States is continuously positive, migration contributes directly to expansion. In the short run, the effect of such additions is more visible than that of births: A large share of all immigrants join the population as working and childbearing adults. Their

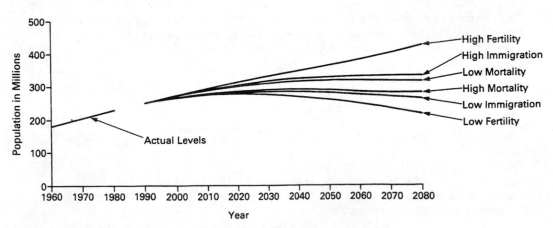

**FIGURE A-1: Total Population Growth Given High and Low Assumed Factor Levels**

*Note:* Assumes middle course, other two factors.

*Source:* Based on estimates in Gregory Spencer, "Projections of the Population of the United States by Age, Sex, and Race: 1988 to 2080," *Current Population Reports,* Series P-25, No. 1018.

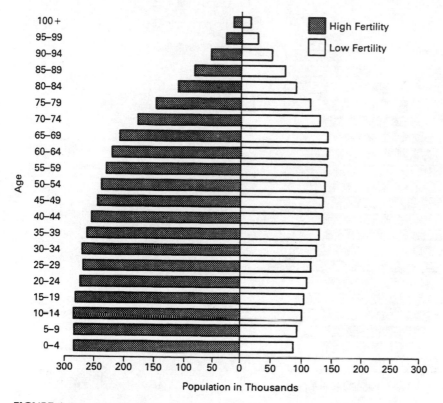

**FIGURE A-2: Age Profile in 2080 Resulting from High and Low Fertility Scenarios**

*Note:* Assumes middle course, other two factors.

*Source:* Based on estimates in Gregory Spencer, "Projections of the Population of the United States by Age, Sex, and Race: 1988 to 2080," *Current Population Reports,* Series P-25, No. 1018.

dispersal over many age groups, however, renders their effect on age structure almost negligible (Figure A-3). Census Bureau projections assume three alternative levels of net immigration: 800,000, 500,000, and 300,000 per year. Although a nontrivial addition to total growth, the number joining the population in this way will be small relative to total births. In the long run, even with the compounding effect of immigrant fertility, this factor can have substantially less impact on total growth than can national fertility trends. The difference between total populations in the year 2080, under

the high and low migration scenarios, is just about 68 million persons.

*Mortality.* In all projection scenarios released in 1989, Census Bureau analysts assumed mortality rates to be dropping and the life expectancies of Americans to be rising. The three mortality assumptions differed only in the pace at which this change would occur. The middle path continues a trend line established in the previous round of projections. It shows a 6.5-year increase in life expectancy between 1985 and the year 2080. The high mortality scenario con-

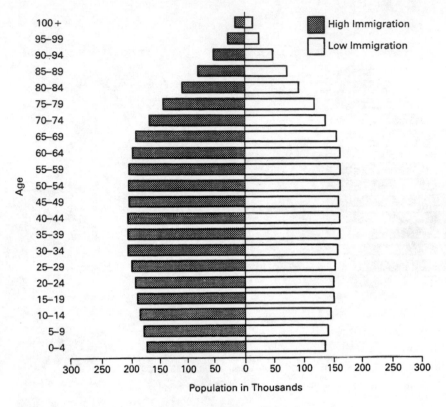

**FIGURE A-3:  Age Distribution in 2080, High and Low Immigraton Scenarios**

*Note:* Assumes middle path, other two factors.

*Source:* Based on estimates in Gregory Spencer, "Projections of the Population of the United States by Age, Sex, and Race: 1988 to 2080," *Current Population Reports*, Series P-25, No. 1018.

strains improvements to just half this rate, extending life expectancy by only 3 years. The low mortality scenario doubles the pace of improvements and leads to more than a 13-year increase in life expectancy. Although at a personal level this may sound like a wide range of variability, over the 90 years being projected these two extremes would result in total populations differing by just 39 million persons.

Mortality is most significant for its effect on age structure (Figure A-4). Under the high mortality scenario in Table A-3, by the year 2080 the share of the population in dependent ages 0–17 would roughly equal the share aged 65 and over: 20.1 versus 21.8 percent, respectively. Given the low mortality scenario, minors would be markedly outnumbered by the elderly: 18.0 versus 29.3 percent, respectively.

*Slow, Middle, and Rapid Growth Scenarios.* The three projection scenarios most frequently cited by data users are the

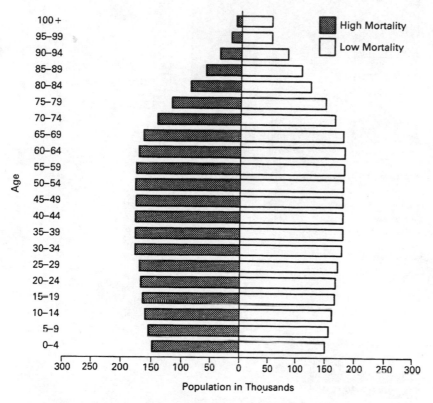

**FIGURE A-4: Age Distribution in 2080, High and Low Mortality Scenarios**

*Note:* Assumes middle path, other two factors.

*Source:* Based on estimates in Gregory Spencer, "Projections of the Population of the United States by Age, Sex, and Race: 1988 to 2080," *Current Population Reports*, Series P-25, No. 1018.

middle growth path, the slowest, and the most rapid. The middle scenario illustrates the combined effects of all three middle assumptions in Table A-3. The slowest and most rapid growth scenarios represent the pooled effects of three reinforcing assumptions—for example, in a scenario assuming high fertility, high immigration, and low mortality, or vice versa. The high and low growth scenarios together span the full range of projected outcomes.

These projections foresee the total U.S. population, which was enumerated by the census to be 249 million in 1990, to be somewhere between a maximum likely figure of 501 million (or a doubling) and a minimum likely figure of 185 million (a 26 percent drop) by the year 2080.

Regardless of which growth path the U.S. population follows, by that time it will probably have aged substantially (Figure A-5). The median age will have risen from 32.1 years in 1987 to between 39.9 and 47.5 years. The number of persons aged 65 and

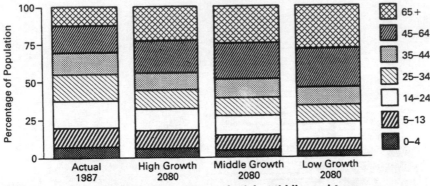

**FIGURE A-5: Age Distribution, 1987 and High, Middle, and Low Growth to the Year 2080**

*Note:* Reinforcing effect of three factors.

*Source:* Based on estimates in Gregory Spencer, "Projections of the Population of the United States by Age, Sex, and Race: 1988 to 2080," *Current Population Reports*, Series P-25, No. 1018.

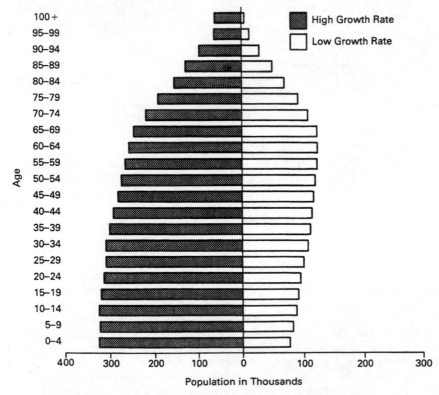

**FIGURE A-6: Age Distribution in 2080, High and Low Growth Scenarios**

*Note:* Reinforcing effects of three factors.

*Source:* Based on estimates in Gregory Spencer, "Projections of the Population of the United States by Age, Sex, and Race: 1988 to 2080," *Current Population Reports*, Series P-25, No. 1018.

above per 100 prime-age adults (ages 18–64) will have risen from 20 to between 42 and 47.

Policies hoping to ward off this aging process through immigration would have little effect unless immigration ceilings were set far above those envisioned in Table A-3. The factor most capable of tempering this aging effect is fertility. Its very dominant role in overall age structure is evident when the projected age profile for the year 2080, based on the highest and lowest growth patterns (Figure A-6), is compared with that resulting from high and low fertility assumptions alone (Figure A-2).

## SUMMARY

This appendix has presented the basic issues, data sources, and dilemmas faced by demographers as they attempt to develop population estimates and projections. Given the complexity of enumerating the existing population, both within and crossing national borders, it should not be surprising that projections of future size and flow often miss the mark.

Even projections that fail in the long run, however, can serve as useful guideposts today. The development of public policy, like the development of population estimates, is an iterative process. New information sensitizes us to different issues. Often it prompts analysts to rethink their use of existing data sources. Analytical techniques are devised to squeeze out more information from that which already exists. When the limits of this process are reached, continued social, economic, or political pressure often results in additional resources being channelled into the collection of appropriate data. Thus in the longrun our very interest in the future enhances our ability to project and shape its course.

## NOTES

1. For a discussion of the formula for determining apportionment, see Poston (1990).
2. The Census Bureau did not release its coverage estimates for 1980 until February 1988.
3. Monthly supplements also explore issues such as changes in educational attainment, work experience, marital and family structure, and fertility. Special CPS supplements on international migration were included in April 1983, June 1986, July 1987, June 1988, and November 1989.
4. The official life table estimates in this abridged table have undergone some additional adjustments. As a result, the formulas discussed closely approximate, but may not exactly replicate, the results noted.
5. Life tables depict events between exact ages (i.e., from birthday to birthday). The average person registered as dying at age $x$ is really halfway to the next birthday—that is, age $x + \frac{1}{2}$. Hence rates obtained from death registration data ($m_x$) are first translated into life table death rates ($q_x$) as

follows:

$$q_x = \frac{2m_x}{2 + m_x}$$

6. In abridged life tables, this calculation is slightly biased, and must be modified by one of several procedures.
7. The term *alien* refers to the nonnaturalized foreign-born.
8. The census data employed were first adjusted for citizenship and nativity misreporting.
9. The main legalization program required that they have been resident in the United States prior to January 1, 1982.
10. It would be impossible to project specific oscillations. Therefore, this path essentially assumes that increases and decreases offset one another in the long run.
11. Assuming a middle path for mortality and net migration.

## BIBLIOGRAPHY

COALE, ANSLEY J., AND NORFLEET W. RIVES. (1973). "A Statistical Reconstruction of the Black Population of the United States, 1880–1970: Estimates of True Numbers by Age and Sex, Birth Rates, and Total Fertility." *Population Index, 39*(1).

HOGAN, HOWARD. (1990). "The 1990 Post-Enumeration Survey: An Overview." Paper presented to the annual meeting of the Population Association of America, Toronto, Canada, April 1990.

POSTON, DUDLEY L., JR. (1990). "Apportioning U.S. Congress: A Primer. In *Population Today*. Washington, D.C.: Population Reference Bureau, July–August.

ROBINSON, J. GREGORY, PRITHWIS DAS GUPTA, AND BASHIR ADMED. (1990). "Evaluating the Quality of Estimates of Coverage Based on Demographic Analysis." Paper presented to the annual meeting of the Population Association of America, Toronto, Canada, April 1990.

SIEGEL, J. S., J. S. PASSEL, AND J. G. ROBINSON. (1980). "Preliminary Review of Existing Studies of the Number of Illegal Residents of the United States." In *U.S. Immigration Policy and the National Interest: The Staff Report of the Select Commission on Immigration and Refugee Policy*. Washington, D.C.: U.S. Government Printing Office.

U.S. BUREAU OF THE CENSUS. (1988). 1980 Census of Population, and R. E. Fay, J. S. Passel, and J. G. Robinson, Housing, Evaluation and Research Reports, PHC80-E4, *The Coverage of Population in the 1980 Census*. Washington, D.C.: U.S. Government Printing Office.

U.S. BUREAU OF THE CENSUS. (1989). Gregory Spencer, "Projections of the Population of the United States, by Age, Sex, and Race: 1988 to 2080," *Current Population Reports*, Series P-25, No. 1018. Washington, D.C.: U.S. Government Printing Office.

U.S. DEPARTMENT OF HEALTH AND HUMAN SERVICES. (1990) *Vital Statistics of the United States, 1987:* Vol. II, Section 6, *Life Tables*. Washington, D.C.: U.S. Public Health Service.

WARREN, ROBERT, AND JEFFREY S. PASSEL. (1987). "A Count of the Uncountable: Estimates of Undocumented Aliens Counted in the 1980 United States Census." *Demography, 24*(3), pp. 375–393.

WHELPTON, PASCAL. (1950). "Birth and Birth Rates in the Entire United States, 1909 to 1948." *Vital Statistics Special Reports, 33*(8). Washington, D.C.: National Center for Health Statistics.

WOODROW, KAREN A., AND JEFFREY S. PASSEL. (1990a). "Estimates of Emigration Based on Sample Survey Data from Resident Relatives." Paper presented to the annual meeting of the Population Association of America, Toronto, Canada, April 1990.

———. (1990b). "Post-IRCA Undocumented Immigration to the United States: An Assessment Based on the June 1988 CPS." In F. D. Bean, B. Edmonston, and J. S. Passel, eds., *Undocumented Migration to the United States: IRCA and the Experience of the 1980s*. Washington, D.C.: Urban Institute Press, pp. 33–76.

# Photo Credits

**Chapter 1** (*a*) M.S. Benedict/U.S. Forest Service. (*b*) Spencer Grant/Monkmeyer Press.

**Chapter 2** (*a*) The Granger Collection. (*b*) Spencer Grant/The Picture Cube.

**Chapter 3** (*a*) Culver Pictures. (*b*) Richard Gill.

**Chapter 4** (*a*) U.S. Department of Agriculture/Monkmeyer Press. (*b*) Library of Congress.

**Chapter 5** (*a*) Michael Serino/The Picture Cube. (*b*) Paul Fortrin/Monkmeyer Press.

**Chapter 6** (*a*) UPI/Bettmann Newsphotos. (*b*) Rollie McKenna/Photo Researchers.

**Chapter 7** (*a*) Prentice Hall archives. (*b*) John Maher/Stock, Boston.

**Chapter 8** (*a*) Frank Siteman/Stock, Boston. (*b*) Greenlar/The Image Works.

**Chapter 9** (*a*) State Historical Society of Wisconsin. (*b*) Culver Pictures.

**Chapter 10** (*a*) Culver Pictures. (*b*) Renée Lynn/Photo Researchers.

**Chapter 11** (*a*) Bettye Lane/Photo Researchers. (*b*) Elizabeth Crews/The Image Works.

**Chapter 12** (*a*) Alan Carey/The Image Works. (*b*) Chester Higgins, Jr./Photo Researchers.

**Chapter 13** (*a*) Joseph Nettis/Photo Researchers. (*b*) Spencer Grant/The Picture Cube.

**Chapter 14** (*a*) Library of Congress. (*b*) Hazel Hankin/Stock, Boston.

**Chapter 15** (*a*) Ulrike Welsch. (*b*) Ellis Herwig/The Picture Cube.

**Chapter 16** (*a*) Michael Siluk/The Image Works. (*b*) Michael Weisbrot/Stock, Boston.

**Chapter 17** (*a*) Prentice Hall archives. (*b*) Alan Carey/The Image Works.

**Chapter 18** (*a*) Library of Congress. (*b*) Mimi Forsyth/Monkmeyer Press.

**Chapter 19** (*a*) Rogers/Monkmeyer. (*b*) Stock, Boston.

**Chapter 20** (*a*) Eddie Adams/Sygma. (*b*) AP/Wide World Photos.

**Chapter 21** (*a*) John Coletti/The Picture Cube. (*b*) Bob Daemmrich/The Image Works.

**Chapter 22** (*a*) Michael C. Hayman/Photo Researchers. (*b*) Frank Siteman/Monkmeyer Press.

**Chapter 23** (*a*) Suzanne Szasz/Photo Researchers. (*b*) Ulrike Welsch/Photo Researchers.

**Chapter 24** (*a*) Arlene Collins/Monkmeyer Press. (*b*) Gale Zucker/Stock, Boston.

**Chapter 25** (*a*) Jim Harrison/Stock, Boston. (*b*) Owen Franken/Stock, Boston.

**Chapter 26** (*a*) Alan Carey/The Image Works. (*b*) Ulrike Welsch.

# Index